Strategic Enterprise Management

An IT Manager's Desk Reference

Related Titles

ATM Network Planning and Implementation, Art Edmonds, Jr. ISBN 1-85032-894-3

Implementing and Operating Switched Local Area Networks, John Roese. ISBN 1-85032-896-X

Network Design Using EcoNets, Roshan L. Sharma. ISBN 1-85032-907-9

Practical Networking with Ethernet, Charles E. Spurgeon. ISBN 1-85032-885-4

The Token Ring Standards Companion, James T. Carlo, Robert D. Love, Michael S. Siegel, Kenneth T. Wilson. ISBN 1-85032-884-6

Strategic Networking, Paul David Henry and Gene De Libero. ISBN 1-85032-203-1

Strategic Enterprise Management

An IT Manager's Desk Reference

Roy T Varughese

International Thomson Computer Press

I(T)P® An International Thomson Publishing Company

Boston • London • Bonn • Johannesburg • Madrid • Melbourne • Mexico City • New York • Paris
Singapore • Tokyo • Toronto • Albany, NY • Belmont, CA • Cincinnati, OH • Detroit, MI

For more information, contact:

International Thomson Computer Press
20 Park Plaza, 13th Floor
Boston, MA 02116 USA

International Thomson Publishing Europe
Berkshire House
168-173 High Holborn
London WC1V 7AA England

Nelson International Thomson Publishing Australia
102 Dodds Street
South Melbourne, NSW
Victoria 3205 Australia

Nelson Canada
1120 Birchmount Road
Scarborough, Ontario
Canada M1K 5G4

International Thomson Publishing Southern Africa
Building 18, Constantia Park
240 Old Pretoria Road
P.O. Box 2459
Halfway House 1685 South Africa

International Thomson Publishing GmbH
Königswinterer Straße 418
53227 Bonn, Germany

International Thomson Publishing Asia
60 Albert Street #15-01
Albert Complex
Singapore 189969

International Thomson Publishing Japan
Hirakawa–cho Kyowa Building, 3F
2-2-1 Hirakawa–cho
Chiyoda–ku, Tokyo 102 Japan

International Thomson Editores
Seneca, 53
Colonia Polanco
11560 Mexico D. F. Mexico

International Thomson Publishing France
Tour Maine–Montparnasse
33 avenue du Maine
75755 Paris Cedex 15
France

A catalog record for this book is available from the Library of Congress

ISBN 1-85032-315-1

Publisher/Vice President: Jim deWolf, ITCP/Boston
Project Director: Vivienne Toye, ITCP/Boston

Manufacturing Manager: Sandra Sabathy, ITCP/Boston
Marketing Manager: Christine Nagle, ITCP/Boston

Production: Multiscience Press, Inc., New York

This book is dedicated to Anna, my partner and friend without whose support and patience this project would not have been possible. It is also for my daughters, Rachel and Leah, who managed for long periods without my company while it was being written.

If you close your eyes
you can see my dream

Rachel Sarah Varughese
(@ age 5 years)

Table of Contents

List of Figures

Chapter 2

Chapter 3

Chapter 4

Chapter 7

Chapter 8

Chapter 9

Chapter 10

Chapter 11

Chapter 12

List of Tables

Chapter 4

Chapter 5

Chapter 6

Chapter 7

Chapter 8

Chapter 9

Chapter 10

Chapter 12

List of Case Studies

Chapter 6

Chapter 8

Chapter 9

Chapter 11

Chapter 12

Navigation

The first chapter is an introduction to this wide area of infrastructure management. The remainder of this book may be viewed as providing three perspectives of infrastructure, namely: *Business, Architectural,* and *Technical*—as shown in Figure P.1.

- Chapters 2, 3, 4 and 5 provide a business perspective of infrastructure management. These chapters cover tools for developing strategy, managing organizational and people issues, and templates for common processes in infrastructure management.

- Chapters 6, 7 and 8 as a group provide an architectural perspective of infrastructure management. Starting with an overview of client/server and intranet building blocks, architected solutions to major deficits in product and solution offerings are defined. Frameworks that automate the implementation of common processes are also defined.

- Chapters 9, 10, 11 and 12 provide a broad technology perspective of infrastructure management covering management platforms, protocol and interface technology, agent technology and software technologies.

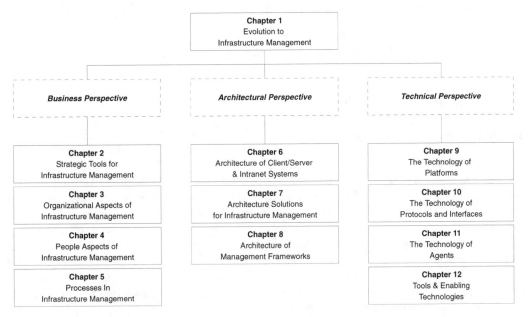

Figure P.1: Three perspectives of infrastructure management

The first part is applicable to a very wide audience, in fact anyone (a manager, end-user or technologist) who is involved with client/server based applications and their enterprise-wide delivery. This "soft" side of infrastructure management is sorely missed in literature in this area. Yet it is the lack of business perspective that stops many organizations from using their current investments in management technology and indeed in IT generally to the full.

The third part is an *inclusive* tutorial on the technology for infrastructure management. While the market has many hundreds of individual products, it is by and large a fragmented one, with most tools and even platforms taking a narrow, parochial perspective of the field. Interworking between tools even built to the same interface specs or protocols is still very limited, making choices for large-scale deployment harder.

The architectural perspective (Chapters 6 to 8) essentially bridges the business and technology portions by providing notions of design abstractions to build solutions using technology while not losing sight of business intent.

This work also contains:

- A glossary of essential terms which define key concepts of infrastructure management, client/server and intranet technology. The chapter and section where the concept is covered in this publication are also shown where relevant.

- 30+ case studies ranging from IT deployment to framework realizations to product descriptions. These can be read as side-bars as they have a flow that is independent of the text.

- 160+ figures help to illustrate many concepts.

Summaries

PART I—Business Perspective

Chapter 1, "Evolution to Infrastructure Management," sets the theme of the book by defining the drivers for marshalling diverse support groups under a single umbrella and a single goal—managing the infrastructure for application delivery. Three models—a business model, a technology model, and an integrative model—define infrastructure management from different perspectives. The following is a brief synopsis of each of the remaining chapters.

Chapter 2, "Strategic Tools for Infrastructure Management," defines a strategic perspective of infrastructure management. Topics define an essential set of management tools to use at different stages of the infrastructure life-cycle. This ranges from developing user awareness to developing business continuity planning to undertaking gap analysis (with respect to current and required infrastructure characteristics).

Chapter 3, "Organizational Aspects of Infrastructure Management," looks at the relationship between an infrastructure management group and other parts of the enterprise as well as external relationships such as outsourcers and supplier's service organizations. A general trend is for at least some parts of the infrastructure to be outsourced. In such a case the continuity from internal service group(s) to external groups needs to be carefully designed.

Chapter 4, "People Aspects of Infrastructure Management," looks at the factors involved in managing the change from a functional view to a team view. The loss of job descriptions in this transition requires new ways of defining and valuing skills and contributions. The shortening of product life-cycles implies a continuous training program for supported areas. It also requires the monitoring of key skills and competencies against requirements.

Chapter 5, "Processes in Infrastructure Management," identifies key infrastructure management processes and develops a prototype of each process. Similar processes are found in most organizations, however they are often implicit. Process re-engineering make processes explicit and visible. Basic tools and guidelines for process re-engineering is included as are guidelines for automation.

PART II—Architecture Perspective

Chapter 6, "Architecture of Client/Server and Intranet Systems," looks at the basic models of client server computing against the models available for managing the supporting infrastructure. The emergence of the intranet as another way of deploying client/server application has an impact on infrastructure management.

Chapter 7, "Architecture Solutions for Infrastructure Management," looks at the deficit between the tools available and the task of building enterprise-wide management frameworks. Architectural solutions provide key pieces, such as resilience, scalability, security, and remote management required for view. Architecture also provides a roadmap in the evolutionary path of strategic technologies such as platforms agents and databases used in building management frameworks. Architecture also helps to contain the capital cost of building such frameworks.

Chapter 8, "Architecture of Management Frameworks," defines scalable frameworks for monitoring (e.g., fault, performance and security events); collecting and storing geographically dispersed information; distributing management information; and remote access to management assets.

PART III—Technology Perspective

Chapter 9, "The Technology of Platforms," looks at one of the three pieces of the current management paradigm (the other two are the agents and the protocol between them). Platforms are complex software products and hence cannot be done full justice in a single chapter. There are a number of types of platforms currently in use. The structure and characteristics of each type is discussed along with representative examples of platforms.

Chapter 10, "The Technology of Protocols and Interfaces," looks at the protocols that enable communication between platforms and agents. The structure of the protocol to a large degree defines the structure and complexity of the agent. A synopsis of SNMP,

SNMPv2, and the OSI model is followed by a discussion of some of the management interfaces relevant to building management applications.

Chapter 11, "The Technology of Agents," looks at the current agent technology—ranging from simple agents that need to be polled by management stations to mobile agents that can be transported to target hosts for execution. The availability of toolkits to build proxy and native agents has accelerated the deployment of agents in areas outside network management. The notion of agent-based computing is undergoing a change with the intranet.

Chapter 12, "Tools and Enabling Technologies," looks at a range of tools and technologies that are relevant to the evolution of the capability for infrastructure management. Over time, infrastructures will become more integrated and new "systems integration" type tools are needed to develop integrated views.

Acknowledgments

My thanks first of all to my editor, Liz Israel, for her enthusiasm about this project from the earliest draft and her continuing belief in the unique approach of this publication.

My thanks also go to Karen Watterson for reviewing this publication and for her many suggestions and comments. I have tried to incorporate most of them into the final manuscript.

My thanks are also due to the team at Multiscience Press Inc.—in particular Alan Rose and Ben Goffman—for keeping me informed and in the loop during the production process.

Part I

Business Perspectives

1

Evolution to Infrastructure Management

Areas covered in this chapter

- The swing from centralization to decentralization and back

- Current state of client/server infrastructures and their evolutionary path

- The changing definition of infrastructure

- The Internet and intranets (I-net) and the growth of the I-net phenomenon

- Convergence of infrastructure management roles

- Stages of maturity of client/server deployments

- Common success factors in deploying client/server projects

- The phenomenon of infrastructure outsourcing

- A business model of infrastructure management

- Technology of infrastructure management

- A composite view of infrastructure

Cycles impact most phenomena known to man, from sunspots to financial markets to politics. IT is also prone to cyclic behavior. One of the most important cycles in IT is that of centralization/decentralization. At any given time, different constituents of IT (applications, operating systems, computing platforms, networks, etc.) are at different points on this cycle.

The term client/server entered the terminology of computing in the 1980s, meaning a decentralized computing model that focused on end-users. The client/server model was seen to center on real user requirements within a workgroup, or within a department, or across a whole line of business spanning functions in several departments.

This introduced an opposite view from that of the centralized *data-center*, from which most mainframe and minicomputer systems and services were delivered to users.

Unfortunately today, the term client/server has no clearly established meaning. It means different things to different people, and is used in different contexts ranging from a technical definition to a marketing term. A selection of current usage of the term is given below:

- To the end-users in a business, client/server means a personal computer (or workstation) attached to servers that store shared resources such as files and documents and provide services such as file management and printing.

- To business managers, it is a method of developing and delivering IT solutions in a shorter time-frame and in a cheaper way than possible with mainframes.

- To the vendor, it is a marketing tool to get the attention of businesses (or individual departments) moving away from centralized IT.

- To the business aware technologists, it is an essential component of realizing business strategies for the millennium.

Many client/server projects were started at a local departmental or operational business level. Such projects largely bypassed the traditional IT function in developing the projects. The main reasons commonly cited for this radical approach were:

- *Business change*—Business and market conditions were undergoing major cyclical upheavals at this time. In many organizations immediate responses, which included IT components, were required to satisfy the changing environment.

- *Long lead time*—The centralized IT function was unable, in most cases, to meet the functional requirements, or where requirements were technically feasible, could not provide solutions in the timescale required by a client business.

- *Inequitable cost model*—The centralized IT function imposed a high cost base on IT development over which individual client businesses had little control. The cost was distributed using opaque and complex "chargeback" models.

Surveys have shown again and again that users of client/server systems (delivered by departmental projects), are by and large happy with the results. Users also remain committed to further development, despite some of the challenges they see. More importantly users believe these systems were instrumental in the expansion of their roles or businesses or sometimes in their very survival.

1.1 The State of Client/Server Infrastructures

On the downside, many of the advantages predicted by the advocates of client/server computing remain unrealized:

- *Cost savings*—Cost savings on medium- and large-scale client/server implementations have largely been mythical. For example, in many cases the cost of support was not considered as a major item. Neither was it realized that keeping pace with application performance needs would require machine upgrades within a 12- to 18-month cycle. Cost of developing new systems has also been underestimated—quality of manpower, need for special facilities such as realistic test beds, need for integrated development tools, the development cycle-time and costs of end-user involvement and training have all been subject to review.

- *Simplicity*—Implementation has been more complex than initially envisaged—especially when scaling up to support more users or to multi-departmental and multi-site levels.

- *Shortened lead time*—Development cycles have shortened. However a culture of continuous delivery involving a series of business driven delivery cycles has developed.

- *Infrastructure level standards*—Issues such as data integrity, high availability and security need to be solved on an ad hoc basis by each client/server system delivering to a wider business constituency in an organization. Infrastructure and system management issues ranging from problem management to performance have been difficult to contain. Incompatibility between platforms in multiple departments, inadequacy of networks and lack of a management framework all contribute to the problem.

- *Leveraging technology advances*—As the power/cost ratio for desktop and server machines improves, making 32 and 64 bit machines affordable, a major software gap is evident: The software technologies used to build the current generation of many departmental client/server applications do not scale to benefit from hardware cost improvements.

Such architectural and infrastructure problems are recurrent in multiple parts of many large corporations. There is a growing recognition across all industry sectors that unlike client/

server application development approaches, where local and ad hoc solutions may work, infrastructure problems require a more strategic approach.

Consequently, there is a general trend for some cross-business function to be invited back to solve infrastructure issues on an enterprise scale. In particular, IT departments are increasingly asked to get involved in assuming responsibility for at least coordinating the IT infrastructure and its management.

Many traditional IT departments, however, have a dilemma: When businesses got the mandate to do local application development, the role and power of the traditional IT departments diminished very rapidly. Over a short period of time they became drastically smaller, concentrating largely on maintaining the data center and taking responsibility for legacy systems development.

Meanwhile, other pockets of expertise have been developed in response to specific requirements of running businesses at the departmental and line-of business levels. The skills required include local area network and communication management, client/server systems administration and client/server application support.

Hence, most traditional IT departments have little or no client/server skills. For an IT-led service organization to bring order to enterprise-wide installations, these diverse fief-doms of wide area communications, network management, systems administration, and the like, have to be brought in line to work in the same direction and under a unified budget. A key question that has faced many organizations is, what core competencies are needed for the new service organization?

1.1.1 Traditional Notion of Infrastructure and its Management

For many IT managers the term "infrastructure" is immediately associated with the corporate network. Enterprise-wide networks consist of different classes of networks.

- Local area networks (LAN), provide connectivity, usually on a building level. A single building may have many LANs interconnected through a backbone LAN.

- Campus or metropolitan area networks (MAN) provide connectivity between multiple buildings in a campus or metropolitan environment. MAN technology typically connects backbone LANs of each building in the metropolitan area.

- Long haul or wide area networks (WAN) provide wider connectivity spanning a country, a continent or the globe.

Many businesses are entirely dependent on the information carried between computers connected by these classes of networks. Disruption of a part of the network often propagates failure of business processes.

Each loss-of-service incident has a cumulative effect on how the business views IT service. In areas such as financial services, loss to the business from network downtime is quantifiable.

For client/server applications, what is termed "infrastructure" consists of the classes of networks described above as well as components and services layered over the networks.

The notion of infrastructure management however begins with network management. This discipline, as understood today, developed in the early 1990s, together with the wide acceptance of the Simple Network Management Protocol (SNMP) and its consolidation as a de facto standard for managing network components.

This by no means implies that this was the first network management protocol. Before this period, however, network management was very much a *black art* tackled only by a small number of network experts. In proprietary computing environments, network management still retains this status. Indeed one of the challenges facing the advancement of infrastructure management as a unifying concept on an enterprise-wide scale, is the integration of such islands of proprietary protocols with the more open SNMP.

Most vendors of networking equipment today support (or promise to support) SNMP in their products. Simultaneously, SNMP management platforms have reached sufficient maturity to be useful in delivering better network service. Maturity is evidenced by the build quality, the pool of trained people on the market, stability of basic standards and the high level of conformance with these standards.

The use of network management technology to minimize or avoid network downtime still forms the most credible of business reasons for the expenditure—on both the technological and the operational function. Other justifications include:

- Automation to cope with the task of managing larger or more complex networks.

- Automation to manage a growing network with a flat (or sometimes reduced), headcount in people.

- Proactive identification of risks and the fixing of emerging faults before they become major crises.

- Ability to handle incremental growth and network changes faster and with fewer errors.

In many organizations, however, the initial cycle of investment in network management technology has not provided tangible payback or quite met early expectations. Many unrealistic expectation levels were set by the vendor's marketing messages.

At the same time, intellectually, better management of the network, ultimately leading to a "self healing" network, is increasingly recognized by IT aware business management as a strategic requirement for growth. In some cases, the very survival of business lines in an enterprise is dependent on the timeliness of network delivered information.

Networks are strategic because they are central to tying together the business areas in an enterprise, providing it with global reach and internal economies of scale. A good communications infrastructure gives competitive advantage in many types of modern business.

1.1.2 Managing the Rest of "Traditional" Infrastructure

Networks, especially the campus or metropolitan level and long haul elements, have long been accepted as "genuine" infrastructure. Local area networks gained prominence as a prerequisite for deploying client/server applications. Hence, the history of client/server computing and the evolution of local area networks have been, and continue to be, intimately linked.

LANs are increasingly designed as infrastructure subsystems. This ensures that other infrastructure components and services dependent on the LAN are able to deliver according to specification.

The current (traditional) view of infrastructure is shown in Figure 1.1. Applications viewing the infrastructure see interfaces for client/server services, such as a database management system, interfaces to common network services such as file systems, and operating system interfaces.

Operating systems, the host or machine level of workstations and servers and the networks may be respectively viewed as a three-layered stack. Each layer uses the services of the layer below.

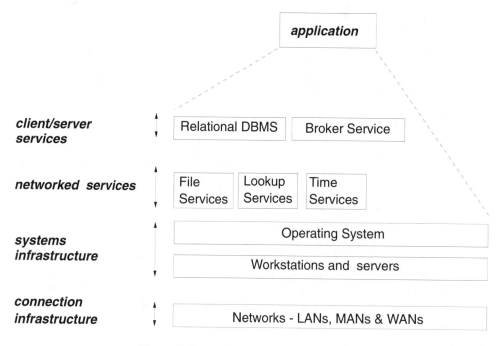

Figure 1.1: Traditional view of infrastructure

In the case of an operating system, it uses the physical resources (processor, memory, display subsystem, and such) of the workstations or servers. A workstation or server uses the interconnection resources of the network (e.g., network protocols, networking devices, network management subsystems).

Closely related to the operating system is a set of common networked services. This includes a *networked file service,* which allows files on different machines to be viewed within one logical hierarchy of files, regardless of where the files are stored. A *networked directory service* to look up the address and resources of other machines on the network and a *networked time service* to ensure all workstations and servers in a corporate network have a synchronized reference about the flow of time.

Above the operating system and above the networked services are a number of services that allow client/server applications to be built. Two common examples are a relational database management system and service to broker communications between clients and servers.

These layers of the infrastructure are managed in a variety of ad hoc ways. The connection infrastructure is considered the domain of network management tools. The systems infrastructure (of the operating system and its hosting machines) also has a whole technology base of management platforms and administrative tools. Client/server services such as a DBMS also have their own administrative toolkits.

Management tools therefore have a very narrow focus and little help is available from that quarter to develop a unified, systems view of the infrastructure. In Section 1.5, we describe a phenomenon where the infrastructure is growing in size, while applications and users that use the infrastructure are also growing. Another more recent phenomenon relating to client/server infrastructure is the growing use of the *intranet* to deliver client/server applications within corporations.

1.1.3 The Growth of the Intranet

The background to the intranet is the *world wide web* (WWW)—a computer network of web browsers and web servers. Users use the browser to request web documents, which reside on the web server. This simple model was initially conceived as a tool for collaborative research between scientists at the European Centre for Nuclear Research (CERN).

The first browsers were primitive and based only on text. This changed with *Mosaic* a graphical browser developed by students at the US National Center for Supercomputing Applications. Mosaic was in effect a revolution in the way information on the Internet could be stored and accessed. Even novices could click on graphical elements on the browser and, as a result, open a connection to a server and request the respective document.

The server returned the referenced document via the same connection and then closed the connection. The browser then processed the document's content for display to the user. The protocol between the browser and the server, Hypertext Transfer Protocol (HTTP) is both lightweight and simple.

The last two years have shown the phenomenal growth in two related technologies of the Internet and the corporate intranet. Both reinforce the client/server model. The growth of the Internet is fueled by a combination of circumstances:

- The adoption of one set of protocols—TCP/IP—by the whole community needing access to the Internet. For the first time in the history of computing, a single standard is universally accepted.

- The technology of hypertext linking and multimedia documents consisting of text, graphics, and even voice, video and small applications has caught the imagination of many non-technical users as well as a whole generation of software developers.

- The technology of a *universal* browser to access and use Internet-based resources has developed from its humble beginnings of a text reader to become an application environment in its own right.

The growth of the intranet is largely fueled by the need for an entity (whether an individual, department, site or an entire enterprise) to access and share information with a larger collection of entities (e.g., an individual with a department, a department with a site, a site with the enterprise level). This is illustrated in Figure 1.2. The growth of the intranet is through proliferation from corporate to departmental and eventually individual levels. Once intranets

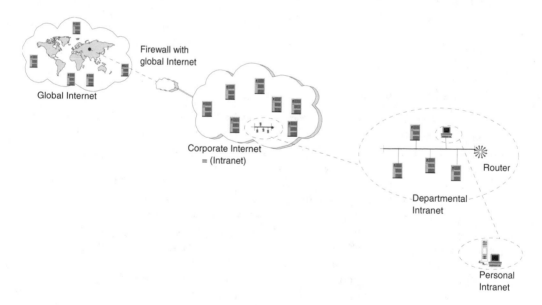

Figure 1.2: *Growth of the intranet from global to personal*

reach the small workgroup and individual level of control, it will re-write many of the current notions of client/server infrastructure.

Drivers and issues, common to both Internet and intranets are shown in Table 1.1. Intranet-based infrastructures are already used in delivering real applications. However several years of maturity are required before they will be viewed as a replacement infrastructure.

Table 1.1: Drivers and Areas of Concern for the Internet and Intranet Phenomenon

	Positive Drivers and Issue Areas	**Description**
Drivers	Low Cost	Browsers and web server software and development tools are all available at very low cost—making deployment cost per desk very low. A relatively simple change management system can upgrade core browser functionality—making service cost low. Because users tend to directly manage intranet resources, production labor is distributed.
	General Availability	Browsers are available for almost all platforms, making them a universal interface to information in the corporation as well as outside it. There are also well-known ways of integrating with legacy data in many environments. This offers new ways of leveraging existing investment in legacy technology.
	Simplicity of Protocols	The protocols that made the Internet possible are scalable both up in size of the Internet and down to the size of the individual. Lightweight protocols are easier to implement and have minimal impact on the network—accelerating their initial acceptance.
	Simplicity of Architecture	The intranet is based on a client/server model. The client environment is the browser, which may have other embedded clients such as e-mail, FTP and directory. The application logic is embedded and distributed in web-based documents. The web server as well as the browser can execute application logic, the latter by downloading the logic into a browser-based engine.
	Ease of Use	The browser has an intuitive user interface into a Hypertext Markup Language (HTML) based document. Pointing and clicking, form-based entry, and other dialog mechanisms are possible. HTML gives the browser control of the appearance of the document.

Table 1.1: *Drivers and Areas of Concern for the Internet and Intranet Phenomenon* (continued)

	Positive Drivers and Issue Areas	Description
	Performance	Because the basic browser and web server communicate using HTTP, the user sees a perceptibly slow response to requests that need more than one document to be accessed. Each point-and-click is a new communications context between the browser and the web server. At the server, incoming requests have to be serialized. The simplicity of the protocol is at the price of performance.
Issues	Security	Exchange of information between the browser and server, transfer of document content to the browser, transfer of applets, etc., are done without recourse to authentication or encryption. This is more of a problem on the Internet, however, intranets also have useful applications where confidentiality is important.
	High Availability	Data in a web server are not replicated easily. Hence, loss of a web site renders access to the documents to be inoperable. If the documents are not just a repository but part of an application deployment, the application essentially fails with the loss of access.
	Administration	The management and administration of a globally distributed infrastructure to deliver enterprise-wide applications is not easy to achieve. Yet intranets will need to define service levels close to those achieved by local applications in problem resolution, change management, performance, etc.

With the constantly changing nature of businesses and markets, information at a collective level is often instrumental in gaining business advantage, in improving business processes, building common business "visions" and in solving daily operational problems.

This is the current challenge in client/server application design.

1.2 The Effect of Success in Network Management

Networks in many large enterprises have undergone major re-engineering with the result that SNMP-manageable components such as hubs, routers and switches were introduced successfully into many production environments.

Many enterprises have also taken the effort to re-engineer within an enterprise-wide architecture or at least with well-defined internal standards. Coupled with investments in network management platforms and tools, this has enabled organizations to monitor these components and understand the traffic flows on the network.

For many organizations this has been the first experience of SNMP based management—and in particular the ability to monitor in a comprehensive way a large part of the infrastructure.

Despite the constant complaints by industry experts about the shortfalls of SNMP, it has made a major difference in many organizations. The service seen by their end-users has improved significantly. Improvements include:

- Low levels of network outage and greater localization of outage.

- Reduced downtime when a failure does occur.

- Faster turnaround for adds, moves and changes to the network.

- Pro-active fixes to capacity and latency problems as they emerge.

- Year on year growth of the network with flat headcount in support staff.

However, the network is only one of the components in delivering client/server solutions to the business. The network's relative stability has moved the focus of attention to the other components that share in the delivery: Namely, the host systems connected to the network, the services and the application components that run on the host systems. At least three classes of applications need to be distinguished:

- *Vertical* applications that provide IT solutions to specific business groups. These often require "domain knowledge" of the business to build and service. Most vertical applications are mission critical. They are often realized using on-line transaction processing (OLTP) models or from packaged software such as SAP R3.

- *Generic* applications such as spreadsheets, word-processors and other document-oriented tools.

- *Horizontal* applications such as a corporate relational database management system, e-mail and document imaging and increasingly, the Internet and intranet-based services.

The remit of the network management group is inexorably widening to encompass generic and horizontal classes of applications. This seems to happen especially in enterprises that have had significant success in controlling network problems—on a "winner takes all" basis. Horizontal applications are viewed in many organizations as infrastructure components used in the development of new business solutions or in re-engineering.

While telecommunication and IT functions have converged in some organizations, the exact opposite has occurred in others. Telecommunications (and its evolution) is to all intents and purpose outsourced.

It is not unusual for the same group to be responsible for the whole network, ranging from LANs to global networks, workstations, servers and horizontal applications. Several enterprises have been doing this for over two years. Management of generic applications is sometimes done under the label of "PC Support."

Infrastructure management may be plainly defined as the management of networks, hosts, operating systems, horizontal applications and core services (such as directory services and file services).

At the current level of maturity, networks can be managed relatively comprehensively, and operating systems and databases can be administered adequately. Other components, including applications and services, are managed in an ad hoc fashion with widely varying success.

Figure 1.3 shows a model for convergence of traditional areas of support through a set of mediums such as common physical framework, use of common technologies, shared databases, mechanisms of information distribution, and so forth.

While the relative success of network management is definitely a factor in promoting its role in related areas, a wider and far-reaching paradigm shift is taking place:

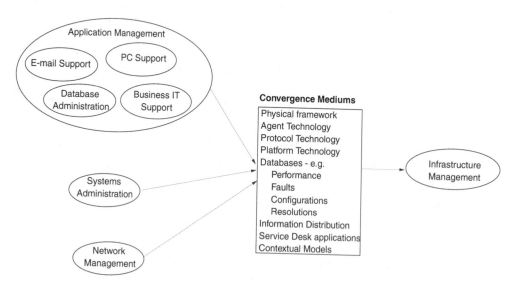

Figure 1.3: Convergence of traditional support groups

Computing is moving away from the technical base of centralized main-frame and mini-computers to distributed processors interconnected by a network. The current generation of distributed computing is widely described in contemporary literature as client/server computing.

Most state-of-the-art application development is (claimed in many surveys) done within this model. Client/server based applications are *network centric*, in the sense that the connectivity between the cooperating computers is of critical importance to the delivery of the application's functionality.

This model has therefore raised the *visibility* of the role the network plays in IT delivery to the business. The availability of the network is just one facet needed to deliver IT: the systems and the application components also have to be managed to a similar *degree*. Extrapolating from this argument, more than network management skills are required to manage the client/server computing environment.

1.2.1 Adoption of the Client/Server Computing Model

As a technical definition "client/server" defines peer-to-peer relationships between one or more *client* software modules and a software module that provides a specific *service to requesting clients*. This is more accurately described as a *request-response* model—where the client module requests a service of a server module, which then satisfies the specific request.

Some of these modules are resident at a desktop workstation while others are resident at a server class machine. There are often chains of such relationships—a module providing a service to a client module may itself be the client of another module providing it with some other service. The variants of the client/server model are discussed in Chapter 6, "Architecture of Client/Server and Intranet Systems."

Implementations of client/server based computing are complex and their underlying infrastructures are difficult to manage for three basic reasons:

- *Extent*—a large number of software components and machines are involved in the delivery of a client/server based application. Delivery may involve connectivity with many sites and over major time zones.

- *Diversity*—the delivery usually involves the integration of state-of-the-art with legacy systems or integration of different operating systems and processor architectures.

- *Changeability*—the software components tend to undergo changes in 6- to 18-month life-cycles. As module functionality is replaced or enhanced, the stress points on the underlying infrastructure changes radically.

Complexity leads to infrastructure management roles coming under pressure for solutions in high availability, coping with business changes and containing cost overheads.

1.2.2 The Blurring of Traditional Management Roles

Network management and systems management functions are separate disciplines in most enterprises. The former was tasked with looking after the network infrastructure of cables, hubs, bridges, routers, switches, multiplexers, etc.

Systems management functions were responsible for server and workstation administration, user administration, software distribution, scheduling across platforms, backup of data and performance tuning.

In general, managing the network increasingly involves system management skills as network and network management components are predominantly controlled by software. By a similar token, managing the connectivity issues of client/server computing environments requires knowledge of network topology and models for server placement.

In specific processes such as fault diagnosis, performance management and security management, expertise of network technology, operating system technology and application technology needs to be combined.

High quality systems management skills are relatively expensive and the duplication of these skills in network management has certainly been a tactical driver for the integration of these two functions.

1.2.3 Investment in Management Technology

As tools and automation investments are being made in both network and system management areas there is increasing pressure for economies of scale in the infrastructure to support these tools.

In general, network management tools have had little in common with system management tools. This has led to the inevitable specialization and duplication of functionality in some areas, such as fault monitoring.

The two groups approach common processes such as fault management very differently. Little scope exists to exchange and integrate management information, or to have common data models and to share training costs.

When management processes such as fault and change management are designed around managing the whole infrastructure, rather than just one component, support groups tend to come up with innovative solutions to the problem of tool fragmentation.

Figure 1.3 shows some of the technology mediums by which convergence to a single framework can occur. As processes and people elements are also viewed from the single infrastructure perspective, other opportunities for cooperation are generated.

1.3 Evolution in Client/Server Deployment

The term client/server has been used rather freely as a marketing term. In Chapter 6, the architectural *dimensions* of the client/server model are examined more thoroughly. Here we look at client/server from the viewpoint of deploying the applications and describe an evolu-

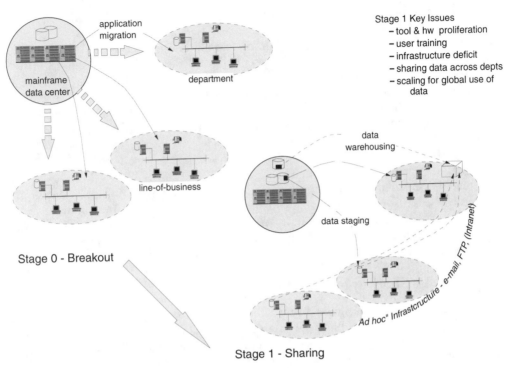

Figure 1.4: *Stage 0 to Stage 1 evolution of client/server deployment*

tionary path seen in organizations that have gone through multiple generations of client/server development.

This viewpoint also serves as an introduction to the business context in which a client/server model is first planned and subsequently evolves. This provides an important outlook on the evolution of the underlying infrastructure.

Client/server based application development has been undertaken by enterprises in almost every business sector. Most of these organizations still have mainframes or minicomputers running large applications and application suites. In addition, there are island PCs and workstations with a rudimentary capability to share printers and file services using a standalone local area network.

To put the spread of the client/server model in perspective, some 40% to 50% of data traffic still flow within networks hosting mainframes and minicomputers (such as SNA and DECNet).

In Stage 0 the break away from the centralized IT department takes place. (See Figure 1.4.) The focus in Stage 0 is meeting the requirements of the departmental or the line-of-business level. Typically, client PCs and workstations are used to install personal productivity applications. A basic LAN infrastructure is built, sometimes with wide area connectivity to similar or smaller remote sites. File servers and Print servers are installed as well as a network operating system to use these services.

Departmental IT budgets although small are still big enough to develop small applications and departmental business procedures. The aim of "departmental" applications is to connect the decision makers within the department to the department's own information resources as well as external resources.

Applications are built using departmental level business knowledge but with specialist IT labor—often contracted for a specific application. Off-the-shelf tools such as spreadsheets, package databases and e-mail are often the building blocks. Some department specific applications move from the mainframe or minicomputer systems, especially those that need re-engineering, thus changing business needs.

In Stage 0, a departmental computing structure has been essentially created within the larger enterprise. Personal productivity gains are claimed but the business benefits accrue largely to the department. The term client/server is largely *unjustified* at this stage. However, many writers and vendors continue to think of this stage of maturity as *true* client/server.

1.3.1 Stage 1—Sharing Information

Departmental (and line-of-business) infrastructures have to be connected as information generated within these systems has to be shared both on a peer-to-peer basis across departments as well as upwards into the enterprise hierarchy. This is achieved largely through rudimentary e-mail, file transfer and more recently, through web pages.

Legacy data on mainframes and minicomputers are still recognized to be important. Development is undertaken to move legacy data. More commonly, legacy data is staged to a departmental relational database. New applications are developed operationally to integrate departmental information with legacy data.

Departmental databases may be distributed and replicated to geographically widespread users. Data warehousing—a concept in looking at information in multiple databases using business specific information *dimensions* may also be prototyped or built using external expertise and specialist software tools.

Decision support systems are designed using information from relational databases. On-line Analysis Processing (OLAP) uses information "staged" in data warehouses and is now increasingly delivered through the medium of internal web servers and browsers.

Increased awareness of the importance of advanced client/server concepts such as security, high availability, and change management occur. The service-cost element and the role of systems and network management tools to manage downtime is considered. Rudimentary standalone network and systems management are often deployed.

Traditional collapsed backbone network architectures begin to feel the strain of cross departmental data traffic. Often the "inter-operability" problems of protocols from the LAN level up to and including the application level become major inhibitors of further progress in sharing information.

1.3.2 Stage 2—Reality of Client/Server

Ease of use becomes a primary requirement as the productivity and ever steeper learning curves for applications become issues. This often results in two departmental (or line-of-business level) initiatives:

- *Training.* Both application specific and general IT training are actively promoted in the department. This is in an effort to increase productivity by using existing tool investments. Collaborative tools are piloted and sometimes used to integrate work-flow across departments. These experiences act as a precursor to the process-centered restructuring in the next stage.

- *Standardization.* Controlling the proliferation of personal choices in tools and applications becomes a major requirement. Information is already made available across departmental boundaries. Office automation tool suite is standardized across a department. Standardization is often done in a cooperative framework with other parts of the enterprise with which there may be close information links. An effort is made to standardize on network protocols—this is often done in response to a visible decline in productivity and service levels in supporting infrastructure elements such as the network.

The strain on the network, help desk and remaining service/support organization becomes unmistakable. Network and subsystem incompatibilities in connecting across departmental boundaries become an issue. Non-scaleability of departmental solutions becomes evident. The performance of systems that cross departmental boundaries begin to deteriorate as infrastructure and service deficits impact delivery.

Service organizations remain in the dark about the nature and structure of the applications being delivered by the infrastructures for which they are responsible. The machine level inter-dependencies of client/server applications make it difficult to track down problems using any linear diagnostic processes. To understand the complex behavior of client/server applications, initiatives in performance monitoring, systems monitoring and fault reporting is often started to provide advance warnings.

Network re-engineering is often begun with a view to simplifying the network and to upgrading to a new network architecture capable of supporting more complex traffic patterns. Element management is deployed as a standard in new parts of the network. Event monitoring of the infrastructure, at least up to the server level is deployed.

Businesses that are still growing while in this stage tend to do so by "globalizing" and as a result make fundamental operating changes. This affects the internal organizational structure. Sometimes, enterprise level mergers with another organization occur. Mergers and acquisitions result in assimilation of both business and IT infrastructures across multiple business areas.

IT infrastructures, however, are rarely pulled down and rebuilt, most changes tend to be piecemeal and produce incremental improvements. This is, however, the time when enter-

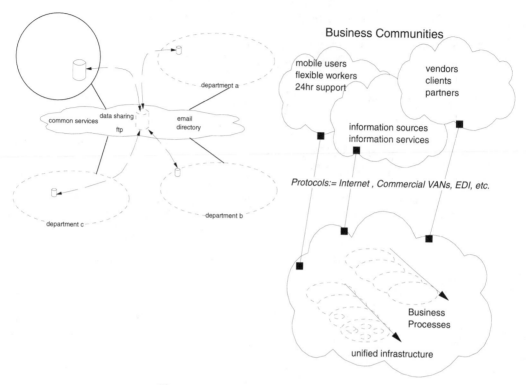

Figure 1.5: Stage 2 to Stage 3 transition

prises seriously consider outsourcing the whole of the service element of running a client/server environment.

1.3.3 Stage 3—Reconsolidation

While restructuring in Stage 2 is due to existing or emerging market pressures, in Stage 3 a deliberate process of restructuring is instigated. Business process re-engineering (BPR) has recently been one of the methodologies used to achieve this. (See Figure 1.5.)

BPR has had bad press, however—particularly with respect to its lack of strategic vision. The purposeful instigation of large-scale change, to gain some perceived business advantage is likely to continue well into the future—maybe under a different brand name.

Large-scale changes offer both opportunities and nightmares in equal doses at the infrastructure level. In its most rational form BPR is a proactive action to focus on the customer, the services or products offered, and the channels by which the customer is reached.

Case Study 1.1: Clash of Infrastructure Cultures

Two retail organizations combined their business operations through an equity merger. The organizations had a mutual need to increase market share as well as diversify in their markets. Hence they were complementary and willing partners. Advising consultants had studied the cost of integrating the technologies of the two organizations and these recommendations had been part of the merger negotiations. The underlying attitudes to technology however couldn't be more different:

Company A had used IT to achieve its market position within a few years and hence from the CEO to the bottom the view of IT was as an enabler for increasing performance. The emphasis on technical innovation and excellence had attracted talented engineers and designers to Company A. For example, the company had defined an internal architecture and IT was bought and integrated in a systematic way. The head of IT was a board member and understood all operational aspects of the business.

Company B was an old established family business that had belatedly used technology and treated IT as an overhead it had to bear. Methods of cutting the IT budget were a major point of debate. IT was represented at the board level by the finance director.

Soon after the merger became operational, the cultural differences regarding technology became apparent. A detailed review of systems by a working party from the two companies concluded that unification of business practices across the two organizations would require an almost total write-off of Company B's systems. Major development would be needed to encapsulate and migrate data from these systems.

The original consultant's conclusions were not based on reality. Company B's system inventory in fact consisted of an ad hoc collection of lowest-cost, point solutions. To build bridges between the two company's environments would have been prohibitively expensive in cost and time. (The consultancy however stuck to its conclusions.)

The initial phase of achieving operational transparency seemed doomed as the scale of unexpected costs and the level of development hit home. Company A decided to bite the bullet and to champion the changes necessary to move forward. This "uncompromising" view damaged the trust and working relationship that had been built up during the period leading to the merger.

Lessons

When information technology is culturally and operationally an intimate part of a business, the migration of IT is a key component of merger negotiations (on a par with financial, people and process factors).

Two cultural extremes in IT cannot be "bridged." The solution often "hurts" one or the other parties. The issue of technical culture and transition needs to be addressed during negotiations.

Companies have little redress when a consultancy makes a major error in judgement or is just incompetent, (other than maybe to get the fees back). More than one opinion is a likely but expensive solution.

BPR attempts to identify and simplify the way work is done from a process-centered viewpoint rather than a functional and departmental view. This cuts across traditional boundaries such as departments, functions, line-of-business, etc.

BPR is perceived to find its targets in people intensive parts of an enterprise. In investment banking, for example, the back office which consolidates and settles the trading done in the front office is a prime candidate: A lot of the work is individually executed, checked, corrected and re-checked.

BPR also highlights functions to which an enterprise cannot add value to be outsourced. Infrastructure management often falls into precisely this category.

Availability solutions for business critical systems, automation of backup, automation of asset management to manage net value and license costs are examples of key indicators of the maturity of an infrastructure that can meet the challenges of BPR.

Key processes such as problem management, change management and configuration management also become established and get followed as *best practice* in significant parts of the enterprise.

Table 1.2: Success Factors in Client/Server Deployment

Success Factor	Description
High level sponsorship	Projects which have a high-level business sponsor tend to be supported through any difficulties. Projects without sponsorship tend not to complete successfully. Regardless of sponsorship, business value to be derived from the project should be clear.
Mid level management buy-in	The buy-in of managers is also important. They are often at the forefront of operational changes within departments and as such need to champion a solution.
User participation	Users who will use the final product as key members of the development team ensure that users share in all aspects of development. Hence the users tend to own the solution long before deployment.
Infrastructure preparation	Knowledge of infrastructure implications on scaling up a client/server application as well as planning for infrastructure support ensures a smoother transition from development to production.
Risk management	Understanding the risks and their active management provides a forward thinking team, and reduces the number of crises that have to be managed. This leads to more productive teams as a side-effect.
Valued teams	Teams that are recognized by the users as valued contributors to their future business tend to take the effort to understand and examine actual user needs. This leads to closer cooperation with users and a better product.

The general dissatisfaction of users with a service organization has changed at this stage to either one of negotiating metrics such as service levels and strategies for cost escalation or to one of handing-off the whole problem to an outsourcer.

BPR often defines a new set of requirements of the infrastructure. Electronic connection with customers and suppliers is at the top of the list. Information received electronically is then expected to be integrated into the organization's processes. Information sent to a customer is expected to be consolidated from multiple internal sources.

1.3.4 Critical Success Factors in Client/Server Deployment

There are many organizations which embarked on the client/server bandwagon in the late 1980s and are now working within Stage 3 as described above and are embarking on a *fourth stage* of maturity. Each stage offers new models and associated building block technologies.

While a few surveys show disappointment with the client/server model, by and large, client/server technology is deemed to have delivered business benefits. A number of common threads seem to recur in the success stories, especially with the earlier stages (Stage 1 and 2) of deployment. These are summarized in Table 1.2.

1.4 Outsourcing the Infrastructure

The emergence of a single *internal* group responsible for the whole infrastructure is not uncommon. However other evolutionary directions for infrastructure management exist. These are in effect a variations on the theme of global consolidation of support groups:

- A trend towards *outsourcing* the operation and maintenance of the network and the systems components of infrastructure. Some organizations have outsourced the whole IT function to a single third party. The idea is to "off-load" the IT function altogether from development of new systems to support and maintenance of production systems. Others outsource part of the IT function such as just the support side and retain IT development. Support operations are often thought of as being a problem area by the IT function itself. IT heads and staff increasingly want to work with the operation, looking at improving its competitiveness rather than worrying about the minutiae of service delivery at the (low) infrastructure level of detail.

- A number of large enterprises have approached outsourcing by first concentrating diverse internal support groups into a distinct entity. This is then "sold" as a management buyout or to an outsourcing organization (or managed as a service by them). "Insourcing" guarantees better continuity of service (at least in the early months of a relationship). This is sometimes reinforced by some equity exchange—e.g., the client enterprise buys a stake in the "enlarged" outsourcing organization.

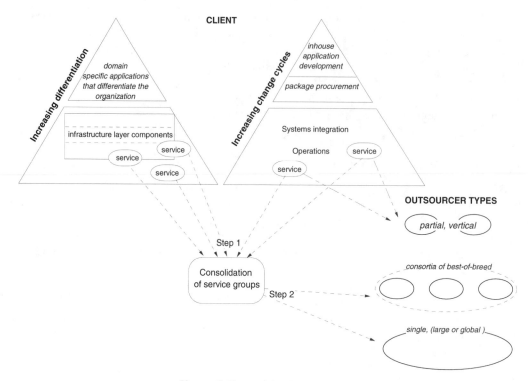

Figure 1.6: *Models of outsourcing*

- Another option open to very large client organizations is outsourcing to a consortia of service companies specifically created to manage the full spectrum of IT requirements of client organizations. This allows best-of-breed in each area of technical and management expertise to work for the client organization. The coordination function is likely to be complex.

These options are shown in Figure 1.6. The main rationale for choosing one of the above outsourcing options is that a business should concentrate on developing its core products and services and not be concerned with managing the technology and infrastructure issues. Year after year, more management attention is spent on technology and service issues such as service failure, security failures, etc.

A fundamental premise underpinning all forms of outsourcing is that the outsourced infrastructure (or at least the part that is outsourced) will have a period of stability—i.e.,

- The technology base will not drastically change.

- The *value* of the current infrastructure to the client will not be any less.

The responsibility for managing generic (office automation, etc.) and horizontal applications (e-mail, etc.) has also tended to move to outsourcing organizations. Outsourcer organizations are also considered especially good at managing PC-based application packages.

Whether it is the whole IT, from strategy to service operations, or just the service side, many enterprises are looking to outsource the future management of their IT infrastructure. Many of these clients are inclined to retain slimmed down, business-aware internal IT groups.

On the service side, just the traditional data center and mainframe operations, or wide area network connectivity may be outsourced, in other cases it may be just one of the systems environments (such as the PC environment).

1.4.1 Advantages and Disadvantages of Outsourcing the Infrastructure

Clearly, from a business viewpoint there are both advantages and disadvantages (to a client organization) in outsourcing the management of the IT infrastructure. Key advantages are:

- *Economies of scale*—An outsourcer able to use its size and market position in negotiating with suppliers and subcontractors in the delivery chain. The outsourcer's experience of the service in multiple sectors can be pooled and best practice developed for all the client's to benefit.

- *Off-load the development of key skills*—Key skills that are in short supply on the general labor market can be developed by the outsourcer—since their utilization across multiple client accounts can be planned well ahead. Acquisition and retention of similar skills by individual clients is often time-consuming and expensive, depending on demand.

- *Develop business knowledge*—Outsourcers look to long-term contracts (more than 10 years) which give them ample opportunity to form strong partnership relationship with each client. It also allows an outsourcer to invest in understanding the business's needs as they evolve at the client organization (if the client organization is willing to share sensitive business information).

- *Customer oriented support*—Outsourcers have a service culture that is often lacking within a client organization's internal service and support groups. Contracts based on service level agreements between the outsourcer and clients is often a means of quantifying the service received from an outsourcer.

- *Off-load cost management*—There has been a general trend in the last few years for costs related to infrastructure to escalate beyond expectations. At the same time, quality has been difficult to maintain. In many organizations senior management has had to take responsibility for bringing infrastructure-related costs under control. Outsourcing frees higher management in the client organization from infrastructure cost issues.

The advantages cited above also form the seeds of potential problems some time in the future. The main disadvantages from a client's point of view of outsourcing are described below:

- *Difficult to differentiate a service*—An outsourcer responsible for managing a client's infrastructure aims to provide the same minimum general level of service to all its clients. While big client accounts may be better resourced, the actual competence and skills brought to the table is more a function of the internal culture of the outsourcer than the culture of the client. Even where an outsourcer has acquired IT staff from the client, the outsourcer is not especially motivated to retain the brightest and the best talent that may have taken the client organization great effort to recruit and retain.

- *Support's remoteness from business strategy*—Businesses that have leveraged the use of IT to gain business advantage can point to the inter-relationship of IT and business strategies. The "post implementation" support of an IT strategy determines the success of a strategy downstream. How the client organization and the outsourcer communicate to make a strategy work is often developed in an ad hoc fashion. Clients in highly competitive industries often fear loss of confidentiality and are therefore inhibited from calling its outsourcers in as advisors in planning to implement a strategy.

- *Lock into an outsourcer*—The long terms that seem to be the norm in outsourcing contracts (10 to 25 years) often leaves the client few options but to continue in any stagnant relationship with an outsourcer. Long-term contracts essentially give an outsourcer the right to monopolize the way service is provided. The economics of IT provisioning is changing all the time, generally in favor of clients. The outsourcer clearly has the upper hand.

- *Risk of the outsourcing organization changing*—The nature of both the client and the outsourcer change over time and however comprehensive the contract, it is unlikely to cover all eventualities that are dangerous to a client. In particular, an outsourcer's core business interests changing, failing, being merged or being acquired by another player can pose real threats to a client.

The key lesson from existing cases of disillusionment is the same: loss of day-to-day control of IT infrastructure operations to an outside organization should be balanced by real *means* to correct future risk to the business. This could be done through a number of means—for example:

- Through safety mechanisms at the contractual level, such as a honeymoon period or continuous review and correction cycles being part of the service level descriptions.

- Through the ability to influence the business direction of the outsourcer as a significant shareholder or board level representation.

1.4.2 Strategic Brakes to Outsourcing

Outsourcing IT functions including infrastructure management has been a phenomenon that has been going on for several years. The level of satisfaction from clients has been mixed. Clients whose needs and expectations from IT have remained at a constant level before and following outsourcing are generally happy.

Clients who have assumed the ability and will of the outsourcer organization to manage change, to be innovative, to re-engineer, etc. (all with respect to the pre-outsourcing technology base) have not been happy.

Across many industries, IT and innovative use of technical infrastructure have allowed organizations, both small and big, to develop new businesses. These giant steps would have been impossible without some critical technology element. The retail industry in the UK and USA where IT has been instrumental in re-engineering the supply chain is a good example.

There is arguably a genuine *lock-step* between technology and process advances on the one hand and business level innovation on the other. The desire to help a business achieve competitive advantage through innovative use of IT is motivationally more likely to originate from within an enterprise, than from the account executive of an outsourcing organization.

Organizations that have outsourced their entire IT function are increasingly finding that they have lost all their brightest IT aware business planners and strategists. This concerns those who view a future where technological nimbleness is a necessary survival trait.

The vertical applications, (or at least the thinking behind them) that a organization uses to compete in any business domain has usually taken years to develop. The continuation of a line-of-business is likely to need continuing development and integration of existing business applications with data in other parts of an enterprise.

It has been unrealistic to assume that an outsourcer organization (even with knowledge acquired thorough influx of people from the client organization) can contribute more than basic maintenance functions for systems it has taken over. This is especially true during the early years of an outsourcer/client relationship.

Outsourcing the management of vertical applications therefore carries exceptional risks to client organizations that are dependent on technology providing an edge (both currently or in the future). Contrary to reported claims, there is currently a dearth of outsourcer organizations that can consistently meet the requirements of enterprise scale management of vertical applications.

Organizations which are also competitors are unlikely to share the same outsourcer. Even within a single organization certain aspects of the business may, by the very nature of the business, be un-outsourceable. The private banking arm of any Swiss bank, for example, is unlikely to let any global outsourcer manage the data storage which includes any information about its client accounts.

1.4.3 Trends Towards Outsourcing Business Processes

The outsourcing of other business processes are also possible in situations where economic reasons outweigh strategic ones. This is a continuing side-effect from downsizing that may

Case Study 1.2: Casual Outsourcing

A medium-size financial services retailer had successfully run PC support and maintenance, predominantly through using contractors from a commercial support organization. Yearly surveys showed that users were generally satisfied with the level of service they were getting.

Following a change in IT strategy (the first phase of which involved the deployment of a packaged application suite), the decision was taken to totally outsource desktop and server support.

The "incumbent" support organization made a bid which included the offer to absorb the client managers who were currently supervising the support contractors. This factor plus the attractive pricing model resulted in the organization getting a five year contract for all desktop and server support.

For six months or so, service continued at a satisfactory level. When the first applications using the new package solution started being deployed, service levels seen by end-users began to take a dive. Despite several attempts to fix the deterioration, in both service and relationship with the outsourcer, the client brought in an outsourcing expert to help it arbitrate a solution. The findings of the expert included:

(a) The service levels expected for each service from the outsourcer were not explicitly specified in the contract.

(b) The key processes of support were not defined, nor the interfaces for management reporting.

(c) The training of the support staff on the package technology of the new IT strategy was not specified.

(d) The pricing/cost model in the contract assumed a constant level of support with no provision for sudden peaks in demand (such as just after a new application is deployed).

(e) The absorption of the client's supervisory staff did not include any long-term incentives for them to stay. With a buoyant market the key staff had left within three months of the outsourcing contract.

In the end the only way to save the situation was either to terminate the contract or to redefine it in realistic terms.

Lessons:

Outsourcing deals should only be undertaken after serious consideration by both parties of the critical success factors. Outsourcing is not a cheap fix for escalating support costs, nor a method for "handing-off" risk.

The outsourcer is responsible for skill development, motivation and retention of all staff, including staff absorbed from the client organization. This responsibility should be specifically stated.

A client-outsourcer relationship is fundamentally different to a relationship with a subcontractor. Outsourcing is more than long-term "body-shopping." An unambiguous framework, including specific services or processes, levels of service, and projections should be part of the contract.

have already occurred or be occurring within an organization. The rationale for outsourcing business processes is very similar to outsourcing the IT infrastructure:

- Any process that becomes capital intensive, or with incremental support costs year after year.

- Any process that has little to do with newly defined or perceived core competencies.

- Any process that is common to all players in a given business sector is likely to be outsourced.

In the case of the process being generic to a business sector, major players in the sector sometimes form a mutually owned company to carry out the process.

The outsourcer for business processes is unlikely to be the current crop of outsourcers. This raises the possibility of different outsourcers for different layers of the business. The coordination of multiple outsourcers is a major management problem.

1.5 *The Evolution of "Infrastructure"*

Components currently regarded as infrastructure include operating systems, hosts, networks and database management systems. This is in fact a reflection of the structure of the current client/server applications developed over such an infrastructure.

Applications, even in the client/server era, still typically consist of large chunks of integrated code with limited use of *common* services. These applications have a task-specific view of data with the data being usable only by the application. Hence many functions are duplicated across many applications rather than as common services.

Future generations of client/server applications will be developed from an information-centric viewpoint. In other words, the data is carried in a form that is not application specific and is consumable by more than one application.

A precursor, at least in the conceptual sense, is the "document" in the emerging generation of Microsoft office automation products. The document is essentially a general mechanism for storing application data. Different applications—word-processors, spreadsheets, and drawing tools can operate and manipulate associated subsets of the data in a document.

A document is in fact a complex information transport structure. For such information containers to be universally appealing, simpler, self describing mechanisms are needed— some think object-oriented components fulfill this requirement.

An information-centric viewpoint drastically changes the structure of applications and the supporting infrastructure. This "evolutionary path" has obvious implications for infrastructure management at every level—technology, organizational, architectural and financial.

1.5.1 Traditional View of Infrastructure

Figure 1.7 shows the relationship between the "size" of the infrastructure and the level of "self-sufficiency" of applications. As more common services get pushed into the infrastructure, the self-sufficiency of the applications, decreases.

In the traditional view the network, the operating system, the hosts, database management systems and other network services are all treated as infrastructure. Applications are largely self-contained and expect only basic services from the infrastructure. These include file services, lookup services (such as name to address translation), and synchronized time.

Other services commonly supplied as a subsystem are the data management services including the database management system itself, data replication and data synchronization services.

As more and more of an enterprise's business applications begin to use a common technology base, the criticality of the infrastructure increases. In other words, if more and more eggs are packed into one basket then the protection of the basket becomes a strategic issue.

A common example is enterprise e-mail. Many organizations use e-mail implicitly in business processes without understanding the service characteristics needed from e-mail. When e-mail delivery fails or slows down, subsequently it is not merely a message that has failed to get through but a process that has failed.

1.5.2 Growing Depth of Infrastructure

In the next stage from the traditional viewpoint, we see generic services beginning to be treated as infrastructure.

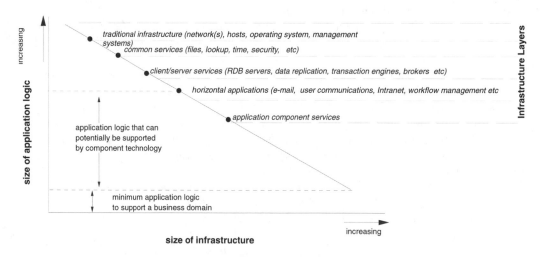

Figure 1.7: *Evolution of infrastructure*

Generic client/server services, described in Chapter 6, "The Architecture Client/Server and Intranet Systems," are other potential "members" of an extended traditional infrastructure layer—these include:

- Broker services which allow clients machines to find server machines.

- Process mappers which allow a complex sequence of server-based computation to be described (outside of the application logic).

- Transaction monitors that allow a computation to be extended over heterogeneous systems.

"Horizontal" applications are also used by multiple groups, starting with obvious ones such as e-mail, or a web and browser-based intranet become treated infrastructure. Less obvious horizontal applications such as document and image management systems, calendar and diary applications, data warehouse and associated front-end tools are all potential candidates to be included as infrastructure.

Business applications now see at the infrastructure level various applications and services useful in developing business solutions. Many organizations already install new products such as groupware and directory services in a form that is shareable.

The number of applications and the number of users the applications will reach will also increase as all parts of an enterprise get connected. This transition shown in Figure 1.8. More users and more applications spell more infrastructure management.

1.5.3 New Infrastructure

Future infrastructure will evolve from this ad hoc collection of services and applications. The way distributed applications behave in peer-to-peer interactions, in defining relationships with subordinates, and the way they process information, the mechanisms they use to distribute information, etc., all have the potential to be standardized.

In addition, a set of "building block services" will allow applications to consolidate and re-form information from many sources. Such an application architecture is already the reality in several cutting edge organizations ranging from utility companies to global investment banks.

Some observers think that applications in the near future will merely determine *context* and *process* and that all the components to build these will be available as component services at the infrastructure level.

Such standardization obviously has profound implications for infrastructure management. Figure 1.9 shows a possible way ad hoc services could consolidate into the infrastructure of the future.

The major challenge is in building an infrastructure management framework that can evolve to meet such future responsibility.

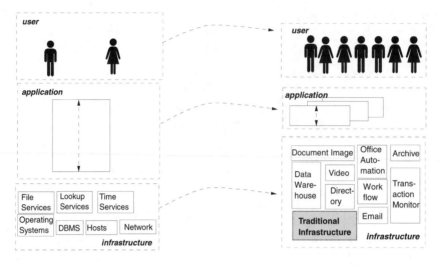

(a) Traditional View

(b) Transitional View

Figure 1.8: *Evolution of the extent of infrastructure*

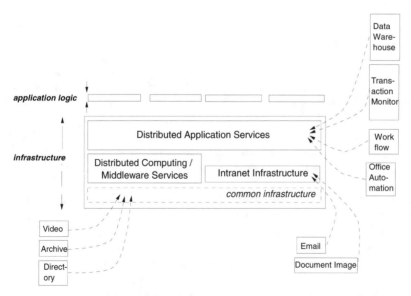

Figure 1.9: *Consolidation of ad hoc services into the new infrastructure*

1.5.4 Models for Viewing Infrastructure as a "Delivery System"

When the corporate infrastructure (of networks, systems, services and applications) is viewed as a *delivery system for the business solutions* it is undoubtedly a critical resource of the organization.

However, to achieve this position involves both IT people and business strategists working together to create such a view. Technologists rarely view infrastructure as a *system* of interdependent components. Similarly, the business users rarely appreciate the risks that the state of the infrastructure, resulting from a historical series of ad hoc decisions, imposes on their business plans and goals.

To develop a more strategic view requires technologists of the various disciplines to provide a unified *front* for the business. Far too often, businesses see fractious technology groups, each trying to protect its turf. This occurs both in crises and in the course of normal interactions.

The remainder of this chapter provides an overview of three models essential to developing such a strategic resource. These three models provide different perspectives of managing the infrastructure's life-cycle. Indeed, the remainder of this book can be viewed as an expansion of these three models:

- The Business model views managing an infrastructure in terms of a service business consisting of a set of generic business areas. This model drives the operational model for infrastructure management and its relationship to other parts of the organization.

- The Technology model views infrastructure management in terms of the technology framework required to execute the management function. This technology is predominantly software-based. The current generation of infrastructure management technology lags behind the needs of the technology of client/server applications. The technology model therefore has limitations for the more complex tasks in infrastructure management.

- The Composite model views infrastructure management in terms of the dynamics between technology, people, and process. Architecture provides a way of developing mechanisms for these inter-relationships. Overcoming the *deficit* of the technology base is another key role for architecture. An architecture approach also provides a roadmap into the future.

1.6 Business Model of Infrastructure Management

Infrastructure management is a complex but relatively self-contained function within IT. Viewing it as a logical business provides a model that is mappable to most enterprises.

The business of an infrastructure management group is to provide a well-defined set of IT services. The actual work done by an infrastructure management group is documented in a number of places, for example:

- *Management process definitions*—that define the operational procedures to manage typical activities handled by the group. These activities define the range of services provided to its clients.

- *Crisis blueprints*—that define operational procedures for *extraordinary* events that have an adverse effect on the clients. Such events are expected to be rare, (compared to normal service volume provided to clients). It is nevertheless a major area for planning.

- *Infrastructure project plans*—define specific pieces of work in terms of a sequence of sub-tasks, delivery expectations, manpower plans and costing.

All work of the business falls into one of these three categories—operational processes of the business, ongoing crisis scenarios, and projects. All work is done within the framework of teams—operational, crisis and project work can all be catered for.

The infrastructure management business's "internal throughput" is aligned to the life-cycles of the organizations' business activities and especially to the sub-cycles that govern their use of IT.

The infrastructure management business consists of a set of business *areas*. These define a functional split of responsibility. Some business areas are closely involved with end-users or clients. Others are intimately involved with the environment being managed and administered and have no direct contact with the clients. A third category of business areas refine and manage information from the preceding two.

The work of a modern business is defined by a number business processes. Business processes are triggered by the occurrence of various conditions. For example a change process is triggered by a change request from a client. A fault management process is triggered by a fault event being detected by the infrastructure management system.

Information flows between business areas, in the course of executing the business processes. The carriers of such information and its structure is also important, because they may be used in more than one business process.

The business model described here allows understanding and developing infrastructure management in terms of:

1. Key processes that define the work of the infrastructure management group. Examples are fault management and performance management.

2. "Information Containers" that flow between business areas in the course of the above processes being executed. Examples are change requests.

3. Interdependencies between business areas (and hence the interfaces between business areas).

4. By inference, the people skills needed to carry out infrastructure management tasks.

1.6.1 Basis of a Business Model

The Network Management Forum (NMF) is a consortium of vendors, standards makers and users active in the network management field. The original remit of the NMF was to promote OSI network management protocols and technology. Lately, the NMF has taken a proactive role in promoting more generic models that are relevant to both OSI and non-OSI viewpoints.

The NMF has defined a logical business model of network management which is applicable to an "average" organization—i.e., one that is relevant to most organizations (regardless of whether OSI protocols predominate in the organization).

Figure 1.10 represents an extension of the original NMF model to cater to the new areas covered by the current definition of infrastructure. It defines a number of business areas with

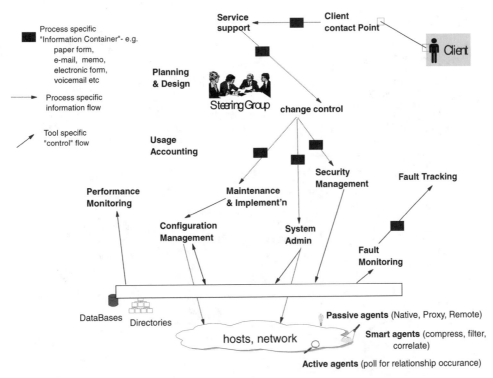

Figure 1.10: Network Management Forum's business model of network management

processes connecting to them. The processes carry information relevant to the process. This model is discussed in detail in Chapter 5, "Organizational Aspects."

1.7 A Technology Model of Infrastructure Management

The business model provides a perspective in terms of business areas and processes. The technology model provides a perspective in terms of the technology components and their inter-relationships. Technology components are used by the business areas in executing infrastructure management processes. Technology relates to the physical and logical information flows.

Management information (in terms of management parameters to change, parameters to read and occurrence of events) is carried in data structures implicit to a management protocol.

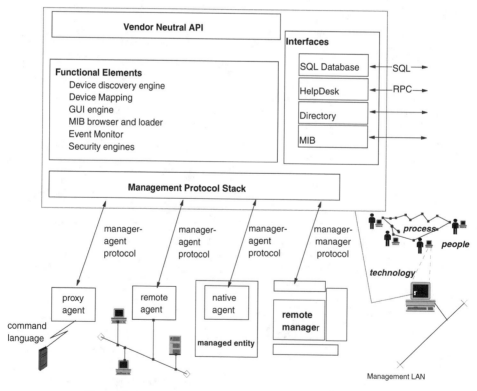

Figure 1.11: *Technology model of infrastructure management*

The technology model for network systems and application management is based on the same general model consisting of a manager station, agents and a communication protocol between the two. Figure 1.11 shows some of these relationships.

Control information flows from the manager station to agents, while status information flows from agents to stations. This is in effect a master-slave relationship. Protocols, however, play the *central* role in this management paradigm. This is because the agent-station model is a closely coupled, asymmetric model with distinct, *rigid* roles for the station and the agent. Some leeway is afforded by making the functionality of the agents more complex:

- Agents which can report on exceptions against a set of baseline conditions configured by the station.

- "Smart" agents that can process, correlate and filter events before reporting consolidated event information to the station.

The efficacy of managing different environments such as remote offices hinge on the efficiency afforded by the protocol. This in turn is related to how much of the work can be distributed to agents.

SNMP has become the de facto standard in network management largely because it is simple to implement. Simplicity as a criterion is contradictory with the notion of a protocol's application in a wide range of situations demanding security, efficiency, functional richness, and so on.

SNMP has on the face of it, limited use in systems and application management. The evolution of network management into infrastructure management, therefore, has been driven by different protocols for different purposes:

- RPC for its functional richness.

- SQL for its data access efficiency.

- CMIP or SNMPv2 for their security and bulk data transfer efficiency.

1.7.1 Role of Protocols in Infrastructure Management

The slow take up of CMIP and SNMPv2 has meant that SNMP based management covers more than network devices such as hubs, bridges and routers.

The SNMP protocol stack and MIB extensions have been widely adopted by high-end host systems (characterized by RISC-based workstation and servers). SNMP MIB variables define not only hardware elements but subsystems such as disk drives and interfaces.

In addition, represented at the operating system level are processes, swap space, network file systems, etc. Most of these management variables exist at the enterprise specific level of the MIB standard and are therefore "non-standard." De facto standards such as the Host Resources MIB, on the other hand, are being supported by several major hardware manufacturers.

The existence of toolkits for building SNMP proxy agents, see Chapter 8, has also allowed the SNMP technology to be adopted in layers above the operating system level, into the application layer itself. There are several successful examples of critical applications being monitored using SNMP.

The ability to integrate information from the device level, through host environments to application entity levels is extremely powerful. It allows *vertical systems views* to be built—for example, showing the subset of computing and network resources used to deliver an application to a specific business area.

SNMP is inefficient in bandwidth terms and totally insecure for adoption as a comprehensive mechanism to control and monitor security sensitive components at the application layer. It is also insecure to control hosts. Hence its use in software components is largely constrained by its simplicity and the safest option is to confine SNMP to providing heartbeat and alarm information from these higher level components.

The inadequacies of SNMP has led to the definition of SNMPv2 as catering to bandwidth and security issues. Availability of stacks and toolkits for SNMPv2 is still in its infancy. The more major constraint is the need of having to support both SNMP and SNMPv2 for compatibility with management platforms.

Toolkit based functionality, see Chapter 8, to build rule-based filters also allows the building of "smarter" SNMP based agents that report only on an exceptional basis against an arbitrary criteria. Proxy agent technology also allows non-SNMP devices, such as multiplexers or modems to send event information to SNMP stations.

SNMP, including SNMPv2, has little to offer as an *information transport* for distributed computing purposes—where the transported data may be used by diverse application components.

While SNMP predominates in the commercial world, OSI's CMIP is prevalent in large Telecom, some defense and government organizations and in some manufacturing related businesses. CMIP is undoubtedly powerful, however, its widespread adoption is constrained by the complexity of the framework and the need for a full 7 layer OSI stack.

The relatively small market for OSI management applications and shortage of application development skills to use the power of its object oriented management information structure show little signs of abating.

CMIP (transported both over OSI protocols and TCP/IP) will therefore continue to have an important and probably slow-growing niche in these markets. SNMPv2 is more likely to be adopted as the successor protocol to SNMP where security and efficiency requirements override simplicity as a criterion of choice. Recent events in the standardization of SNMPv2 has cast doubts on this projected role.

The Desktop Management Task Force (DMTF) desktop management interface (DMI) provides yet another information structure, *Management Information Format* (MIF), to carry asset type information and other proprietary information.

This is targeted at the largest population base attached to a network—namely, the Intel microprocessor-based platforms, networked printers, the network interface cards in peripherals such as scanners and mass storage devices. The DMI specification covers other product types—management consoles, management applications, hardware and software subsystems.

RPC is the de facto standard in client/server–based management applications. For example, more than one top end SNMP Remote Monitoring (RMON) agent provides the option to transport over RPC real-time monitoring information (to server-based applications). These applications process the raw data received from the RMON groups, display and archive the data. This is far more efficient, secure and scalable that using SNMP.

RPC is also the protocol of choice in database synchronization. Global infrastructure management architectures require management databases of event, configuration, ticketing and resolution information to be maintained globally to a known level of consistency (see Chapter 6). The database technology used in conjunction with a management platform is a strategic decision. One of the reasons for this is that one or more SQL based infrastructure management applications are likely to be developed in-house.

1.7.2 Relationships in the Technology Model

Figure 1.11 defines the relationships between the environment being managed and other components of the management paradigm. The technology model of infrastructure management is defined by a relatively small number of relationships. Some of these are examined below.

Agent with the Managed Entity. Architecturally, agents are meant to have a core set of functionality plus "value added" functionality. This core functionality in the case of SNMP is defined by MIB II compatibility.

An agent may be embedded into the software of the managed entity, in which case the interface between the agent's MIB data structures and its relationship to the managed entity's internal variables is not distinguishable. This internal interface may be procedural, which in more complex entity architectures map to internal inter-process communication mechanisms between the agent process and the entity process.

A special case of this is the so-called *proxy* agents which allow ad hoc enterprise specific MIB variables to be defined and procedures to be attached to the variables. These procedures then "translate" to and from the native protocol of the entity being managed. This native protocol could, for example, be a scripting language such as Perl or a command line language such as Digital's DCL—in any case, one that is specific to the entity.

Proxy agents allow non-SNMP entities to be managed from an SNMP station and hence to participate in an SNMP based management scheme. Proxy agent toolkits that support SNMPv2 are also beginning to appear.

Agents are traditionally viewed largely as passive components, pre-defined structures resident in one place. Passive agents therefore have a fixed functionality allowing specific MIB variables to be read, written to, or to flag pre-defined trap conditions. In all cases the communication is with a station entity.

An *autonomous agent* periodically polls external entities using the entities' native protocol, processing the result of the poll against baseline conditions with which it has been configured. It reports exceptions to this baseline. This is a class of agents that is especially needed in large complex environments. Other simpler, autonomous agents may check on the *liveliness* properties of entities, such as the ability of a database engine to execute a sample SQL script, or at the network level to respond to a TCP/IP "ping." The results produced by autonomous agents are sent to the manager station using a management protocol or using RPC.

Mobile agents have "no fixed abode" and may be distributed from a server to temporarily reside on a node, executing some audit function or search criteria and then de-commission from the node with the result. It is for example useful to build some audit agents in this way. The delivery mechanism for mobile agents and their results is independent of low-level management protocols such as SNMP or RPC. Instead, application protocols such as privacy enhanced e-mail may be used. This greatly improves the reach of such agents.

Agent with Station. This is briefly addressed in Section 1.7.1. This is a management protocol such as SNMP or for efficiency RPC may be used. The structure of information carried in RPC is ad hoc and only the participating entities are likely to be able to make use of it. Information carried in SNMP, although much simpler, can be understood by any SNMP station.

Protocol gateways that provide translation before delivery to the station is another emerging possibility. This is driven for example by the need to deliver management information from managed data networks in CMIP dominated Telecom provider's environment to SNMP based client sites.

Agent with Dual-Role Agent. The agent-station model defines a single level hierarchy. When a large population of agents need to be managed, the problem of scaleability becomes apparent.

To manage large numbers of agents requires a modification of the simple agent-station model. A successful solution has been to define a second level in the hierarchy through dual-role agents. To the traditional agent it looks like a station and to the traditional station it looks like an agent.

This scaling agent can then be defined with functionality not possible with the simpler model. This is described in greater detail in Chapter 8.

With Management Processes. The information flow between agents and its hierarchically higher entities (station or intermediary agent) is largely determined by the configuration of event thresholds (for event notification) and the number of read/write commands sent to the agents. The interface between the agent-station model and the process-people model is of some importance. This is treated in greater detail in Chapter 6.

Raw information (events and replies to read commands) enter network management applications for further processing or display on GUI based representation or for compression, storage and archive, etc.

Automation technology can take raw information in event notifications and provide the linkage to infrastructure management processes. Automation involves filtering against a list of expected events. When an event on the expected list is found, re-packaging of the event information takes place for input to the relevant management process.

Another function of automation tools is to package information into human process-able forms, and to use these consistently in human interaction in the course of network management process execution. An example is the generation of a *trouble ticket* when a fault event is received from an agent. Hence, trouble tickets, change requests, change orders, or security alerts may all contain information that originated from or is destined for the management framework.

1.7.3 State of Management Technology

As managed infrastructures become more complex and user expectations harden, the inadequacies of vendor offerings in areas ranging from management platforms to applications becomes more evident.

To lessen the complexity of the management framework itself, the framework has to become more distributed. The essence of distribution is that the structure and content of management information should be the center of focus rather than the task-oriented management applications.

Each application (even from the same vendor) has taken its own view of information structure. Some attempts are currently under way to define an object-based common repository standard. This is being attempted with a view to vendor dominance rather than *common good* and is therefore several years away.

The basic need is to be able to take management information from any source, transform it in real-time into any application specific form and define common services to distribute the information. Many useful services such as routing from any source producer of data to any destination consumer of data, data translation, filtering, correlation, etc. can be provided in a platform-independent manner.

Some platform vendors have second generation offerings in the pipeline that begin to address distribution of data and computing resources. There are still many areas of distribution not addressed by vendors. Some of the more essential areas, especially for survival of large infrastructures, are discussed in Chapter 6, "Architecture of Client/Server Intranet and Systems."

Network management and system tool vendors continue to follow different drummers. Increasingly, these tools sit side by side at the infrastructure business process level. An organization has finite limits to the number of consoles it can train for—resulting in the under-use of most tools and their eventual disposal. This is good for vendors, bad for consumers.

Even within the sub-field of network management, the degree of integration between tools and hosting platforms is very basic—sometimes to the point of being pointless. Unfortunately, some of the dominant vendors of management technology have little interest in listening to user requirements that don't subscribe to their "marketectures."

If history is to repeat itself, this points to a major *paradigm shift* in the near future. Meanwhile, architecture, innovation and a systems approach are the only weapons available to architects and managers having to cope with large complex environments.

1.8 A Composite Model of Infrastructure Management

Looking at the field of infrastructure management from the single perspective of technology has neither led to best utilization of the technology nor provided the full benefit to the organization. The reasons include:

- Linkage between the management framework (of agents, platforms and protocols) and the people involved in the management function is not often designed. Issues include getting the right skills and developing organizational structures for teams to work well.

- Linkage between the management framework and the management processes is similarly not designed. Issues include how and where in a raw event's "path" automation should be applied.

- Deploying infrastructure management technology without considering the people who use it and without defining basic service processes provides advantage only to a certain point.

Figure 1.12 shows infrastructure management as an intersection of people, process and technology facets. Such a model helps to highlight the mutual interdependency of these three areas.

Important components are shown outside each circle within this facet. For effective infrastructure management these three facets must be aligned to the needs of the business users being supported, the nature of the organization's business and with each other.

The key processes in infrastructure management are relatively well documented, and include *Fault* and *Change* management. People operate these processes. There is, therefore, an iterative relationship between processes and people—processes may have to be redesigned for available people to perform efficiently or people may have to be re-skilled to make processes more performant.

Infrastructure management tools and applications underpin the people and process facets. These tools may also have a constraining effect on people and processes. Key among constraining influences is the fact that infrastructure management is, in fact, an amalgam of three distinct "cultures" of networks, systems and applications.

Even within a single area such as network management, the lack of any data engineering standards results in each tool vendor inventing proprietary data architectures.

On the technology-process front, therefore, careful design needs to be done on common database tables, common trouble ticket storage and key formats, etc.

Infrastructure management architecture plays the role of aligning three facets of process people and technology. Its effect is most potent at the points where at least two of these facets intersect. Hence the design of physical frameworks with specific properties such as resilience and high security are problems for an architect to solve.

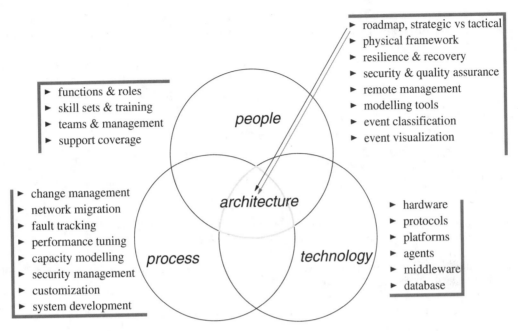

Figure 1.12: *Infrastructure management = architecture + people + process + technology*

1.8.1 The People Facet

Processes can only operate as well as the people who operate them. Whenever people get together for a specific purpose, organizational structures are formed. With maturity, *organizational cultures* or a shared value system can be encouraged. If managed well this culture leads to adding value, to innovation, to pulling together in crisis. This team effort is the essence of people management in an infrastructure management group.

Many organizations have strong remnants of the mainframe operations culture. This is often not characterized by a user facing or service-oriented approach. Since at least part of the infrastructure management group usually co-existed with this culture at one time, little time may have been spent on planning changes appropriate to integrated infrastructure management.

Achieving an appropriate work structure within the political realities of the organization is often complicated by:

- Existence of multiple "management" groups. Each with responsibility for one area of the infrastructure, or only for a small part of the infrastructure. Each may be under different reporting lines.

- Existence of multiple cultures with irreconcilable views and priorities on service provision, investment levels, training programs, etc. to be applied to the management function.

- Parts of network operation may be outsourced. This is usually accompanied by mismatched levels of service skills of the outsourcer and that of the internal management capability. This leads to service variance.

- For various reasons low morale, low skill levels and low service quality.

Because infrastructure management staff play such a central role in the management of IT delivery, several personnel policies specific to infrastructure management staff is likely to be needed:

- Establishing an on-call principle as part of the job contract. Managing round the clock in 7 x 24 hour patterns is becoming the norm.

- Skill based re-numeration to encourage re-skilling on a continuous basis and to limit poaching by rival organizations.

- Special security practices to ensure that the people most positioned to damage IT delivery are "risk-managed."

People in the infrastructure management function are responsible for negotiating with and managing people on several levels—these include:

- Setting, reviewing and monitoring Service Level Agreements (SLAs) with clients.

- Managing external supply chains—services, vendor support, outsourcers, on which the function may be dependent to deliver its own services to the business.

A management-style appropriate to process orientation of the group needs to be developed. Achievement is more likely due the "cross-functional" (network, systems, security, application knowledge) team effort rather than just individual expertise.

This requires new ways of assessment and valuing work done by the group. Given the strategic importance of infrastructures to application delivery, a steering group of business users and line management is key to keeping the evolution of the management services in line with business changes. Steering of the infrastructure is often subsumed to IT steering for the organization.

1.8.2 The Process Facet

The second facet in the composite model of infrastructure management is that of process. Complex infrastructures require standardized ways of doing things, otherwise quality variance occurs when different people do the same job.

Case Study 1.3: Attracting Top People

A company in the fashion design and consultancy field saw the concentrated use of IT allowing it to leapfrog its competition in delivering its services on a global scale. The strategy required both a high quality team of dedicated IT professionals as well as high quality service support. The IT design capability however would have a realistic lifetime of only 18 to 24 months with the company. Technical consultancy would then be needed only on an ad hoc basis.

The alternatives were to outsource the initial design to a technical consultancy or to attract a top technical team. After a short period of discussion with technical consultancies there was a strong feeling that all of the technical consultancies did not represent the fashion sector and would be likely to disseminate the company's innovative ideas to gain a foothold in the sector. It was felt that this was also likely to happen before the company could start to gain advantage from it.

The company moved to explore the second alternative by commissioning a "head-hunter" to find a senior IT manager. From a shortlist, a senior manager from investment banking seemed the likeliest fit to the company's needs.

The company defined its vision in full as well as its willingness to set up the new IT function as a separate operating entity (with its own profit center). It could after a period of 24 months begin to offer vertical IT consultancy in the field as well as continue to provide both technical consultancy and IT support services to the company.

The company discovered that the manager was looking for a change of pace and would be willing to bring over a core team that provided all the skills needed for the early phases of the work. The remainder of the team would be built up over a period of 6 months. The core team would have equity share in the new company.

Lessons

When going into new areas like IT, identify a real expert to take responsibility for recruiting IT skills. Look for clusters of skills or expertise rather than just individuals.

Look to these skills in areas where delivery and application of IT is highly valued (such as investment banking).

Provide both short-term and long-term incentives for good IT people to be attracted, grow and contribute within its culture.

Since infrastructure areas such as networks constantly evolve through addition and moves of network components and people, a protocol is needed to control how any change is undertaken. This is the essence of change management—probably the most important process in infrastructure management. Most organizations that have been the victims of catastrophic network failure, for example, have traced the origins of the problem back to unauthorized or unsafe change practises.

Another key process is the fault management process. Many infrastructure management groups have invested heavily in monitoring their network and systems environments. Yet when a fault is detected there is no explicit process to manage its resolution. The same types of faults end up being handled differently by different people.

Processes are initiated on explicitly defined conditions being recognized (e.g., a type of request being received at a helpdesk, a problem being detected by a monitoring framework, and so on) and are terminated when an explicitly defined sequence of activities is performed:

- Company structures and politics of group rivalry.

- Groups with intersecting operational responsibilities.

- The company structure itself in terms of autonomy of business units, for example, in procuring IT services.

The existence of explicit processes allows the measurement of their effectiveness in terms of service quality and productivity (efficiency). Metrics allow users to understand the work of the group. They also need to be established before targets for improvement can be set and/or achieved.

Moving from a functional to a process model highlights the need to have backups if the process's underpinning mechanisms fail. For example, if the ticketing system fails for any period of time, a fault management process can come to a standstill, since all relevant information is carried in the tickets. Process recovery in the event of failure of the supporting mechanisms is a key part of architecting the processes.

This architecture needs to provide resilience at the physical level as well as alternative, manual implementations of the process. This may in reality only be invoked in a contingency site following a major disaster at the primary site.

Process architecture requires knowledge about the pattern of demand for the process in terms of:

- Volumes that need to be handled over the management framework.

- Time-of-day related variations on the pattern.

- Time-expectations for various stages of the process's execution.

- Diversity of what the process has to handle in terms of distinctions in input.

- Exceptions it has to handle in input.

1.8.3 The Technology Facet

The technology facet is the most familiar of the different areas of the composite model. The marketing of management technology by major vendors has focused the minds of line managers on how the technology can help them manage systems and networks for which they are responsible.

Infrastructure management technology may be defined in terms of functional components such as the hosting hardware, management platforms, protocols, agents, databases and graphical user interfaces.

The platforms currently defined by the market for network and systems management, respectively, vary to the point that they have very little in common. A key decision is from which of these platforms the management of applications should be undertaken.

Some technology components are strategic in nature, in that their impact is long term and persist beyond the point of its specific usage in a management framework. A prime example of this is the database technology. Information in the database has multiple usages during its lifetime, by different management processes and applications.

Moreover, databases have to be actively administered if they are not to become unstable. This in turn implies that the relevant skills are needed in the organization. Once skills are available database applications can be developed fairly easily. Several major network management platforms don't allow a choice of database and several other management platforms don't have an interface for a relational database.

Other strategic technologies are the host platform and operating system—both of which require administration skills. Different organizations will consider different components to be strategic. For example one may decide to standardize on SNMP, while another may prefer the flexibility from having multiple protocols which together can fulfil the inadequacies of SNMP.

Infrastructure managers are constantly having to make decisions about buying management applications and other technology without having the opportunity to evaluate these in depth. An internal scoring system for application and equipment selection is an essential tool to be developed by each organization. The criteria used is often tied in with realities in different organizations. In Chapter 5, "Processes in Infrastructure Management," a staged method for selecting equipment is developed.

An area at the forefront of many buying decisions is the obsolescence factor. By and large, new technology is waiting to replace current technology choices in six to twelve months rather than the familiar three to five years. Planning for obsolescence includes examining how components may be de-coupled as much as possible, so that replacement at one point does not lead to changes at many other points.

Most major network and systems management platform vendors are finding ways to increase and maintain market share by making proprietary technologies attractive to the line mangers responsible for infrastructure management. The general trend towards reduced software product development cycles has resulted in vendors actively selling the benefits before the product is shippable.

Not getting pulled into vendor "marketectures," and evaluating the risk of "waiting out" until an upgrade or a new feature has been actually proven in the field is one of the disciplines that is ideally developed in this era of rapid change.

The reason for caution is that changes to the infrastructure management framework is probably just as dangerous as ad hoc changes to the managed environment. This is especially true if the management framework and the managed environment are closely coupled topologically.

Finally, there are classes of applications and technology which can play the role of *enabling integration* between diverse platforms or environments and a class of applications that enables the automation of processes.

These application classes are not always differentiated from the mainstream of management application, with the result that full use is not made of these powerful tools. For example, ticketing applications can be used much more effectively when their use is customized to automating the workflow in a specific process, i.e., the process is designed first and then mapped to the application.

Tools are likely to be developed by an infrastructure management group to fulfill inadequacies in the tools market. The skills and environment to achieve such development needs to be attracted to the group.

1.8.4 The Architecture Facet

An infrastructure management architecture provides the roadmap for developing the management framework. It deals with a number of concerns around the critical role of the infrastructure management to the delivery of business services over it.

Of these, survival of infrastructure management function in scenarios of component failure is probably foremost. Other issues are managing a large number of nodes, security, tools to understand traffic changes that occur with application mixes changing.

An infrastructure management framework is itself a network of systems and applications. It is essential to separate this framework from the managed network. The industry is full of anecdotes about how network and systems management tools that could have saved a crisis situation became unusable because their protocols could not reach the points that needed to be controlled.

A contingency framework for out-of-band management of the network is needed for situations where the infrastructure management framework itself fails, say in the event of a major disaster. This second framework usually uses a terminal access protocol via a connection to a serial port on network devices. This is especially relevant to managing remote sites, where loss of *in-band* management connectivity cannot be fixed until device replacement can be arranged for the site.

As the number of points from which information may be gathered increases, the problems of dealing with large populations of event sources increases. These problems include:

- How a large population of agents can be configured and re-configured in the light of systems failures or the failure of the infrastructure management framework.

- Filtering event outputs, rate limiting, etc. to stop network traffic being an excessive overhead.

The current state-of-the-art is still defined by the agent-station model, which while simple in concept does not scale in large or complex environments. In effect this has led to infrastructure management architectures having to be built over the simple agent-station "building block."

One of the reasons that event sources are proliferating is because agents are being deployed to report events from the operating system and application levels in addition to the device management role originally envisaged. The take-up of agent technology at the operating system and application layers has highlighted security concerns over the simple agent-station approach.

Foremost is how an agent may authenticate the source of commands to it and how to secure the integrity of information in control streams to agents. Again, infrastructure management architecture is needed to build solutions.

Remote node management is another area where security and bandwidth concerns exist. Increased intelligence is required to filter events at local agents, forwarding only selected conditions to the primary management site. Managing a large number of remote sites requires an architectural framework for event collection, remote configuration, dynamically redefining filtering criteria, etc. Information engineering outputs from architecture role include:

- The classification of events by severity levels.

- Combined patterns of events that intelligent agents need to match against.

- Threshold values to set baselines for remote monitoring.

As the managed environment becomes complex, change management over existing classifications occur over shorter life-cycles. At a certain size of the "event volume," automated tools are needed to define and propagate these changes. Some of the other areas where architected solutions are needed are summarized below:

- While SNMP is a de facto standard for network management, there still are significant population of devices which cannot be managed or monitored using this protocol. Several organizations have chosen, for various historical reasons, multiple management platforms. The integration of such devices into a single framework is of considerable importance.

- When "vertical" systems views (for example, the portion of the network relating to service to a specific business in the organization), are needed there is a role for an abstract entity to describe the required views. This may be achieved by relational-joins across multiple-event databases Another model is of an entity that collects and processes information from non-SNMP environments, diverse management tools and platforms that may be in place.

- This "integration" of information from heterogeneous environments and platforms is increasingly achieved through a class of software called middleware. Given the resistance of the major platform vendors to make their respective applications and tools to *interwork* across platforms (through the ability to exchange of information), middleware has a major role to play in providing the low-cost solution for such integration.

- When events such as a fault alarm occur, or performance thresholds get triggered, it is useful to map the event to different contexts. This allows the visualization of any event across different contexts such as security effects, business area(s) affected, effect on the status of contingency resources, and so on. For such contextual maps to

Case Study 1.4: Impact of Automating without Architecture

A large trading company with facilities and a presence in 140 locations worldwide re-designed and consolidated its help desks to two centers.

As part of its consolidation it deployed a ticketing system for automating helpdesk calls. This was the result of a project undertaken by the vendor of the ticketing tool. The project approach followed a classical model—with phases for requirements definition, prototyping, piloting and finally, deployment.

Consolidation resulted in a large volume of calls into the helpdesks. Each call was logged using the ticketing system and routed to teams supporting different areas of technology. Each ticket was subsequently closed or remained open until escalated solutions were executed. The ticketing system also provided the means for providing feedback to the callers.

Following the consolidation, a number of major IT system upgrades occurred. This introduced sudden peaks in the number of calls to the helpdesk following each change. These calls could not be classified by the routing system. These tickets tended to become ignored while other more "tangible" problems were dealt with.

In other words, problems that were not recognized by the system were implicitly given lower priority.

As a result the helpdesk could not effectively cope with the demands for support following any change to the environment. The ticketing system was designed in such a way that it could not be easily modified for supporting new technology bases.

The affected users associated the service problems as being the direct consequence of the helpdesk consolidation.

The ticketing system was seen to be cumbersome by the helpdesk staff and different groups gradually began to use the ticketing system differently. The utility of the ticketing system is therefore set to diminish.

Lessons

While a ticketing project can be defined and executed competently, the wrong problem can easily be solved. Automation should be with respect to processes delivered by the helpdesk (such as problem reporting, change management, IT ordering, etc.) and not the helpdesk function itself.

Both large scale changes and combinations of minor changes are a natural part of the life-cycle of a client/server environment. Changes to a production environment need to take into account the impact on the helpdesk and its management to ensure that the helpdesk is not caught off-guard.

be dynamically drawn on a relevant event occurring, a knowledge representation is required of the relationship between a set of possible events and a set of contexts in terms of systems, network components, applications, and business groups.

1.9 Books for Further Reading

Bancroft, Nancy H. *Implementing SAP R3* (How to Introduce a Large System into a Large Organization). Prentice-Hall, 1996.

Butler, Janet G. *Mainframe to Client/Server Migration* (Strategic Planning Issues and Techniques). Computer Technology Research, 1996.

Cronin, Mary J. *Internet Strategy Handbook* (Lessons from the New Frontiers of Business). Harvard Business School Press, 1996.

Enck, John. *A Managers Guide to Multivendor Networks.* CBM Books, 1997.

McConnell, John. *Managing Client/Server Environments* (Tools and Strategies for Building Solutions). Prentice-Hall, 1996.

Scheer, August Wilhelm. *Architecture of Integrated Information Systems* (Foundations of Enterprise Modelling). Springer Verlag, 1992.

Vaskevitch, David. *Client Server Strategies* (A Survival Strategy for Corporate Reengineers). IDG Books Worldwide, 1995.

2

Strategic Tools for Infrastructure Management

Areas covered in this chapter

- Success factors in deploying infrastructure management

- Use case and actor model of infrastructure management processes

- Use of risk management as a discipline to control the development and operation of client/server infrastructure

- Gap analysis as a technique to relationship between a current state and an ideal state or "best practice" state

- Using simulation tools and results in gap analysis

- Proactive use of financial criteria in infrastructure management

- Importance of business continuity planning and data in infrastructure recovery strategies

- Importance of "user awareness" and how users "consume" IT resources and services

A client/server infrastructure consists of networks, hosting systems, application services and management frameworks. Such an infrastructure has a complex life-cycle. Successful infrastructure deployment depends on the understanding and management of this life-cycle.

An infrastructure's life-cycle is determined by the interaction between the various layers of the infrastructure as well as the relationships between the applications using the infrastructure:

- Each "layer" of the infrastructure has a finite capacity to provide services to a higher layer.

- At the same time each higher layer requires a minimum level of service from the lower layer services in order to be considered "performant."

- The relationship between the various layers change over time. This makes parts of the infrastructure incapable of delivering the required levels of service, over time.

- The relative requirements of applications using the infrastructure changes over time.

Seemingly minor changes have profound effects in service delivery. The main reason for this is that the infrastructure is a highly "leveraged" structure. There are many service delivery dependencies in existence at any given time in a common infrastructure that supports many applications. Hence changes in one part can inadvertently impact performance in another.

Managing the life-cycle of the infrastructure requires management tools that allow re-alignment of the infrastructure with the changing world around it. This chapter defines some of the tools to manage the infrastructure's lifecycle. These definitions should be viewed as "strawman" models. The strawman is essentially a prototype from which enterprise specific tools can be designed:

- Experience with life-cycles of multiple client/server deployment point to some general rules for success and common barriers to success. These points should drive the planning of client/server based projects and building client/server infrastructures.

- Process engineering is a tool to examine and re-align the management group's activities with the goals of the organization. Process engineering is applicable in life-cycle management on several fronts. To be successful processes should have a precise view on meeting user requirements.

- Risk management is a tool to forecast events that can impact a project or an existing infrastructure and then manage the events' impact in terms of time, quality and costs aspects.

- Contingency planning is a planning tool to ensure that the business does not stop in the event of catastrophic events such as a natural disaster or a terrorist bomb.

- Gap analysis is a tool to focus on the needs of the infrastructure relative to wider goals of the business or in terms of business benefit. Associated with gap analysis are the tools to collect data for analysis.

- Financial management of the infrastructure ensures that investment and benefit from the infrastructure is seen within the context of financial best practice.

- User awareness is an information based tool which allows the infrastructure management organization to understand the operational use of the infrastructure by the business and to maintain sync with business changes affecting infrastructure.

These tools help to identify a reference point in the current "alignment" of technology, people, processes and architecture—and to use that to establish a roadmap to manage the changing infrastructure.

2.1 Deploying Client/Server Infrastructures

Infrastructures exist to support applications delivery. Many aspects of the life-cycle of an infrastructure for client/server and intranet-based applications is determined by factors that are unrelated to the infrastructure, its technology, or even the applications and systems deployed over the infrastructure.

There are relatively well-known barriers to successful deployment into production of enterprise-wide infrastructures for client/server based applications.

Where deployment has been successful, a number of simple rules seems to have been consistently applied. This section looks at both barriers and success factors of deployment and provides a checklist tool to manage the progress of client/server applications and infrastructures to a production status.

2.1.1 Barriers to Successful Deployment

Studies of client/server application deployments across several organizations show a number of key service and infrastructure technology oriented barriers. Barriers also exist for successful deployment of infrastructures:

- Processes and service organization structures to manage the infrastructure end-to-end (desktop to server) are still not widely available, even on a departmental level. The inability to develop infrastructure management services on an enterprise scale is a strategic barrier. This leads to serious questions about availability and maintenance of the infrastructure that support business critical systems.

- Departments within an enterprise have often made separate technology decisions. Different departments also have different generation infrastructures, realized from different base technologies. Building a client/server infrastructure that spans different generations and types of technology requires specialist skills and considerable budgets for internal standardization.

- Building client/server applications that span different computing technologies such as mainframes, packaged systems and in-house applications requires application architecture and development skills that are in short supply.

- Lack of end-user training programs for both packaged and internally developed client server applications often lead to poor realization of results. The "front line" affected by the consequences of a lack of user training is the helpdesk.

- Users have a very poor understanding about support and maintenance cycles that affect application usage.

Other barriers exist when the intranet technologies form the client/server application platform. Intranet-based application architectures are still in their infancy. Real applications are being built and real business benefits are being realized through the power of this new architecture.

- There is however indiscriminate blending of fact and fiction. This tends to create wrong expectations among users about the intranet as an infrastructure.

- Problems also stem from the inadequacy of the infrastructure itself (and the lack of intranet infrastructure management) to cope with such a central role.

- The intranet technologies themselves are in a state of evolution: To view the intranet as an application infrastructure means that a number of technologies have to work together in a cohesive manner.

- An enterprise's chosen vendors in technology areas such as security, directories, e-mail, backup, etc. may not scale or inter-operate on an intranet scale. The wider physical distribution of intranet servers places new demands on end-to-end services such as user authentication.

- The core technologies of the intranet—HTML, HTTP, browsers, etc., as they currently stand, all impose performance limitations. There are both classes of applications and "segments" of users, where performance is not a major issue. Performance expectations from using the world wide web in a wider Internet context, etc., have already prepared user expectations at a low enough level. The very availability of a new service that genuinely aids normal work is often enough to get the support of such users. Other classes of applications and user segments will find the low performance and access to intranet-hosted applications a throwback to a previous era of computing.

2.1.2 Success Factors in Infrastructure Deployment

The experience of a number of organizations suggests that there are a number of high-level rules to successful development and deployment of large-scale infrastructure projects. These high-level rules for success suggest that they should be part of the strategic planning for infrastructure projects (as well as deployment of client/server applications). Table 2.1 shows a checklist of questions as a guide in developing a strategy in each of the success factors areas.

Of these, the solidity of management sponsorship is a primary factor. Sponsorship comes through a fundamental understanding of the benefits to be accrued from the infrastructure, infrastructure cost models, performance and organizational dependencies.

While a high-level champion is necessary, the buy-in of managers closer to the users is also essential to broaden the support base. The lack of "critical mass" of support, or the business sponsorship not continuing for the full duration of an infrastructure project is a major risk. Its impact gets bigger with the size of the infrastructure project.

Leading on from the critical mass of management support, is the level of user participation in the functional definition of what the infrastructure needs to deliver. User dissatisfaction with the result always overrides any excellence (e.g., technical, cost containment, managing to schedule, etc.) that may have been achieved.

Achieving user satisfaction starts with setting and managing expectations. However expectations have also to be managed throughout the life-cycle of the project. This involves continuous communications. An infrastructure group has several constituencies of users—two of the most important being end-users and IT development/integration.

The third major area is in managing vendor and third-party relationships. Most large infrastructure projects require the integration of technologies from a number of vendors. Vendors in the infrastructure field are notorious for their inability to help in integration problems. This affects the whole infrastructure stack from the network up.

2.2 Process Engineering

Another aspect of the infrastructure life-cycle is the relationship between:

1. its technology base,

2. the processes that use the infrastructure,

3. the people responsible for the infrastructure's integrity and

4. the architecture that defines infrastructure solutions

This relationship is highly dynamic. Many organizations have introduced the current generation of infrastructure management technology without a fundamental look at the way information from this technology is disseminated and processed within the management group.

Case Study 2.1: Amplification of "Simple Change"

A business unit of an insurance company decided to make a "simple" change in an infrastructure: The standard workstation for a whole department was to be upgraded to one with more memory and a state-of-art processor.

Such upgrades are common in many enterprises, e.g., to cope with new releases of office automation application suites. This case study summarizes experiences across several organizations of the same "simple change."

The new workstation is usually expected to run existing client/server applications very much faster. The processing speed and the extra buffering allows the workstation to access services at a higher rate. However, depending on where the respective infrastructure "service level curve" is at the time of the change, a number of things may happen:

The performance at the local network segments that are based on "shared media technology" (such as Ethernet) will deteriorate as each workstation competes harder for the finite bandwidth.

If the local network segment has sufficient spare capacity (e.g., because each segment supports a very small number of users), then the aggregate traffic to "infrastructure" application services such as a lookup service will increase. Such servers may be placed on a "backbone" portion of the network and may even be supported by a high-bandwidth technology such as FDDI. The point-of-connection of such servers will become relative "hot-spots." Depending on the backbone's structure, packets may be dropped as bursts of traffic all destined for the same point hit the backbone.

If the backbone can deliver the packets from the workstations without dropping packets and without introducing delays, then the respective server(s) can be expected to receive a larger volume of requests. Moreover, if the workstation LAN and the backbone LAN are both performant enough to make them "transparent" to the traffic from the workstations, then the requests arriving at infrastructure servers will also be bursty. Servers are likely to have to be re-sized or duplicated to cope with the new demand patterns.

This above scene is at least a situation which can, with fore-knowledge, be analyzed. As the applications using the infrastructure get updated (and *continuous update-until-replacement* is the rule of the game), stresses on the infrastructure are both difficult to predict or analyze, even when the effects are observable.

This is because changes in application protocols, that tie together clients and services, map to multiple lower-level mechanisms. The potential numbers of chains of cause-and-effect through the layers, set up by a change, are too numerous. In addition, the condition that triggers off an infrastructure crisis is often too transient to capture through observation.

Table 2.1: Checklist to Develop Success Criteria in Infrastructure Deployment

Area	Key Questions
Sponsorship and management buy-in	Does the project have high level sponsorship?
	How is the relationship with the sponsor maintained?
	Does the sponsor embrace his/her role and its projection in the organization?
	Is there a high-level steering body for the project?
	Are any process changes associated with the deployment of the infrastructure known and supported by the users and their management?
	Is there a thorough understanding in the project of the business benefits critical to the different constituencies of users?
	Is there agreement and understanding of the timescale of the project?
	Is there an understanding of the complexity and risks being managed?
	Are there going to be any cost surprises, has the overall cost model been presented?
	Is there documented agreement on any factors being compromised (time, quality, functionality, cost, etc.)?
User Participation	Are users with "real" process experience involved in each stage of the project?
	What tools are being employed to ensure user requirements are being captured?
	How are the users involved in testing and usage trial stages?
	Are the views of technically knowledgeable users being captured?
Managing User	Are user requirements for availability and performance understood, are they explicit?
Expectations	Are these requirements being met in the first deliverables? If not, are the users aware?
	Is there any incremental strategy to meet availability and performance criteria?
	Is there any strategy for global deployment, do the users know the plans?
	Is there a process to communicate the issues of total cost?
	Are the past experiences of the users known, and what effect does it currently have?

Table 2.1: *Checklist to Develop Success Criteria in Infrastructure Deployment (continued)*

Area	Key Questions
Infrastructure Preparation	Has the infrastructure been surveyed and benchmarked?
	Has the work required for any re-engineering been costed and communicated?
	Do plans exist to sequence infrastructure deployment and any application work?
	Are there enterprise-wide standardization initiatives the project could benefit from?
Managing Vendors and Third Parties	Are the vendors and partners chosen on the basis of matching the needs of the project?
	Is a multi-vendor solution required, how is the liaison managed?
	Is there a lead partner who manages and integrates the efforts of subcontractors?
	Is the partner experienced in client/server related uncertainties such as re-sizing?
	How are vendors and partners integrated into the overall project management?

This is one of the reasons why only limited successes have been gained from investment in the technology.

Infrastructure management groups must first and foremost recognize themselves to be service-oriented groups. The work of the group can be defined in terms of a set of *natural* processes. A process is essentially a sequence of predefined activities executed to achieve a pre-specified outcome or result. Management processes are geared to provide service

Common examples of such processes are those for *adding* users, *changing* versions of an application/operating system environment, *moving* the location of a group of users and their computing resources and *fixing* a user reported fault.

Such processes define a controlled, pre-tested way of achieving a specific service. As such they also specify a form of quality measurement for achieving a specific result.

Organizational structures and job specifications often obscure or fragment processes so that they are perceived to be *implicit* practises that an individual or subgroup undertakes. Processes define such practises *explicitly*—enabling critical analysis. The first job of process engineering is to identify the key processes in a given business.

Chapter 5 defines the set of core processes in infrastructure management and treats the area of process engineering in considerable detail. Processes should be designed very much along the lines of systems, without losing sight of the process's users and the process's goals.

Here we look at a tool to align the features of a designed process with the users of the process and the goals to be achieved by that process. It is essentially a tool to define enterprise-specific processes.

2.2.1 Process Development

One of the most important elements of any process design involves capturing the user requirements in a clear and unambiguous form. Users in this case are individuals in the infrastructure management group.

Without understanding requirements in the local context of each enterprise, it is simply not possible to develop a process successfully. It does not matter how elegant the work analysis model is or how sophisticated the design, if the process does not meet the needs of the users of the system.

An *actor* is an abstraction of the various entities that interact with a process. The concept of an actor can include users of the process, other processes, as well as systems or tools the process uses.

Use-cases & actors is a method that represents the user requirements as a series of operations that are performed on a process by various actors. Use-cases & actors essentially allows a conceptual bridge between processes and the organizational structure.

The interactions with a process is described by a series of discrete use-cases, each of which consists of a sequence of steps that are performed by an actor, to carry out some role in a process. The use-cases are organized into a hierarchical structure, which represents the complete set of operations that can be performed with the process.

2.2.2 Actors

The interactions between an actor and a process typically involves the exchange of information or the actor influencing the behavior of the process in some way. Examples are:

- An end user submitting a problem report to the user requirements.

- A project manager accessing topology information prior to planning a change.

- An inventory database that holds up-to-date user asset information.

In practice, actors can be divided into categories according to their characteristics such as the types of operations they perform, their access rights, their patterns of usage. When considering human users these categories frequently correspond to the various job titles or job functions that exist in the organization that is being served by the system.

If each category of actor is considered as a separate class of user, then each actual user can be viewed as an instance of the corresponding actor class. This is demonstrated in Figure 2.1(a).

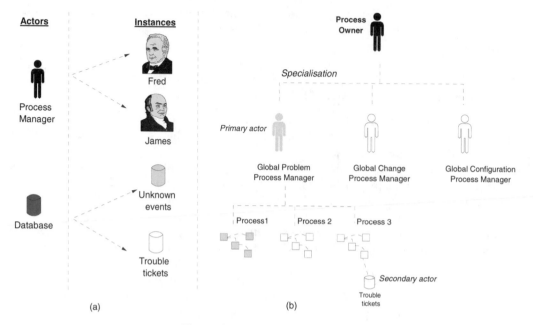

Figure 2.1: *Actors and processes*

Actors may be divided into two main types: primary actors and secondary actors. Primary actors are the entities for which the process is being built; typically the users that it directly empowers. Secondary actors exist to support the system in order to facilitate the actions of the primary actors.

One technique for clarifying the relationship between these two categories is to note that without primary actors there is no need for secondary actors. Hence an inventory database is not needed if none of the processes endeavors to manage the database.

An important aspect of actors is that their behavior is non-deterministic, that is they are able to perform any action of which they are capable, at any time and in any order, regardless of any previous actions that may have been performed.

One category of actor may be a sub-class of another or the specialization of another. This allows common attributes of a group of actors to be factored-out and placed in a parent actor class that represents features that are common to all derived actors. This is shown in Figure 2.1(b)

When identifying actors it is important to note that actors are not individuals, but classes of entities that interact with the process. The most common form of actor in many infrastructure management processes is that of its human users. Each such actor therefore refers to a single role that a user (or a category of users) can play.

Although an individual human user can adopt the role of several different actors during their use of the system, they may only perform one such role at any given time.

One technique for identifying actors is to consider the objectives set for the process and to identify the various actors that are needed to meet these objectives. It should be possible to assign each objective to one or more actors; if this is not the case then either an actor needs to be created or the list of objectives needs to be more clearly defined.

The roles and responsibilities of each actor should be documented as they evolve, since this will help when it becomes necessary to partition the processes into sub-processes. It is usually more difficult to identify machine and systems actors than human users, due to the problem of determining whether or not the exchange between the actor and the process is of a sufficiently high level of "intelligence."

2.2.3 Use-Cases

A use-case describes a generic sequence of interactions between a given actor and a process—the result of which is some service-related result.

Specific interactions may be generated by replacing the abstract parameters in the use-case with actual values. The use-case is thus a template for the complete range of possible interactions that may be performed when the process is executing.

Each use-case can be viewed as having behavior—defined by the steps within the use-case and a *state*, which is defined by the current position within the use-case.

An instance of a use-case is created as a result of the process receiving a particular stimulus from a specific actor. The relationship between actors and use-cases is shown in Figure 2.2. Few process requirements can be expressed by a single use-case. It is therefore necessary to employ some mechanism for decomposing the user requirements into a series of separate use-cases, which must be connected together by some controlled relationships.

The most important relationship supported by the use-case concept is that of one use-case extending another. This allows a use-case to enhance the functionality of another use case, in a manner that is transparent to the use-case being extended. The transparency of the *extension* relationship is important since it implies that the original use-case may be executed in both its extended and non-extended forms. It also means that the original use-case does not need to be modified, even if more extensions are defined.

The concept of extension can be used for a number of purposes, including:

- Modular decomposition of use-cases (particularly when complex alternatives are possible).

- Indicating optional behavior.

- When a large number of choices are available.

- Representing exceptional behavior and error handling.

A second type of relationship between use-cases is when a sub-sequence of operations is shared by two or more use-cases. Such sequences typically perform horizontal process functions such as systems administration. This situation is represented by the *uses* relationship.

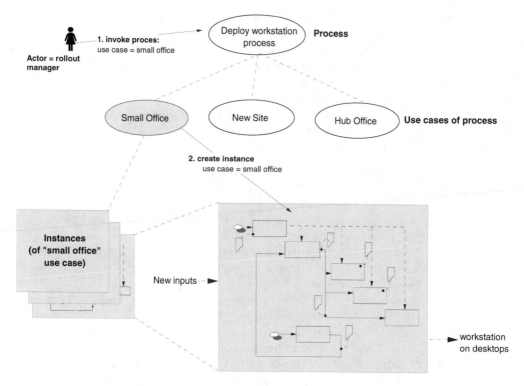

Figure 2.2: *Relationship between actors and use-cases*

The common sequence is said to be *used* by all of the other use-cases that include it in their sequence of operations. Note that this relationship differs from the *extends* relationship described previously, since a use-case will become incomplete if the uses sequence is removed.

Use-cases are refined as follows:

- Each of the different operations that may be performed by the actor when interfacing with the process.

- For each such operation, consider the stimulus that starts it, the events that occur during the operation, including any parameters that may be associated with these events.

Document each such operation as a use-case, including:

- The name of the use-case and the associated actor.

- The inputs and outputs of the use-case.

- A brief description of each of the steps within the use-case that are performed by the actor.

Name the use-case by placing the noun first—this will make it easier to identify the objects that are operated upon by the different use-cases and to group them according to the process related objects that they manipulate.

Initially, the description of use-cases should be restricted to the normal process flow. The handling of exceptions can be considered during the later stages of the development. Ensure that each use-case only involves one actor. If more than one actor appears to be required, then a combination of the following two approaches should be used:

- Define an *abstract* actor that factors out the common elements of each of the actors involved in the use-case, and substitute this for each of the different actors.

- Divide the use-case into a series of distinct use-cases, each with its own actor.

A use-case should be subdivided if:

- The users do not consider that it represents a cohesive flow of events in the process.

- Events within it are separated by long periods of time.

- Several actors are responsible for different portions of the use-case.

- An external event splits the use-case into clearly identifiable parts with different goals.

When most use-cases are defined, extract common sub-sequences and document them as abstract use-cases. These should be connected to their "sub" use-cases via *uses* relationships. This operation should only be performed in those cases where it leads to a significant simplification of the use-cases.

A process should be validated by considering the overall objectives of the infrastructure management group, to ensure that use-cases exist to support all of these objectives.

For example, if one of the high-level objectives is that inventory should be controlled, this implies that there should be interfaces between all the processes which can change the asset status to an asset database actor, asset database management and asset search use-cases.

2.3 Risk Management

A risk defines the possibility of a future adverse event which can impact something of value to an enterprise. Risk management is a means of tackling risk by:

- Avoiding it.

- Off-loading it to a third party.

- Containing the severity of impact.

- Reducing its probability of occurrence.

The concept of risk management is a general one, applicable to many situations. Risk and its management is especially relevant to two levels in infrastructure management:

- As a management tool for infrastructure projects through all the phases from planning through to "production" (i.e., the results of the project being used).

- As a tools for developing an *infrastructure-at-risk model*—a model to track continually the risks impacting the infrastructure from various inside and outside factors.

The relationship between these two levels is shown in Figure 2.3. Risk management is increasingly used as part of program management and project management methodologies. It is described here as a stand-alone tool.

Risk management is a process-driven tool to ensure that all risks are predicted as early as possible and to develop *strategies* to eliminate or minimize their impact.

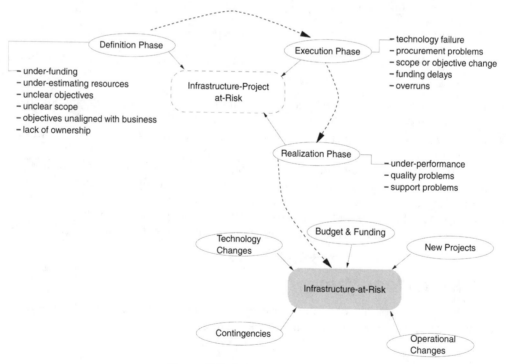

Figure 2.3: *Risk in infrastructure*

Risk management is increasingly important in infrastructure management due to the infrastructure's increasing complexity almost every year. Changes of any sort have the potential to impact as critical issues later in the life-cycle of the infrastructure. The cost base of client/server infrastructures is sufficiently large to absorb the cost of risk management. Risk management is generally a lot less expensive than dealing with the future impact of an unmanaged risk.

In this sense, aspects of operational infrastructure management such as a fault management framework and business continuity planning have similar justifications. There is therefore a *continuum* between risks that can be identified and conditions that suddenly occur—to impact the infrastructure.

2.3.1 Infrastructure-at-Risk Model

Client/server infrastructures are at constant risk from a set of internally and externally generated factors. Identification of individual risks and executing a risk management program is a key part in viewing the infrastructure as a strategic resource. Some of the common risk categories associated with a complex infrastructure are defined below:

- *Contingencies*—Catastrophic failure which has the potential to impact a large number of users. The cause can range from a single "central" component failing to concurrent failure of multiple-components. Failure can be at the hardware level, at the software level or at the protocol level (connecting separated components). Contingency can also refer to a major degradation of service which impacts on business processes.

- *Disasters*—Large-scale incidents whether natural or man-made render significant parts of the infrastructure to be unusable for a long duration. Business may have to relocate. The basic infrastructure for the business to continue its operations needs to be rebuilt. Although this may be on a smaller scale, the key issue is to ensure that the correct data is available.

- *Operational failures*—These are small-scale incidents which can be handled through well-known procedures. The failures of a server or a hub card are relatively common occurrences in a large infrastructure. Both the quality of the repair and the management of the downtime period itself is essential.

- *Operational changes*—Additions, moves and changes are often the precursors to major incidents later on. Most infrastructures have performance "hot spots." These limit the amount of operational change possible without re-engineering parts of the infrastructure.

- *New applications*—Introducing new client/server applications is a special case of operational change. New applications comprise a major risk factor since they often change the traffic profile at the network level, usage patterns of infrastructure services and other common services. The new applications category should also include major version upgrades of software packages. The trend is for new versions of familiar software to demand orders of magnitude increases in basic resources such as memory, compute power and network bandwidth.

- *Obsolescence*—Over a relatively short period of time (3 to 5 years) significant parts of the infrastructure becomes candidates for re-engineering. This is only partly to do with the pace of technology. Infrastructure obsolescence is more to do with being unable to deal with the growth in demand, change in business direction and change in scale. Also, if disparate technologies have to be integrated, the service cost element in the future will increase.

- *Wrong choice of technology*—The current state of many consortia and quasi-standards bodies driven by vendors or even genuine standards bodies unduly influenced by vendors are pushing key infrastructure products onto a relatively naive market. Recent examples where organizations have made the "wrong choice" are 100 MBit Ethernet and ATM to the desktop. Backing out of wrong choices is equivalent to re-engineering with all the cost and disruption involved. Wrong choice as risk is likely to accelerate in the infrastructure arena.

- *Budgetary and funding*—Money for infrastructure upgrades often dries up depending on external factors such as business cycles, perception that the infrastructure management organization does not provide value for money, and so on.

The key lesson on managing infrastructure-related incidents, whether large (disasters) or small (operational failures) is that the infrastructure should have the architectural qualities to survive failure. These qualities include spreading the risk so that, for example:

- A single operational failures does not cause a whole department or business process to come to a standstill.

- The ability to change components without having to "power down" the infrastructure.

Table 2.2 shows typical strategies and actions for managing an infrastructure-at-risk model.

2.3.2 Risk Management of Infrastructure Projects

In more and more organizations, infrastructure needed for client/server applications is re-engineered on an enterprise scale. Infrastructure projects are often complex due to reasons of technology, multi-site and multicultural team structure. The geographic extent of the

Table 2.2: Components of an Infrastructure-at-Risk Model

Risk	Containment Strategy	Ongoing Actions
Disasters	*Develop* business continuity plans *Develop* architectural solutions such as mirroring critical servers offsite, using a mainframe as a data repository, etc.	Communicate plans to business Refine plans as business changes Test plans
Operational Failures	*Establish* blueprints for recovery for common use throughout the enterprise *Establish* post mortem procedures *Develop* high availability architectural solutions	Communicate, train and refine within infrastructure management functions Execute post mortem after each incident and distribute findings Use high availability solutions across enterprise and enable discussion of experiences
Contingencies	Use solutions from business continuity and operational failure blueprints as starting points	"Scenario" training to cope with unknown events Establish potential crisis teams
Operational Changes	*Establish* a change management process and include an impact analysis step *Establish* a risk management plan and ownership for execution	Get high-level sign off about potential risk
New Applications	*Establish* a piloting phase *Establish* a costing exercise as part of new application rollout	Communicate and manage expectations of users about large-scale change
Obsolescence	*Develop* architecture-based standards compatible with client/server model's evolution *Develop* modular solutions *Develop* re-engineering business cases based on known and anticipated business changes	Understand business direction and anticipate requirements from the infrastructure Update business cases
Budgetary and Funding	*Use* financial tools to communicate cost and quality of service and benefits to the organization	Communication

Table 2.2: Components of an Infrastructure-at-Risk Model (continued)

Risk	Containment Strategy	Ongoing Actions
Organizational Differences	*Develop* a process-oriented organization *Use* metrics to demonstrate effectiveness	Communication and establishing commonality of purpose
Others		

change resulting from an infrastructure project may be large, depending on the size of the user population impacted, and the cost of the project may also be large.

Until they are completed (or cancelled) all infrastructure projects are at risk. Complexity is the main contributory factor to risk. Some other contributory factors are:

- Ambiguity of purpose—Infrastructure projects often span multiple communities of interest, each with conflicting definitions and expectations for benefits as well as for success.

- Degree of change—Infrastructure projects often cause major changes below the application level. Errors or lack of quality at the infrastructure are amplified across multiple application clients using the infrastructure.

- Time-related uncertainty—Infrastructure projects have a tendency to be long-lived, hence cost and delivery schedules are impacted.

In many cases the perceived complexity of infrastructure projects is reduced by partitioning the work into distinct streams that meet specific business goals. This portfolio of work is often called a *program*.

The discipline of programs management is somewhat different to project management. A work delivery model, clearly defined information interfaces between the streams, minimized dependencies between the streams and a risk management framework for delivery are all activities in a program's design.

Within such a multi-stream view allied to specific business goals, many large infrastructure programs are in fact *change* programs that change the working environment of the enterprise.

Unfortunately, in many program and project management circles, the term *risk* (and its active management) carry one or more negative connotations to be associated to any proposal of risk management. This includes the following:

- As not fully grasping the problem to be solved, its scope or its dependencies.

- As pre-emptive reasoning why the project will not succeed.

- As expressing a pessimistic view on the possible results of the project.

- As imperilling acceptance of a project proposal by a funding body (which may construe that a set of risks diminish the probability of success).

Another more worrying attitude to risk management is that *managers control risk to a considerable degree as a matter or course.* By implication therefore managers don't need any special tools or approaches for an explicit risk management function. Nothing could be further from the truth. There is a direct correlation between disciplined risk management and the success of large infrastructure projects.

Table 2.3 shows some common categories of risk to infrastructure programs and some questions to drive risk identification.

2.3.3 Process for Risk Management

Risk management is a process-based tool. Figure 2.4 shows a process flow model with the inputs and outputs from each activity. Each enterprise has to develop a risk management process that fits in with the enterprise's culture. The process defined here is a good prototype for this.

Risk identification is a group activity which is often conducted in a workshop setting. Participants to the workshop should include the project sponsor (or delegate), project managers and technology specialists relevant to the program or project. Information needed from the workshop activity are:

- A documented set of risks and their consequences as agreed by the group.

- For each documented risk, values representing classifications of (*a*) the probability of occurrence, (*b*) the level of impact on the program level (*c*) the level of impact on the project level, (*d*) the priority for planning containment.

- A risk owner for each documented risk who will be responsible for developing containment strategy and actions, their subsequent execution, and a review of the risk's status.

Development of a containment strategy, costing for the strategy, communication of the strategy and its sign-off by the project sponsor are prerequisites to building the mechanisms for the execution of the containment strategy. The output of this phase are:

- A consolidated risk management plan built from individual plans developed in the previous phase.

- A risk control framework defined by review meetings (frequencies and key agenda items for these risk management meetings should be developed).

Table 2.3: Common Infrastructure Risk Categories

Risk Category	Typical Questions to Identify Risks
Business sponsorship and buy-in	Is there direct or indirect sponsorship from the business for the infrastructure program?
	Is there a well-developed and published business case for the infrastructure program?
	Is there a steering body for the program?
	Is there any internal competition for the whole program or parts of the program?
Business Requirements	Are the business application(s) requirements understood to a point where they can be analyzed?
	Can the business sponsor verify the actual operational use of the business application?
Technology	Are new products being proposed?
	Are product lead times understood?
	Are the relationships between software and hardware technology bases understood?
	Are testing and piloting methodologies for the products understood?
	Is innovation needed, if so who provides the lead?
	Are complex products being proposed, if so who provides support?
	Are the limits of the technology known?
Skills	Are system integration skills important, if so who provides it?
	Is external recruitment necessary for this program?
	If third parties are involved, what is their financial and resource stability?
Delivery	Are actual deliverables and their time-scale defined?
	Are there sufficient quality checks?
	Are the dependencies defined and published? Does the sponsor know them?
	Are there any legal or legislative barriers to delivery?

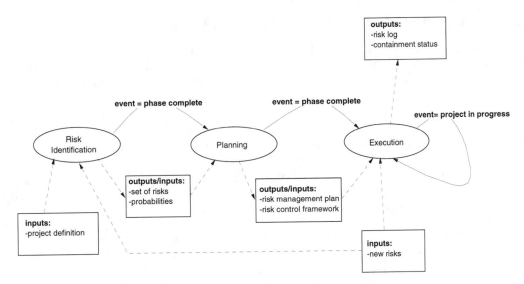

Figure 2.4: *Risk management as a process-based tool*

- A workflow for the execution, review and tracking of risk by each risk owner. The workflow may be a paper trail or a new component in an existing workflow automation system.

- Tools such as enterprise specific forms to capture information, a web page to distribute information and collect comments.

The next phase of the process is one where the risk management plan is executed. Progress needs to be reviewed on a regular basis and any adjustments and revisions agreed. The risks themselves need to be tracked. This phase executes until the project or program is completed. The output from this phase are:

- A risk log identifying key actions against risks. This log is updated as the activities in this phase are reviewed. It holds the current status regarding all risks being managed.

- If an identified risk does become an issue despite the containment plan being executed, then the risks have to be revisited, to re-align with the new situation.

- If new risks are identified then these have to be added to the risks being managed.

- At the end of the project the cost, benefits and lessons gained from the risk management exercise need to be identified by the participants. This is sometimes communicated to a wider audience.

2.4 Gap Analysis and Benchmarking

The difference between a current value of a characteristic metric and the "required" value of the metric defines a gap. When the metric relates to the infrastructure or its management, it is often part of a set of characteristic metrics used to profile the infrastructure.

An example of a characteristic metric for a client/server infrastructure is its *ability to cope with bursty service requests*. An example of a characteristic for infrastructure management is the *hours of helpdesk coverage*. The current value of the first is "measured" by analyzing the network and system topologies, the value for the latter is determined by questioning helpdesk personnel and looking at helpdesk logs.

The *required* or *ideal* value, against which the current value is compared, may be from a number of sources. The choice of the value's source is important because the resulting gap defines different things. Common sources for the required value are:

1. *An industrial or sector average.* This information is gained from a benchmarking organization or from an experienced consultant with access to a database of industry-wide measurements. This source is used for comparison with the current value when the goal of gap analysis is to examine current values against industry averages.

2. A site within the enterprise which is considered to have *enterprise best practice.* The values for enterprise best practice are measured values. The goal of gap analysis using this source of data is to show internal variance or differences within the enterprise itself.

3. An *industrial best practice.* This information is also supplied by benchmarking organizations or an appropriate database. Gap analysis using this source of data shows difference relative to the "best" in industry.

4. A value that *could be achieved with state-of-the-art* technology or process. Such values are generally speculative and are often supplied by an experienced consultant. Gap analysis using such values aims to go beyond industry best practice.

Benchmarking is a technique of comparing measured values of a set of characteristic metrics with values measured for a significant number of other *peer* enterprises. The values relating to other enterprises is provided by an organization with a large benchmarking database. Most of the "major league" management consultancies such as IBM Consulting Group or Andersen Consulting have IT practices that undertake benchmarking assignments (or provide benchmarking data in some cases).

Although these databases hold data from real enterprises, their identity remains confidential—even to the staff of the benchmarking organization. Such organizations would not survive otherwise.

Benchmarking differs from gap analysis in the sense that the questions answered are different. A gap defines a potential goal to be fulfilled. Benchmarking provides a tool for understanding where the enterprise would be ranked in a peer group. Benchmarking is therefore a higher level executive tool to understand issues such as the current investment and cost levels, efficiency, skills base, technology employed, etc., through peer comparison.

Layers of the infrastructure, its management, client/server technology, the application portfolio are all individual areas for benchmarking. This is discussed in Section 4.4.4.

2.4.1 Use of Gap Analysis

The results of gap analysis is used to illustrate and quantify a goal to be achieved, highlight a problem area or to demonstrate improvement or deterioration over a time period (over which successive "gaps" have been measured).

The choice of *what* to measure is determined by the set of metrics available from the sources described in Section 2.4. Hence sets of data may be envisaged for network performance, organizational structure, operational structure, and so on. Such sets are useful for defining a profile of a specific area (i.e., network performance, etc.)

The suppliers of data for gap analysis also define *how* the current value is to be measured. This is as a control for the quality of measurements. Measurements may include both physical tools as well as interviews and request for information. Figure 2.5 shows a flowchart of gap analysis using Quality metrics such as those described in Chapter 3, Sections 3.3 and 3.4. Gap analysis with quality metrics results in outputs useful for different planning purposes—for example:

- Analysis of the infrastructure management framework.

- Cost and skills analysis.

- Project plans for process level or infrastructure improvement.

- Service levels for negotiating with outsourcers.

Gap analysis can be applied to a wide range of situations in the infrastructure management context. Some examples where gap analysis has been successfully applied are described below:

- Performance characteristics of an existing network with respect to characteristics empirically determined to be required for the roll-out of a new client/server application. (Client/server based, highly distributed applications place heavy stresses on the network, as the number of users scale up.) The gap analysis helped to identify the areas for infrastructure re-engineering prior to deployment.

- Organization characteristics of a set of autonomous management groups (responsible for different parts of the infrastructure), with respect to a new global infrastructure management organization. The gap analysis helped to identify the structure for a management organization and the goals to be set for each group to achieve best practice.

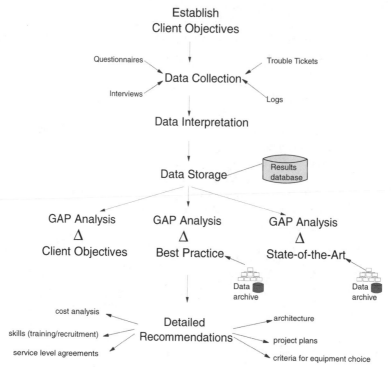

Figure 2.5: *Stages in a gap analysis of quality indicators*

Gap analysis is also undertaken on an ad hoc and qualitative basis in some key infrastructure management processes:

- The methodology for making equipment or software choices is one common example where a form of gap analysis is undertaken between a defined set of features and each vendors' set of features.

- Defining skills required for using a specific application suite in a business process, identifying current skills, doing a gap analysis and establishing a training plan as a consequence is another common example.

2.4.2 Gap Analysis with Network Characteristics

The concept of gap analysis can also be applied to a set of network characteristics. Such an analysis is appropriate, for example, to define the ability of an organization's network topology to support a planned application upgrade, or a new corporate application.

Case Study 2.2: Skills Deficit

A country-wide brewery and liquor shop chain with a steadily increasing market share decided that the use of IT was important to its future and especially in improving the efficiency of its supply chain. The managing director commissioned a recruitment agency to hire two IT managers, one to develop new systems capability and the other to consolidate current office automation and database-based IT solutions.

The brief for the recruitment agency described the greenfield nature of the position as well as how business and IT would drive each other. After some three months of search and interviews, two young managers joined the firm as well as a small team of PC developers. None had direct experience in the supply chains involved. The two managers however had experience in developing PC-based systems for wholesale retail businesses.

The managers developed a plan guided by the managing director's vision. While the new systems were being developed or integrated, current solutions were cleaned up to provide higher quality management information about sales and volumes. Over a period of another year new on-line analysis and information delivery systems were made available. Over the next year, the company however began to miss opportunities that allowed both traditional competitors and copycat operations to gain market share.

An internal debate about the usefulness of the IT systems was started. A task force of internal managers and external consultants concluded that some of the sources and quality of information used to develop the management information were not adequate for the purpose.

In addition, the IT managers had neither the industry contacts nor the operations experience to validate the vision pursued by the managing director. Hence there was no real means of identifying gaps between the information needed and the information being delivered.

Lessons

While good technical knowledge is essential in such a greenfield site, business knowledge and more importantly the dynamics of the business are essential to develop for gaps in IT systems.

A steering group rather than a single individual should be driving major IT initiatives. Also prototyping and piloting should be part of the IT delivery scheme.

Recruitment agencies rarely have contextual knowledge of a vertical business. When they do have the knowledge it is unlikely to be in how business and IT work together.

Such analysis is appropriate in many organizations where the "evolution" of the network topology has not kept pace with the use of application suites, process automation technology and indeed the change of business flows.

Gap analysis in this case provides conclusions relative to measurements of commonly used performance metrics utilization, throughput, and response time. From these primary metrics inferences can be made about the three network characteristics of latency, bandwidth and the ability to handle burstiness—required at an application transaction level.

The measurement of these metrics, for the data collection phase, however, requires modeling tools. Discrete event simulation is one such tool, which is certainly useful to provide *insight* into the scale of the gap between what the network is capable of at a given point in time and what it needs to be capable of.

2.4.3 Discrete Event Simulation and Gap Analysis

Simulation can be used to build models of the current infrastructure to *approximate* current values for key metrics. Simulation can also be used to model future needs in terms of new deployments, scaling the number of users or new client/server topologies and how this affects the current infrastructures. Simulation is particularly useful in understanding LAN/WAN interfaces.

The gap is the difference between what the current infrastructure can support and what the future needs are. The main areas for investigation in this type of gap analysis are shown in Table 2.4 and are briefly described below:

- *Segment analysis.*

  To approximate the delays and utilization of specific type of media and mode of use (shared or switched). For each identified "channels" in the infrastructure, the effect of varying users and application load can be seen.

- *Application message end-to-end delay.*

  To approximate delay in a given client/server topology and the effect of varying the number of users.

  To approximate delay in a traversal across multiple nodes over a wider topology and the effect of varying the number of users.

- *WAN sizing analysis.*

  To approximate application transaction response, link delays and utilization by link speed. This is relevant for sizing WAN links and components.

  To approximate application transaction response, link delays and utilization by users. This is relevant for capacity planning the deployment of client/server applications in remote offices.

  To approximate application transaction response capacity to support additional users and applications. This is relevant for backbone and router sizing.

- *Server sizing analysis.*

  To approximate application transaction response, server processor, and disk delays and utilization by server processor power and disk speed. This is relevant for server sizing.

To approximate application transaction response, server processor, and disk delays and utilization by number of users. This is relevant for capacity planning.

Common Errors in Using Simulation Techniques. Simulation tools have been around for many years, yet have found little favor in planning corporate infrastructures. Until recently, simulation models had to be built using a high-level language.

Table 2.4: Summary of Simulation Results by Simulation Purpose and Variable

Purpose of Simulation	Simulation Result	Variable
Single segment throughput analysis	Channel Delay	Number of users
	Utilization	Number of users
	Channel delay	Application load
	Utilization	Application load
	Application Message End-To-End Delay	Number of users
	Application Transaction End-To-End Delay	Number of users
Router/Bridge/Switch sizing for intersegment throughput analysis	Application Message End-To-End Delay	Intermediate System Throughput
	Application Transaction End-To-End Delay	Intermediate System Throughput
WAN sizing analysis	Application Transaction End-To-End Delay	Link Speed
	Link Delay	Link Speed
	Utilization	Link Speed
WAN capacity analysis	Application Transaction End-To-End Delay	Number of users
	Link Delay	Number of users
	Utilization	Number of users
Server sizing analysis	Application Transaction End-To-End Delay	Number of users
	Application Transaction End-To-End Delay	Server Power

For modeling infrastructures and client/server topologies, several high-quality packaged tools currently exist. These allow models to be "wired" together from relatively well-built modules. Modules exist, for example, for most types of network media and WAN technologies.

These have an immediate use if a level of realism is attached to their purpose. Some common pitfalls that have been met by several previous generations of simulation tool users are still germane—and are briefly discussed below:

- *Invalid models.* The models that are built are invalid, due to inaccuracies in topology details, bugs in the tool or modules, etc. Another reason is that simplifying assumptions are sometimes made which don't scale up.

- *No specific goals.* Each simulation model should be built with a specific set of goals. Certainly for gap analysis, many small models, each with one or two goals is preferable to a large model which meets a significant number of approximation requirements.

- *Inadequate simulation language/system.* Simulation packages vary greatly in price and quality. Some don't scale more than a few hundred end points and others have low-quality modules. However, even when packages are used, careful design and planning activities are needed to build anything close to a realistic model. This can only be done following a significant degree of training with the package.

- *Too short simulations.* Complex topologies require longer simulation runs to get better results. Simulation is not a "real-time" what-if tool. Long runs require faster processors. This is the reason that the top end of the simulation tool market has not been available for PCs until recently.

- *Inadequate participation by model developers.* Even with packages this is still a danger. The developers must be able to understand the subtleties of the environment they are modelling. For this reason the models are best built by an architect or senior technical designer.

2.4.4 Benchmarking

Benchmarking is a collection and comparison exercise. Common types of data collected are:

- Costs—including operational costs, capital employed, present value and investment models, cost ratios such as infrastructure technology costs per head and application portfolio costs per head, and technology costs such as helpdesk costs.

- People—including skills and competencies, investment in training, staff morale and turnover and personnel policies.

- Technology—utilized MIPs of technology employed, communications capability, strength of architecture.

The best benchmarking models do not normalize the data collected. Formula-based normalization usually introduces errors which skew the comparison. Actual data from previous profiling of a significant number of peers are more appropriate. The number of peers in a peer group should be in the order of 17 to 25. In order to do such a straightforward comparison, however, previously profiled data needs to be organized into peer groups on a turnkey basis.

Hence an enterprise being benchmarked may want the peers to be in the same industry and to be of similar size and to be in the same country. Another client may want the peer group to be just in the similar industry and anywhere in the world.

The best benchmarking models also have a healthy skepticism of ranking. Ranking tends to ignore the constraints such as legislation under which a company being benchmarked has to operate.

The *difference* with the peer group (whether above or below the peer group), needs to be examined in a knowledgeable way and examined to see what the underlying meaning is and whether any change is implied. Such knowledge is most often found with a large consultancy or within specialist benchmarking organizations.

Quality metrics such as those described in Chapter 3 and collected over a large number of assignments are relevant for benchmarking. With respect to infrastructure areas of architecture, technologies, people and processes a major upheaval is to be expected every 3 to 5 years as business changes.

The validity of benchmarking using data from a highly volatile environment has been questioned. The purposes for which the results of the benchmarking will be put, including its time-frame should be clearly understood.

2.5 Financial Criteria in Infrastructure Management

Conventional financial criteria such as present value are important in developing business cases for investment decisions. Financial tools are also important in the prioritizing the development of infrastructures and its management.

Conventional financial tools are very difficult to use in benefit analysis of infrastructure. This is because infrastructure is rarely visible as a contributor to the bottom line of a business. While cost of ownership of applications can be linked back to business advantages, the underlying infrastructure cannot be explicitly attributed in adding benefits.

2.5.1 Valuing Infrastructure Management Services

The work of infrastructure management groups needs to be sufficiently valued in the organization for the group's work to gain credibility as an essential part of the application delivery chain.

IT managers increasingly dislike the role of managing "nuts and bolts" of infrastructure technology. Rather, they want to work with the business in developing IT based solutions. Leading from this is an internal driver to outsource.

Complete outsourcing of all infrastructure management while not common is no longer rare. While a successful enterprise might want to outsource its infrastructure operations, it is unlikely to let the outsourcer close to its business thinking.

While the debate for outsourcing versus the internal ability to respond to changes continues, infrastructure management groups can benefit from being more financially aware, This includes:

- Getting credit for being service-oriented (or making measurable progress towards becoming service oriented).

- Use of financial criteria in submitting proposals involving capital spent for the infrastructure and infrastructure management functions.

- Putting a monetary value on the processes and information inherent in infrastructure management. Treating information in infrastructure management databases as an *intangible* asset.

2.5.2 Applicability of Common Financial Criteria

Return on Investment (ROI), *Present Value* and *Payback Analysis* are financial criteria used in examining investment opportunities. These are commonly applied in most areas of investment. All have well-established formulae.

Capital budgeting is the process of planning capital investments in selected areas of a business based upon:

- An analysis of the cash flows associated with the investments.

- An analysis of the benefits likely to be gained from the investments.

The underlying premise for capital budgeting is that any investment made today will result in a larger amount being received back over time (Return on Investment). Capital budgeting therefore frequently requires choices to be made between areas for investment.

ROI. Using the ROI criterion for infrastructure and infrastructure management investment decisions has, however, generally failed. In the case of infrastructure it is because it is difficult to establish beneficial effects directly affecting the business, stemming from infrastructure investment.

In the case of infrastructure management, cause-and-effect is removed even further: investment in infrastructure management directly benefits infrastructure, which in turn assists in meeting business goals is a chain that is difficult to construct.

Present value. The present value defines a value to the current infrastructure. Different organization use different methods to calculate present value. Some methods are determined by local internal revenue guidelines.

- *Capital Assets.* Examples of assets with residual value as assets include:

  Computers—ranging from mainframes to servers to desktops.

  External storage and archive subsystems.

  Networks—consisting of hubs, local backbone structures, infrastructure management infrastructure, cable/fiber plant, etc.

- *Intangible Assets*—The following are all increasingly important intangible assets (relevant for example in specifying net value when considering outsourcing infrastructure services).

  Goodwill of the user community.

  Capabilities (any system of processes, technology, people and architecture) that increases availability of the infrastructure.

  Service reputation in sector (relevant in attracting top technical talent).

2.5.3 Valuing Information as Knowledge Assets

The infrastructure management processes create many forms of data which if organized and processed properly have properties of being knowledge assets. Typical value of these knowledge assets are:

- Monetary Value in terms of reducing time—to achieve recovery, to achieve an infrastructure change.

- Monetary Value in terms of reducing (probability of) loss—protection from loss of business assets, increasing probability of business survival after a major disaster.

- Service Value in terms of ensuring that a third-party service is being provided to expected levels and negotiated price/value. This also extends to equipment procurement. Many large organizations negotiate global discount on capital items such as workstations and network hubs, but rarely track to ensure that the discounts are actually delivered in different countries.

Such information is complex enough to need databases and directories technology to store the information in a safe and accessible manner. Documentation should be an integral part of infrastructure management processes. Prime generators of information which such assets value include:

- *Fault management process*—which provides the means to learn from past fault resolution experiences and to spread the knowledge to the whole enterprise by sharing this information.

- *Configuration management process*—which provides a "wiring diagram" of how the infrastructure assets are put together and is therefore a crucial process for rebuilding the infrastructure for whatever reason.

- *Change management process*—which ensures that the impact to the current infrastructure is controlled and managed.

Quality of information.   Most information in the infrastructure field that has value has a finite shelf life. Beyond a certain time the information may be useless and sometimes even dangerous. Consider the case of an out of date network map being used during an infrastructure crisis. Hence such information assets need to be managed. Some of the activities this implies are defined below:

- Responsibility for timeliness of information.

- Review periods to establish validity of information.

- Storage and archiving of information in a safe and accessible way.

- Recovery of the information in the event of a disaster.

- The methods of sharing information with other sites.

- The methods of access of the information from different platforms by humans and programs.

- Security implications of storage and unauthorized access.

2.5.4 Activity-Based Costing

Conventional financial tools can only go so far in convincing higher management about targeting areas of the infrastructure for investment. When all is said and done, infrastructure still looks like an overhead item in accounting records.

Activity-based costing (ABC) is a methodology that provides cost information on the basis of work performed by an activity or a process. It is of considerable relevance to managing the infrastructure.

Different processes and services within the context of a client/server infrastructure have a highly diverse cost dynamics. Averaging them as happens today results in significant cost distortions ABC provides the ability to model cost behavior by defining four classes of cost patterns:

- Unit activities—which occur for each unit. For example, adding a user, putting in a new cable run, answering a helpdesk call.

- Batch activities—which occur for batches. For example, putting in a naming service for client/server deployment, putting in a helpdesk, putting in a LAN.

- Product activities—which support a product line or line of business requirement. For example, security engineering for a negotiation team, intranet for a sales team, planning an office move for a department.

- Sustaining activities—which support the infrastructure. For example, the fault management and tracking processes, performance and security monitoring processes, the network management framework.

Figure 2.6(a) shows the link that is possible between costs and their attribution to the activity classes described above. By tracing costs to activities, ABC provides information about processes that conventional cost accounting cannot do.

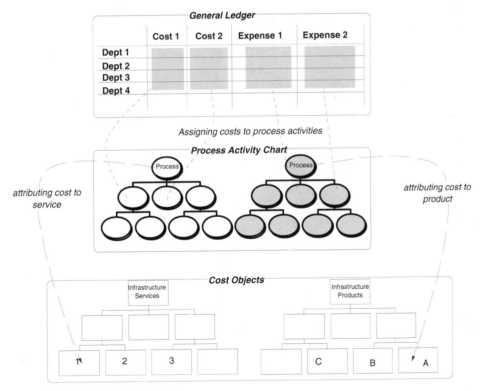

Figure 2.6: *Assigning costs to activities and combining process/cost views*

Case Study 2.3: Activity-Based Costing in Project Management

A utility and services company deploying a new generation of e-mail based application globally, became alarmed at the cost overrun of carefully costed estimates. A small project was started to develop an analysis of the problem based on an activity cost model. Some of the components of the derived model are shown below.

1.   Base desktop upgrade
2.   New desktop sourcing and delivery
3.   New desktop staging with standard software suites
4.   Office level infrastructure procurement
5.   Office level infrastructure deployment
6.   Training for new applications
7.   Per user mailbox migration
8.   Per user staging with non-standard applications

The breakdown of costs on an activity allowed an end to end view of the project's historic spend. The major "unexpected" cost overrun activities were upgrades and new desktops needed to deploy the new application, training, infrastructure set-up costs and resources for migration of individual mailboxes to the new system.

The senior managers were so impressed with the quality of the analysis that the project was extended to integrate with the resource management for the project, allowing a "real-time" view of cash flow within the project.

Lessons

The breakdown of costs on an activity basis reduced the "semantic gap" between cash flow within the project and the accounting view of the project.

Management information improved so that the delay between "cost generating" events and corrective decisions was reduced. This improved the conduct of the project.

Activity-based costing is a relatively easy tool to be integrated into a general purpose spreadsheet and can be integrated into most project management disciplines.

ABC allows an infrastructure manager to quantify the cost of processes. By adding a cost dimension to a process, the combined evaluation of architecture, people, technology, process and cost is possible. This is shown in Figure 2.6(b).

From an infrastructure manager's perspective, ABC's ability to assign cost more logically and its ability to map costs to actual management processes rather than as a cost bucket is an important tool in showing the true role of infrastructure in supporting the business.

ABC is a relatively new concept and not widely accepted by the accounting community. ABC has been implemented as a *supplementary* information source to existing financial systems in several large infrastructure management groups. These groups see ABC as an *enabler* in achieving the large-scale change they are committed to.

Setting up for ABC in an infrastructure group requires specialist consultancy resources. Several tools are available to "establish" its benefits through inclusion in infrastructure management processes.

2.6 Business Continuity

Many businesses require 100% availability of key IT systems and services. Infrastructure management groups are often asked to deliver high availability as a specific capability of the infrastructure.

A common reason for the 100% availability criterion is that many businesses are run on a global scale or at least have components that are widely spread. An IT infrastructure is needed to tie together the flows of information and even capital between departmental or geographic entities.

Another viewpoint says that the availability requirement is a sign that IT infrastructure is accepted as both "mature" and ubiquitous enough to be viewed much as a *utility*—rather like power or telephones or road transport infrastructures. The IT infrastructure is therefore integral to the environment in which business is conducted in many sectors.

Availability is usually formalized in service level agreements between users and the infrastructure management group. Developing a high availability strategy for a client/server infrastructure rarely goes far enough to address how actual client businesses survive a major contingency such as a natural disaster. Availability and business continuity are therefore related by being at the two ends of the scale in terms of their business impact. This is shown in Figure 2.7.

2.6.1 Availability

Network availability is therefore the first stage to a more comprehensive scheme. A strategy for managing availability of the whole infrastructure as an application delivery system involves a multi-faceted approach. The main components are defined below:

- *Architecture.* Unifying the notions of disaster recovery, which defines recovery following a catastrophic failure, with the notion of "smoothing" out availability problems of a lower degree or scale.

- *Development of service delivery paths.* As part of deployment of all new applications a map should be produced of the "paths" defining the infrastructure elements required by the application. This should be maintained by the change management process. Analysis of the deployment of older applications will result in their respective maps. This should be done as part of contingency planning for these applications.

Degree of failure

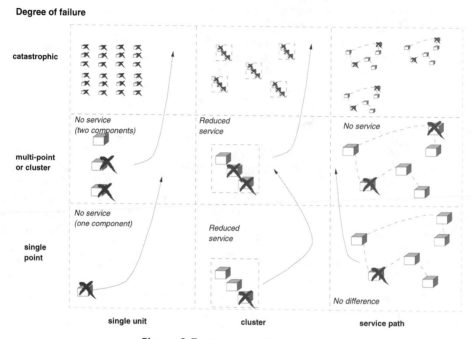

Figure 2.7: *The availability continuum*

- *Detecting change-of-state in criticality.* This defines the viability of resilience mechanisms. Requires frameworks for monitoring and visualizing problems that specifically affect the availability of business applications. For example, RAID subsystems should be monitored so that modules can be replaced as soon as possible after failure—(for the subsystem to revert to its "redundant" status). Others failures such as a software process, a member in a server cluster, or failure of a redundant network component are all candidates for monitoring from this special viewpoint.

- *Communication service solutions.* In metropolitan areas high-speed network connectivity services are available to develop an offsite facility with contingency resources (see the discussion in Chapter 7, Section 2.2). Other services allow dial-up "out-of-band" links to remote locations.

- *Technology solutions.* An availability solutions catalog would include mechanisms in the following categories: (1) Autoconfiguration, (2) Network resilience (physical), (3) Network resilience (protocols), (4) Server replication, (5) Disk mirroring, (6) Software Process Groups. Examples of actual solutions are RAID subsystems for storage, software for mirroring servers and data, vendor specific server clustering products. Choice of both categories and actual products should be driven by wider architectural requirements, cost/benefit and ability to manage the solution.

- *Process.* Availability monitoring should be a background activity to keep an eye on contingency resources in terms of its state of "readiness." Periodic review of contingency plans or as part of planning cycles should also be attempted. Operational process should prioritize "repair" work relating to events affecting availability.

2.6.2 Management Infrastructure Availability

With business expectations of 100% availability of systems and services, infrastructure management groups are looked on increasingly to providing the active management of resources to be used in the event of a contingency.

As described above, this involves a multi-faceted approach. In the era of business systems running on a relatively small number of mainframe or mini-computers, disaster recovery plans focused heavily on having the data regularly backed up and stored offsite. The major decision points in this scheme being *what data* is important, the *frequency* with which the data is moved offsite and the *mode or mechanisms* to execute the transfer offsite.

With client/server application architectures, computing environments have evolved from the processor-centric view of the mainframe to a *network-centric* one. The resources needed for a singe business service (or to achieve a single business level transaction) are dispersed across multiple servers. The servers may be platforms running different operating systems.

Each infrastructure element that a client/server based business service is dependent on for connectivity, processing or storage is vulnerable to failure. and with each failure the outage of the entire business service becomes a possibility. The data essential for a business function or process may therefore be spread across multiple machines.

Management of contingency resources for client/server applications requires a special analysis of dependencies. The identity of the application data to be moved, its source and target location, frequency for the move and the mode of movement need to be known in contingency planning of client/server systems. Rather than simple enumeration of data-files to be moved offsite, a more sophisticated tool is required to capture this information—one such tool, Service Graphs is described in Section 2.6.4.

Client/server systems introduce a second more serious complication—the *heterogeneity* of the data required for recovery of a process. End to end from user to systems this could include an operating system specific file, a relational table, an object oriented structure, a document. Each is likely to have to be captured in its native form.

Hence there are multiple *container* types (file, table, object, document, etc.) for data to be recovered on a contingency basis to re-enable a single business service. The problem now is to specify how these map onto a scaled-down environment at a contingency site, to have tested and verified the mapping assumptions.

This leads to a sizing of the client/server infrastructure to be duplicated at a contingency site. The size of the infrastructure is directly related to the number of business processes that need to recover to their planned check-points.

Metrics for Availability of Infrastructure. Infrastructure management in many organizations manage more than just the network elements. Hosts, operating systems, disk subsystems and horizontal applications such as e-mail and its associated support services are increasingly the responsibility of one group.

The user is usually not able to differentiate between an application failing and a network segment supporting the application failing. All failures of service tend to be blamed on the management group and reflect badly on IT in general. Developing a set of metrics for measuring and presenting actual failure patterns is a useful management tool. Table 2.5 shows a prototype of such metrics covering the main areas of infrastructure.

2.6.3 Infrastructure Management and Contingency Planning

The infrastructure management function plays a major role in contingency management of the business. Management architectures designed with this mission in mind can contribute greatly to the capacity for an organization to prevent small crises becoming disasters and in recovering from genuine disasters. As such the infrastructure management function should have a clear, proactive contingency management role:

- In contingency planning—developing a methodology that will work for the given enterprise and working with the business to develop plans by business lines.

- In the day-to-day monitoring and providing feedback on the contingency plan's operational status.

- Once a contingency site is permanently active, in transparently using contingency site resources for normal business.

- In the planning and advance placement of infrastructure resources to cope with different types of data—so that business recovery is not compromised through under-resourcing.

2.6.4 Service Graphs

Service graphs are a means of representing the inter-relationships between resources that participate in the delivery of a business service. Figure 2.8 shows the prototype for a service graph.

Table 2.5: Indicators for Availability of Network and Systems

Indicators	Sub-indicators	Best Practice	State of the Art
1. Availability of managed structure	MTBF per network		
	MTTR per network		
	Total downtime/month per network		
	No. of times/month/network redundant capability invoked		
	Total downtime per month per PUT leased link		
	Total downtime per month per data service connection		
2. Failure of network management infrastructure	No. of times secondary connection capability invoked		
	Critical management servers failures		
	Critical management database failures		
3. Failure of infrastructure services leading to business disruption	Class of Infrastructure Service per month by location		
4. Failure of infrastructure services largely unnoticed by business users	Class of Infrastructure Service per month by location		
5. Failure of infrastructure subsystems	Servers		
	Printers		
	Disk and archive		
	Workstations		

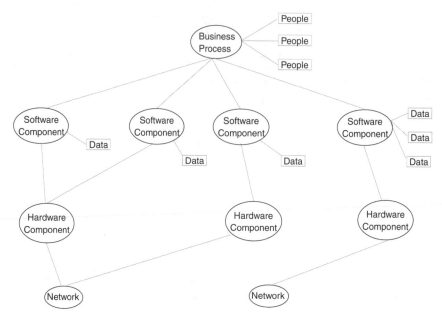

Figure 2.8: *Use of a service graph to capture service delivery information*

For each service the graph defines the following metrics:

- The *Recovery Time Objective.* This defines the elapsed time from a point-of-disaster to a point that restores a business service to full operations status. The capacity in terms of the number of users to be supported at the recovery point is also defined. For a "core" business service, a "sequence" of recovery time objectives may be appropriate—each successive element in the sequence defining increasing capacity.

- The *Recovery Point Objective.* This defines the condition and point to which the data refers to after recovery. All the data required and their location is enumerated and the mechanism by which each type of data can meet its recovery point objective is defined.

- *People involved in the process.* This defines the people in the current business process with data ownership responsibilities. The roles and responsibilities of these people should be periodically reviewed.

- *Technology.* The equipment classes, physical connections, network functionality used, circuits used, application and system software used by location for delivering the service is denoted in the graph to show relationships.

2.6.5 Steps to Contingency Planning

1. Identify all key business processes (for a line of business or business unit) and the business applications used in the processes.

2. Identify all resources participating at a business service or business application level.

3. Understand the implication of failure of any of these resources—i.e., the relationship between the resources and a business process.

4. Identify single points of failure in a given deployment of the identified resources.

5. Develop a business impact analysis in conjunction with the business.

Business Impact Analysis. The methodology for business impact analysis has to be developed together with the business. The organizational model in Chapter 3, Section 3.4.4 describes a business alignment role—this function is ideal to represent infrastructure management in this business "partnership."

The business case for contingency resourcing for a given business unit is developed from the results of a business impact analysis. The results of business impact analysis across business units allows an overview of the important business processes. Senior business management (very often at the board level) then has to define the priorities to be implemented for contingency resources.

As the nature of businesses changes in an organization, new impact analyses need to be undertaken. This is likely to result in new priorities and re-planning on how contingency resources are planned to be used.

2.6.6 Infrastructure Recovery

A major disaster may involve the loss of major parts of the infrastructure, including multiple LANs and LAN backbones. The steps to recovering the infrastructure involve the following activities:

1. Identify a new location. Invoke a pre-laid LAN or invoke the plan for building the contingency LAN in a contingency site. This should support the equipment and people identified by the contingency plan (for the affected line-of-business).

2. Arranging voice and data services or invoke pre-arranged services provisions from telecommunication vendors. Acquire computing and office equipment or invoke pre-arranged lease provisions from specialist disaster recovery suppliers.

3. Refine the contingency plan and install additional equipment, cabling and office equipment as required and capacity allows. Install computing equipment and appli-

cation software to configurations from a *master* user information base. Reload application data and execute pre-defined functional tests.

2.6.7 Quality of Contingency Plans

The quality of contingency plans determines an organization's readiness for disaster. The following set of questions define indicators to assess this quality:

1. Was contingency planning approached from a business perspective—specifically from a business impact viewpoint?

2. Does top management know the contingency strategy and is it publicized? Was the purpose of the contingency planning understood by the business?

3. Does senior management receive reports on contingency and disaster recovery status? Is middle business management advised on changes to the availability and contingency status (as monitored by the management framework management)?

4. Is contingency planning viewed as a process and not a one-off project? Is impact analysis going to be periodically executed to verify that business functions remain adequately covered?

2.7 User Awareness

User awareness is a conceptual tool. It allows an organization charged with managing an infrastructure to understand the business usage of the infrastructure. The concept covers the area of gathering and maintaining information about the IT assets used by the user community, serviced by the organization.

Ideally, the concept should also cover the continuous process of gaining and maintaining knowledge of the business-lines and their relative importance to the organization.

Enterprises with multiple business-lines that are globally organized are inevitably complex. There are three dimensions to consider when viewing a global enterprise from the infrastructure perspective:

- The number of business-lines themselves. Different business lines have different requirements from the infrastructure. A retail-type operation has different needs to a service-type business-line.

- The number of locations that the business-line consists of. If a business-line stretches across multiple locations, then there are likely to be fundamentally different infrastructure management needs—e.g., between a "hub" site and a smaller "satellite" site.

- The key business processes related to each business-line. Many businesses have reorganized along process lines. Some processes have to remain local for regulatory and taxation purposes, while other processes may span across both locations and business-lines.

2.7.1 Mapping Enterprise Reality to Infrastructure Needs

Until now this complexity has not been a problem since even within a single business-line "local autonomy" created islands of computing. As these separate operations are brought together for business reasons—to share data, to create economies of scale, to implement the results of business process re-engineering initiatives—infrastructure is expected to scale.

Figure 2.9 shows the relationship in a global enterprise between infrastructure and the three basic dimensions of business-line, location and process.

The mapping between business and infrastructure is most "natural" at the process level. At the business process level, an accurate requirement specification of key metrics of importance to the business is possible. Examples include:

- The nature of the application, its architecture, its support requirements, its requirements from the networks and systems.

- The performance needed end-to-end to satisfy a process.

- Types of transparency (the concealment from the users of the separation of process components) to be provided by the infrastructure. Failure transparency, location transparency of both users and systems, replication transparency.

Maintaining almost "empirical" information about the businesses which use the infrastructure does not come cheap. Knowledge of the business-line, its market evolution and tracking of internal reorganizations are essential. Two common methods of achieving this knowledge are through a business alignment staff position in infrastructure management or through an interface with the IT "account" managers into each business-line.

Many experiences show that IT account managers are often unwilling partners of infrastructure management. Organizations that choose this path should get clear buy-in about the purpose of the relationship directly from the business. They should also establish explicitly the roles and responsibilities of the account managers.

2.7.2 User Information

Accurate information about the user community is critical to many aspects of infrastructure management operations. Figure 2.10 shows the role of user information relative to some of the components of the organization model of infrastructure management in Chapter 3, Section 3.4.

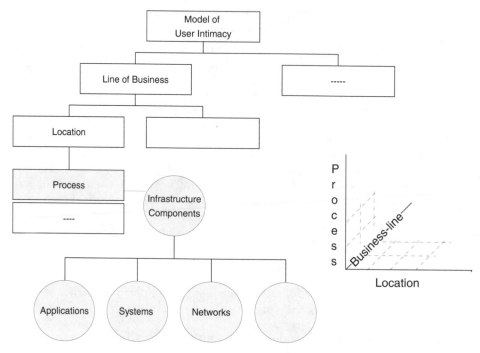

Figure 2.9: *Three basic dimensions of global business*

An infrastructure management group can get a clear edge from having intimate knowledge about the business areas and the users within each line-of-business within their domain.

This knowledge can be fed into the design of the key processes and associated technology used to provide services to end-users. Users should access services of the infrastructure management group through a single point on contact (called the service desk in the organizational model). This point of contact needs to be staffed with people trained to have customer serving skills in addition to technical competencies.

At this contact point, knowledge about contacting users can play significant dividends in providing a service-oriented image. Key pieces of information useful at this point include—where each user fits into an organization, which business areas or processes the user is involved in, knowledge of IT resources consumed, preferences, etc.

Another general principle of service is to keep the user informed of progress of any outstanding requests from the user to the contact point. This can extend to providing advisories of situations that may affect the users in a certain area. Such service is relatively easy if information is classified by the user.

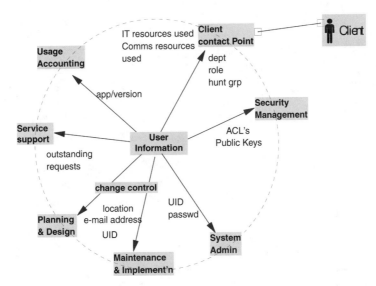

Figure 2.10: *Use of user information to infrastructure management functions*

Surveys of users attitudes to IT have shown again and again that users are more upset by not being informed about what is happening rather than failures in service or other problems occurring in the first place.

The infrastructure management group is unlikely to be the only technology group with relationships with the business users. Other functions that provide IT development services and internal IT "account" management roles are two that are commonly found in many organizations.

One of the important roles of the infrastructure manager is to establish peer relationships with these technologists and cascading to the rest of the group "intelligence" gained about users, impending changes, etc. from these sources.

Figure 2.11 shows the use of a directory-based database to hold user information. Directories were designed for just this purpose. A directory service can be used to satisfy imprecise queries and search for specific information with only partial knowledge of the structure or content in the database.

Availability of packaged LDAP/X.500 type directory technology now make enterprise-wide user information service to be feasible. The characteristics of X.500 that make it ideal as a user information database include:

- Built in resilience through replicating its data across multiple servers.

- The ability to maintain information close to its users.

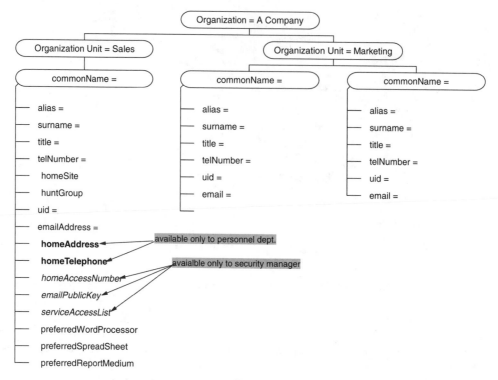

Figure 2.11: *Part of X.500 directory with arbitrary user attributes*

- Secure from both access and administrative points of view.

- An application programming interface allowing simple gateways to be built to import information from other management databases.

LDAP/X.500 is considered as an enabling technology in Chapter 12. The growth of the Internet and intranet have also created a demand for robust and scalable directories. In the above example, each entry in the directory consists of a name and a set of attributes. The values of the attributes may be populated by imports from, for example:

- Ticketing database—for outstanding requests from users and their status.

- Asset database—for applications and versions used, workstation details, services allowed, etc.

Some useful classes of information about users from an infrastructure management viewpoint are defined:

- *Role(s) in organization*

  Title, location/phone number, personal assistant details, whether member of any IT crisis committees, associated IT account manager

- *User preferences*

  Word-processor, spreadsheet and presentation tools
  Active e-mail user or paper reports required

- *IT resources used*

  Workstation/software
  Information feeds directly into workstation
  Specialized communication links with outside world
  Consumer of value added services from network management

- *Security related information*

  Frequency with which system passwords need to be changed
  Number of authentication keys held and type
  Enumerated access levels to all systems managed by service function
  Instances and types of security breaches

- *Status summary of outstanding user transactions*

  Equipment order
  Problem reports
  enquiries

2.7.3 Requirements of User Data

Building infrastructure management processes around user information places a major requirement on ensuring the quality and completeness of the information. Solutions such as X.500 only allow a focal database to be built. Information from other databases and other processes (such as human resource recruitment and termination processes) have to input data.

The quality of the interfaces, the quality of the importing processes and the quality of the data itself impact on the information in the user information database.

Another issue is that certain types of information about users may have to be kept relatively confidential. This requires at least a rudimentary confidentiality hierarchy to be developed.

2.7.4 Service Levels

The establishment of service level agreements (SLAs) with user groups is now widely practised—this is largely driven by end-users because of infrastructure's central role and infrastructure management's visibility as a cost center.

In all organizations there are groups of workers whose work is more critical to the business than others. Knowledge of such priorities are invaluable in the event of multiple crises affecting diverse user groups. The priority for the management of crises can be driven by previous agreements with the business.

SLAs allow the end-users and the service staff to have a common understanding of what is important to the business being supported. SLAs have a particular role to play when all or part of the infrastructure is outsourced. SLAs are often given in detail on such contracts and have to be carefully drafted. When multiple outsourcers are involved, SLAs have to "line up" so that end-to-end service delivery does not suffer.

2.7.5 Helping Technology Awareness

Technology Awareness programs bring together end-users and IT staff. Key areas where infrastructure management function can add value for its IT development clients is to provide information on:

- The effect of usage patterns on traffic flow and any extrapolations that may be made as to future capacity requirements.

- Models of projected usage of network in terms of latency, bandwidth and burstiness characteristics of applications.

- Remotely supported applications' impact on local metrics.

- Security and risk issues.

Such information helps IT development and infrastructure management to forge new relationships.

2.8 Books for Further Reading

Boar, Bernard. *The Art of Strategic Planning for Information Technology* (Crafting Strategy for the 90s). John Wiley & Sons, 1993.

Carson, Ewart R., and Robert R. Flood. *Dealing with Complexity* (An Introduction to the Theory and Application of System Science). Plenum Pub. Corp., 1993.

Kasser, Joe. *Applying Total Quality Management to Systems Engineering.* Artech House, 1995.

Lewis, Ronald J. *Activity-Based Models for Cost Management Systems.* Quorum Books, 1995.

Stalick, Susan K., *et al. Business Systems Engineering* (The Survival Guide). Yourdon Press Computing, 1994.

Vacca, John. *Intranet Security and Disaster Recovery Secrets.* IDG Books Worldwide, 1996.

3

Organizational Aspects of Infrastructure Management

Areas covered in this chapter

- Impact on infrastructure of organizational changes

- Concept and use of service delivery chains to analyze inter- and intra-organizational relationships

- Using quality metrics to determine and improve quality of infrastructure management

- Prototype organization functions in infrastructure management

- Key client-facing management functions and operational functions

- Concept of horizontal (or cross business) application services

- Security functions in infrastructure management

For client/server infrastructure to function as an *application delivery system,* skilled individuals need to fulfill specialist functions. For an infrastructure to function as a delivery system on a global scale requires an organization that is specifically designed for the role.

The part of the IT organization that is charged to manage the infrastructure may be integral to the enterprise or may be a third party—typically an outsourcer organization.

If infrastructure management is part of the IT function, the infrastructure is "owned" by the enterprise. Some outsourcer organizations provide only a service, while others also gain possession of the client's infrastructure.

In both cases the organization responsible for managing an infrastructure provides a number of services, some direct to end-users (such as a helpdesk, adding new users and moving users). Results of other services such as capacity planning or fault tracking are only indirectly seen by end-users.

Most infrastructure management organizations have grown almost as "organically" as the infrastructures they are asked to manage. They may have undergone a number of internal "mergers," downsizing and reorganizations. The logic and necessity of such corporate activities is seldom understood by those on the ground.

As responsibilities for different parts of the infrastructure are added, or concentrated into one organization, the opportunities to stand back and re-examine the overall workings of the organization diminishes.

The *prototype* of an infrastructure management organization is a useful baselining tool. The templates in the prototype define typical infrastructure management functions in an "average" enterprise. This definition of the prototype organization includes the key tasks of each sub-function and the information flow between them. Within such a prototype, centralized and decentralized models of support can be developed.

Another stabilizing tool is provided by developing and measuring against a set of quality metrics. These metrics refer to the services provided by the management organization. A management organization embarking on a program of change can find metrics a useful method for setting internal standards and goals.

Metrics can be used purely internally within the management organization for the ongoing development of the components of its services. Metrics are also a powerful communication tool in explaining and building business cases for developing infrastructure management.

The infrastructure management organization, because of its responsibilities, has a number of business relationships with other organizations. These relationships result in a flow of information between the parties. Examining this information within the context of a service delivery chain provides a starting point in understanding and improving key relationships.

3.1 Organizational Structures

As a side effect of downsizing in the late 1980s and early 1990s, many large enterprises ended up with more direct departmental responsibility for computing directions. Each business unit developed its own associated networks, helpdesks, and different ways of hiring and working in the various technology management disciplines.

While this was successful when the downsized businesses were self-contained, as soon as integration of businesses was attempted organizational practices within these islands effectively became constraints on speedy integration. When integration was attempted on a global scale, other organizational constraints became evident.

From the mid-1990s onwards there has been a slowdown of decentralization of infrastructure management functions. In many cases there has been an effective reversal to central IT control of the function. This is often accompanied by an explicit recognition of the infrastructure's relationship to business delivery. The new centralized function is given the mission of re-aligning the infrastructure's evolution to meet business goals.

An alternative to centralized functions has been partial or complete outsourcing of the infrastructure's management. Complete outsourcing is still uncommon. Partial outsourcing (for example, the WAN factor or all structures from the backbone LAN up to and including the desktop) is likely to gain popularity.

In either case, multiple teams with different reporting lines and with specific responsibility for the network, or systems or applications, etc. were and still are the norm. Sometimes a specialized, complex application, such as a market data system in an investment bank, was also delivered to the business—adding another support group.

Other causes of organizational diversity in the infrastructure management function are the widespread mergers and acquisitions that have taken place across most business sectors. A challenge is to rationalize such organizational diversity in the light of:

- *Lack of common management frameworks.* Each part of the enterprise is likely to have developed some technical and people framework for management functions. The mapping over dissimilar frameworks of common processes such as fault reporting and tracking is difficult if not impossible. Another area of disconnect is in disaster preparedness, where different business units have different viewpoints.

- *Lack of clear boundaries of responsibility.* Infrastructure often spans geographic and political boundaries. Where any IT service has to be delivered across boundaries, responsibility rarely resides with one group.

- *Different reporting lines.* Different groups usually have different goals and agendas. In most organizations there is a level of healthy rivalry between groups with similar remits in different locations. A level of competition also often exists between groups with different remits such as systems management and network management. Beyond a certain point, however, competitiveness stops essential cooperation between groups and between locations.

In general an infrastructure management organization has the following types of work activity:

- *Control operations* that manage the superstructures and enabler services that make service delivery in service operations possible.

- *Service operations* that provide "tangible" services to consumers, whether they are the end-users or other internal service functions. Many such services are accessed from a helpdesk.

- *Development operations* that provide the evolutionary force for the managed environment changing in an ordered way.

- *Security operations* that manage the IT security aspects—independent of the other three areas in order to avoid any conflict of interest.

The organizational model in Section 3.4 provides the function level "prototype" to define a common framework applicable across an organization. The business areas need to map to generic organizational units. Figure 3.1 shows an example of this mapping of business areas to activity types.

3.1.1 Going Global

During the late 1990s many enterprises undertook a global view of their business. When an enterprise decides to reorganize as a global business, information flow over the infrastructure generally increases. Information sharing becomes of paramount importance.

Infrastructure management has to be organized along new lines to support the new patterns of business flow. Organizational design requires a fundamental understanding of the business and the information "assets" of importance to the business. Some of the key organizational issues raised by globalization of business are briefly discussed below:

- Business units are likely to consist of more dispersed groups of people—including a "nomadic" population, widely different sizes of offices ranging from a few thousand per site to one or two in remote offices. Infrastructure management needs to have the "reach" to meet the requirements of a dispersed group while maintaining consistent service levels.

- Connecting offices together of widely differing sizes raises its own special set of challenges: the structure of the helpdesk to support the range of offices, delivery of "local" IT support to small and remote offices, design responsibility and funding for an infrastructure management framework to provide management across the range of offices—are common concerns.

- Business processes in a globalized business spans the geographically distributed groups. The current generation of client/server applications, commonly used in enterprises, is unlikely to have been designed with high availability in mind. Providing availability solutions that work across major time zones, contingency planning that spans cultural and political boundaries, phasing physical re-engineering activities are common difficulties facing infrastructure management.

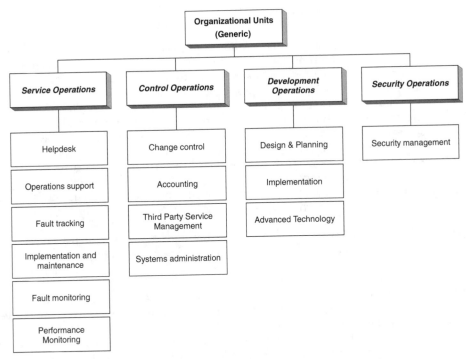

Figure 3.1: *Mapping business areas to generic organizational areas*

- There are often multiple lines of business in an enterprise. The high cost of infrastructures for client/server applications makes their sharing by different businesses likely. Infrastructure management, however, now has to understand the workings of multiple businesses if business-aware support is to be provided.

In reality, much of the above is still in the class of a wish list. Many compromises have to be made today. As experience of managing global infrastructures grows, however, organizational design will make a major contribution to solving such problems.

3.2 *Service Delivery Chains*

The infrastructure management organization is only one component in delivering IT services to an enterprise. Client/server and intranet-based application services are likely to be only a small part of the portfolio of IT services brought to the enterprise.

The delivery chain, with an infrastructure management organization as the central component, is likely to be relatively complex. A delivery chain describes relationships necessary

Case Study 3.1: Bureaucracy and Project Delivery

Company A and Company B merged after a period of negotiation. This resulted in an ad hoc re-engineering of Company B's IT operations (Company A was the larger, dominant partner). A number of new cross company IT initiatives were started to build the new organization.

Company B had actively encouraged a project-oriented culture where successful project delivery was rewarded both financially and in company-wide recognition. This had over some years attracted competent and focused individuals who were used to being given total responsibility for delivering business-oriented results. Architecture and internal standards played a major part in the culture of delivery.

Company A had a more centralized "methodology," that had been in place for over 10 years. Under this method each project went through many review cycles starting with a resource and cost review panel. Project proposals were often pared down with the result that in Company A, delivered solutions which were "just adequate." Many projects had historically failed to deliver.

The analysis by Company B's project managers concluded that while Company A was good at controlling costs it did not have the capability to control project requirements. Secondly, Company A's methodology deliberately added resources to a late project. Many late projects eventually became failed projects.

When projects were run by Company B's managers under the new scheme and began to fail, a major campaign was begun to abandon the old methodology. The reduction of bureaucracy was supported by the business users, and a joint presentation was made to the board.

The board was convinced by the evidence that bureaucratic mechanisms had to be dismantled if the company was to both retain key skills as well as benefit from the program of change.

Lessons

Projects should be started with realistic resource requirements. "Negotiating down" resources on a per project basis tends to inflate requirements. Successful project managers know that managing requirements (input) controls how much resources are consumed.

Any campaign to change the culture of delivering IT should be driven by end-users (consumers) of the results.

IT methodologies should change with the changing needs, and need to be pertinent to the technologies deployed using it and add value to the delivery.

to deliver the whole management function. A "functional" delivery chain consists of many smaller delivery chains linked together.

A delivery chain is "held together" by information flow. Developing a delivery chain (or chart) is an essential part of understanding how a function such as infrastructure management is related both internally and externally within an enterprise.

Figure 3.2 shows infrastructure management function in a central position. Common categories of functions (such as application users), with a "direct interface" to infrastructure management, radiate from it. A further level of functions radiate from, for example, "Sys-

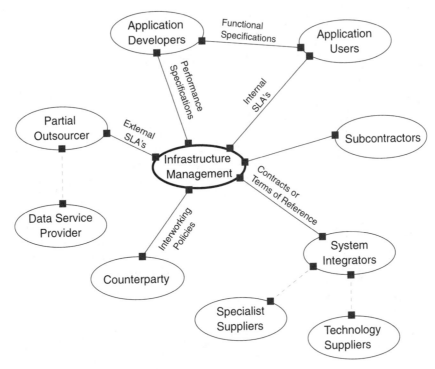

Figure 3.2: *Infrastructure management as one link in the total service delivery chain*

tems Integrators." These second-level functions have no direct interface to infrastructure management; however, the systems integration service (continuing the example), seen from the infrastrucutre management perspective, is dependent on the quality of dilivery by these second-level functions.

- *Third parties* such as systems integration services or specialist service providers. Such relationships are most often formalized through legally binding agreements such as contracts and service level agreements (SLAs). The content of these formal documents is often negotiated by the parties involved and are specific to the parties. Professional input, such as from a legal team, is often necessary to ensure interests are being met.

- *Internal users.* Managing the service expectations of users through formal and informal service level agreements and performance specifications. These are not legally binding but nevertheless are likely to be questioned if expectations are not being met. The relationship between the people responsible for infrastructure service delivery and the users varies widely between enterprises and even within enterprises.

The levels of user intimacy and the competencies available for communicating with the businesses determine the information content of this relationship.

- *Counter-parties.* Several management "domains" often exist in an enterprise spanning a global extant or major time zones. Relationships are through interworking agreements. Examples include the timetable for out-of-hours monitoring and a security policy that all relevant counter- parties subscribe to. In some cases counter-parties may exist with respect to a distinct specialty area.

- *Outsourcer organizations* which have responsibility for managing the whole or some part of the infrastructure. This is also often managed through formal contracts. In addition, one or the other organization subscribes to or interfaces to the working procedures of the other.

Figure 3.2 shows the infrastructure management function having direct interfaces to the different types of organizations described above. These *primary* organizations have relationships to other organizations shown by the different links. Although not shown, these secondary organizations have relationships with other organizations further down the chain.

In addition to identifying and defining information flows, a service delivery chain also defines a dependency graph. The graph helps to design processes that defines activities that go outside an enterprise's management boundaries.

For example, a new-technology rollout process, aimed at changing the desktop technology of thousands of users globally in an enterprise, has to be cognizant of all the smaller delivery chains involved in planning. Time related and other dependencies from the secondary chains feed into the performance of the larger (rollout) process.

Third-party relationships are especially critical during periods of infrastructure crisis. Hence as part of a wider relationship strategy, strong bonds approaching "partnerships" are often to be recommended. Partnership involves sharing information at a planning stage about major projects and emerging requirements.

Developing and maintaining a service delivery chain is one method of analyzing such requirements.

3.2.1 Inter-Organizational Dependencies

A service delivery chain defines dependencies on other organizations in order to deliver infrastructure related services to local users. Some of these dependencies are formally defined through service level agreements. Others are defined by shorter-term commercial contracts such as an equipment order for services or equipment.

Time elements are common to all types of dependencies. Two common, subjective criteria in establishing long-term partnerships (whether with a vendor or an outsourcer) is how "responsive" the party is and the "turnaround" time from request to delivery.

Responsiveness and turnaround are both determined by the capacity of the supplier organization to deal with the requests—seen across their client interface. Relationships between an infrastructure management organization and a supplier organization should be through well-defined interfaces. Client interfaces have both human and information technology aspects. A key activity in developing long-term partnerships is the "design" of this interface:

- Most supplier organizations now have a concept of a client manager—an individual or a team whose job is to understand and service the requirements of a specific client. From the client viewpoint, managing multiple relationships with service and product suppliers constitute the wider role of vendor management. Depending on the "quality" of the respective people on both sides of an interface, both the client and supplier organizations can form long-term working relationships.

- Informational interfaces between the client and supplier organizations (e.g., through their respective intranets, inter-connected via the external Internet), defines a longer term view of the relationship. In certain industries such as shipping and investment banking there are third-party organizations selling information connectivity as a value added service.

The actual information that flows across the client/supplier interface has to be designed in the case of bilateral relationships. E-mail is one informal mechanism for information flow. Web-based pages and forms offer a more specific and structured means of communication.

The information that flows across industry-specific value added services are often predefined at the interface to the service. Sometimes a "black box" solution may be available to convert to and from the value added service's conventions to more common formats such as spreadsheets.

3.2.2 Inter-Organizational Processes

Section 3.4 defines a business model of infrastructure management. Chapter 5 elaborates on some of the key internal processes within the business model. Internal processes often have to *handover* across an interface with another organization.

For example, a problem tracking process often depends on close interaction with a vendor's product experts. In a case of problem resolution, information about the problem is likely to be sent to these external experts. Information also flows into the management organization—for example, a bug fix from a vendor or a report from a consultancy.

A key point about inter-organizational processes is that the end originating the information flow effectively loses control of the process once it exits its IT boundaries.

Agreements on standards between organizations at either end of a process relationship determines how well constructed incoming information is for organizational consumption.

Consider the case of an e-mail-with-attachment medium used by two organizations for communication within a delivery chain. Unless the recipients of the e-mail can read the attachment, it has little utility in information transfer.

Because the organization at either end of a chain can change internal IT standards without recourse to the other, assumptions about communication mediums have to be periodically re-visited. In the above example if one organization decides to standardize on a package that is not available to the other, then the current communication method effectively terminates.

Similarly, internal reorganizations and business re-alignments with new external parties may also affect the conduct of inter-organizational processes.

This loss of control at an organization's IT boundary affects the design of processes with external interfaces. The "reliability" of the outside organization and the longevity of the relationship often determines how defensively the dependency needs to be managed. Dependencies in outside supplier organizations may be managed as a *risk* affecting the client organization—as defined in in Chapter 2, Section 2.3.

Case Study 3.2: Changing Outsourcers

An insurance company had outsourced its PC/server environment of some 5,000 users to an outsourcer on the basis of the lowest cost bid that significantly reduced the company's cost base.

A "design & transition" phase of 3 months was followed by a subsequent "honeymoon" period of some 6 months. During the latter it became obvious that the outsourcer could not cope with the support needs of the company. Despite the outsourcer pouring people into solving the defect—service seen by end-users actually deteriorated. This deterioration was determined by quality metrics for key functions.

At a checkpoint at the end of the honeymoon period the contract was suspended and the outsourcer was given a further 3 months to pull its act together.

When the outsourcer still had not achieved any significant improvement in 2 months, the insurance company started negotiation with another outsourcer. A strategy based on managing transition risk was worked out by technical staff who the company had retained.

At the end of the 3-month notice period, the transition was executed and the new outsourcer took over all responsibility for the service portfolio.

The maturity and capability of the new outsourcer was obvious from the beginning and over some two years both the overall cost base and delivery quality have improved.

Lessons learned:

While cost cutting is the commonest motivation for outsourcing, the lowest cost bid is not a sound basis for choosing an outsourcing partner.

The client company had developed a number of risk management factors into the contract—including measurement of delivery quality metrics, "honeymoon" and "cooling-off" periods. This allowed it to make hard decisions without undue compromise of "operations integrity."

The company had retained enough technical expertise to ensure that it was not totally at the mercy of the outsourcer.

The company had set internal expectations with users in terms of there being genuine risks and how the risks were being managed.

3.3 Quality Metrics for Infrastructure Management

An indicator of the degree service ethic in any service organization is shown by the importance given to providing a high quality of service. Quality as a service goal is essential to managing complex systems such as client/server infrastructures.

The notion of quality is made concrete by identifying the metrics relevant to infrastructure management and defining the methods for collecting and measuring each metric.

Metric collection, organization and storage should be automated as far as possible. Apart from labor savings on the manual procedures, automation has the added value that the resulting metrics are often more believable to people outside the infrastructure management organization. Being able to explain the methodology of collection, measurement and reporting implemented in the automation scheme gives potential subscribers greater confidence in the results.

A taxonomy of infrastructure management quality indicators and key metrics within each area are defined in Section 3.3.2. This provides a total of some 150 metrics. Not all are relevant to every organization.

There are external benchmark consulting organizations that can provide data about best practice and what is possible with state-of-the-art tools in each of the areas that the metric covers.

3.3.1 Using Quality Metrics

Once collection and measuring has begun it needs to be stabilized as a normal activity. The metric data's most important use is as a tool to identify areas for improvement within the infrastructure management organization.

The prioritizing of actual areas to be tackled for improvement is best driven by a preceding gap analysis against sound business goals. Hence if specific services such as the hours of coverage need improving, as part of specific business goals being achieved, that area is likely to be justified as an area for improvement.

Subsets of quality metrics may be used for different purposes—specifically:

- To define the infrastructure management organization goals in terms of achieving change, driven by best practice or what is possible with state-of-the-art tools. Once goals have been set in terms of improvement that will be measured over a period of time, the group achievements over the period can be reported.

- As input to a gap analysis exercise aimed at prioritizing short-term budget spent to improve service delivery in focused areas. For example, to reduce the lead-time in a specific process such as change management or the range of functions offered by the helpdesk. The gap may also be defined by a new business goal such as "expansion to a new overseas office within a specified time window."

- To profile an infrastructure management organization's operations against best practice. The data for this is provided by an external agency specializing in benchmarks in this area. Although gap analysis is still used to identify areas for improvement, the motivation for profiling is different. Profiling helps longer term, strategic investment decisions to be made. It also helps to identify infrastructure dependencies of strategic business goals.

- To demonstrate increasing or decreasing effectiveness in infrastructure management operations over a period of time—through the difference in measured metric values. The period in question may represent the course of different events—such as downsizing, merging functions or a major business move.

- To define the requirements and set the expectations for outsourcing in whole or in part of the infrastructure management operation. Metrics allow the client enterprise (outsourcing the operation), to enter into negotiations about service level agreements and other contract details from a strong position. The metrics and the associated operations costs provide a baseline relative to which the outsourcer needs to show value.

3.3.2 Key Quality Indicators

The following sections define a set of key quality indicators relevant to a typical infrastructure management organization. (These are shown shaded in Figure 3.3.) Each indicator category expands out to define several specific metrics in the area. Those shown here should be treated only as examples in each area.

Supersets or subsets of these metrics are likely to be relevant to individual enterprises. In fact, an enterprise may also have other quality indicators to add to these prototype metrics.

A set of metrics tailored for an enterprise may be used for the various purposes described in Section 3.3.1. These quality metrics are compatible with the business model described in Section 3.4. The information tree for these quality indicators is shown in Figure 3.3. The three main categories of quality discussed are:

- *Organization quality*—which examines how well the management organization "fits" to its mission.

- *Quality of design*—which examines how specific functional components match the needs of infrastructure management's operations.

- *Quality of processes*—which examines the quality of the processes that define the management organization's operations.

Each of the indicators shown in the information tree is expanded in the tables that follow—one table for each leaf of the information tree. Each table shows the value for each

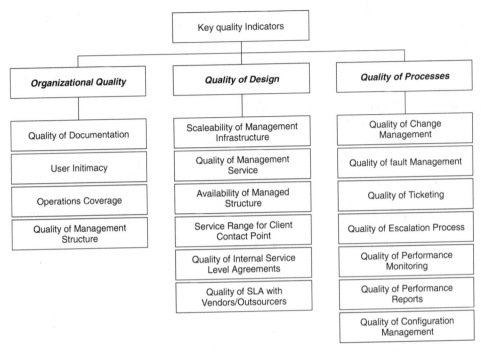

Figure 3.3: *Information tree for common quality indicators*

metric on a *best practice* basis taken across eight organizations, and also with respect to what is possible with the current *state-of-the-art* in the field.

3.3.3 Organizational Quality

Organizational quality is a measure of how the organizational structure favors the scope and nature of the tasks in the infrastructure management portfolio. Many organizational structures are remnants of the *datacenter/communication* split environments of the late 1970s.

These were characterized by the rigid roles assigned for people and hierarchical management structure in controlling it. Such delineation of responsibility is an "inhibitor" in infrastructure management, where cooperation between individuals and groups is required to fulfill even ordinary operational duties.

The datacenter and glass-house cultures (centralized power and remoteness from the user base), have in many cases survived into the "downsized" enterprise. Such a culture is likely to re-emerge in some enterprises as infrastructure management becomes a more centralized function or is even outsourced.

Re-training and re-skilling can alleviate some of the shortfalls in large-scale infrastructure skills. Viewing the infrastructure as an application delivery system, however, requires a high degree of technical education levels, as well as skills in abstract thinking, diagnosis and problem solving and working in multi-disciplinary teams.

Quality of documentation. The availability of up-to-date information "immediately" to hand, very often determines the fine line between success and failure during an infrastructure crisis. Table 3.1 shows examples of metrics in this area. Core infrastructure management processes should output high-quality information for this reason.

Table 3.1: Quality of Documentation Indicators

Indicators	Metrics	Best Practice	State of the Art
1. Documented information	Security guidelines	Yes	
	Backup plans	Yes	
	Escalation procedures	Yes	
	Physical network	Yes	
	Logical topologies	Yes	
	Common fault recovery blueprints		In modular nets
	Roles and responsibilities	Yes	
	Organization chart	Yes	
	Maintenance contracts	Yes	
	Internal and External SLAs	Yes	
	Consultancy contracts	Yes	
	Outsourcing contracts	Yes	
2. Identifiable responsibility (at functional level/ process task level) for documentation	Checking accuracy, completeness		
	Control timeliness of update		
3. Availability of documentation "to hand"	Accessible on a backed-up file server	Yes for all	
	Kept instantly available as hardcopy	Yes for some	

A key role is that of a librarian who takes responsibility for controlling this information, including checking for accuracy and completeness. Each type of service-related document should therefore be produced to an internal standard. The document standard should specify the tools to use, naming and storage conventions.

Information should be made available in such a way that it is viewed within the infrastructure group as a "common" resource. This could be through an in-line document access server. Private databases should be banned as a matter of policy.

User intimacy. This defines the level to which the infrastructure management group understands its customers. Table 3.2 shows examples of metrics in this area. Ironically, this concept flies in the face of what many infrastructure management groups think their remit to be—which is to manage the technology.

In a client/server environment an end-user is likely to require access to many services on the infrastructure to complete a single business transaction. Infrastructure management groups can quickly become out of touch with the pace with which business systems change. Once knowledge about the end-user becomes obsolete, there is usually a downward spiral of deteriorating relationships between the infrastructure management groups and the users of their service.

A widely accessible repository of user information, maintained to be up-to-date by management processes such as the change management process is a major information asset.

Table 3.2: User Intimacy Indicators

Indicators	Sub-indicators	Best Practice	State of the Art
1. Central repository for user information	User preferences	Yes	
	IT resources used	Yes	
	User service priorities	Yes	
2. Feedback or status updates provided to users for	Progress of user change requests		Tracking system
	Progress of user reported faults		Tracking system
	Progress of enquiries	Yes	
3. "Quality of Service Delivery" user survey	Done annually		
	Done more frequently	Yes	
4. Access to systems that are similar to users		Yes	

Other aspects of this metric are user satisfaction surveys and a framework to provide users with progress feedback on user requests. Infrastructure service personnel should have access systems that are equivalent to ones users report problems about.

Operations coverage. The use of computing systems has reached a certain level of maturity that many businesses view it in terms of a plug-and-use "utility" similar to electric power. In many business sectors there is a need for "non-stop" availability of systems. Secondly, many businesses are global in nature where information flows from somewhere in the world throughout the day.

Wider operations coverage requirements result from the needs for 24-hour non-stop working and non-stop systems availability. Table 3.3 shows examples of metrics in this area.

The current generation of management protocols unfortunately do not allow "safe" remote management practices for mission critical applications. Systems can be monitored at sites which have shut at the end of day, from remote sites that are still open.

While many organizations apply 24-hour monitoring of "common" infrastructure resources, few envisage extensions to processes to remotely fix any complex problems at the

Table 3.3: Operation Coverage Indicators

Indicators	Sub-indicators	Best Practice	State of the Art
1. Normal hours covered and compatibility with business needs	Weekdays		
	Weekends		
	Out-of-hours per 24 hours/ 7 days		
2. Coverage scheme	Holidays		
	Sickness		
	Out-of-hours		
3. Non-local coverage	Remote offices		
	Handover with another management domain		
4. User satisfaction with coverage	Normal hours		
	Out-of-hours		
	Remote offices		
	Cooperating management domain		

monitored site. Hence, all large sites have recourse to people who can be called out when "simple" fixes don't work.

Coverage is an issue close to users. If users start work very early or stay very late, support is fully expected during the whole period. User satisfaction surveys should examine user perceptions on coverage.

Quality of Management Structure. This is a quality measure of staffing and its appropriateness to management tasks. The level of empowerment is against each management process. See Chapter 5 for details on the extent of empowerment possible for the key infrastructure management processes.

Large infrastructure management organizations inevitably have an administrative overhead. A goal of any such organization is to keep control over this overhead. Another goal is to have multi-skilled people with at least one secondary area of expertise. This is often achieved through training.

The helpdesk is the key interface with the business users, hence its efficiency is directly seen by these users. Table 3.4 shows examples of metrics in this area.

Table 3.4: *Quality of Management Structure Indicators*

Indicators	Sub-indicators	Best Practice	State of the Art
1. Administrative to experts ratio		1:20	
2. Level of empowerment by process:	Fault management	Hit team	
	Change management	Multi-disciplinary team	
	Security audit	Individual	
	Network migration	3rd party	
3. Single-line expert/multi-skilled expert ratio		1:1	
4. Efficiency of helpdesk (HD)	Contacts handled/number of HD persons	30 per person	
	Contacts handled/resolved at HD	70%	
5. Staff turnaround at helpdesk	Over 6 months	0	
	Over 12 months	5%	

3.3.4 Quality of Design

Quality of design metrics define how well the systems and frameworks used for management meets the needs of a specific enterprise. Most items in the group are systems related and technical.

Increasingly, the quality of design of the infrastructure management framework is as important as the quality of client/server environment being managed.

Scaleability of Infrastructure Management Service. These define the level of scaleability inherent in the architecture of the infrastructure management service. Scaleability defines the degree to which the service can be scaled up or down (e.g., by site size or by the number of computing environments supported). Service architecture minimally includes frameworks for monitoring events that indicate fault, performance or security problems.

The architecture also determines the efficiency with which capacity on the network is used up for management purposes. The use of open protocols is another key indicator of scaleability. The consistency with which security is applied in local and remote operations indicates whether safety is a consideration.

The architecture also defines how different platforms may be used in different parts of the infrastructure. Table 3.5 shows examples of metrics in this area.

Table 3.5: *Quality Indicators for Scaleability of Infrastructure Management Service*

Indicators	Sub-indicators	Best Practice	State of the Art
1. Level of scaleability	By adding framework "modules"	Yes	
	By adding OS level framework		Yes
	By making framework larger/smaller	Yes	
	By including framework at external locations	Yes	
2. Bandwidth efficiency for management operations	On LAN/MAN as function of (Number of managed nodes and subnet)	1 pkts/sec per node, 5 pkts/sec per subnet	
	On WAN as function of (management traffic/business traffic ratio and time-of-day)	5% during business hours, 20% out	

***Table** 3.5: Quality Indicators for Scaleability of Infrastructure Management Service (continued)*

Indicators	Sub-indicators	Best Practice	State of the Art
3. Use of "open standards"	SNMP	Yes	
	SNMP V2		Yes
	CMIP/CMOT		Yes
	ANSI SQL	Yes	
	RPC	Yes	
4. Consistency in security practice in local/remote management operations		Yes	
5. Architecture "type"	Best-of-breed	Yes	
	Single vendor		In subsets
	Ad hoc	80%	
6. Management platforms	Network management		
	Systems management		
	Multi-function or manager of managers	Yes	
7. Web/intranet use in management	for deploying in-house management applications		
	for distribution of management information		
	for staging and processing from operating system utilities tools		

Quality of Infrastructure Management Service. The services offered by infrastructure management organizations can be described in terms of general efficiency and measures. Throughput defines the capacity of the organization to handle different categories of work.

The ability of the organization to complete work to user satisfaction is shown by a ratio—new work/re-work. Another set of metrics is provided by the time it takes for the organization to respond initially to service requests. Variance here is immediately felt by the users. Table 3.6 shows examples of metrics in this area.

Table 3.6: Indicators for Quality of Infrastructure Management Service

Indicators	Sub-indicators	Best Practice	State of the Art
Work throughput (for problems and fault fixes,	Per month		
user add/moves, new projects,	Peak over 12 months		
maintenance projects, etc.)	Average over 12 months		
New work/re-work ratio	Per month, average over 12 months	8:1 jobs	
Variance of initial response time	To fault reports	± 10%	
	To add/move/change requests	± 10%	
	To equipment orders	± 10%	
	To information requests	± 10%	

Quality of Service Level Agreements. Service Level Agreements define contracts between the network management group and the users of the network managed by the group. SLAs also define contracts between the organization and outsourcer organization. Table 3.7 shows examples of metrics in this area.

Table 3.7: Indicators for Quality of SLAs

Indicators	Sub-indicators	Best Practice	State of the Art
1. With internal users	Expressed in business terms	Yes	
2. User responsibility awareness	Virus guidelines	Yes	
	Password guidelines	Yes	
3. With external parties	Drawn up by legal counsel	Yes	
	Penalty terms explicit	Yes	
	Confidentiality terms explicit	Yes	

3.4 Organizational Model of Infrastructure Management

The Network Management Forum's model briefly discussed in Chapter 1, Section 1.6, is a good starting point for viewing infrastructure management as a services business. It is, however, inadequate for a business with a broad technology scope. It also does not cover the geographic extent of infrastructure management and realities of interacting with the business users who are widely dispersed. Figure 3.4 shows an augmented model with an additional number of strategic functions:

- **Infrastructure Steering** is a group of infrastructure managers, end-users and other IT and business function heads that define the strategic and tactical directions for the infrastructure management group. Steering is a strategic function.

- **Horizontal Services Administration** is a group responsible for the administration of applications such as corporate databases, client server database engines, corporate e-mail as well as services such as directory services and middleware. Such services increasingly span the whole enterprise and enable users to share information and resources.

- **Inter/Intranet Services Management** is a group responsible for the enterprise's electronic interface with the outside world. Such services have to be actively managed as a means of connecting with clients, partners, suppliers and increasingly as market channels. The same group or a sub-group is responsible for managing internal, intranet services. Intranets are increasingly important for mass, cost-effective applications to be deployed.

- **Business Alignment** is a group responsible for understanding business goals and directions, to interpret these goals to drive the development of the infrastructure. Ensuring that the services available in the infrastructure are aligned to business requirements becomes more important as infrastructures grow bigger.

This model has an interface with the management technology components used to access or process raw information from the environment being managed. This model also provides the means to define relationships between management processes and people. The business areas of this model also help to "stage" process flows. Exercises such as profiling or benchmarking and gap analysis are much easier within an organizational structure.

Some business areas provide functions closely related to the users of the infrastructure and hence may be termed "front-office" in a traditional business sense. The "back-office" defines functions that are intimately related to the structure of the environment being managed and the infrastructure management technology used.

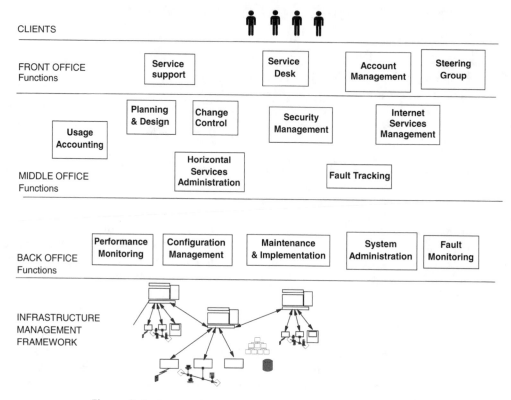

CLIENTS

FRONT OFFICE
Functions

MIDDLE OFFICE
Functions

BACK OFFICE
Functions

INFRASTRUCTURE
MANAGEMENT
FRAMEWORK

Figure 3.4: *An organizational model of infrastructure management*

A third category of functions play a "middle-office" role of consolidating information from the front and back offices. Figure 3.4 shows a classification of the business areas in these categories. The key activities within each area are defined in the subsections below.

Steering, service desk, inter/intra net management and horizontal services administration span across geographic and time boundaries. This is shown in Table 3.8. Infrastructure "content" is directly related to office size. A enterprise may consist of multiple "global" businesses that are geographically distributed across different size offices. Figure 3.5 shows the relationship between office size, infrastructure and management

Table 3.8: *A Simple Classification of Offices and Infrastructure*

Management Function	Large/Hub Office	Medium-size Office	Small-size Office	Affiliate Office
Steering	|-----------------group spans all offices----------------------|		
Service Desk	on site	on site/virtual	virtual/3rd party	3rd party
Service Support	on site			
Business Alignment	|-----------------group spans all offices----------------------|		
Fault Tracking	on site	on site		
Change Control	on site			
Planning and Design	on site			
Performance Monitoring	on site			
Fault Monitoring	on site			
Internet Services Management	|-----------------group spans all offices----------------------|		
Horizontal Services Administration	|-----------------group spans all offices----------------------|		
Systems Administration	on site			
Security Management	on site			

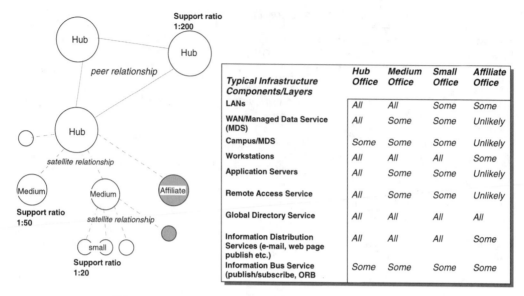

Typical Infrastructure Components/Layers	Hub Office	Medium Office	Small Office	Affiliate Office
LANs	All	All	Some	Some
WAN/Managed Data Service (MDS)	All	Some	Some	Unlikely
Campus/MDS	Some	Some	Some	Unlikely
Workstations	All	All	All	Some
Application Servers	All	Some	Some	Unlikely
Remote Access Service	All	Some	Some	Unlikely
Global Directory Service	All	All	All	All
Information Distribution Services (e-mail, web page publish etc.)	All	All	All	Some
Information Bus Service (publish/subscribe, ORB	Some	Some	Some	Some

Note:
- Typiclal number client/server support people needed for user population changes with size of office.
- Larger offices give better economies of scale for internal support

Figure 3.5: *Relationship of types of offices, service relationship, and infrastructure*

3.4.1 Steering

In infrastructure management at an enterprise level, the steering function is the key to ensuring the infrastructure develops to meet business expectations. In enterprises that are geographically distributed, a steering group may have subsidiary groups working at either a business level or by a primary location.

The general role of the steering group is independent of whether the infrastructure management function is an internal corporate function, or if it is partially outsourced or fully outsourced. Steering for infrastructure management covers the following activities:

- Ensuring that the infrastructure management group's direction is coordinated where necessary across geographic and "political" boundaries.

- Coordinating the policy issues of managing the infrastructure, including ratifying service-level agreements with internal users and external suppliers.

- Resolving conflicting requirements from different user groups and in prioritizing projects to be delivered to different user groups.

- Prioritizing investment and funding requirements and representing these at the enterprise funding fora.

Given its coordinating role, steering needs to meet periodically to determine the overall direction of the infrastructure management group's work.

Steering members have individual roles to play in representing the work of the infrastructure management group to the business and in providing early intelligence on major business activities that will affect the infrastructure.

Sub-groups of steering sometimes have a mediation role to play in the resolution of service related issues between the infrastructure management group and business users.

3.4.2 Service Desk

The help or service desk is a logical point of contact for all users of the infrastructure. It is logical in the sense that the physical location and structure of the service desk is transparent to the "contacting" user. Global business also implies mobility across offices. A single service desk number maintains continuity.

Business users increasingly prefer to have a single point of contact to articulate all their IT needs. The service desk on the other hand may not be able to handle the full range of needs. The service desk personnel should have a high enough level of product or service training to answer common questions for the full range of services offered.

The services supported by the service desk depend on the enterprise. From a process viewpoint the service desk plays a key role as it is the sole interface for the business users and therefore represents the service organization. Service desk personnel skills should therefore include client interaction skills.

In large enterprises there is a trend towards consolidating the service desk at a small number of locations, usually on a regional and time zone basis. Typically, two to three such primary service desks exist in a global enterprise such as an investment bank.

A number of subsidiary service desks may be located at offices that with a "critical" mass of people and systems. A central service desk is responsible for delegating low level service functions to the subsidiary service desks.

Service desks are often outsourced, or in smaller offices may be subcontracted to a third party. Table 3.9 defines generic quality indicators for the service desk function.

The sub-indicators column expands on the generic area. The best practice shows whether the area is implemented in any of the sample of eight organizations surveyed for this publication. The state-of-the-art column shows whether technology is available to implement the area.

3.4.3 Service Support

Service support is the main support group. Problems that are not solved at the service desk result in a trouble ticket being created, which by default becomes the responsibility of this

Table 3.9: Quality Indicators for Service Desk Function

Indicators	Sub-indicators	Best Practice	State of the Art
Services supported	Troubles/Faults reports	Yes	
	Add/Move/Change requests	Yes	
	Equipment orders	Yes	
	Advice/general enquiries		
Special services requested through service desk	Application traffic modeling		Possible
	Event maps by business area		Possible
	Technology piloting		Possible
	Performance studies for application groups		Possible
Access methods to service desk	Helpdesk phone (well-known "global" number)	Yes	
	Voicemail	Yes	
	E-mail	Yes	
	Direct from workstation		Possible
Feedback/status info to user	Phone/e-mail/voicemail	Yes	
	Direct to workstation		Possible
Skills training	Customer awareness	Yes	
	Depth in IT subject for 1st level diagnostic	Yes	
	Horizontal applications	Yes	
	Network and Telecommunications	Yes	

support group. In some enterprises service support may be a "virtual" function—staffed on an as-needed or rota basis by personnel with other mainline responsibilities. Examples include developers contributing time to support applications on a part-time basis.

Processes in which service support is operationally involved include fault management and provisioned-change management. With infrastructure management, given its technology scope, problem diagnosis is often difficult. Converging on the area of the infrastructure where a problem is actually occurring is difficult.

For example, a fault reported as a slow network may in fact be a server thrashing because it is running out of memory. Diagnosis is complicated also because the right skills within service support need to be focused on the problem from the earliest possible time.

A key requirement for service support of infrastructure management is that the whole function needs to be multi-skilled and knowledgeable in network, systems and applications. Another alternative is to build service support using small "hit" teams which collectively have the required skills. Service support usually includes a second level of expertise.

Problem escalation within this function therefore involves the contribution of time from internal experts. Vendor service departments usually work on a peer level with the first level of service support. Exhaustion of the escalation process within service support results in the services of external parties such as vendor experts or technical departments needing to be invoked. Service support's main activities are described below:

- Identifying or determining the problems described in trouble tickets. Trouble tickets are generated by one of several sources:

  The service desk which creates one in response to contact from end-users.

  An end-user who may directly report through filling in an electronic problem report form.

  An automated monitoring framework which generates trouble tickets for specific recolonized events.

  "Non-ticketed" events communicated by stand-alone tools.

  Trouble tickets forwarded by other service support centers in an enterprise.

- Diagnosing problems—Infrastructure problems are often difficult to diagnose without detailed "drilling" through the layers. Performance related problems and certain classes of security events can also be handled by the service support function. Some of the most difficult types of problems to solve are intermittent performance problems. These usually require specialist analytical tools and lab work or out-of-hours work—to recreate the problem and develop fixes.

- Taking corrective actions—The service support function concentrates skills and competencies required to manage a network to user-expected service levels. Associated with this is some degree of empowerment to correct problems quickly and efficiently. Problems at network and systems level are often solved by reconfiguration.

- Repairing and replacing equipment—Many repair activities are achieved through reconfiguration. In architectures that are designed to be resilient structures, the redundant components need to be replaced as soon as safely possible to re-instate the designed levels of resilience.

- Referencing problems to third parties—Some problems will require specialist help from vendors or a consultancy. In addition, there may be service contracts that could be invoked to get specialist help. Increasingly, the Internet provides a medium for accessing people who know the answers to generic problems in a specific area.

- Reconfiguring—Problem resolution and upgrades require reconfiguration of the network or other components on the infrastructure. Reconfiguration also refers to the management of the monitoring frameworks. Information is collected by remote agents and processed according to thresholds, polling frequencies and other configured criteria. Information is also polled by a central point such as the network management platform, based on configured parameters.

- Recovering from crises—In the course of crisis resolution, temporary fixes sometimes have to be executed to provide "best effort service" during business hours. More permanent fixes may have to be implemented outside business hours.

- Updating original problem descriptions—Trouble tickets used across the infrastructure management "layers" provide logs of how the problem was resolved. This is useful as a "solution template" for solving similar problems anywhere in the enterprise. Many problems that are handled may not have a trouble ticket. A key activity is to "normalize" the description of such problems so that a consistent record format is maintained in the event and problem resolution databases.

- Information inputs to the function include:

  Trouble tickets that are already opened by the client contact point.
  Trouble tickets generated by automated monitoring frameworks.
  Trouble tickets forwarded from peer-service support centers.
  Visual input from maps and other management tools.

- Information outputs include:

  Change requests for further processing within the change management process.
  Problem resolution "advisories" for distribution within the enterprise's service support function.
  Contact-log entries which detail ongoing contact with third parties involved in specific problem resolution.

3.4.4 Business Alignment

Business alignment is a function to help reduce the communication gap between the business and technologists—a business alignment person usually has responsibility for a subset of the business areas. In large organizations there is likely to be at least one such alignment manager per organizational business area. In smaller organizations one alignment manager may support multiple businesses. The likely activities in this area are described below, however, these are subject to variations between organizations:

- *Evaluating tactical impact of business plans.* Applied on a short- to medium-term horizon. While the steering function should give strategic direction, the alignment manager should be the infrastructure management group's "interpreter" on the requirements for executing business plans. Ideally, the alignment manager should be included in business planning from the earliest point. Hence alignment managers need a good knowledge of the enterprise's business.

- *Impending change requests.* To review and publish for the infrastructure management group, impending changes in the use of the infrastructure. This includes all the adds, moves and changes as well as new requirements for which the infrastructure management group may need to plan, pilot or test new solutions. Some types of changes are provisioned for in an infrastructure's design, others may need migration to a different technology base.

- *Business development.* The infrastructure management group can often provide significant input to business plans to deploy and exploit IT. The alignment manager can bring together the appropriate parties as well as play a liaison role. Business can access technical expertise through the one interface. Alignment management also has a responsibility to market the infrastructure management group and examine areas where the infrastructure management group can help to help solve business problems.

- *Status update and conflict resolution.* Alignment managers also play the role of business level interface to the operational functions. For example, they may be responsible for providing feedback on outstanding requests with the infrastructure management group. Similarly, alignment managers are the first point for complaints about the infrastructure management group. Internal processes should then escalate to conflict resolution. Another responsibility is to represent the business when prioritizing infrastructure resources that are limited.

3.4.5 Fault Tracking

Fault tracking is a function ensuring that all fault events reported in the system have a closure within guidelines set by the fault management process and with respect to any service level agreements with users. This function is closely related to the service desk and service support and is sometimes executed as a sub-function within service support.

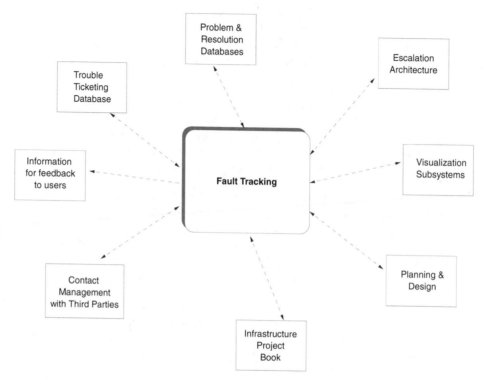

Figure 3.6: *Fault tracking interfaces*

Fault tracking introduces a notion of continuously housekeeping the managed environment. Figure 3.6 shows typical interfaces the function has within an enterprise context. Key activities within the function are:

- *Tracking manually reported and monitored faults.* There is a natural tendency within any fault management function for higher priority faults to constantly supersede lower priority ones. This activity helps to limit this tendency and ensures that when it is unavoidable, it is only done under controlled circumstances.

- *Managing escalation.* The escalation procedure is one of the most important procedures in infrastructure management, and needs to be clearly documented. Sometimes a new project has to be started to resolve a problem permanently. Managing the progress of the fault resolution following escalation is essential, especially when there are long lead times to a conclusion.

- *Referring problems.* Escalation of problems outside the infrastructure management group to external parties, such as vendor service organizations, also needs active management.

- *Distributing information.* Knowledge gained in problem resolution at one site is often useful to other parts of the enterprise. The release of such information into an enterprise-wide domain, however, has to be preceded by ensuring the safety and general applicability of the defined solution.

- *Information inputs include:*

    All open or escalated trouble tickets.

    Visual input from maps and other management tools.

- *Information outputs include:*

    Summary report of outstanding faults and state of resolution.

    Resolution database entries that detail resolutions to specific problems.

    Contact logs entries that detail ongoing contact with third parties involved in specific problem resolution.

3.4.6 Change Control

In an era where user requirements can change overnight, infrastructures should be designed so that a considerable degree of change can be accommodated by the underlying structures. Changes range from users and services being moved from one part of the network topology to another to users and applications being added. Adds, moves and changes nevertheless alter the traffic flows and stress-points on the underlying components.

Another class of changes involves parts of the environment having to be expanded or redesigned. Examples include replacement of one server with a higher specification and upgrading network topology.

Large-scale changes should be done under projects specifically started for the purpose. A development methodology (encompassing the network, host, operating systems and other infrastructure components) needs to be followed to manage the risks associated with any large-scale change.

Unauthorized or poorly planned changes inevitably result in weakening the infrastructure's integrity. The change management process is a key process that ensures that all changes have been planned and are safe.

Training all staff on the importance of change management from the infrastructure integrity perspective should be an ongoing part of developing a management culture.

There are two different types of change management process; one for provisioned changes and one for major changes. The change control function handles both these processes and has the following primary activities:

- *Processing change requests*—Initial processing of change requests to decide whether it involves provisioned changes or non-provisioned changes. Eliciting information from the originator of the change request and discussion of timescale and other risk factors is part of the account manager's remit. Depending on the type of change management process involved, the new change request has to be added to any existing list.

- *Managing and tracking change requests*—Consolidation of change request. Tracking the state of all change requests being handled by the group. Providing feedback information periodically or on request to users. This is done via the service desk or the account management function. Planning timescale and flow of the request through the change management processes. Managing resources required for a change request sometimes involves prioritizing change requests. When conflicting requirements have to be resolved, escalation is required to higher management levels as defined by the change management process.

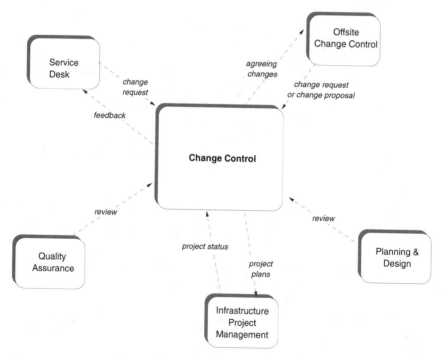

Figure 3.7: *Interfaces for change control*

- *Cooperative servicing of orders*—Execution of some change requests involve the cooperation of several sites or groups. The change control functions within the respective groups need to be geared for cooperative working. This includes the tools for sharing and distributing information and controls for distributed project management.

- *Supervising the execution of changes*—The change control function needs to have "real time" knowledge of how the changes are progressing. Any intervention and escalation needs to be timely. All projects relating to execution of changes need to be reviewed on a periodic basis. Figure 3.7 shows the key interfaces between the change control function and other infrastructure management functions discussed in this chapter.

3.4.7 Planning and Design

Planning and design is a key function, especially in large or complex environments, to ensure that a consistent level of expertise is applied to technical issues such as changes, network-related IT purchasing and maintenance of quality.

This is essentially an engineering function and likely to be staffed with more "experts" in respective areas than any other function in the infrastructure management group. As the patterns of service delivery over enterprise infrastructures become complex, more analytical skills are needed in planning the evolution of the network and other infrastructure components, and in managing the risk associated with making changes to it.

- *Analyzing needs*—All changes need to be analyzed with respect to the flexibility offered by the infrastructure's architecture and current knowledge about the capacity, latency and traffic characteristics of infrastructure components. This involves the use of tools ranging from "educated-intuition" to quantitative tools such as simulation.

- *Projecting application load and sizing resources*—When new applications are added, or indeed when seemingly simple changes are made (such as upgrading user workstations), the traffic characteristics of the network changes. Resulting bottlenecks may occur at network components or at servers. Use of models to understand traffic flows, server loading and sizing, etc. before a change is executed is the key to managing the risk associated with changes. This also applies to building new infrastructures and introducing new technology.

- *Authorizing changes and long-term tracking*—Analysis and traffic projection activities help to minimize the risk-to-business inherent in the change process. Measurement of traffic flows during subsequent stages of the change management process helps to ensure the validity of the original analysis and projections. Over a period of years an infrastructure inevitably evolves, and usually migrates to new technologies. Changes are sometimes undertaken only in parts of the infrastructure, in which case different technology bases have to co-exist. Long-term effects of change therefore need to be systematically tracked.

- *Raising major purchasing orders*—Many IT purchases today have *connectivity* and *manageability* elements to them—which in some cases determines the actual usability of the equipment or software in a given environment. The involvement of the engineering function in specifying and understanding these aspects, as well as providing analysis, aids in improving the quality of purchase decisions.

- *Producing implementation plans*—The concentration of engineering skills within this function means that it is likely to have a comprehensive understanding of the enterprise topology and resource deployment. This function is therefore ideally suited to develop the implementation "sequences" involved in both provisioned changes and well as the infrastructure's migration to new technologies.

- *Establishing enterprise standards*—Standards ensure that enterprises can limit the diversity of IT systems. The specification of enterprise standards for applications and operating systems has to be balanced against providing the best tools to satisfy the business's needs. Standards for "building blocks" for the infrastructure and infrastructure management structures provide uniformity across the enterprise. This provides a major payback in reducing management costs. As current infrastructures or parts of it, such as the network migrate, simplification is a primary driving goal.

- *Maintaining quality assurance*—The "quality of the design" of building blocks used for infrastructures and that of procedures for provisioned changes are the main areas for quality assurance responsibility within this function. Quality assurance also extends to the services provided by the infrastructure to users. In this case quality metrics need to be collected for analysis and review.

3.4.8 Performance Monitoring

Performance monitoring is usually undertaken at a layer or subsystem level (e.g., network, application, database, etc.). End-to-end performance monitoring is a result of assembling constituent information from layers and subsystems and is still in its infancy.

Before performance monitoring can be done, a baseline of *normal* performance levels for the requisite area needs to be established. Exception conditions and value thresholds are ideally expressed against this baseline. The definition, configuration and distribution of exception conditions is a key part of performance monitoring.

Performance exception and threshold events raise alarms at the network or system management platform. Alarms are most often filtered, correlated and consolidated at the management platform level. The main activities in this function are:

- *Usage metering*—Some parts of the infrastructure or a specific networked service may be sensitive to costs or may need to be shared between multiple parties on the basis of usage.

- *Infrastructure performance monitoring*—Each subnetwork and "topological units" within it may be remotely monitored. Topological units include *segments* and *virtual LANs* in the local area and *circuits* and *public switched service* in the wide area. Individual hosts and application components may also be viewed as units for performance monitoring.

  Standards such as the RMON MIB (in SNMP), define remote monitoring of LAN protocols. RMON II extends this up to the application layer traffic flows.

  A framework may be shared for monitoring performance and for monitoring faults since the same agent may cater to events for both areas.

  The per-unit performance metrics however needs to be combined in different contexts to understand infrastructure performance. This is usually done by applications closely coupled to the monitoring agents.

- *Monitoring service level agreements (SLAs)*—Another viewpoint of performance is in terms of characteristics that are expressed as parts of SLAs. SLAs define what the users of the network may expect to experience, for example, in terms of network availability and how quickly users can be added or changed (which is related to the level of network modularity).

- *Monitoring vendor and third-party performance metrics*—In complex enterprises part of the infrastructure operation may be outsourced to one or more third parties. In order for the in-house management framework to inter-operate with these parties, quantifiable levels of service have to be met by these parties. Service contracts with service vendors usually carry premiums for enhanced response times. In order to get value for money, provision of these services needs to be meticulously monitored and metrics captured. These are then points of negotiation with the outsourcer.

- *Optimizing and tuning*—Infrastructure management increasingly involves traffic engineering where network hot-spots are eased through redeployment or duplication of affected services. Performance monitoring helps to anticipate the next hot-spot and proactively manage it. When network performance data is correlated with performance data from hosts and application level data (executing on hosts), more sophisticated tuning of hot-spots can be achieved.

- *Modeling*—Infrastructures that are designed as application delivery systems need to be modeled, so that planned enhancements and changes in the application and user profiles can be matched at the topology level. A tool that is used successfully for traffic modeling is discrete event simulation. Captured and generated traffic may be used to drive simulation models to understand impacts of topological changes or application changes without physical changes being necessary.

- *Reporting on performance statistics*—Information capture, processing and distribution of performance metrics are important activities in enterprises where the network is recognized as a critical component of the business. Automating capture, processing and distribution helps to make the information easily auditable and helps to give greater credibility to the contents of such reports. Increasingly, web servers are used for distribution. This allows a wider audience to access such information without recourse to special tools.

- *Trending and analysis*—The capture and storage of performance data for off-line processing is an important part of this function. Much of this needs to be automated to ensure integrity. Such archival data is most often used in capacity planning and in periodic studies to understand emerging hot-spots on the infrastructure. Figure 3.8 shows the key interfaces between the planning and design function and other infrastructure management functions discussed in this chapter.

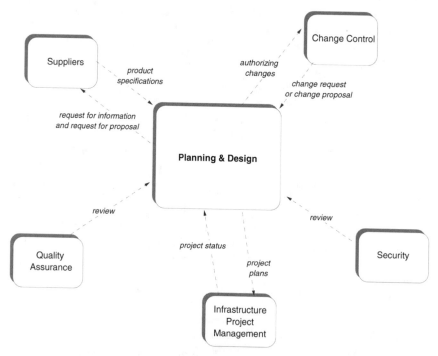

Figure 3.8: *Interfaces for planning and design functions*

3.4.9 Fault Monitoring

Fault monitoring is a complex area of infrastructure management. This is especially so when it is approached from an application delivery viewpoint. Fault monitoring is largely an automated function, executed by a fault monitoring framework. An architectural perspective of a fault monitoring framework is covered comprehensively in Chapter 8, Section 8.2, and Case Study 8.1.

The complexity in fault monitoring is driven by the monitoring *extent*—in terms of both the number of monitored nodes and number of points of monitoring within a single node. This potentially results in a large number of agents having to be managed.

Large-scale monitoring is increasingly done by remote agents that have "local intelligence" to filter events and pass back information only on an exception basis. The definition, configuration and distribution of exception conditions is a key part of fault monitoring.

- *Monitoring application, systems and network faults*—Increasingly, the same fault management framework is used to monitor the network as well as systems and application level faults.

   In some organizations, application level faults are also monitored using pattern recognition agents scanning application log files and console messages. These are then converted into a common format for presentation at an interface with the management platform.

   Many network components such as hubs and switches have native agents that provide information about the component. In the case of SNMP the agents have to be polled and the polling engine needs to be "relatively local" to the agents being polled. Locality of polling schemes is a key part of a fault monitoring framework. It reduces traffic overheads and distributes polling responsibility as the number of agents increase.

- *Correlating events for speedy problem detection*—Since the current communication models are based on protocol stacks, problems in one part of the stack usually results in secondary alarms. A common problem is that of higher level application protocols that time-out due to loss of connectivity at a lower level of the protocol stack.

   The isolation of the primary or causative event from a potentially large number of secondary events is aided by pre-processing all events—looking for known failure dependencies, and for known patterns of failure.

- *Automated opening of trouble tickets on detection of alarms*—Trouble tickets define a uniform way of expressing infrastructure problems and subsequently for tracking problems to a conclusion. Events are first classified, and when a matching event is detected an automatically generated trouble ticket, indicating the problem, gets routed to the associated service support group.

- *Referring trouble tickets*—When relationships with vendor service organizations and outsourcers exist, a key interface is the ability to refer trouble tickets outside the enterprise. Although this may sometimes involve development work to interoperate between dissimilar trouble ticketing systems, it allows internal processes such as fault management and change management to remain "continuous" when external groups are involved. The ability to extend key infrastructure management processes have a major payback when several groups are responsible for different parts of the enterprise infrastructure.

3.4.10 Internet Services Management

Internet services is a distinctive set of services that has become a key toolset for developing business solutions for many organizations. The term *intranet* services is used to distinguish internal usage, and this is indeed the higher growth area. Primary distribution services used on the intranet are web and to a lesser degree news. E-mail is already treated as part of the infrastructure in many organizations. A whole host of cooperative applications can be deployed over these basic services. Such applications are increasingly being leveraged by business users.

The systems administration function traditionally takes responsibility for these services. This class of services has an important "business channel" role in providing critical internal distribution mechanisms as well as projecting the organization to outsiders. This role points to a functional responsibility distinct from mainstream systems administration. A key difference is the high level of specific expertise required in these services. Key areas of activity are:

- *Server engineering*—The demand for intranet services in technically mature organizations often outstrips capacity within short periods of initial deployment. The function of server engineering is to build and monitor sizing models. As intranet services are used for production solutions, issues such as server performance and availability need to be addressed.

- *Technology tracking*—A rapid evolution is taking place in the base technologies for providing some of these services. An important role for this function is to understand emerging services, development methods and protocols. It demands the need to take a hard look at new technologies in server design and application development tools.

- *Enforcing security policies*—The security function within an organization needs to clearly articulate security policies to apply to intranet and Internet services. This function needs to apply these policies and monitor violations. Violations are managed through the respective security escalation process.

- *Server data management*—As intranet services get taken up by business users, the respective servers become major points for storage of corporate data. This function develops a model for the provisioning of storage resources on a demand basis. This may include setting and enforcing quota systems or developing archival criteria.

- *Application consultancy*—The ability to deploy business applications over the basic intranet services is likely to accelerate. This may range from developing pages for distribution via the web server to sophisticated subscribe/publish applications using internal news servers. Of particular interest to business users is the notion that browsers and readers have become sophisticated environments for developing applications.

- *Usage monitoring*—Usage statistics of deployed servers and services on offer provide feedback to users. It also helps in the early days of deployment to define accounting models for paying for the intranet services. Accounting reports can then be generated for cost-allocation purposes.

3.4.11 Horizontal Services Administration

Horizontal services are services used by a wide variety of applications and groups in the organization. They are treated as part of the infrastructure and managed individually but within a common management process and technology structure. Common processes for fault management, performance management, security audit, etc. ensure quality of operations.

Use of common frameworks for monitoring events, visualizing events, and collecting contextual help information, help to simplify fragmented tool usage. Using common trouble ticketing conventions and databases ease training requirements and help reduce human error.

Some key common areas of responsibilities are installation, monitoring, fine tuning, managing user accounts and ownership, trouble shooting and monitoring performance and faults, managing disk storage, and managing specific user contexts. Some areas administered under this common framework are:

- *Relational database administration*—This function has in many organization evolved independently of other support functions and is one of the most difficult to integrate into a common framework. Many client server applications have a major relational database component. Database administration is a key function given the central role of the database engine and the database management system (DBMS) to client/server applications. It requires an understanding of the business application domain as well as the structure of the databases. The function is one of applying knowledge about one application (the DBMS) in the support of a business specific application. Many DBMS provide rudimentary management tools. These can often be augmented, especially in monitoring, by third-party tools.

- *Managing object repositories*—As object oriented tools, languages and methodologies are used in many modern software development projects, the need to organize and manage the output of the projects, namely, objects is a critical function. In most large projects an object librarian has a well-defined role in managing object versions and environments. On an enterprise level, re-use of objects as well as "mining" for larger scale "frameworks" is becoming part of best practice. Such activities are ideally staffed centrally, rather than within individual teams.

- *Managing client/server database products*—Database products other than the database management system are often used in developing client server applications. Examples include products that provide gateways to different DBMS and products that provide data replication. These are essentially other applications in a suite including the DMBS. Such components often provide key functions to a client/server application and hence need to be treated as infrastructure applications.

- *Managing corporate e-mail*—Enterprises tend to have a variety of e-mail packages. An early result of integration at the business level is to enable e-mail connectivity. This is often done by building an e-mail backbone that can transport and translate between the various e-mail clients. The commonest complication in managing the backbone is the management of e-mail addresses. This is especially true when remote and roving access is needed. The architecture of the e-mail backbone has a significant impact on the ease of administration as well as the e-mail services that are available at each of the different types of desktop.

- *Managing directory services*—These are often associated with e-mail but in fact have a much wider use in managing the infrastructure. Their role is as a centrally managed and distributed repository of people and service-related information. This information includes preferences, public cryptographic keys and organizational relationships. Directories are distributed applications in their own right and sometimes map onto a commercial relational database engine. Directory administration requires specialist knowledge and security privileges.

- *Managing middleware services*—Many products claim to be middleware. These may be better described as services that provide various types of *transparency* to participants in distributed computing. The commonest of these are location transparency that allows a service to be requested without knowledge of its location, and access transparency that allows local and remote services to be accessed using identical operations.

These are used by client/server applications to cope with issues of diverse platforms and operating systems, and reduce coupling between the various components.

This is another class of software that requires specialist knowledge. Middleware products are often closely coupled with the operating system on the one hand and the programming language level on the API side. This close coupling makes life difficult operationally, especially because middleware products rarely have "hooks" or tools for operational management.

3.4.12 Systems Administration

This has long been a distinct function with relatively clear boundaries of responsibility. However, such isolation is not appropriate to client/server environments that depend on leveraging services from the different layers. Close cooperation between disciplines and teamwork is required to understand and solve client/server infrastructure problems. Key areas of responsibility include:

- *Software version control*—Client server applications are built using development technology that can produce incremental enhancements in 3- to 12-month cycles. This makes software version management across the multiple components a high risk activity and requires development of a clear methodology that specifically works for the enterprise.

  Other parts of the infrastructure such as network hubs, switches and routers are increasingly software controlled, the inter-dependencies between different versions in different components impact the function of these components. A more structured approach of controlling versions across inter-networking components ensures the risks inherent in such changes are better managed.

  By a similar token the management of software versions of network management tools and agents also impacts the ability to manage a network. In this case the large number of agents involved (running into tens of thousands of units in a large enterprise), challenges traditional methods of migrating from one version to another.

- *Software distribution*—As the number of software driven components in an infrastructure increases, the method of distributing software to them has to be made more efficient. This is often done with software distribution tools. A key issue is the potential volume of traffic when changes are undertaken. Associated with software version control and software distribution is the need to tag and store the software itself in a secure software archive. The platform diversity and location of the distribution targets often requires specialized distribution architectures to be developed in each enterprise. These architectures then have to be maintained.

- *Systems management*—As the size and complexity of the environment being managed increases, the systems resources used by client/server applications need to be actively monitored for performance. A structured approach is needed to get the optimum performance for a given *mix* of applications.

  Other areas of monitoring are for fault and security events. Many of these are reported by the operating system in internal system logs.

  Standardization of platforms and having specific configurations for different use-cases reduces platform diversity to a small number of standard machines. This helps to reduce complexity for the support organization.

Another class of systems that need to be proactively managed is the specialized hardware on which remote infrastructure management agents are distributed in the enterprise.

- *Contingency management*—Newer generations of client/server applications are built with resilience as a key feature. Managing high availability is however still an art form. High availability is essentially a set of mechanisms and protocols (Chapter 8, Section 8.2, discusses high availability from the perspective of an architectual model). Each client/server application needs to be reviewed in terms of its availability during infrastructure failure.

The infrastructure management capability needs to offer 100% availability to support the infrastructure as an application delivery system. This is done through a resilient infrastructure management framework and redundant resources. These contingency resources and resilience mechanisms, however, need to be proactively managed so that failed components are fixed. If any part of the management framework fails, systems administration is the most essential skill set required for managing recovery.

- *Maintaining configuration and directory databases*—The infrastructure and its management framework are complex in their own right. Complexity demands for a more centralized and disciplined approach to holding and maintaining configuration information. This includes replicating the information at more than one site to guard against local disasters.

The documentation and updating of configuration information relating to the infrastructure is defined as part of the respective management process (e.g., provisioned change, non-provisioned change, network migration and so on). The following classes of configuration information are relevant for centralized maintenance:

- *Device level*—Every component that is software configured in the "domain" of the infrastructure management group, including the management infrastructure itself. In a "follow-the-sun" management scenario, component configurations of remotely monitored network domains need to be accessible from secondary sites.

- *System level*—All workstations and servers used at a site should be clones of a small number of "master" configurations. Servers and workstations may have to be rebuilt speedily in the event of failure.

- *Application level*—The software components and tools that are part of the infrastructure. Details of their configuration are kept in such a way as to speedily rebuild the application environment in the event of a contingency within the infrastructure.

- *Infrastructure management group directory*—Showing all infrastructure management and related personnel on an enterprise level with various levels of detailed information on job functions, areas of expertise, skill level with tools used, preferred modes of communication, etc. For the local group, more detailed information on the resources used, vendor relationship, etc. may be kept.

- *Asset/inventory management*—Client/server applications consume considerable amounts of capital in terms of assets and inventory. The effective management of software licenses, maintenance contracts, amortization and cost allocation of capital equipment is an increasingly important function. Assets in the infrastructure also need to be tracked and equipment may need to be upgraded or services duplicated when their usage exceeds original design goals.

- *Data management and backup*—Policies must be developed to define storage of production data on servers. This is defined by quotas, identities and time windows for production data that needs to be retained. The use of hierarchic storage to store older data on least-cost media is not uncommon and aids the development of such policies.

Client/server applications potentially creates large amounts of data as information is cached and moved around the participating servers. In the event of a major disaster, the data required to a defined "roll-back" point has to be available and easily identifiable.

Most organizations backup every production server as a matter of course. This usually has considerable manual overheads to ensure availability. When the infrastructure has a large number of servers, the extra volume of traffic (for a significant duration) caused by automated backup and verification procedures is often an issue in many networks. This is because application aarchitectures often expect access to production servers, regardless of the time of day that backup is undertaken. This usually leads to backup strategy based on a business impact analysis. This defines a data priority on the basis of its importance in a disaster scenario.

Large amounts of data are also generated in the course of monitoring the infrastructure components and in the course of executing infrastructure management processes.

The backup and storage management of data from infrastructure management processes require intimate knowledge of the management applications. Backup should be organized with a view to disaster recovery of the management infrastructure. Hence a business impact analysis is required to understand which of the infrastructure management processes would be affected. Loss of capability for a management process such as change management quickly leads to infrastructure instabilities and failure.

3.4.13 Implementation and Maintenance

The infrastructure being managed and the management framework itself is constantly undergoing changes. Some changes are due to change requests, others are due to managed upgrade programs and provisioning, and some are due to detection of emerging problems such as service hot-spots. The implementation and maintenance function executes the physical changes to the infrastructure. This involves networking devices, hosts and software changes:

- *Implementing provisioned changes*—Provisioned changes should be done using pre-defined blueprints for adds, changes and moves. This procedure-based approach reduces the risks associated with changing the infrastructure as well as ensuring a consistency in quality.

- *Migration*—Because infrastructure technology is advancing with shorter development cycles, within one to two years of building an infrastructure, pressure begins to build to use improved or new technology.

  The triggers for such pressures include requirements to meet the increased loads on the infrastructure, to reduce service latencies or to increase availability.

  Migration is a planned, systematic move to a new technology base for layers of the infrastructure, such as the network or the hosts, while co-existing with the older technology for the duration of the change process.

  Associated with migration of infrastructure layers are changes to the infrastructure management framework, often to cope with new management criteria. In some cases migration has to be preceded by retraining infrastructure implementation staff in one or more new technologies. Using external expertise in specific new technologies during the migration process contributes to "ramping" up internal knowledge.

- *Provisioning*—This is essentially the extension of the infrastructure to accommodate larger scale changes. The ease of provisioning is largely determined by the modularity inherent in the infrastructure's architecture. For example, if the network is designed as a modular structure consisting of backbone substructures, business group substructures and other topological abstractions that map well to application delivery, then provisioning consists of building more of the appropriate set of substructures.

- *Upgrades and maintenance*—This defines the fourth type of change. Because of the complexity of many of the components used to realize modern infrastructures, many upgrades are done in response to bugs found in the components when put under certain loads or within a certain configuration or in previously untried combinations with other vendors' equipment. Most of such problems cannot be anticipated. Maintenance is likely to be a planned activity. As a general rule, maintenance type upgrades should only be undertaken when the target version is known to have been stable. Debugging vendor offerings should not be part of the process, if at all possible.

3.4.14 Security Management

In general the security function should be provided by a group which is not directly influenced by the infrastructure management group's line of management. This is in order to avoid conflicts of interest between security and expediency that are likely to arise. In many organizations, however, the systems administration staff also provide security functions.

In general, if a specific security policy exists for the infrastructure management group, then it should be implemented. Some enterprises are less security conscious than others and don't see a need for stronger standards of security to be applied to the management group. Key activities in the security management function are:

- *Threat analysis to the infrastructure*—The network, the hosts and systems and the whole management framework need to be methodologically analyzed to understand threats to it. This needs to be done as part of the change management process—since new security holes usually appear after changes have been made to a previous "status quo" that was known to have been secure. Results from the analysis are fed back into a corporate security policy review activity. (This may be part of the remit of a high level IT steering committee.)

- *Administration of security services*—Securing the infrastructure and the management framework involves the use of security services hosted on one or more dedicated servers in the infrastructure and the management framework.

  Strong authentication is usually needed when business users and infrastructure management staff dial in from offsite locations. An authentication server is part of a scheme that implements a physical token-based mechanism, (such as a smart card based identity algorithm plus a personal secret such as a password) and cryptographic certificate-based mechanisms.

  Access control services define the systems and services that may be accessed by business users and each member of the management staff. For the latter this is directly related to the roles each member of staff plays in the group. In addition, access control define management staff's access across internal firewalls to business networks and systems.

  Encryption allows applications to exchange information with the assurance that the information remains confidential. Encryption is sometimes a feature of the application—such as privacy enhanced e-mail. In other cases it may be treated as a utility available to encrypt at a data object level such as a file. Encryption services are also relevant to several operations in management:

— (I) When storing backup data "offsite" whether in the form of physical data media or directly onto offsite-based storage media. In some enterprises all data held offsite is encrypted as a matter of policy.

— (II) When exchanging management information between sites and with third-party service providers. Encryption in this case is a mechanism for ensuring that only persons with the matching keys at external locations have the opportunity to view the information.

- *Administration of security tokens*—Security tokens include passwords, cryptographic keys used in encryption, and secret values used in message integrity schemes and access control lists. Such tokens are especially relevant in large enterprises with a global network management organization. Administrative activities include:

Enforcing adequacy policies associated with each type of token—such as those relating to the structure of passwords and change frequency for passwords.

Transferring instances of tokens between sites—such as the transfer of a private key to a remote group using public key encryption.

Storing tokens offsite and defining contingency access to these (including access from another site), in the event of losing the normal site.

- *Review of security policy*—A security policy defines the basis for security mechanisms in the enterprise as a whole and sometimes with a special case for the management framework. The policy itself has to be periodically reviewed by a competent authority to ensure that it continues to satisfy the current requirements of the enterprise.

- *Detection of breaches and recovery*—Detection is a mixture of monitoring and proactive search for patterns of behavior (such as a single host trying to systematically access a protected file system). The infrastructure management architecture should provide a monitoring capability for security events. The main use of this monitoring capability is in a real-time security audit process which includes:

- Detecting change in configuration of host, operating system functions and network resources in the production as well as the management framework.

- Detecting known patterns through regular expression-based search of firewall logs and system logs.

- Matching remote access to the management framework against staff rota.

3.4.15 Relevance of the Business Model

This organizational model is an essential tool to define infrastructure management processes, the information flow between the business areas and for defining skill-sets in each business area. This is done in Chapter 4, "People Aspects of Infrastructure Management," and Chapter 5, "Processes in Infrastructure Management."

This model also helps to define the functional requirements of the technology to support the management processes as well as requirements of the organizational structure for the infrastructure management function. The nature of the organization to which the management function is applied can diminish the usefulness of this model:

- Very small organization—multiple functions across several business areas may be done by the same people.

- Multiple infrastructure management groups with their own "turfs" with no overall direction or cohesion between the groups.

- An infrastructure management group remote from the service desk, making the loop to other functions difficult to control.

3.5 Books for Further Reading

French, J. Alfred. *The Business Knowledge Investment* (Building Architected Information). Yourdon Press Computing, 1990.

Imhoff, Claudia, *et al. Building the Operational Data Store.* John Wiley & Sons, 1995.

Schermerhorn, John, *et al. Basic Organizational Behavior.* John Wiley & Sons, 1995.

Simon, Herbert A. *Administrative Behavior* (A Study of Decision-Making Processes in Administrative Organizations). Free Press, 1976.

4

People Aspects of Infrastructure Management

Areas covered in this chapter

- Issues in building cross-technology management teams

- Organizational models for staffing an infrastructure management organization

- Building and managing multi-disciplinary teams

- Developing training models for infrastructure management teams

- Classification of infrastructure management skills and roles

- Special issues with infrastructure management roles

- Managing the skills portfolio of an infrastructure management organization

- Typical tasks in infrastructure management

- Skill and knowledge attributes to achieve infrastructure management tasks

Year after year, people costs typically represent 40% to 70% of the operating budget of running a client/server infrastructure. Over a three-year cycle, people costs account for over 60% of the operating costs for an IT infrastructure.

Operating an effective and competent infrastructure management organization requires a wide range of expertise and skills. Competency areas include technical skills, skill sets for "interfacing" with business users and vendors, as well as well-developed administrative and managerial capability.

Achieving excellence in infrastructure management is not possible without developing the people aspects. The people that staff an infrastructure management organization and the culture within it ultimately determine what is achievable by that organization.

In most organizations, infrastructure is managed by multiple groups organized along technology lines, each group with its own management structures. There are several drivers for a single infrastructure management organization:

- The need for a single point for end-to-end responsibility for the delivery of IT support services. In most organizations multiple support groups are involved in day-to-day operations with no overall control.

- The need for consistency in competence across all the disciplines to support client/server applications. In most enterprises there are major deficits in skills that become evident especially when a crisis has to be managed.

- The need for flexible organizational structures to cope with changing support needs of the business.

Infrastructure management viewed as a set of processes helps to build a "unified" perspective of management that cuts through the traditional layers of technology. A problem management process is just as applicable whether the problem is a workstation that has stopped working or a network component that has failed. In both cases the process defines a sequence of activities. The details of a very small number of activities will be different for the workstation and the network element.

Although a process focus is mainly advocated in this publication for infrastructure management, there are complex technology areas that have still to be viewed within a functional structure. This functional view is relevant within infrastructure management because:

- It provides a focus of expertise and specialization with which to build teams. Teams for infrastructure management need to be built with specialists that work well in a team, rather than generalists who can put their hand to "anything."

- It infuses thinking in a specialist field from outside the organization. For example, good systems administrators will continually keep abreast of bug status and fixes for operating systems they are responsible for, without this activity being explicitly defined as part of their job specifications.

Traditionally, job descriptions have defined specialist functions. Job descriptions, however, imply that the definition of the function is static. The environment for which the function applies and the associated technology base making up the function changes at a relatively fast rate. In other words it is difficult to keep changing somebody's job titles and job descriptions on short life-cycles.

Job descriptions also do not fit well with the process model. Processes define actors who participate in very specific ways with in its activities. An individual is therefore likely to participate in a number of processes. Also, individuals are likely to be rotated through the infrastructure processes, so as to gain different types of experience and learning opportunities. An individual therefore plays a number of roles.

The notion of roles defines a method of defining an individual's job. A role-based view allows the necessary flexibility to build organizational structures to meet the challenges of infrastructure management. The organizational building block for infrastructure management is a multi-disciplinary team. Such teams are both flexible.

4.1 From Decentralized Control

During the late 1980s and early 1990s businesses underwent decentralization under management umbrellas such as "rightsizing" and "business process re-engineering." This also resulted in decentralization of responsibility for the new components of IT. This is described in Chapter 1, Section 1.3, as a "path" through increasing levels of maturity in the deployment of client/server systems.

Maturity does not necessarily imply increasing levels of expertise in the components—networks, the systems deployed over it, common services, etc. Expertise and skills were in many cases brought in as short-term contracts. In other cases responsibility has been outsourced.

By and large, businesses have expanded since rightsizing. In infrastructure terms this means:

- Infrastructures that are larger or global—to deliver to a wider user base across local area, metropolitan area and wide area technologies.

- Infrastructures to meet the diverse operational needs of businesses—Different business have chosen "point" or tactical solutions to meet their specific needs without recourse to any "common framework."

From a people viewpoint, decentralization has created special interest groups which support some narrow part of the infrastructure. Figure 4.1 shows typical support groups involved in end-to-end delivery of IT support. The picture therefore shows that managing client/server systems, especially in a business critical environment, requires a large support structure.

The trend of decentralized control has slowed down and reversed, as the level of integration between businesses increased in "globalizing" businesses. This is described in Chapter 1. Integration is essentially leading to a centralized IT support function in many enterprises.

There is however little similarity between the new notions of centralization and the remit of previous central IT functions:

- Infrastructure management has recognized the need for a professional understanding of the businesses that depend on it and their operational cycles.

- The linkage between the business and the infrastructure services offered is fulfilled by a "steering" function. Steering committees consisting of users usually exist at each geographic level and coordinate with counterparts to ensure that business needs are met.

- Infrastructure management defines many operational policies and processes globally. This allows development of best practice and a greater flexibility in moving people and skills between locations.

- Another global theme is the mutual dependency for 24 x 7 support with critical business systems being monitored on a follow-the-sun principle (the working day "cycles forward" from Europe to the U.S. and to the Far East).

- Responsibility for the infrastructure is more likely to be outsourced—another form of centralized control. The business justification for outsourcing is that infrastruc-

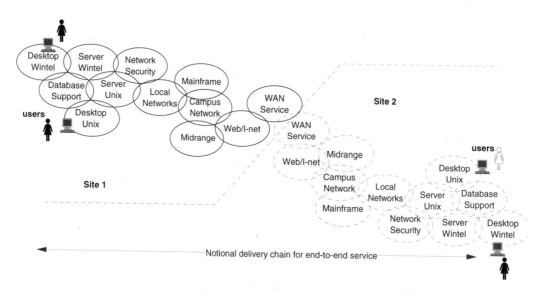

Figure 4.1: *Support groups involved in client/server infrastructure management*

ture management is not a core competency (except some service companies), and is therefore not worth developing internally.

4.1.1 The People Dimension

The wider enterprise's view of infrastructure management people is likely to be in terms of hierarchies defining different functions. Viewed in a global context, within a decentralized organization, the management functions are duplicated at both business unit level and at each location.

Infrastructure management is a relatively new concept that aims to bring together the functional groups operating in isolation into a single framework. The "pillars" of this framework, discussed in this publication, are the technology and architecture, people and their organization and management processes.

This chapter looks at the people dimension of infrastructure management from the following perspectives:

- *Internal organization* defines the management and control structures—taking into account the global remit and the infrastructure-as-a-delivery-system viewpoints. The traditional hierarchic model, the process-centric and an architecture-centric models are considered.

- *Roles* define the major types of work in infrastructure management and is independent of the internal structure of the organization. An individual may "play" one or more roles, each for varying lengths of time.

- *Teams and teamwork* define the model for the smallest organizational units. The purpose of teams in infrastructure management is to ensure that all the required skills and competencies match the internal organization.

- *Competency-based recruitment* is based on identifying competencies required by an internal organization and targeting recruitment to fulfill the requirements.

- *Training* is the key to the continual development of skills to manage an evolving infrastructure. To manage technologies that have relatively short life-cycles requires re-skilling within similar time cycles.

One of the problems in infrastructure management is that technical skills are often separated from business competencies. Hence the technical and business decision-making processes remain disconnected.

Communications between upper management and infrastructure management often need to be improved. Upper management needs to appreciate that technical details are important in any business transaction involving the infrastructure. Technical management needs to understand the concerns of upper management.

4.1.2 Internal Organization of Infrastructure Management

Different enterprises favor different organizational structures for infrastructure management. The organizational model of infrastructure management described in Chapter 3, Section 3.4 (Organizational Model of Infrastructure Management), is a prototype showing the key infrastructure functions. The groups of people that execute these functions can be organized in a variety of ways. Three basic models of organization—by product/technology, by architecture and by infrastructure process—are shown in Figure 4.2 and are discussed below.

The commonest view of infrastructure management is based on supporting the different product/technology areas that make up the infrastructure (both operationally and in engineering capability when required). Examples of product/technology commonly found are *mainframe, Unix or NT RISC based servers, Unix or NT RISC based workstations, and Intel based PCs.*

Support of each product/technology area is set up along the lines of multiple levels of expertise ranging from the first tier of support at the helpdesk to the highest tier of support often within an engineering team. The main role of the first tier of support is to solve end-user problems. Higher tiers of support deal with infrastructure issues such as server sizing as well, work in the functional areas (problem management, performance tracking, security, etc.). Similar organizational "substructures" are found in each similar-sized sites or location. Larger sites may support satellite sites.

The second model for internal organization of infrastructure management is end-to-end architecture led by a strong emphasis on application to infrastructure integration and an inti-

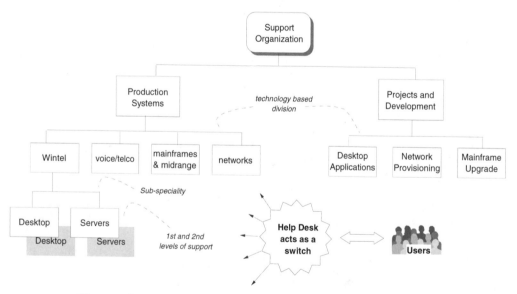

Figure 4.2: *Traditional organizational model for infrastructure management*

mate understanding of how each business line uses the technology. Strategic interfaces with the businesses ensure that the support remains aligned with business needs. The day-to-day interface with end-users is through a client contact point through which all support services on offer by the organization are made available to end-users.

In an end-to-end architecture setting much of the work is achieved through different projects of different durations. Projects that are of very short duration (e.g., less than 3 days) are often treated under a special term (e.g., a work-package). In addition there are often "crisis teams" to handle any ongoing situations.

Project teams are formed under the leadership of a team leader, to meet specific goals, and are staffed from a pool of skills available to the internal organization. Some project teams may have specific focus areas such as security or server engineering.

In this model the infrastructure management organization can span across geographic (as well as business boundaries) without having to duplicate organizational substructures.

The third model of internal organization views infrastructure management in terms of process-centered teams. Teams are responsible for each infrastructure management process from the beginning to the end. Team staff are rotated through the pool for retraining and for changing team sizes.

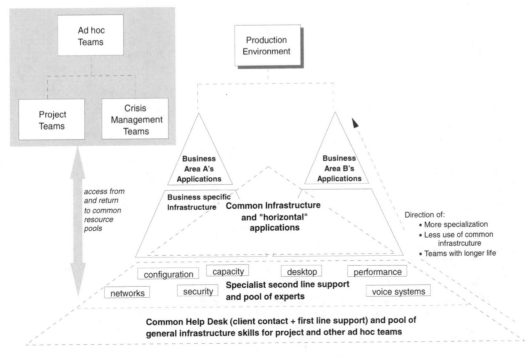

Figure 4.3: *Architecture-based organizational model of infrastructure management*

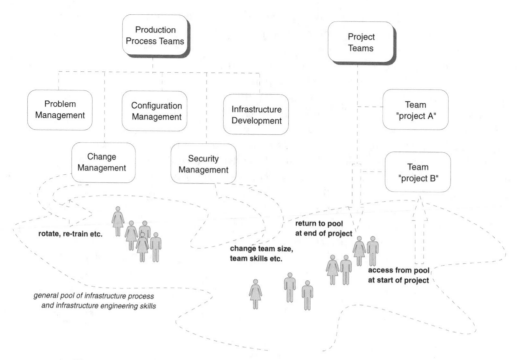

Figure 4.4: *Process-based organizational model of infrastructure management*

Non-process work is undertaken as different-sized projects. The number of projects at any given time varies as does their duration. The staff for the projects are taken from a general but highly skilled pool of skills.

Over time both engineering and process skills are gained, as are career paths through support and engineering.

Resource models of skill pools have been successfully used by engineering consultancies for many years. This is another model that is scalable for global infrastructure management. A team can extend over several sites and still work to a common purpose and standard.

4.2 Multidisciplinary Teams

Managing a client/server infrastructure requires access to multiple disciplines covering the range of technologies and levels of sophistication used to build the infrastructure. Hence teams are multidisciplinary by definition. In many organizations the "component" competencies are found in individuals or small specialist groups spread geographically across different offices.

Work done in an infrastructure management organization relates to planning, executing "standard" management procedures and processes, project work or incident management. In enterprises that have undergone business process re-engineering (BPR), infrastructure support teams may be organized to support key business processes. This is however very rare and its efficacy is currently not well understood.

A team is a group of people with a high level of interdependence geared to achieving the relevant tasks and goals. Hence teams may be thought of as management teams, process teams, project teams and incident teams. Teams are formed for different durations for each of these work types: incident teams are formed on an ad hoc basis to manage through an incident or crisis. Project teams should also be formed to do a specific project. Process teams and management teams are longer lived.

Far too often however the notion of teams does not go beyond that of an administrative convenience. Culturally, many enterprises are not ready for teams. Being a team player in infrastructure management is the opposite to being individualistic and "doing your own thing." Appraisal and other ranking systems in common use tend to pit team members against each other and do not help the development of teamwork.

To be effective in each of the above types of work, all the skills covering the infrastructure areas required for the situation need to be focusable without additional managerial effort. This often implies two things from individuals:

Individuals can no longer work for years on end as specialists in one area. They must develop a portfolio of competencies that span more than one role or technical area of infrastructure management. This is achieved through formal training and through rotation through different roles and different teams.

Secondly, individuals need to learn to work in a cooperative mode, contributing their relative strengths to the task at hand. Cooperation requires fundamental organizational and cultural changes to be enacted, which rewards cooperation, however it also requires individual changes of attitudes.

Teams viewed as multidisciplinary organizational units need to "cut through" the traditional hierarchical manager-worker barriers. Effective teams in infrastructure management usually consist of between 5 and 10 people:

- The team is responsible not only for executing the tasks, but also for planning, controlling and improving the tasks. In addition the team has some responsibility for internal training.

- The team leadership is rotated and shared and is largely on the basis of knowledge and experience. The team is accountable to supervisory levels of the organization for quality, costs and achievement of goals.

- The team contains the multiple skills to perform all the steps in the team tasks. Specialization is often inevitable given the technical nature of client/server infrastructures.

4.2.1 Advantages of Teams

Multidisciplinary teams provide advantages to an infrastructure management organization that is charged with managing the infrastructure as an application-delivery system:

- Increase in overall productivity as each individual's involvement with tasks become focused. Control and ownership over the tasks often result in an improvement in morale and creativity and innovation is often a result. In many cases however there is a lead time before productivity gains become apparent and sometimes even an initial drop in productivity. End-to-end responsibility, for example within a problem management process, also provides a comprehensive view on how the infrastructure is used to deliver specific services to the business.

- Better internal communications from sharing information within teams and between teams. Teams often provide a single point of knowledge with respect to a process or an incident or a project—depending on the purpose of the team. Team dynamics lead to learning from contributions from different team members and skills to solve problems in a cooperative way.

- More effective use of resources by cutting across traditional lines of "segregation" such as mainframe, telecoms, PC support, server administration, etc. that may all be components in a service delivery path delivering an application or service to a business. The "territorial" barriers of different technology support groups is a common cause of service levels deteriorating.

- Higher quality decisions through integrating knowledge of different backgrounds in technology, mindset and approaches. This however requires high-quality leadership skills pertinent to multidisciplinary teams (rather than traditional management skills).

4.2.2 Barriers to Team Building

There are however a number of real barriers to both building and succeeding with semi-autonomous teams in the field of infrastructure management. Barriers apply to all stages—set-up, operations and ultimately the stability of the team-based organization.

The first problem is one of expectations. Most successful team-based operations have taken at least 2 years to become mature enough to provide the benefits cited above. Teams go through several stages of development.

The initial stage is often one of optimism, training and goal setting. A second stage is usually one of conflict where disagreements about leadership and control become apparent. In the following stages the conflicts are either resolved and the team finds constructive ways to achieve goals or may change, adding and losing members or establishing new goals. Once constructive ways of working together are found, the team moves on to team development.

Barriers also exist in more mundane forms. A key problem is the unavailability of suitably numerate staff—increasingly required in the strategic management of client/server infrastructures where modeling and analysis are increasingly important. Infrastructure management unfortunately does not attract top problem solvers despite the challenge of problems in it. The field is not racy enough, has a reputation for high turnover of staff, stress and lack of career paths compared to other engineering and technical fields.

Looking at teams from the perspective of global management, different parts of an enterprise are likely to have different levels of buy-in into the team concept and the organizational structure that implies. This results in conflicting "ownership" of responsibility for infrastructure, which in turn makes the building of motivated teams very difficult to achieve. Changing ownerships of responsibility across each business or geographical boundary also makes it difficult to define team goals.

Infrastructure management teams fail in achieving goals, in working cohesively, and in delivering benefits due to a number of fundamental causes:

- Teams are made up of people. Hence personality conflicts and individual agendas are almost inevitable. Team managers can (often inadvertently) allow these to interfere with team goals, especially in the course of executing day-to-day tasks.

- The team is not clear about its goals, and doesn't know where it is going. The team focuses more on the team itself rather than the required outcomes to meet well-defined goals. People in a team may also have come together because they like each other or feel they can work together. This leads to similar ways of thinking and to the suppression of conflict.

- Accept ideas only from certain quarters, often related to the status of the person or group giving the advice. This hinders internal generation of ideas within the team that is essential for continuous improvement of infrastructure management processes. This also misses out on opportunities for individual recognition which is probably the greatest motivator for innovation within teams.

- Poor leadership is another common cause of failure. Leading teams require special communication skills to communicate vision and values. It also requires facilitation and conflict resolution skills. It requires consulting skills and feedback skills for maintaining the trust of the team. Very few organizations recognize or act on the need for special leadership training.

4.2.3 Building Winning Teams

Teams are collections of people working together to achieve well-defined, common goals. However, just bringing people together is not enough to make them function as a team. For example, if a team owns a major infrastructure management process, it often requires specialists to work cooperatively across the relevant functions. The conditions for such cooperation need to engineered.

There are several enterprises where the infrastructure management groups have succeeded in using team-based approaches in gaining major benefits for its business users. Infrastructure management at an enterprise level is a horizontal function and should be viewed in terms of a "global" service business. Teams should be part of an overall strategy for the organization. Wining teams have a number of common factors:

- Clear about goals within the group as a whole and within other teams or subgroups within infrastructure management. This means that the goals and aims of each team are being communicated and reinforced repeatedly. The whole group works to an articulated vision. Goals should be realistic and expectations need to be managed.

- Clear understanding about the business being supported, with user-intimacy and user-relationship being a high priority. Upper management support and creation of specific organizational mechanisms such as team-sensitive reward policies.

- Amenable to receiving input for improvements from any source—keeping an open mind, communication and mutual trust. Investment in developing the team through a steering committee, a design process and pilot leads to better quality teams.

- Developing team leadership to overcome and manage conflict, manage diversity in the team and competition without undermining individuals. Also active leadership to generate mutual respect, trust and support among team members. Member roles and responsibilities need to be clearly defined and ground rules for behavior well documented.

Infrastructure management teams will consist of people who are different in fundamental ways. They want different things, they have different motives and values and needs. They believe differently and act differently. Yet the belief that people are fundamentally alike seems to drive the formation of many infrastructure management teams.

The different roles in the infrastructure management function hint strongly at different personalities almost by definition. There are several psychological tools that provide valuable understanding about inner personalities. Myers-Briggs Type Indicator is commonly used in many big enterprises to identify character and temperament types and to match these to organizational roles.

The payoff to the organization of using such tools is that individual differences can be viewed and used positively as one of the inputs in the staffing of teams. Less formally, many process-based teams in infrastructure management need the following mixture of people:

- *Big-picture* people who understand the whole infrastructure and/or all its dimensions. Such people often make good architects and are good in planning functions.

- *People* people are essential at the helpdesk as well as in all negotiation and vendor management roles.

- *Analytical* people are essential in key functions such as problem solving, performance management and planning but often need to be complemented with doer's.

- *Doer* people should form the bulk of the teams. Doer's are often task oriented, dependable and organized.

4.2.4 Team Performance

Team-based environments require new metrics and reward systems for team performance. The team becoming the primary focus often upsets individuals who were considered star performers. This sometimes leads to loss of talented individualists. In the long term, teams provide a *hedge* against the risk of loss of key staff leading to disruption of services.

Rewards also need to become focused on the performance of the team. A team-centric reward system may include one or more of the following components:

- *Pay-for-learning*—Rewards and recognizes the continuous training required to cope with the technology life-cycles in the infrastructure.

- *Pay-for-productivity*—Rewards team productivity in the context relevant to the team. However, productivity as a team goal is only triggered if assurances are given that a boost to productivity will not lead to job losses.

- *Profit-sharing*—This is common in engineering and IT development areas. When tied to results of a team it is increasingly relevant to service and support functions.

- *Individual recognition*—This is still relevant in a team context but recognition is for participating and contributing in a team context.

- *Self assessment*—Teams should assess themselves periodically to examine how well they are functioning and what constraints they are working under.

Many aspects of processes can be monitored automatically as described in Chapter 5, Section 5.5.4. While such automation focuses on the performance of the process itself, teams executing a process play the most important part in identifying problems and improving processes.

Hence positive deltas of process metrics are useful for measuring team performance. Use of automatically collected metrics for process performance provide direct and early feedback to process teams, allowing analysis and corrections to be made with the minimum of delay. Longer term trends in the metrics also allow planning for capacity changes, process improvement, etc.

4.3 Training

Within the engineering disciplines that make up client/server infrastructures, some 20% to 40% of knowledge used in day-to-day work is obsolete within 12 to 18 months. This is largely due to the effect of product life-cycles. Hence to build and maintain "educated" infrastructure management teams requires the design of a continuous program of training.

A key responsibility of infrastructure managers (and their management teams) is to make a make a priority of establishing systematic training that is targeted at specific infrastructure management roles. Continuous training programs are often best approached within the context of a training process which takes a proactive view from developing training requirements to implementing the training.

Most technical training is likely to be sourced from external training organizations. Specialist consultants (for example in security) also provide courses tailored to the organization. Tailoring requires knowledge of an organization's architectures and its level of maturity in using key technologies.

A common source of training is from vendors—who provide training for specific platforms and tool-kits. A point of note here is that many vendors run excellent courses at their home sites. These get diluted or deteriorate when held in other geographic areas due to the lack of suitable trainers.

There is a growing trend in high quality on-line training systems—especially in desktop applications and using IT facilities—to develop business solutions. Other areas related to training for infrastructure management staff include:

- *Communication and interpersonal skills*—This is increasingly important in the context of teams that have end-to-end responsibility that includes direct contact with the business users. Infrastructure management also needs to have communication skills to interact with business management and in negotiations with outside parties.

- *Working knowledge of key applications*—A general policy should be for all infrastructure management staff to have a working knowledge of key applications and technologies used by the business.

- *Visits to seminars and exhibitions*—These are often springboards for new ideas and services. There are also opportunities to understand how other organizations deal with similar problems or apply similar technologies.

- *Provision of professional journals*—Free provision of high-quality journals and a quiet area for reading and access to on-line services send clear messages about the value being placed on keeping up-to-date on technology and operating issues related to the infrastructure.

4.3.1 Strategic Skill Sets

Some infrastructure management roles are strategically important to the enterprise and hence the skills associated with those roles are also strategic in nature. Strategic skills in infrastructure management are recognized by the following:

- Skills that represent a long-term view that has taken in a technology or a discipline, e.g., service management on a global scale and knowledge of management processes used by the enterprise.

- Skills that are hard to come by on the market (or difficult to develop internally within a realistic time-scale)—e.g., relational database administrators with domain knowledge of infrastructure management databases.

- Knowledge which is essential for the maturity level of the organization or due to the business nature of the enterprise, e.g., in an investment bank, knowledge about the business applications used day-to-day is essential.

Unfortunately, existence of rare or strategic skills implies that other organizations at a similar maturity level are also likely to have similar requirements. Hence there are individuals within service organizations who will have an inordinate impact if they were to leave.

In general there should be a systematic attempt to reduce over dependence on key individuals in the provision of infrastructure management services. One way is to *disperse* such skills into processes that are executed by teams. A sustained effort to raising the general education levels and to have multi-skilled team members reinforce dispersal of strategic skills. Use of standards-based solutions also increases the probability of being able to recruit from the technical job market.

Most skills in infrastructure management change are over periods ranging from 12 months to 2 years. Some of these changes can be accommodated by upgrading the level or scope of skills. Existing skills often provide a basis for new skills when the new skills are not related to a paradigm shift.

The term paradigm shift comes from Thomas Kuhn's observation that in many scientific disciplines there is an *established science* or accepted techniques for achieving the intentions of the discipline. The established science is backed up by products, seminars, training courses and by experts and consultants.

In the meantime, on the outer fringes of the discipline, radically different techniques or approaches are being tried and perfected by individuals. At any given time there are several such revolutionary approaches with varying levels of following. These practitioners keep in touch through more informal networks and by word of mouth. Radical approaches with a critical mass of following are termed paradigms.

Thomas Kuhn went on to observe that almost overnight one of the paradigms shifts so as to overturn the established science of the discipline. The practitioners of the established science have almost no other options than to follow the new rules of the discipline.

Paradigm shifts are particularly relevant to client/server infrastructures and their management. Currently, much of the basis of building client/server systems and their management is likely to undergo a paradigm shift. The paradigm itself is the computational model opened up by the technology and economics of the *intranet*.

A paradigm shift invariably results in a scramble for acquiring new strategic skills. In the area of infrastructure management the depth and scope of the new skills are often not understood by early adopters of the resultant technology. This often results in inadequate or inappropriate training. Generally, all training should be aligned with information maintained about individual and team competencies and built on current strengths.

4.3.2 Re-skilling Existing Staff

Many organizations, new to managing global client/server infrastructures, often start with people who were previously responsible for administering a global *mainframe* environment or managing enterprise-level telecommunication services.

Re-skilling staff with a background in an older perspective of infrastructure poses several difficulties. These backgrounds often bring with them a number cultural characteristics that need to be changed:

- Both cultures lack the level of customer awareness required to service client/server infrastructures. Awareness of the business and the way the business uses infrastructure resources, the key players in the business are often prerequisites in an environment where support staff are expected to be more visible than the voice at a helpdesk. Lack of business life-cycles, lack of ability to understand and act on business priorities are often major handicaps

- The relatively invisible, backroom roles of mainframe administration and telecommunications rarely encourages the development of skills to interact with end-users or the development of a service culture. End-user interaction skills have often to be learned by most technicians. Higher technical competence as well as higher service awareness are needed for infrastructure management.

- Another area of interaction that infrastructure management staff have to deal with is the software or application development staff. Most large enterprises undertake software projects whose results often use the infrastructure being managed. Lack of confidence for peer interaction with development staff always leads to a risk that the infrastructure will be unable to support new projects.

Efforts in several large organizations systematically to re-train and re-skill staff from a mainframe administration or telecommunication background for new roles in client/server infrastructure management have met with limited success in terms of their eventual effectiveness in the new roles. For example, in general only about 30% of COBOL programmers are able to make a transition to object-oriented techniques.

While specific individuals in all organizations are successful in picking up a new technology area and thriving in it—these are by and large exceptions rather than a rule. Today, and increasingly so in the future, to manage infrastructures and the systems dependent on them effectively requires new *combinations* of knowledge far removed from both these backgrounds.

Lack of context between the old and new infrastructure worlds is further complicated by the fact that legacy systems are unlikely to be totally replaced in many organizations that embarked on a transition to client/server. This is largely because of the critical data repository and data processing roles mainframes continue to play in complex businesses.

Moreover, in many organizations the designers of the mainframe-based systems have left without any continuity of their knowledge being apparent. Hence the skills for the maintenance of legacy systems is unlikely to be retainable until a complete transition away from these systems is accomplished.

Generally, the best of the people from a mainframe background (i.e., with the best chances of making a transition to new systems) are key resources in maintaining these systems—often to their frustration. From another perspective, an area where organizations have had considerable success in outsourcing is the mainframe and legacy systems. As a result, the best staff in this area have often been lost in the outsourcing deal.

In general, without long-term technical re-education, re-skilling staff from a traditional mainframe and telecommunications technology background is a hit and miss affair. Such re-skilling is therefore increasingly undertaken as part of an enterprise's social policy and not as a strategy for skills upgrade.

4.3.3 Managing Change

Re-training, re-skilling, and process engineering all imply large-scale change to people's working lives. People can only handle a certain amount of change at a time in their working practices. There is considerable anecdotal evidence that large-scale changes that are suddenly imposed often lead to failure in meeting expected goals.

People need time to adjust. However, a certain level of pressure is required to ensure change is occurring in the right direction. Without a momentum being built-in, people revert to their old ways very quickly. The balance therefore is in phasing change versus gaining momentum to the desired end. Change tends to bring out the negative in people. This is largely caused by instinctive factors.

Change makes people feel self-conscious and awkward because it puts them in unfamiliar situations. Most people also instinctively think of change in terms of losses they may incur rather than gains that may be made. In times of change internal communications break down and a news grapevine invariably grows. People instinctively hide their true feelings about the change and often end up feeling isolated when the changes are implemented.

The process of change can however be managed with a number of simple rules being applied:

- Ensure the change is managed by a team, get critical mass in the team and support from outside, get a high-level management champion.

- Leadership should be visible; communicate the vision and lead in providing solutions through the inevitable barriers to change.

- Plan the change and publish the plans. Phase the change so as to keep the necessary momentum; keep changes within each phase simple.

- Maintain a communication program; be open with information, create positive images of change.

4.4 Infrastructure Management Roles

Infrastructure is traditionally viewed in terms of the product/technology layers, and infrastructure management is viewed in terms of the functions to support the layer technologies. Functions are usually duplicated across the layers, hence one job title may define responsibility for planning at the network layer, while another job title may define responsibility for planning server deployment and yet another for sizing databases.

An integrated view of infrastructure and its management requires a different perspective of responsibilities rather than just accumulating job descriptions from the component layers. With infrastructure management the focus moves from single-layer management to an integrated management of the infrastructure.

Hence new models of working are needed at an organizational level. These models need to support the multidisciplinary nature of infrastructure management as well as support the notion of dynamic teams (teams that last for a relatively short duration—e.g., for a project).

Figure 4.5 shows a more flexible way of defining jobs within infrastructure management. A job is viewed here as consisting of several roles that need to be "played" concurrently. Each role has a duration. Roles are applicable regardless of the internal organization for infrastructure management:

- In a process-centered setting, the set of roles that people play are directly related to the processes and projects they participate in.

- In a traditional product/technology setting, functional responsibilities (such as membership of a first tier support team) as well as project tasks are described in terms of roles.

- In an end-to-end architecture setting, membership of teams and the tasks undertaken within each project are described as roles. These roles are more dynamic.

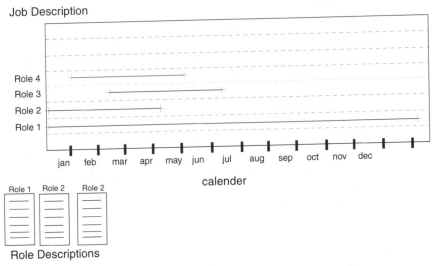

Figure 4.5: *Relationship between roles and job descriptions*

The notion of roles separates an individual's job title from the set of activities that the individual participates in. The duration that an individual undertakes a role is independent of the job title.

In infrastructure management, role-based definitions of an individual's responsibilities allows development of flexible team structures. Teams can be formed on relatively short lead times, staffed from a pool of competencies available to the internal organization.

The ability to form new teams dynamically is important when managing infrastructures that are constantly evolving in size and because of the product life-cycles of component systems.

There are several generic role types that are especially relevant to infrastructure management and applicable across the three internal organizational settings:

- *Supervisory roles* define day-to-day overseeing responsibilities. Supervision may be with respect to the standard infrastructure management processes, implementation projects or situation management (such as an infrastructure crisis that may be current).

- *Coordination roles* define roles that manage across technology, organizational, process or project boundaries. Coordination roles ensure that the necessary skills are available and are applied consistently to deliver start to finish service.

- *Security roles* are often separated out from other operational roles in many enterprises, since there is often a conflict between operational and security requirements. Security should be driven by business-defined policies.

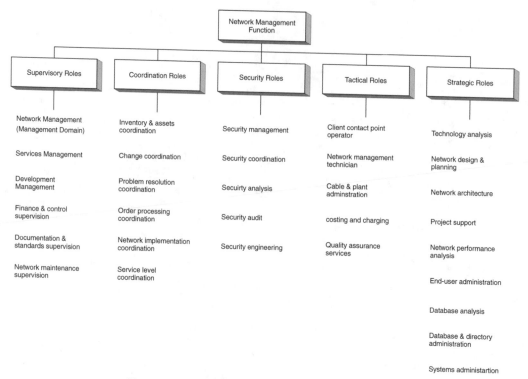

Figure 4.6: *Generic roles and examples of actual roles*

- *Strategic roles* are roles which take a long-term view of the infrastructure and its management. Strategic roles ensure that the infrastructure evolves in a way that is aligned with the business goals and so that risks to the infrastructure are managed.

- *Tactical roles* take a day-to-day perspective of managing the infrastructure. They include managing all sizes of infrastructure crises. The biggest volume of work is undertaken within these roles.

Figure 4.6 shows examples of the above role types. No general assumptions can be made about which type of role belongs to which job title. Each organization will assign these roles differently, depending on internal organization. The roles themselves should be treated as prototypes.

4.4.1 Process Ownership

Organizing infrastructure management based on a process-centered setting is described in Chapter 5. *Ownership* of infrastructure processes is described by the roles that individuals play. Process ownership usually resides with a team, rather than an individual. The team is responsible for all aspects of the process including planning, execution, management and improvement.

A large proportion of the day-to-day work of infrastructure management is undertaken by core processes such as problem management and change management. The roles of individuals in a team should collectively be able to cover the role of the team. Sometime role coverage at a team level is only possible by the inclusion of individuals for the duration of the requirement for the specific role.

A process-centered setting for organizing infrastructure management should be able to encompass the full depth of the infrastructure. Hence the management of a fault reported by a user about a specific application results in several levels of expertise having to cooperate. Multiple areas of knowledge ranging from LANs to middleware and operating systems are often needed to solve common problems in the client/server world.

The team owning the fault management process should either carry all the expertise as part of a fixed team or have the capability to access expertise dynamically for short durations. Organizing around processes however is not easy both from a manager's and individual team member's perspectives and often takes some time before bugs can be smoothed out.

Issues of team formation relating to the ownership of some of the key processes is described below.

- Change management is probably the single most important process because a production infrastructure, if allowed to be changed in an ad hoc manner by different teams, is bound to fail. Infrastructure design should make provision for a degree of change required by the dynamics of a specific business. Provisioned changes should then be relatively low risk and self-contained to a relatively long-lived team. Non-pro-

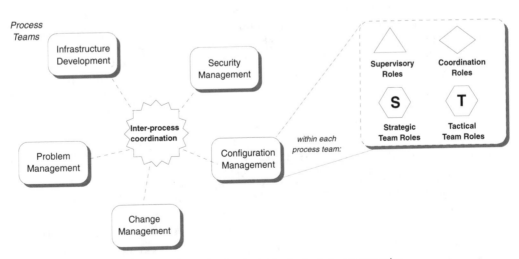

Figure 4.7: *Collecting individual roles into process roles*

visioned change requires co-option from the strategic roles to ensure that architectures remain in alignment and for analytical and modeling expertise. In addition, security often has to be re-evaluated and re-validated. In older infrastructures, application life-cycles determine the need for non-provisioned change. In this case coordination is needed with development teams or with application vendors.

- Problem management process is likely to be invoked with the highest frequency on a day-to-day basis. Problem management on an infrastructure scale needs expertise in a wide range of technology. In general however fixing the majority of end-user reported problems requires application knowledge. Fixing many instrument-reported problems on the other hand requires intimate knowledge of the infrastructure's design. Some of the latter skills are likely to be found within strategic roles. Coordination is required to track a problem until its completion and in getting multiple parties to work towards a solution.

- Configuration management process is related to initial commissioning and subsequently in executing other processes such as change management, performance tuning, and as a result of background work such as trend analysis and modeling. A key part of configuration management is management of the databases holding configuration data. These databases have "consumer" processes. The standards used for configuration of various layers of the infrastructure need to be aligned with any evolution of the processes. This requires coordination across multiple process teams to ensure that configuration data remain aligned with the needs of consumer processes.

- Security management procedures are aimed at developing an independent perspective on the security of the computing environment supported by the infrastructure. Security management procedures range from expert evaluation of configurations of devices such as firewalls to monitoring for specific patterns of activity. Security management procedures such as a security audit and validation need to be applied following many processes, including change management, re-configuration of any part of the infrastructure and following any infrastructure recovery. Both strategic and tactical security roles need to have close cooperative relationships with the relevant process teams.

4.4.2 Special Issues with Role-based Teams

Several roles in infrastructure management are in uniquely privileged position to cause damage to an organization. Types of damage range from financial loss through fraud, loss or damage to information resources, loss of technology leads and loss of reputation. Roles should be combined in such a way as to minimize the concentration of such opportunities within individuals. Where it is inevitable then supplementary procedures should be put in place as a check and balance.

Studies have shown for example that most security threats to an organization are perpetuated by internal sources. The basis for the threats range from pathological personalities to grudges that build up while the individuals are in employment.

This suggests that the starting point for any special personnel policies for infrastructure management staff should start with the recruitment process. In many organizations, however, there are no special procedures to verify the backgrounds of potential employees, and managers sometimes even bypass the elementary checks that are possible.

The personnel management part of the organization should be fully involved in the design of the recruitment process for infrastructure staff and their subsequent management. The organization should in general be stringent about checking staff backgrounds and references.

Psychometric testing specifically designed for positions involving a high level of trust is also available as a tool in the recruitment and selection process—although this should not be the only factor. Internal audit procedures to ensure that staff are operating within acceptable guidelines are common in sensitive roles such as security.

Some organizations have found it worthwhile to develop human resource processes specifically for managing complex global infrastructure staffing needs. The goals of such a process are:

- To develop global policies for infrastructure management staff covering organizational prototypes for different types of offices, training and remuneration.

- To attract and retain the level of skills required and to ensure that an adequate pool of people with the right skills is available for global needs.

- To develop models for performance evaluation of teams and individuals, including formulae for compensation and career planning.

- To develop feedback and monitoring mechanisms to assess staff morale, performance levels and for analyzing any trends which may lead to staffing problems.

4.4.3 Geographic Distribution and Out-of-Hours Support

In most businesses that are global in scope, the infrastructure has always to be in a state where it is capable of providing business services. Business processes "connected" on a global scale are always active and hence resources and information located at any point in the organization may be needed at any time.

To ensure global availability of services 24 hours x 7 days a week, support staff working on a shift basis have been the norm in mission-critical data centers. This is feasible with skeletal staffing levels outside business hours and when the number of data centers are in the order of two or three. Shift-working to support a client/server infrastructure in a distributed environment is a prohibitively expensive proposition—both due to the large number of potential peer sites and the minimum staffing required to make support viable.

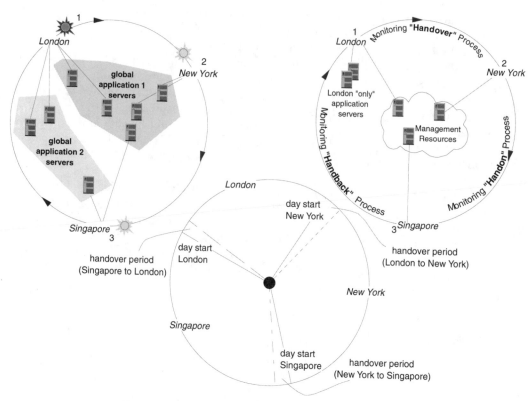

Figure 4.8: *Follow-the-sun monitoring of critical systems*

Within distributed environments an alternative to 24-hour staffing is to devolve responsibility for monitoring of critical resources out of normal hours to a remote site in another time zone. This is shown in Figure 4.8. The remote monitoring is augmented by local "on-call" staff (at the monitored site) who continue the diagnosis and fix the problem. In many cases the monitoring site may be able to safely re-start failed systems.

There are clearly limits to the number of sites and systems at each site which can be included in a remote-monitoring scheme. Two common limiting factors related to people are:

- At each monitoring site there are staff and systems resource overheads for remote monitoring. Usually, only the most critical systems can be monitored.

- At each monitored site local staff need to be placed on a "on call" rota. This has a negative effect on morale as it is seen to extend working hours.

In scaling infrastructure management processes globally, team members who have never met need to work cooperatively within the context of the process. This raises the issue of applying winning tactics of teams to a distributed context:

Some important aspects building global teams include:

- Having one global head for the infrastructure management function, so that the same vision and same goals are shared globally.

- Cycle key people through different sites so that they become accepted as global team players.

- Establish similarity in working practices, career structures, training and compensation so that a global organization is discernible.

- Establish regular seminars and technical meetings between regional teams so that local experiences can be shared and learned from.

4.5 Managing the Skills Portfolio

An infrastructure management organization needs to track both the set of skills it requires as well as the level of competency required in each area. Hence an organization which supports desktop applications needs a high level of competence in the desktop applications area. An organization which outsources desktop support requires few or no skills in the area.

The "heterogeneity" in large infrastructures (i.e., the different types or families or generations of systems that are integrated to build the infrastructure) continues to mushroom. Heterogeneity places a burden on the range of skills that need to be retained.

This is despite attempts at the corporate headquarters levels to mandate single-vendor solutions and enterprise-wide architectures. Individual business areas still have ample scope to make good business cases for choosing alternative choices and to claim resultant advantages to improve the bottom line of the business.

The proactive management of the portfolio of skills required to support a corporate infrastructure ensures that service delivery is not suddenly impacted.

Steps and drivers in active management of the skills portfolio are shown in Figure 4.9 and main activities are described below:

- Review the current skill portfolio in terms of skills and skill sets, an estimation of the competency level.

- Identify current (or known) skill requirements in terms of the actual skills or skill sets, the competency level for each skill or skill set, and the number of people required for each of the levels and the geographic distribution of the people.

- Produce a projection of skill requirements covering the requisite planning period.

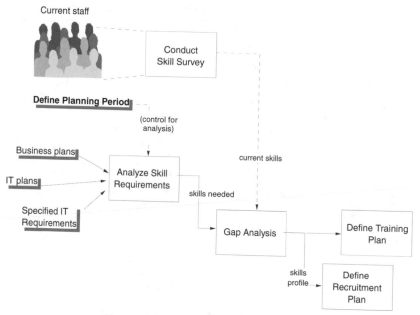

Figure 4.9: *Managing the skills portfolio*

- Match and compare skill requirements (both known and projected) with the current portfolio in the dimensions of skill sets, competency and geographic distribution. Define the gaps between requirements and the current portfolio.

- Evaluate training versus recruitment options and define respective skill acquisition plans using each option—to fill the analyzed gaps.

Maintaining an inventory of skills is essential to tracking and managing changing skill requirements. Keeping a skills inventory up to date is often best done within the context of a formal process. This would typically update a skills inventory on events such as new hires, completion of training and following performance reviews.

Linking the management of skill portfolios with bonus and reward schemes (for gaining new skills) sets up a positive feedback loop in a group or organization. Results, in terms of an emerging "learning" organization, are usually visible within 6 months to one year.

4.5.1 Components of Job Satisfaction

The main motivators for job seekers in infrastructure management is similar to other high-technology service areas and has changed little over the last decade. In general, however, surveys show that there is a relatively high turnover of experienced staff.

Part of the reason is that there is a global shortage of experienced staff to satisfy the needs of all the organizations that are scaling up client/server environments.

Understanding what is likely to motivate people is a prerequisite to developing working environments that actively reduce staff loss. Some organizations survey their staff directly to get such answers. There are also cultural factors to motivation—this is often a problem in the global management organization.

The following are common components that contribute to job satisfaction and should be considered:

- Salary and financial benefits. Skills that ensure that the corporate infrastructure continues to run are currently in high demand and therefore offer a premium at all levels. Financial incentive is often assumed to be the reason for staff changing jobs. Surveys have shown that financial incentive in itself does little to make staff feel good or creative about their jobs. However it creates substantial dissatisfaction if pay and benefits are seen to be inadequate.

- Job security. In the wake of downsizing most people are realistic about the limits of job security. The trend to outsource infrastructure operations complicates the notion of security—very often an individual is forced to work for an organization with a different culture. Neither size nor economic prowess of the enterprise contributes to job security. Security is related more to how strategic and appropriate specific skills are to the business operations of the enterprise. Gaining business knowledge, becoming multiskilled and continuing further education are typical strategies that contribute to job security.

- Challenge and empowerment. Being given responsibility and the means to achieve results attracts talented individuals. If measurable milestones and deliverables are set for individuals, then the freedom should also be provided to develop the associated tasks and budget time to produce the deliverables.

- Continuous training. One way for individuals to ensure the marketability of their skills is by having their skills and competency levels upgraded to reflect state-of-the-art in infrastructure technology. The provision of structured programs for training is a major factor in retaining key staff. Training programs send a message that the individual's skills are highly valued. This is often reinforced by incentives to become multiskilled.

- Career paths. In flatter organizations, traditional career paths are not as relevant as in hierarchic organizations. Instead, recognition should be provided in other ways. For many technical staff recognition by their peers is an important factor.

- New projects and job rotation. In addition to a training program, the focus of individuals should be challenged through job rotation. This should be part of the individual's appraisal and training plan. Participation in new projects is another method by which skills and knowledge can be developed.

4.5.2 Skill Definition for Infrastructure Management

The skills required for supporting the infrastructure are derived from the tasks that are executed in each of the roles required in its management. The actual tasks depend on the internal structure of the infrastructure management organization and the actual roles defined by the internal structure. Figure 4.10 shows the dependency between skills and the other related concepts described below.

A task relative to its importance in underpinning the internal structure of the infrastructure management organization determines the level of competency required. Competency is essentially a measure of the breadth of experience. In most cases only three levels of competence are needed:

- *Expert*—one who can improve and adapt the related set of tasks to the internal structure of the infrastructure management organization, can teach others or extend the state of the art—e.g., through automation or systems integration.

- *Practitioner*—one who has successfully executed the related set of tasks a number of times, has all the skills and attributes required and feels generally comfortable in executing the tasks under the internal structure of the infrastructure management organization.

- *Aware*—one who has exposure to the tasks, has some of the skills and attributes, sees the relevance but has not executed the tasks.

Once skills are defined then the attributes associated with the skills can be identified. Attributes are useful in both descriptions for recruitment as well as in identifying training to gain the skills.

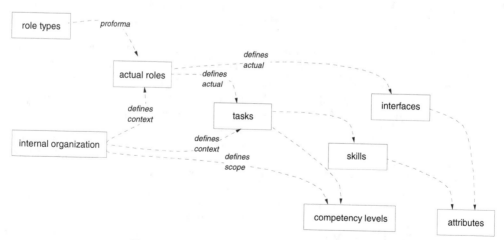

Figure 4.10: *Dependency chain for skill definition*

The actual roles defined in an infrastructure management organization also determine the interfaces between different internal roles as well as with different parts of the enterprise and outside parties. These interfaces also contribute to the required attributes.

4.5.3 Skill Portfolio Reviews

Once the skills have been defined then the skills inventory (relative to the technology base of the client/server infrastructure) can be built. The skills inventory shows the distribution of skills in terms of the level of competence and geographic distribution of the people with the skills.

"Bootstrapping" the skills inventory is usually achieved through questionnaire-based surveys and interviews. The information in the inventory is best updated through a formal process to ensure the timeliness of the inventory information and to guarantee the integrity of the information.

Review of the skills inventory is an essential first step to developing recruitment and training strategies. The inventory is also essential in internal organizational structures in which teams are put together for the duration of projects from a pool of resources with the requisite skills. Hence the skills inventory is a major resource and likely to be under "continuous" review as project managers create new teams.

Skills inventories are sometimes extended to hold "state" information about allocation of the persons with a skill to projects (or to management processes) and to show the level of spare capacity in a skills area.

Managing skills inventories for a global infrastructure management organization poses problems in buy-in and coordination if the overall leadership of the organization is fragmented.

4.5.4 Changing Skill Requirements

Recruitment and training based on specific skill requirements creates a structured framework for activities that are often disconnected and chaotic in many enterprises. Such a framework and an associated skill management process is essential to make global management organizations work efficiently.

In operational terms the main purpose of such a framework is to ensure that the human resources organization can take a proactive role in ensuring that skill deficits do not occur in infrastructure management. It is therefore important to understand the key factors that cause skill deficits in this area:

- An individual is likely to have multiple roles to play in the course of a period and hence flexibility in terms of the relative priorities of each role is required. Expansion of roles and taking on of new roles are likely to cause the inability to use some of the skills of an individual.

- Business requirements of IT based on client/server technology are driven by business, technical and fad factors. Change of strategic direction often results in the need for different types or levels of infrastructure skills.

- Businesses have recently tended to think globally or at least to integrate multiple operations for economies of scale. This requires a different set of IT skills in architecting and scale of the infrastructure.

Both tactical skills (required for day-to-day operations) and strategic skills (required to manage the growth of the infrastructure) are needed in infrastructure management. Tactical skills can by and large be outsourced without damaging service delivery. Hence outsourcing whole skill sets is an alternative to recruitment or training.

Strategic skills on the other hand need to be applied within the context of the wider goals of the organization and hence are ideally retained within the enterprise—especially when viewed long-term. Long-term, strategic skills are likely to play a part in leveraging the infrastructure for competitive advantage.

Infrastructure staff have traditionally pursued vertical specialities. As more flexible team structures are introduced, the need to become multi-skilled and better trained are important. Some types of teams, such as process-centered teams, cannot function without team members being multi-skilled.

In addition to developing skills in specific areas, an infrastructure management organization also needs to develop generally high levels of competency in key subject areas related to the discipline. This should be within the context of its application in the enterprise. Some example subject areas are defined below:

- *LAN, MAN and WAN topology.* Client/server applications are entirely dependent on the different types of networks connecting users to information resources. A good general understanding of the network architecture of the enterprise and the deployment of resources is essential to supporting client/server systems. General distribution of status information about the networks allows an ongoing appreciation of the topology to be maintained.

- *Telecom and data services.* Client/server based systems are often used in conjunction with other communication services. Typically, the telephone and video conferencing are used increasingly in augmenting communication information from applications. In other organizations real-time information such as news and financial data are critical to the business. An understanding of the services and service providers of all key services is needed to field queries from end-users.

- *Operating system and middleware services.* Operating systems are often the most complex pieces of software in an enterprise. This is often considered the province of experts, however, a general understanding of operating system issues relating to end-

Table 4.1: Competency Matrix by Selected Functional Area*

Selected Area	Selected Tasks	Network Topology	Telecoms & Services	Operating System	End-user Application
Client Contact Point	receiving problem reports	aware	aware	aware	expert
	general enquiries	aware	aware	aware	
	change requests	X	X		X
	IT equipment require-ments	X	X		X
Fault Tracking	tracking faults	aware	aware	aware	practitioner
	tracking progress	aware	aware	aware	aware
	tracking escalation	X	X	X	aware
	distributing fault information		X	X	X
	referring problems to management	X	X	X	X
	generating fault metrics	X	X	X	X
Security Management	threat analysis	expert	practitioner	expert	practitioner
	key administration	X	practitioner	X	practitioner
	reviewing security policy	expert	practitioner	expert	practitioner
	detection of breaches	expert	expert	expert	expert
	security audit	practitioner	practitioner	practitioner	practitioner
	security recovery	practitioner	practitioner	expert	practitioner
	logging events	X	X	X	X

*Level X = Don't Care

users is relevant at all levels. In particular there should be a general familiarity with the user interface tools. Where feasible the operating system should be used within the infrastructure management organization. Middleware services are increasingly important as unifying mechanisms in tying together different technologies and different parts of the enterprise. This is another area for experts.

- *Applications used by end-users.* Horizontal applications like e-mail and office automation that pervade across the enterprise are often handled by special sectors of the helpdesk or even outsourced. Knowledge of client/server application architecture is needed in functions or processes involving problem diagnosis, analysis, projection, etc.

Another area where general competence needs to be developed is in the use of infrastructure management tools. Proficient use of the tools used in the infrastructure management organization is an essential part of a multi-skilled staff. Tool usage should be treated as part of general competency requirements rather than skills. Common examples of tools relevant to infrastructure management are shown below:

- Helpdesk and trouble ticket application (1).

- Office Automation Suite including e-mail (2).

- Event monitoring tools including information bulletin boards (3).

- Directory and database search tools (4).

Table 4.1 shows a competency matrix for a small sample of functional areas described in Chapter 3, "Organizational Aspects of Infrastructure Management." The tools used are referenced by the respective number in parentheses. The competency level that is needed is defined in terms of the expert/practitioner/aware classification discussed in Section 4.5.2.

4.6 Developing Skill and Competency Requirements

Some tasks that need to be done in an infrastructure management group are generic while others are dependent on the internal organizational structure (and the actual roles defined within the structure).

In the following tables, sets of tasks have been collected together and have been aligned with actual roles in supervisory, coordination, strategic and tactical areas (as described in Section 4.4).

In a "traditionally" structured infrastructure management organization these tasks get executed by individuals responsible for each function. In a "process-centric" organization these tasks are executed within processes (by the actors participating in the process). In an "architecture-centric" organizations these tasks form the subject of on-going projects and are executed by the various teams.

Once the tasks are identified then the personal attributes required to execute the task and the competency levels required can be defined. Definition of these three areas provides inputs for people-related processes and activities:

- To identify current skill deficits.

- To target recruitment and define requirements.

The following tables describe the infrastructure management roles in Figure 4.6 with key attributes required for the role.

4.6.1 Tasks in Supervisory Roles

Supervisory or management roles are found regardless of the internal structure of the infrastructure management organization. Examples of actual supervisory and management roles and the tasks related to these roles are shown in Tables 4.2 to Table 4.7.

Common external interfaces for these roles include: (*a*) Managers of other IT functions, (*b*) other domain network managers, (*c*) key users, (*d*) consulting company partner level, (*e*) training/recruitment companies, (*f*) senior vendor management, (*g*) account management from telecom suppliers.

General management. Role which carries overall responsibility for the infrastructure management function.

Service management. Role with overall responsibility for aspects relating to the services provided and services bought by the infrastructure management organization.

Project management. Role with overall responsibility for the delivery of projects relating to the infrastructure or the execution of multiple work packages.

Finance and control. Role with overall responsibility for developing and maintaining financial control models in infrastructure management.

Standards control. Role with overall responsibility for the definition and maintenance of internal documentation and standards

Maintenance supervision. Role with overall responsibility for all maintenance activities relating to the infrastructure.

Table 4.2: General Management Tasks

Tasks	Attributes Required
Ensure overall "quality" of infrastructure management function	Graduate in numerate discipline, training in administration, budgeting, strategic planning, project management
Human resource planning	
Planning of product delivery	Knowledge of statistics
Develop and implement internal operational standards and discipline	Ability to delegate
	Good communication skills
Recruitment of senior and specialist infrastructure management staff	Excellent team management skills.
	Excellent negotiation skills
Performance evaluation of processes, technology, people, architecture	Knowledge of network technology and telecom trends
Performance review of staff	Knowledge of business
Membership of steering committee	
Direct development projects	
Negotiation of major purchases	
Financial review of forecasts and budgets	

Table 4.3: Service Management Tasks

Tasks	Attributes Required
Review of external service level agreements	Training in business administration or administrative management
Negotiation of internal service level agreements	
Preparation of training programs for service operations area	Financial administration training and experience
Spending forecast and budget preparation for service operations area	Supervisory experience of technical staff and contractors
Tracking inventory and equipment order status	Communication skills with sales and services from vendors and suppliers
Manage escalation point for complaints about problem management, order processing	
Review security plans and security status (with security functions)	Good knowledge of organization's business
Stand-in for infrastructure management for operational issues	
Responsibility for operational cover	

Table 4.4: Project Management Tasks

Tasks	Attributes Required
Business case development for network projects	Graduate in engineering discipline
Project planning, estimation and project review	Training in project management and estimation techniques
Report to network domain management on project status and risks	Understanding of products and technology used
Liaison with users or application development staff and end-user departments on network requirements and timescale	Team leadership qualities
Preparation of training program for development operations area	Knowledge of infrastructure related risk

Table 4.5: Finance and Control Tasks

Tasks	Attributes Required
Manage unified account model for voice and data circuits	Accountancy qualifications
Develop criteria-based billing	Analytical
Develop activity-based cost models	Good communication skills
Input network accounts to company accounting system	Knowledge of activity-based costing
Participate in budgeting and forecasting	Knowledge of company accounting practices
Participate in financial negotiations with vendors and outsourcers	Knowledge of equipment life-cycles
Participate in costing part of equipment selection process	

Table 4.6: Documentation and Standards Tasks

Tasks	Attributes Required
Develop and review documentation standards	Graduate
Run quality program for documented information	Training in use of IT for archives
Participate in directory attribute definition	Appreciation of global directories and web-based distribution
Participate in maintenance of automated event collection	
Keep track of status of external standards used, documentation distribution	
Prepare budgets for documentation process	
Maintain latest vendor documentation for reference	

Table 4.7: Maintenance Supervision Tasks

Tasks	Attributes Required
Develop implementation and maintenance processes and status	Technical training in infrastructure areas
Manage contractors	Appreciation of procedural/process mechanisms
Manage phased upgrade programs	Product training in key areas
Assess physical risks—security, facility and utilities failure	Experience in managing short-term contractors
Participate in product selection from maintenance perspective	Experience in long-term project planning
Maintenance of physical security measures	

4.6.2 Tasks Associated with Coordination Roles

Coordination roles span across infrastructure management areas, sometimes into the end-user communities and into functions such as the facilities management. Such roles require interaction skills and the ability to work in "virtual" teams. The interfaces are with other internal groups.

Table 4.8: Asset Inventory Tasks

Tasks	Attributes Required
Responsible for population of assets database and its frequency and method of update	Understanding of technology assets in environment
Review of accuracy of automated capture mechanisms	Knowledge of how license servers work
Maintain and backup infrastructure configurations	Knowledge of techniques to optimize licenses
Maintain context relationships between assets and business usage by business process	Understanding of licensing models for different classes of software
Track equipment deliveries and state of usage and any security issues	Understanding of client/server life-cycle models
Develop software license tracking	Knowledge of maintenance contracts
Responsible for inventory control through life-cycles of equipment	Knowledge to set up a Wintel re-cycling process
Responsible for access to maintenance contracts and periodic review of contracts	Understanding of issues in re-cycling of Wintel equipment
Track received service levels against maintenance contracts	
Budget input for maintenance element	

Table 4.9: Change Coordination Tasks

Tasks	Attributes Required
Schedule and prioritizes all change activities	Understanding of cross-technology areas
Ensure quality of change "package" including implementation plan, test plan, resource plan, documentation plan, project leadership	Knowledge of service level development and implementation
Maintain status of all changes currently in progress and signed off for implementation	Knowledge of processes used for change management
Ensure all changes occur according to defined implementation plan	Understanding of project management
Responsibility to call and manage change meetings	Knowledge of escalation models
Provide management reports on changes and status including risk profiles of changes to existing operations	
Develop and review change management procedures with respect to service levels	

Table 4.10: Problem Resolution Coordination Tasks

Tasks	Attributes Required
Review and maintain routing matrix of expertise for problem classes—including management of holiday season and illness	Degree or equivalent education
Monitor existing problems and their status. Assists in prioritizing on the basis of service levels and systemic criticality views	Understanding of technology dependency areas
Coordinate opinions and resources from strategic engineering functions for managing major crises	Understanding of complex inter-process flows
Maintain crisis skill sets and contact methods	Knowledge of escalation models
Manage distribution of current problems to co-respondents on other management domains	Knowledge of best practice in problem management
Define automated collection of problem status and summary	Knowledge of statistical models for problem management
Assist in escalation of problems and managing crisis meetings	Knowledge of ticketing and workflow products
Define cross-functional resources required for managing crises	
Report problems in business terms and provide feedback for end-user consumption	

Table 4.11: Implementation Coordination Tasks

Tasks	Competencies and Attributes
Ensure change process has been applied to each work order	Project management and tracking skills
Schedule implementation work	Contract negotiation skills
Document all events in executing a work order	Understanding of testing philosophy and models
Responsible for configuration data reflecting implementation	Facilitation skills
Responsible for coordinating with external subcontractors	Technology analysis skills
Responsible for reporting on work quality of subcontractors	
Evaluate test plans and coordinates test observation and reports	

Table 4.12: Order Processing Coordination

Tasks	Attributes Required
Prepare and distribute vendor listings and cost to organization	Knowledge of generating and managing an internal product catalog
Assist in consolidation of orders on a periodic basis	Understanding equipment life-cycles
Manage order status	Skills to manage vendors and sales people
Define impact of order replacements on internal standards	Understanding of end-user business requirements
Liaise with users, change and strategic roles on internal standards	
Manage inventory levels	
Ensure strategic requirements and internal standards are understood by potential and current vendors	
Liaise with vendor representatives	
Prepares and distributes vendor evaluations	
Provide information for inventory management and configuration management	

Table 4.13: Service Level and Risk Coordination

Tasks	Attributes Required
Negotiate service levels with external suppliers of communication and other services	Understanding of IT risk methodology
Define service parameters and educate on internal service levels	Knowledge of building charging models allied to service delivery
Negotiate with internal groups on charging, delivery and reporting of service levels	Knowledge of building service level measurement framework
Set up monitoring and reporting frameworks for service levels	Knowledge of risk management techniques
Evaluate delivery risks across security, contingency and resilience to define overall risk measures for application delivery	Good communication and presentation skills with end-users
Distribute requirements from service levels to capacity and performance planning activities	Knowledge of developing monitoring of high integrity client/server systems

4.6.3 Tasks Associated with Security Roles

Security is often managed outside the scope of IT so that there is no contention between security related decisions and IT delivery. Security related escalations needs to be resolved at a higher level than IT management who may not agree with the urgency of actions.

Table 4.14: Security Management

Tasks	Attributes Required
Evaluate security risks, security plans and escalation procedures	Knowledge of corporate security standards
	Knowledge of security standards work
Manage security monitoring and security event distribution	Understanding of activities in security area for each operating system supported by the organization
Create and reports on threat matrix by business area	
Review security recovery plans	Understanding of security products
Define security education for end-users and participate in security awareness programs	Understanding of security features of IT service offerings (e.g., web content hosting)
Keep up to date with security threats in generic areas	
Define security product selection criteria	Understanding of consequences of using security products in cross border scenario
Define and manages security framework for network and systems management staff	
Decide actions against security violation	

Table 4.15: Security Coordination

Tasks	Attributes Required
Real-time monitoring of security events	Understanding of business processes using security services
Management of security sweeps	
Management of authentication and authorization keys or passwords	Knowledge of corporate security policies and their actual execution
Escalation of violations	Knowledge of contingency plans regarding security
Responsible for single logon across heterogeneous systems	

Table 4.16: Security Analysis

Tasks	Attributes Required
Security threat analysis by business area	Degree in numerate or engineering subject
Define security plans	Technology analysis skills
Define security characteristics by business area	Knowledge of security techniques and skills
Evaluate and review security of network and systems management field	Knowledge of evaluating security products
Evaluate and report on performance and resilience aspects of security services	Knowledge of role of security in application delivery
Quality assurance for security products implementation	Understanding of legal and country implications of security techniques used
Define authentication and authorization mechanisms by business area	
Define procedures for network and systems management personnel	

Table 4.17: Security Audit

Tasks	Attributes Required
Evaluate daily security events	Knowledge of audit procedures
Define sweep frequencies	Knowledge of audit procedures and criteria used by external auditors
Assist in estimating real-time security threats	
Assist in deciding actions against active threat or intruder	Knowledge of current best practice in security audit
Defines portfolio of physical and IT defenses	Knowledge of relative merits of audit methodologies
Defines violation thresholds	
Scan sources for state of security threats in relevant operating systems	
Associate with security management bodies for latest risk profiles and procedures	

Table 4.18: Security Engineering

Tasks	Attributes Required
Implement security measures	Operating system expert
Evaluate security products for efficacy and robustness	Security API expert
Design solutions for managing identified risks and threats	Knowledge of security algorithms
Develop resilience for security implementations	Knowledge of engineering models for security implementation
Provide consultancy for application development activities	
Configuration of security instruments	

4.6.4 Tasks Associated with Tactical Roles

These are non-specialist in nature and the primary skills for most day to day activities. Such skills are the most likely to be found on the job market. many of these roles are interchangeable from organization to organization.

Table 4.19: Helpdesk Tasks

Tasks	Attributes Required
Liaison and primary interface with end-users	Knowledge of desktop applications
First level problem diagnosis and use of escalation procedure when unsuccessful	Skills for dealing with end-users
Use process guideline for opening trouble tickets, change orders, queries and purchase orders	Helpful attitude
Network supervision using infrastructure management maps for fault, performance problems, security, change in contingency status, etc.	Knowledge of processes used at helpdesk
Review status of changes in currently operation	Understanding of single point of contact model and its evolution
Review agent generated faults	Understanding of feedback processes to keep users informed
Review fault and change management processes' databases to provide feedback to end-users	Understanding of escalation and end-user communications models
Provide feedback on end-user sentiment to infrastructure management function	
Data entry activities where appropriate to update contextual relationships	

Table 4.20: Technician Tasks

Tasks	Attributes Required
Provide second level diagnosis	Technical diploma or degree in technical area
Network supervision using infrastructure management maps for fault, performance problems, security, change in contingency status, etc.	Knowledge of escalation procedures and models
Use of intelligent tools for rapid problem "root-causes"	Knowledge of engineering processes
Maintenance of intelligent tools	Team working skills
Implement pre-defined bypass or recovery procedures	Understanding of technical infrastructure for client/server systems
Perform network shutdown during maintenance	
Define network start-up check sequences	
Liaise with database and performance experts on solving related problems	

Table 4.21: Higher Technician Tasks

Tasks	Attributes Required
Provides third level in-depth diagnosis	Technical degree or diploma
Technical interface to vendors and vendor information services	Knowledge of technical infrastructures for client/server environments
Distribution of vendor specific information on problems	Team player in cross technology team
Design recovery or bypass procedures and distribute it to second and first levels where appropriate	Team leadership skills
	Crisis management skills
Technical interface with application developers	Methodological approach to problem solving
Assist in network problem resolution	
Supervise network start-up, configuration and re-configuration	
Define proactive diagnostic mechanisms	
Propose ways of automating diagnostics	

Table 4.22: Cable and Plant Administration

Tasks	Attributes Required
Define criteria for front end and database ends of cable management tools	Knowledge of plant architecture models
Define processes' use of tools	Knowledge of cabling and connection advances
Selection of tools	Knowledge of tests for selection verifications
Population of databases of tools	
Review database for trends	Knowledge of testing rigs for post implementation verification
Maintain tool interfaces to exchange information with other systems (such as the configuration system)	Knowledge of tools for cable management
Develop cable/fiber testing criteria	Understanding of cable labelling and identification schemes
Develop cable/fiber selection criteria	Skills for spot checks of cable implementation
Spot supervision of testing and review of test results	
Develop inspection and test plans	
Develop cable/fiber run architecture and cable/fiber distribution scheme	
Define storage criteria and tests for spare parts	
Define labelling standard for cable/fiber runs	
Provide maps for cable to equipment connections for generation of topography maps	
Provide status reports on the state of cables/fiber runs	

Table 4.23: Costing and Charging Tasks

Tasks	Attributes Required
Define charge-back policies for infrastructure management and network services	Understanding of accounting models for infrastructure
Define cost components and develop model following corporate guidelines	Negotiation skills with internal users and external suppliers
Collect information on cost attributions	Understanding of IT delivery cost models
Monitor vendor pricing and impact on new plans	Understanding of outsourcing models
Develop accounting policy and check accounting accuracy of produced information	
Balance service level to charges equation	
Training end-users on charging and cost components	

Table 4.24: Quality Assurance Tasks

Tasks	Attributes Required
Defines quality levels	Knowledge of quality methods to apply to infrastructure
Defines internal company standards	
Manage implementation of standards and migration to standards	Understanding of quality versus delivery time trade-off
Monitor measurement methodology of service levels with internal users	Understanding of setting up a quality framework
Monitor service levels with external parties and invokes penalties on violation	Training and communications skills
Report on quality results to end-users	Understanding of quality at process level
Monitor any quality indicators relevant to current improvement programs	Knowledge of benchmark techniques
Evaluate quality in infrastructure management processes	Knowledge of gap analysis techniques
Establish education programs on quality for infrastructure management staff	

4.6.5 Tasks Associated with Strategic Roles

Strategic roles deliver benefits on a longer term basis in that they deliver to a longer term IT vision. Strategic roles are important, especially when "applied" to areas of the infrastructure that tend to evolve slowly as opposed to being replaced.

Table 4.25: Infrastructure Design and Planning Tasks

Tasks	Attributes Required
Feasibility studies for network changes	Degree in numerate or computer science related field
Evaluate effectiveness of network structures for application delivery	Knowledge of fundamental network algorithms
Network design to meet architecture definitions	Knowledge of network standards
Characterization of current work-loads	Knowledge of network and system architecture development
Develop network migration plans	Understanding of application architecture and development process
Develop implementation plans for unprovisioned changes	Good communication skills
Evaluate risks in all change situations	Practical skills in developing networks through an engineering process—design, prototype, pilot, full-scale development, etc.
Develop testing and evaluation methodologies	
Supervise system testing	
Perform hardware and software selection	
Evaluate risks in adopting vendor upgrades	Project management experience
Produce impact analysis reports for major changes	Risk analysis experience
Planning for new release or upgrade of software	
Version upgrade strategy for remotely sited equipment	
Educational program on design, performance, vendor offerings	

Table 4.26: Network Architecture Tasks

Tasks	Attributes Required
Develop a roadmap for network evolution	Degree in numerate or computer science discipline
Model current network usage and projected usage	
Evaluate communication services	Knowledge of state of the art in network technology
Visit reference sites	
Evaluate vendor and standards architectures and protocols	Debates in network design
	Knowledge of vendor offerings
Develop feasibility studies of applying technologies to meet business demands	Knowledge of client/server stack and layer inter-relationships
Develop criteria for pilot installations	Intellectual curiosity about other technical architecture areas such as object oriented frameworks
Prepare design alternatives and fallback situations	
Train in technology trends at subsystem and services levels	
Develop infrastructure management strategies	
Develop criteria for hardware and software selection	

Table 4.27: Project Support Tasks

Tasks	Attributes Required
Implementation of vendor software packages	Understanding of administration procedures for requisite operating systems
Environment set-up for internal projects	
Testing environments for internal and pilot projects	Understanding of software development models
Release control and release strategy	
	Understanding of development tools used

Table 4.28: *Performance Analysis Tasks*

Tasks	Attributes Required
Define performance indicators and metrics for network and systems levels	Understanding of client/server performance models
Define, build and review baseline performance models for LAN, WAN and MAN	Knowledge of building performance management frameworks
Define and perform performance tests on LAN, WAN and MAN	Knowledge of performance management instrumentation
Define and perform tuning	Understanding of performance management limitations and advances
Analyzes data in performance database for trends	
Define data collection parameters including frequency and data compression variables	
Select instruments and software for performance work	
Assist in "third level" problem diagnosis and fixing	
Define and package performance tests for non specialists	

Table 4.29: *End-User Administration Tasks*

Tasks	Attributes Required
Registers user complaints	"Customer facing" skills
Liaison for managing users leaving or changing within the organization	Understanding of user business areas
Develop statistics for metrics end-users are interested in and their distribution	Understanding of business context for use of IT services and resources
Define user profiles	Understanding of business processes run over IT resources
Identify and "deconstruct" user processes	
Distribute details of end-user processes for understanding in network management group	

Table 4.30: Data Analysis and Architecture Tasks

Tasks	Attributes Required
Perform selection of database components based on architecture defined selection criteria	Relational database product knowledge
Sizing of databases	Client server applications
	ORB object definitions
Define database schema for performance, fault, ticketing and configuration databases	Java object model, distribution, security, etc.
Define performance analysis criteria for adequacy test during database operation	Understanding of client/server architecture models
Define data replication criteria and protocol	Understanding of client/server architecture models
Define directory structures for end-user configuration information	
Definition of schema for equipment configuration	Understanding of distributed corporate application development processes
	Understanding of application database lifecycles and performance requirements

Table 4.31: Database and Directory Administration Tasks

Tasks	Attributes Required
Configuration of databases	Knowledge of database vendor's product set
Definition of filtering	
Design of archiving and back-up policies	Knowledge of directory architecture and design principles
Design of resilience mechanisms for high availability of infrastructure management databases	Understanding of competing products and current debate in the field
Establishment of test and reference infrastructure management databases	Understanding of SQL and its usage
Definition of existential criteria for infrastructure management databases	
Performance tuning of databases as growth or changes occur	
Define access rights to databases and access authentication mechanisms	
Define user privileges for directory front ends	

Table 4.32: Systems Administration

Tasks	Attributes Required
Responsible for administration of all computing assets in network and systems management function	Graduate in numerate subject
Management of software versions and their distribution	Knowledge of requisite operating systems and its development history
Monitoring and management of resilience structures and mechanisms for infrastructure management	Knowledge of best practice in configuring the operating system
Coordination of dependencies between vendor and internal software and execution environment	Knowledge of implementing administration procedures
Software inventory management	Knowledge of applications and toolkits for implementing administration processes and procedures
Management of software version migration in interdependent execution environment	Understanding of software and operating system life-cycles
Review of security and other risks in infrastructure management architecture	
Implement back-up and archives operations for all infrastructure management function's workstations and servers	

4.7 Books for Further Reading

Graham, Morris A., *et al. The Horizontal Revolution* (Re-engineering Your Organization Through Teams—Jossey-Bass Management Series). Jossey-Bass Publishing, 1994.

Gross, Steven E. *Compensation for Teams* (How to Design and Implement Team Based Reward Programs). AMACOM, 1995.

Pokras, Sandy. *Rapid Team Deployment* (Building High-Performance Project Teams—Fifty Minute Series). Crisp Publications, 1995.

Varney, Glenn H. *Building Productive Teams* (An Action Guide and Resource Book—Jossey Bass Management Series). Jossey-Bass Publishing, 1989.

Processes in Infrastructure Management

Areas covered in this chapter

- A process view of infrastructure management

- Difference between process engineering and re-engineering

- Common tools for process engineering and re-engineering

- A pragmatic approach to process engineering for infrastructure management

- A pragmatic approach to process re-engineering for infrastructure management

- Common success and failure factors in process re-engineering

- Process flows and components of key infrastructure management processes

- Quality metrics that can be applied to measure the efficacy of key infrastructure management processes

- A process automation model for use with infrastructure management processes

- The importance of process monitoring and process life-cycle

The Shorter Oxford English Dictionary defines a process as *"A continuous and regular action or succession of actions, taking place or carried out in a definite manner."*

The organizational model described in Chapter 3, Section 3.4, defines the main functional areas in infrastructure management. Functional and departmental lines often obscure the roles and responsibilities of groups and individuals responsible for delivering the actual infrastructure services.

Most infrastructure management groups have to justify their existence on the basis of doing value added work. The process view is used in this chapter to define the way in which work is done within an infrastructure management organization and also to define how work is distributed between management organizations in a global enterprise.

Functional or departmental views only provide a subset of the process view. Without the whole picture it is difficult make improvements that provide lasting benefits to both the infrastructure management organization and its clients.

A process perspective allows delivery of support services to be viewed in terms of information flow across the functional boundaries. The activities of a group viewed across *process* lines provides an end-to-end view that focuses on the recipients of the service. Two major benefits of viewing infrastructure management from a process perspective are:

- The roles and responsibilities of groups and individuals become explicit. This in turn provides a better basis for developing human resources.

- The costs associated with each activity in a process become amenable to being modeled and measured.

Most organizations have some procedural framework in place for key activities such as adding a new user, although these may not have been developed end-to-end (e.g., from a request to add being received to final sign-off by the user). Process *engineering* is a discipline to identify these partial processes and fix broken parts or build the missing parts.

In organizations where a framework for infrastructure management processes already exist, process *re-engineering* identifies and changes the way services are delivered or executed in an organization.

Process re-engineering can occur without a preceding engineering step. Re-engineering aims to deliver binary order of magnitude improvements while process engineering aims to deliver incremental improvements. Both are based on a similar set of basic principles. The payback from process re-engineering, when successful, is considerably more.

This chapter looks at process engineering and re-engineering from the specific perspective of infrastructure management. The infrastructure management field can be viewed as a set of core processes with another set of more secondary processes. These processes are as defined in Section 5.3.

In many organizations, the introduction of management technology is an event that also offers an opportunity to revisit the way support services are fundamentally delivered.

Another rationale for developing a process-based definition of infrastructure management work is to identify areas for automation in information flow. Information level automation has the potential to improve the effectiveness of an infrastructure management organization dramatically.

Automation should however always follow a process engineering or re-engineering exercise to ensure that the organization gains maximum benefit from automation.

This chapter aims to provide the basic tools to undertake a process-level definition of the infrastructure management organization.

5.1 Process Engineering and Re-engineering Tools

Many organizations approach process engineering and re-engineering in infrastructure management with the impression that a complex methodology is required to undertake the exercise. This illusion is maintained by many consultancy organizations who like to "help" organizations re-engineer.

Every consultancy, whether in the major league or not, has developed a business process engineering (BPR) methodology. Such methodologies are however too heavyweight and inappropriate for re-engineering in the infrastructure management context.

Process engineering and re-engineering efforts that endure are in fact undertaken by local infrastructure management, using a commonsense approach, and through leveraging the comprehensive understanding of a given organization's needs.

Process engineering and re-engineering activities are helped by a number of simple tools. This section looks at a number of such commonly applicable tools for process engineering and re-engineering within infrastructure management organizations:

- *Process matrix tools*—The *performance-importance* matrix is a planning tool to help prioritize work on engineering or re-engineering current processes. The *process-organization* matrix is a tool to identify key actors of an existing process.

- *Process mapping tool*—defines a set of symbols and a simple form-based approach to capturing, documenting and reviewing the higher levels of a current process. It is also a communication tool in proposing changes to a process.

- *Process decomposition model*—defines a method of decomposing a process into any constituent sub-processes and shows the information flows relating to the process, including the conditions that start and complete the process.

- *Process activity model*—shows actual steps or activities and their descriptions and the roles and responsibilities of actors relating to the activities. Flows show transition of responsibility between actors in a process as well as information flow end-to-end in the process.

The process decomposition model leads to a process activity model. The process matrix tools are process planning and evaluation tools. The process mapping tool is used as a documentation as well as a design tool.

5.1.1 Process Decomposition Model

The process decomposition model provides a view of the internal relationships of a process. The process decomposition model is a high-level representation of an infrastructure management process. It is graphically shown as a set of linked boxes in Figure 5.1. Each box defines a sub-process.

- *Inputs* enter on the left-hand side of a sub-process box. The inputs can be information which come from an external source to the process or they may be the output of a sub-process within the same process. Inputs that are from external sources (to the process) are often shown consolidated in a separate graph.

- The *output* exits on the right-hand side of the process box. An output defines information which is the result of the sub-process activities being executed. The output of the overall process being depicted is shown on a separate consolidated graph.

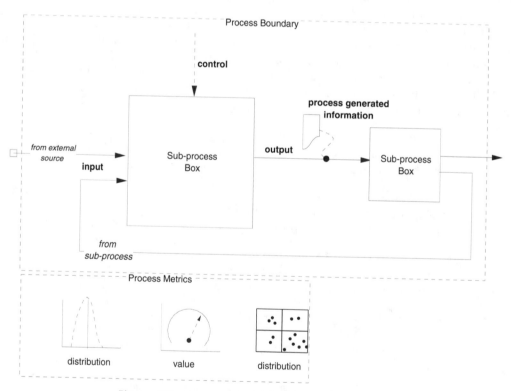

Figure 5.1: *An example process decomposition model*

- The *control* enters on the top side of the sub-process box. The controls define criteria for measuring activities within a sub-process or for controlling the activities in the sub-process box. Controls are often outputs of sub-process boxes, but can also be from sources external to the process being depicted.

- *Information mechanisms* define explicit mechanisms used to carry information in inputs and outputs of sub-process boxes. Mechanisms define the actual means used to transport this information.

Process decomposition models can be developed independent of an organization's internal structure. They are therefore useful in developing and communicating generic definition of processes.

A process may be decomposed into other (sub) processes. Decomposition can occur to an arbitrary depth (or number of levels). An activity is a process that cannot be further decomposed. An activity is defined by start and finish conditions and a set of executable actions.

5.1.2 Process Activity Model

The process activity model is a representation of the relationships between all the actors in a process. The actors that participate in any given infrastructure management process are determined by how functions are distributed within an infrastructure management organization.

Process activity models are therefore organization specific. One method of analyzing existing process-to-organization relationships is by building a process-to-organization matrix as shown in Figure 5.2. This shows the degree of process involvement by the management functions in an organization.

The example in Figure 5.2 uses the functions described in the organizational model in Chapter 3, Section 3.4. The functions shown in the column participate in executing steps or activities of the process shown as rows. The process actors are those with strongest involvement in executing activities.

The organizational model of infrastructure management defined in Chapter 3, Section 3.4, provides a set of *prototype* actors for use in developing process activity models. The actors form the nodes through which process activity "flows."

Figure 5.3 shows a process flow for a fault management process. The actors in the process are shown as columns and the activities executed by each actor is shown as rows within each column. Lines with arrows show the activity flow both within a column and across columns.

The process activities are usually numbered for reference purposes and are described separately. The responsibilities of each actor in a process is determined by the activities in the respective column.

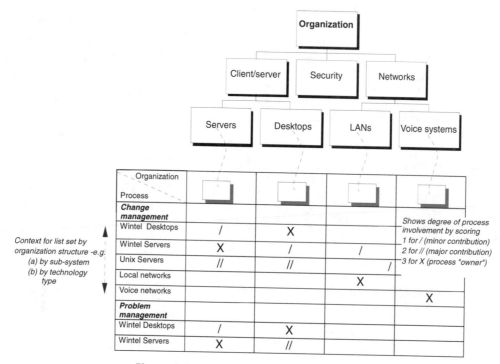

Figure 5.2: *An example process-organization matrix*

As activities are executed information is consumed or generated by the actor executing the activity. Hence process activity flow also defines information flow between actors. Each process has a set of information "artifacts" that transport the information between actor/ nodes. Documents such as forms, reports, a rule book, etc. are examples of information arti- facts commonly found in most infrastructure management processes.

Other artifacts are specific to the process. An information artifact specific to the fault management example is a *trouble ticket*. A trouble ticket is a record of a problem starting from its initial logging at a helpdesk to the problem's final resolution. The trouble ticket is then moved to the resolution database for future reference.

Process specific information artifacts such as a trouble tickets are inseparable from the process definition, i.e., the data structure of the artifact is determined by the process. Chang- ing the process will require changes to the data structures of process-specific artifacts.

Information generation within an activity consists of information being added or changed. Information that can be added or changed as part of the process activity has to be explicitly identified in the activity description. The actor executing the activity is then respon- sible for the information update.

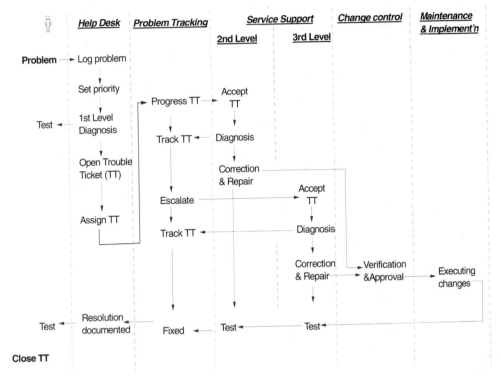

Figure 5.3: An example of a process activity model

The process activity model also defines how an instance of a specific artifact gets created and transported and how the information in it is stored.

Many infrastructure management processes need to exchange information. This requires a commonality of information conventions, especially for storage, retrieval and usage. Sometimes closely related processes also share artifacts, in which case the requirements of both processes drive the data structures of the artifact.

5.1.3 Process Matrix Tools

The *performance-importance* matrix helps to identify candidate infrastructure management processes. An example is shown in Figure 5.4 for a process-mature enterprise that was about to undertake process re-engineering of the infrastructure management organization. It highlights areas for prioritizing work on process development. The highest priority, exclusively from a performance-importance criteria, are the processes that populate the upper-left quadrant.

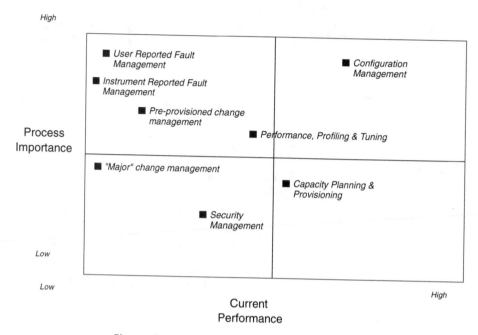

Figure 5.4: *An example of a performance-importance matrix*

Information for current levels of performance were provided by quality indicators such as those defined in Section 5.4.

Another source of data on process performance is from surveys. Although such data is likely to be subjective, it does provide a valuable new perspective on which areas process engineering is likely to get internal support. Surveys can be targeted at the following constituencies:

- End-users—to gain information on how the NM organization is viewed by them.

- Infrastructure management staff—to elicit how the service provider sees improvement.

- Independent reviewer—to gain an industry viewpoint on service delivery.

Each survey needs to be planned and designed to gain answers to specific questions—i.e., the survey should not just be a general gathering of viewpoints. Survey data often lead to new conclusions on both performance and relative importance of processes. Conclusions and justifications gained from surveys on processes of importance to the business are key components of infrastructure management business plans.

The process-organization matrix is another matrix tool which is useful in making re-engineering decisions. After an infrastructure management process has been put in place, it often evolves to fit in with day-to-day realities in an organization. Hence after a period of time the process is likely to have changed to a point where different functions to those originally designed have become parts of the way the process is currently executed.

A major cause of processes changing to fit the organization is the re-organizations that seem to plague infrastructure management groups. Process activity flows are very sensitive to re-organizations. Hence, in theory, each infrastructure management process is a potential candidate for re-engineering after a re-organization.

The process-organization matrix is valuable as a before and after (re-organization) measurement tool to evaluate the impact on each infrastructure management process. Used at any time the matrix shows the differences between the designed actors and the current actors.

The process-organization matrix is also designed to grade the level of interaction with the process. All actors should show the highest level of interaction, while lower levels of interaction indicate "process-creep." Lower levels of interaction imply less association with the process. Actors of processes that don't feel ownership can easily destabilize the process. The reasons for lower level interactions therefore have to be questioned.

5.1.4 Process Mapping Tool

The process activity diagram shows the activities categorized by the management function responsible for the activity, the transition of responsibility between the functions and the logical flow of information.

The process mapping tool is a simple tool that allows annotation of process activities and flows. This tool is of use during the requirements definition and during the design of a process. The process activity diagram is the result of process design.

The process mapping tool provides a number of symbols for shorthand annotation. Figure 5.5 shows an annotation of the problem management process defined in Figure 5.3:

Key annotations are described below. Other annotation sets can be added on an ad hoc basis, as the tool is an informal one, designed primarily to add information value to process activity flows.

- *Operation*—defined by a single step or a sequence of steps.

- *Decision*—a point at which a key process specific decision is made.

- *Delay*—a delay at the point between completion of one activity and start of another.

- *Supervisory*—a deliberate stop-and-examine operation defined by one or more steps.

- *Flow*—a transition of responsibility from one function to another as well as the flow of information from one activity to another.

- *Data storage*—a mechanism to store the data, allowing the stored item to "persist" in the future of the process.

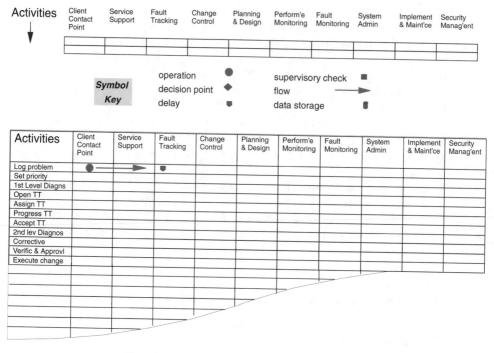

Figure 5.5: *An example of process mapping tool*

- *Control*—a criterion or rule which drives a decision, a delay, or supervisory annotation.

- *Metric*—a point at which a process metric is measured.

These annotations provide considerable expressive power in mapping current processes as well as in designing new processes. The visual nature of the annotation also allows process patterns to be seen easily without formal analysis.

5.2 Principles of Process Engineering

Process engineering in the infrastructure domain can be approached in the context of a number of general principles. The aim of both process engineering and re-engineering is to understand the current status quo and create changes in the way support services are delivered. The following are general principles applicable to both process engineering and re-engineering:

- *The process view must be developed from the user's perspective.* Some infrastructure management processes provide services directly to users. The focus in these processes is on users. Their needs from the initial contact point with the infrastructure organization, providing useful feedback, and being sensitive about the business processes the users work with are key considerations.

- *Capture information once only and at the source.* Information relevant to a process originates from different sources, both human and systems. Technical solutions are often available to ensure that information that is generated, whether human or system, is usable at all the points where it is needed, without re-entry. Ensure that once information is captured its integrity can be guaranteed throughout the process and that it can be audit trailed if required. Captured information should be "instantaneously" available to all parties that need to know it.

- *Involve as few people in the execution of a process.* This is done through eliminating as much work as possible. Work to be done by people is reduced through simplification of individual steps, automation of the process steps, eliminating activities that don't add value and eliminating layers of management and supervision. The reduction in management and supervision can be achieved through establishing clear roles and responsibilities for the participants.

- *Perform all the steps in a process in as natural an order as possible.* Considerations include eliminating "loops" where a work item re-visits previous execution points, and "compression" of time taken to execute a process step—through doing steps in parallel, making steps simpler or "smaller."

- *Perform the work where it makes the most sense.* Some activities may be done centrally, while others may be decentralized to individuals or sub-teams which may need to get closer to the user requiring the service. This division also applies to the wider organizational centralization versus local for processes that span global boundaries.

- *Reduce manual controls.* Empower people at the "front line" when possible without compromising the quality aspects of the process. Delegate decision-making to them as much as possible (again within well understood guidelines).

5.2.1 Process Engineering

The main rationale for process engineering at an "established" site is to fix current practices with a minimum of disruption to organizational and operational structures. In a "greenfield" site on the other hand, process engineering is about building a core set of processes.

Infrastructure process engineering is often best started with a documentation of the current practices and procedures that are used. The people currently responsible for individual infrastructure management functions need to be involved in this documentation and its review. Documentation should minimally capture the key "actors" and the high level steps in each "procedure" that is currently used.

Review consists of a walk-through each documented procedure, correcting any inaccuracies and refining any descriptions. Following this a consensus needs to be generated about the areas that can provide the greatest improvement to the delivery of support services.

These identified areas then have to be analyzed in terms of more detailed activities that make up the area. Processes are then developed with existing parts forming key components.

The core processes described in this chapter provides a useful checklist of processes to identify and contrast with respect to current practices.

Different organizations have different priorities for areas that need fixing. A key consideration in assigning final priorities is the actual improvement to be gained from fixing a part of the process. Three common perspectives for improvement are:

- *Increasing user satisfaction*—through better levels of services seen by end-users. "Better" is measurable through metrics such as a more responsive helpdesk and the quality of the response from support staff being better.

- *Making the cost base explicit*—through building a realistic process-level cost model. A cost model is a powerful communication tool in directly attributing support service costs with a business activity and streamlining process activities from a cost basis.

- *Making support capacity explicit*—through automation. Outsourcing or building up the support structure allows the correct level of support to be applied to levels of business activity.

Process engineering is very often followed, sometime later, by a decision to re-engineer the identified processes. This is because order of magnitude benefits require fundamental changes to be made.

5.2.2 Process Re-engineering

This section defines an approach to redesigning infrastructure management processes. Key processes are defined in Section 5.3. The most important considerations when planning process re-engineering in the network management context are:

- Whether an existing process or processes form the basis of the re-engineered process *or* whether a virgin process is to be created from scratch.

- In the case that there is an existing process, whether it changes or migrates at some pace to the new one *or* whether the existing process is replaced in one step by the new process.

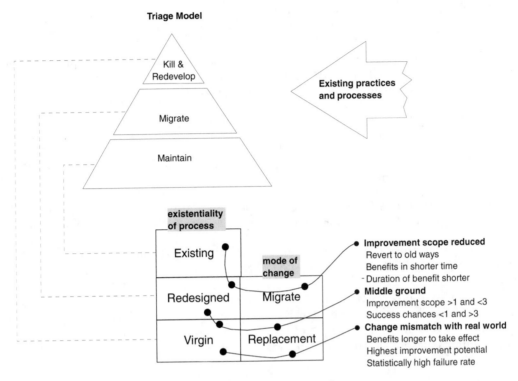

Figure 5.6: *Paths to re-engineered process*

If an existing process is to be redesigned, then an understanding of the current process to an appropriate level of detail is a prerequisite to the redesign activity. If a process is to be designed from scratch then a fundamental re-think on how the service is to be delivered is necessary.

Figure 5.6 shows three paths from a "current" situation to the re-engineered process. The paths are:

- There is an existing process which is redesigned. The existing process then migrates to the redesigned process.

- There is no discernible existing process or the current process is incomplete (i.e., some parts of the process may exist). The process is designed (using existing parts where relevant), which then displaces all current activities in the area.

- There is no current process in the area or no parts of the existing process is considered. The new process replaces the current "vacuum" in the area or replaces an actual process if there is one.

The path that is chosen has a characteristic risk and benefits as shown. For core network management processes such as problem and change management, a middle ground (path 2) seems to work best.

While a new process created from scratch replacing an existing vacuum or process promises high improvement potential, the risks of failure in real life have been shown to be considerable. New process design is needed in the following circumstances:

- When the current process is incompatible with the infrastructure management technology deployed.

- When new "foundation" areas are added (for example a security audit process in a client/server environment).

- When radical improvement in organizational performance is required (for example, to manage a larger or more complex user base with the same number of people).

Redesigned processes on the other hand tend to carry forward organizational constraints such as lack of the skill sets and requisite competency levels in key areas of infrastructure management.

If an existing process is changed to a redesigned one then the *least* benefits may be expected. This is however a model of incremental improvement which may be applied multiple times. Incremental improvement of management processes is appropriate to organizational cultures that are already at a high level of "process maturity."

5.2.3 Problem Indicators in Existing Practices

Whether there already are explicit processes or merely equivalent implicit functions in an infrastructure management organization, a number of problem indicators are often seen. These highlight areas for targeted improvement:

- *Complexity in the operation of a service.* Complexity invariably leads to a low degree of understanding of the constituent activities by infrastructure personnel. Alternatively, the operation may be understood by just one or two people in the organization. In multi-team infrastructure management, complexity is sometimes a defense mechanism created by some functions to protect job titles.

- *Information gets bounced between subgroups or with respect to groups outside of the infrastructure group.* Each time the information crosses a boundary it ends up in a new queue. A typical situation in multi-team infrastructure management is that problems that are especially complex get bounced from team to team. With each team transition the original context and priority of the problem gets lost.

- *Follow up telephone calls and memos written before tasks can be completed.* This again is common in multi-team infrastructure management structures because there is no effective internal tracking. Again, it is most often the hard to fix problems that fall into some organizational black hole. From a user perspective this equates to long waiting times before results are seen.

- *Re-work and re-submissions are common.* This is a common occurrence when there is no means of end-to-end tracking of submissions and hence there is no single point of responsibility. Sometimes the bottleneck is at the point at which end-users submit the work, which has inadequate procedures for collating and logging the original request. Another variant of this is that work waits due to "inadequate" information to progress it any further. This is a sign that the related procedure has broken down and parties on either sides of the divide are not aware of the need to fix it.

- *Re-keying of information at multiple points in the activity chain.* Most infrastructure management organizations develop in an organic manner, eventually bringing together diverse cultures. Internal practices often develop from basic office management procedures. As the work of the infrastructure management organization gets more integrated, simple office procedures begin to break down. Another example of appropriate procedures is that checking, supervision and reporting within the organization is done without adding any real value.

- *Exceptions and special cases are common.* Lack of internal standards on the services offered to end-users and lack of understanding by the end-users of any process for common requests are the commonest causes of this situation. User requests enter the infrastructure management organization in a multitude of ways, ranging from memos to phone calls to e-mail. The point of contact used by the end-user may also vary, often depending on who is calling. Variability in both the mode and point of access results in an inability to control and manage requests. This eventually leads to having to treat specific requests on an exception basis to deliver.

5.2.4 Steps to Process Re-engineering in Infrastructure Management

Process re-engineering is only applicable in a relatively process mature organization. The current process maturity level of the infrastructure organization can be assessed from the answers to two questions: Whether there is a process culture among the support staff and whether there are discernible, documented processes or procedures in day-to-day use?

Process re-engineering at the local scale can be proceduralized as a series of steps. This procedure is described briefly below:

- *Collect data* on the current state of key infrastructure processes or procedures. Data about the current processes is gained from a variety of sources, including surveys, any quality metrics that are being collected, and results of any profiling. The method for collecting data has to be designed.

- *Identify candidate processes.* The performance-importance matrix and process-organization matrix tools are two tools for process identification. The first shows processes that are of high value to the organization but perceived to require higher performance. The second shows the degree of "disorder" in a process from an ownership and participation viewpoint, and hence may contribute to the lack of performance.

- *Identify the approach for re-engineering.* Options are redesign versus virgin and migration of an existing process versus replacement of the existing process. Often practical considerations such as being able to use the information in existing databases determines the re-engineering path.

- *Present business case and establish steering group.* Before beginning any re-engineering work, develop a business case and ask for a business led or business appointed steering group to guide and help manage the execution of the re-engineering. Re-engineering efforts that don't have sponsorship from the end-user community have a high failure rate.

- *Assemble a re-engineering team.* Re-engineering often requires skills that are not commonly found in infrastructure management originations. However, a lot of the knowledge that can drive a successful re-engineering exercise is found within the organization. Small groups of outside process expertise and internal knowledge is a successful team structure to adopt. Such teams however have some lead time before they can start working as a team.

- *Analyze and redesign.* Once the team is up and operational analyze the collected data, augmenting it where necessary with further information gathering or measuring activities, then diagnose and redesign the process. The process has to be tested using a use-case method (described in Chapter 2, Section 2.2) to ensure that the process is applicable across all the uses it will be put to. If the re-engineering is on a purely local scale, use-case testing is less important. Often however in a global infrastructure organization, buy-in to a re-engineering effort occurs after some initial result has been shown. The design team should therefore be ready to extend use-cases for the process following piloting.

- *Pilot the solution.* Before a process is used in production it is judicious to pilot it so that bugs can be ironed out. In most organizations this is done at a pilot site, often side by side with the current process. An alternative that is increasingly becoming reality is to simulate the process on a process simulation tool. This reduces risk and set-up time, but the conclusions often lack a sense of reality and completeness which a hands-on pilot provides. Pilots should lead to an assessment of the process's viability and should also be a laboratory for any obvious changes and improvements.

- *Restructure systems infrastructure.* Process re-engineering very often requires investment and re-engineering of the systems infrastructure supporting the process. The choice of technology should be driven from the requirements of the process. Process infrastructure however needs to support more than one process both from a skills and training point of view and for distributing the cost across multiple processes. Restructuring the systems infrastructure therefore is only possible after the requirements of all the candidate processes (and non re-engineered processes) have been evaluated.

- *Restructure organization.* A similar situation to systems infrastructure exists for organizational restructuring—it affects multiple processes and needs process requirements to be known. In the case of organizational restructuring there are usually additional constraints such as getting the right skills within a required time-frame. Organizational changes often affects morale and therefore should be undertaken within a program of communication for the support staff to understand the benefits of the changes.

- *Rollout.* Rollout occurs to a wider audience or across a number of sites. The re-engineering approach determines how a process is introduced into different sites. When multiple processes are introduced at the same time then further planning is required. In general, core processes should be followed by control processes and finally, secondary processes. Within each category however there are information relationships between processes that may stop a deployed process from being fully functional, or having to redesign information input. A dependency graph is a useful tool to analyze the sequence for deploying multiple processes.

- *Assess and report.* The final step is to assess the full-scale rollout using pre-defined success criteria. An essential part of process re-engineering is to provide feedback to the steering group on the lessons learned from the exercise and to set expectations for service improvement.

5.2.5 Success and Failure Factors

Analysis of infrastructure management related process re-engineering across several "process mature" organizations indicates a number of key success factors:

- Process re-engineering requires a high-level sponsor from the user community. Without linkage to business advantage, re-engineering can quickly run out of steam.

- Select processes that are already in trouble but seen as important to the conduct of a business process as initial candidates for re-engineering. Aim for quick hits and incrementally build on success.

- The scope of the initial work should not be too large or complex. The scope should be "enveloped" by the roles key processes, defined in Section 5.3, play in infrastructure management.

- Select subsequent processes on the basis of major impact with the users such as those which would show dramatic cost-effectiveness over a period, or improve key service levels. Candidate processes should be from a list similar to the key processes in Section 5.3.

Process re-engineering efforts are also liable to fail for a diverse set of reasons. Common ones are discussed below:

- The re-engineering effort attempts to fix existing activities rather than change them. Consequently, the major expectations from re-engineering are never realized.

- The scope of the re-engineering is too large or prior management constraints are placed on the problems that *may be* solved and those that are hands off for political or other reasons.

- The re-engineering is attempted by people running the existing processes, without recourse to uninterested parties and outside re-engineering expertise. As a result, difficult issues are avoided or not enough knowledge is available to solve key issues.

- Resources assigned to re-engineering is inadequate in skill, are part-time or inadequate in numbers. Resource under-estimation is a common cause of project cancellation.

- The core processes (e.g., those defined in Section 5.3) are not focused on; instead, process activities are viewed in terms of current roles and responsibilities.

- Senior management and the business does not provide the commitment to the change, buy-in to the vision or provide support for the results of the exercise.

5.3 Key Infrastructure Management Processes

Infrastructure management processes fall into three general categories. Core processes define processes that are the most frequently used in the management of infrastructure. Core processes define core skills that need to be in place. Secondary processes are often identified and implemented after core processes have been established. Control processes form a third category and define procedures for the internal control of the infrastructure management organization. Processes in each of these areas are described below. Core processes described in this chapter are:

- *Problem management*—Manages the way problems (events automatically detected by infrastructure management frameworks and those reported via a helpdesk) are handled so that their immediate and future impact on users is minimized.

- *Change management*—Manages the way changes to the infrastructure are executed so that risks to current users of the infrastructure are not escalated and new risks are not introduced.

- *Performance management*—Defines the way the performance of the infrastructures, viewed as an application delivery system, is monitored and managed both in short and long time-frames. This is to ensure that the infrastructure does not become a potential inhibitor in running a successful business.

Secondary processes define infrastructure management skills at the next level of "sophistication." Key processes in this category include:

- *Infrastructure recovery*—Defines the generic procedures for recovering from infrastructure failure. The scale of the failure covered by the process may range from a user workgroup to an entire site. Infrastructure recovery is distinct from problem management in the sense that problem management is more centered on a single user.

- *Capacity management*—Defines the procedures for monitoring, analyzing and managing the capacity of an infrastructure. This is especially important for the traffic dynamics of client/server architectures, where capacity hot-spots can suddenly appear.

- *Configuration management*—Defines the procedures and mechanisms needed to organize and control the data used in many infrastructure management processes. Processes include those for building new machines, moving users, replacing failed network components, etc. Configuration management is also responsible for monitoring changes to standard "builds" of workstations and servers, and unusual traffic on the network.

Control processes define control skills internal to the infrastructure management organization. This category includes processes for controlling the interfaces with the outside world.

- *Internal procedures*—These are a collection of procedures for control activities within infrastructure management. Key areas covered are the different types of management reviews, planning and managing service capacity, managing service budgets and managing customer relations.

- *Helpdesk management*—The helpdesk is a critical interface between the infrastructure management organization and the end-users. In global organizations there are often multiple, hierarchic helpdesks.

In the following sections each of the above processes is described in a standard format—consisting of the goals of the process, a process decomposition diagram and a description of the sub-processes.

5.3.1 Provisioned Change Management

All production infrastructures built to support client/server applications need to be able to support a specified degree of adds, moves and changes. Provisioned change refers to changes done to the infrastructure within this "envelope" of possibilities. When a change is outside the capability of the infrastructure to absorb, some significant level of redesign or migration to a new environment needs to be planned.

The difference between provisioned and non-provisioned changes is that the former aims to be non-disruptive while the latter is definitely disruptive. The goals of the provisioned change management process are:

- To enable introduction of changes to a production environment with no disruption to existing users. When disruptions are unavoidable they are actively managed—e.g., through scheduling as out-of-hours work, to have minimum effect on users.

- To identify and plan for high-risk changes. Planning includes developing tactics for roll-back in the event of the change failing. High-risk changes have to be communicate to and signed off by business management.

- To assign responsibility for change activity and to subsequently track accountability for changes. This includes communicating recognition for successful change activity and conducting post mortems when failure occurs.

The main sub-processes shown in Figure 5.7. These are described below:

1. *Define and maintain change management policies*—The change management process is probably the most important of the core processes. This is because all changes to a stable environment introduce potential risk to the infrastructure and hence to the businesses dependent on the business. Change management policies define the kind of changes that are possible under production level change management, the turn-around time and the sign-off required for each type of change.

2. *Evaluate change request*—Change requests are submitted by users to the infrastructure management organization through the designated helpdesk. Change requests are ideally evaluated in a committee context so that a wider set of perspectives can be applied to the requested change. This also allows the infrastructure-at-risk model to be managed more explicitly.

3. *Planning*—Once a change request had been evaluated and the risks understood, further impact analysis may need to be carried out. This depends on how much provision there is in a given infrastructure for change. Following a decision, some degree of planning and work scheduling is required to ensure the production environment is not disturbed.

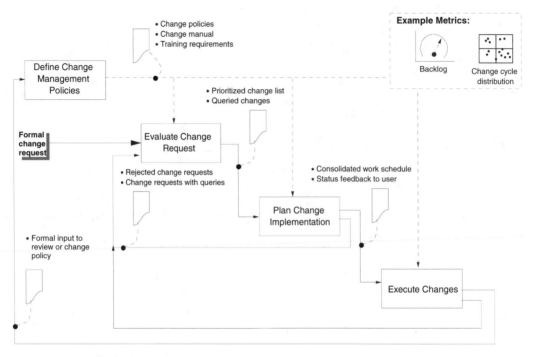

Figure 5.7: *Process decomposition for provisioned change management*

4. *Execution*—The execution of changes is always accompanied by a definition of how roll-back to the pre-change condition will be carried out in the event of failing to complete the change. Execution of change is also followed by a testing and quality assurance step that ensures the production environment has not been impacted in reality.

5.3.2 Problem Management

The problem management process reduces the impact and duration of faults and other damaging events affecting users. The process defines steps to identify, diagnose and analyze problem events. Once the extent, nature and the fix for a problem is identified the problem is tracked until resolved. The problem management process directly affects end-users' perception of the effectiveness of the infrastructure management organization. The main goals of the process are:

- To minimize the impact of a problem in terms of duration and cost.

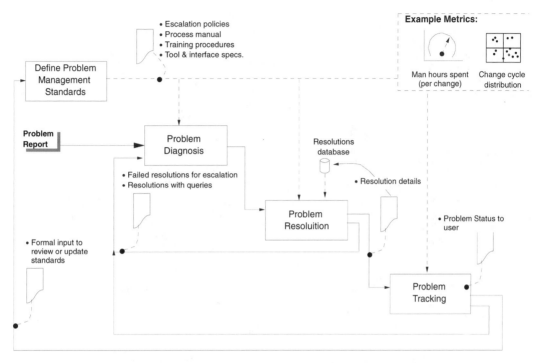

Figure 5.8: *Process decomposition for problem management*

- To reduce the probability of recurrence through analysis and permanent resolution.

- To meet metrics in service level agreements with end-users. Service level metrics define the level of service.

Notification of a problem occurs through system generated events, calls to a helpdesk or as a result of using management tools by infrastructure management. Figure 5.8 shows a process decomposition model for problem management.

The main sub-processes of problem management are:

1. *Define and review problem management standards*—Define corporate best practice in training and procedure, the local and global escalation structure, error thresholds, support level assumptions and blueprints to bypass common problems.

2. *Define problem management interfaces*—The problem monitoring framework collects and transports faults and exceptions from the parts of the infrastructure monitored by the framework. The problem management interfaces define the tools and the means by which information from different sources are integrated and distributed in a global infrastructure management organization.

3. *Problem diagnosis*—Problem diagnosis begins at the helpdesk. Unresolved problems get escalated to more skilled service support levels. Problem determination and analysis in client/server environments requires a multi-disciplinary approach, where experts in the infrastructure sub-specialities need to work in a cluster until the problem is solved.

4. *Problem resolution*—Many problems have relatively simple fixes. Such fixes, once entered into the resolutions database can be accessed and used by lower level support functions. In other more complex resolutions, a plan is required for problem resolution that covers impact analysis, change management and execution in a production environment.

5. *Problem tracking*—Tracking a problem through the different escalation levels until its sign-off is the key control sub-process within problem management. Tracking also involves understanding problem trends and producing supporting metrics.

5.3.3 Performance Management

Performance management is a process to ensure proactively that the infrastructure is performing to designed criteria or to levels agreed within service level agreements. Performance management is an end-to-end discipline, covering all the component layers of the infrastructure. The main goals of performance management are:

- To ensure that service level agreements on end-to-end performance are being achieved.

- To develop performance decomposition models showing the components that make up the end-to-end values and to track these as the infrastructure evolves.

- To provide a monitoring framework to enable performance components to be monitored and performance data collected in an automated fashion.

- To provide tools in a ubiquitous form such as spreadsheet models to analyze performance levels and for *what-if analysis* for planning for performance tuning.

A process decomposition model of performance management is shown in Figure 5.9. The sub-processes shown are:

1. *Define requirements*—Evaluate business application requirements on infrastructure performance and create or update infrastructure plans.

2. *Develop performance models*—Models are required for each application whose performance service level agreement is being tracked. Each model defines the components contributing to each of the relevant performance metric.

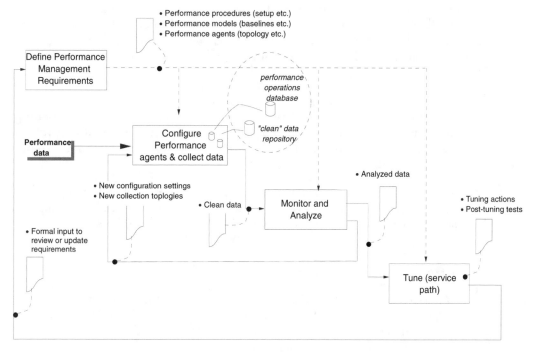

Figure 5.9: *Process decomposition for performance management*

3. *Develop a performance management framework*—The performance management framework allows the automated collection of performance information in a time-series. In the case of client/server systems performance measurement involve the integration of more fundamental values. Measuring end-to-end delays within different layers of a client/server infrastructure requires sophisticated measuring algorithms.

4. *Monitor and analyze collected metrics*—Monitoring for exception conditions can be automated. Analysis of collected metrics for predicting emerging conditions is often a manual procedure. Collected metrics are also analyzed to fix performance problems.

5. *Tune performance*—Analysis highlights problem areas and an understanding of the causes. Sometimes, performance problems can be solved by changing user behavior or resetting user expectations. Fixing the problem often involves changes and hence should be done under change management. Performance tuning may involve simple additions or complex moves and changes.

5.3.4 Configuration Management

Configuration management involves managing the data used in configuration, distributing the data within an organization and monitoring to ensure that key configurations do not change.

Configuration data is used by many infrastructure management process activities, ranging from building a new workstation for a new user (a possible activity of the change management process) to replacing a network component (a possible activity of infrastructure recovery process). Configuration management ensures that the relevant data is distributed and available at the right place in a global management context. The main goals of the configuration management process are:

- To organize and catalog all data used in configuration purposes by different processes.

- To identify and manage the life-cycle of individual data items, including ownership of data.

- To maintain the means for distributing the data in a global context so that all parts of the enterprise have current data.

Configuration databases are essentially file-level repositories. An industrial strength file versioning and tracking system are essential. Sub-processes of configuration management are shown in the process decomposition model in Figure 5.10. These are summarized below:

1. *Define internal standards.* Internal standards set the requirements and expectations from the configuration management process. Standards also define how distribution of configuration data should occur and the tools and systems to manage the data. In addition the types of data to be monitored for change should be identified. The policies for managing configuration data should also be communicated and buy-in bought from infrastructure management staff.

2. *Develop systems.* Make build versus buy decisions for data organization, data capture, data distribution and data monitoring. Choose vendors and products or defined development work. Build and implement the tools and systems.

3. *Populate configuration database.* Capture and store the different types of files used as the configuration database and execute interfaces with other management processes that generate data for storage in the configuration database.

4. *Provide configuration data to consumer processes.* Provide access to processes that use the data in the configuration database.

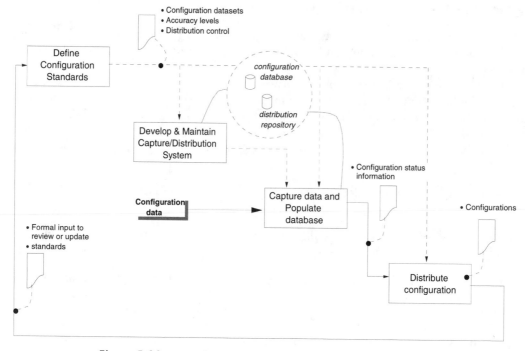

Figure 5.10: *Process decomposition for configuration management*

Figure 5.10 shows some of the relationships between the configuration management process and consumer processes.

5.3.5 Capacity Management

Capacity management provides an understanding of how current capacity is used, allows emerging capacity trends to be identified and to have extra resources in place before the demand exceeds "supply." Capacity also has a direct bearing on service levels commitments and investment strategies. The main goals of capacity management are:

- To develop a map of the infrastructure showing potential and emerging bottlenecks down to a service and component level.

- To take a longer term view on developing the capacity of the infrastructure to meet business needs.

Capacity management requires an architectural framework for the automated collecting, storing and distributing capacity data.

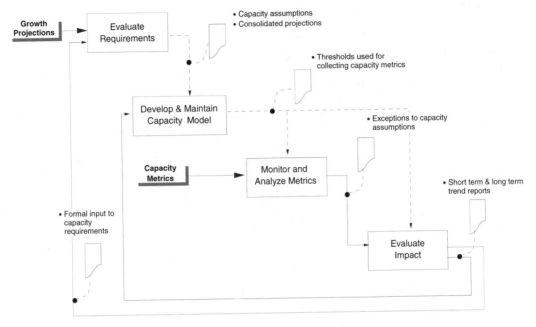

Figure 5.11: *Process decomposition for capacity management*

Figure 5.11 shows the main sub-processes of capacity management. The sub-processes are:

1. *Evaluate* business requirements, and associated infrastructure plans. Evaluate and develop a capacity management framework to enable capacity measurement of required metrics.

2. *Develop a capacity model* of metrics for each infrastructure technology. Some metrics will define end-to-end measurements that are constituted from more basic ones. The integrity of the capacity metrics are therefore important. In addition to metrics, a system of capacity thresholds will allow automated monitoring and reporting on an exception basis.

3. *Monitor capacity metrics* using the capacity management framework. Process to compare metrics against the defined thresholds. Provide exceptions and trends for control purposes.

4. *Evaluate exceptions and trends* and match against current capacity plans. New plans may have to be created or capacity plans updated. Provide capacity metric summaries for infrastructure steering.

5.3.6 Infrastructure Recovery

Infrastructure recovery is the process that restores failures in the infrastructure. Infrastructure failure can be classified to cover a wide spectrum of failure types. For example, in Chapter 2, Section 2.3.1, on the infrastructure-at-risk model, a prototype classification is provided. The main goals of the infrastructure recovery process are:

- To plan for the recovery from failure of all business critical systems and to provide the actual means to meet specific business objectives of recovery.

- To prepare for different classes of failure as a part of risk-managing the infrastructure. Preparation also requires training for efficient recovery.

- To influence future engineering design to add automated failure recovery.

- To ensure that business critical data is backed up in such a way that its integrity for recovery is maintained. In the case of client/server systems this requires a model of how data flows across the distributed system of servers and workstations.

Figure 5.12 shows the sub-processes of infrastructure recovery.

1. *Identify business requirements*—Identify from a business perspective the requirements for data and systems recovery. Data recovery requirements include those for backup as well as longer term archiving. Systems recovery requirements define the type of recovery (on a range of a non-stop system to one which will incur down-time while the system is logically or even physically replaced).

2. *Develop recovery procedures*—Plan, design and test recovery procedures for each business requirement identified. Train staff to develop crisis management skills within the infrastructure management teams.

3. *Develop a recovery framework*—For backup and archiving including monitoring for successful backups, and exceptions. The framework also often provides security for backed-up and archived data. Daily management reports on the viability for recovery is an essential output from the framework.

4. *Execute backups*—For data backup, execution is at different frequencies for different business systems as identified in the business requirements. Each backup operation should be logged and any exceptions or problems notified through the problem management framework. System backups may be automatically invoked or manually invoked depending on the solution.

5. *Execute recovery*—Use recovery procedures where relevant and execute recovery actions and manage the crisis until normal operational status is gained.

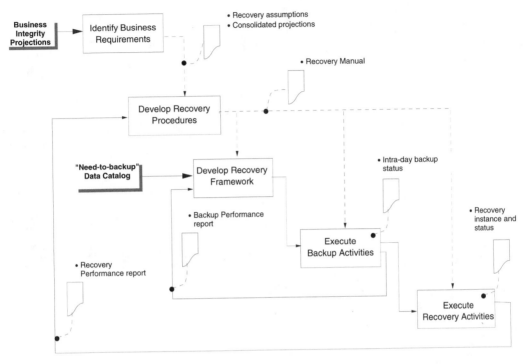

Figure 5.12: *Process decomposition for infrastructure recovery management*

5.3.7 Internal Management

Internal management is aimed at ensuring that the infrastructure management organization is able to meet its customer obligations and to deliver these services within budgetary constraints.

Demands for infrastructure services can take unexpected peaks as business conditions and requirements change. A major challenge of infrastructure management is matching resources to demand in the short term and ensure resources are available in the longer term.

Other sub-processes are required for the internal management and control of the infrastructure management function itself. (See Figure 5.13.) These processes define some of the relationships between different management functions described in the infrastructure management model in Chapter 3, Section 3.4.

1. *Business case definition* defines a structured approach to defining the problem, the solutions, the costs, the tangible and intangible benefits as well as any return of

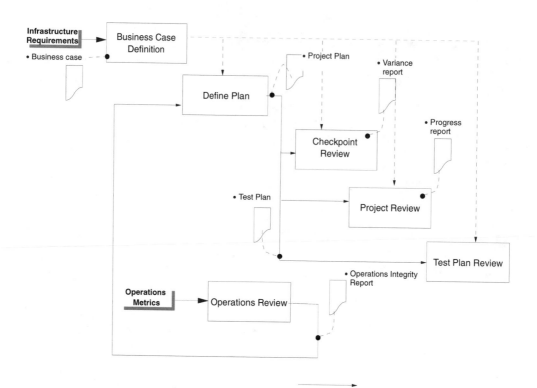

Figure 5.13: *Process decomposition for internal management*

investment or payback analysis relevant to the organization. Its primary readership is the steering group described in Section 3.4.

2. *Checkpoint reviews* define a formal process of review which take into account whether the goals are being met, variance from plan, cost problems and skill-deficit reviews. Its primary use is at the infrastructure manager level.

3. *Design review* examines a functional design specification of an infrastructure solution against architectural goals and design criteria such as cost and redundancy. Outside parties such as consultants can provide non-partisan views on choices. Design specifications should reflect decisions made at such reviews and should be signed off by a designated authority other than the designer, so that ad hoc changes or implementation cannot be made by authority of a single person.

4. *Project review* examines a project plan from the delivery viewpoint, assess risks, personnel issues, progress reporting structures. Many organizations organize all work

above a certain size (typically over 10 man days work) as a project. Projects allow users on the steering group to prioritize work on the basis of benefits to the users. Projects also show the personnel cost and skills requirements explicitly.

5. *Test plan review* examines how a design or change can be tested and evaluates the plan against it. Many organizations separate the production network from networks for piloting or development. Test plans may refer to the feasibility phase, piloting phase, or acceptance phase of technology deployment. Depending on the phase, different criteria apply depending on the technology.

6. *Operation review* is a mechanism for understanding outstanding operational issues and to see if any patterns are emerging. Operations review should be done on an exception basis and the purpose is to find solutions. Outside parties can bring specific expertise or a methodology to approach the problems. Users can bring a user perspective to the problem. Some problems may require initiatives that need to be implemented over a period of time. The progress of such work can be reported.

5.3.8 Helpdesk Management

In large global enterprises, there are often a network of helpdesks which cooperate to provide services to end-users on a global scale. Helpdesk management is a distinct process for ensuring that end-users, services are maintained. The goals of helpdesk management are:

- To ensure that end-users have unambiguous lines of communication and ensure they are aware of the services available from the helpdesk.

- To provide feedback to the infrastructure steering on the delivery of services to end-users relative to their expectations, especially in complex helpdesk networks.

- To ensure that end-users are kept informed of the status of any emerging or current crisis which may impact their ability to perform business.

- To ensure that all feedback to end-users regarding outstanding requests or problem reports are handled in a consistent way.

The sub-processes of helpdesk management (see Figure 5.14) are described below:

1. *Marketing and communications*—Market the services of the helpdesk to end-users. Provide training or information on the modes of communication possible with the helpdesk.

2. *Plan staffing and training*—End-user and technology support requirements change every 12 to 18 months in enterprises with significant client/server technology. Help-

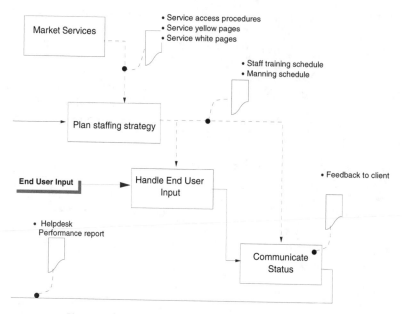

Figure 5.14: *Process decomposition for helpdesk management*

desks are at the front line of these changing requirements. Staff require skills to handle end-users, proficiency in any workflow automation systems in use and training in giving any "product" type information that may be asked for by an end-user.

3. *Handle end-user input*—Dealing with and logging end-user calls and electronic communications such as e-mail. The range of end-user requests that the helpdesk deals with ranges from asking for information to problem reports to change requests.

4. *Communicate status*—Provide feedback on existing crises to status of outstanding requests. This may be over the phone or using electronic media such as e-mail or workflow automation tools.

5.4 Quality of Processes

The quality of key management processes are measured using metrics specifically associated with the process. Each process has a set of metrics that are unique to it. This section defines a sample set of measurements for several areas of the infrastructure management processes and procedures described in Section 5.3.

Metrics should be seen as a mechanism to understand the execution of processes and as providing information to improve them. Improving processes, especially of the core processes, is evident to end-users as improvement in service.

Many quality metrics described here are derived from more primitive data that is collected in the course of process execution. Hence there is a set-up cost for collecting metrics and the cost/benefit of collecting and processing metrics. Aspects of process quality covered in this section are:

- Quality metrics for change management process.

- Quality metrics for problem and fault management process.

- Quality metrics for ticketing.

- Quality metrics for automated escalation procedure.

- Quality metrics for performance monitoring.

- Quality metrics for configuration information.

5.4.1 Quality of Change Management

Change management is the single most important infrastructure management process. It is also a process whose effects are directly visible to end-users. Quality of change management metrics define how well the process is functioning. Table 5.1 shows examples of quality metrics in this area.

The data are organized to show any change request patterns. The key metric for change is the duration between the request and the change being executed. Some types of changes can be achieved very quickly while others have a lead time. The time-bands ranging from less than 1 hour to more than 1 month are used to develop a distribution (number of changes falling into each band).

5.4.2 Quality of Problem and Fault Management

Problem management is another core process whose effects are directly seen by end-users. Table 5.2 shows examples of quality metrics in this area. Quality of problem management metrics define how well the problem management process is functioning. Some enterprises make the distinction between *problems* that are reported by end-users while *faults* are reported automatically by the fault management framework.

Some metric details differ between the two, however no such distinction is made in the descriptions below, the term *problem* refers to both user and framework reported problems.

Table 5.1: Indicators for Quality Change Management

Indicators	Sub-indicators	Description
1. Change request backlog	Weekly time series	Measures the backlog of change requests that have not been yet been executed. Expressed as a series by week.
	Actual changes/ planned changes	Measures the success rate of attempted changes from the end-user perspective.
2. Distribution of change duration	Less than 1 hour 1 to 10 hours 2 to 10 days 11 to 31 days Greater than 1 month	Defines a logarithmic distribution to see any patterns over a period. The change duration is measured from the time a change requested at the client/service point (help-desk) to its closure by the execution point.
3. Number of change back-out	Less than 1 hour 1 to 10 hours 2 to 10 days 11 to 31 days Greater than 1 month	Number change requests that needed back-out from. Expressed as a duration time log distribution.
4. Successful changes/ total changes ratio over a week	Weekly time series	Ratio of successful changes to total number of changes applied. Expressed as a series by week.
5. Total manhours in executing change requests	Weekly time series	Maximum number of manhours spent in executing change requests. Expressed as a series by week.
6. Priority distribution of change requests	Weekly time series (priority 1 - priority 2 - priority 3 -)	Enterprise level change request priority distribution (priority 1, etc.) expressed as a weekly time-series.

Table 5.2: *Indicators for Quality of Problem Management*

Indicators	Sub-indicators	Description
1. Problem type classification	Weekly time-series (application, common services, systems, LAN, WAN)	Classification of problem types and number of problems per week in each category. Captured as a series.
2. Total manhours spent problem fixing	Weekly time-series	Maximum number of manhours spent in executing change requests. Expressed as a series by week.
3. Priority distribution of problem fixes	Weekly time-series (priority 1 - priority 2 - priority 3 -)	Enterprise level problem priority distribution (priority 1, etc.) expressed as a weekly time-series.
4. Duration distribution for fixing a problem	Less than 1 hour 1 to 10 hours 2 to 10 days 11 to 31 days Greater than 1 month	A logarithmic distribution showing the time it took to fix problems. Duration is measured from the time the problem is logged to the point at which the problem ticket is successfully closed.
Problem maps	By event type By business area By geographic area	Problem maps are a powerful way of summarizing problems affecting a certain group or interest.
Distribution of problem information	Management groups Business groups IT groups	The groups to which problem maps and reports are distributed.

5.4.3 Quality of Ticketing

Ticketing is a means of logging an event or condition that causes a process to be invoked. The ticket provides a record of the end-to-end flow through the process. At the end of the process the ticket persists in a database for future analysis. As such, ticketing is a critical information transporter and represents process automation in most organizations. Table 5.3 shows examples of quality metrics in this area.

Ticketing technology comes at a variety of "strengths" and cost breaks. The quality of the technology chosen will determine the quality of the automated processes.

Table 5.3: *Indicators for Quality of Ticketing*

Indicators	Sub-indicators	Description
Integrity of ticketing technology	Audit trail Resilient servers Replicated database Enterprise database SQL API	The integrity of the technology is an important consideration. The ticketing system should have resilience features such as those shown by the attribute set. Another consideration is that SQL-based tools can access information stored in tickets so that metrics can be derived. Skills for this are likely to be in the "enterprise" database.
Routing of tickets	Attribute-based Severity-type based Time-of-day based actions Multicast to other sites	Another facility of packaged ticketing technology is the ability to route the tickets through various "stations." This is a mapping of the actors of the process. Routing can be done on the basis of several parameters carried in the ticket. These are mapping from the "policies" in the process.
Cryptographic facilities	Ticket signature Access authentication Encryption	Security is increasingly important in ticketing. Three areas where strong security is needed are in signing a ticket, accessing the ticketing system and in transferring secrets such as cryptographic keys to external sites.
Attribute-based searching		The ticketing database is a rich source of information. Research is encouraged if there are good database search facilities.

5.4.4 Quality of Escalation Procedures

Escalation is central to process-based management, especially in problem resolution. Escalation refers to actions that are to be taken when certain exception conditions occur. Escalation procedures are often key points in service level agreements.

The escalation process can be automated to a high degree. This is particularly important when faults are automatically reported from a management framework. User-reported problems often still need a human decision-maker. The rules for human-related escalation and training is a separate issue.

These quality measures for automated escalation therefore define how dependable escalation is for electronically reported faults using criteria such as a severity-level event remaining unallocated for a period of time.

Automation of this process involves "configuring" the people element such as holidays and backup procedures in the event of the automation tools failing. Table 5.4 shows examples of quality metrics in this area.

5.4.5 Quality of Performance Monitoring

Performance monitoring of client/server based systems is one of the most difficult areas of infrastructure management. Performance measurement in a client server environment requires relatively "intelligent" agents to generate application-level test packets as response time "probes," to analyze packets and to filter measurements against threshold conditions. The best known family of performance agents is defined by the RMON and RMON II standards. (These are described in Chapter 11, Section 11.2).

There is however a significant overhead in managing distributed intelligent agents in that they have to be programmed with thresholds and other configuration parameters. Because changing the patterns of a performance monitoring framework is time-consuming and error prone the performance "net" gets out of step with changes in the client/server environment. Table 5.5 shows examples of quality metrics in this area.

The quality indicators in performance monitoring define how capable and relevant to client/server computing is performance monitoring.

5.4.6 Quality of Configuration Information

Keeping configuration data in a "fit" state—where it is known to be up-to-date (as checkpointed within management processes that change the data) is important in client/server environments. Managed configuration information is a primary indictor of a successful infrastructure management organization.

Table 5.4: Indicators for Quality of Automated Escalation Procedures

Indicators	Sub-indicators	Description
Pre-defined thresholds for automated escalation	Severity type Source of event Source of event Infrastructure area	Ordering of problems is normally by severity type. Escalation rules define how to override severity-based ordering by other criteria such as source-of-event by business area and source-of-event by infrastructure area.
Threshold review	Monthly Quarterly Annual	Escalation rules and thresholds need to be reviewed periodically as part of managing the escalation procedure.
Automated paging on "hunt" group	In-hours Out-of-hours	Part of the automated escalation framework is paging of process actors on a "hunt" group basis which increases the chances of problems being allocated earlier.
Exceptions reporting to management	As it occurs based on severity Consolidated (daily, weekly)	Both infrastructure and business management have an interest in infrastructure events that may impact business operations. Most businesses have critical times of the day, month or year when loss of service is more serious. Regular exception reporting helps decision-makers manage a crisis better.
Quality of escalation procedure	Actor awareness Actor adherence Percentage of faults automated Event-type automation Multiple escalation procedures Review on holidays/absences	The quality of the automated escalation procedure can be evaluated through a number of indicators as shown. Often ambiguity is caused by there being more than one escalation procedure. Also, normal staff changes such as holiday and other absences have to be tracked with respect to the escalation procedure.

Table 5.5: *Indicators for Quality of Performance Monitoring and Reporting*

Indicators	Sub-indicators	Description
Unresolved perfor- mance issues	Weekly time series (end-user reported framework reported)	The number of problems reported that are performance related. Classified into end-user reported and framework reported and stored as a weekly time-series.
Delivery time		
End-to-end response time	MMM hourly time series (application 1 application 2 application 3)	End-to-end response time calculated by appli- cation-specific test probes. Sent out periodi- cally from pre-defined measurement points. Stored as a three value—maximum, mini- mum, mean—hourly time-series for each application measured.
Utilization level	MMM hourly time series (common services, systems, LAN, WAN)	Collection or calculation of utilization of com- mon resources used to deploy client/server applications. Stored as a three value—maxi- mum, minimum, mean—hourly time-series for each resource measured.
Level of measurement granularity available	Message level Packet level Byte level Bit level	Defines the level at which performance data can be captured. Application message level, network packet level, and network byte level indicate the capability of the performance monitoring framework.
Method of collection	RMON probe RMON II probe stand-alone	Another indicator of the capability of the per- formance monitoring framework. Managed probes allow the performance measurement criteria to be changed with new requirements.
Performance report to clients	Daily Weekly Monthly	The frequency with which performance reports are generated and distributed. Reports can be automatically generated from stored data.

Table 5.6: Indicators for Quality of Configuration Information

Indicators	Sub-indicators	Description
Technology base	File system Database Web Directory	Defines the technology used to store configuration information. File systems are the most primitive and directories offer the most features. Databases offer the most for accessing and processing the data. Configurations may initially be held in multiple formats.
Level of organization	By component By layer By application	The level at which configuration information is organized.
Application programming interface	SQL LDAP	The method for writing applications to access the configuration data.
Change authority	Process owner Application owner	The change authority for information in the configuration database. The configuration management process owner.
Coverage and completeness	Application level Common services Server systems Workstation systems Local networks Campus networks Wide area networks	The coverage of configuration information can cover the whole client/server stack and all applications. This metric usually improves only overtime as configurations are centralized as a matter of policy.
Requests for configuration information	Weekly time-series	The number of requests for information from the configuration database. Stored as a weekly time-series.
Problems caused by configuration information	Weekly time-series Out-of-date data Missing data	The number of problems that may be attributed to the configuration database-held information.

The mechanism of storage, access to the information, etc. all contribute to enhancing the quality of data. The centralized management of configuration information allows different processes to change and update information safely, using the safety of automated mechanisms such as database locks to guarantee the integrity of the change. Table 5.6 shows examples of quality metrics in this area.

5.5 *Process Automation*

A fundamental process engineering exercise conducted with the tools defined in Section 5.1 gives a complete end-to-end work perspective of infrastructure management in an organization. This often leads to analysis of current problems within a specific infrastructure management context, such as moving to a new site, and possible options for fixing the problems. Process engineering often results in incremental improvements.

Process re-engineering is usually conducted in an organization that already has a level of maturity in process-based approaches for common areas of infrastructure management work. Re-engineering seeks to provide a order of magnitude improvement rather than incremental improvement.

Process "designs" of infrastructure management (whether as a result of fundamental engineering or more ambitious re-engineering) can be implemented without underlying workflow technology to support it. Workflow technology essentially recognizes information types relating to a process and transports it according to rules defined for the process.

When the process design is mapped to workflow solutions, however, the potential benefits are maximized. Many organizations typically introduce components of workflow technology, such as ticketing and helpdesk management systems, without first developing an organization specific process model as suggested above. These solutions are often implemented with "low-level" vendor-led consultancy that tend to use generic models from a box.

Implementations undertaken from this basis invariably deteriorate in effectiveness over time and often contribute to service delivery problems in the future.

Process automation is a system-based representation of a specific process. An automated solution includes manual and workflow components as well as interfaces with the management framework.

Some architects define process automation as a transport component within the management framework itself. Others define process automation systems as a bridge between the organization and the management framework. These two views are shown in Figure 5.15.

The main difference between the two models is one of ownership and are hence driven by different development and maintenance responsibilities.

5.5.1 A Model for Process Automation

Process automation marries the model of a specific process developed using the techniques and tools described in the above sections with systems concepts such as workflow and databases. The key components of a process automation model are:

- *Business model*—Defines the infrastructure management function as a business, including its resources and processes. Process definition at this level defines rules for initiating and terminating the process, routing of process information within the

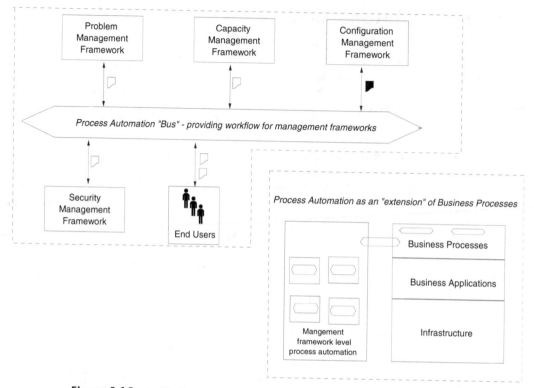

Figure 5.15: *Positioning process automation within a management framework*

organizational structure and scheduling and escalation within each process. Other definitions include the success criteria for each process.

- *Process model*—Defines the decomposition of each process to the level of "atomic" activities of each process and a process map showing all the human and systems actors touched by the process.

- *Process controller*—Controls the process using the criteria defined in the business model for initiating and terminating the process. Other control functions include collecting defined quality metrics.

- *Human actors*—Individuals or groups who have a specific role to play in executing a process. A human actor often plays more than one role in the same process. Human actors are likely to have responsibility for more than one process.

- *Artifacts*—Electronic "entities" that are produced as a result of process activity. Artifacts represent the "work" in workflow. Artifacts have to be transported to different

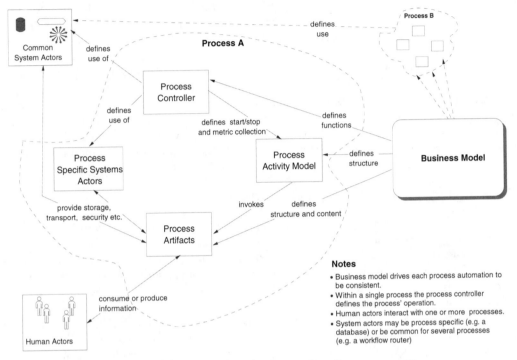

Figure 5.16: *Relationship of process automation components*

actors shown in a process map and sometimes on an inter-process basis. Examples of artifacts are forms, reports, files and business objects. Artifacts such as forms and reports also play the role of human-computer interfaces in a process.

- *Systems actors*—Systems components such as databases and a transport protocol for artifacts play obvious roles in automation. Programmable software components such as message-routing mechanisms are less visible actors.

Figure 5.16 shows the relationship between the above components. The business model plays a central role. The process controller refers to the business model for rules regarding control and flow through process activities. The start and termination conditions for the process are defined in the business model. The artifacts are a link between the human actors and the business model, in the sense that human actors interact with the business model through the artifacts. Artifacts are invoked and modified by the execution of process activities.

Each process is initiated when a start condition is recognized by the process controller. Such conditions are carried in discrete events. The process controller creates a new instance of a process on detecting an event. A process instance lasts until a terminating event causes it to stop. During the lifetime of a process, artifacts are modified or generated, and often persist in a database after the process instance has been terminated.

External events that are start conditions for a process are likely to be generated by end-users (e.g., a change request) or the management framework (e.g., a detected fault). Terminating conditions may either signify a successful outcome (such as a fault being fixed) or an error condition (such as a change having to be rolled back).

Artifacts used in infrastructure management processes such as a change request or a problem report are essentially the user interface to the process. An instance of the artifact is generated per process instance. In this respect the artifact is also a "state machine" for the process instance. The artifact carries an audit trail of all the states it transitioned through.

5.5.2 Basic Principles of Process Automation

An infrastructure management process such as change management viewed in isolation may depict little business value. However, viewed as part of a "value chain," where an efficient change capability is an enabler to operate in, say, a new business environment, change management takes on a different perspective. Infrastructure management processes therefore have relationships to the wider business processes in a value-chain model. Value-chain models are valid in enterprises that run their core businesses on a process model.

The infrastructure management business model is the "rule book" for defining all aspects of process definition and usage within the infrastructure management organization. The business model specifies each process to a point where it is a complete specification for designing the automation of the process.

Automation of infrastructure related processes is relatively straightforward once the processes have been comprehensively defined. Using process definition information in the business model a number of new design activities need to be undertaken:

- The artifacts for use by both human actors in executing the process activities need to be defined. These artifacts are user interface components and as such require close work with the users of the artifacts.

- The artifacts for use by systems actors are data and interface definitions and require information about the target systems.

- A state model needs to be derived from the process specification. An abstract state machine for each process needs to be defined. This is the representation of a process for its workflow automation.

- The state model definition allows a requirements specification for choosing workflow products to be specified.

- The abstract state machine and the artifacts need to be mapped to a chosen workflow product, designed and tested.

5.5.3 Process Life-cycle

Processes start operating on recognizing a start condition and terminate on recognizing a termination condition. These conditions are defined as part of each process's definition.

For example, the start condition for the change management process is a change request and a terminating condition is the successful completion of the change. Other terminating conditions may include an error resulting in roll-back. A process's life-cycle may last for a period ranging from seconds to weeks or months. This may be determined by the nature of the process. For example, infrastructure recovery would define a finite duration for a specific type of recovery (plus or minus 15% or thereabouts).

In the case of the problem management process, a problem may be fixed at the end of a call to the helpdesk or may require the execution of a major process to fix it, giving a large range for the life-cycle.

When a process is automated, life-cycle has a more specific meaning. Life-cycle refers to a distinct instance of the process. A new instance is created each time a start condition is recognized. In addition to start and terminating conditions, other conditions signal progress through the process activities. In automating a process, the system recognizes the different events that are "milestones" in the process life-cycle.

In an automated infrastructure management process the related artifacts are essentially carriers of state information. This state information is used in several ways:

- To define where the process instance is with respect to the process state machine (derived from the process definition on automation).

- To hold an audit trail of the states through which the process instance has gone through.

- To hold any text annotations entered by a human actor in the course of participating in the process activity.

The artifact then persists in an infrastructure management database as a record of a specific event. The record has value in the generation of management metric and often also as "intellectual property." For example, where there is a global infrastructure in an enterprise, problem resolutions relating at one site in an enterprise have value to management groups in other sites.

5.5.4 Process Monitoring

Processes need to be measured if they are to be controlled. Most process measurement can however be automated. Process measurement should focus on measuring the performance of the process rather than the people performing the work.

The metrics to be measured and the use for the metrics should be defined at the time of process design. Typical process metrics are:

- *Queue length*—There are likely to be several points in a process where queues of work items are formed. Identifying these points and measuring the length of each queue is a measurement that directly relates to the throughput of the process.

- *Productivity*—This is defined as a percentage of output-value/input-cost Input cost is largely people costs in the case of infrastructure management processes. Output value is difficult to evaluate. It nevertheless defines how much work (classified by relevant "types") has been achieved by the process team.

- *Cycle time*—Defined as the difference of the finish-time (or date) and the start time (or date). This is a measure of the efficiency of the process. To be meaningful as a performance, metric cycle time should be normalized for the number of "resources" executing the process.

- *Quality index*—A consolidated measure showing "defects" as a percentage of total process instances. The process metrics in Section 5.4 shows potential candidates.

It is not uncommon for processes to "deteriorate" over both short terms (up to 3 months) and over longer terms. Process monitoring provides the means to identify such trends in an organization. Tracking long-term trends is important as it indicates the capacity to achieve the process goals.

5.6 Books for Further Reading

Martyna, B., and Bruce R. Elbert. *Client/Server Computing* (Architecture, Applications and Distributed Systems Management). Artech House, 1994.

Ould, Martyn A. *Business Processes* (Modeling and Analysis for Re-engineering and Improvement). John Wiley & Sons, 1995.

Peppard, J., *et al. The Essence of Business Process Re-engineering.* Prentice-Hall, 1995.

Simon, Alan R. *Network Re-Engineering* (Foundations of Enterprise Computing). AP Professional, 1994.

Traeger, Lisa, and E. C. Ericson. *Expert Systems Applications in Integrated Network Management.* Artech House, 1989.

Part II

Architectural Perspective

Architecture of Client/Server and Intranet Systems

Areas covered in this chapter

- Architecture in the context of client/server based computing models

- Client/server models and their possible evolutionary paths

- Key communication protocols used in client/server communications

- Message-based communication models for client/server applications

- Major issues in client/server architecture and its evolution

- High-level application communication

- Intranet concepts and its building blocks

- Scaling the intranet

- Major issues in intranet architecture and its evolution

- Using intranet architecture to enhance traditional application delivery

- Impact on desktop clients of intranet evolution

- Network considerations for client/server application developers

- Basic characteristics of client/server and intranet application traffic

A rchitecture is a term that is most commonly used in the context of buildings and other civil engineering structures. An architecture's most tangible form, in this sense, is a physical model or a set of detailed engineering plans. Modern architects however are beginning to use IT mediums such as a virtual reality model to give realism to the plans.

The architecture of computer systems is, like its counterpart above, essentially an approach to partition a large system into a set of subsystems. The "architectural approach" is strong in areas such as processor and hardware subsystem design. Its use in other areas, such as client/server systems and software product design, is still in its infancy and approached in an ad hoc fashion. Few computer systems in existence today have a formal architecture as such. Most have grown "organically" over time.

Table 6.1 contrasts the meaning of *architecture* as used in the conventional sense and in the context of computer systems.

Another take on architecture is as a method of managing complexity in any large computer-based structure. Unfortunately, complexity in computer systems is often mistaken for "fitness-of-purpose": "*We have a complex !@?~# system to handle our accounts.*" is meant to imply quality and a measure of the technical competence which delivered the system.

In reality, and especially in the case of computer systems, gratuitous complexity does not provide long-term value for an organization. And the cost and effort needed to produce modern computer systems demand that such a long-term view is taken.

Table 6.1: The Term "Architecture" in Conventional and Computer Systems Modes of Usage

Conventional Usage	Computer Systems Usage
Pertains to any complex physical structure	Pertains to any complex structure with both logical as well as physical dimensions
Usually uses pre-built subcomponents made from well-understood materials	Almost invariably builds subcomponents from scratch using a variety of tools and languages at various stages of maturity
Usually uses well-understood rules, even in unconventional designs	Usually develops rules on a project basis. Rules may get re-used on an individual architect level
Architects are a distinct, recognized profession	Almost anybody can be described as an architect
Usually has an aesthetic element which distinguishes a design. Fitness-of-purpose is another qualitative measure widely applied	Elegance is recognizable in the best designs, simplicity, "doing-most-with-the-least," flexibility and scaleability are all hallmarks of a good design
Usually related to a wider context such as surrounding structures, landscape or geological factors	Environment in which the system operates, relationships with existing systems, tools used to build the systems all define the wider context

Complexity is however inevitable in large computer-based structures. The management and control of this complexity is the single most important role of architecture in large systems design today.

The commonest technique to manage complexity, whether in a civil engineering structure, a piece of literature or a computer system is the successive breakdown of the "big" problem. This results in an interrelated set of smaller problems which is again broken down. The process of breakdown continues until the problem size is something that can be handled in a system-development project.

The very basis of the client/server model is the breakdown of the functions of large mainframe-based systems into smaller pieces. The pieces could then run on smaller, cheaper and more personal computers.

The term *client/server* is widely used by vendors to describe their products, by academics and journalists to describe the current *thing* in computers.

In the client/server model, a program, the *client*, requests a service that another program, the *server*, provides. A server has a *client interface* that specifies the individual services supported by the server. A client may only request services that are supported at the client interface. The server performs the requested services and returns the results.

Software architecture designs the top-level rationale for a computer system based on the client/server model. Hence the architecture decisions made at the software level percolates through the rest of the computer system.

In effect the hosts for the software and the network connecting the hosts together are merely the skeletal framework for software. A software architecture defines the interfaces of the software subsystems and the rules for using them.

At the current state-of-the-art prefabricated subcomponent software does not exist for mainstream computing platforms. Applets and OCX controls offer the beginnings of component technology for browser-based platforms. Even worse in most cases, the architectural framework itself as well as the subcomponents start life afresh for each project.

This state of affairs is being addressed by the gradual move of the software industry to objects and object-oriented development tools. However, it is still several years before industrial strength software components will become available. There is then another period before they will be accepted as off-the-shelf components.

The motivation for an architecture-based design of computer systems, and especially client/server based systems, is summarized by the following points:

- To define the overall objectives of the system and its *design-center* with respect to (*a*) financial constraints, (*b*) resource constraints and (*c*) any technical limitations such as the need to interwork with existing systems.

- To define the tools used to construct the system, including development protocols, languages and operational management techniques.

- To define the hardware and software elements used as building blocks and their respective contribution of risk to delivering the system.

- To define the degree of maintainability in terms of the ability to modify, and extend the system to meet changing requirements (and also to correct faults).

- To define the operational manageability in terms of service as a production system.

- To define the criteria for *fitness-of-purpose* of the system for its end-users and within its user environment.

6.1 *Client/Server Computing Models*

Client/server architecture defines the basic building blocks and the way in which these building blocks are logically and physically distributed. We examine architecture here for two reasons:

- The first is to identify the diversity of design of the applications being described as client/server.

- The second is to understand how the structure of an application relates to its management.

Client/server architecture may be viewed in two ways: (1) in terms of how the application's functional components are distributed; (2) in terms of an implicit data hierarchy that defines how the data maps to its users.

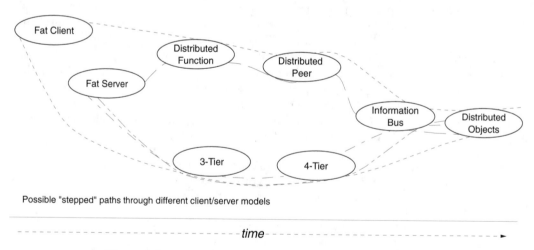

Possible "stepped" paths through different client/server models

Figure 6.1: An evolutionary progression of the client/server model

6.1.1 Client/Server Modeled in Terms of Functional Distribution

Software used to build the client/server model consists of different types of application logic—each of which has distinct functional properties:

- *Presentation Logic*—Responsible for the user interface through which the user conducts a dialog with the application. Layers of this component are also involved in translating between data conventions for presentation between different parts of the application. This is especially important if the application is spread across multiple types of platforms. In particular the data convention sent out on the wire may be standardized.

- *Application Logic*—Responsible for the unique set of computations relating to the application's specific domain or function. Hence a trading application will have various calculators, a word-processing application has text manipulation tools and so on. Computations provided by the application logic often relates to the interpretation of data in the specific domain. Application logic therefore has embedded knowledge about the nature and structure of data.

- *Data Management Logic*—Responsible for manipulating data objects relevant to the application, usually through the medium of a language-based structure. The commonest language medium is structured query language (SQL). Data objects in a relational database include tables, indices, triggers (defining conditions to be recognized), stored procedures (defining procedures to be executed by specifying the name of the procedure). This logic is closely related to the application logic since it is the usual consumer of the data.

- *Database engine*—A database server responsible for managing the relational tables representing the schemas pertinent to the application. It usually includes administration tools and interfaces for database administration. Industrial strength databases engines include those from Oracle and Sybase. Database engines may also provide capabilities such as replication or parallel searches that may be utilized by the data management logic to add value to the application logic

Functionally "divided" software may be viewed as a set of specialized software components that cooperate to deliver the services seen by the user. These functional components ideally reside on different classes of machines (often called workstations and servers respectively). Table 6.2 shows the qualitative difference between these two classes of machines.

Deciding on the class of machine to distribute a functional component is largely driven by factors such as the computing culture in an enterprise, and the experiences of using different generations of the client/server model.

There are several models for "splitting" the application logic components, described in Section 6.1.1 across workstation and server-type machines. Four such models are discussed

Table 6.2: Some Qualitative Differences Between Workstations and Servers

	Workstation	Server
Cost	Lower cost, sometimes 10% of server costs in some cases depending on processor power, memory and storage features. Most workstations are either Intel (Wintel) and RISC based processors.	Generally offers higher specification for a higher price/performance ratio. Dual power supplies and power filtering are sometimes standard with non-stop power as an external option.
Expansion	Generally offers minimal expansion capability due to enclosure and motherboard limitations.	Greater expansion capability, with different internal bus technology and peripheral connection options.
Memory	Generally in the order of 16 MB to 32 MB for most operating systems. "Upgradeability" of memory possible to some maximum that changes with each generation of machine.	Error correcting memory. Several binary orders of magnitude memory are not unusual depending on operating system (e.g., 128 to 256 MB for Unix). Usually upgradeable to a higher "ceiling" than workstations.
Storage	Ranges from diskless to 1 GB disk storage. Unlikely to be (Redundant Array of Inexpensive Disks) RAID. Likely to hold only application and operating system executable, with data on a network disk drive (i.e., on a server machine).	Greater disk storage capacity, with options in secondary storage technology. May be part of a hierarchical storage scheme. Also RAID storage common.
Processor	Ranges from low end to top end of processor family. Upgradeability of the processor often an option.	Tends towards higher end of processor family. Depending on operating system supports multiple processors, math co-processors, etc.
Network connect	Usually Ethernet or Token Ring. Very few with higher bandwidth technologies such as ATM. and FDDI over copper. Keeps network interface costs low.	Ethernet and Token Ring common, with greater take up of FDDI, 100 MB Ethernet and ATM. Connection to switching hubs becoming commoner.
Availability	Availability not generally a key feature. Breakdown results in replacement. If no data files are on local drives then minimal loss of data occurs.	Availability a serious concern since loss affects many users. Data file repository needs replication and backup depending on the type of business supported. Processor fault tolerance is through clustering servers.

below: *Fat Server, Fat Client, Distributed Function,* and *Distributed Peer.* These models are shown in Figure 6.1 in terms of one of the strands of evolution or progress of client/server based computing.

6.1.2 Fat Server

The Fat Server model, as the name implies, distributes a large proportion of the application logic in the server. This is the simplest type of function distribution. Figure 6.2 shows the simplest type of distribution of function in a client/server application. This was a common model in the earliest days of client/server—during the "corporate downsizing" era when smaller mini's replaced mainframes. In a more modern context, this model offers major advantages when there is a long distance between the "point of viewing" and point of data management:

- It ensures that raw data does not have to traverse an Internet or wide area network, potentially saving bandwidth, and avoiding issues of potential loss of data in traversing a network.

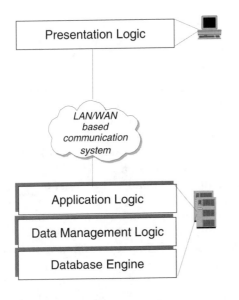

- In this model only the presentation logic runs on a local workstation. The application logic, data management logic database engine runs at the remote server(s).

- Not many commercial cient-server applications follow this model of distribution any more, although it is still relevant to deploy a "bursty" application over the WAN.

- This model is relevant to infrastructure management applications, since it allows remote management servers to collect the data and execute application programs in each "local" context. The results of the remotely executing mangement applications are used at a management client.

- Low cost RMON platforms are often distributed in remote offices using this model. Instead of raw data from the RMON monitor traversing the network to a central point of management, the data is first processed and only summary or exception information is sent.

- Similar diagnostic applications for systems management, application services management, security auditing, and availability management are feasible.

Figure 6.2: Fat Server model

- It ensures that the delay from execution to viewing the results is minimized since much of the processing is done locally, with the results of the processing being of higher informational value than the raw data.

A common protocol between the presentation component and the remote application component is the X-11 protocol. X-11 uses RPC as its underlying transport protocol, making the presentation logic—application logic link reliable. Variants of X-11 have been optimized for use across low-speed WANs.

In a modern variant of this model, the presentation logic is split across server and workstation. The presentation logic for user dialog resides in the workstation while presentation logic for back-end processing resides at the server end. This is a complex split, however, many applications being designed for cooperative use by humans need to consider consistency of presentation to each client. Splitting the presentation between a front-end and back-end provides consistency of views seen by all parties.

The Fat Server model is probably the weakest in terms of scaling. As more consumers of the data are added, the bottleneck moves to the data server. There is little scope for alleviating the bottleneck, other than to use a more performant server.

6.1.3 Fat Client

In this model both the data management logic and the database engine reside remotely. This is a common architecture in many business applications and is probably the commonest realization of the term client/server. Figure 6.3 shows the logic distribution.

This model works well for applications where the traffic between the workstation based logic and the data server is not bursty and therefore the server characteristics can be accurately sized. The workstation bears the major burden of computation, while the server provides a centralized repository for the data, and ensures its integrity and security.

As the client code gets "fatter" as more functions are added, more powerful workstations are needed. Adding more users always means adding workstations of the respective power.

The server is also responsible for performing backup, checkpoint and transaction logs. A common protocol between application logic and the data management logic is SQL, which is also a language for data manipulation. Most commercial database management systems (data management logic) interfaces interpret SQL queries and handle queueing of requests.

A potential problem exists with the protocol architecture between the application logic and the data management logic. Unless the interface at the data management logic can manage multiple sessions, the access to the data repository is serial, with throughput implications for a set of users concurrently accessing the data. This model works best when the data transfer requirement is relatively low.

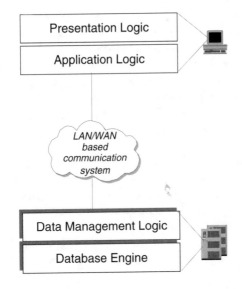

Presentation Logic
Application Logic

LAN/WAN based communication system

Data Management Logic
Database Engine

■ In this model both the presentation logic and the application logic reside on the workstation while all the database components reside on the server(s).

■ This architecture is suitable in a variety of departmental decision support applications, where different departments use "common" data, but in a department's own specific context.

■ In such decision support applications the client end typically generate SQL queries for processing by the database end. Results from the database are processed for display by the client end.

■ This model is also popularized by several of the current generation of development tools such as Power Builder (Powersoft Corp).

■ Performance problems often arise when users try to access across a WAN. This is mostly because SQL is sensitive to latency in the intervening WAN.

Figure 6.3: *Fat Client model*

6.1.4 Distributed Function

The distributed function model is a direct evolution of the Fat Server and Fat Client models, aimed at overcoming their respective shortcomings. Figure 6.4 shows the distribution of application logic in this model. The model allows processing overheads for the application to be more equitably shared between workstation and server class machines.

The model is often used by software package vendors, where the first generation of the application uses a Fat Client architecture. Subsequent releases place additional features into the server. Development tools in modern Computer Assisted Software Environments (CASE) allow an application to be configured differently across client and server machines for different market segments.

An example of this development is seen in PC based e-mail packages. Over 3 years or so these have moved from being a predominantly client based application to a server based application with a much smaller client (i.e., relative to new features which have been added).

In a more complex use of this model, the workstation hosts a full application in its own right—including rudimentary data management or transactional logic. Data management's main task is to manage access to the application sources for its data. The server application acts as one component that the client application accesses and integrates together.

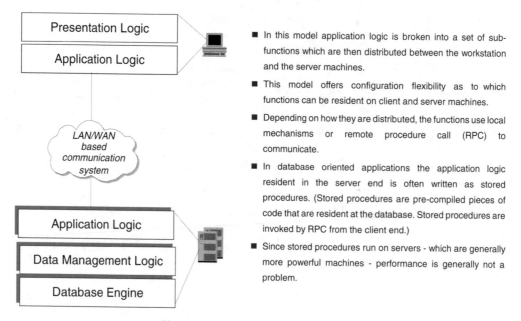

Figure 6.4: *Distributed Function model*

Its major disadvantage is that the two pieces of application logic are coupled and little scope exists to enhance one part of the logic without affecting the other(s). The application logic to application logic protocol is usually based on a framework such as RPC.

6.1.5 Distributed Peer Model

The Distributed Peer model is another evolutionary point in distributing functions across machines. Figure 6.5 shows the logic distribution between workstation and server class machines.

Here the application components are distributed across multiple servers. Each server provides a specialized application service or provides redundancy. This model has unprecedented scaleability to add and change the application's functionality, provided the peers are connected using a standard framework.

Another advantage is that this model works well as a distributed object oriented model—under some circumstances. Objects encapsulate data as well as function. Access to the objects services are through a well-defined interface. The peers may be seen as very large objects with well-defined interfaces connected together by a connection framework.

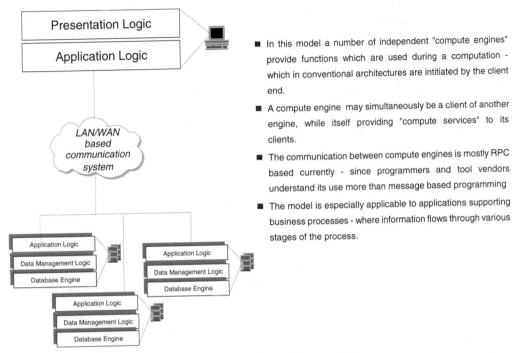

In this model a number of independent "compute engines" provide functions which are used during a computation - which in conventional architectures are intitiated by the client end.

A compute engine may simultaneously be a client of another engine, while itself providing "compute services" to its clients.

The communication between compute engines is mostly RPC based currently - since programmers and tool vendors understand its use more than message based programming

The model is especially applicable to applications supporting business processes - where information flows through various stages of the process.

Figure 6.5: *Distributed Peer model*

6.1.6 Client/Server Modeled in Terms of Data Hierarchy

Another way of looking at client/server models is in terms of a data hierarchy. This has origins in the classical two-tier master/slave model of computing. Usually a mainframe (the master) communicated with terminals (slaves) over a network.

A common architecture in migrating from mainframe based computing to client/server is the so called three-tier model. In the simplest case, the top of the hierarchy is still the mainframe (or mini-computer clusters). The terminal tier is replaced with servers class machines which act as clients of the mainframe. The third tier consists of desktop workstations, which are in turn clients of the servers.

The three tiers of the hierarchy are also one of graduated computing power and price—where the top of the hierarchy has the powerful mainframe and the last level has the least powerful PC.

The mainframe, servers and the desktop machines are connected together by a local area network, although the mainframe may also be accessed across a long haul network. Above the basic network and transport protocols, there is a protocol for moving data from

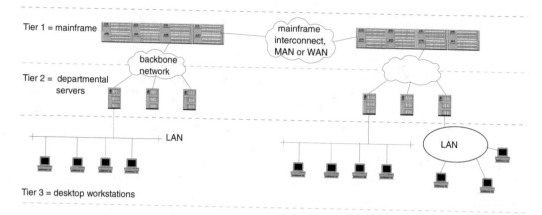

Figure 6.6: *Horizontal scaling of the three-tier model*

one tier to another. Most database management vendors provide products to bridge between the different class of machines in the tiered model.

The three-tier model has been successful in migrating computing power to the desktop. The model is scalable horizontally in each tier. As more users are added at the lower tier or more demand is placed on the data in the highest tier, additional servers can be added to the second tier.

This is shown in Figure 6.6. Mainframe to mainframe connection between co-sited machines is usually over some proprietary high speed interconnect technology. If the machines are more widely distributed then connectivity may be over a local area network, a campus network or much more commonly, over a wide area network (e.g., linking two geographic data centers). Server to server connectivity is likely to stay local or campus wide.

Horizontal extension of the basic three-tier model, however, is not without its problems. For a start it becomes more complex to build—as data integrity, performance and availability across machines in a tier become major operational issues.

Secondly, a data architecture is need to decide the distribution of data across machines in a tier. If new applications are being developed using the data, then application logic distribution also becomes an architectural issue.

6.1.7 Three Tier Plus

A consequence of the wide adoption of the three-tier model (by in-house applications, software package vendors and general software vendors) is that the second tier as well as the third tier gets "bloated."

The usual cure for this is to upgrade the machines in the affected tier to faster machines with more memory. An alternative is to scale vertically by adding an extra level of servers. An extra tier of servers plays one or both of the new roles as follows:

- As a means of dividing the mainframe database into multi-departmental and departmental classes of data. The new server then plays the part of a *staged* data framework.

- As a new level of application server, allowing the migration of application logic usually from the client end to make the client thinner in the process.

Updates are a particular problem with staged data, as either the updates must be replicated "down the chain" in real time or must be stored and forwarded as a batch.

Real time updates involve heavy network traffic. Batched updates bring into question the timeliness of the data being forwarded and hence its usability. The capability of the network to cope with such traffic volumes and the use to which the data is put determines which type of mechanism is used.

The extra tier as an application server has particular problems in terms of the extra level of coupling between the two server tiers. The three levels of coupling place severe limitations on the ability to maintain incrementally an application with new features and functions. As the flexibility to move with changing business requirements is a major rationale for developing client/server style applications, this is a risk to be managed when choosing this architecture.

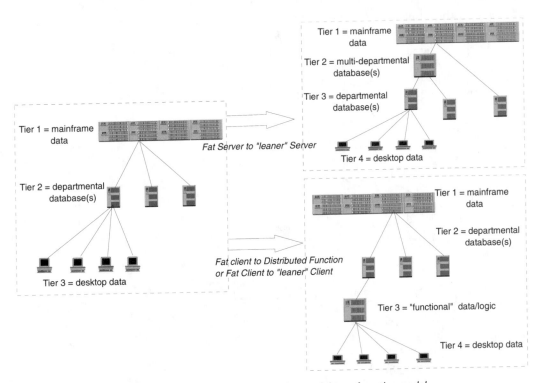

Figure 6.7: Transition of three-tier model to a four-tier model

6.2 Client/Server Communication Mechanisms

Communications between components of a client/server application are dominated by two mechanisms *remote procedure call* (RPC) and *messaging*. Of these RPC is by far the most widely used. Figure 6.8(a) shows the communication stack between application components. Table 6.3 compares RPC with messaging, in terms of the positive and negative aspects of each in building client/server systems.

RPC is provided as a service in most distributed computing toolkits. Chapter 10, "The Technology of Protocols and Interfaces," Section 10.6.2, provides a comprehensive overview of the protocol structure of the RPC mechanism. Here we look at RPC from the perspective of application architecture.

The simplest execution model of a client/server application is of two processes, a client process and a server process. RPC is then primarily a method of inter-process communication. Conceptually, it extends the basic procedure-call mechanism, available in all high-level programming languages, to work across a network.

RPC essentially allows synchronous control: a process invoking a remote procedure waits until the invoked procedure returns with the results of its execution.

Extensions to the basic RPC mechanism allows an invoked procedure to call back the invoker with the results. This frees the invoking process to continue with other processing

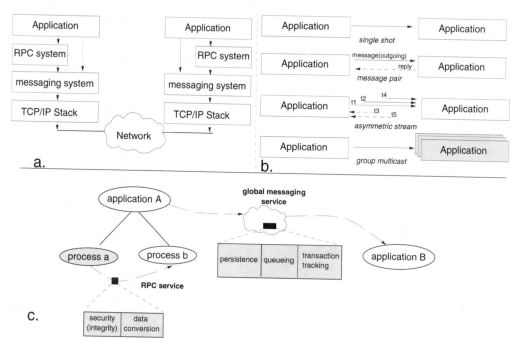

Figure 6.8: Features of RPC and messaging

tasks. These extensions are however quite complex to program and de-bug. Consequently they are rarely used.

When the invoking process and the invoked process are physically separated by a network, the latency of the network drastically limits the throughput of RPC.

Table 6.3: RPC versus Messaging in Client/Server Communications

RPC	Messaging
Widely used and understood due to its long and stable history (5-10 years). Widely taught in courses as a programming mechanism.	Message-based programming is still not part of mainstream computing. Message-based skills are relatively rare.
Primarily a synchronous mechanism. Asynchronous behavior is achieved at the cost of complexity.	Supports both synchronous and asynchronous communication. Well suited to all client/server models and supports event-driven computing. Provides time independence between sender and receiver through queueing.
Supported as a *base technology* in distributed computing environments. Multiple standards (e.g., OSF RPC & OSI RPC) exist—which is a problem in enterprise-wide standards setting.	"Value added" services can be added between sender and receiver. Examples include information persistence and transaction-level integrity checking. These services are needed in certain classes of applications such as banking.
Needs pre-compiling of interface definitions before transfer.	No need for any pre-compilers.
Available for many platform architectures.	Product availability across platforms is still patchy.
No need to define new API when distributing application logic. Well suited to many client/server applications.	Standards are still emerging or in early stages. Multiple vendor-supplied APIs all tend to be incompatible with each other.
RPC is primarily suited for communication between application components. A state of the art RPC toolkit includes basic data format translation and basic security as features. Services such as queueing for inter-application communication are difficult to add on.	Messaging is especially suited in application-to-application communication. A number of additional features such as message queueing, message persistence and availability-based routing are easily realizable. Its use in inter-component communication is often less performant than RPC.
Support across heterogeneous environments allows RPC to be powerful building blocks in applications that span across multiple platforms.	Usable as a building block in new application messaging models and information flow patterns—e.g., see Section 6.4.1.

Messaging, as the name implies, is a method of transferring information between applications or between application components. Figure 6.8(b) shows common types of message flows. Information in a message is usually data but may include control information.

Messaging is built from a set of lower level protocols and mechanisms close to the operating system. Basic messaging is a "building block" mechanism, used as transport by application level messaging solutions and RPC (see Figure 6.8(a)).

Both RPC and messaging depend on underlying protocols for transport between two points. The characteristics of the underlying transport protocol (such as flow control and "reliability") affects the throughput of messaging.

Application level messaging mechanisms typically provide a high level API for posting messages to outbound queues and for retrieving from inbound queues. This design tends to push additional behavior such as flow control into applications, impacting the distributed systems modularity, maintainability and extensibility.

Using messaging between application components is, generally speaking, less performant than RPC. This is because the application has greater overheads in the logical management of message-based communications.

6.2.1 Basic Message Communication in Client/Server Models

Messaging is a mechanism for transferring data as well as control information. The client/server model is driven by communications between the client and server entities. The information content of these communications is defined by application level message "units"—which are both generated and targeted at application logic. The sending and the receiving entities are "peers" in a communication model.

These message units are then transported by lower level protocols such as UDP and TCP which in turn map to network layer protocols such as IP and then into data frames such as Ethernet. This is shown in Figure 6.8(b), which also shows a classification of application level messages. This is described below from the viewpoint of the application logic of the sending and/or the receiving entities:

- *Single shot*—the sender sends a message and does not expect a reply or response from the peer entity. If the underlying transport protocol is a reliable one (e.g., TCP), the sending application entity will receive "feedback" on both successful and unsuccessful delivery to the peer application entity.

  If the transport protocol is an "unreliable" one, the sender only receives notification of the local transport layer's failure. There is no trace of the message once it has been successfully accepted by the local transport layer.

- *Message pair*—the sender of a message always gets a reply message. This is one way of using an unreliable transport protocol and still confirming the receipt of each application message by the remote peer entity. Message pairs imply that the sender and receiver entities have synchronized communications.

- *Asymmetric stream*—two peer entities establish bilateral communication paths. Asynchronous message pairs may exist in either direction—i.e., The sender of a message expects a reply message some time in the future and need not idle waiting for the reply. A single reply may confirm receipt of multiple messages. Each stream is however active independent of the other.

- *Group multicast*—this is a "one (sender) to many (receivers)" form of a single shot message. A special form of address called a multicast address is used to achieve this. Each multicast address defines a unique group of entities subscribing to any messages sent to the address. The address is therefore essentially a handle for the group. The group can be joined and left at will using a protocol. A message is distributed to all the current members of the group.

6.3 Issues in Client/Server Architectures

The client/server models described in the preceding sections all evolved to solve specific problems.

Developing client/sever applications on conventional platform is both expensive and risky from the perspective of the business user. Some of the widely cited barriers to starting new application initiatives using a client/server model include:

- Difficulty in recruiting and keeping critical skills needed to meet time-to-market and quality requirements.

- Poor internal coordination between different departments (or business lines) leading to incompatibility at software, hardware and application functionality levels.

- Lack of training programs for internally developed applications leading to poor realization of benefits.

The alternative to client/server application development is evidenced by the phenomenal growth of packaged client/server applications such as SAP in manufacturing and resource management. Interestingly, these packages themselves are beginning to hit the barriers cited above—as they move to a client/server technology base. The global deployment of packaged applications generally take several years to complete.

Client/server architectures still offers the best time-to-market characteristics of currently available options. These architectures however suffer from a number of issues which are discussed in the following sections.

6.3.1 Issues of Coupling

Coupling between software components defines the content and method of information flow between the programs. The degree of coupling determines the degree to which client/server application programs can be maintained to meet changing requirements over time. Maintenance includes activities to change the logic of existing functionality, to add new business functionality and to interwork with new components.

In general the more coupled a system of software components is the more difficult it is to change any component in isolation from the others. There are however different types of coupling between components:

- *Content coupling*—coupling where the logic of one component manipulates the content or structure of another. This is supposed to be impossible with modern languages. However, it is not impossible using pointer manipulation. It is still possible with some types of commonly used scripting languages.

- *Data coupling*—coupling between data structures used by two or more application components. Such coupling is largely a thing of the past in commercial software. Both training and programming language semantics discourage data structures to be shared other than across explicitly defined interfaces. All operations on the data have to be conducted through the interface.

- *Control coupling*—coupling where explicit control parameters links two components. An example is a master/slave relationship component where a master defines the slave's operations. The slave has no autonomous behavior other than through the commands. The master is essentially a bottleneck.

- *Format coupling*—coupling where the lowest level data format or representation needs to be used by all communicating components. Format coupling was solved very early in distributed computing protocols such as RPC, which introduced a low-level translation protocol for common data types.

- *Semantic coupling*—a common coupling at the application level, where an application level protocol links the different components. Application protocols determine the future extensibility of the application in terms of high-level functions. This type of coupling is more an issue in defining the architecture.

- *Temporal coupling*—coupling where two components in a client/server environment are linked in a time-related sequence. A simple example is the synchronous communication between two components, where one component has to wait until some result is passed. More complex couplings exist in transactions that span across different platforms. Temporal coupling is both a performance issue and a major cause of failure.

6.3.2 Scaling and Complexity Issues

The client/server model is scalable in a number of dimensions. Within each of the client/server architectures discussed in the preceding section, some leeway is possible for upward scaling.

In general there are three options for upward scaling that are discussed below. The impact of each of these options on the client/server models, discussed in the preceding sections, is shown in Table 6.4:

- Increase server size and power of servers. Depending on the client/server model, different effects may be seen. An alternative is to increase the number of servers and introduce a mechanism for the new servers to share the load.

- Increase the workstation's power. This works in a client/server model where the client is compute intensive. This has been a common phenomenon with stand-alones, each new generation of an application demanding machines with more power and memory. This is also applicable to the respective client/server models.

- Increasing the levels of hierarchy. This works up to a point as shown by the evolution from the three-tier model to a four-tier model. As hierarchy increases, the complexity of the model increases. The transition from an n-tier to an n+1 tier architecture is more difficult to achieve. Unless re-engineering is feasible, increasing hierarchy is difficult.

Table 6.4: Impact of Applying Different Scaling-Up Options on Client/Server Models

Model/Option	Increase Server Power	Increase Server Number	Increase Workstation Power	Increase Server Hierarchy
Fat Server	major			
Fat Client			major	
Distributed Function		major		
Distributed Peer				major
Three-Tier	major		major	
Three-Tier Plus		major		major

Scaling down is also an important consideration when deploying a client/server application into different size offices. In most cases scaling was never considered as a design objective of client/server applications. This results in applications having to be deployed over ad hoc infrastructures in different size offices. Global enterprises embarking on new client/server projects should define scaleability as a design criterion. This has major paybacks in both operational costs and infrastructure costs.

One of the reasons for deployment complexity creeping in is when scaling is attempted. In other cases the application is itself trying to achieve a complex job and the associated systems architecture is complex. Complexity is manageable at both design and deployment levels by thinking in terms of building blocks.

Complexity has major operational implications—from performance problems to difficulty in tracing faults. If a client/server deployment model gets complex then new architectural options have to be considered.

Historical records of problem resolution help to detect trends of increasing complexity. These impact operational effectiveness in delivering the applications.

6.3.3 Reliability and Manageability Issues

Reliability is a function of many factors. Client/server computing was once described as a "fault-probable" environment. Despite this, *high availability* of an application is often secondary to getting it built in the first instance.

The requirements for reliability also creep up—as the application becomes a critical business system. A relatively reliable application used in a local area context appears to be unreliable when scaled to remote offices or at a large number of offices. This is true of even stable applications such as e-mail.

The client/server infrastructure can provide some retrofitted solutions in this area. Increasingly, high availability toolkits are available to use in the architecture and design of client/server systems. Reliability has to be built in top-down.

Manageability is the ability to control the life-cycle of a client/server application once it has entered production. Technology elements such as agents play a major part in this ability, however, other "softer" areas such as processes, people and architecture collectively play a larger part.

In most enterprises, application developers give little thought to downstream management of applications they are building or integrating. Management is often thought about just before deployment.

Manageability is another design criterion that needs to be considered at architecture and design time. If the "use-cases" of the application are known then the management issues can also be identified. More importantly, manageability should be part of the design methodology, and should be prototyped, tested, training provided, etc.

6.4 Evolution of the Client/Server Model

The client/server model has undergone major changes since the early implementations. In the first generation of client/server implementations the network address of the server that a client machine connected to had to be configured as a control parameter of the client code. It was configured during installation.

The client and server were "control-coupled" so that changing a server or the underlying network topology involved a large number of error-prone configuration changes in the clients.

Transparency is the notion of concealing the consequences of the *separation* of client and server components. Transparency services allow clients and servers to be viewed as a cohesive system rather than as a collection of components. Transparency addresses different aspects of component separation. Transparency is implemented through transparency mechanisms, services or protocols:

- *Location transparency* allows components to be accessed without direct knowledge of their address. Hence in the case of client and server machines, a *location transparency service* would allow the client to specify to it the name of an application service. The transparency service returns the current address of a server providing the application service. Lookup services such as NIS available with Unix and Domain Name service in Microsoft NT provide location transparency.

- *Access transparency* allows an application component to access local and remote components with identical operational semantics. This allows components to be built that can reside on either the client or server with equal effect. Access transparency is provided by application-level procedures and protocols which can be layered over different lower level transport services. Examples include messaging protocols.

- *Failure transparency* allows a client/server based application to continue operation in the event of failure of hardware and software components. The mechanisms for hardware failure transparency include server clustering—where any member of a set of identical machines can provide an application service. The mechanisms for software transparency include process groups—all processes in a group hold the same state and any process can continue if one of the processes dies. Server clustering is provided by many server vendors. Toolkits for software transparency need to be layered over the operating system.

- *Replication transparency* allows multiple copies of data to be maintained in a way that is transparent to the users of the data—whether human or software. Replication transparency is important in enterprise critical systems such as a global directory. Replication products are produced by major database vendors. Replication is often justified on the grounds of performance—keeping relevant data close to its users, rather than on the grounds of reliability.

Tools for the operational management of client/server environments are getting better in an incremental fashion, however the rate at which client/server application are being deployed suggests "auto-configuration" and transparency are key concepts.

6.4.1 Application Level Communication Models

Section 6.2.1 looked at basic message communications in the client/server model. Here we look at messaging from a higher, application level perspective. This level of messaging maps directly to the use the basic messaging in Section 6.2.1 as building blocks. Four such application-level models are considered here: Request-Response, Publisher-Subscriber, Anonymous-Messaging and Scatter-Messaging.

Client to server communication starts with a person invoking an operation at the user interface, resulting in a sequence of messages between the workstation on which the user is operative and the associated servers. Such communication is termed *client centric*. The service is provided as a result of an explicit request for the service.

The communication between client and servers machines may in fact be initiated by either party. There are therefore also a number of *server centric* models of communication where a service "provider" initiates the transfer of information to potential consumers of the information.

Request-Response. This is the commonest and oldest form of client server communications. The client requests a specific operation available at the *client interface* of a server. The server responds to this request by executing the requested operation. Most client/server applications built today use this model and a number of infrastructure mechanisms support this as a general purpose communication model.

An enhancement of this basic model is that of a *request broker* providing address and location transparency services. It allows a client to request for a service rather than a specific server's name. The client is also freed from having to know the servers' address or location. The broker maps the service name to an appropriate server. The broker keeps up to date with servers that are available and may also provide basic load-balancing capability.

Other basic services such as data translation free the client from having to know about the basic data representation used by the server.

Publisher-Subscriber. In this model one or more servers publish information to a community of clients that have previously subscribed to an interest in a subject. Clients specify the subject of interest, and in some cases can even qualify what kind of changes to the subject content would be of interest. This is called subject-based addressing. Clients can de-register interest in a subject as well as register interest in new subjects.

A common use of this model is in distributing financial market data. Data about different types of financial instruments are brought by data "feeds" into a publisher (server). The publisher software categorizes the raw data into a subject hierarchy and processes updates against a client register of interest in specific subjects.

Clients explicitly subscribe to specific subcategories of information or entire categories. When information matching the subscription becomes available, the publisher server forwards the information to all the registered subscribers.

This is termed server-centric because, the communication between the server and the respective clients is driven by information events occurring at the server. The publisher-subscriber model is also a general building block to distribute real-time events to many recipients. It is usable as a means to build a distributed computing framework—see Case Study 6.1. The criteria for using the publisher-subscriber as a general purpose mechanism are:

- The available richness of its subject-based addressing scheme. This includes a scripting framework to define the subject hierarchy and the syntax for both publishers and subscribers to use.

- The second requirement is one of performance in the distribution protocol. If a large number of clients are serviced by a publisher or the frequency of the updates is high, then with the increase in volume, the publisher-server become a potential bottleneck.

- The third requirement is to guarantee that a client actually receives an update. Delivery should include sequence guarantee and timeliness of delivery.

Anonymous-Messaging. Anonymous messaging is a type of application-level messaging where the producer of a message (which is usually an application component but can be a whole application) is not aware of the potential consumers of the message. Consumers are also either applications or an application component.

This model was invented to build large-scale business processes which span multiple business systems and applications. Information and events originating in one application flows through a number of systems in a global business till some *closure* on the use of that data is achieved. This messaging model is therefore a means of integrating systems.

In anonymous-messaging the producers and consumers of a message are freed from having to know the higher level business processes. Neither do they have to know the business rules related to the flow and actual use of the information at its point of consumption. In effect, this model de-couples the actual participants in a process (in the sense that their respective information requirements do not have to be published).

This is only possible because the medium which connects the producers and consumers has "intelligence" to do all the required processing defined by business rules.

Scatter-Messaging. In scatter-messaging a server initiates the sending of messages to a set of candidate participants. The candidacy is determined dynamically. This is different from group multicast which is distribution of a message to a set of clients by virtue of their membership of a group.

A common example of scatter-messaging is a "computation" server parcelling out parallel streams of computation to a number of workstations with idle capacity. The state of idle-

Case Study 6.1: A Distributed Computing Environment

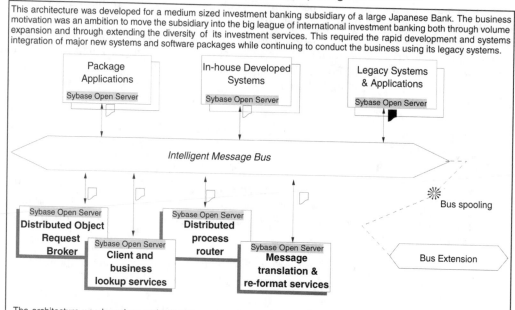

This architecture was developed for a medium sized investment banking subsidiary of a large Japanese Bank. The business motivation was an ambition to move the subsidiary into the big league of international investment banking both through volume expansion and through extending the diversity of its investment services. This required the rapid development and systems integration of major new systems and software packages while continuing to conduct the business using its legacy systems.

The architecture was based on an intelligent message bus providing a number of intelligent services as shown. The bus supported anonymous messaging to integrate the different applications, request/response messaging (through an ORBIX object request broker) for client server applications. All systems connected to the bus using Sybase Open Server interface as a connector technology (Open Server was available for all the required platforms). Messages were structured using Sybase Tabular Data Stream as a common message standard. The bus allowed messages to be exchanged between package systems, in-house developed systems and legacy systems. The ORB and process router gave advanced distribution capabilities to new applications. The bus could be extended to external sites through a bus spooling service.

ness is determined prior to the sending of the message. Each workstation, in this example, that is still idle works on a parallel stream of the computation. Workstations that are no longer idle at the time the message is received, effectively reject the parcel of work by indicating they are no longer idle.

If a participating workstation's processor becomes less idle, the parcel of computation is withdrawn from the workstation by the server. The withdrawn stream may be submitted to another workstation that is idle. Monte Carlo simulation is a candidate for this type of computation—and it is widely used in financial engineering and other decision-support tools.

6.4.2 Information Bus-Based Client/Server Model

The N-Tier architecture is not extensible beyond four tiers without causing complexity and maintenance problems. If more than four levels of processing are needed on some data item (i.e., the data hierarchy is deeper than four levels), then a bus-based model is more appropriate.

The general structure of the bus-based model is that a system of servers process the data by communicating over a bus. The application level communication models in Section 6.4.1 are best supported on a bus. They however need the bus to provide some communication-enabling services. The most important of these is described below:

Request Broker. This is a dedicated service that mediates between client applications needing a service and the servers capable of providing them. Brokers free the clients from having to maintain information on where (i.e., the name and location) of servers. Some types of brokers also have information on the how to obtain particular services.

All applications that belong to a "brokered" environment register their services, their location and client interfaces with the broker. Typically, the broker uses the storage facilities and interfaces of a directory or naming service to hold such information. Services are normally registered dynamically during runtime. They can also dynamically de-register for graceful shutdown of a service. Figure 6.9 shows two different models of mediation.

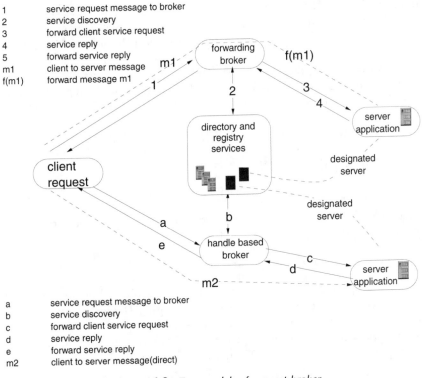

1	service request message to broker
2	service discovery
3	forward client service request
4	service reply
5	forward service reply
m1	client to server message
f(m1)	forward message m1

a	service request message to broker
b	service discovery
c	forward client service request
d	service reply
e	forward service reply
m2	client to server message(direct)

Figure 6.9: *Two models of request broker*

- *Handle-based broker*—Returns to the requester a handle which contains the information, such as name and network address of the server application. The requester uses the received information to contact the server directly.

- *Forwarding broker*—Relays the client applications's service request to a server application, gets the response of the server and relays this reply back to the client. A forwarding broker is capable of hiding the message formatting and semantics of a server application from a requester.

Some brokers can also play a dual role as specified by the requester, and defaults to one of the models. Several commercial brokers are available. Brokers, especially forwarding brokers, provide a central point of control in terms of detecting interactions, logging activity against time, etc.

Forwarding brokers are likely to have performance problems since all client/server traffic goes through them. Handle-based brokers, get over the bottleneck problem, sometimes, by caching handles that are commonly requested.

Process Mapper. This is a dedicated service that allows an implicit service request to be mapped to a number of server applications. If the component services are mutually independent, (and non-blocking communication is possible), then the mapper can invoke the services concurrently.

When there are inter-dependencies between the component services a specific sequence will need to be defined, including the conditions for progression through the sequence. The process mapper exhibits a basic behavior shown in Figure 6.10 and described below:

- Map a client's implicit request into component services and identify the scripts which define the dependencies between the component services. Establish a context or execution record for the specific request.

- Identify the servers that provide each of the application services.

- Execute the script to complete all service requests to the server applications, updating the execution record. Assemble the final results.

- Send a reply to the requesting client.

Process mappers support the anonymous messaging (an arbitrary message is mapped to the component services that process it) and scatter messaging (a client request is dynamically mapped to a set of servers) described in Section 6.4.1.

Process mappers allow the business process to be described centrally through a scripting language. Scripting languages that can be used by non-technical people enhance the use of process mappers.

Separating the flow and control of information flow from the functional logic of an application, de-couples applications that participate in a business process. This allows

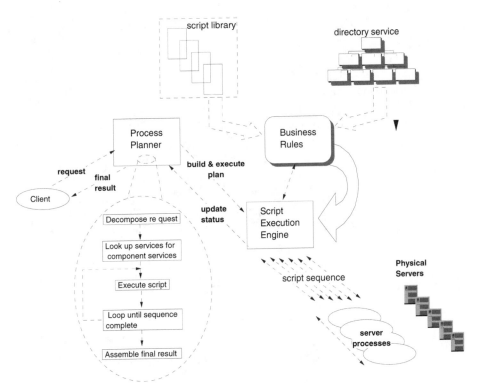

Figure 6.10: *Process mapper function*

changes to be defined in a business process, in the same time-frames as business cycles rather than IT development cycles.

6.5 Intranet Concepts

The architectural components of the intranet and some of the key protocols between them are shown in Figure 6.11. Each component is briefly described below and the protocol components are described in Section 6.5.1:

- *The web server*—A specialized file server that acts as a repository for web documents. The documents that are accessed are usually "hyperlinked pages" of hypertext markup language (HTML). The server manages requests from the browser (clients) for the content of pages. Contents are addressed using a Universal Resource Locator (URL). Each hyperlink in an HTML document points to some place within the same document or points to a resource outside the document.

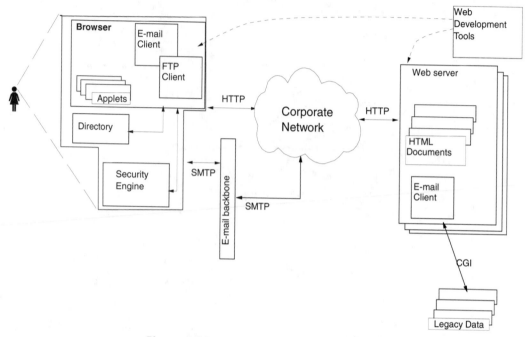

Figure 6.11: *Intranet architecture components*

A hyperlink consists of: (*a*) an anchor (such as text or a graphical element), which triggers the hyperlink when clicked on; (*b*) the Universal Resource Locator (URL) which defines a description of the resource and how to reach it. An absolute URL consists of the protocol, the server name and the path to document. A shorter form called the relative URL is used to reference other documents on the same server as the current document. URL supports protocols other than HTTP allowing resources other than HTML documents to be accessed through other protocols, e.g., FTP, Telnet, etc. URL defines a powerful uniform naming mechanism for accessing almost any type of resource using any type of protocol.

- *Web browser*—The web browser defines the user interface to the web through which the user controls the interaction with the web server and other network resources. The browser uses a referenced URL to get an HTML document from a web server and to display the document to the user in as rich a way as the user interface allows. The browser will render it differently on a character-based terminal than it would on a Motif-based workstation. When a hyperlink is selected by the user the browser uses the URL associated with the hyperlink to start the process again. As URLs can reference resources other than HTML documents, the browser may act as an FTP client, an e-mail client, a Telnet client, etc. as the URL demands. HTML does not contain any native graphics formats. Graphics, audio and other media may be embedded in an HTML page. When a browser client encounters a tag such as an *image* in a page it is rendering for display, it sends another request to the server to download the named image.

- *The directory*—A directory is essentially a specialized, server-based database. Read operations from a client (human or program) exceed writes by many orders of magnitude. Hence the mechanisms for read access are highly optimized. A directory service in the intranet is accessed through a browser-based client. The client uses a protocol such as LDAP. The term directory covers two meanings in the intranet context: (1) As a technology that human clients use (via a user interface) to look up the attributes of a person, user, service, etc. A program can also use the directory for attribute lookup through a directory-access protocol; (2) As a catalog of intellectual assets such as documents, image libraries, video-clips, etc. (Confusingly, however, LDAP can refer to the protocol as described above as well as a type definition of the associated directory.)

- *Web development tools*—Tools to develop, distribute and maintain intranet based applications. These range from (1) authoring tools to create HTML documents from word-processor files; (2) scripting tools to build logic at the browser and server ends; (3) full scale system development environments for web languages such as Java.

6.5.1 Protocols and Interfaces

The protocols and interfaces used in the intranet model are briefly described below:

- *LDAP*—Light Weight Directory Access Protocol—this is a protocol used to access the directory. It is described in Chapter 10, "The Technology of Protocols and Interfaces," Section 10.7.4, as well as Chapter 12, "Tools and Enabling Technologies," Section 12.5.2. (Note that in current usage LDAP can refer to the protocol between a client and a compliant directory as well as describing the associated directory itself.)

- *CGI*—Common Gateway Interface is a standard interface to invoke server-based scripts or applications as a result of client request. The script can be written in any scripting language (e.g., Perl or TCL). Application may be any previously compiled program (e.g., written in "C" or BASIC). Scripts and applications provide "dynamic content" to a document. The CGI itself may be viewed as an engine that is invoked by HTTP every time a client requests a CGI supported service.

- *HTTP*—Hypertext Transfer Protocol is the standard protocol for communication between two parties on the intranet. It defines the four steps in an intranet browser client—web server connection—how the client and server establish a connection, how the client specifies a request to the server, how the server responds to the request and how the client and server disconnect. HTTP is a stateless protocol.

- *HTML*—Hypertext Markup Language is an international standard (maintained by the Internet Engineering Task Force). HTML is the means by which the content of web pages are defined. HTML defines the fundamental mechanisms by which users interact with web documents, navigate through the documents, to other web sites and to other resources anywhere on the network. HTML allows the representation of many kinds of content within the same document, ranging from text in the simplest case, to voice and video clips, to applications of any complexity. The actual display formatting of the document is decided by the web browser which reads the document and the target environment on which it is displayed. HTML documents can be manually authored using any text editor, dynamically defined at runtime by a web server script or converted from other document formats by filters. HTML also allows the building of simple user dialogs through forms and textual input.

- *SSL*—Secure Socket Layer is an open Internet protocol that is layered below HTTP to provide security in the communications channel between the client and the server. SSL provides three services; message encryption (which keeps the message confidential, mutual authentication of client to server and server to client (which verifies the identities of the two parties) and message integrity (which guarantees that the message content and sequence has not been altered).

6.5.2 Scaling the Business Use of the Intranet

The business value of an enterprise-wide infrastructure is increasingly determined by how well it can integrate with the enterprise's "business network" of clients, suppliers, regulatory agencies, professional service providers, etc.

One school of thought says that this will occur only as a set of bilateral relationships using the electronic data interfaces relevant to specific industries such as airlines or functions such as regulatory reporting. Another school of thought favors the more open approach afforded by the global Internet and popularized in the minds of many by the notion of the information highway.

In this publication we favor this latter view, not least because there seems to be widespread acceptance by end-users of Internet mechanisms such as web browsers.

The key to integrating enterprise networks is to make the internal technologies scalable up to Internet scales. While this is technically achievable, in a business sense, two infrastructure services are indispensable components for communications with the wider world.

The first is a Directory service to lookup people or to act as a corporate catalog of information sources and services. The second is a service to enable secure communications with external people. These two services are in fact brought together by the concept of directory services. Directory services are treated in detail in Chapter 12, "Tools and Enabling Technologies," Section 12.5.

6.5.3 Applets and Browser Plug-ins

Browser plug-ins are pre-compiled applications that are installed and configured for an individual browser. (See Figure 6.12.)

Plug-ins may have been developed in any language, since only the complied image is relevant. Plug-ins are likely to be browser and sometimes operating system platform dependent.

Applets, in contrast, are mini-applications downloadable to a browser from a web page. Java is probably the best known of languages specifically designed to develop applet-based software. Java applets are automatically downloaded to a Java enabled browser whenever a visit is made to a web page containing the applet. The applet then gets executed within the browser environment.

Applets are executed on a virtual machine in the browser environment. A virtual machine is a software emulation of a machine architecture for executing the applet language. When a browser encounters an applet tag, it sends a request to download the named applet. The browser then executes it on a virtual machine or compiles the applet and executes it on the native hardware—all within the browser environment.

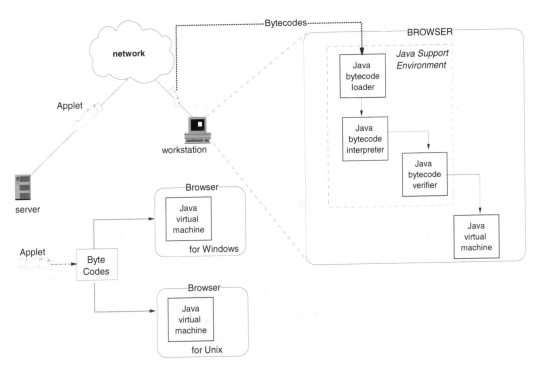

Figure 6.12: *Execution environment for applets*

6.5.4 Deficits with Intranet Server Architecture

As the Intranet becomes an important infrastructure for deploying enterprise-wide applications, the intranet servers need to be scrutinized closely. The web, FTP and e-mail services field the vast majority of service requests from clients on an intranet-based infrastructure.

Operating systems used in servers, such as Unix and Microsoft NT were originally designed to support only up to a few hundred simultaneous users. These operating systems timeshare the computing resources so that multiple connections from users can be supported at the same time.

Timesharing in this instance works under the premise that a user will use the processor cycles and other allocated resources for a long enough period to justify the cost of switching between connections.

This premise however does not hold for intranet service like the web. A typical session between a browser and a server involves retrieving a set of pages. Figure 6.13 shows a train of requests from a browser resulting in a train of responses from the "originating" server or its cache. In all events the connection is broken after the session is completed.

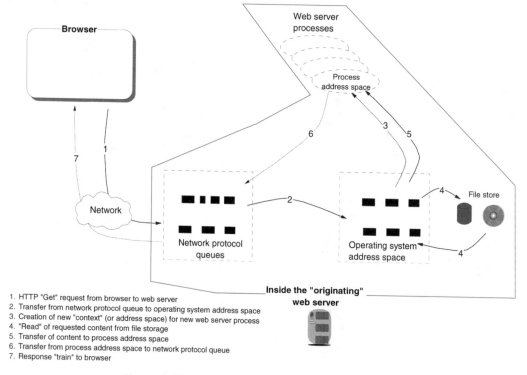

1. HTTP "Get" request from browser to web server
2. Transfer from network protocol queue to operating system address space
3. Creation of new "context" (or address space) for new web server process
4. "Read" of requested content from file storage
5. Transfer of content to process address space
6. Transfer from process address space to network protocol queue
7. Response "train" to browser

Figure 6.13: *Lifecycle of a browser to web-server session*

Browser connections are numerous but last for brief periods of time. During the lifetime of an HTTP connection the processing resources are for getting a single request and generating a response, which usually involves moving a file to or from the machine.

While the processing required is low, the operating system still has to spend time context switching from the previous connection. This involves cleaning up after the last process, allocation of an address space and manipulation of control tables to define a new, unique process. Context switches can run into thousands of machine instructions. The time it takes to context switch is longer than the lifetime of the process.

As memory gets used up by individual address spaces, the operating system begins to swap out, or page, process address blocks to disk to make room for new connections. Paging can bring server functions to a halt as application protocols time-out waiting for a response from the server.

Some versions of Unix support a concept of lightweight processes known as "threads." This allows multiple activities within a single process and a single address space. Threads though lightweight compared to processes, still require operating system overhead to switch. The time taken to switch threads is comparable to the lifetime of the thread, hence it does not offer much benefit.

The server is overloaded when the thresholds for number of processes, number of sockets or number of open files is reached. These are operating system level configuration parameters, however, each operating system has its own scaleability guidelines for such parameters.

6.6 Intranet and Selected Application Areas

As described in Chapter 1, one of the main reasons users abandoned the centralized IT department for localized client/server application development was the IT department's perceived unresponsiveness to changing business requirements.

The rate of change of business requirements has accelerated in the meantime. Client/server application groups adopted a model of incremental delivery to cope with the new cycle of business change. It turns out that six monthly or even three monthly increments may not be enough.

Businesses find that there are small but useful additions to applications that significantly add tactical value to the application—especially within a real business process. Such add-ons however have little payback for mainstream client/server development groups who therefore prioritize—e.g., on the basis of maximum benefit.

Several organizations have found that another tier of development using intranet development tools can provide many useful small applications both quickly and at low cost. These applications sometimes revolutionize the way their users work and should be viewed more in terms of IT being ubiquitous to a business environment.

The intranet architecture is particularly suited to re-engineering the delivery of several types of business applications commonly found in most enterprises. We look at three such selected areas—*document management, decision support and data entry* and *data warehousing*.

6.6.1 Intranet Based "Value Adds" in Selected Application Areas

Document Management. The most common use of the intranet is as a document repository. The web server is especially suited to storing documents that hold the intellectual capital of an organization. A network of web servers scale to hold the intellectual capital of individuals to workgroup to departments to a whole corporation.

While web servers form ideal repository mechanisms, the browser is an ideal environment to develop search, retrieval and display engines into the repository mechanism. These engines can also be specialized with minimum effort to suit the needs of specific practices or processes within an enterprise.

Material that forms intellectual capital often requires security features for the contributors of this capital to feel comfortable. Existing hardcopy and "softcopy" documents can relatively easily be converted to the new document structure suitable for web storage. Enlacement can be made which, for example, allows specific parts to be viewable only when a certain cryptographic key is used, or users may need certain access rights to see certain types of documents.

Many tools exist to convert existing word processed documents into web pages. Using the intranet to manage intellectual capital however needs to be approached from a project perspective with specific goals, timescale budgets and payback periods.

Decision Support and Data Entry. Another class of application, with a "natural affinity" with the intranet architecture, is found in the area of decision support. Here the browser is an ideal interface for humans to specify queries and to display most forms of returned data. In addition, the browser can be easily "connected" to e-mail, spreadsheets, word processors and presentation tools. This allows a form of application integration that leverage existing investments in office automation technology.

Use of the web is particularly attractive when a workgroup or department has a significant mobile population. The ability to access information regardless of a person's location is a powerful concept. For example, allowing all staff to participate in daily events at key locations.

Detractors point that the speed of access is relatively slow. This is however far outweighed by the fact that the solution is "open," has a "skinny" client end (i.e., the browser) which can be accommodated on almost all existing laptop platforms.

Data entry, via a browser-based front end (using forms and point-and-click widgets), is another general class of applications suited to intranet technology. Browser scripting languages allow small applications to be built for formatting and validation of input. Validation is often driven using the relevant business "rules," and usually change over time. These applications and the rules need only be downloaded from the web server on connection for a data entry "session." This ensures that all accessing users work to the latest set of rules.

The browser and the web also offer a means of modernizing the front end of existing decision and data entry applications, without re-writing the whole application or staging the data in relational databases.

Several projects have shown that upgrading the front end helps increase end-user productivity without taking any of the risks in re-engineering the application or data. Figure 6.14 shows two common ways in which the intranet connects to legacy environments.

Data Warehousing. The development of client/server computing at the departmental level created databases that were literally groaning with operational data. Converting islands of operational data into useful information, and the distribution of this information to decision-makers are the two underlying concepts of data warehousing.

Data warehousing is a technology used to hold historical data—organized by business dimensions. The number of dimensions can sometimes run into hundreds. Each warehouse summarizes data in each dimension in a time series.

State of the art in data warehousing allows the historical data to remain current in "almost real-time"—through automation of the collection and entry of the raw data into the warehouse. Delivery of the information in a data warehouse to decision-makers throughout a large organization, however, is expensive. Costs associated with developing the analytical cli-

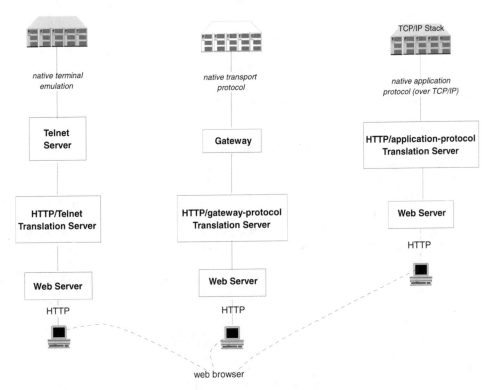

Figure 6.14: *Connecting to legacy environments*

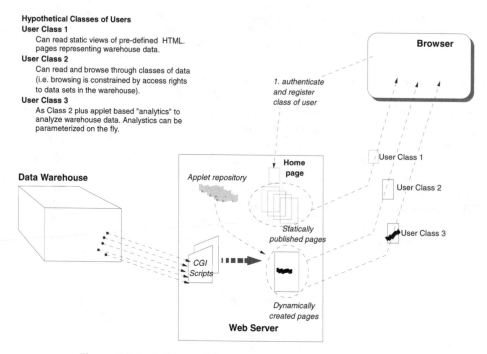

Figure 6.15: *Delivering different data views to different user classes*

ent software, its distribution with changing business conditions, training, etc. add up to significant support costs.

The intranet offers a method of lowering the cost of distribution as well as the ability to view the data using generic office tools such as spreadsheets and presentation graphics. Another advantage is that the intranet allows multimedia content to be integrated to the structured data from a data warehouse. See the case study in Figure 6.15, which shows how intranet web pages deliver different levels of analytical data from the warehouse to different management layers.

Another capability contributed by the intranet is the ability to collaborate in decision-making through web-based discussion tools.

6.6.2 Intranet in the Client/Server Application Development

Many in the computing industry view the intranet as having a unique part to play in new client/server application architecture. A key architectural property of the intranet is that it is highly scalable from an application architecture perspective. Application functionality can be partitioned within the Intranet components as follows:

- At the web server through specializing for a specific application or a specific sub-function of an application. Hence several web servers may support a single application. Alternatively, web servers can be made to load balance for any of the applications functions being supported.

- Functionality can also be partitioned between the browser and the web server. In the browser, computation and control flow can be embedded using applet or plug-ins. New display components are needed to display new types of data.

At the web server, scripts are one of the means of developing server-side functionality. Languages such as Java also allow server-side logic to be built to communicate with client-side applets. This is described in Chapter 12, "Tools and Enabling Technologies," Section 12.7. The web protocols are transparent to the type of data it carries. Support of new types of data is straightforward.

The second architectural property of the intranet is its ability to integrate data from multiple sources. A fact of life in client/server based application development is that a "big bang" delivery approach is unlikely to be viable for any large application. More often application functionality is delivered incrementally. Hence, often the data for use by a client/server application at some stage of its delivery cycle is resident on one or more systems that is "incompatible" with the client/server platform.

A part of a client/server applications functionality may be to "blend" data from multiple sources and of multiple types for delivery to the client. Depending on the volume of data that needs integrating and its frequency, data integration can occur at the client or server end.

The data, regardless of origin and regardless of the processing it has undergone, is available through the single browser interface. Using a browser as an application environment allows client-side integration of multiple data sources. Figure 6.16 shows use of intranet components to enable the integration at the server. Examples of different data sources include relational databases, object-oriented databases and network file system (NFS) files.

6.6.3 The Intranet's Relationship to Client/Server Models

The web model of client/server application is a client which can download varying parts of the client logic from the web. The browser is an execution environment for the downloaded logic. The logic executed in the client therefore varies from that of a "thin" client to that of a "fat" client. The browser may act as a thin client for one protocol and as a fat client for another protocol.

"Gut reaction" by some packaged client/server application vendors has resulted in a class of web-enabled "fat-clients." The evolutionary model for these clients is unclear.

By a similar token the web server takes on different "shapes" for different applications. The availability of languages such as Java which allow server and client resident application is still very new. It is too early to say how their performance will scale.

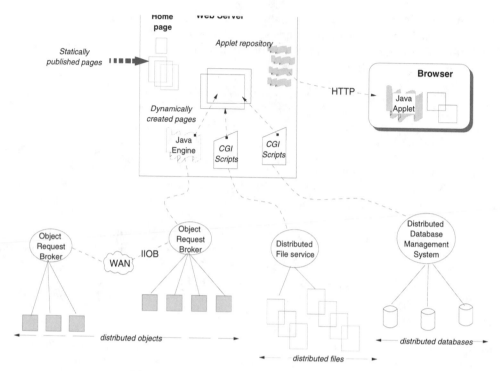

Figure 6.16: *Intranet in a "data integrator" role*

6.6.4 Issues in Intranet-Based Infrastructures

The use of intranet in delivering applications is still very new. Many of the current issues are related to the technology deficits. The following are some of the major areas of concern. Advances are occurring in both protocol development and products to fix many of these problems:

- *Availability of web resources.* There is currently little defense against a web server becoming unavailable. Infrastructure-level solutions such as clustering, RAID, and mirroring are possible. The operational viability of such solutions with the intranet protocols is currently not widely understood.

- *Performance of web services.* This is limited due to the way HTTP works at a very small transaction level which have very short lifetimes. Current operating systems such as Unix and NT used to realize web services are inadequate for supporting high rates of access from clients. Access is generally slow. The utility and availability of the information has overridden concerns such as speed until now. However, web-based infrastructures cannot compete with conventional client/server infrastructures.

- *Administration.* The management of resources that have a major impact on the business requires to be approached from a different perspective to that of non-critical use. Roles such as web-masters currently are ad hoc and need to be subjected to work within the roles and responsibilities of more conventional infrastructure management disciplines. Any enterprise investing in intranet-based infrastructures needs to define explicitly the operational policies for its conduct. It should not be left to the mercies of a "web-master."

- *Change control.* The responsibility for changing the contents of the web pages, managing access rights to web contents, quality assurance, web development methodology, piloting applets before release into an enterprise may be considered by the experts in the field to be far too conventional a view. While the document and network-centric models of the intranet is new, safety practices still need to apply if any part of the business is dependent on it. The change management process is the key in intranet administration and may have to be specially modified for the intranet's administration.

- *Scaling the intranet.* Other than duplication there is a severe limitation to the scaling of the intranet's resources. The problems of reliable software distribution to geographically distributed servers is a major administrative burden and new process steps may have to be developed in the change-management process.

6.7 Network Considerations in Client/Server and Intranet Development

Network performance has the biggest impact on user perception of how well the infrastructure is managed. *Variance* in performance is probably more damaging than a slow network which is still working above the expectation threshold.

The relationship between network engineering and software development groups is often limited by the lack of a common language. Application requirements of the network are rarely specified and therefore rarely understood by network engineering groups. Network groups often get involved just before, or more often as applications enter their final cycles of testing.

In far too many enterprises the first indication of a deployment is when some associated change request is received. Here we look in detail at the role of the network in support of deploying client/server applications.

6.7.1 Key Network Performance Characteristics

Since infrastructure management is to a significant extent about managing LANs and WANs, it is useful to characterize these managed structures in terms of performance.

The primary metrics of interest (in a LAN viewed as an application delivery system) are latency, bandwidth and ability to handle burstiness in application traffic. With client/server architectures these metrics have to be derived from more basic metrics.

Metrics with greatest impact on the WAN are more qualitative—security, type of the links, delay and bandwidth properties of links and routing topology are some examples of note. The basic metrics applicable to networks and systems is briefly defined below:

- **Response time** is the interval between a request by a user or a system of a system and the response. To be more precise, however, it is the interval between the end of a request submission and the end of the corresponding response. The time between submission of a request and the beginning of the execution to provide a response is called the *reaction* time—this is however possible to measure only if there is instrumentation with access to internals of the system. The response time of a system increases as the load on the system increases.

- **Throughput** is the rate at which requests can be serviced by the system. The throughput of a system generally increases as the load on the system increases. After a certain load however the throughput stops increasing and then generally deteriorates. The bandwidth of a system defines the maximum achievable throughput under an ideal workload. In some cases the response time at maximum throughput is too high. Hence of more use is the usable bandwidth of a system—which is a throughput value delimited by a response time. The ratio of the usable bandwidth to nominal bandwidth is called efficiency.

- **Utilization** is the ratio of time that a resource is busy servicing requests against the elapsed time over the measured period. The not-busy period in the elapsed time is called the idle time.

The *service type* of a performance metric determines the ideal values for the metric in a system. The three common service types and examples are described below:

- *Higher is better*—Throughput is an example of the higher the throughput value the more it is valued. (Low throughput is a sign of poor performance.)

- *Lower is better*—Response time is an example where the lower the value the better it is. (High response time is equivalent to poor performance.)

- *Nominal is best*—Utilization is an example of a metric where the middle ground is preferred. (High utilization tends to increase response time while low utilization indicates non-usage.)

6.7.2 Application Characteristics Affecting Management

While performance metrics such as response time may be used in defining service-level agreements with user or by users in describing problems, the causes of performance problems are sometimes difficult to isolate.

One of the reasons for this is that network engineers rarely have a grounding in the ways that application designers (especially of client/server and distributed systems) end up using the network. Application designers for their part by and large assume that there will be adequate capability in the network for their needs. Hence traffic analysis is rarely undertaken as part of the application's design methodology.

Latency in the LAN. In client/server computing, server-based application services are sensitive to latency. The greater the latency, the less efficient these services are as networks provide less opportunity for the server to output at its designed maximum throughput. The greater the variance in latency, the greater the probability that there will be performance problems—as dependency chains in distributed services "stretch." Common examples of such services include (see Section 6.4.1):

- Subscriber/publisher service which distributes (publishes) events to clients that have subscribed to the specific information.

- "Scatter" processing manager service which parcels out work onto unused client machines, collecting and collating the results generated.

Such servers require points on the network topology that *guarantee* (a) low latency (independent of load on the LAN); (b) a narrow variance between minimum and maximum. Without such guarantees client/server applications can display intermittent performance problems.

Network management (specifically the planning and design function) should establish the best case (theoretical) and worst case (design center) for latency that may be experienced by a server at each point of deployment on the network.

Bandwidth classes in the LAN. With current network technology it is possible to have a range of bandwidth options available within a local topology. A bandwidth hierarchy is a useful concept to adopt in evaluating LAN topologies.

- Define the range of bandwidth available to a server on a per deployment point basis.

- Is there a discernible backbone in the topology? If so, what technology base is used to realize it?

- For shared media technology (such as Ethernet) the number of shared segments and minimum/maximum users supported per segment, architecture of the hub technology used.

- Are there switched connections for end-users? If so, what technology and architecture are relevant?

Ability to handle burstiness. Distributed computing is built on the principle of *divide and conquer*—which means that a number of (distributed) services cooperate in order to deliver a primary business service to the end-user. This is called a service-dependency chain. This chain has to be able to handle some "design center" value of peak of throughput. This peak value maps onto a physical network, and means the network has to be able to handle the associated traffic.

- Peak throughputs defined at end-user sources and "sinks" of the network shed little light on bursts of traffic that occur at the associated points within the service dependency chain inside the network. A key function of the network management design and planning function is to understand how well a LAN meets the demands of applications to be deployed over it.

- A key characteristic of modern development methodologies for client/server systems is that the functionality is incrementally delivered. With each increment the requirements on the physical network change. Cumulatively, several increments can suddenly introduce failure modes, sometimes when parts of the network suddenly become bottlenecks, sometimes when latency requirements can no longer be met.

A LAN's ability to handle bursts of application level traffic is related to whether it can make latency and bandwidth guarantees.

6.7.3 Client/Server Network Traffic Profiles

Bandwidth over-engineering is one tactic that is commonly executed by network groups undertaking an upgrade of the network levels of the infrastructure to deploy the client/server applications. The reason this tactic has worked is because network bandwidth is critical to the current generation of clint/server applications. These applications are based on the two-tier (desktop machine and database server) or the three-tier model (desktop machine, database servers and mainframe).

Figure 6.17 shows why increased bandwidth can be used by more powerful workstations and servers. One point to note is that as network media is upgraded, the bandwidth (or throughput) of connecting components such as routers and switches also need to be considered.

When client/server applications are distributed across many more than two machines, increasing bandwidth provides little additional benefit. This is because a single message originating from say a client-end results in many other messages being generated. The various types of delays add up to slowing down a roundtrip of a request-response cycle.

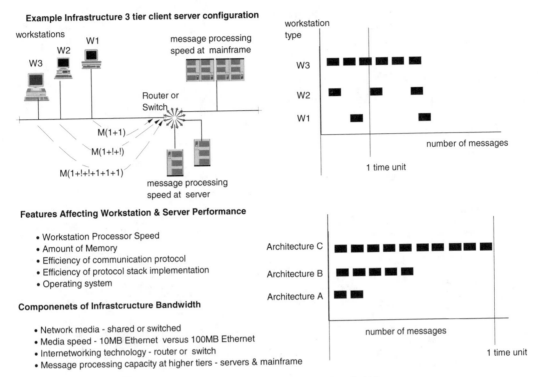

Example Infrastructure 3 tier client server configuration

workstations

message processing speed at mainframe

Router or Switch

M(1+1)

M(1+!+!)

M(1+!+!+1+1+1)

message processing speed at server

workstation type

number of messages

1 time unit

Features Affecting Workstation & Server Performance

- Workstation Processor Speed
- Amount of Memory
- Efficiency of communication protocol
- Efficiency of protocol stack implementation
- Operating system

Componenets of Infrastcructure Bandwidth

- Network media - shared or switched
- Media speed - 10MB Ethernet versus 100MB Ethernet
- Internetworking technology - router or switch
- Message processing capacity at higher tiers - servers & mainframe

Architecture C

Architecture B

Architecture A

number of messages

1 time unit

Figure 6.17: *Machine power versus bandwidth use*

This is called latency and is a major concern in the network architecture to suit distributed applications. An existing architecture or any infrastructure technology contributing to latency will need re-work before any significant deployment of distributed applications can take place.

Figure 6.18 shows the partial infrastructure for a distributed application—consisting of a number of cooperating applications servers: A workstation sends out a single request message to a server. This results in a series of message exchanges between the servers associated with the processing of the request. A response is finally received at the workstation. The components of the round trip time for the request-response is shown.

High performance machines can generate packets at higher rates. If several of such machines are on a shared network media then the utilization of the network media will increase. Architecture should consider the use of switches and also how to distribute the placement of the machines on the network.

If an application is distributed across multiple servers, then latency is the key factor to control in the infrastructure's architecture. Several network building blocks such as routers

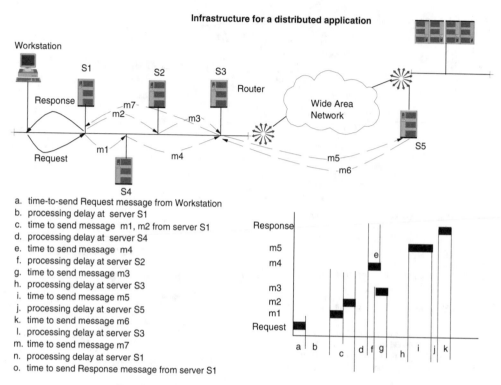

a. time-to-send Request message from Workstation
b. processing delay at server S1
c. time to send message m1, m2 from server S1
d. processing delay at server S4
e. time to send message m4
f. processing delay at server S2
g. time to send message m3
h. processing delay at server S3
i. time to send message m5
j. processing delay at server S5
k. time to send message m6
l. processing delay at server S3
m. time to send message m7
n. processing delay at server S1
o. time to send Response message from server S1

Figure 6.18: *Secondary message sequence generation*

and switches that need to convert between one media format to another add to the latency problems. The time to send a packet between two points is determined by the speed of light. In a global application deployment scenario the distance between cooperating servers is a common cause for slow responses.

Case Study 6.2 shows the consequences of not fully understanding the service requirements of a distributed application. Latency-like effects can be created.

6.7.4 Components of Latency at the Network Level

Latency experienced by a client/server application is in part contributed by the network. Latency consists of the following types of delay:

Insertion delay. This is the delay experienced by a device that has a packet to put onto a link. If the link is "unable" to accept the packet at the precise instant required, then the machine has to wait until the link can accept the packet. When the link is able, the speed at which the

Case Study 6.2: Mismatch Between Use of a Common Service and its Topological Position

A European insurance company re-engineered its local area networks to a new corporate standard. The main rationale was the migration of its IT infrastructure to Microsoft NT. The applications to be run included the Microsoft Office application suite, a number of packaged applications, a terminal emulator for access to its mainframe, in-house developed Customer Relationship Management and Underwriting Risk Management applications. The basic network architecture is shown below: Key characteristics are a single level FDDI backbone for servers, a collapsed router backbone connecting subnets of 20 users via a standard Ethernet hub.

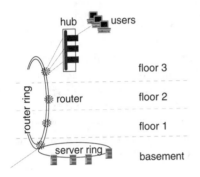

FDDI was chosen for sound business reasons: Mature technology, minimal premium on card and media costs, ready availability of expertise, manageability, high bandwidth. Two events occurred:

- The risk management application designers chose to develop a n-tier client/server model which resulted in a number of NT application servers distributed at the workgroup and corporate levels.
- One of the main package vendors sold a client/server version which also shared some of the servers with the risk management application.

The servers all ended up on the FDDI server backbone. As more users were migrated to the new environment, response time became noticeably slower. Several solutions were tried, including a faster router and multiple FDDI segments off a router - both of which gave some relief. The trend of a gradually slowing network continued. Empirical analysis showed that an infrastructure server on the ring was being hit with bursts of requests from all workstations. The server had the capacity, but due to the collapsed backbone and shared medium architecture, and the server position, it could not service the requests fast enough. Consequently one of the in-house developed application protocols reset itself in reaction to the low throughput. The choice was then one of changing the backbone architecture or changing the loading on the server.

packet can be put onto the medium is determined by the bandwidth of the link (the slower the link, the longer it takes to transmit the packet).

Links may be logical such as LANS and public Frame Relay Services or are "real" such as a leased line between two cities. If the device is a workstation or a server then it is likely to be connected to a LAN medium such as Ethernet or Token Ring. If the device is a router then the link is a LAN or a WAN.

If a shared media LAN technology is used, then the utilization of the medium determines the wait that a station has before it can insert a packet onto the LAN. If switched LAN technology is used then insertion may be a problem in a different way:

While the switch may accept a packet from the station, the packet may subsequently get dropped internally due to sudden and unsustainable demand for switch resources (such as memory and CPU cycles).

A second phenomenon of internally dropped packets occurs if many senders send packets to a single destination station. In this case the packets may get dropped from outgoing queue waiting to be collected by that station.

In both cases the packet has to be re-inserted by the originating station Dropping packets, after acceptance by a network device, has drastic performance consequences in a client/server setup.

- **Propagation delay** is determined by the physics of propagation of light and radio waves. Hence the longer the distance between the source of the packet (its sender) and the destination, the longer the propagation delay. This applies to both real and logical links.

- **Roundtrip delay** has two propagation delay components—one on the outgoing and the second on return. The roundtrip delay of a terrestrial circuit is at least 100 milliseconds for a 5,000 miles circuit, regardless of bandwidth. The propagation over a satellite is in the order of 500 milliseconds. When high bandwidth medium is used between two machines separated by a large distance, the only way to use the bandwidth effectively is to keep the "pipe" full. The higher level protocols (usually at the transport or application layers) need to be windowed, i.e., the window determines how many packets may be in "flight" and the maximum number of packets before an acknowledgment needs to be received from the receiving end.

- **Queueing delay.** Queueing delay is the delay experienced by a packet within a network device that internally queues packets till outbound links can accept the packet. Queuing is possible in routers as well as switches. Queuing in networking devices occurs due to congestion. Congestion is triggered by peaks of demand that are beyond the throughput of the network device (or within a "chain" of interconnected devices forming a path for a packet). When the peaks are short-lived, internal buffering provides the necessary elasticity. When congestion is sustained for a characteristic period (depending on the packet structure and actual buffer resources of the device), packets get dropped.

- **Processing delay.** Processing delay is the delay experienced by a packet as it is processed within a network device—specifically as a packet is moved from the input ports to the output port. Different device architectures have different philosophies on how to scale processing power—ranging from a plug-in of a family of increasingly powerful processors to modular and multiple processors.

6.7.5 WAN Characteristics Affecting Management

The global nature of many businesses means that a single business application may be deployed on a global basis. In many cases some aspect of the business such as profit and loss accounting may be done at one central location for the whole business. Other businesses may by their very nature be global—such as investment management.

The wide area network is therefore an integral part of business delivery. There are however fundamental differences between managing the wide area and local area parts of a *business delivery* network. The fundamental discontinuity is in:

- *The ownership of WAN resources*—Key questions are based on which organizational unit controls and owns it, how politically transparent is it, are public data services used, and if so, are the end-to-end contingencies for service failure adequate?

- *Connection bandwidth*—Key questions include whether the application is designed for global deployment, are infrastructure sizing, cost and service limits at the remote offices understood, are there discontinuities of performance, and if so, is it accepted by the users?

- *Propagation distance*—Key questions include whether the application is split at the right places, does the split affect the modularity of management, what are the configuration issues, what are the issues for normal maintenance?

Together these discontinuities conspire to make the client/server application delivery over an enterprise highly problematic. A key consequence of the discontinuity of resource ownership is that very few enterprises are sufficiently mature to have the same management policy applied across the globe.

Most remote offices involve some external infrastructure service agency which is given responsibility for application delivery. The degree of control or influence over the conduct of such an agency is important.

Connection bandwidth is between two to three decimal orders less in the WAN connection than in LAN "connections." Round trip delays play a significant part in slowing application performance. When non-windowed protocols are used (at the application level), performance is seen as a major problem.

Security in WAN Connection Management. Remote offices of global enterprises will (a) will have a suitable group of staff capable of taking on management responsibilities, (b) not have technically able staff, or (c) the service is outsourced at the remote site. The main management group responsible for application delivery needs to have solutions for the following basic security issues:

- *Management domains*—in terms of precisely who is responsible for each function and what equipment the multiple groups control. This is the pre-cursor to defining variants of network management processes such as change and fault management for remote offices. When changes are done at the WAN level, strict quality controls are needed to ensure that security holes have not been left open.

- *Topology change coordination*—in terms of how does the cooperation of multiple sites get coordinated for different infrastructure management processes. Some of the key processes this affects are fault and change management, any large-scale cross-office rollouts of client/server applications.

- *Security policies for reconfiguration*—Consider the case where an autonomous management domain accidently or maliciously alters routing level parameters that end up affecting the flow of information outside the domain. Most management protocols and systems are based on insecure control mechanisms. For example, in the case of SNMP, most network managers turn off the SET function so that inadvertent changes cannot be made. Architecture of a two-level router or switch backbone helps to identify which tier is which group's responsibility.

- *Defenses to stop virus propagation*—Viruses cross WAN links just as easily as within local networks. With the advent of intranets the opportunities for propagation of viruses has increased considerably. Business critical systems should be kept within internal firewalls. At the firewall, virus and protocol checkpoints can be built. Viruses can however be transported by being piggy-backed over legitimate traffic. E-mail and other types of traffic from the external world should in general always pass through a firewall.

- *Confidentiality of data*—Crossing international boundaries with confidential business data is already a well-known problem. Many organizations encrypt such cross-country traffic as a matter of course. The interception of commercial data for product, economic and market intelligence gathering by national agencies is not just fiction.

- *Authentication of remote accessors of data*—A mobile workforce inevitably leads to requirements to access data sources and for use of e-mail and other connection services. All users of corporate resources should be subject to strong authentication. A major problem in client/server environments is authentication of remote servers to corporate server access.

WAN Network Structure. The structure of the WAN can determine the feasibility of deploying some client/server architectures over the WAN. A WAN is essentially built from leased lines or by accessing public-switched services.

Client/server applications are normally very sensitive to latency as discussed in Section 6.7.4. Many of the current public switched services such as public frame relay are prone to latency problems. There is also no guarantee of the bandwidth if a client/server component generates bursty traffic. Client/server application designers rarely design the application protocol from the viewpoint of having to recover from data loss incurred by "lower" communication layers. LAN-based connectivity is by and large reliable.

Leased lines provide better latency characteristics although the bandwidth is still limited by cost in many parts of the world. Service providers continue to exploit their monopolistic markets. Public-switched services on the other hand are cost effective, especially as service providers try to encourage the move away from leased lines.

WAN delay and bandwidth is made worse by the overheads of network monitoring, unless controlled SNMP type monitoring can use significant amounts of bandwidth.

Most TCP/IP based global networks are built using routers. Routers have several roles to play as an enterprise backbone technology. The mixing and matching of routers from different vendors is, however, not to be recommended. If "all" parts of an enterprise need to be connected, but use different router vendors, a major investment is to re-engineer the router backbone to use a common router family.

Managing a router backbone is complex, and without the consistency of components and configurations, geographically distributed teams cannot manage such a backbone.

6.7.6 Fractal Nature of Client/Server Traffic

The discovery, around 1993, that network traffic has "self-similar" or fractal properties has a major impact on the way networks are designed and deployed for high performance client/server applications.

Self-similarity means that the statistical properties at a time range of milliseconds, seconds, minutes, hours, days, weeks and beyond are all broadly similar. Self-similarity appears not only in Ethernet traffic, the original subject of the discovery, but also in web traffic, traffic relating to distributed objects, ATM traffic and network management traffic (under certain configurations).

The implications of self-similarity are that network designs have to cope with sudden surges of traffic. Moreover these surges tend to occur in waves.

Observed from inside a switching device, there are relatively long periods of inactivity or nominal activity followed by a heavy surge on a majority of the ports. Before internal-buffering schemes can clear the backlog, another period of peak activity occurs.

Switches in conjunction with high input/output, (I/O), performance workstations or PCs connected to them conspire to induce the conditions for this kind of wave phenomenon.

The bottom line is that not only do client/server application architects need to communicate how distributed resources are used, but network architecture has to be taken seriously. Network architects need to be more conservative in their assumptions about switch-based network performance.

By understanding the roles and functions of distributed resources in a client/server application, a network architect can map designs to cope with the clustering of traffic peaks.

Clusters themselves tend to cluster as the time range is increased and as the client/server stack is traversed. Application architects need to be aware of this phenomena when deploying client/server applications globally where "natural" bottlenecks will exaggerate the duration of peaks. Hence server deployment strategies are often affected.

6.8 Books for Further Reading

Berson, Alex, *et al. Sybase and Client/Server Computing.* McGraw Hill, 1995.

Corbin, John R. *The Art of Distributed Applications* (Programming Techniques for Remote Procedure Calls). Springer Verlag, 1991.

Coulouris, George, *et al. Distributed Systems* (Concepts and Design). Addison Wesley, 1994.

McGovern, D., *et al. A Guide to Sybase and SQL Server.* Addison Wesley, 1992.

Minoli, Daniel, *et al. Client/Server Applications on ATM Networks.* Manning Publications Co., 1996.

Tsai, Thomas C. *A Network of Objects* (How to Lower Your Computing Costs and Improve Your Applications Delivery). Van Nostrand Reinhold, 1995.

7

Architecture Solutions for Infrastructure Management

Areas covered in this chapter

- Use of architecture in a discipline for developing infrastructure management solutions

- Common technology and product deficits in developing infrastructure management on an enterprise scale

- Key complexity factors in deploying client/server systems

- Looking at high-availability solutions from an architectural perspective

- Looking at security solutions from an architectural perspective

- Model for identification and classification of events in an infrastructure

- Visualization of events for infrastructure management

Architecture, viewed in high-level terms, provides the glue to fit together technology, process and people aspects. If infrastructure management is viewed as a service business, then architecture plays the following roles:

- There are major deficits in the technology available for infrastructure management—especially when viewed from the perspective of a global or enterprise-wide scale. The role of architecture in this scenario is to provide solutions for this shortfall. Architected solutions often involve technology elements as well as organizational and process elements.

- Different areas of infrastructure management technology are changing and evolving at different rates. The role of architecture is to allow explicit separation of the technologies that are strategic to infrastructure management from technological features that are assimilated, when available. Again, change at any level of technology often affects organizational and process aspects

- Technology vendors are clearly in the business of making money, while consumers of the technology want cost-effectiveness and proven value for money. Vendor-defined solutions are often too expensive, especially viewed from the perspective of the technology's life-cycle. The true cost of ownership often becomes apparent well after the buy decision. Architecture can show the relationship of the process and people aspects to the technology and hence allow better models of ownership to be built.

Each enterprise involved in managing client/server infrastructures should have a clear roadmap of what and how it is going to achieve its goals. Architectural abstractions or models provide the tools to develop this roadmap independently of vendor-marketing visions and products.

Chapter 6 looked at the nature of client/server and intranet systems and issues that arise in the use of an infrastructure to support client/server applications. In this chapter we look more closely at the nature of the client/server infrastructure. Architecture is also re-visited in Chapter 8 to define the frameworks for key areas of infrastructure management where technology deficits are apparent. These frameworks are essentially prototypes for enterprise architectures in monitoring, control, remote access, etc.

7.1 Scoping Architecture Solutions

High-level decisions in developing an enterprise-wide management architecture include the following:

- The choice of platform vendor(s) with whom to establish "strategic" relationships. By implication this defines the management platform to form the *enterprise standard* for some time into the future. In the event of multiple existing platforms a plan is required to migrate to the standard without reducing the service provided by each platform in its current role. The role of platforms in managing infrastructures is currently under a state of rapid evolution due to the possibilities offered by web technology.

- Two philosophical issues related to platform choice are first, whether a single vendor should supply most or all infrastructure management needs versus whether best-of-breed systems should be integrated. The second issue is whether for integration of best-of-breed systems, external vendors should supply the integration technology or whether in-house architecture and software development should drive the integration.

- Bringing the roles and benefits of infrastructure management into the perception of the business users. The adequacy of the infrastructure to be considered before business solutions can be reliably delivered. Application development often gets the attention of the business due to its direct impact in running the business. The post-delivery part of the application's life-cycle is rarely understood, even by application developers.

- Recognition of infrastructure management as a mission-critical function within the organization and planning investment. Engineering an infrastructure management environment capable of supporting client/server applications within a mature framework involving resilience, service guarantees, contingency plans and so on requires talented people, resources and time.

- Choice of software tools and the methods for acquiring software for the management environment. Until recently, only organizations with deep pockets could afford to develop their own management applications. the power of web technology has opened up a new economics for software development.

- Inevitably, there are politics in defining a global infrastructure management organization. The constituent domains, organizational responsibilities, scaling within domain, topology where management servers are to be sited, the architecture for management servers to communicate are all subject to politics.

- Development and global agreement on key metrics for quality of service for infrastructure management. How to gather, process, store and distribute these. How to define and review baseline thresholds for metrics.

Table 7.1 shows the areas covered in this publication by architected solutions. These are common areas of engineering that are needed to manage a large client/server infrastructure. All the solutions involving frameworks are treated in Chapter 8.

Table 7.1: Deficit Areas Covered by Architecture

Architecture Area	Why It Is Considered
High availability. Refers to the ability for the client/server infrastructure and its management frameworks to be as close to 100% available. A mixture of physical redundancy and logical resilience mechanisms are used to guarantee access under different failure scenarios.	Client/server computing is used in building management frameworks. The model is inherently fault probable and failure of critical components such as servers and databases in the framework can lead to critical events being missed in the managed environment. High-availability solutions architected for the management framework are applicable generally for any client/server application.
Visualization. Refers to the ability to filter useful information from a "sea of events" and present the information using visual mechanisms. Humans have a massively developed visual cortex, which if presented with appropriate images can diagnose and process at higher speeds than logical reasoning. Maps are the commonest method of presenting relationships.	The client/server environment is dispersed across platforms as well as geographically across locations. Each event needs to be understood within the context of its impact or relevance rather than as an isolated occurrence. This understanding has to occur speedily to be of use in managing a potential crisis.
Security. Refers to a set of policies and mechanisms to ensure that the management framework itself is not usable to subvert the managed environment.	The degree of "coupling" required between the management framework and managed environment introduces new threats from the former. This is exacerbated by the extent of the client/server environment.
Event classification. Refers firstly to an exercise in classifying events relative to an enterprise's infrastructure and other resource deployment. The events are likely to be of diverse structure and from disparate sources. Secondly, when an environment is in failure, large numbers of events are generated. A classification of which events cause secondary events helps event-filtering software to zoom into primary causes.	As more and more of the client/server environment gets instrumented with management agents, there are potentially tens of thousands of different events. While prioritizing these in terms of impact to the managed environment is a first step, to be useful contextual relationship between events need to be computable as they occur.
Monitoring framework. Refers to a framework for monitoring events from a variety of sources that make up the client/server environment. Given the numbers involved, this has to be done economically. The events themselves may refer to different functional areas of management—the key ones being faults, performance thresholds being breached, and security conditions.	Client/server environments with thousands of dispersed agents cannot be controlled centrally. A scaling component needs to be introduced. As the managed environments often support global business operations, 7 x 24-hour monitoring is required. To achieve this at least, people cost is often a corporate goal. Hence scaling involves number of agents, number of operators and escalation of management traffic.

Table 7.1: Deficit Areas Covered by Architecture (continued)

Architecture Area	Why It Is Considered
Basic control framework. Refers to the ability to securely change parameters that control the infrastructure. The first class of parameter controls the monitoring thresholds. The second class controls system states. The latter class has more stringent security requirements.	Even in client/server environments where only monitoring is considered, threshold parameters that control monitoring have to be changed. There can be a large number of these. The second problem is one of security. The change capability should not be exploitable to attack the infrastructure.
Framework for managing remote offices. A management framework deployed in secondary offices. Characteristics include assured security, ability to survive unattended, and ability to conserve bandwidth.	Client/server environments often extend to remote offices with limited support facilities. A primary support center is responsible for monitoring, configuring and recovery activities at such sites.
Framework for contextual reporting. A framework is required to provide infrastructure related information to a wide audience which may not have access to management platform applications.	The extent and platform diversity in client/server environments make the collection and reporting of management metrics difficult. SQL based front-end tools can be applied to relational databases holding management data, however this does not scale.

7.1.1 Service Model of Client/Server Infrastructure

Infrastructure may be viewed as a service delivery system for client/server applications. Infrastructure management encompasses the management of all tangible assets such as workstations and servers as well as more abstract assets such as protocol stacks. Within such a service context, infrastructure may be modeled as a layered structure. Each layer's "interfaces" provide services which are accessed by a higher layer.

This is shown in Figure 7.1, where in addition to the horizontal layers, an infrastructure solutions layer provides solutions to support these horizontal layers. Table 7.2 shows examples for the structure of the horizontal layers and Table 7.3 shows infrastructure solution components that apply to each layer.

The lowest layer in this model of the client/server infrastructure is the enterprise network. Enterprise network management covers Local Area Networks (LAN), Metropolitan Area Networks (MAN) and Wide Area Networks (WAN). Client/server applications supporting a "global" business extend to multiple sites, linked by the networks. In service terms, networks provide logical connectivity between client/server components. These "connections" have specific characteristics such as bandwidth and latency (as discussed in Chapter 6, Section 6.7, "Network Considerations in Client/Server and Intranet Development").

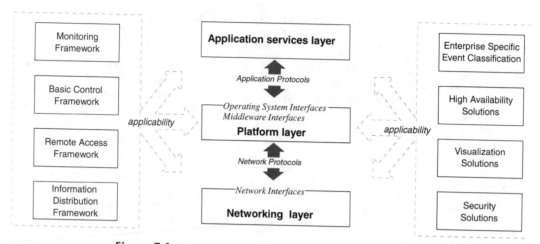

Figure 7.1: Service access model of client/server infrastructure

Traditionally, LAN management and WAN management have been handled with fundamentally different processes, tools and skills. As client/server deployment has spread across WANs, WAN management has had to learn more about client/server and SQL traffic characteristics. This is essential to provide management solutions that are sensitive to these needs. Assets managed in this layer include hubs from port level right through backbone topology components and traditional inter-networking components such as routers, bridges and switches.

The next layer from networks defines the subsystems. These include the actual hosts, the operating system, basic services such as naming, network time, protocol stacks and network interface elements that allow the hosts to connect to the network. It also includes the various subsystems associated with a host or that are connected directly to the network. Examples include networked mass storage, networked subsystems for backup and archiving, and printing.

The highest layer in this model is the application services layer. The content of this layer, which is variable depending on the organization, comprises applications and services that support some significant proportion of the user population. E-mail, document imaging, groupware and office automation packages increasingly fall into this category.

The assets, services and interfaces managed in each layer and the interface between the layers are detailed in Table 7.2.

In strict business terms investment in infrastructure management provides payback only indirectly through better delivery of applications and services to business users. Business applications, including mission-critical applications, are increasingly deployed using client/ server systems. Many popular package systems such as SAP are also delivered over client/ server systems.

Table 7.2: Examples of Assets, Services, and Interfaces in Service Model of Infrastructure

Model Element	Network Layer	Subsystem Layer	Application Services Layer
Infrastructure sets	hubs for workstations hubs for servers backbone components MAN inter-networking components WAN inter-networking components	workstation hardware server hardware host network interfaces host peripherals networked subsystems	vertical applications
Infrastructure services	network time host name/address lookup domain name network communication (e.g., multicast) network file	host protocol stacks process communication services (e.g., RPC) broker services distribution services (e.g., web) administration services (e.g., backup, licensing)	corporate messaging corporate groupware corporate office automation corporate WEB sites
Interface to layer above	physical interfaces— fiber or copper. media access protocol	Application Programming Interfaces Inter-Process Communication mechanisms	

However, the current generation of client/server applications are merely precursors to true distributed computing in the near future. With distributed computing, more services will come under the purview of infrastructure management.

Many enterprises already do business on a global scale. The extent of a client/server application's environment refers to the geographic bounds of its deployment. Geographic extent is a key factor that drives the complexity of infrastructure management for the client/server model. Figure 7.2 shows some of the intervening network structures between clients and servers in different offices.

"Global" applications are therefore deployed into multiple offices of the enterprise around the globe. Offices are likely to be of different size, with different infrastructure technologies, different in-house IT capability, users with different IT maturity and culture.

Therefore, the management problems that the extent of delivery produces are some of the most challenging in the field.

Table 7.3: Infrastructure Solution Components Supporting Service Model Layers

Infrastructure Solution	Network Layer	Subsystem Layer	Application Services Layer
High availability	spanning tree dual-homed Ethernet	RAID server failover operating system partitions	process groups auto configuration
Security	firewall dial-back modems encrypting firewalls	authentication server encryption key server	smart cards (for authentication tokens)
Management frameworks	MIB-based agents— embedded agents in devices, RMON agents in devices, proxy agents	MIB-based agents— native agents such as host resources MIB, add-on agents at operating system, proxy agents for peripherals pattern-matching agents management platforms	management protocols management tools and applications
Remote access and information distribution	physical interface media access protocol	application programming interfaces inter-process communication mechanisms.	

Specific management difficulties the "extent" produces are:

- Expectations of seamless service across different network technologies. In particular, managing performance, problems, add-moves-and-changes will have different service levels for different type offices.

- Proliferation of the management agents and their remote management in terms of configuration, monitoring their "heartbeat" is difficult.

- Synchronized upgrades of client/server applications and management tool applications.

The number of components involved in the delivery of an application in a global client/server environment is a problem exacerbated by extent. The whole point of client/server architecture is to "divide-and-conquer" the application function, hence to deliver a business solution involves more machines in the delivery chain.

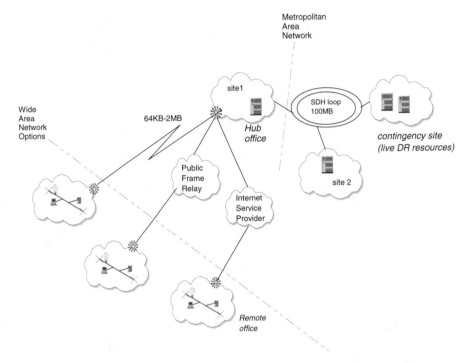

Figure 7.2: *Extent as a complexity factor inherent to client/server models*

Some of these machines play more critical roles than others. Some are involved in all transactions, while others are invoked only for specific conditions. Some are needed at every location, others can be centralized.

The placement of servers over a given network infrastructure is therefore a key activity in managing the performance and resilience characteristics of the client/server environment.

The second factor that drives the complexity in managing infrastructures supporting client/server applications is the discontinuity in the network topology used in their deployment.

Figure 7.3 shows two sets of numbers. One is the bandwidth or network capacity available at the desktop workstation, backbone and wide area link. in Mbits (per second). The second set of numbers denotes the relative number of systems at the desktop, at the application server level and at the infrastructure services level. The large number of total systems involved and the bandwidth differences at different points in the topology mean that application traffic has to be carefully managed in the infrastructure as client/server application change in character.

The management frameworks therefore require different mechanisms to manage systems (monitor, measure, control, report) at the end of a wide area link, at a desktop LAN, or at a switched backbone LAN.

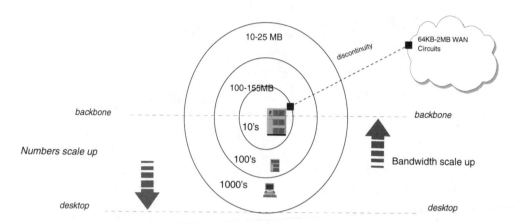

Figure 7.3: *Topological discontinuity as a complexity factor of client/server model*

Infrastructure management frameworks therefore have to be viewed in the context of the expanding and changing natures of client/server deployment. The technology areas of protocols, management platforms, and agents provide building blocks for developing management frameworks.

7.2 High Availability

High availability is a set of concepts, technologies and protocols. High availability aims to minimize the effect of infrastructure failures on end-users. In the best case, failures will be transparent to end-users.

Investment in high availability can be thought of as an insurance strategy. In most businesses today commercial insurance cover is mandatory, specifically designed to cover downtime caused by acts of God, large-scale accidents, etc.

High availability is of particular importance to the client/server environment since multiple systems and components have to cooperate in providing application services to end-users. Failure at the client, failure of network components, failure of a data or application server, failure of network service can all result in failure of service seen by an end-user. Figure 7.4 shows points of failure in delivery paths that client/server-based applications are typically dependent on.

High availability cannot protect against application failure, human error, corruption of data (or whole databases) and impact of failure due to viruses. These type of failures will still demand traditional backup and recovery procedures.

High availability is also applicable to the infrastructure management frameworks to ensure that framework failure does not compromise the ability to manage.

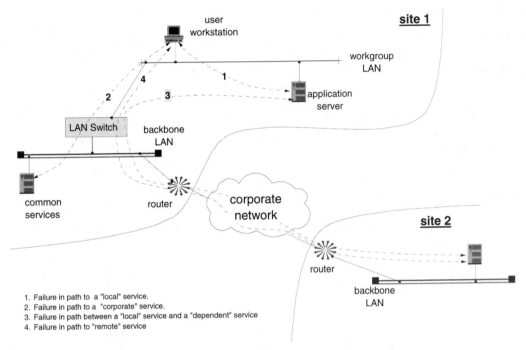

user
workstation

site 1

workgroup
LAN

4

1

2

3

application
server

LAN Switch

backbone
LAN

common
services

router

corporate
network

site 2

router

backbone
LAN

1. Failure in path to a "local" service.
2. Failure in path to a "corporate" service.
3. Failure in path between a "local" service and a "dependent" service
4. Failure in path to "remote" service

Figure 7.4: *Typical failures in a simple client/server environment*

The responsibility in an enterprise for providing high availability solutions is often ambiguous. Application development teams, application vendors, operating system vendors, workstation and server vendors all provide some part of the solution.

The responsibility for managing availability, on the other hand, clearly resides with the infrastructure management organization. Consequently, high availability mechanisms are often bolted on without much thought about how the mechanisms themselves will be managed.

An architecture based solution applicable across the enterprise needs to be defined if the benefits of high availability are to be realized. Managing high availability entails the following:

- Monitoring specific parts of the infrastructure from the specific context of detecting change of availability state. This is done by having specialized agents.

- When change of availability state occurs, the end-users that are affected by the change of state need to be understood to prioritize operational decisions.

- Have the repair blueprints and strategies to repair the failure as well as have the skills (or access to skills) to undertake the repairs.

7.2.1 Rationales for High Availability

Centralized systems have traditionally provided various means of providing high availability. For example, hardware fault tolerance through processing modules in mainframes and clustering in mini-computers have been available since the 1980s.

In the case of client/server systems a number of individual systems have to cooperate to provide an end-user with some service. Failure of any of these subsystems in the service delivery path (or in the connectivity between the systems) results in a failure of the service to the end-user. High availability is of particular relevance when "mission critical" applications are deployed using client/server systems.

Well-designed client/server systems have a degree of natural redundancy—for example, through the ability to load share requests. The term failure therefore needs qualifying from an end-user's perspective. the impact of failure can be any of the following:

- *Inability to do further work*—actual loss of the system, use or loss of connectivity despite repeated log-on attempts, etc.

- *Deterioration of ability to do work*—perceived as a performance problem—relative to a nominal or expected level of performance.

- *Loss of work already done*—actual loss of work done within a preceding period. The time-frame of this period which can range from minutes to years depending on the application domain. (The low end of the range is due to failure to complete an operation. Higher up, the ranges could be due to the massive data loss or inability to restore lost data.)

The concept of high availability should therefore be thought as being essential in providing mission critical end-user services. Providing high availability across the multiple architectures of network, systems and applications requires a clearly defined framework. High availability solutions are built from commercial off-the-shelf mechanisms integrated together as building blocks.

Well-designed client/server systems built within a quality-oriented framework and using high-quality components are relatively reliable. In 7 x 24-hour scenarios, 99.5% availability is possible without any high availability mechanisms being used.

The key questions that a business has to answer are the cost to business of downtime and the amount of downtime that can be tolerated by the business.

7.2.2 Scope of High Availability Solutions

High availability solutions normally applies to surviving small-scale failures such as disk crashes or server failure. High availability uses redundant components in the infrastructure. The redundant components are capable of mirroring functions or replicating data.

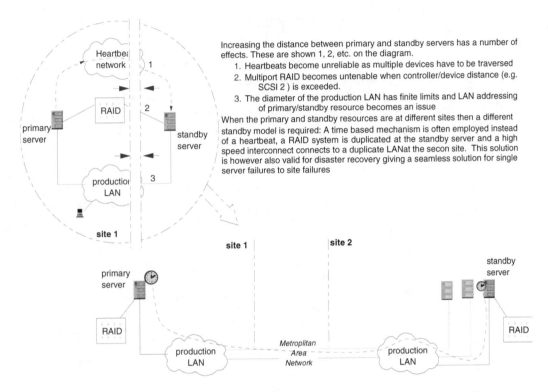

Increasing the distance between primary and standby servers has a number of effects. These are shown 1, 2, etc. on the diagram.

1. Heartbeats become unreliable as multiple devices have to be traversed
2. Multiport RAID becomes untenable when controller/device distance (e.g. SCSI 2) is exceeded.
3. The diameter of the production LAN has finite limits and LAN addressing of primary/standby resource becomes an issue

When the primary and standby resources are at different sites then a different standby model is required: A time based mechanism is often employed instead of a heartbeat, a RAID system is duplicated at the standby server and a high speed interconnect connects to a duplicate LANat the secon site. This solution is however also valid for disaster recovery giving a seamless solution for single server failures to site failures

Figure 7.5: *Effect of separating redundant components from primary components*

The proximity of the redundant components, relative to their respective primary components has a bearing on the scale of failures that can be handled by the redundant components.

Figure 7.5 shows that by placing the redundant components in a different physical site, the loss involving any or all of the respective resources at the "primary" site can be survived. Loss of a site is often classed as a major disaster. If site disaster can also be covered by a high availability solution then the value of the solution to the business is considerably increased.

High availability solutions introduce a major cost element to building client/server infrastructures. Clearly, not all parts of the infrastructure need high availability.

In parts where high availability solutions are deployed the capital cost of the infrastructure can increase between 2 and 3 times the nominal cost (without the solution). High availability is therefore often applied on a selective basis to support mission-critical applications.

Two other factors limit widespread deployment of high availability solutions:

- High availability solutions tend to have an impact on systems performance. If high availability is to be part of the production environment, then all acceptance testing of the client/server system should be done with the actual high availability mechanisms.

- If mission-critical systems are supported with high availability solutions, then it is only useful if there is a framework to detect and act on events that change the availability status. This implies that monitoring (and acting on failure) of high availability environments is required outside business hours as well.

7.2.3 Basic Principles of High Availability

Components of particular relevance to applications of high availability are the servers, server-based software and network elements. High availability may also be applied to logical services. The use of high availability technologies is targeted at achieving the following abstract notions of resilience:

- *No-single-points-of-failure*—Generally a single component failure should not completely stop the provision of a service or application delivery. Points of failure are defined relative to a service delivery path—i.e., all the physical components and infrastructure services needed to deliver a service. The more "common access" there is to the service (or the more "infrastructural" it is in nature), the stronger the reason to ensure it is highly available. (When dissimilar classes of components in a service path fail concurrently, and provided each class has redundancy, the combinatorial effect of the multiple failure should be examined.)

- *Limited impact of failure*—Component failure in a service path in the worst case should affect only a relatively small proportion of end-users. This can be done though "hard" partitioning service paths across sets of users, specialization of resources so that multiple services are not affected by a single component failure.

- *Criticality*—A criticality of zero defines the availability state of a service in terms of all the components, services, etc. required for its delivery having redundant backups ready to take over in the event. In a "no single points of failure" scenario, the criticality value increases by one for each failed component anywhere in the service delivery path. An increased criticality value indicates that another failure in the path increases the probability of total failure of the service. In particular, the failure of a backup component that has already kicked in will cause the service path to fail.

- *Repair without disruption*—Mechanisms that allow redundant components transparently to take over when a failure occurs should be augmented with the ability to repair the failed component without disrupting the working environment. The longer a failed component remains in place, the longer the criticality of the system (for a given service) will remain high. By the same token if a failed system cannot be replaced for a prolonged period of time after initial failure, then depending on the importance of the service, more than a single-point-of-failure class of redundancy may be required.

7.2.4 High Availability Through Topographical and Deployment Tactics

Before looking at off-the-shelf products for building high availability solutions, it is worthwhile considering a set of tactics that ensure minimum impact of failure. These techniques are based on leveraging topographical (i.e., dependent on where in a network topology a service is located), service relationships and service distribution (i.e., dependent on being deployed in a certain proportion) options:

- *Workgroups*—most modern enterprises work on the basis of organizing people into workgroups or teams, members of which do related work. Connecting alternate workgroup members to different wiring hubs ensures that hub-related failures (a common cause for LAN service failure) does not impact a whole workgroup. The maturation of mechanisms such as virtual LANs allow configuring individual users so that they are part of the same virtual LAN regardless of their physical connection to the LAN.

- *Splitting users in a workgroup* across multiple servers is another method of limiting the risk of a single server failing. Depending on the type of server, multiple servers may dynamically share the load of processing requests, or different users may have their data resources on different servers. The ability dynamically to move data resources helps to manage add moves and changes of workgroup members, without affecting the tactic.

- *Centralizing home directories* on servers ensures that failure of desktop machines minimizes data loss. The high performance and reliability of the LAN is a prerequisite to gaining benefit from this tactic. This tactic has to be used in conjunction with the previous one of splitting users across multiple servers. Depending on the operating system at the desktop, there may be bottlenecks on the LAN, for example, when users log on at the start of day, or as automated backups occur during the day.

- *Standardized desktop configurations* minimize the delay between a machine failing and a replacement machine being made available. A single standardized desktop is often hard to achieve when there are very different needs from IT.

- *Specializing servers*, i.e., not mixing file services with application packages and databases ensures that multiple services are not wiped out in the event of a server loss.

7.2.5 Off-the-Shelf High Availability Systems and Protocols

High availability solutions are built from off-the-shelf systems and protocols. The main categories for these are at the file storage, server and LAN protocol levels. Some advanced middleware products for building client/server software provide redundancy at a software process level:

File Storage. RAID—or Redundant Array of Independent Disks is the most common subsystem. It uses a concept of distributing parity bits for every byte of data on a disk across multiple disks. Failure of any single disk is transparent. Failed disks can be swapped out without power down. RAID is commonly used as a high availability mechanism. Table 7.4 shows the classes of different RAID systems.

Server Failover. Mechanisms and protocols for tracking the "heartbeats" of a server host so that in the event of failure of a tracked host, the tracking machine can transparently take over from a failed host. Clients of the server however have to re-log to the new host. A tracking machine may be able to track several server hosts (depending on the hardware slots available for interface cards, etc.). The tracking host requires access to the disk subsystems of the host being serviced.

Failover schemes have to be carefully evaluated, configured and managed. For example, the method by which the system that takes over acquires a network address can determine the efficacy of a failover solution.

Server shadowing is a concept that is related to failover, however, each standby server shadows only a single server. Both servers are configured exactly the same. Shadowing is at a byte-write granularity. Server failover and RAID are usually combined high availability implementation.

LAN Failover Protocols. Failure "resistant" protocols include:

- *Spanning Tree*—a network protocol used to detect loss of connectivity, bypass a failed path and find an alternative pathway within a finite time period.

- *Dual Attached FDDI*—a networking interface protocol consisting of two counter-rotating rings that provide resilience in the event of the failure of one of the attachment points for the FDDI connection. In the event of the failure, the second ring takes over, generally without loss of any packets.

- *Dual Ethernet Transceiver*—a hardware device that has primary and secondary Ethernet links (typically to different hub devices). The device detects the failure of the Ethernet port, the primary link is connected to and switches over to the secondary link.

High availability is often incrementally deployed so that it "propagates" over some period of time from the backbone part of the topology to the desktop. High availability is perceived in

Table 7.4: Classes of RAID Systems

Description	Application Note	Key Metrics
RAID 1. Provides disk mirroring by copying all of the data from a primary disk to an identical disk in the RAID array. If the primary disk fails the mirrored disk takes over.	Expensive since each disk has to have a backup disk. Usually justified for truly critical data. Fast disk read performance and moderate disk write performance with hardware controllers, slow otherwise.	*Array Capacity*—Gbytes to Tbytes range. *Cost per Mbyte*—$0.50 to $3.00 depending on performance. *Sustained transfer rate*—5 to 70 Mbyte per second. *Burst transfer rate*—20 to 500 Mbyte per second. *Management interface*—variable, ranging from (1) visual indicator or LCD panel, (2) GUI tool, (3) serial ASCII text message output, (4) serial command input, (5) SNMP.
RAID 0+1. Disk mirroring as in RAID 1. In addition "stripes" data across all disks in an array so that the whole array works in parallel.	Disk mirroring with better reliability and improved write performance over RAID 1. Although more expensive than RAID 1 and offered by fewer vendors, RAID 0+1 is more ideal than RAID 1 in a high availability scheme.	
RAID 3. Data is stored across multiple disks in an array using "striping." Generates and stores parity data on a single disk so that data can be regenerated on an array member failing.	RAID 3 has a single point of failure, the parity disk, the failure of which kills the whole array. Also RAID 3 has low performance for random access I/O, commonly required in client/server systems.	
RAID 5. Similar to RAID 3 except parity data is written across the whole array.	RAID 5 is the most commonly used level in high availability solutions. It provides reasonable I/O in all types of disk access.	
RAID 7. An advance on RAID 5 where the array functions as a single virtual disk.	RAID 7 provides high volume, high performance read and write operations. Performance fall is minimum even when a disk module fails.	

a network topology in terms of an environment where LAN failover protocols such as those above work together.

A point to note is that these different protocol and related mechanisms work at different reaction speeds.

Software Process Redundancy. Process groups define a set of processes that offer similar services. Each process member is typically resident on a different server—the effect of which is

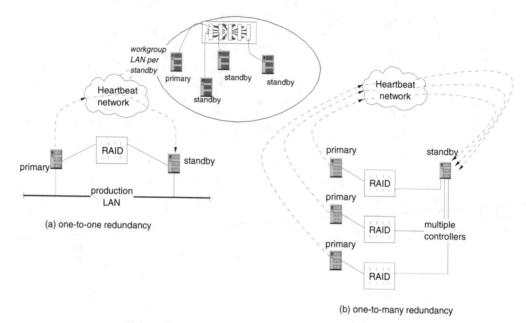

Figure 7.6: *Combining failover and storage redundancy*

to replicate a service. Processes can leave the group, for example, if a server crashes, and new processes can join the group. Leaving and joining is done dynamically.

Redundancy is invoked through a software and protocol-based mechanism (offered through an application programming interface over the operating system). Messages from a client requesting a service are multicast to all members of the process group.

Figure 7.7 shows a client which is "bound" to a group of servers, any of which can provide the particular service. The client's request for a service is multicast to all the servers in the group. When the server that is processing the client's request replies, the reply is multicast to the whole client/server group. The other servers in the group are able to update their state in a synchronous manner.

This allows any alternative server in the group to take over transparently in the event of a failure. Software process level of high availability is increasingly used in safety-critical client/server systems including energy distribution, capital markets trading systems and mass transport management.

Databases and Persistent Information Assets. Information that persists—whether software programs or more complex objects should have copies in multiple places. Persistence is a concept in data architecture that ensures not only the survival of the data but that it survives in a usable form. This is a form of redundancy that is often not managed. It can however be bought as complete systems (e.g., Tandem's NYSE).

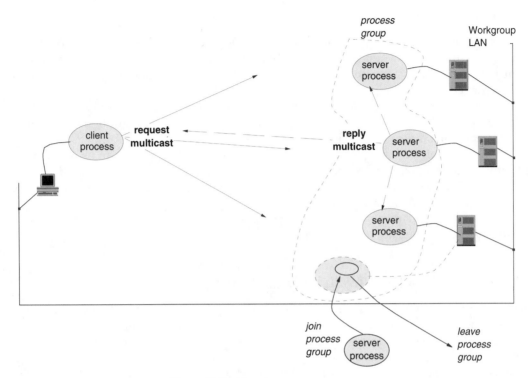

Figure 7.7: *Client/server process groups*

More generally, systems concepts that can be integrated into an architecture for protecting data and information assets include::

- *Storage protection*—Data assets should be assured of protection from loss regardless of the scale of a disaster. This includes databases, file-based information, transactions and messages.

- *Data restoration*—Data loss in the worst case should be recoverable from backup (within a predefined nominal and maximum acceptable "loss band" for a business). Server installation design should include secondary networks specialized to automated backup and restoration.

- *Replication*—Relational database management systems offer replication at the database table level that is often used to ensure that data relevant to local contexts by a client application are replicated. Replication is a key concept in operational management of directories.

7.2.6 Hot Swap

Transparent resilience mechanisms such as RAID, FDDI, server clustering and process groups are often highly valued as high availability mechanisms because it is possible to swap out failed components at the relevant failure point—without powering down the components that are still working.

While "hot swap" avoids disruption to the business, there is still a risk that introducing new components will cause working components to fail. Hence hot swap should be applied with caution in a production environment.

When modules are stored for hot swap, the processes that upgrade the revisions of the relevant systems should ensure that the redundant modules are up to spec. Also, spare modules should not be left till a crisis, but should be regularly used by swapping out working modules in a controlled maintenance schedule.

Figure 7.8 is a map showing where in the infrastructure "hierarchy" the high availability mechanisms described above would apply.

7.2.7 Managing High Availability Environments

In most organizations high availability environments are confined to business critical systems—due to the cost and operations overheads. For these environments to be effective, special consideration needs to be given to them in terms of applying management processes such as fault management and change management.

The business case for a high availability should include an understanding for the extra management overhead. Managing a high availability environment is a "use-case" of some key infrastructure management processes. (see Chapter 2, Section 2.2.3, "Use-Cases"). As an example, the use-case for the problem management process is driven by the following considerations:

- When a failure occurs in a high availability environment, it needs to be treated with the highest priority and given the necessary resources for resolution. In service-level terms this class of failure gets the highest level of attention. This may seem non-intuitive (since in a well-provisioned environment the failure may have been transparent to users). A basic principle of supporting high availability is that its status quo is maintained as soon as possible.

- One of the reasons a high level of service is accorded to a failure in this environment is that its real and potential impact needs to be evaluated as soon as possible. However, manual effort is not always necessary. Automation scripts (agents) can be executed to gather and present the necessary information. Some types of failure require an explicit set of actions to be invoked following a failure (for example, safe shut down of the failed system).

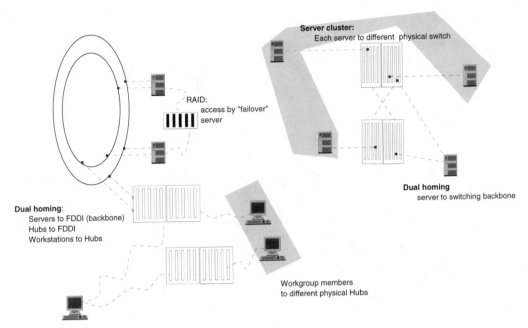

Server cluster:
Each server to different physical switch

RAID:
access by "failover"
server

Dual homing
server to switching backbone

Dual homing:
Servers to FDDI (backbone)
Hubs to FDDI
Workstations to Hubs

Workgroup members
to different physical Hubs

Figure 7.8: *Application of high availability mechanisms*

- Users need to be appraised of the change of high availability status. Users also need to be updated on both change back to high availability as well as any deterioration, for example, through further failure in the respective service delivery path for a system. Some organizations use an escalation scale of alerts (yellow, orange, red) to indicate events. The web is an increasingly common method of distributing this status information.

- High availability solutions are available for most operating system environments (Unix, Netware, Microsoft NT) used for client/server systems. A high availability environment supporting a critical business function often spans several platforms. Managing high availability in a heterogeneous environment is likely to require specialist skills from each area. Crisis-team forming and coordination are needed.

Reaction speed refers to the time taken for a mechanism or protocol to react to the failure of the component (being "protected") and for the alternative component to be brought into service.

The high availability environment defines a collection of high availability mechanisms that include LAN failover protocols along with other high availability mechanisms. Each component of high availability operates at a different "granularity" of reaction speeds. The impact of the differences should be analyzed.

7.3 Security

Security is another area of IT, (like high availability described in Section 7.2) where the responsibility for providing security solutions is often unclear. Developers of client/server systems have traditionally not worried about security any more than basic file-system security and the use of passwords.

In many organizations the responsibility for security solutions has de facto become a role for an engineering function within the infrastructure management group.

Security is also an area which requires high capital investment as well as time and technical talent. These costs can push up the cost of the infrastructure significantly. Until recently, justifying such high costs was almost impossible. Two trends have changed perceptions about the need for security solutions within client/server infrastructures:

- The general acceptance of the Internet and the need to connect to the Internet as a future channel of communication and business has opened up the possibility of hackers having free reign over an unprotected infrastructure.

- The need for a lot more of corporate staff to be mobile and to access corporate resources remotely has raised the need to manage access to corporate information and resources.

As client/server applications take over from traditionally secure centralized environments there is also a need for strategic security solutions which scale in global client/server infrastructure.

As the infrastructure management function continues the trend to manage more business-critical systems based on client/server, the security within infrastructure management operations itself needs to be explicitly examined. This is done here within an architectural framework, the primary focus of which is to develop solutions for use in infrastructure management. From a security perspective, infrastructure management is a set of client/server and intranet-based systems. Similar solutions are viable for business-related client/server applications.

Security within the infrastructure management function is by and large a cultural problem, and as such, it is intimately tied into policies for managing people:

- The prerequisite is a security policy that specifically covers the operations of the network management staff.

- Associated with this is an operations manual that defines security procedures related to specific infrastructure management processes.

- Another task is categorizing resources and applications in terms of use by different parts of the enterprise.

Together, these provide the guidelines for security awareness within the group. The discussion of security and its continuous improvement is very much a part of the leadership and strategic "visioning" provided by the network manager.

7.3.1 Measures for Enhancing Infrastructure Security

The security within the infrastructure management group is significantly enhanced by the following measures:

- *Standardized workstation and server builds.* All servers and workstations used by infrastructure management staff should be built to a known standard. Part of the security management function is to track security-related enhancements to the operating systems and to deploy systematically these into the standard workstations and servers.

- *Monitoring changes to builds.* As part of deploying servers and workstations for infrastructure management, continuous monitoring of changes to the last build level can be implemented. One technique is to develop a database of configuration signatures of standard builds. The signature of each machine is periodically computed by an agent and compared against an externally held signature database. Several high quality public domain software is available for this, for example, based on one-way hash functions.

- *Client authentication levels.* Different roles require different levels of authentication "strength." For the management of local resources from the infrastructure management may only require password-based authentication. Managing remote resources or remote offices may as a matter of policy require stronger token-based authentication and authorizations mechanisms. Similar strong authentication mechanisms may be required as part of the policy for managing business specific resources such as transaction and database servers.

- *Discussion of security policies.* A specific forum for the quality improvement of security measures helps security to be at the forefront of infrastructure management thinking and operations. Regular briefings on the state-of-the-art for security related to the operating systems and network areas in the infrastructure management framework helps to maintain vendor recommendations on security.

- *Monitoring firewalls.* Many enterprises are partitioned using firewalls. Most common are one or more external firewalls between the enterprise and the global Internet. Firewalls can also be deployed internally between different networks. A firewall between a software developers' network and production networks is common in many enterprises. Firewalls are configured to provide a controlled access between the respective networks. A policy of continuously monitoring the configuration and logs of the firewall systems is needed to ensure that the firewalls aren't being internally breached.

- *Configuration and script files.* The security of files holding configuration information, configuration signatures and configuration scripts used to execute configuration are critical information areas to be protected. Such files should be held in an encrypted form and backups should be available as part of the respective infrastructure management processes.

7.3.2 Building Security Solutions

Strong security solutions for client/server infrastructures are developed from off-the-shelf systems, products and concepts that are made to work together. The key building blocks are:

- *Access management products*—these include corporate and internal firewalls, authentication servers and authentication protocols.

- *Encryption products*—these include products that encrypt data that flows in point-to-point links and for encrypting data files for "confidentiality."

- *Intranet security protocols*—As the browser becomes the universal mechanism to access all types of information, the secure socket layer (SSL) and secure hypertext transport protocol (SHTTP) are protocols for secure transfer of information between browser and server.

- *Intranet safety mechanisms*—related to the intranet model where application code (or applets) are downloaded over the network to be executed locally. "Safety" refers to ensuring that downloaded code cannot "run amok" in the local environment.

- *Segmentation*—a topographic tool that develops secure perimeters around systems and users on the basis of need-to-communicate relationships.

These building blocks and their use in developing security solutions are described below.

Access Management. The first line of defense are systems and protocols that control access to the infrastructure. Mechanisms in this category are firewalls and dial-back modems that provide logical entry to the infrastructure. The next level of access is provided by an authentication mechanism that aims to provide surety of the identity of the user or system that has gained access.

In general, current access management schemes can be made to work for "known" groups of users. They are difficult to implement for authenticating "strangers." A simple method of making "strangers" to be "known" is to implement registration before access.

Once the user is accepted at the network perimeter, further security consists of application level protocols. One of the problems with access management products is that there are no standards. This means that scaling security solutions, or building solutions with coverage of the whole enterprise, usually requires products from the same vendor for inter-operation.

Because there is a real need for industrial-strength access products, there are currently a lot of vendors selling products with partially developed architectures. The actual safety of many firewall products has not been independently evaluated. Choosing access products without expert guidance is therefore relatively risky.

While firewalls are placed as a matter of course between the corporate network and Internet service points, many organizations do not provide the same protection for dial-in access. Also, strong sanctions are needed to stop ad hoc access via local modems in workstations or laptops that are also connected to the corporate LAN (i.e., dual homed).

While firewalls are supposed to manage access to the infrastructure the actual activity at the firewall needs to be continuously monitored. It is a common practice to develop scripts or agents to search for suspicious patterns in the firewall-event logs. For example, an external firewall being flooded with lengthy e-mail messages or a high frequency of DNS requests are likely to be denial-of-service attacks on the firewall. Once a pattern is recognized, an event should be dispatched to the monitoring framework.

Figure 7.9 shows the use of access management to protect infrastructure management resources. Resources include information in management databases. A secure web server can produce HTML data on the fly from relational databases and SNMP for caching at general websites in the network. The information in these websites is for corporate consumption.

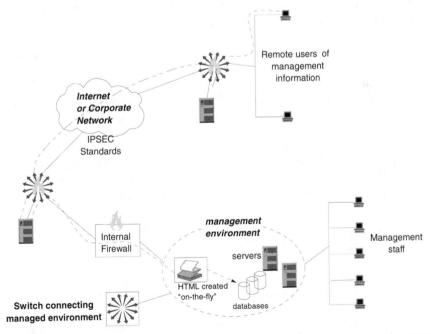

Figure 7.9: *Access management to protect the infrastructure management environment*

Specific browsers may also be able to access the secure server directly, using an application specific secure access protocol. The use of internal firewalls is described under segmentation below.

Encryption. Another class of products that is aimed at providing secure communications end-to-end are encrypting firewalls. These products encrypt either at the IP packet level or at the application level.

Encryption at the IP stack level can be of just the IP packet's data payload or it can be the entire IP packet (which is then encapsulated in a second IP packet that is addressed to the other end of the IP link).

Encrypting just the payload enables valuable information to be gleaned from the IP headers (of multiple captured packets)—such as the location of routers and firewalls and addresses of protected devices. Encapsulation of an encrypted packet can cause the resultant packet to exceed IP packet-size limits set at routers and firewalls. This is turn leads to fragmentation and re-assembly with the consequent loss of performance.

With application level encryption the management function allows encryption of application traffic on a selective basis. Some traffic can be send in the clear. This level of control introduces a configuration management overhead. Since the configuration has to be synchronized globally across all sites, this is a non-trivial task.

Encryption and decryption are compute intensive and the architecture of the product will determine its impact on packet throughput. Some products use a special encryption chip while others share the general purpose processor. Client/server traffic often tends to be bursty. Also, packets used in client/server communication tend to be relatively small (at least in one direction depending on the client/server architecture).

Several vendors of encrypting firewalls are beginning to support the IETF standard-based IP Security (IPSEC) scheme. This theoretically allows different vendors encrypting routers to communicate.

The second application of encryption is in encrypting data files to ensure that the data in them is protected. In a client/server infrastructure, encryption is of particular relevance when:

- Information, whose confidentiality is linked to the credibility of the business. Examples include patient records in a clinic, architecture of a corporate floatation in an investment bank, design of a drug in a pharmaceutical firm.

- Information which resides offsite, where the site is un-manned or is shared with other organizations. In this case additional classes of information need to be made confidential.

- Information which can be used in attacking the infrastructure. Passwords, keys, configuration details, internal addresses, etc.

- Some organizations recommend all files holding any corporate information on laptops to be routinely encrypted. Also all e-mail sent to trading or business partners are candidates for encryption. Pretty Good Privacy (PGP) is a public domain software which supports a public key encryption. Several such public domain mechanisms are commonly beginning to be specified for use in file transfers and in e-mail communications involving commercial transactions.

A major headache for global enterprises that have sites throughout the globe, is the U.S.-led restriction on the type of keys that can be globally used with products such as encrypting firewalls. This is currently an area of major public debate within the U.S., that extends to freedom of choice for legitimate businesses to protect their assets. There are potential compromises in the pipeline which may benefit different types of organizations in different ways.

Another problem relates to countries, such as France, where the use of encryption technology for commercial purposes is illegal. This poses some challenging problems in developing global security architectures.

A fact of life in the current state of global peace is that a lot of effort is spent by government agencies in gathering commercial intelligence, citing national interests in areas ranging from trade negotiations to corporate takeovers to product design.

Using low quality keys (such as the 56 bit keys allowed for export from the U.S.) to protect confidentiality of strategic resources, including those of infrastructure, is often a waste of money. It provides a false sense of security while in reality even well-equipped hackers can compromise the privacy.

Some organizations have implemented encryption-based solutions using non-U.S. equipment running non-U.S. encryption protocols. There are an increasing number of such products. One downside is that the integrity of such schemes has usually not been verified—since major scrutiny by a wide expert community has not been possible.

Intranet Security and Safety. Much of the future evolution of infrastructure management tools and systems is likely to involve an intranet-based architecture. A key part of this scenario is the access to information from any part of the infrastructure using a universal browser. The browser can also access application repositories, downloading application components for execution in the local browser platform.

A dominant language in this area (with several management-related standardization initiatives for using it underway) is Java. The Java environment is described in some detail in Chapter 12, Section 12.7.

Java has a robust security model that addresses the issue of ensuring downloaded code is both safe and guaranteed not to cause havoc in the environment in which it is executed.

- The language is designed so as not to use pointers and to allocate memory dynamically at runtime. These two features make it impossible to infer the physical memory map of a Java class by studying its source code.

- The Java runtime environment maintains a separate name space for each source of Java class. This makes it impossible for classes from one source (e.g., downloaded over the network) to masquerade as classes from another source (e.g., the local base classes).

- Java's runtime environment verifies the Java code by subjecting it to a language theorem prover before executing it. This ensures that a rogue complier has not created any non-standard code.

- The network interface of Java's runtime environment can be configured to control network access—such as disallowing all network access or allowing access only to the host from which the code was downloaded. This controls all external relationships.

The secure socket layer (SSL) and secure hypertext transfer protocol (SHTTP) are two other protocols to ensure secure browser/server communications.

SSL is a per-transaction level scheme that provides server authentication, encryption and client authentication. SSL however uses 40 bit keys (which are considered unsafe by many security experts). SHTTP uses public key technology (with key sizes of 64 bits and above), and is applied to an entire browser-server session.

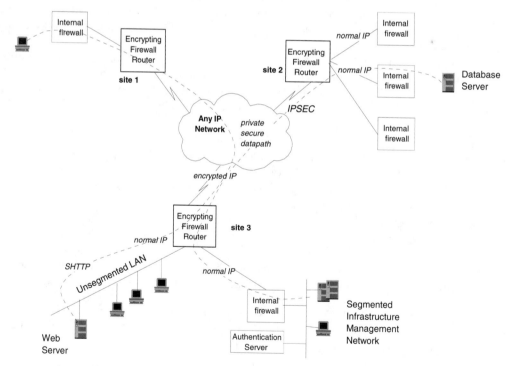

Figure 7.10: *Protocols and mechanisms secure end-to-end communication paths*

These protocols allow insecure networks such as the Internet to be "traversed" when accessing confidential information using a browser. Figure 7.10 shows the deployment of mechanisms and protocols to provide end-to-end security.

Segmentation. An old military tactic involves dividing up a large territory into smaller but better defendable pieces. A common case in large client/server infrastructures is that many parts of the infrastructure don't need to communicate with each other. For example, an environment for in-house software development does not really need direct communication with the production environment. Code release, upgrades, acceptance testing, etc. should be done through indirect processes to protect the integrity of the production environment from both deliberate and accidental damage.

Internal firewalls segment users into business zones or on the basis of client/server applications that need to communicate with each other. Some applications such as e-mail need to be able to traverse all zones.

Such segmentation makes it much harder for both external and internal attackers to "run amok" and also makes its easier to detect illegal entry. Limiting general access is often anathema in organizations which are proud of open, free networking and hence may present a cultural barrier in some cases.

Internal firewalls need not be commercial products, they can be realized from high-quality workstations and public domain code. The downside of internal firewalls is that there needs to be an efficient administrative procedure to change filters in the firewalls. Reconfigurations should be expected if a protected segment has users that are mobile and need access to protect resources. Graphical tools often help to minimize reconfiguration errors.

7.3.3 Virus Protection

Protecting the infrastructure from viruses is probably the security area of greatest concern to most people. Virus protection should be covered under the security policies. Education of all staff on virus awareness is an essential component of virus protection. In addition:

- Deployment of an industrial strength virus scanning package on all systems.

- Development of boot-up configurations so that virus checks cannot be by-passed.

- Development of operating system shells so that reading from a diskette drive always invokes the virus checker.

- Reporting of virus detection into centralized logs, automated scanning of logs and event generation on virus detection.

The key problem with virus packages is that they need to be frequently updated with new releases covering new viruses. Top vendors distribute new releases every month or so.

Given that vendors need lead time to develop virus recognition software, from the time when the virus first appears, the virus is prevalent by the time the virus software has been upgraded. Its deployment is therefore fairly urgent.

When thousands or tens of thousands of workstations and servers need to be upgraded globally within the shortest time-frame, there is often a logistical problem in distribution. When such upgrades have to be done every month or so, then the operational costs of virus management escalate.

One way of automating the timely distribution of security-related information is through mobile agents to carry the information payload for the upgrade.

Another area where virus checking is increasingly relevant is before files are backed up. Usually, a second virus checking package using a different technology to the mainstream virus checker used on the file system being backed up. This increases the probability that all backed-up files are free from viruses.

Viruses can also be transported through messaging systems such as multipart e-mail. Viruses can be embedded as part of a mail message and get executed in the receiving mail gateway or the mail's recipient.

There are firewalls which also run virus checkers for all traffic. Given the overhead of administration and management, virus checking at the firewall is however likely to be more effective when provided as a service by an Internet service provider.

7.4 Classification of Events

Figure 7.11 shows parts of a simple client/server environment that may be instrumented with monitoring agents. Monitoring can cover a whole range of issues—fault or exception conditions, high availability, security, performance are common examples. Monitoring can be implemented at the different layers (application, services, network) in both workstations and servers. The number of potential events classes from these sources is large.

On an enterprise scale the number of types of events increase with increased instrumentation. A classification system is needed to identify the important single events from the potential set of events. The rationales for an infrastructure-wide event classification are:

- To ensure that all infrastructure management staff can maintain a common understanding of what are the key events received by monitoring frameworks.

- To ensure that the relationships between events are analyzed and the understanding is maintained with the changing infrastructure.

Once the event classification scheme is developed, "second order" information related to events can be developed. Important information includes:

- *Known dependency chains between events.* For example, loss of connectivity from a sub-net (router interface) will cause known secondary events at machines connected to

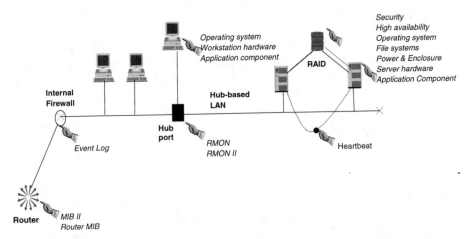

Figure 7.11: *Instrumentation points in a simple client/server environment*

the subnet. Documenting such event dependencies between two (or more) events in "a chain," provides the basic information for both manual and automated search for "primary" events from a large set of event occurrences presented at a management framework during an infrastructure failure.

- *Thresholds (or search patterns to set) for event generation.* Events are generated on some predefined condition being detected. Thresholds define a point above or below nominal "within-band" conditions that should result in an event. Similarly, search patterns define text message patterns to be recognized in log files—which should result in an event being generated.

- *Type of agent the event "emanates" from.* Given the key role that agents currently play (and continue to play) in infrastructure management, new types of agents are likely to be created and deployed. The type of agent determines how the event should be pre-processed. For example, the method to use in uniquely identifying or naming an event from the agent, uniquely identifying the physical source of the event and whether any check should be applied to verify the event.

- *Path to where event instances are stored.* Defines where or how instances of the event may be found in a database or MIB.

There are three important classes of second order information relating to events: (*a*) information about how to pre-process the event, (*b*) configuration information which specifies the parameters to be set at the originating entities of the event, and (*c*) operational information about the impact of the event. A web database allows these connections to be centrally defined and managed.

7.4.1 Developing the Schema for Event Classification

A model or schema needs to be defined before any classification framework can be built. Two common sets of criteria for classification that are especially relevant to client/server infrastructures are by infrastructure layer, and by business application. Figure 7.12 shows how these sets of criteria are related. They are described below:

- *By layer.* The service model of client/server infrastructure defined in Section 7.1.1 is a starter model for classifying events. Events from network devices, hosts and operating systems and from within applications can be viewed on a layer basis. In addition, events from infrastructure solutions can be accounted. Within each layer the events can be further broken into the classic areas of infrastructure management—Performance, Security, Configuration, Fault and Accounting. This is the simplest classification model, and allows events to be cataloged and is necessary for the catalog to be maintained. Such maintenance should be an activity in the change management process that controls all changes to the infrastructure. However it is very technology-centric in that it does not factor in any information about the business-level importance of the events.

- *By business application.* This is a further step-refinement using the events cataloged in the layer model classification above as a baseline. Service delivery paths are drawn by connecting events developed for the layer event catalog. The events from the participating components of a service delivery path are collected together. Such an event collection is defined for each application used by a business. This brings a business application perspective to the event classification. Event collections should capture redundant paths in high availability application environments. Monitoring high availability events should be a step-refinement over these event collections.

- *By business area.* This is a linear refinement of the business application model above. The events relating to a business area essentially define a virtual infrastructure for the business area.

There are two further classes of events that need to be treated differently:

- "Existential" events are events such as "heartbeats" messages from systems to indicate that they are functionally operational. Existential events include results of protocol level utilities such as "ping," in TCP/IP, which echos back a message from a "live," targeted system (to which the ping message is sent). Such events can also confirm application level "liveness." For example, a database engine able to respond to an existential "trigger" message can be assumed to also be capable of normal database operations. Absence of an existential event for a specific time period, that is characteristic of the event, indicates a problem. The absence of an expected event has often got to be confirmed by specific confirmatory, proactive action, such as a "test" message that always elicits a response from a live system.

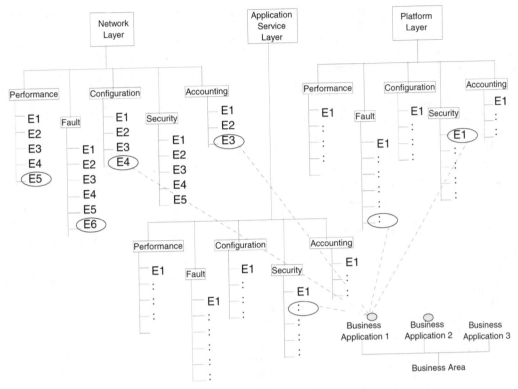

Figure 7.12: *Criteria for classifying events*

- "Prognostic" events provide an indication of some condition occurring in the infrastructure. For example, a sudden and sustained increase in traffic at a router interface with the Internet may indicate some form of attack. If this correlates with constant size packets then the hypothesis is strengthened. Such events are usually generated at a correlation engine.

7.4.2 Managing Event Classifications

The event classification model is a key resource, it should therefore aim to catalog and capture all potential events likely to arrive at each "event management point" in an enterprise. These points are provided by event monitoring frameworks.

An event classification is often used as a global event dictionary and distributed within infrastructure management groups as the definitive specification on how the respective events are treated.

The event catalog which results from capturing the event details is an important database. Information in this database is useful both as a stand-alone information resource accessed by infrastructure management staff or information may be used as input to in-house management applications. Developing this database from scratch should be done as a project with the eventual goals for the database as a key requirement in the database design.

Event gathering is likely to be distributed between autonomous agents, such as RMON agents, pattern recognition agents, mobile agents as well as through polling of systems by the management platform (acting as an agent). Events cannot be generated by agents without being configured with specific parameter values that define event-generation conditions.

Hence the configuration information for the agents is intimately related to the events the agents generate. As the infrastructure changes, the maintenance of event classification includes the maintenance of configuration values.

7.4.3 Operational Information about Events

Another class of information about events relates to "what to do" when the event is detected at a monitoring framework. These define information relevant to an operational context when an event is monitored.

The "output" of event classification is an important piece of work because it defines those events that will be recognized at the interface to the monitoring framework. In other words it defines the events that will be recognized versus events that will be filtered out when a mixture of events are seen at the interface. This is a common occurrence when some part of the infrastructure is in the process of failing:

- *Event severity.* The severity assigned to an event or class of events. These are defined as part of classifying the event. Some events (especially from the application layer) may merely denote warnings, while others may denote exceptions and others imminent failure. Events entering a monitoring framework should result in a ticket being generated. The pre-assigned severity levels allow ticketing software to assign agreed priorities for the event automatically. The severity is also displayed in maps. Infrastructure staff responsible for the processes that follow the event to its closure can then work to simple rules.

- *Severity of impact.* The specific origin of an event sometimes determines the severity or level of the impact on the infrastructure. In most infrastructure management organizations events that affect a large number of users pre-empt other types of events. An operations manager continuously has to re-prioritize on how resources are used for problem management. A common principle is based on *triage*—problems which affect a large number of users get the highest level attention, secondly—problems in areas with service level guarantees get the next biggest slice of attention, thirdly—all other problems are solved on a first-come-first-served basis.

- *Time-of-day impact.* Many business processes have a strict time-of-day requirement for completion of locally related activities or for the closure of the process. This is reflected at the infrastructure level in that some events are more critical-dependent on the time of day. This needs to be codified into the event definition for infrastructure management to be successful. It allows prioritization decisions to be made from the perspective of business impact. It is common for many business organizations to develop their service level agreements precisely from this perspective.

7.5 *Visualization of Events*

Developing a framework for capturing events from the client/server stack is relatively straightforward (see Chapter 8). Making sense of the instances of events that occur from a real world is quite another matter.

When distributed agents generate events, they are transported to a management platform for display. What is done next is dependent on many factors, in particular the internal organization of infrastructure management, (for example, whether process-based or crisis-team based).

The efficacy with which events are acted on is again dependent on several factors, including the knowledge about the event itself (layer or product), the skill and training in using the application.

Event visualization is an advanced class of application that allows events to be viewed through different contexts. Event visualization helps to de-skill the first level of processing on first seeing an event being displayed and hence reduces the variability with which events are handled. The commonest method of visualizing an event is to depict it in a map. Maps can be built for almost any relationship—physical, logical or semantic.

For example, any member of the infrastructure management staff could tell whether a particular component failure could affect a particular business process by seeing if the failure is being shown on a *process map* of the business operation. The process map of the business operation defines one *context* or perspective from which to consider an arbitrary event. The same event can be concurrently viewed from different contexts. Figure 7.13 shows how a single event may be mapped to different viewpoints.

Visualization allows the highly developed visual cortex of the human brain to be used most effectively in understanding patterns of multiple events.

Visualization is particularly important to infrastructure management due to the huge volume of events generated in a fully instrumented management environment. Given the ability to filter out "noise," the remaining events have to be processed and distributed to enable decisions to be made on their relevance.

Any aid to decision-making is especially important when the infrastructure is under stress during a crisis. Multiple secondary events generated as a result of even a single "root cause" can quickly swamp the infrastructure management capability both in terms of systems bandwidth and the human ability to handle inputs.

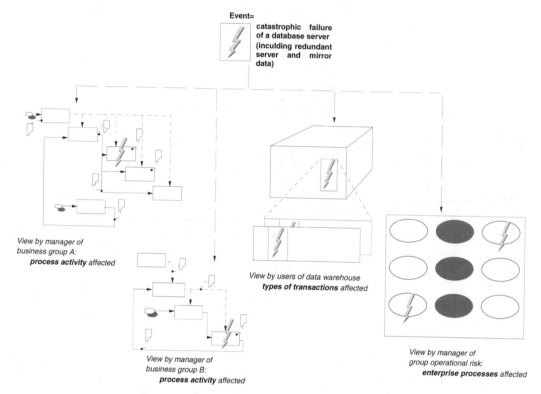

Figure 7.13: *Mapping events to different viewpoints*

7.5.1 Common Visualization Contexts

An arbitrary event from an agent in the managed environment may be viewed within several useful contexts:

- *Physical*—Location of the component the event refers to, with any unique "address" for the component, including any labelling or code assigned to the component. Maps of physical location help find the correct component. For example, most organizations keep their infrastructure components in special equipment areas. Often the layout of such areas is not widely known. Knowing where to look may be critical in a crisis.

- *Management area*—The type of event as classified in enterprise management—by layer and management area within the layer (e.g., as defined in Section 7.4 to include Fault, Performance threshold, Security violation, Configuration violation, Quota violation, etc.)

- *Risk factor*—Combination of events at multiple points on the infrastructure often compromise the integrity of the infrastructure. One scenario where this often happens is when there are over a certain number of events with high severity impact and the infrastructure management organization is unable to cope with the volume or uniqueness of the events. The risk factor increases as some part of the infrastructure has or is likely to collapse.

- *Business area*—The business areas (or the business processes within one area) affected on the basis of "consumption" of affected infrastructure resources. This context is common when service-level agreements are in place with specific business areas. The map defines an unambiguous specification of the resources and services covered by the agreement. Severity of business disruption in terms of number of people affected.

- *Impact extent*—The geographic extent of the areas affected by the event. For example, the loss of access to an un-replicated corporate database may affect all users in an enterprise.

Within each context the severity of the event is also displayed—usually in the form of a color or numeric code.

Concurrent contexts allow an event to be evaluated across multiple dimensions concurrently—although this is often done by different people with different interests in knowing the information.

Ideally, such contexts and the information available through them should be widely available to as large a constituency as can use the information usefully. The "channel" of distributing this information and the media for its visualization are therefore key issues.

7.5.2 Visualization Media

Until recently, representing events in contextual maps were the exclusive province of management platforms. Indeed, auto-discovery of and map-drawing capabilities (to denote simple physical and logical contexts) have been a heavily promoted selling point for platforms.

Network maps on network management platforms and resource maps on systems management platforms are the best known of visualization tools. These maps are used successfully to show the simpler contexts such as the "Physical" and "Business area" contexts described above. Severity levels are shown through color or textural changes.

Mapping logic is closely integrated into the platform tool's functionality. As such the efficacy of this media in terms of maintenance of the maps, (within a wider change management process for the infrastructure) is determined by the openness of the platform's map API. Communicating the information in maps to a wider audience has been more or less impossible without gaining knowledge of the map representation structures used by a platform. Similarly, viewing the maps without at least remote access to the platform user interface has been impossible.

Another more recent notion for building maps is through web pages. A web page for each context allows different representations of an event (through a separate web page for each context). Part of each web page can be an applet (loaded into the browser on first access), which periodically updates a users page display with any change of state. The information can be represented graphically or in more textual form. The applet would be responsible for any user-authentication scheme.

At the web server end, the server would more than likely generate the maps "on the fly" for each request from a browser client. The web server would access the sources for the event from databases and possibly at the interface to event-monitoring frameworks.

The use of "non-management" platform mechanisms (web servers and browsers) for visualization is a major paradigm shift in distributing infrastructure management information. It allows non-technical people, without any special tools other than a browser, to engage with management information relevant to the conduct of their business.

7.5.3 Architecture for Visualization

An architecture solution for developing visualization capabilities is helped by some of the advances in protocol technology such as configurable thresholds in the RMON specification. Figure 7.14 shows a logical chain of processing of an event leading to visualization.

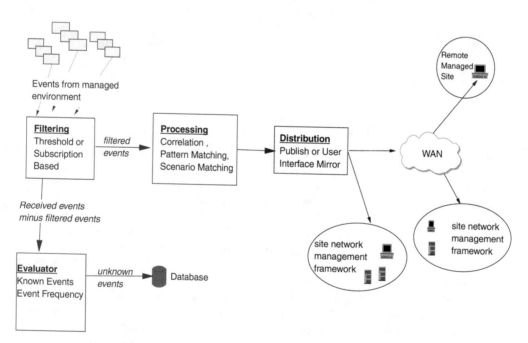

Figure 7.14: *Basic architecture of visualization solutions*

Events from the managed environment enter the event-monitoring framework. The event-monitoring framework should use information from the event catalog as a dictionary to identify events that "go forward" into the monitoring framework for further processing. Other events are recognized but not processed any further. At any given time the event catalog should be considered to be out of date. Hence a subset of received events are likely to be unknown.

Part of the maintenance process for managing the event classification and the resultant catalog is to examine information in the unknown events database.

Events that go forward are processed in the event monitoring framework and in the simplest case to display the event in all the relevant maps or logs. Basic processing includes assigning a severity code, and filtering out multiple instances of the same event.

Functionality also exists within different management products to process events further—for example, to correlate an event with other events or a model of events, or to identify a known sequence or pattern in an event stream.

The result of the processing is available within the monitoring framework and can also be distributed to a wider audience as data for display. Files of "map data" may be shipped offsite or the maps may be made available through a remote access method. Unfortunately, there aren't any widely available visualization products that go beyond maps.

7.5.4 Use of Maps for Visualization

A map whether management platform or web based, allows event information and in particular the source of an event, to be viewed from a static, a prior-specified perspective.

For example, an arbitrary *Fault* event may be shown on the following maps: (*a*) within a floor/rack level physical layout to define where the "event source" is located, (*b*) on subnet map to identify the logical network for the equipment, (*c*) on an end-user dependency map to show the actual end-users or group potentially impacted, (*d*) on a process flow map to show how it affects a known business process.

Different people in the organization view an event from different viewpoints. To a network manager the location and logical network details may be relevant, to the operations manager the business process impact is of relevance and to a relationship manager the end-user impact map is of relevance.

The collection of maps, or the "atlas" built for an organization allows events such as faults, security breaches, application exceptions, performance warnings, etc. to be viewed by different groups in the organization.

Maps define perspective essentially through defining relationships between sources of events and the *concepts* driving the perspective (e.g., event to *location* or event to *address* or event to *users*). Maps in a management frameworks can be categorized into:

- *Network level maps* that show the relationship of the event source to MAC layer and network layer concepts. At the network, *segments* and *subnets* respectively are the predominant concepts. These maps are native to most management platforms. Apart from manually re-ordering and collating map elements in terms of some predefined map hierarchy, little value can be added to the maps.

- *Service delivery maps.* These are arbitrary collections that define the usage of different components, resources and services in delivering an application service. Hence the proper functioning of resources in an arbitrary number of layers is needed to deliver the service. Such maps have to be developed by each organization.

Handcrafting of maps to represent individual contexts is relatively crude in the sense that there is a maintenance overhead as the infrastructure details change.

Many infrastructure management organizations which have embarked on map-based visualization have neglected maintenance of the maps as the infrastructure changed. This is true even with relatively simple network level maps where contrary to vendor claims, platform discovery algorithms are still able to populate only 70% to 80% of a map. The remainder have to be manually entered. Out-of-date maps results in inaccurate and incomplete information being used daily for operations management.

There are however examples of knowledge-based systems being used as a central change control point for event classifications, relationships within contexts and other infrastructure relationships. Maps are built dynamically using the relationships when an event matching any the contexts are received.

These were built in-house within large organizations that depend heavily on complex client/server systems for their business. While such investment is justifiable only in a minority of organizations, the payback is in terms of intelligence to manage global delivery systems. Chapter 12, Section 12.6.3, "Knowledge Bases," defines a knowledge representation method suitable for developing an infrastructure knowledge base.

7.5.5 Synchronized System Views

Enterprise-wide infrastructures and application delivery systems have several areas where a consistent view of the system is required regardless of the "point of observation." This is shown in Figure 7.15 where *exactly* the same information regarding a set of state variables is seen from multiple points.

The observation points need not be physical locations, but in fact may be logical. For example, global "value-at-risk" that a trading house is holding viewed from trading, accounting and decision support viewpoints. Common requirements for logical synchronized views are driven by distributed functions that concurrently execute a part of a business process.

Examples of more concrete topologies that commonly need to provide consistent views across multiple observation points include:

- The state map of WAN connectivity end-to-end, showing the delivery paths into the local area networks at each site (from the local areas networks of the other participating sites). In a meshed, routed environment this is the WAN interface map of all the routers used in WAN. In a managed (virtual) data network environment (such as

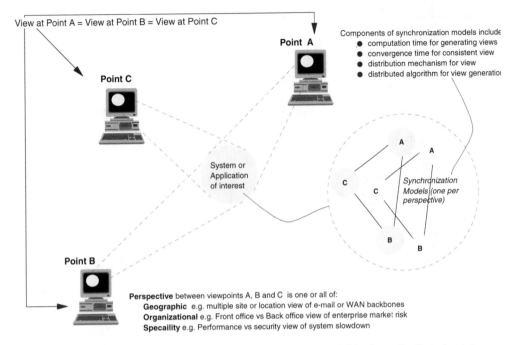

Figure 7.15: *Consistency in viewing state of subsystem variables from distributed points*

using a public frame relay) this is the state of the PVCs and the local area side of router interfaces.

- The servers required in the service delivery paths for an enterprise-wide application and the network "paths" to those servers end to end. The application can be a horizontal application such as e-mail and global intranet services or vertical business applications used by a distributed business group.

Synchronized views allow the computing and network environments to be "chunked" into meaningful abstractions. Such views are also essential to developing 7 x 24-hour network control centers. Monitoring responsibility for global applications and business systems can be rotated on a "follow-the-sun" basis.

More than one large global securities investment house and most utility companies have the ability to achieve this today.

Synchronized views are usually achieved through exploiting database technology. A database application "assembles" subviews replicated from external sites and distributes the views.

Other technologies such as multicast of application-level messages are also applicable and used in publish/subscribe-based trading floor applications in investment banking.

7.6 *Books for Further Reading*

Beekman, George, *et al. Computer Confluence* (Exploring Tomorrow's Technology). Benjamin/Cummings, 1997.

Buschmann, Frank. *Pattern-Oriented Software Architecture.* John Wiley & Sons, 1996.

Muftic, S., *et al. Security Architecture for Open Distributed Systems.* John Wiley & Sons, 1993.

Neilson, Robert, R. *Collaborative Technologies & Organizational Learning.* Idea Group Pub., 1997.

Architecture of Management Frameworks

Areas covered in this chapter

- A framework-based approach to developing infrastructure management technology

- Limits of scaling current management solutions to an enterprise level

- Structure and case study of a monitoring framework for infrastructure-wide events

- Principles for developing a basic control framework

- Options for developing an infrastructure management information distribution framework

- Structure and case study of a remote access framework

- Building capacity management capability using multiple frameworks—expressed as a "long" case study

- Principles for deploying frameworks

I n Chapter 7 two roles were defined for "architecture" in infrastructure management: (*a*) providing solutions for the current technology deficit in key areas, and (*b*) defining an enterprise-specific roadmap for the deployment and evolution of management technology. This chapter looks at solutions from the perspective of building such a roadmap.

These solutions are called "frameworks"—and define "prototypes" in four main areas— monitoring, information distribution, basic control and remote access. (See Figure 8.1.) A set of management frameworks essentially defines a service level architecture for management. Conventional management areas such as fault and capacity management use the services of the frameworks for execution of their functions. This mapping is shown in Figure 8.2.

In the simplest sense each framework is a collection of network, hardware and software resources dedicated to the purpose of providing a set of services for managing the infrastructure. Frameworks define the skeleton of the functional behavior required to develop infrastructure management functions. Every framework is defined by a set of components with specific roles.

An enterprise-wide management architecture is built from "connecting" together the frameworks. In this sense frameworks are the building blocks of the architecture. For the

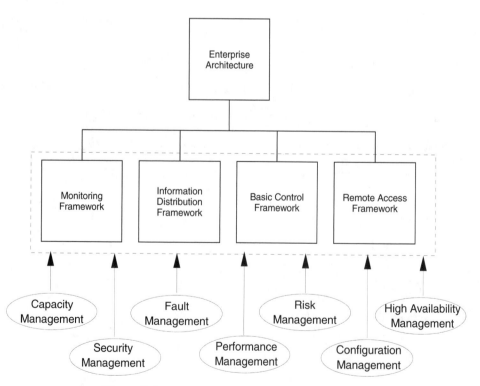

Figure 8.1: *Key frameworks for enterprise architecture*

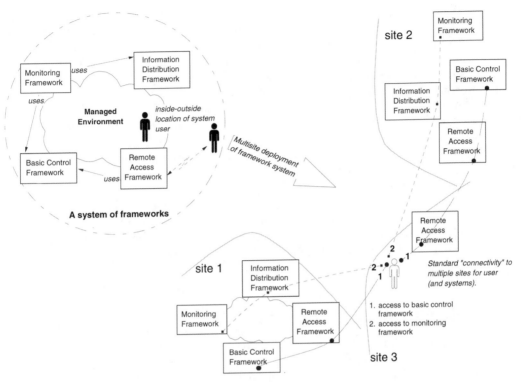

Figure 8.2: *Enterprise architecture in terms of using framework services*

actual "realization" of each framework in an enterprise, off-the-shelf products and sometimes bespoke software are used as actual components. At the current state of product fragmentation these components may have to be specialized depending on the part of the infrastructure being managed. Hence different schemes are needed for managing networks, systems and applications components.

In most enterprises this is also reflected in distinct management groups being responsible for network, systems and applications. Each of the groups have a complete "culture" centered around specific platforms, tools, agents and protocols. This has also led to extremes in skill specialization in each area.

In Chapter 1 we look at the drivers for the evolution in the way client/server infrastructures are managed, which combines the services provided by these three areas into end-to-end services. A goal in defining a management framework is to provide common solutions and systems capability for these distinct groups to "merge."

Looked at from a computational viewpoint, the significant autonomous processing done in agents (such as RMON agents, smart agents and scaling agents described in Chapter 11) have the effect of distributing the processing across many entities.

The results of these agent-level computations are events signifying some occurrence and sometimes data. Both events and data have to be processed by higher level functions (often by multiple applications) before any meaning can be attributed to the results. This "reality," of infrastructure management itself being a distributed application, is however rarely recognized when designs for network, systems or application management are considered.

In distributed computing more components have to cooperate together to do anything useful. Hence, for example, thought needs to be given about how the management function will survive failures of "subsystems" in its service-delivery chain (in supporting the management function).

The biggest threat to most management frameworks in use today is that there is no separation of management resources. The environment being managed and the resources used for management share the same infrastructure.

Strategically, without a physically separate structure to "house" management resources, infrastructure management will have limited effectiveness as it gets impacted by the very failures it is trying to fix. Developing a physical infrastructure management framework does incur cost, typically 10% to 15% of the capital cost of management resources (platforms, agents, tools, databases).

8.1 Drivers for Frameworks

For better or worse SNMP is the only standards based protocol that has wide acceptance in the industry. This ubiquity makes it available for managing almost all parts of an infrastructure's stack—from network devices to application components.

SNMP as the "lowest common factor" (between the managing systems and the managed environment), determines to a large degree, the technology deficits that need to be "made up" through architecture.

The station-agent model (described in Chapter 1, Section 1.7) is used in network management, systems management and increasingly in applications management. In control terms this is a model of the master (station) controlling a number of slaves (agents). A central station controlling a number of agents in a sense reflects organizational reality of a centralized group managing resources in its domain—and is therefore one with a significant "emotional" appeal.

It is however totally outmoded for applying to the task of managing client/server infrastructures—which consist of many components stacked vertically while being distributed horizontally. There is therefore a massive defect in the manger-agent model in areas like scaleability, data-models, control and security to deal with the reality of managing client/server systems.

Infrastructure management technology has not progressed much in the 1990s. Many promising visions such as OSF's Distributed Management Environment (DME) and even SNMP V2 have fallen by the wayside. Vendors have by and large been content to boost sales revenues which have burgeoned with the global take-up of client/server-based computing. Innovation has taken a back-seat.

Instrumenting a client/server environment involves using different types of agents, each of which has a very narrow focus. Balancing the economics of instrumentation with the need for unified end-to-end management (desktop to desktop and everything in between) is one problem. Given the rate at which the remit of infrastructure management is expanding, enterprise's need a roadmap to help plan the investment in management technology.

Enterprise architecture is needed to help in both design and operational aspects of infrastructure management. The lack of scaleability of current models for client/server environments and lack of a unified model for representing the whole infrastructure are the two top reasons stopping many organizations today. These are described in detail below:

Lack of scaleability. As the size of the managed environment increases current management schemes reach their limits of effectiveness. The size of the managed environment increases as the number of computing resources (workstations, laptops, servers, network printers, etc.) in an organization grows.

The increase in mobile computing and information distribution using a corporate intranet has brought a heightened "democratization" in expectations of service from the infrastructure. Now everybody expects a 7 x 24-hour uptime. The problem of scaleability affects several areas of management.

- A "fully" instrumented client/server infrastructure results in increased management traffic. Significant volume and burstiness of management traffic can affect normal business traffic if the two share a common backbone.

- Client/server infrastructures often span several types of offices (ranging from a campus to a single mobile user). Management solutions that are economically viable across this range are difficult to find.

- Lack of secure and reliable control of the instrumentation. As the number of instrumented points increase control activities take up significant time. The security and reliability with which activities such as reconfiguration of agents and upgrading of virus scanning packages determines the effectiveness of management.

Another area where scaleability is an issue is when dealing with a crisis situations such as the failure of a network component. Once a centralized manager's resources is being used for crisis management in one area, its ability for providing normal services for the unaffected areas is often compromised. Handling of multiple crises often have to be serialized.

SNMP agents have to be to polled for conditions other than events to be collected. Also, since SNMP traps use an unreliable transport protocol, any loss of trap messages remain undetected. Polling to capture change of state of some set of variables is a second line tactic to catch important events.

The case with SNMP agents is that as their numbers increase, the basic manager-agent relationship becomes untenable for adequate monitoring. This is because a single manager can only poll a finite number of agents before bandwidth usage escalates. Secondly, the computational capability of the manager will be exhausted on polling some finite number of agents. Before such exhaustion, however, the frequency of polling will be too low to be meaningful in management terms.

Piecemeal focus of the manager-agent model. In each main area of infrastructure management—networks, systems, and application services, the manager-agent model is a de facto standard for tool development.

One of the reasons why these areas look fragmented from each other is that, in the absence of any standards, vendors in each area have unilaterally developed their own manager-agent model. A large enterprise often ends up with 20 to 70 different technology bases for agents. Moreover there is usually a special console to manage each type of agent. The fact that console applications can be launched from a common management platform adds little value.

In Chapter 7, Section 7.1, the *extent* of deployment of a client/server application is shown as being a prime reason of making its management a complex affair. Application extent essentially forces an increase in the diameter of the management domain. The greater the diameter the greater the diversity of the resources that need to be managed and the greater the discontinuity of technologies used to realize the management structure.

The inadequacies of the manager-agent model in dealing with extent is across all three areas of monitoring, control and reporting:

A typical centralized manager usually works only with its own agent family. Centralized managers for networks and systems management handle agents differently. While schemes such as auto-discovery are available for one layer, they often have undocumented gaps in what is discoverable. Such discontinuity results in gaps in the way a dispersed environment is enabled for monitoring. Gaps create uncertainty about whether the true picture is being seen by the centralized manager.

In a small management domain different types of agents can be mixed and hand configured. The more dispersed the environment the less likely this is. In many organizations the initial configurations remain in place because it is too hard to change.

Since different managers deal with different areas and even different families within the same area, consolidating information about resources from the different areas is impossible. In a local office, information can be gathered by looking at different consoles. In a dispersed environment visual consolidation is less feasible.

8.1.1 Methods Available for Scaling the Manager-Agent Model

Platform vendors have belatedly started to provide some capabilities for scaling. Figure 8.3 shows three methods currently available for scaling the manager-agent model.

With the first method the manager's console can be logically separated from the manager and database "servers." This allows the manager to work independently as a central server for monitoring and event management while multiple console clients can access the services.

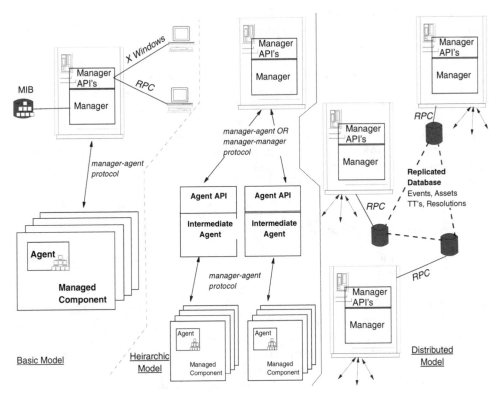

Figure 8.3: *Currently achievable manager-agent scaling models*

The second method uses the concept of introducing a hierarchic level by an intermediate agent or "middle manager" which looks like a manager to the agents and like an agent to the manager. Middle managers field local monitoring and event management. Only predefined events are escalated to a central manager. The central manager may view the middle managers as peers in which case a peer-to-peer protocol over RPC is used. When the middle manager is viewed as an agent then SNMP is likelier. Middle mangers are sold as products or can be realized from development kits. Low-cost monitoring platforms can be attached to developed middle managers to view local events.

The third method provides scaling by distributing managers and providing communication protocol (e.g., CMIP or SNMP v2) between the managers. Information such as the management domain is "unified" at the database level This allows management information to be viewed logically rather than being manager or location specific.

The three methods can be mixed and matched. Caution is needed however when attempting to scale-up using vendor supplied solutions:

- The cost of high-end network and systems management technology (which is already prohibitive to many organizations with client/user) gets pushed up even further when scaling features are added.

- Easy to get long-term lock-in into a single vendor's solutions. It is likely to be difficult to mix and match vendors scaling architectures as well as re-engineering existing management set-ups.

- The dominant network and system management technology vendors have been short on product innovation for managing "mature" client/server based computing environments. (Vendors depend instead on the increasing new adopters of client/server technology for market share.)

8.1.2 An Architectural View of Scaling

To manage (i.e., to monitor, report and control) on a large scale requires "repeatable" solutions to a number of issues. These issues are discussed below:

Proliferation of agents. The number of types of agents, especially resident in hosts is increasing. There is also a trend for static agents to be more and more specialized. One for inventory, one for security audit, one for monitoring operating system resources, one for monitoring a database management system, one for distributing software, and so on.

When client/server infrastructures first geared up, the cost and convenience of specialized agents looked attractive. Managing a typical set of some five to eight static agents across a large number of geographically distributed hosts is not viable in the longer term.

First and foremost is the cost element of agents as a client/server environment is geared up. In many enterprises, agents are usually first deployed on servers. For many types of management tasks, however, information from the desktop systems is also needed. Deploying agents on desktops drastically changes the economics of this approach. A consequence of this is that many deployment programs are curtailed.

The second longer term viability issue is one of change management. To track and change agents individually as their features get enhanced, or as the version of the component being managed changes, is a logistic nightmare in large environments.

Large volumes of events. An average client/server environment today contains several thousands points that can be instrumented with agents. A device such as a server or a workstation used in a client/server application may have multiple points of monitoring (by the same or multiple agents). Hence the number of points that are monitored within a client/server environment could well be in the tens of thousands range.

Significant bandwidth of the managed device's CPU and communications bandwidth can be consumed by local agents in the course of computing and sending events. Communication requirements effectively get aggregated over the network. Architectural mechanisms have to be deployed to minimize both these overheads. After detecting an event, the decision point at the agent end is whether the event should be forwarded to the next level in real-time or is locally logged.

Events are also going to go missing. For example, SNMP is carried in the transport protocol UDP. If a UDP packet is lost, the event is not known by the sending or receiving end since UDP packets are not acknowledged by the receiving end.

Auto-configuration. As the number of managed agents become large, configuring each individual agent from a central point becomes impractical. This is true in both initial deployment of an agent technology into a client/server layer and in subsequent reconfiguration of the agents.

Auto-configuration is the ability to discover the necessary relationships: agents need to discover the target for their output streams and sources for their control parameters. In a scaling-up architecture based on mid-level managers, both agents and the mid-level managers need to discover their respective targets and sources.

Auto-configuration is essentially a protocol executed by these components, and a key point of design is whether the hierarchically lower or the hierarchically higher component is responsible for initiating auto-configuration.

Auto-configuration is especially relevant for establishing service after failure of a component. Redundant components need to be available, so that dependent components can reconfigure to use the alternative path.

Redundancy and security. Agents and agent intermediaries are bound to fail. Redundancy ensures that there are alternative components to service dependent components. The availability of redundant components and an auto-configuration protocol are key requirements in large-scale management. The ability to auto-configure raises a number of security issues. In particular any new relationships set up between components on auto-configuration should be verifiable as being with genuine components. In some cases message integrity is also important.

8.1.3 Relationship to Processes and People

Deployment of infrastructure management technology should be related to how it is going to be used. Far too often the (human) managers responsible for infrastructure give little thought to how a set of tools are going to be used. The fact that one or two individuals are keen to use a tool is taken as sufficient evidence that the tool will be used productively. In small or local environments this probably still works.

In a large or complex client/server environment (where thousands of agents of different technology bases have to be offered) a more structured approach to tool selection and development is required. Ensuring adequate training of all the staff likely to use the tools is also essential.

Most large organizations have therefore ended up with a portfolio of network and system management products, none of which can be productively made to work with each other (within processes).

Even in organizations where significant investment in tools has been made, it is worthwhile revisiting the area to analyze:

- Compatibility between the tools and the organizational structure.

- How day-to-day processes (or procedures) actually use the tools.

- Whether individual tools are adequate for actual use.

- Where the pressures for automation are.

In many cases the relationship between technology, processes and the people using the tools have to be engineered—for example, using the tools described in Chapter 4. Management frameworks can be viewed as a set of building blocks for building the technology.

8.2 Monitoring Framework

The main goal of a monitoring framework is to allow events and data from the different parts of the client/server infrastructure to be collected, filtered and presented for further processing. Further processing may entail:

- Display of the actual event received (or a representation of it). Typically, a received event such as a trap from an RMON agent will get displayed in a map depicting the RMON "device." A human being then acts on the information.

- "Integration" of the actual event received, transforming the information "value" of the original event. Information value is increased by combining in some way information in multiple event instances. A common function is *correlation*, which is essentially a search for known relationships between the sources of two or more events. Once a relationship is discovered then inferences (such as the "root" event causing "secondary" events) can be made. These conclusions can be displayed in addition to the actual events.

- Triggering an action by the framework to collect more comprehensive information. Sometimes events received at the monitoring interface don't carry much information other than indicating that any one of a whole set of conditions exist. Typically, SNMP traps from devices carry information as a value which identifies the area in which something interesting has happened. Further MIB values have to be evaluated to pinpoint/verify the cause.

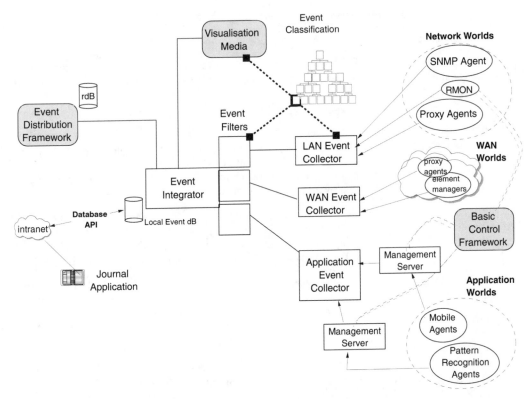

Figure 8.4: *Abstract components of an event monitoring framework*

Figure 8.4 shows an event monitoring framework as a set of abstract components. The function of the components is described in more detail in Section 8.2.1. The event monitoring framework interfaces other frameworks:

- With the event distribution framework for distributing event related information.

- With the visualization subsystem for display/presentation of events.

- With the control framework for reconfiguration of remote agents.

The monitoring framework also provides access to an event database through an off-the-shelf database related API. Access to a relational database allows web-based applications to be developed at relatively low cost.

There are some important considerations for building an event monitoring framework for a client/server infrastructure. These are summarized below and Table 8.1 shows how the requirement is supported by the event monitoring framework described here.

Table 8.1: Supporting Client/Server Requirements for Monitoring

Requirement	Support for Requirement in Framework
Coverage of whole client/server stack	The monitoring framework needs to support all the types of agents found in the different layers. This includes the capability to deploy and configure these agents. An event classification system ties together the events from different agent classes with operational use of the event.
Heterogeneity of client/server environment	A universal agent architecture is needed to coordinate access to event information "natively" available in log files, in console message streams and other sources of status information in systems. Intelligent proxy agents are needed to convert from one protocol to another, including from text output on a system to SNMP traps.
Extent of client/server environment	The framework components need to be distributable in an "economic" manner (cost and network bandwidth) in an enterprise with hub-site managing satellite offices. Event classification defines the priority of events. Data engineering defines how information is stored and used.
Tuning the monitoring framework	Predefined templates in the form of graphical front ends are needed to reconfigure devices and systems safely and easily. Use of one control framework ensures consistency and reduces training needs.

The first point is that events from all the layers in the client/server stack have to be monitored. For example, the networks, subsystem, application services infrastructure model described in Chapter 7, Section 7.8.1, is one possible layer model. End-to-end views are not possible without integrating events from the whole stack.

Secondly, client/server infrastructures are likely to be heterogeneous in one or more layers. Similar events from similar components have to be collected and "normalized." For example, any two similar inter-networking devices from two vendors are more than likely to use different SNMP trap values to signify the same type of event. Similar events need to normalized before "semantically higher" processing such as correlation can be made scalable for a large infrastructure.

Thirdly, a client/server infrastructure is likely to be widely distributed. Events from widely separated components have to be "normalized" in a different sense. For example, a time-stamp is often attached to events received from different locations, so that the receive order is captured. Also, monitoring frameworks in different locations is likely to have to be "connected" in some way. In a large enterprise, event monitoring frameworks may need solutions for small office, mid-size and large offices.

Fourthly, a significant proportion of the agent technology is likely to have to be reconfigured and tuned on a regular basis—for operational control of the generation of events. Such reconfiguration is often a result of the wider change management. Adding new users and applications, upgrading an application component, re-engineering part of the infrastructure—are all often followed by tuning the thresholds for monitoring. Tools for such operational re-tuning need to be well integrated as a function for the monitoring framework.

8.2.1 Event Monitoring Components

An event monitoring framework for a client/server infrastructure can be built from a set of abstract building blocks. The main functions within each of the event monitoring framework components are shown in Figure 8.4 and are described below:

Agents. Management agents that are runtime resident in systems to be managed. These provide monitoring and control capabilities at different layers of the client/server model. Agents are generally specialized to specific sub-problems of system management. Hence different agents may be required for performance management, for configuration management and security management. The initial use of agents is for reporting events to the tools on the system management platform. Proxy agents are software components which on one side can communicate with the management platform (using SNMP) and on the other side interface with non-SNMP components such as legacy systems.

Local management servers. These provide a local staging post for collecting information provided by local management agents and providing the means to hold software for distribution (upload) to agents. Examples includes software code for security audit agents, scripts for defining threshold configuration and filter configurations to the local agent. Use of such servers decreases the management traffic that needs to otherwise traverse the network.

Collectors. Collect management information staged by local management servers. This introduces a two-level hierarchy for collecting information—allowing global system management structures such as a rolling, 24-hour, system management center to be designed. The hierarchy also allows redundancy to be designed at relatively low cost.

Integrators. Integrate management information (through combining, conversion and filtering) from specific perspectives—these allow sets of information from the distributed sources to be viewed from physical (which hardware is involved and where it is located) trading systems (which software services and relationships are involved), business area (which business area, which group of people, which trading activity). New perspectives are designed and programmed as the needs arise and as the environment changes.

Visualization subsystems. These are software mechanisms to present information from the system management framework into a human-digestible form. Typically distributed agents produce information overload if their raw data is viewed without pre-processing—this is especially evident in a crisis mode when the information flow generally increases. Visualization mechanisms include maps, surface and volume geometry and more mundane techniques such as instrument panels and graphs.

Databases. Relational databases are used to hold historical information received as events from the distributed servers. This information can then be used by external applications for reporting, queries, status updates. Modern relational databases such as Sybase allow use of the open server interface and triggers to realize integration to applications such as a distributed ticketing system and object oriented journals (for classification of assets, alarms, etc. on a temporal or other basis).

Other frameworks. Event monitoring is dependent on a number of other frameworks including the data in the event classification scheme, a visualization mechanism to present event information and the basic control framework.

8.2.2 Monitoring Remote Offices

Monitoring of multiple client/server applications at remote offices, in a consistent way, is one of the major problems that face infrastructure management.

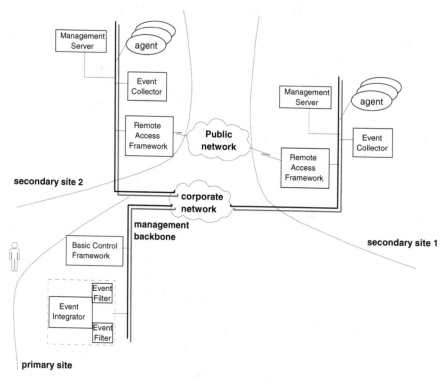

Figure 8.5: *Remote office monitoring*

An event monitoring framework has to be "distributable" so that different-size offices can be integrated. This is made easier by the building block approach. Communication between the building blocks transfers information to a more central point.

The organization of management responsibility determines the information architecture for managing the information. This responsibility is usually in terms of a hierarchy of a primary office responsible for the management of a number of secondary offices. The distributed building blocks of the monitoring framework connect together through the corporate network. Figure 8.5 shows how the monitoring framework is distributed—with the event integration and basic control and information distribution functions at the primary site. At the secondary sites event collection and agent management functions are deployed. The remote access framework provides out-of-band access if the corporate network becomes inoperable for management. In some organizations there is a third level of small or "affiliate"

Case Study 8.1: A Monitoring Framework in a European Investment Bank

Monitoring frameworks are built from commercial off-the-shelf systems and products. The following is a case study at an organization which built a monitoring framework to monitor its mission critical client/server environment and a large proportion of its other infrastructure. Figure 8.6 shows the products used to realize event monitoring in terms of the abstract components described in Section 8.2.1. This framework was built and deployed over 18 months and therefore used products available at the beginning of the period.

The components are briefly described below:

- Low cost SunNet Manager platforms form the collection and agent manager mechanisms at remotely monitored offices. The hardware platform is also shared for: (a) RMON based software agents, (b) a proprietary event dictionary utility, (c) a proprietary event filter driven by the event dictionary. This system of software collects events from RMON and proprietary log reporting agents and forwards specified events (in event dictionary) to the management center.

- The Command Post platform from Boole and Babbage forms the centerpiece of the monitoring framework at a primary management center. It integrates different classes of events including logs from local mainframes, application servers and database servers, "pre-correlated" wide area network events, as well as events from remotely monitored sites (that the management center is responsible for).

Event visualization is provided through Command Post's event lists and maps. In addition SunNet Manager's event display capability was driven by a map drawing tool which created business level contextual maps using information from Command Post's event database.

- Event information distribution to local infrastructure management staff, for use in management processes is through a ticketing and workflow system (Remedy Action Request System). The same system is used in help desk creation of trouble tickets.

- Exchange of information with other management centers is through replication of event and ticketing databases.

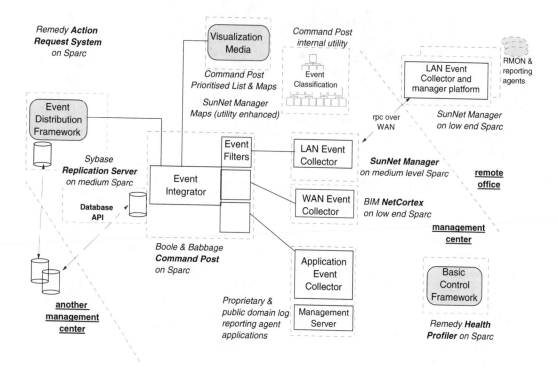

Figure 8.6: *Case study of a monitoring framework*

offices that need to be considered in a monitoring framework. Depending on the number of such offices, monitored information can be staged either at a secondary level or communicated directly to the primary level. An alternative is to treat this third level of offices as a "mobile" population and apply fault reporting scheme for mobile workers.

Building blocks for monitoring at a secondary office are sensitive to two major issues—which should be contained through specific business criteria:

- *Cost.* As resources are being duplicated at each office, the overall costs can escalate with each office. Maintenance and support costs for these resources should be minimized.

- *Bandwidth.* As communication is required between primary monitoring centers and secondary centers, the actual bandwidth "lost" to business traffic needs to be minimized—through filtering events based on the event classification and also through staging events in a temporary event database. These can be examined from the primary center out-of-hours when bandwidth requirements are low.

8.3 *Basic Control Framework*

Many third-party network management applications are integrated to management platforms, mostly in name. Other than being able to launch the application from the platform, integration such as information sharing between applications is unlikely to have been implemented.

As management platforms get burdened by more and more applications, the redistribution of applications across multiple platforms is a reasonable alternative to "collected data" traversing an inter-network to a point where it can be processed at the platform.

This is especially the case when the information from an application is not shareable with any other applications at the platform. Required result sets can be extracted by automated database processes in batch or triggered modes.

Data analysis and configuration tools associated with autonomous agents (such as RMON and RMON II) described in Chapter 11, are other candidates for redistribution and redeployment as the managed environment changes.

These two types of redistribution are commonly undertaken as reengineering activities. Redistribution ought to be possible through dynamic control of the management environment as a normal part of its evolution.

A basic control framework is a collection of generic tools and (where it is unavoidable) product-specific tools. These are used as an environment for controlling a managed environment. Geographically dispersed management groups can share the same environment. Activities that are control-oriented include:

- *Configuration of devices and systems.* Infrastructure management starts with the set-up of individual elements—network devices, hosts, operating system software and service components. These work together as an infrastructure. Management, however, involves constant tuning and changing of individual elements. Different parts of the infrastructure use different technologies—e.g., Telnet for some network components, TCL/TK scripts for the operating system, a proprietary command language for each service component. Networking device vendors usually have specific tools to configure and tune. Product specific applications are an important part of the management toolkit. These applications are increasingly delivered as "stand-alone" on low-cost Windows-based PCs or for execution in a web browser. A basic control framework should have an environment for such tools to be launched on an as-needed basis.

- *Configuration of framework components.* Frameworks such as monitoring framework in Section 8.2 have distributed components that need configuration and tuning. Here, a template-based approach that captures all the variables into a single-user interface context works best. Such templates can be realized using TCL/TK as well as Java. Changing values through the template is an error-free way of configurations.

- *Automated polling.* Much of what happens in a client/server may be captured and logged locally. It is by and large impractical to transport anything but a small proportion of these as events. Nevertheless the dynamics of a client/server infrastructure is often locked in "counter" type variables. When accessed at an adequate frequency, these values provide important prognostic information which can be turned into a class of event that provide a prognosis. Automated polling is a script-based "thread" of execution to poll or get a set-requisite variable value. The script stores the result in a database, or passes the values to another piece of logic which correlate the results from several such threads.

- *Automated responses to events.* In SNMP a trap merely indicates that a closer look is needed. Every trap should have a set of variables that need to be examined on receipt of the trap. In some cases the variables can be examined and further action taken. Other events can trigger corrective or preventive actions.

Figure 8.7 shows the relationships between key components of a control framework. The above control mechanisms involve the use-scripts to define the logic for automated polling and responses. Configuration of devices and framework components can be "fronted" by a graphical user interface, with logic behind the user interface to test the validity of parameters entered through the interface.

TCL/TK is one environment for developing management interfaces and powerful scripts. The emerging Java Management API (discussed in Chapter 10, Section 10.7.5) is another environment.

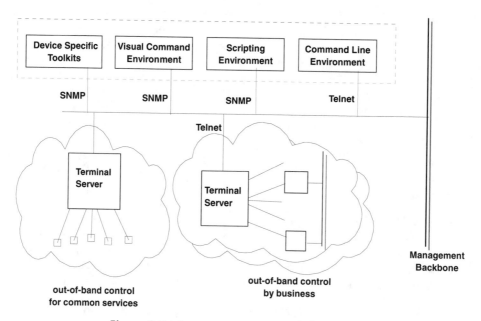

Figure 8.7: *Components of basic control framework*

8.3.1 SNMP Sets

Many devices on the infrastructure can be controlled through SNMP sets. Sets have generally not been used with inter-networking components such as routers and switches largely because of security fears. (See Chapter 10, Section 10.2.4, "Security Threats with SNMP.")

These threats are lessened considerably when the infrastructure is segmented through internal firewalls. Firewalls protecting SNMP enabled systems need to have policy-based control over the pass-through of SNMP traffic from outside. Developing logic to monitor, capture, analyze and create security alarms when SNMP traffic enters a protected segment is another tactic to improve use level security.

Proprietary MIBs are developed by many organizations to support parts of the infrastructure, such as "middleware"—which is a set of services that sits above the operating system and below the application layer. Middleware is important in "gluing" and coordinating together distributed application components.

The realization of multi-layered client/server applications has resulted in a resurgence in the use of SNMP sets. It is especially relevant in "concurrently" configuring different parts of the infrastructure.

Sets involving variables with application level relationships, however, need a graphical front-end to enable their use. In fact anything but the simplest case of configuring requires a user-interface abstraction if the sets are to be done consistently and without error.

A front-end designed for a specific management task can be distributed as an internal standard tool doing the task for different parts of the management organization.

Such front-ends can be developed relatively easily, for example, within TCL/TK or Java-based environments. The front-end developed in TK or JavaScript should include logic to validate parameter entry and parameter relationships. Both TCL/TK and Java offer SNMP "aware" extensions for transformation to SNMP commands.

Hiding the details of SNMP sets from the user reduces the opportunities for both accidental and malicious mis-configurations.

8.3.2 Out-of-Band Management

Out-of-band management enables management in the event that the infrastructure management resources fail. Examples of failure that can render normal management to be ineffective include:

- A "central" management server (or server cluster) failing can stop the management platform applications or databases.

- An inter-network component such as a router or a switch failing can stop connectivity to the managed environment.

In addition to building in high availability solutions, explicit strategies should exist for managing such contingencies. A management alternative is required while recovering from such failures.

Access to devices and systems is possible via the operator interface available with most network devices and server systems. This allows command line access from a terminal or terminal emulator software to key status information and the ability to configure parameters using command. Telnet is a common terminal protocol.

Part of the basic control framework should include an independent substructure to access operator interfaces (from the infrastructure management LAN). This is often achieved by using a terminal server connected to a separate segment. Generally, two classes of systems need to be accessed in the event of normal infrastructure management systems failure:

- Access to managed resources of mission-critical applications.

- Access to common or "backbone" infrastructure resources.

Having a second method of access to the infrastructure clearly raises issues of securing the channel until an emergency occurs. A simple tactic is to "power-up" the channel only when it is needed.

The out-of-band management capability is immeasurably enhanced by having on-line help about the command set of devices and systems accessible through the structure. This is possible by scanning in a basic manual for each system. A further step is to have graphical templates for common commands likely to be executed through the out-of-band structure.

8.4 Information Distribution Framework

Event classification described in Chapter 7, Section 7.4, results in the definition of events of importance to infrastructure management in a specific enterprise. Monitoring frameworks allow the gathering and storage of this event information. In both network management and systems management the management platform is the key component in event capture and storage. Collection of events from application components is more than often through bespoke solutions.

For a long time management platform vendors have been insisting that relational (SQL) databases are not critical to managing information received from network and system elements. Various proprietary and unstructured data storage (such as flat files) have been widely deployed.

In a framework-based architecture SQL databases play a central role largely because as a standard many vendors support interfaces to SQL databases and because SQL data can be transported easily.

Figure 8.8 shows two examples of event distribution where the SQL database technology provides off-the-shelf solutions:

- Information from an SQL event database can be "mined" dynamically by a web server according to a context specified by a web user.

- Information from an SQL database from remote sites can be collected at a central location through simple scripts.

An information distribution framework quite simply allows management information to be used more productively. Often, constituencies outside the management team can also find use for the information. For example, information in a trouble-ticket database can be analyzed by a department tracking global service-level conformance with service providers. Three major categories of information distribution schemes are:

- *Ticketing/workflow based.* Usually provided by a software package that interfaces with the management platform's event database, filtering and generating tickets for recognized events. Tickets can also be manually generated. Tickets are then distributed to "clients."

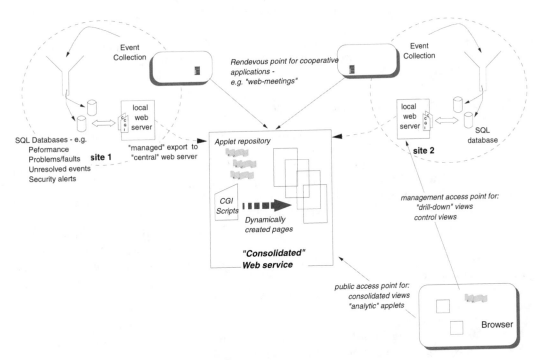

Figure 8.8: *Examples of SQL database in distribution roles*

- *Web and intranet based.* Provided through advanced web servers that "mine" data from one or more SQL databases (for which the web server has rights access to) using criteria defined at the browser by a requesting user. The mined data is converted to web pages for display to the requesting user.

- *Mobile agent based.* Provided usually by made to order technology that transports an executable entity with a specific purpose to one or more target hosts. The usual purposes for the executable are to collect data from, or to configure the target host's environment.

The first two are used to distribute information to users while the last is normally used to distribute systems information. All three may be present side by side in an infrastructure management organization. In most organizations however only ticketing/workflow based systems are likely, however, web/intranet-based frameworks are becoming more common especially to distribute infrastructure status to end-users.

Mobile agent-based frameworks have been used for highly secure transport of systems information including cryptographic keys and for global upgrade of virus scanning software. (Other uses are described in Chapter 11, Section 11.5.)

Table 8.2 compares the three types of frameworks. All three are described in the following subsections.

End-users are a part of the rationale for information distribution frameworks, hence a comparison of the usage of the three frameworks is shown in Table 8.3.

8.4.1 Ticketing and Workflow Based Framework

Largely used to distribute information within an infrastructure management organization, the most common type of information carried is encapsulated in a "ticket." The ticket represents an event that needs resolution (or may be almost any other type of communication that is relevant as input to the infrastructure management organization).

Automatically generating a ticket when an event is recognized in effect makes the event "persistent." Event classification described in Chapter 7, Section 7.4, should drive what is actually recognized at the event. Once generated the ticket records the event's effect and its resolution path. A ticket continues to persist not only in an active portion of a ticket/resolutions database but also is usually archived. Figure 8.9 shows the components of a distribution framework for tickets.

Once a ticket is generated it is transported on a determined route—often by the execution of simple rules:

- An information field in the ticket is used to index into a lookup table which matches the type of event to some subgroup of the infrastructure management organization. Hence different types of events can be routed to specific groups—e.g., a security event to a security group or high availability failure to a crisis team.

Table 8.2: *A Comparison of Information Distribution Schemes*

	Ticketing/Workflow	Web/Intranet	Mobile Agents
Cost	Submit clients are low cost. Relatively expensive when a large number of "clients" need to manage ticket flow (write licenses)—i.e., true in a large infrastructure management organization and in most process-centered organizations.	High-end web server (with dynamic interface to SQL database) and browser licenses.	Largely recurring development costs as new executables are created.
User interface	Submissions via bespoke client or via a web browser at a platform. Form-based dialog. Bespoke clients usually provide two-way communication.	Web browser based—hence open and accessible from potentially any platform. Form-based dialog (data validation is an option).	Not applicable.
Scaleability	Scales well within a "single site" management organization. Multi-site reach requires replicated database.	Enterprise-wide so long as web can be accessed.	Enterprise-wide so long as transport mechanism has reach.
Security	No particular notion of security.	Both browser and server level security through the web security extensions (SSL and SHTTP).	Safe interpreter. Encryption and digital signature over executable payload and optionally, the data.
Maintenance	Initial set-up costs are considerable as package has to be tailored to environment. Further changes often need specialist product configuration knowledge.	Scripts or (code using database APIs) corresponding to new query contexts have to be developed. The language used is likely to be commonly used—e.g., Perl & TCL for scripts and Java for applets.	New executables need to be developed for new functions. The language used is likely to be commonly used—e.g., Java or (Safe) TCL.
Technology Dependency	SQL database. Software package mostly self-contained otherwise.	SQL database interface.	A transport mechanism (e.g., e-mail or HTTP). Security mechanisms (e.g., PGP).

Table 8.3: *A Comparison of Usage*

Ticketing/Workflow	Web/Intranet	Mobile Agents
Used to "connect" monitored events to management processes through generating and tracking tickets representing the events to closure.	Used as a secure method for end-users to access management information specific for a given end-user's consumption.	Used for the secure transport of information using e-mail as transport. Special purpose agents can be developed for any party.
Used as a method for users to communicate service requests to the infrastructure management organization. This can include problem reporting through this media.	Used as a secure method for infrastructure management staff to access management data from remote devices and relational databases.	Used as a secure data distribution and remote execution mechanism—for example, to remotely upgrade security mechanisms such as virus scanners.
Used as method for infrastructure management staff (primarily the helpdesk function) to generate trouble tickets identifying a problem which has not been submitted by either of the above means.	Used internally, especially by an infrastructure management team for communicating fixes, etc. globally. The web is used to distribute management data internally.	
Used to distribute information back to end-users—either on a specific user basis or as a broadcast message.	Used as a general method for mass distribution of information such as infrastructure bulletin boards.	
Used by infrastructure management organization to automate process activity flow. Hence the path a potential ticket takes is predicated by the definition of the process handling the ticket.		

- Time-of-day rules determine the method of "announcing" the event. Outside normal hours a pager is likely to get better attention. Different offices may have different mechanisms for accessing support staff.

- Escalation and backup rules define what to do if a ticket is not picked up within a given period.

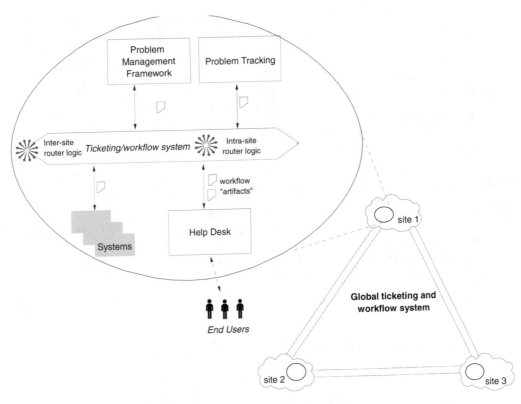

Figure 8.9: *Components of a ticketing/workflow-based information distribution framework*

Once a ticket gets owned by a group, the results of any work done relating to the ticket are recorded in the ticket. A ticket can be manually re-routed to specific individuals or other groups. The ticket therefore holds all state information about the work, including the path (or workflow) it takes through different groups.

A ticketing/workflow system distributes information from the managed environment to the infrastructure management teams. In some organizations information can be submitted into the infrastructure management ticketing/workflow subsystem by end-users.

In this case the system also offers a method for submitting any type of work request from the users. Examples include purchase requests for IT equipment, or change requests for adding or moving users.

In this case the ticketing/workflow system transports information from users to the infrastructure management group. Once the information enters the infrastructure management domain, it goes through the various "stations" representing the internal organization for doing the related work. Information can also be sent back to users—usually faster and more reliably than e-mail:

- Information may be specifically related to a user. For example, the acceptance of a previously submitted purchase order or the schedule for a requested change.

- Information may be broadcast to some or all users—for example, about any infrastructure status changes affecting the users' business.

8.4.2 Web/Intranet Based Framework

Static web pages are pages that have been created by a web page creation tool usually under the direction of a human being. Created pages are posted to a web server—for subsequent access by browser based users.

A web site consisting of static HTML pages needs to have its content continually maintained. Typical maintenance activities include:

- As information changes, web pages have to be created and installed on the web sites (supporting the information distribution).

- Outdated pages have to be deleted or changed.

- Hypertext links have to be changed to point to current sources.

Such maintenance has turned out to be expensive, time consuming and error prone in most organizations.

Static web pages are a "one-way" communication mechanism (from web server to user) and hence have limited use as an information distribution mechanism. The overhead of maintenance makes it useful only for relatively slow-changing information.

Dynamically created web pages are pages created on the fly, with the creation criteria being driven by the accessing user. Hence the user gets just what is asked (delimited by what is "askable"). The "raw" material for pages creation resides in a relational (SQL) database or it may be an SNMP MIB accessed from a system or device.

Information in a relational database can therefore be "mined" and the results distributed a web/intranet based framework. The framework also works in the opposite direction. Data entered into the framework can be placed in a relational database.

Dynamic creation of web pages "from real-time mining" across a relational database is made possible by advances in web servers that have the capability to create HTML from a stream of SQL data and vice versa.

The information seen by the user is a representation of the current data in the database (at the time the pages were created). Hence updates of the database get reflected in a web page the next time that the information is accessed and the page is created.

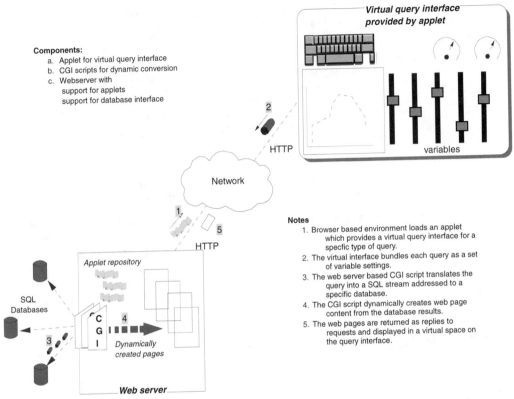

Components:
a. Applet for virtual query interface
b. CGI scripts for dynamic conversion
c. Webserver with
   support for applets
   support for database interface

Notes
1. Browser based environment loads an applet which provides a virtual query interface for a specfic type of query.
2. The virtual interface bundles each query as a set of variable settings.
3. The web server based CGI script translates the query into a SQL stream addressed to a specific database.
4. The CGI script dynamically creates web page content from the database results.
5. The web pages are returned as replies to requests and displayed in a virtual space on the query interface.

Figure 8.10: *Components in the dynamic creation of web pages*

Dynamic web pages are two-way communication mechanisms in the sense that a dialog between the user and a web page artifact (such as a form or a query interface) can get translated to SQL commands (or database-specific API calls) the relational database interface understands or an SNMP sequence a device or system understands.

This translation logic may be downloaded and resides at the browser. Alternatively, the browser resident logic may only validate user input and web server based logic may generate the SQL or SNMP sequences.

Information from relational database systems are accessed by the web server using two common methods, Common Gateway Interface (CGI) scripts or the "Web API" developed by major database vendors. A brief comparison of these two methods are in terms of portability, security, performance and ease of development is described in Table 8.4.

Given that powerful server-based logic can be developed, it is relatively easy to develop an executable definition of a map for visualizing events within a specific end-user context (as described in Chapter 7, Section 7.5)—provided the event's "existence" can be accessed by the web server.

Table 8.4: Comparison of Database to Web Server Interface Techniques

Comparison Point	CGI Scripts	Web API
Portability	Written usually in TCL or Perl. Portable to any platform with the respective interpreter.	Pre-compiled and therefore depends on vendor support. APIs are proprietary.
Security	So that safety mechanisms to ensure CGI scripts cannot run amok. However, "Safe" interpreters are available for TCL.	Pre-compiled—hence barring bugs, is more secure.
Performance	Interpretation is generally slower and dependent on script size.	Generally higher performance than script interpretation.
Development	TCL and Perl have powerful string manipulation functions that are needed in transforming database information. CGI development tools can speed up applications.	No special tools needed. The API often supports specific database vendor's special features.

8.4.3 Mobile Agent Based Framework

A mobile agent based framework is discussed in Chapter 11, Section 11.5. Mobile agents can provide innovative solutions to agent proliferation and the change management problems. Whole classes of agents such as inventory agents, security agents collect and carry information and don't have to be resident all the time.

Many commercially bought agents merely collect and re-package data freely available in the system. These sources can be directly accessed. Reducing the number of agents simplifies management.

The downside is that mobile agents have to be built in-house as there is little commercial activity in this area at present. However good tools such as Safe-TCL are available for this purpose.

Unlike the other information distribution frameworks described here, mobile agents play a role as an information processing program. Two such examples are given below:

- *Integrating state information.* Client/server environments in large enterprises are rarely built with a homogeneous computing environment. Many factors including legacy data and deployment economics mean that heterogeneous operating systems and platforms are involved in the delivery of business applications. To manage the "health" of such environments therefore requires the integration of state information from heterogeneous operating systems and platforms. Often the quality of data from each point is limited by the absence of agent support for a needed operating system or platform. Mobile agents provide a way of collecting or distributing "equivalent" types of state information from different platforms.

- *Enterprise dynamics.* Enterprise wide environments change relatively fast. New users are added, new offices are opened, remote offices get scaled up or down. The ability for an infrastructure management framework to reflect business dynamics is increasingly critical in the client/server era. This is because infrastructure management is linked to the quality of business delivery. Long lead times between the change and actual inclusion of a changed environment into the management framework (and errors when changing) are less tolerated. Mobile agents allow faster reflection of adds, moves and changes in areas where they are the transporters.

8.5 Remote Access Framework

The remote access framework represents the interface with the outside world. The framework provides remote access services for safe access to management systems. The main uses of a remote access framework are for:

- Infrastructure management staff to remotely access: (*a*) management systems out-of-hours, and (*b*) systems at remote offices.

- Access for "expert" support from vendors (of infrastructure products as well as business software packages).

- With a country domain, "connecting" remote access frameworks at different sites provides secure method for the remote management of sites.

Remote management is an essential part of normal infrastructure management. It allows networks, systems and client/server application components at remote locations to be configured, monitored, diagnosed and controlled. This capability is essential for:

- *Managing satellite offices.* In geographically dispersed enterprises service support staff may be concentrated in a few "primary" centers. The management of remote offices is achieved through remote monitoring from a primary center and "invoking" a local outsourcer to provide maintenance "in situ" when problems are diagnosed.

- *7 x 24 management.* In global enterprises with business cycles approaching 24 hours, hand-over of responsibility for monitoring key systems (and providing first-line support activity on any problems that arise) can be rotated between primary support centers on a "follow-the-sun" basis. Hand-over includes responsibility for resources in satellite offices (associated with the primary support center being handed over).

- *Managing during a disaster recovery phase.* Major disruption of service to satellite offices during loss of service at a primary site can be reduced by handing over responsibility for the satellite offices to another primary site.

8.5.1 Requirements for Remote Access Framework

The key architectural issues of remote infrastructure management on an enterprise scale are:

- *Security*—A key part of the architecture is to ensure that change and control functions can only be carried out by authorized support personnel. This includes strong authentication, confidential communication between the primary and satellite sites, as well as use of communication protocols to ensure message integrity in communications. Given that a remote access framework provides services to callers from the outside world, well-administered mechanisms are needed to ensure the security of access.

- *Modularity*—When many satellite offices have to be supported, a standard framework will ensure that primary centers can manage any remote office in a uniform way. Without this level of standardization the processes for remote management from primary centers can become complex and error prone.

- *Traffic bandwidth*—Monitoring using the current generation of management protocols can result in major bandwidth consumption, which can impact normal business traffic. This is especially relevant in relatively low speed, wide area links between primary and satellite centers of business. A key part of the architecture is a solution for cost effective polling and event filtering locally at each satellite site. Also, high-speed dial-up links may be part of the solution for removing the impact of management traffic.

- *Management*—Given the security implications, management is a major concern. Several special management contexts exist for remote access. Requests for access result in user profiles being added for access. When users who have access leave the organization their access rights have to be revoked. Also, special monitoring contexts exist. Dial-in access points are primary points for attack and automated monitoring for unusual activity is needed.

8.5.2 Components of Remote Access Framework

Figure 8.11 shows the components for a remote access framework:

- *Remote access server.* A class of inter-networking device that combines a modem pool with a router. On one side it accepts connections from the outside world and on the other side interfaces to a LAN.

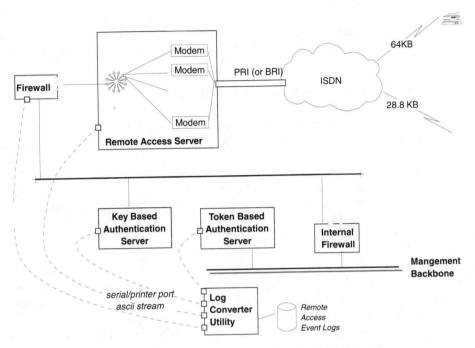

Figure 8.11: *Components of a remote access framework*

- *External firewall.* An access control device that makes a pass or stop decision on a per IP packet basis. The decisions are controlled through configuration parameters— that specify the criteria for the types of traffic that may cross through the remote access server in each direction. It also keeps a log of activity at its interfaces.

- *Password-based authentication server.* A server that authenticates the identity of a user usually using a key or a password that the user knows. The server also maintains a log of call activity through the server. In addition it is a repository for profiles of users allowed through that point-of-access.

- *Internal firewall.* An access control device to access a specific backbone LAN (such as infrastructure management). The LAN is segmented by the firewall.

- *Token-based authentication server.* A stronger authentication scheme than a password-based one as the user also has to have a physical token that provides some unique characteristic. Used here to provide access to segmented parts (so that entry into the corporate LAN does not give total access).

- *Log converter utility.* A mechanism, usually proprietary, to access logs from each component—through a serial operator interface or printer port. The messages from a log are parsed and consolidated in a "secure" database. Information correlated from the firewall logs and the authentication server log are key sources of information in security management. Converting the logs to an SQL database aids the development of security applications.

To have useful bandwidth for infrastructure management purposes, the connections from the outside world are typically through ISDN or channelized T1. Telecom suppliers offer a single physical connection onto which are reverse-multiplexed a number of channels. An ISDN pipe (PRI) would consist of between 23 and 30 ISDN B channels. A T1 pipe would have 24 DS-0 channels.

The power of this scheme is that the channels can be dynamically aggregated through using the multilink point-to-point protocol (MLPPP). Hence during some period of the day an ISDN pipe can be used by up to 30 callers simultaneously while at other times multiple channels can be combined for information transfer, leaving only the remaining capacity for callers. Moreover, Telecom suppliers can mix ISDN calls with normal asynchronous calls in a single pipe.

In most organizations that have deployed mission-critical client/server systems, there is increasing pressure to provide remote access to business users. Remote access is likely to be needed for each site. An obvious way of justifying the cost of a big pipe at a site is to share the remote access framework with business. Bandwidth requirements for management on a day-to-day basis is relatively limited. At sites where a big pipe cannot be justified, just the requisite number of ISDN channels need be purchased.

Currently, such big pipe scenarios work only on a country-by-country level and too often only in or near big cities and business centers.

8.5.3 Multiple Functions of Remote Support Framework

The global nature of many businesses and their operational structure demand that systems are operative on a 24 hour x 7 day basis. For example, in a global investment bank, a trade done in the Far East may be accounted and "settled" in New York in an automated fashion, regardless of the hour in New York.

Several alternative support solutions exist to ensure such availability requirements, including: (*a*) 24-hour manning at each key site, (*b*) automated paging of "on-call" support personnel at a local site, (*c*) remote monitoring from a global "network" of service centers on a "follow-the-sun" basis.

In many organizations out-of-hours support of the latter two types is done from the home environment for a first line of support. This essentially means dialling into the site and gaining access to tools and data in the management framework. Regardless of the model chosen, serious problems at a remote site will require the attention of the nearest local experts who may also need remote access.

By and large for remote support to be feasible in global client/server infrastructures, the physical and logical infrastructure should be duplicated at the respective sites. This includes standardization of:

- LAN, workstation and server architecture.

- Management frameworks and personnel policies.

- WAN connectivity architecture.

- Security frameworks and policies.

Deploying remote access frameworks across multiple locations provides features for managing a dispersed client/server infrastructure. When dispersed resources need to be accessed for management purposes, the initial choice is to use the corporate network.

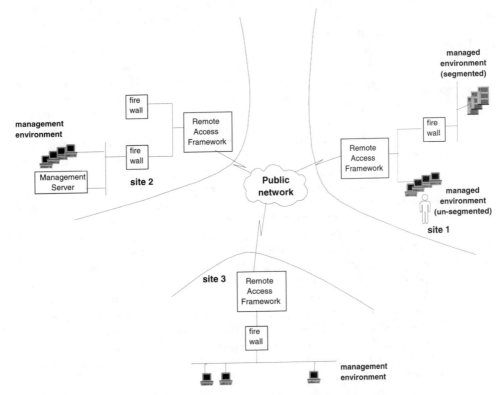

Figure 8.12: Remote management of enterprise sites

However, this often results in a contention with business traffic, especially in activities such as software distribution. When out-of-hours work is not an alternative, then additional bandwidth needs to be "switched in." The remote access framework can support this role as shown in Figure 8.12.

Multiple authentication at each site ensures that the accessing staff are authorized to access the remote site.

Remote management also often entails extensions to infrastructure management processes to enable infrastructure management of dispersed resources. Most issues surround "handover" of responsibility to an external group. These are often solved only by developing related policies.

Case Study 8.2: Remote Management Framework in a Consultancy Organization

The following is a case study of a remote management framework developed by a second-tier management consultancy firm. The primary use is for some 200 consultants on "engagement" across the world at any time to access intellectual assets, share information and use e-mail based consultancy business processes on its ConsNet. The framework is also used for out-of-hours support and for project work with external partners. Figure 8.13 shows the actual components used in realizing the framework. These are briefly described below:

- *LANrover Access Switch* from Shiva Corp. provides dial-in access from analog modems. Modem speed is variable and determined by the local Telecom conditions the consultants find themselves in. Multiple LANrovers provide capacity for some 150 concurrent calls. Shiva's management utility is used to configure and monitor all the LANrover units from a secure management station. The same management station has access to user classifications and policies associated with each legitimate user.
- *Borderware Internet Firewall Server* from Border Network Technologies Inc. provides the external firewall. Address and packet level filtering ensures that only a known set of users can access the ConsNet service. An out-of-band process involving "trusted persons" allows ad hoc requirements to be turned around within 4 hours.
- *Remote Access Dial-in-User Server (RADIUS)* from Livingston Enterprises, Inc. provides the first-level authentication to the ConsNet service. This provides access to downloadable material and HTML pages that are of the first-level security classification. (Loss of this material would not compromise the consultancy or its client's business.)
- *SecureID* from Security Dynamics Inc. is used as a second-level authentication mechanism to access deeper resources, including discussion groups and business processes. This is termed Level 2 information. Some Level 2 information is held encrypted.
- A security hardened Solaris kernel-rebuild on a SunSPARC machine from Sun Corp. and running public domain firewall software is used to segment the internal practice backbones.

This framework combines multiple layers of technology with operational policies on the use of remote access as a service. This provides a winning combination.

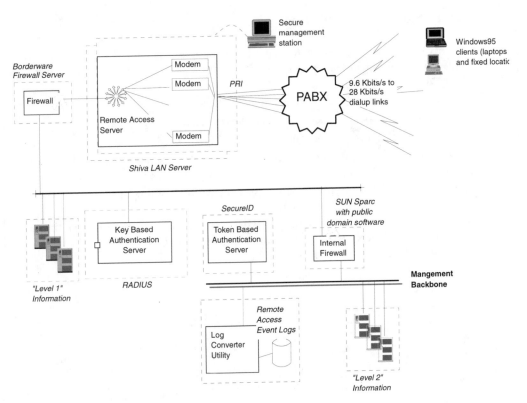

Figure 8.13: *Case study of a remote management framework*

Case Study 8.3: Capacity Management Using Frameworks

Capacity management is one of the mainstream areas of infrastructure management. This "long" case study looks at the deployment of capacity management in a British, country-wide retail bank.

The Environment. The retail bank provides banking and currency services directly to the public (including small businesses) through branch premises. Branches are supported by regional offices that provide batch operations for processes such as consolidating checking accounts. The bank had replaced its leased line-based country network and instead linked its business sites through a public Switched Multi-megabit Data Service (SMDS) provided by a country-wide Telecom services vendor. The tiered structure of the bank's business network is shown in Figure 8.14 along with typical issues that the capacity management framework is expected to solve.

Case Study 8.3: Capacity Management Using Frameworks *(continued)*

Requirements Definition. Information for capacity planning was defined as a *standard* set of capacity planning metrics. These metrics are independent of whether LAN, MAN or WAN service technologies are involved:

- *Bandwidth utilization* (in each network technology).
- *End-to-end delay* (with respect to an application's service delivery path).
- *Hurst constant* (a measure for burstiness of traffic measured at a point).
- *Packet loss*—in modern networks packets loss is more often than not a consequence of "underpowered" components.
- *Capacity related events*—from inter-networking component due to capacity problems such as lack of memory in a router.

Metrics are "derived" from "raw" data through processing. Raw data is collected from the relevant points in the multi-tiered structure. Collection is by sampling (therefore absolute values of the raw data provide little information).

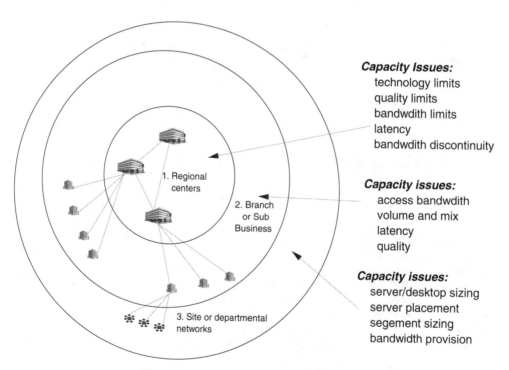

Figure 8.14: Key issues in capacity planning

Case Study 8.3: Capacity Management Using Frameworks *(continued)*

Because of the size of the bank's network, a tacit assumption is that the network topology will not remain static. Technical requirements included the following:

- Capacity management framework should be applicable to any network topology.

- Solutions should be modular with a low unit-cost (given the potential scale of deployment).

- High degree of automation should be achieved in data collection processing to derive trends. Also easy maintenance of the whole framework.

Use of Metrics. Capacity planning is to be developed as a decision support type application (rather than an operational application).

A number of requirements are identified regarding the use of the capacity related information:

- Capacity information is of relevance for work in different management and business contexts—network planning, negotiation of SLA contracts, accounting, budgeting and departmental billing. Information is also to be distributed in a "small" number if standard reports.

- As small in-house applications were likely to be developed over time, the "raw" information is to be accessible to ubiquitous tools, in particular spreadsheets and web browsers as well as in-house SQL based query and report tools.

- The framework needs to provide guarantees on the accuracy, timeliness and reliability of the metric values produced. The framework needs to provide *reliable trending functions* that stand up to empirical analysis. Absolute values from sampled data should be treated to display trends over a time period. (Such averaged or trend information have higher confidence levels.) Examples of trending functions relevant to capacity planning in the bank are: (a) moving average for different periods and time of day windows, (b) rate of change, (c) delta (change) against a baseline, (d) minimum-maximum value history for different periods.

Defining and Using Frameworks. The approach to developing capacity management is based on the use of standard frameworks as building blocks. Similar building blocks are deployed in the bank's sites. The activities and the framework components required for each activity are described below:

- *Step 1*—Collect the raw data from a set of sources of data. This requires a *collector* to automate the collection of data from each source.

- *Step 2*—Process the collected raw data using a defined set of *trending functions* (to derive operationally useful information). Trending functions are developed for a low-cost platform (such as Windows PC) and together they are treated as a single framework component.

- *Step 3*—Storage of the information output by the trending sets into a *relational schema*. Within the database information *consolidation functions* provide summary views of the "whole" bank's network, exception recognition functions compute exceptions occurring in the datasets.

Case Study 8.3: Capacity Management Using Frameworks *(continued)*

- *Step 4*—Distribute the information to a central point using a distribution framework. This includes generation and forwarding of predefined exceptions as alerts to a management framework.

- *Step 5*—"Export" of selected data sets to parties outside the management framework as standard reports or software tools (such as simulation models to enable longer terms *what-if* analysis).

Framework components can be deployed in different ways. Table 8.5 shows design options in collection, storage and metric generation. The options offer different cost and performance trade-offs.

Raw Data Sources. The long-term justification for capacity planning is to manage the "integrity" of office to office interconnection through the SMDS (and point-to-point) links.

Routers are used to connect subnets. The router's switching role makes it the primary source of raw data for capacity planning. Wellfleet (Bay Networks Inc.) routers are used in the bank. Its management software provide a rich abundance of reliable router state data. Table 8.6 shows the source collected data.

Collector and Distribution Building Blocks. Figure 8.15 shows details of two variants of the collector building block for building a capacity planning framework. The building block consists of:

- Hardware platform with a dedicated interface (Ethernet) to routers that connects local network to the SMDS cloud.

- Intelligent "agent" to poll and collect raw data from the routers. This is built from a proxy agent toolkit.

- An SQL database engine to organize processed data.

- WAN probes to decode and measure traffic on individual links.

- RMON probes to provide LAN performance metrics.

Components of the distribution building block are:

- Dedicated web server (or access to a corporate intranet one) to distribute processed data.

- Interface for decision support tools' access to stored and summary information—e.g., web browser.

- Interface for export to other tools.

Case Study 8.3: Capacity Management Using Frameworks *(continued)*

Trending Building Block. The trending functions provided are *(delta, rate of change, moving average(s), min-max history)* for each of the following classes at the regional center level:

- Outgoing packets into the SMDS cloud.
- Incoming packets from the SMDS cloud.
- Total volume of packets handled at router.
- Router incidences of internal memory and buffer faults.
- Router ratio of outgoing packets into SMDS cloud/sum of packets presented at router (excluding packets from the SMDS cloud).
- End-to-end delay through SMDS cloud (collector to collector).

At the "branch" level the following additional levels of trending information can be derived:

- Bandwidth utilization for SMDS access.
- LAN/SMDS traffic profile (protocol mix carried, time-of-day peaks and troughs).

At the LAN level:

- RMON group data.

Figure 8.16 shows how summary information is presented, how a relational database will hold consolidated information and access to this information.

Table 8.5: Design Options for Capacity Management

Metric Processing Node	Storage	Metric Generation
1. Processing node at site.	1. Local storage of raw data.	1. Local processing—central consolidation, exception generation at central point.
2. Processing node supporting *n* sites.	2. Local storage as relational data (in an SQL server).	2. Local processing and consolidation, exception generation locally.
3. Processing node shares a platform.	3. Remote storage.	3. Remote processing—central consolidation, exception generation at remote point or central point.

Table 8.6: *Sources of Raw Data for Capacity Management*

Source	Description
Site LAN to SMDS Router	Router Private MIB variables relating to SMDS DXI and frame sizing
	Router private minor traps relating to internal sizing (memory, buffers, page faults)
	Router Interface MIB II statistics at packet and octet levels
	Incidences of Router Interface traps
	RMON groups' data in the case of LAN capacity
ICMP Ping and Trace Route packet injection	Results of ICMP PING and TRACE Route in IP enabled routers
Burst pattern injection	Results of canned burst patterns

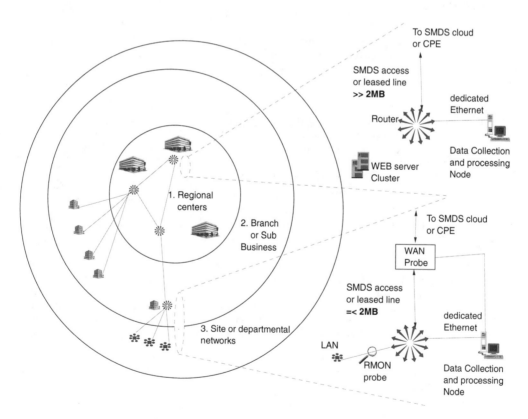

Figure 8.15: *Capacity management framework*

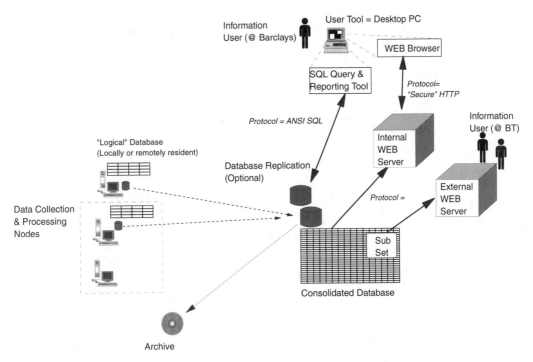

Figure 8.16: *Distributing capacity information*

8.6 Principles in Deploying Frameworks

Infrastructure management capability can be incrementally built using frameworks as building blocks. The final section in this chapter looks at some practical principles to apply to make a framework-based approach successful.

The general principles for developing an infrastructure management frameworks are:

1. To keep the management resources separate from the infrastructure being managed. The management resources should be engineered to cope with projected worst case scenarios—such as the number of events that may occur in a crisis. This is when the infrastructure management should not fail.

2. Have capabilities set up for contingency scenarios capabilities such as out-of-band management, backups of configuration and other critical data, and blueprints to use in the event of loss of the management resources at a managed site. Periodically test and practice the use of these capabilities.

3. Have single logical points to collect management information. Loss of infrastructure management resources should not impact future management (e.g., having to regress to pre-framework period).

More specific principles are covered under the following categories:

- *LAN architecture* dedicated for infrastructure management. The network architecture needed to manage a highly instrumented client/server infrastructure needs to provide characteristics such as high bandwidth, security and ability to cope with bursty traffic.

- *Systems resources* for infrastructure management. Systems should be dedicated to infrastructure management. Even in small environments, resources should be as specialized as possible.

- *Infrastructure management databases.* Databases should also be dedicated to management, be of industrial strength with interfaces to write in-house applications using generally available programming skills.

- *Resilience* in infrastructure management network and resources. Resilience should be designed as part of the architecture. Once procedures and processes start using a management framework, loss of framework capabilities (even for a short period) will result in corresponding loss in the ability to manage.

- *Data hierarchy.* Data generated by instrumentation in a large client/server environments have to be processed to be useful for infrastructure management at different levels—local office, regional or management center level and global level. Data architecture defines what data are used at each level of management.

8.6.1 LAN Architecture for Infrastructure Management

A separate infrastructure management network is almost a prerequisite for successful management at a management center and hub site. Advantages of having such a network are:

- Much of the management traffic is confined to this structure—hence normal working segments can be guaranteed not to be overloaded even under conditions of stress.

- Better security as the network can be segmented from the other networks. Users allowed access to the systems on the management framework must be strongly authenticated.

- Management traffic enters other user segments only for control purposes and hence cannot easily be tracked by a listener.

The downside is that it incurs a cost, especially since high-quality components need to be considered in this critical role. The framework for network management should ideally consist of a pair of separate hubs cross-segmented to provide physical redundancy. This allows the basic physical framework to cope with single points of failure.

Management servers and management stations are connected to this physical structure using high bandwidth connections (such as 100 MB Ethernet). Points of access to the managed environments and devices also "radiate" from this structure. The infrastructure management network is connected to:

- On production hubs one of the internal buses is dedicated to management traffic and is connected to this network. The hub's internal management module is accessed through this bus.

- A dedicated port on each of the routers and switches is connected to this network. RMON data is often provided by switches.

- Servers which run proxy agents or RMON agents are also homed onto the network through a dedicated interface.

In addition there will be a number of database servers on the management subnet; a capacity information database, the alarms and fault database, the ticketing database, configuration database being the key ones. These can be accessed by users and applications from outside the infrastructure management network—ideally through strong authentication.

The management subnet should also implement a basic control framework as described in Section 8.3.2 to provide an out-of-band management mechanism. This is especially required for managing the router backbone through the technician's interface. This is primarily used for managing routers under conditions where the network management network is non-operational.

An infrastructure management network is shown in Figure 8.17. A terminal server is used to connect to:

- Legacy systems through the respective terminal emulator and command language.

- Systems that do not support SNMP. The text messages these systems produce can be processed into events.

8.6.2 Infrastructure Management Databases

Infrastructure management requires a number of key databases. In general, data architecture has not been widely applied. Platform vendors in particular have downplayed its critical role.

Organizing information into industrial strength databases is however the cornerstone of developing global infrastructure management capability. Hence the extra development effort and expense of databases is well justified.

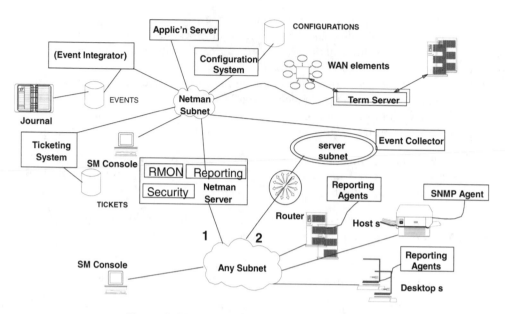

Figure 8.17: *Infrastructure management network*

In general a single database server can support several databases. Thought should however be given to the value of information held in databases and the deployment of the servers. The key databases are described below:

- *Event database.* This is a relational database that holds events that have been filtered, integrated and/or shown on a visualization system. Its primary value is if responsibility has to be handed over to another operational group. The database holds a summary of events over a period, typically a week or to a quarter. A second part of the event database holds events that have not been recognized at the filters. This is used in maintaining the event classification.

- *Ticket database.* This is a relational database that holds outstanding tickets. It is used by tools to manage workflow and to generate service level reports. A second part of the database holds resolutions to previous problem. The resolutions part of the database is browsed when new problem tickets are generated—to see if similar problems have been solved before. They are also used for training, updating other sites for handover.

- *Configurations database.* This holds application specific configuration data. These data are often organized as a file system rather than a relational database. The information in these files are often scripts. Examples include configuration scripts for routers, hubs, and other devices. The whole files system should be held encrypted and access rights should be carefully designed as it holds information that is invaluable for a potential hacker.

Other databases may be justified depending on the structure of the organization. Databases can be accessed through web servers and browsers. Web servers can create views of the databases on the fly. Hence databases can also be used as repositories of information of interest to a wider population. For example, the event database can provide the raw material for context-specific views to be created on the fly using criteria defined at the browser.

8.6.3 Workstation and Server Resources

The infrastructure management network is likely to have a relatively heterogeneous collection of workstations and servers ranging from PCs to RISC-based engines. In small management domains, it is not unusual to find a single machine playing multiple management roles—centralized management console, application engine, database engine, event collection engine, etc. Multi-user operating systems allow multiple operators access to the system.

In larger management environments machines need to be specialized along functional lines. Even in small environments sufficient computing resources should be assured to deal with peak requirements in a stressed or crisis scenario. Analytical work is required to "size" peak requirements and specify worst case scenarios that the management environment can cope with.

There is often a choice of using high-end machines to play multiple, concurrent roles versus lower-end machines dedicated to single roles. Generally, operational cost of the lower-end machines is proportionately less due to their relative simplicity. The problem with having specialized servers, is that these servers themselves have to be managed, significantly raising the overheads for managing the management framework. Typical server specializations are described below:

Application servers. Industrial strength applications in infrastructure are produced for a small number of operating systems, typically Unix and increasingly NT. Management applications in these environments are becoming increasingly complex and consequently require more computing cycles and internal memory for performance reasons.

It is not unusual for several applications being needed concurrently in the course of normal processes as well as in crisis scenarios. Application servers allow application level computation to be separated from the control and command aspect.

Use of distinct machines for management applications provides greater deployment flexibility when amalgamating network, systems and application level management. Application servers are usually higher-end machines, with robust hardware features such as error correcting memory, environmental monitoring and dualed power supplies. Also, performance enhancing capabilities such as support of high-speed network interfaces, a high bandwidth internal bus architecture, and large amounts of memory are key requirements.

Management servers. These servers play the role of providing services to local agents, usually on a per sub-network level. They also provide the role of being platforms for remote monitoring and control agents—such as RMON and RMON II agents and agents based on the HOST Resources MIB for hosts.

As agent platforms, a high-end machine may be used to monitor multiple sub-networks or smaller and lower-cost machines may be dedicated to single subnets. The capital and operational costs of the two are roughly the same, therefore the choice is often dependent on the architectural philosophy prevailing within an organization.

In the role of being an intermediary between local agents and central points of management control, such servers are the key to scaling a management environment. This means that these servers are an *enabling* component when deploying infrastructure management on an enterprise scale.

Database/file/web servers. Databases increasingly play a central role in infrastructure management. Many management applications have tended to use flat file structures often as an optimization for performance when only a single machine supports all the management functions. Databases are essential in more mature environments and where infrastructure management is viewed as having a strategic role.

File servers hold information and executables as files. A common practice is to build all workstations and servers to be "clones" of a small number of machine types. The machine image for each type is stored and maintained centrally so that multiple versions of an image do not occur.

Web servers have an increasing number of roles in infrastructure management, ranging from being an obvious method for developing in-house applications for infrastructure management to providing the means to disseminate information.

Specialized servers are available for all three areas and have an impact on performance and easing access to the information they hold. Databases, file systems and web servers all provide cross-platform support allowing the details of the platform to become unimportant.

Management workstations. These are likely to range from portable PCs to high-end workstations. In general there are likely to be several operating systems in use, ranging from "Windows 9X" to Unix. In general they should be standardized with as few types as possible and all workstations should be built as clones.

Management is an area that usually employs a high number of contractors and consultants. Use of industry standards usually helps in finding the skills easier. Another key point in this regard is that the highest standards of security should be developed and actively maintained for management workstations.

8.6.4 Resilience

The availability of a dedicated infrastructure management framework is a prerequisite to management on an enterprise scale. Resilience is an applied concept which, through the use of a portfolio of technologies and techniques, can reduce the probability of the total loss of the management framework.

Infrastructure management is dependent on several centralized services. A common example is authentication and access control service—loss of which can render the whole management framework unusable.

Deployment of resilience is mostly determined by common sense or failing that, budget constraints. The types of resilience possible in a management framework are:

- *Server resilience.* In the event of a key management server failing, another server needs to be booted up to take its place. The duration of loss of service is dependent on the resilience technology. In a server-cluster or "process-group" configuration, the loss might be imperceptible as alternative servers can take up the extra processing load without further action. In looser coupled, switch-over type solutions, the alternative processor has to detect the fault and boot-up with the correct applications. Some part of the previous state including events in the pipeline are invariably lost. Server resilience technology applicable in a given environment is usually determined by the operating system used on the server.

- *Workstation resilience.* Key network management staff may have more than one workstation. A useful policy is to have no data files on the local disk. All workstations are built to be clones of a known master. Home directories are mounted on the network file system, so that any workstation failure is solved by a quick swap-over with a pre-configured workstation.

- *Database resilience.* Some database vendors provide the ability to mirror database writes onto a second image of the database resident on another server. A secondary mechanism is to use Redundant Array of Independent Disks (RAID) technology to provide resilience at the disk level. Replication is a capability provided by some database vendors where part of a database is replicated in almost real-time on another server. The database server, if separate from the management server, needs to be part of the server resilience cluster.

- *Network resilience.* Both servers and workstations in the network management framework can have two points of access to the physical infrastructure management framework through dual transceivers or two physical ports. Loss of the primary path is detected by driver software and the secondary path is invoked. When servers are connected to the network management framework using dual path technology, such as FDDI, then resilience occurs at wire-speeds and is transparent. Network protocols such as the spanning tree algorithm are aimed at computing alternative paths in the event of a device failure. Spanning tree has a recovery time in the order of 15 seconds and is used as part of the infrastructure management framework architecture.

- *Agent level.* Agents collect and distribute state information from one or more entities in a client/server layer. In the case of remote agents, the agent process in the operating system or the hardware platform itself on which the agent resides can die leaving the management framework blind on that part of the network. The ability to recognize loss of an agent and dynamically reconfigure a replacement agent is critical to managing remote (satellite) sites. The method for doing this is however dependent on the operating system in question.

In the deployment of resilient architectures, the state of resilience needs to be actively monitored. When some part of the infrastructure management structure fails in the first instance, redundant resources minimize downtime. However, the "criticality" of the system has increased. This means that a second failure may not have redundant resources to fall back on, until the original failure has been repaired.

This change of criticality and the status of using redundant resources sometimes needs to be notified to the users, depending on agreements with a specific business.

Finding the cause of failure is also important: When a component fails due to factors involving "age" or a specific configuration bug, the redundant component, which is likely to be similar may also be a candidate for imminent failure. Resilient structures need to be repaired with the same urgency as non-resilient structures.

8.6.5 Data Hierarchy

Hierarchy is a method of managing complexity and organizing management data. The data hierarchy influences the logical design and deployment of infrastructure managers, managers for remote offices, database servers, software agents and remote monitors. Hierarchy can be introduced at an infrastructure management level on several bases—one common rationale based on data usage is described below:

Hierarchy based on data consumption. Management data produced in a given part in the infrastructure is *informationally relevant* only to a subset of the management organization—i.e., mapping data to organizational consumption. A secondary hierarchy defines which parts of the organization has ownership of and responsibility for specific subsystems.

Figure 8.18 shows an example model for data hierarchy based on organizational consumption. The hierarchy consists of:

- *User level data* (such as per user traffic statistics) as the leaves of hierarchy. Manageable remote monitors RMON agents on LAN segments and SNMP agents on the hubs/concentrators on user segments are used to collect data relating to end-users. Local management stations provide functionality appropriate to network management groups supporting end-users.

- *LAN backbone data* (such as server performance statistics) and application segment data (such as peak utilization) is at the next higher level. High-power platforms con-

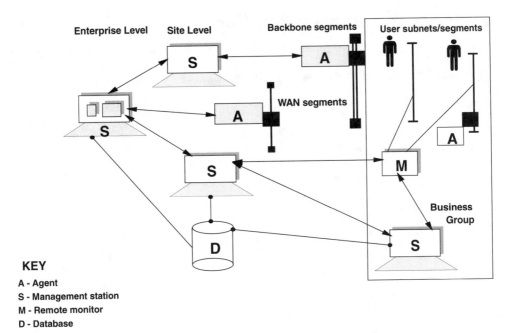

Figure 8.18: *Network management data hierarchy*

KEY

A - Agent
S - Management station
M - Remote monitor
D - Database

solidate user segment-to-backbone data and data from monitored backbone server segments. Management applications at this level also consolidate alarms and events from the physical infrastructure; set-up configuration and performance monitoring. Also, key management databases with a local context (such as faults and resolutions) are found at this level.

- *WAN segment data* (such as point-to-point circuit statistics, and information provided by services providers) are at the next higher layer. At this enterprise level are management stations and applications that can access from the site databases, control WAN circuits and backbone elements such as the routing backbone, etc. (In fact the same class of functionality as found in the site level above is required. The difference is that this environment has to manage a wider geography—this raises issues of the timeliness of the data—not found in single site management environment.)

User-level data is of relevance to groups that support desktop systems, backbone data is of relevance to support groups responsible for site-wide services, while WAN data is primarily of use to groups with inter-site responsibilities.

8.7 Books for Further Reading

Hare, Chris, and Siyan Karanjit. *Internet Firewalls and Network Security.* New Riders Pub., 1996.

Kershenbaum, Aaron, *et al. Network Management and Control.* Plenum Pub. Corp., 1990.

Spencer, Kenneth L. *NT Server Management and Control.* Prentice-Hall, 1995.

Wymore, W. A. *Model-Based Systems Engineering* (An Introduction to the Mathematical Theory of Discrete Systems). CRC Press, 1993.

Part III

Technical Perspective

The Technology of Platforms

Areas covered in this chapter

- Evolutionary nature of platforms and possible "trajectories" for current platforms

- A classification of the types of managers

- Selection criteria and lightweight methodology for selection

- Cost of ownership components for managers

- Characteristics and case study of a "system manager" type of platform

- Characteristics and case study of an "open network manager" type of platform

- Characteristics and case study of an "integrated manager" type of platform

- Summary characteristics of other common types of platforms

The history of modern platforms begins with the adoption of SNMP by vendors of inter-networking devices, such as routers and bridges. This resulted in each vendor (such as Digital Equipment Corp.) developing a management console in-house (or "re-badging" an external, third-party console), to host some basic applications to manage a specific device such as a new router.

From a user or "consumer" point of view this quickly became untenable as one management console supported the hubs, another the routers, and so on.

The recognition that there were too many management consoles (each providing applications only for a single vendor's devices) led to the concept of a general management *platform*—from which any SNMP compatible device could be managed.

One further evolution of a general platform is that management applications should also be unaware of the underlying management protocol (SNMP or CMIP) used. There is however not much call for dual-stack platforms at present.

Management platforms cover network management, host and operating systems management and to some degree applications management. In most organizations the management platform forms the focal point for the whole management function.

Infrastructure management is largely based on the *platform-protocol-agent* model. Tools available "off-the-shelf" for managing networks, systems and application/services still tend to be specialized for the layer.

The main reason for this fragmented state of the market is that there still is no technology, acceptable across all three layers, for modeling management objects. However, several vendors now offer proprietary solutions which go a long way to having a single data model for the infrastructure.

After a recent shakeout, some four or five platform vendors currently dominate the whole infrastructure platform market. The market size is however expanding with the take up of client/server as a technology base by corporations of all sizes. These surviving platform vendors therefore have actively pushed their proprietary architectures.

From the user side, the platform to manage a client/server deployment is often selected under pressure and usually only after the infrastructure has been built. User input into platform evolution has therefore been poor and the dominant platform vendors have been deaf to demands, given their rising sales in the expanding market.

The evolution of client/server deployment (discussed in Chapter 1, Section 1.3) provides the typical drivers for user requirements for the management environment changing over a period time.

9.1 Directions in Platform Evolution

Platform vendors have also been removed from the life-cycles of client/server applications and inter-networking components. In Figure 9.1 life-cycle is shown as a progression through different versions. The scale of the difference between the platform's advance and the evolu-

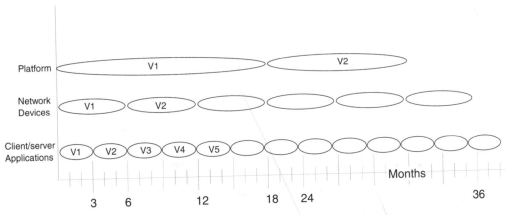

Figure 9.1: *Life-cycle comparison of different parts of the client/server infrastructure*

tionary cycles within the network devices and client/server applications layers is quite stark. By the time a platform has significantly improved, the managed environment has iterated through several steps. This is impacting the platform's current position a the focal point of management:

For example, configuration of network devices and hosts is a common operations activity—as systems, users and applications are added, updated, changed or "moved." Until recently many inter-networking device vendors tended to offer their specialized management tools in this area for three or so of the management platforms with the highest market share.

Device vendors however work in 6- to 9-month product cycles and platform vendors work on 12- to 18-month cycles. This means that platforms are not the ideal delivery mechanism for product specific tools.

The current trend is for device vendors to bypass management platforms and deliver for ubiquitous operating systems such as Microsoft Windows. This trend is fast leading to making the application even more platform independent. The web is likely to be the universal platform for this class of application.

There is a general frustration, especially with the leading edge users of infrastructure management, with the lack of technical advance in current platform products.

The cost of platforms is prohibitive for many organizations extending their infrastructure management to encompass multiple sites. The general cost of software on Unix/RISC machines has always been high and management platforms (other than Sun, possibly) have exploited this in their pricing.

Cost is also leading to web-based solutions, especially in information distribution. Platforms will still continue to play a part, however, its dominance in the strategic sense is on the wane. When platforms are ported to an NT/Wintel base, current prices are unlikely to be

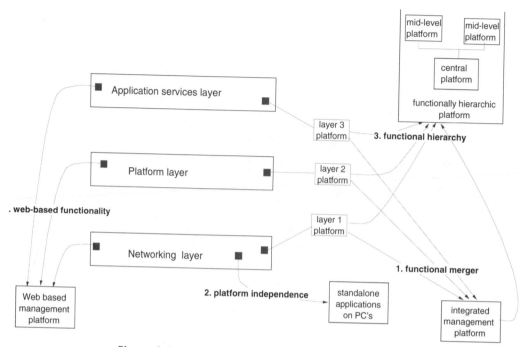

Figure 9.2: *Evolutionary paths for management platforms*

sustainable. Hence future "value" of current buy decisions are likely to be unfavorable. The changes in strategic value and capital value are important points to consider when making decisions about platforms.

A management platform minimally consists of a protocol engine to communicate with agents, a graphics engine for communicating with the user, some form of data storage and a core set of management applications.

The notion of the management platform as the central component of infrastructure management is undergoing a major change. A platform tended to focus on one layer, typically the network level or the systems level. System level managers often offered some limited form application monitoring as well.

A number of major evolutionary paths are evident. This is shown in Figure 9.2:

1. Functionality of platforms previously aimed at the separate layers are merging to a single platform. A single API, database, managed-object model support the infrastructure.

2. Third parties such as internetwork device vendors are increasingly choosing not to develop applications for network management platforms. These new applications are instead developed to run directly on standard PCs.

3. Platforms are being used more as collectors and repositories for events. Events are stored in SQL databases. Applications are independent of the collection platform. Information in the SQL database can be "mined" in real-time by a web server and presented at a browser.

4. The web-based enterprise management (WEBM) initiative is an attempt to develop a single set of standards for managing the whole infrastructure. It consists of an object model called the hypermedia management scheme (HMMS), a hypermedia management protocol (HMMP) an HTTP-like protocol and Java Management API (JMAPI) to develop management applications.

9.1.1 Web Futures for Platforms

The last two paths have an important impact on the future role of a management platform especially in a multi-site deployment. Where multiple platforms were needed earlier (usually one per major site), lower cost "midlevel" managers can now act as local collectors.

SNMP events and data are collected and converted to SQL data and then to HTML as requested from a browser. Alternatively, SNMP can be directly converted to HTML on the fly. The main benefits are:

- Lower costs of large scale deployments.

- Greater flexibility in building in-house applications.

- De-coupling from the platform's life-cycle.

- Greater distribution of management information.

The other side of the coin is the immaturity in the concept, tools and a lack of deployment experience. Also there are security concerns over long-range control using the intranet.

Figure 9.3 shows an architecture comparison of conventional deployment in multiple sites versus the use of mid-level managers.

9.2 Platform Structure

The platform's functional subsystems are shown in Figure 9.4. Characteristics and relationships between the components are defined below:

- *CPU power*—this should be the in the higher end of the MIPs' range for the chosen hardware/operating system combination. The machine is ideally of a server class, with the associated duplicate power supplies, error correcting memory, environmental monitoring, etc.

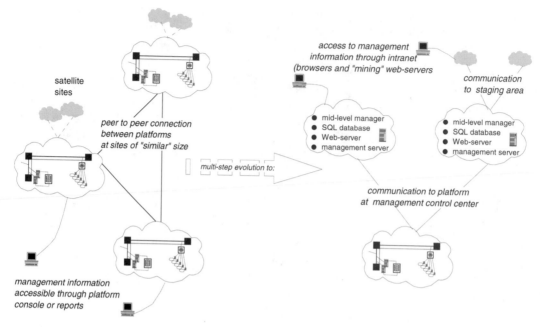

Figure 9.3: *Conventional versus new deployment architecture*

- *Memory*—in the hundreds of megabytes range to cope with several tools being concurrently operational (especially during a crisis when computational overhead peaks).

- *Secondary storage*—in the gigabyte and above range of memory, RAID based disk system, dedicated CD-ROM and tape drives.

- *Database engine*—an industrial strength relational database. Ideally, third-party tools should be available to develop database applications for the chosen database server.

- *Workstations*—high resolution, multihead workstations connected over a LAN. Workstations can be in the mid to high range of the chosen hardware/operating system (which should belong to the same CPU family as the servers). Workstations should be configured to off-load from the server as much of the computation for management applications (as each application's architecture allows).

- *Network connection*—connected to a dedicated LAN, with high bandwidth, latency and modularity determined by the central role of the platform to a site's management capability.

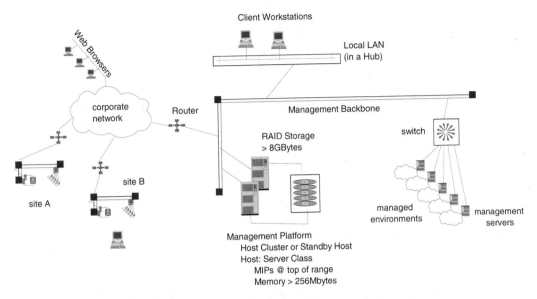

Figure 9.4: *Functional breakdown of management platform resources*

- *Resilience of server*—the platform server should ideally be part of the switch-over or cluster type resilience mechanism offered by the chosen hardware/operating system.

The deployment of a platform involves its own infrastructure costs. This is shown in Figure 9.4. Infrastructure includes resilience for the server and the connectivity to managed environments. As the platform is centralized it has to be able to cope with worst case conditions.

9.2.1 Classes of Managers

Before embarking on a discussion of current management platforms it is useful to classify platform products. Each product is aimed at specific market areas. Figure 9.5 shows the classification and Table 9.1 shows the market segment characteristics for platform products. Each "leaf" of the classification in Figure 9.5 is briefly described below:

- *Systems managers*—are aimed primarily at the UNIX systems and relational database administrators to automate common administration procedures such as software distribution and managing security tokens, to scheduling jobs on database servers. Supports a traditional view that tools and resources for systems management have a different profile to network management.

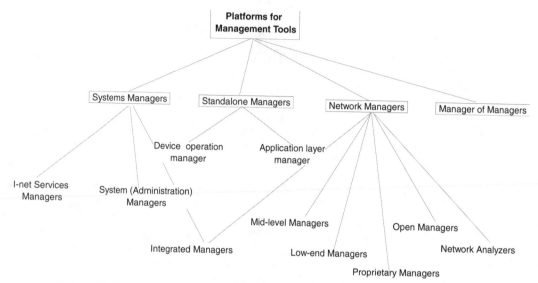

Figure 9.5: *A taxonomy of management platforms in terms of market segmentation*

- *Int-net services managers*—are an emerging class of managers aimed at out-of-a-box administration of Internet and intranet (Int-net) services. Managing these two areas consist of supporting a number of generic services including browsers, web (HTTP) servers, naming (DNS) servers, news and FTP. These managers support software-based servers from specific vendors—such as the Microsoft Internet Information Server 2.0 in the case of web service management. Managers allow monitoring, configuration and control of individual services.

- *Open managers*—are aimed primarily at network management using SNMP and to a very small degree CMIP. Still aimed very much at the device management level but increasingly accommodates host, operating system and application levels through SNMP agents.

- *Manager-of-managers*—are aimed primarily at distributed environments that need to integrate SNMP manageable devices and subsystems, with existing management tools in legacy mainframe and minicomputer environments, network element managers for non-SNMP devices such as modems and multiplexers and so on.

- *Integrated managers*—are aimed primarily at newer environments and combine the capability of open managers with systems managers, providing commonality at several points including user interface, the ability to share databases for systems management and network management data, better integration of user interface.

- *Proprietary managers*—are aimed primarily at the evolution within an existing vendor specific environment. IBM's established user base of SNA evolving to open systems is a clear focus for IBM products in network management which covers the full spectrum of its mainframe, minicomputer, PC and Risc operating systems.

- *LAN managers*—are aimed primarily at Wintel desktop and server-based environments. Uses SNMP and SNMP proxies to provide a consistent set of tools for single-site (and in some cases multi-site) LAN management. Being based on a Wintel technology base, it offers a single platform for LAN operating systems administration and LAN management. Scope for integration of monitored information and development of tools on a single scripting language.

- *Stand-alone managers*—have an "application layer perspective" and can appear on a spectrum of technology bases: (*a*) when based on a Unix platform (or possibly NT in the future), the manager applications may be packages of console and software agents to manage subsystems such as databases and middleware components, (*b*) when based on a Wintel platform, the manager applications are likely to be provided by device vendors to handle relatively infrequent jobs such as configuration for "clusters" of devices.

- *Network analyzers*—are aimed at LAN and WAN protocol management, particularly in a trouble shooting phase where physical portability realtime analysis is the primary concern. Network analyzers provide sophisticated protocol decoding applications as well as the ability to generate traffic.

Table **9.1:** *Market Segment Characteristics for Managers*

Manager Type	Applications	Cost Per Manager (Site)	Protocols/ Agents	Examples
Systems/Services Manager	Monitoring operating system variables, administration of users and resources. Performance, configuration, security, backup, software distribution part of suite.	$20,000 to $75,000	RPC for manager to manager, SQL for database, SNMP or RPC for manager to agent.	Tivoli Management Environment—IBM

Table 9.1: *Market Segment Characteristics for Managers* (continued)

Manager Type	Applications	Cost Per Manager (Site)	Protocols/ Agents	Examples
Network Manager	Monitoring network devices and systems with native or proxy SNMP agents. Performance/ configuration, ticketing, etc. available from 3rd parties.	$20,000 to $40,000	SNMP mostly. Some CMIP in Telecoms (sub) market.	Open View Node Manager—HP Spectrum 4.0—Cabletron Systems
Integrated Manager	Covers network and system managers areas plus integrated views of the infrastructure layers.	$40,000 to $250,000	Combination of system/network managers. Sometimes includes an agent-scaling framework.	Unicenter TNG—Computer Associates ISM/Openmaster—Groupe Bull
Manager of Managers	Monitors output from systems managers, any element manager or network manager.	$75,000 to $200,000	Varies. Ranges from ASCII text stream to SNMP to CMIP through a gateway type interface.	Command Post—Boole & Babbage
Proprietary Managers	Covers proprietary operating systems hosts and network architecture.	Variable. Sometimes bundled free with HW.	Proprietary agent or software modules.	Netview—IBM
LAN Manager	Covers some desktop administration, server administration and network monitoring and SNMP interface for small networks.	$1,000 to $2,500	Usually native agents in devices and proxy agents in servers. Some support DMI.	Openview for Windows—HP SNMPc Network Manager—Castle Rock Computing

Table 9.1: Market Segment Characteristics for Managers (continued)

Manager Type	Applications	Cost Per Manager (Site)	Protocols/ Agents	Examples
Stand-alone Manager	"Application" layer management—monitoring, configuration and changes. Complex devices (and clusters) management— e.g., routers and switches. Configuration and performance.	$25,000 to $40,000 Note: cost loaded on agents.	Agent with "knowledge" of application domain as well as specific product within domain (e.g., Sybase SQL server or Tuxedo). Use of "non-standard" protocols not uncommon.	Patrol—BMC EcoSYSTEM— Compuware Ciscoworks— Cisco, Inc.
Network Analyzer	Covers measurement of network management traffic performance.	$15,000 to $30,000	Distributed collection components, some based on the RMON standard.	Network General

Different managers cover different parts of the infrastructure. Figure 9.6 shows the extent of the coverage of the different types of managers defined here. The manager-of-managers by its nature can cover the most ground. However, its application is largely in monitoring and automating fault management. Performance management, security configuration, account management, etc. are not covered since its data model is primarily based to hold events.

Integrated managers also cover a lot of the ground although the cost and a single source for the whole portfolio of tools is not suitable for many organizations that believe in integrating best-of-breed products.

9.2.2 Platform Cost of Ownership Components

In an enterprise infrastructure, management architecture often defines more than one platform type. Selecting one or more platforms for infrastructure management is a difficult task, since it impacts almost all downstream operational activities. Capital cost of the platform forms only one part of the cost of its deployment and forms even a smaller part of the cost of

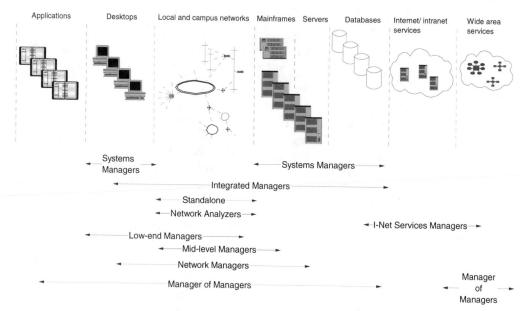

Figure 9.6: *Coverage of infrastructure by manager type*

ownership over about 5 years. Key components in the costs of ownership are briefly described below:

- *Non-enterprise standard*—Platform vendors do not often support an enterprise's standards in areas such as database, user interface and operating system. Choice of a platform hosted on or using what is non-standard technology components for the organization, leads to the platform being viewed as a "black box." The ability to tailor and integrate using internal skills is compromised. Some work is inevitably required over a five-year term that will have to be provided by the vendor. Often in countries outside the technical homebase of the product, such skills are likely to be very expensive.

- *Deployment*—The amount of infrastructure required to deploy a platform in each site may vary according to internal architecture. However, a platform which requires hosting on top-end servers and workstations is likely to evolve to an even more powerful host in a five-year period. Under the current state of flux for the role of the platform, large-scale deployments have to be risk-managed so that excessive dependence on conventional platforms is not the only option. Capital cost of deployment should also be viewed from the perspective of different size offices.

- *Development effort*—Deploying a management platform involves considerable development effort. Development effort is related to how the platform is going to automate or integrate with management processes such as problem management. Common areas of development are in:

   (a) Ensuring enterprise level operating system standards are maintained.
   (b) Systems integration with databases, ticketing and agent systems.
   (c) Building maps.
   (d) Building event classifications and requisite filters.
   (e) Developing threshold settings for agent systems.

- *Training*—All personnel using the platform need adequate training before being able to use it. Far too often only one or two individuals learn to use a platform. When these people are absent, the platform tends to fall into disuse. Training costs are related to the number of people to be trained, the amount of staff turnover and the depth of training required.

- *Maintenance*—15% to 20% of the price paid for the platform is usually a yearly expense for vendor maintenance and support. The support provided by vendors is very variable depending on factors such as service culture of the vendor, country in which service is needed, and the size of the client. The managed environment in a client/server environment is likely to change significantly every 12 months or so. Many changes are reflected at the management platform—at the database, at the event filtering interface, at the map level, etc. Hence there is likely to be ongoing projects in keeping abreast of changes.

9.2.3 Platform Selection Methodology

Platforms and the applications they host are expensive and decisions regarding an enterprise-wide platform have long-term consequence. Each organization has to develop a method for assessing and choosing products. Most of the time this is left to the discretion of one or two individuals. Key principles in developing an enterprise-specific methodology are:

- Map technical requirements for the platform from an enterprise architecture viewpoint. Secondly, "weight" technical requirements according to its need in the architecture.

- Identify technology risks. Some of the key risk dimensions are described in Chapter 2, Section 2.3.1. Especially in the fast evolving fields, product vendors and their wares can disappear. Hence often a number of options may have to be attempted in parallel.

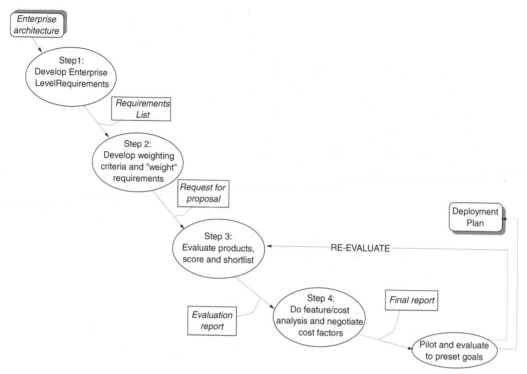

Figure 9.7: *Stepped approach to platform selection*

- Capital cost is usually only a small part of a platform's cost. Hence separate technical aspects from cost aspects. Often what looks like an expensive platform may provide better operational value when other costs of ownership factors are taken into account.

- Pilot before buying. Try out a platform for some time before making the final-buy decision. While this incurs an expense, hands-on experience with the platform and close work with the vendor can provide "confirmation" of the platform's suitability in the enterprise.

As platform choice is likely to affect almost all operational aspects, time is well spent on developing a rigorous approach to selection. Figure 9.7 shows a multi-step methodology which is described below. Before applying a methodology it is useful to establish the basis for comparing platforms. Table 9.2 shows general criteria for platform comparison. The applicability of individual criteria to selection for a given enterprise is dependent on the architectural role to be played by the platform.

Ideally, before platform selection is attempted, each enterprise needs to develop an architecture for infrastructure management. In phase 1 the enterprise-level requirements are developed. Technical requirements define the characteristics needed to implement the architecture in an enterprise. The platform plays one or more roles in the realization of the building blocks of the architecture. The platform may be the central component in the smaller environment or multiple platforms may be distributed across multiple sites.

Requirements will vary with the role. In general the more central the role the more features or functions are needed at the platform. When there is a hierarchy—central platform, mid-level platform, stand-alone—platform "power" tends to be distributed.

In step 2 the features are given a relative weighting. This weighting is based on the relevance of the feature or characteristic to the enterprise architecture. In general, vendors define product characteristics within their own "worldview" of management. For example, in an enterprise with several sites, and a platform at each site, an industrial strength SQL database is essential in several areas such as problem management of global applications. Because database management requires expensive resources, a key qualification may be that the SQL database should conform to the enterprise's own database standard. Hence the enterprise standard SQL database would get a higher weighting than one that may be imposed by the platform vendor.

In step 3 the "weighted" requirements are compared against product offerings. This is done through sending a request for proposal (RFP) to vendors or by in-house/external consultant research. Developing weighted requirements allows all parties to see the important drivers that will be used in deciding the platform.

In step 4 the cost implications are analyzed. Having identified a shortlist of suppliers in step 3, ownership costs over the life-cycle of the platform are evaluated against the offering. This leads to a round of negotiations with one or more vendors on price and delivery of different aspects of the platform.

The final step before deployment is the piloting of the platform in a realistic setting. Piloting requires help from the vendor. This is best negotiated on a fee-paying basis to keep control of the pilot, as well as its integrity and quality. Piloting is the first real chance at evaluation in the enterprise's own setting. This opportunity allows confirmation that:

- Technical characteristics are implemented by the vendor and work in a correct way.

- Life-cycle cost assumptions previously made are either valid or need to be re-visited.

- The platform can be integrated into the internal procedures or processes (that use it).

The result of the pilot is the development of full-scale deployment plans for the platform, or if a failure a reiteration through from step 2.

Table 9.2: Common Criteria for Platform Comparison

Criterion	Description
Infrastructure areas covered	The infrastructure areas covered by the platform. This can range from application and service elements at the top layer to network elements at the bottom layer. Figure 9.6 shows the coverage of common types managers.
Management areas covered by applications	Platforms usually support a set of core applications and secondarily, through partnerships or third parties, support a portfolio of other applications. The relevant management areas will vary with the infrastructure areas covered. However, fault management and configuration management are common to all layers of the infrastructure.
Hosting operating systems/servers	The platform is often supported on more than one operating system. Until recently Unix was the operating system of choice for high-end platforms. Unix servers are usually an expensive item. NT is increasingly likely to be important due to better price/performance.
Operating systems managed	In a heterogeneous systems environment multiple operating systems are found. The platform may have interface technology for more than one operating system. Interfaces typically interface at the console message and error message level.
Agent technologies supported	The platform may be able to interface to agents through multiple protocols such as SNMP, SNMPv2 CMIP, RPC. Platforms may also have a system for developing agent code or for scaling deployment.
Database technologies supported	The database technologies that the platform interfaces to. Platforms typically support some form of flatfile structure and/or a SQL database. Access of the interface to the SQL database is important for developing internal applications. Ideally the same database (i.e., from the same vendor) as the corporate standard should be supported by the platform.
Database vendors that are partners	SQL databases play an important part in deploying platforms across multiple sites. Database technologies such as replication and server to server security are important tools in this respect. The relationship between a platform vendor and the database vendor of choice determines the future evolution of the database-related functionality.

Table 9.2: Common Criteria for Platform Comparison (continued)

Criterion	Description
Compute scaleability	Over time the platform may have to deal with increasing numbers of input events. In a crisis a large volume of events may be generated. The platform should be able to handle worst-case volumes without being overloaded. Compute scaleability defines the way the computing capability of the platform is increased. This may be through more powerful servers or by having concurrent servers.
Multi-site scaleability	In a large organization, platforms are deployed across multiple sites. The architecture of the platform determines the limits and the cost effectiveness of multiple platforms being able to share information such as events.
Multi-operator scaleability	In most organizations multiple operators will need to access concurrently the data as well as use applications. Multi-operator capability is usually provided by client/server architecture or through the multi-user capability of the host operating system.
Console emulation	All major operating systems have a command line console through which system services can be controlled and managed. Emulation of this console allows a direct interface into the operating system level of hosts being managed. Command scripts can often be executed across the interface.
Correlation method	Correlation is the ability to examine whether there are any relationships between events (being) seen by the platform and to filter the "root" event(s) from the "caused" events.
Automation method	Automation is the ability to execute pre-defined actions when a specific event or specific pattern of events is recognized. Actions are defined by executing a script. The logic to determine which script to execute is also defined by a platform level scripting language such as TCL/TK, Perl, REXX or Javascript.
Interfaces to other managers	Some managers, especially manager-of-managers allow other managers to be invoked as well as information to flow between the two manager systems.

Table 9.2: Common Criteria for Platform Comparison (continued)

Criterion	Description
Interfaces to ticketing products	Ticketing is a key mechanism to tie together the technology of platforms and the human aspects of process management. Events seen by the platform need to enter the human process chain, so that events can be acted on. Tickets are one method of enunciating and tracking the progress of events. Ticketing is sometimes an integral application with the platform and sometimes provided by one or more third parties. ARS from Remedy Corp is an example of a ticketing package that integrates to many management platform.
Vendor experience in management products	Platform vendors have entered the platform market from several backgrounds—mainframe tools, Unix systems vendors, start-ups, network analysis tools. Consequently vendor background is evident in product functionality and design. Product architecture that complements enterprise management architecture is a major advantage.
Vendor commitment to open standards	Standards defined as part of the enterprise architecture may need to be supported. A number of de facto standards dominate the platform market. The willingness of the vendor to support standards where they are available is an indicator that the platform is likely to evolve with user requirements.
Vendor's country support organization	Vendors provide variable levels of support in different countries and even within regions in a country. In a multi-site environment, it is important to understand the vendor's support structure and to factor these into operational processes.
Third-party tools for platform	The number of third parties that have tools for the platform is a statistic that is often quoted by vendors. In reality most of these products turn out to be very loosely coupled. Often the platform's user interface merely allows a tool to be launched. See Chapter 12, Section 12.1.1, on the degrees of integration between tools and the platform.
Financial stability of vendor	Platforms deployed in strategic roles (of the enterprise architecture) have long lifetimes, in the region of at least five years during which their capability should be expected to grow. The financial stability of the vendor defines whether the vendor will be around for this period and the degree of product development that will take place over that time.

Table 9.2: Common Criteria for Platform Comparison (continued)

Criterion	Description
Client reference sites	A key prognostic metric is the number of similar clients the vendor can identify. The opinions of users at these reference sites are an important input, and should be viewed within a local context. The lack of any reference sites should be worrying.

9.3 Systems Managers

System managers are aimed at managing hosts at the operating system and some aspects of application software layers. System managers are generally speaking "proprietary" systems. Their vendors' motivation is to sell the base platform and the remaining functionality through a set of separately priced applications and tools.

Availability of genuine third-party products for such platforms is rare. The platform vendor sometimes enters into partnership with specific tool vendors to port a tool or toolset for a specific area.

System managers are probably best described in terms of typical functions since the architecture varies from vendor to vendor. The major functions offered by a vendor is likely to a subset of the following:

- *Software distribution*—Provides the ability for a systems administrator to package binaries at a source and distribute them to specific hosts on the network. An enhancement of this is the ability to stage the package at intermediate servers for local distribution from that point. At the installation targets the software installation is automated as much as possible, with exceptions being reported. With client/server applications having 3- to 12-month software development cycles, software distribution constitutes a major part of systems administration.

- *Monitoring system parameters*—Provides the ability to monitor specific events at the operating system and application level through scanning log and console messages output by the respective software. When an event is recognized at a managed node, it is reliably transported to a central console, where it may undergo further transformation.

- *Managing security services*—This ranges from front-end tools to administer end-user passwords to managing a single sign-on scheme. Other security services include managing access to system resources based on policies for different classes of users. Auditing workstations and servers to ensure that their operating system builds have not been tampered with.

- *Managing printers*—Printers are important end-user resources, but more often than not they are not proactively managed. Top-end printers and many workgroup printers increasingly have the ability to report their status over the LAN. This allows intelligent agents to detect and display printer events (such as low toner and service warnings). A printer management module is available with some managers.

- *Managing storage*—Storage deals with managing large (or increasing) volumes of data produced by the end-user community in a cost-effective way so that the less important or less-used data is archived onto less expensive media than disk storage. Much of the archiving activity is also policy driven. Managers provide the front-end applications to set and apply policies across user groups.

- *Managing backup*—Backup relates to the systematic storage of current data for use in the event of a major disaster or more commonly in the event of a contingency such as a server failing. (In both archiving and backup some intelligence is required to verify that the stored data has not been corrupted by the respective mechanism or process during transfer.)

- *Scheduling and workflow*—The automation of job "streams" that occur repeatedly is a key part of systems management. In a client/server environment, scheduling "milestones" are usually based on meeting a set of dependencies (of which time-of-day may be one). Scheduling is often achieved through executing a script. Front-end tools to define scheduling parameters graphically are available on some managers.

System manager vendors fall into two broad categories: those from the UNIX inspired open systems school and those that were previously mainframe tool vendors who have now turned their expertise to open systems management.

Those from the former category have a better understanding of the problems of distributed management that is reflected in their architecture. Their tools however are generally not as functional or performant as those from the second category. Most of these however have little architectural merit in issues of distribution—such as scaling for example.

9.3.1 Pros and Caveats of System Managers

System managers have, in one form or another, found their way into most big enterprises. The factors in their favor are:

- They provide a set of tools to automate a significant number of labor intensive and error-prone system administration procedures.

- They offer integration of previously disjointed procedures, allowing management processes encompassing multiple procedures to be better mapped to management tools.

- The integration of tools allows the enterprise to develop automation in a shorter timeframe, than otherwise possible with different tools having to be chosen, piloted and integrated with enterprise resources.

- The tools often have a common look and feel that eases training and allows quicker take-up of the toolset.

Viewed strategically there are several negative factors which need to be considered. System manager vendors like everyone else, have finite development capabilities. The complexity of the product set often impacts development cycles. Vendors will take a strategic view on prioritizing their efforts with respect to target environments and tool functionality:

- The cost of system managers is related to the number of systems being managed through it. When scaling up, costs escalate dramatically. Since all the necessary extras have to be bought from the vendor, the balance of power is with the vendor.

- To manage distributed systems requires close coupling between the vendors' technology and target operating systems and applications that are likely to be from other vendors. When for example, new operating system versions become available, the lag before the tool vendor reacts can slow down and in the worst case stop migration to newer versions of base software.

- Often, proprietary protocols and mechanisms are used—hence there is little scope for in-house enhancements or development of the platform into areas that may be uniquely required by an enterprise.

Case Study 9.1: Case Study of a Systems Manager

The Tivoli Management Environment (TME) is undergoing a transition from being a system and services manager to being an integrated manager. This is being achieved through the functional merger between the TME and IBM Systemview.

This case study looks at the Tivoli Management Framework (which is also the foundation of the new TME 10) as a Unix systems manager—which is its primary function in its current user base.

A key part of TME's attraction is the support for policy-based administration. Hence different resources such as servers can be viewed from different grouping perspectives. Similarly, different classes of users can be managed under different policies. Tivoli's second attraction is its powerful object oriented data model of the resources it manages. This database is distributed and can be accessed from multiple TMEs. This allows a global system management environment to be developed. TME consists of a suite of applications and their related agents that are separately priced. The application areas are summarized in Table 9.3. TME's power is that it offers a simplified, graphical view for Unix system administration. This in turn allows less-experienced people to be used productively in this traditionally very expensive skill set.

Table 9.3: Tivoli's Application Elements

Tivoli Application	Description
Systems administration	The platform discovers managed resources such as user accounts, host configurations and NIS domains. Resources are modeled and actual instances are reflected in the object database. The database may be distributed across multiple TME systems. The object database can model and track a comprehensive set of Unix resources. Each resource is fully modeled in terms of its generic attributes. For example, attributes for a *host* includes name, IP address, aliases, netgroup membership and NIS tokens. An instance of a resource can be grouped into "policy region" and responsibility for policy regions may be delegated to different administrators.
Fault and performance monitoring	Sentry agents can monitor several categories of events that occur when predefined thresholds have been crossed. Thresholds can be set through the application—e.g., to monitor the activity level of file systems, memory/paging levels and the "liveness" of common Unix daemons to name a few criteria. When the pre-set thresholds are crossed and event is communicated as defined by the associated action to be taken. The options include a message to be sent to a file or device or via SMTP e-mail, or a script to be executed. Unix performance parameters are also monitored—such as the sizes of the print queue, disk space and swap space.
Software distribution	Courier agents allow software packs to be distributed to a set of target machines. Courier application controls allow system managers to specify machines groups according to predefined policy. Distribution can taken place as it is invoked or on a schedule basis. In both cases the "push" model is supported.
Security	Users can be authenticated using Kerberos—which is the primary authentication mechanism. Kerberos is also used to authenticate administration staff. Kerberos realms are managed as resources. The Network Information Server (NIS) is also managed as a resource. Tivoli provides a graphical front-end for both services and ensures the safety of changes to NIS and Kerberos realms.
Backup and archival	Backup can be automated to provide baseline backups. The backup schedule is updated with new file systems as they are created. Archival criteria can automatically copy respective file systems to less expensive storage (than disk).
Scheduling	TME provides a comprehensive development environment for application developers. In addition the function of any Tivoli application can be customized and extended through scripts or by attaching executables.

- While most system managers are likely to do an adequate job in the functional areas they support. Best-of-breed products in specific areas will always provide better functionality and often performance—especially over a period of 12 to 24 months or so from purchase. This is unlikely to be exploitable without retiring the system managers functionality for the particular area.

9.4 "Open" Network Managers

Essentially, the SNMP station of the early 1990s was developed by (or OEM'd to) a specific device vendor (such as a hub or router vendor). These stations typically provided rudimentary MIB browsing, trap processing and the ability to interpret the device-specific MIB extensions.

The management of the device-specific variables was of greater interest to the users as they allowed the device to be "managed." Yet each device vendor of (hubs, routers, bridges, etc.) ended up defining a new SNMP station.

This limited the markets for each SNMP station while leaving the users with the headache of having to buy an SNMP station for each vendor and sometimes one for each class of device from a vendor.

This proliferation was obviously unsustainable both for the vendor and the users in terms of return on investment (ROI) in management stations. The notion of *open platforms* originated as a marketing concept for improving ROI on SNMP-based product development by vendors and product investment by users.

Open platforms by definition need to adhere to certain principles of "openess":

- The first of these was the active support for applications from different device vendors. These applications needed to conform to one of the levels of integration the platform offers. Hence device vendors entered into business relationships with platform vendors and the third-party application builders were attracted to a platform rather than spending resources developing in-house management stations.

- Use of standards-based management protocols and industrial strength protocol engines allowed device vendors and application vendors to track the evolution of the platform.

- Use of standards-based APIs and full disclosure of proprietary APIs used by a platform vendor allowed various levels of integration with the platform's "services." Hence a device or application vendor could concentrate on developing applications rather than be concerned about lower layers of the management stack.

- Provision of toolkits for application developers resulted in third-party applications vendors gaining expertise in developing software for a platform.

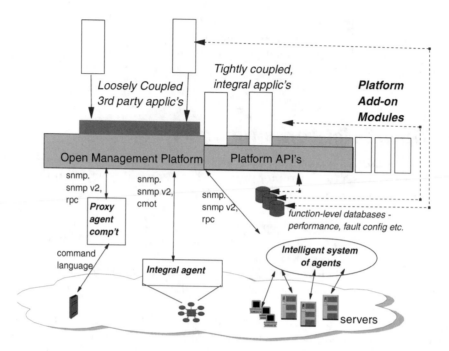

Figure 9.8: Functional model of open platform

- Modular architecture of the platforms allowing accommodation of new protocols, etc. by hiding low level details from application view. The level of abstraction to which applications write code is gradually getting away from protocol and data structure details and more towards an object-oriented model.

Adoption of the open platform concept by the user community has resulted in a major "shakeout" of the SNMP station market.

Some of the original device-specific station vendors are trying to make the transition to the platform "label." A second shakeout is currently on the way which will result in some two or three platform vendors remaining.

Open platforms provide a set of basic services. These are gradually extended in scope and depth of functionality as the platform market matures. A set of such basic services available on each of the major open manager platforms would be element discovery, iconic map and graphics interface, status message and alarm capability.

9.4.1 Element Discovery

Elements in the network being managed are "automatically" discovered, largely through the discovery of IP addresses of connected hosts and extraction of information from router tables and ARP tables.

Element discovery in a complex or highly subnetted topology is however a complex, distributed algorithm. The current state of the art cannot guarantee *timely* discovery without high bandwidth cost involved in such primitive techniques as frequent PING broadcasts. Current discovery algorithms also have problems with:

- Discovery of non-IP devices.

- Discovery within network topologies involving bridges.

- Discovery within abstractions such as switch-based *virtual LANs*.

The natural effect of autodiscovery is the discovered element's inclusion into a map. Such maps if left unedited tend to become cluttered and after a threshold of some 100 or so elements fairly useless as a visual tool.

Hence a common post-autodiscovery action is to re-edit one or multiple maps to show the discovered element.

Auto discovery also has a finite bandwidth overhead over the network. For this reason autodiscovery can be scheduled as a lights out or background activity that occurs only during periods of low network usage.

The use of ICMP to access elements introduces vulnerability that can be exploited to attack the network. ICMP attacks are primarily used to corrupt information selectively, introduce widespread denial of network service and selectively leak information.

Since most current algorithms use router tables, autodiscovery can result in discovering too many elements for the platform to cope with. The extent of the discovery search needs to be settable.

9.4.2 Graphical User Interfaces

Most platforms use standard user interfaces based on Motif and X Windows. Discovered elements are placed as icons in some connectivity relationship. These are called maps and the icons can be referenced by pointing.

Maps resulting from auto-discovery get very confusing as the number of elements increase. Most platforms allow a large map to be partitioned manually into smaller maps. Multiple maps may be related to each other through a drill-down hierarchy.

The data used to draw a map is held in some program "writeable" form in a file or data structure. This offers the ability to trigger re-draws from new data entered into the data structure.

Many auto-discovery algorithms can recognize the difference between routers, bridges (inter-networking components) and hosts (end systems). In some cases they can recognize the manufacturer from the MAC address code translation. Key aspects for this service to be generally useful are:

- *Partitioning* big maps into multiple maps. An element may appear in more than one map. Any state change associated with an element gets displayed on all maps that the element is represented. Some platforms allow an element to be represented by different icons in different maps. This is however a manual operation.

- *Direct manipulation*—where the icon representing a device can be referenced as an addressable element to which commands or management instructions can be sent. The menus should only show the commands that may be sent to the element. This ensures the safety of such operations.

- Grouping of multiple icons where a set of icons represent a context such as the resources for a business process. Grouping these resources either into a separate map or as a named "building-block" is a useful visual tool.

9.4.3 Status and Alarms

Events from devices are put through a staging mechanism provided by the platform. This mechanism can be programmed by the end-user (either through a platform tool or third-party tools):

- Capture protocol alerts (such as SNMP traps) and execute any confirmatory polls of MIB variables.

- Poll for MIB variable value and execute simple functions such as range checking to generate status values.

- Set thresholds for MIB variables. When the variables are polled and the threshold is crossed an internal event notification is generated.

- Filter incoming alerts and internal event notifications and place them into a rudimentary classification based on fixed severity levels such as "informational," "warning," "urgent," etc. The events to be displayed and the events to be logged can also be defined.

- In some systems simple hysteresis models can be set for individual MIB variables (usually based on the count).

- Send Internet Control Message Protocol (ICMP) "Pings" and returns to indicate whether the target of the Ping is "alive"—and if not to raise an internal event notification.

The event and status management subsystem is relatively compute intensive. The event management system is therefore a natural function to execute on one or more separate processors. The output of event management is closely linked to the user interface tools and platform configuration tools.

9.4.4 APIs and Other Interfaces

Application Program Interfaces (APIs), provide transparency of internal details of the platform architecture—allowing application developers to write applications without intimate knowledge about the platform. The publication of APIs has been the major reason for calling such platforms open. Vendors usually develop applications on the basis of:

- Size of a platform's market share relative to an application.

- Ease of use and quality of the APIs.

- De facto standards—e.g., ratified by international bodies such as IETF or ISO.

In addition to publishing APIs, platform vendors also supply developer toolkits which provides additional resources such as templates for interface definition. Platform vendors sometimes provide certification services.

Use of management APIs is however not intended for in-house development. Each platform vendor's set of APIs is different and developers have to port their applications.

The difficulty of developing multiple APIs has resulted in most third-party applications being only trivially integrated to a management platform. Often only joint ventures with the platform vendor result in applications that exploit the platform's data resources.

Two other interfaces between the platform and its "outside" world are the database links and the modules for communicating with the managed environment.

- *Database links*—Platforms have tended to use ASCII flat-files internally for storing device-related data. This has been attributed to reasons of internal performance. Some platforms have an integral object oriented store. Others use an integral relational database engine from a third party. Relational (SQL) databases allow sophisticated, data mining and report-generation tools to be deployed to extract information without recourse to platform tools.

- *Modular management protocol stacks*—Platforms have to convert data transported from devices into internally usable forms. Similarly, control and data from applications have to be transported to devices. Many platforms develop an abstract layer that can translate different management protocols without having to modify internal logic.

9.4.5 Mechanisms for Scaling

Platforms are by and large developed for a centralized architecture, hence in large environments scaling is an important consideration. Platform-level scaling mechanisms are ideally needed to address:

- *Multiple operators*—Managing a large environment often requires more than one operator having to access and use its tools concurrently. Operators may specialize along functional or process lines. The platform needs to be separable into a server (applications and data) and multiple client parts to access these services. This is achieved through a real client/server architecture but may be as simple as "detachable" consoles with access right to specific views.

- *Multiple sites*—Centralized platforms at each site need to communicate and exchange information about devices and systems being managed. (This is especially true when global client/server systems have geographically distributed parts.) This is achieved through the management protocol (such as SNMPv2 and CMIP) or through synchronized, replicated databases. Synchronization and replication are features of most industrial strength relational databases.

- *Volume of events*—The volume of events that a platform has to deal with increases as the size of the managed environment increases and during times of failures in the infrastructure (when a lot of secondary events occur as a result of each primary failure). Event volume can be handled by specializing event management functions (such as collection, filtering and correlation) to be separately hosted on different servers. Alternatively, the server power can be scaled up using the technology appropriate to the server platform—e.g., quad-Pentium based platform or a load-sharing architecture.

- *Resilience*—Resilience is achieved usually by using RAID and server fail-over or cluster technology. A consequence of "load-sharing" architecture is that resilience is improved. When a server in a load-sharing configuration fails the other server continues working. Hence a service is maintained at the price of performance (the failed server cannot participate).

9.4.6 Pros and Caveats for Open Managers

"Open" managers are still riding a wave of expanding sales as more and more LANs are developed. The primary advantages are that the platforms are mature with wide availability and support. Market dominance by platform vendors ensures continuing improvements (although at a pace that is too slow for many device vendors who are looking at alternatives such as web-based consoles).

Table 9.4: *"Open" Manager's Characteristics by Platform Design Center*

Design Center for:	Open Manager Characteristic
Monitoring	Fault, performance threshold violations, security events, operational warnings. 70% to 95% auto-discovery of elements and topology details. Filtering of events using "crude" classification into priority-classes.
Control	MIB Variable Sets from a browser or dialog tool. Console launch of pre-defined scripts or command line interface to enter commands directly.
User Interface	Predefined icons and maps for display. Use of visual cues to show status of elements or subsystems represented on the display. Direct manipulation of icons, and menu-based dialogs. Command line interface to enter command language statements.
Network Extent	Local Area Networks and to a lesser degree Metropolitan Area Networks are directly monitored. Also consolidation at the data level for LAN/MAN. The Wide Area Network is rarely monitored directly using open managers, more likely to manage "mid-level" managers.
Management Interface	"Open" protocol standards. "Open" standards-based APIs for providing transparency to applications. Proprietary but published APIs for third-party application integration.
Target Environment	Protocol "stack" up, to and including the network layer. Some ad hoc monitoring of other parts such as host systems.
Managing change	Expects a changing environment with *adds, moves* and *changes* of devices. Recompiling MIBs and address information. MIB compilers, MIB browsers and application-level dialog interfaces.
Interworking with manager-of-managers	Launch *from* manager-of-manager console (as a lower level manager) and launch *of* manager-of-managers open platform console.
Platforms	Integration at map level and icon reference and sometimes through use of a common database vendor.

There is probably sufficient expertise worldwide to plan and deploy the platforms—especially at single sites. Platform vendors are likely to be better supported by third-party consultancies in their home countries—hence to achieve global deployment and integration will require in-house talent in design and project management.

On the minus side the following are concerns to keep in mind when planning for new platform or changing platforms:

- Coverage of the infrastructure spectrum is limited largely to the network. Focus is on single devices rather than subsystems.

- Centralized architecture—unsuitable for distributed environments, scaling usually expensive as multiple platforms need to be bought and supported.

- The role of the platform is undergoing a major revision in terms of managing inter-network components and devices that increasingly need a subsystem management approach.

- Lack of integration between tools means the usefulness of a tool rarely extends beyond a narrow usage.

- Only SNMP (and CMIP in some cases) environments can be supported.

Case Study 9.2: Case Study of a Network Manager

Spectrum 4.0 from Cabletron Systems is an example of a state-of-the-art network management platform. One of Spectrum 4.0's unique characteristics is its Inductive Modeling Technology which is a method for modeling any physical or logical device it can manage. The abstract model is used to define relationships between managed devices. This tool can be used to develop correlation models to manage any network device.

The platform is based on a true client/server architecture. The application server is called the SpectroSERVER. The client application is called SpectroGRAPH and is resident on workstations (i.e., separate from a Spectro SERVER). Information access to the servers is relatively efficient as the presentation logic is in the workstation.

Several SpectroSERVERS are connected together to form a distributed server network. Spectrum 4.0 based management services can be geographically distributed as the server parts can be logically connected over a wide area network. Hence application and models can be developed that are enterprise-wide.

Spectrum 4.0 is also unique in that it has recognized the value to users of providing management event information in different contexts (or "views" in Spectrum parlance). The main architectural elements of the product, including the set of pre-defined views it provides are shown in Table 9.5.

Spectrum includes a protocol translation layer that makes the support of new management protocols relatively easy as the core applications are not affected by the change.

The platform also provides user-level tools for creating and editing models, customizing icon and graphical views. More advanced tools are available in the form of a system developers kit.

Table 9.5: Spectrum 4.0's Component Applications

Core Application Element and Views	Description
Auto-discovery	Maps the network by identifying IP addresses. As devices are added or removed, auto-discovery is invoked to update the network map.
Control panel	A user interface for the launch of Spectrum applications.
Watch	A filter-based tool to "watch" for and log any attribute of a model in the database. Calculation can be done on the variable.
MAC address locator	Finds the location of the device from its MAC address. This is used to determine the physical details (such as the hub and port of a workstation whose MAC address is known.
Data export	Allows data to be exported for access by third-party applications.
Database backup	Automatically backs up the database at defined intervals.
Report generator	Provides automated generation of reports from report templates.
Scheduler	Provides automated execution of scripts and jobs on the server.
Location view	Shows where a device is placed relative to a background map. Status shows alarms and events relative to location.
Topology view	Shows a device relative to a topology map. The connectivity of the device relative to the topology is shown. Status shows alarms and events relative to the logical topology.
Organization view	Shows a device in terms of usage (or ownership) within a specific organizational context. Status shows alarms and events relative to the effect on users or departments.
Event log view	Provides a list of events and alarms that have occurred.
Performance view	Shows network statistics from managed devices in a single logical view.
Alarm view	Shows the currently active alarms relative to the models that generated the alarm. The possible causes and actions to take can be annotated to the alarm model.

9.5 *Integrated (Network and Systems) Managers*

Network management and systems management have been separate disciplines in most organizations. The first was deemed to be responsible for the network infrastructure of cables, hubs, bridges/routers, switches/multiplexers. Systems management on the other hand was responsible for application, workstation, and server performance, workstation and server administration including software upgrades, user administration, software distribution, scheduling across platforms, and backup of data at the file level.

There is now however a very definite trend for integrating these two functions at an organizational level. The main drivers for this trend are:

- Experiences with the deployment of client/server based applications have highlighted service interdependence within the infrastructure stack. This is reflected in the close working relationships needed between network and systems management staff—e.g., in fault diagnosis, managing security alarms and performance problems.

- At the high end of the client/server deployment maturity model in many enterprises—hosts, databases, and middleware services are viewed as being part of the infrastructure. (Databases and middleware are viewed as part of the application when such technology is first deployed.)

- Network management tools and platforms require a high level of skill in systems administration. These skills are usually fulfilled in an ad hoc fashion.

9.5.1 Platforms in Transition

Such drivers have in turn created a market for integrated network and systems manager technology. These managers provide a merger of the functions provided by system management platforms and network management platforms. There are several advantages to integration out-of-a-box rather than integrating best-of-breed solutions:

- A well-architected platform—for example, based on an object model that unifies the infrastructure layers—can provide end-to-end, desktop to desktop views of all the service paths in an infrastructure. This can also lead to an event-driven model, irrespective of the management protocols used.

- The cost of integration is "capped." Often integration of best-of-breed products run into unexpected difficulties that cause overruns at best or sometimes even failure of the original aims.

- The technical risk is limited, provided the vendor is stable and continues to develop the product to support evolving areas such as web management and firewall management.

- The platform's APIs can provide a stable set of standards for developing in-house applications that cover end-to-end management.

Several manager platforms that previously fitted into being either systems or network managers are currently trying to make the transition to integrated managers. Table 9.6 shows examples of platforms that are making or recently made the transition. Some such as CA-Unicenter TNG (Case Study 9.3 in Section 9.5.1) have completed the transition—and have done so through engineering a unifying object framework and acquiring agent technology. Others such as HP are bundling multiple products together to span the layers.

In fact, a common object model is a key part of the architecture to integrate network and systems management. Figure 9.9 shows how the object model allows layering and as a place for storing object status.

Table 9.6: Examples of Platform In-Transition to Integrated Management Platform

Original Name/ Original Area	Post Transition Name	Transition Strategy	Current Status
HP Openview Node Manager (network manager)	HP Openview IT/ Operations	Bundling existing product lines Node Manager and Operations Center.	In transition, level of product integration remains to be seen.
Tivoli TME (systems manager)	TME 10 Global Enterprise Manager	"Merger" with IBM SystemView platform. Leveraging off TME's object model.	In transition, combined product suite and direction unclear.
CA-Unicenter (systems manager)	CA-Unicenter TNG	Around a new layered architecture with an object repository and layered agent technology.	Transition completed.

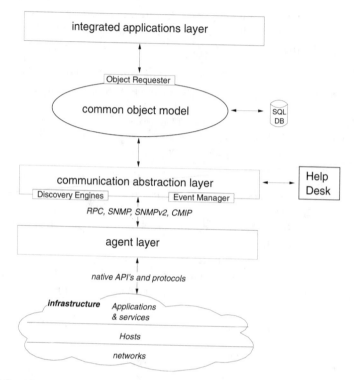

Figure 9.9: *Object model as a unifying concept for integrating network and systems*

Case Study 9.3: Case Study of an Integrated Manager

CA Unicenter TNG is an integrated manager in that it combines management capability for networks, systems, databases and to some degree applications.

Unicenter TNG has an internal object-oriented management object repository called the Common Object Repository at its center. This is used to normalize the end-to-end views spanning the infrastructure layers it supports. Also, all the tools have access to the same data model, the tool functionality is much more integrated and event oriented.

The repository also drives interfaces for visualization, such as 2D maps and 3D models. Change of state to an object in the repository are automatically seen by all views that include that object.

Another unique feature of the Unicenter TNG is the intelligent agent layer which allows many computational functions to be encapsulated in agent logic and shared with peer-level agents or hierarchically higher level agents.

Unicenter TNG bundles a number of powerful applications centered around the concept of the object repository—these are shown in Table 9.7.

Table 9.7: Unicenter TNG's "Component" Applications

Core Application Suite Functions	Description
Auto-discovery	Auto-discovery spans resources in application, database, system and network parts of the infrastructure. Extensible to discover new classes of resources.
Event management	Provides a comprehensive event filtering and correlation system based on the agent layer and the object repository. Event management rules can be defined at either or both points.
Web-server manager	Provides monitoring of web server status and event logs and utilization statistics. Monitors HTML page usage for migration of least-used pages off-server. Supports SSL and SHTTP as well as audit of access.
Software distribution	Software distribution across heterogeneous platforms using customizes fan-out and distribution schedules. Offers alternative distribution models. Supports large-scale environments with audit and tracking of installed software.
Security management	Provides a single sign-on based authentication, resource authorization. Also eases administration of user IDs and passwords including enforcing password policies. Resources such as file-systems and servers can be grouped and authorized for use at a business process level and users participating in the process. User authorization can also be at an application level. Audit facilities allows a process to screen for violation of security policies.
Storage management	Provides backup and restore across a heterogeneous client/server environment through support of open standards. In addition functions such as encryption, compression and error correction are provided. Hierarchical storage management with automated restoration of off-line files is provided through a third-party product.
Desktop management	Provides inventory management of hardware and software as well as a configuration of desktops. Supports the open desktop management interface (DMI)—that allows DMI capable systems also to be monitored.
Schedule management	Supports distributed scheduling and flow of jobs over a heterogeneous environment. Scheduling can be controlled through policies. Shared calendar objects allow changes to be reflected across all related schedules and job flows. The progress of distributed job schedules can be monitored and presented at a business process level. Triggers for generating exception events can be specified and managed through the event management system.
Performance management	Provides agent-based instrumentation for performance management across a heterogeneous environment. Performance metrics can be collected through the infrastructure layers (networks, hosts applications and services). Can establish response time baselines for service delivery paths and can check for exceptions against the baseline.

9.6 Manager-of-Managers

The reality even as we approach the millennium is that the open manager platforms manage only a small proportion of the devices that an enterprise depends on to do its business.

Almost all Fortune 1000 organizations run mission-critical networks that use components pre-dating the open network management protocols and interfaces. Such components are managed by proprietary protocols between *element managers* and the components. Element managers usually consist of a control program that is executed on a host and can send commands to, and elicit responses from the components being managed. The comand-response sequences are in effect a protocol.

A single such protocol is unlikely to manage more than one vendor specific set of components. Examples of such components include modems, multiplexers, mainframes and minicomputers. The newer generation of some of these components may support SNMP agents or it may be feasible to build proxy agents. Organizations depending on such components have by and large not wanted to disrupt these networks for such an upgrade.

Hence improvement of management capability at a low risk to the organization has defined the order of importance in evolution of this scenario.

The manager-of-managers platform precisely fills this requirement. It integrates information from multiplexers of element managers, allowing simplification of procedures as more events get processed in a standard way. It also allows simplification through reduction of the types of management technology in the environment. In many cases simplification of technology allows staff reduction.

Low risk to the enterprise because the manager-of-managers vendor customizes the platform for the element managers is of interest to the client. This is often in the form of a module that can be modified if necessary without affecting other areas of a manager-of-managers'-based framework.

Provides state of the art in workstation technology for the user interfaces—a far cry from single line command interfaces. This improves morale and productivity of staff entrusted with managing "legacy" networks.

The high cost of manager-of-managers can often be justified in terms of the level of automation and the "completeness" of the solution supplied by the vendor for managing individual element managers.

Retains a high probability of being able to co-exist with open platforms through the efforts of major manager-of-managers' vendors to integrate their products with open platform partners. A typical example of a manager-of-managers is Command Post from Boole & Babbage, Inc. Until about a year ago Command Post had at least two competitors. This market is currently undergoing a shakeout.

Figure 9.10 shows the typical relationship between a manager-of-managers' platform and element managers. Typically, the manager-of-managers provides two interfaces, one to emulate the command stream to the managed components and one for text input from the managed components.

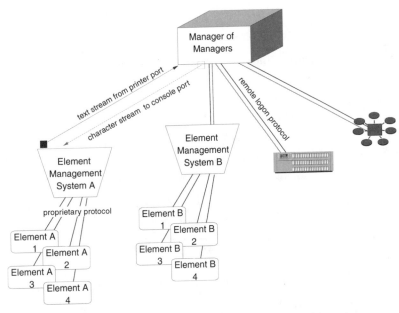

Figure 9.10: *Manager-of-managers in a manager hierarchy*

9.6.1 Scaleability

Manager-of-managers' platforms tend to use a client/server architecture with greater understanding than other types of managers. One of the areas where this has produced results is in the scaleability of products.

Scaleability is of particular importance with such a manager-of-managers because they tend to be more firmly embedded into the managed environment. It is often impossible to move away from a manager-of-manager environment once it has been deployed.

The very reasons for choosing the manager-of-managers' platform—reduction of risk of deployment failure, coverage of multi-generation, heterogeneous environments—also locks users in a "life-cycle embrace" with the vendor.

An evident danger exists in that a vendor that is losing market share is unable to develop the product at a sufficient pace to be useful to a large enterprise.

Also, the vendor holds all the intellectual property rights to key filtering and interfacing solutions. The quality of the vendor's technical and consultative capability changes with its market position. This is likely to impact the user's environment.

Table 9.8: Manager-of-Managers' Characteristics by Platform Design Center

Design Center for:	Manager-of-Managers' Characteristic
Monitoring	Devoted almost entirely to fault management. Conversion rules for incoming text messages to alarms. Filtering of text messages to minimize "noise." Consolidation of alarm and their relative priorities.
Control	Automated response to alarm conditions. Opening session to element manager via window. Automated polling for "existential" criteria.
User interface	Color coded alarm lists by alarm priority. Explicit relationships between alarms. Clearing and stand-down of alarms.
Network extent	Predominantly in WAN. Some uses in monitoring legacy systems in LAN and MAN.
Management interface	Bespoke by vendor for each element manager or system. Vendor sells a portfolio of such interfaces or undertakes to build one-off interfaces. Interfaces maintainable by vendor.
Target environment	Collecting information from multiple stand-alone systems or centralized environments.
Managing change	Assumes little change in each target environment—adding new environments or replacing environments is possible. Accommodating evolution of an environment involves the manager-of-managers vendor. Little evidence of element managers' vendors cooperating with manager-of-managers vendors.
Interworking with open platforms	Assumes future product integration between a specific manager-of-managers' vendor and specific open platform vendor through support on the manager-of-managers of additional open protocols.

The following types of scaleability are important from a user's "survival" perspective:

- *Multiple types of clients*—the number and types of clients that can access and act on the information from the manager-of-managers tends to change over time, especially as mergers, downsizing, global expansion, etc. occur.

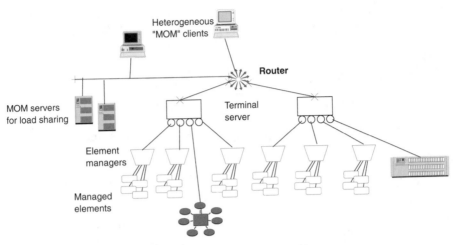

Figure 9.11: *Scaleability in manager-of-managers*

- *Load balancing*—As the volume of one type of events diminish and others increase, extra capacity is often required. Some vendors support multiple servers for load balance, some balance the load by distributing the CPU intensive function across "specialized" servers.

- *Interface to database used*—the manager-of-managers' event database is a rich source of enterprise-wide information. Access using off-the-shelf tools would increase the use of the data in other management contexts such as capacity management and distribution of key events using web-based technology.

Figure 9.11 shows framework changes as a manager-of-managers' environment is scaled up.

9.6.2 Interoperation with Open Managers

A comparison of manager-of-managers' platform and open manager platform characteristics show little overlap. In organizations with a large installed base of legacy systems as well as requirements to manage substantial client/server systems, then each has a role to play, particularly in fault management. To this end several manager-of-managers' vendors have alliances with specific open platform vendors.

Manager-of-managers'-type architectures also have a role to play in integrating multiple open platforms. In large enterprises decentralization during the early 1990s resulted in different management strategies being followed by different businesses. These same enterprises look to reintegrating the management of the infrastructure when moving to a global perspective.

Such a situation is also common as a result of the mergers and acquisitions followed by business integration. Changing from one platform to another is difficult to achieve.

9.7 Other Management "Platforms"

Other types of management platforms include:

- Proprietary managers developed in the heyday of manufacturer architectures ruling corporate facilities.

- LAN managers developed to address "small" or uncomplicated Wintel environments.

- Stand-alone managers that are essentially applications that address the needs in a niche area.

- Network analyzers—strictly speaking not "yet" a platform, however, still important to managing any large network.

These are described below.

9.7.1 Proprietary Platforms

Proprietary management platforms are developed for vendor-specific network environments. IBM's Netview is perhaps the best-known example with its very large installed base. It was originally developed to support all the tasks in its System Network Architecture (SNA). Other proprietary "platforms" that survive include those for DECnet.

Mainframe Netview is characteristic of such platforms and has in some organizations been given a new lease of life with new roles being found for mainframes (e.g., as a corporate "information" server) in some organizations.

Mainframe Netview is a host-based network management system consisting of a group of software programs that monitor and report on network operation, and supports mainframe, PC networks as well as non-IBM devices.

Mainframe Netview is an example of a centralized management system. It allows different products using the SNA protocols to communicate and share management information using Mainframe Netview as the management focal point. Figure 9.12 shows two means of achieving this.

In the first, Netview is a hierarchically higher entity that uses a proprietary protocol to communicate with other Netview environment managers. In the second the SNMP, CMIP and SNA environments use their respective native protocols to communicate with the central manager.

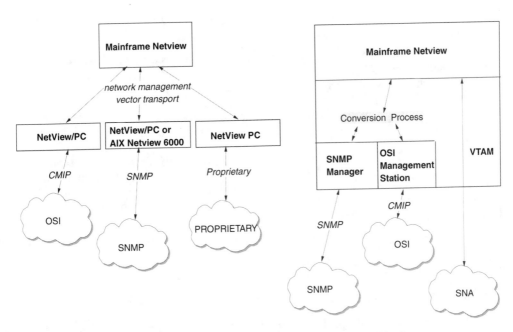

Figure 9.12: *Proprietary management in Mainframe Netview*

9.7.2 LAN Managers

Most organizations with PC LANs employ one set of tools for local management and another set of tools for managing, at the corporate level, the "internetwork" of PC LANs.

The former is usually through DOS/Windows utility-based tools while the latter usually depends on Unix based platforms. (In the future, vendors may migrate from Unix to NT in which case differentiation between low-end and corporate level managers will diminish.) Low-end managers are largely aimed at integrating these two aspects of PC LANs and servers.

With many organizations working on a global basis with international offices of various sizes, this kind of platform has an important role to play in integrating infrastructure management processes across an enterprise. The main characteristics of low-end SNMP managers are:

- Low-cost PC based platform and low cost of software.

- Manage 100 to 500 nodes environments.

- Integrate PC administration functions with network management on one platform.

Case Study 9.4: Case Study of a LAN Manager

Openview for Windows (OV for Windows) from Hewlett Packard is a network management product aimed at small LANs of a few hundred nodes in total. It provides SNMP management capability for network devices or systems with native SNMP agents (as well as devices or systems supported by proxy SNMP agents).

A unique feature of OV for Windows is its Visual Basic based controls to develop front-end applications using SNMP Gets and Sets. Such applications can be developed without much programming effort.

A hierarchy of OV for Windows managers can be set up with a central console having alarms forwarded to it from "secondary" consoles. OV for Windows allows the central console to remotely "takeover" consoles that are in a "forwarding" relationship to it. The console that has been taken over can be manipulated as though it were local. The main features of HP Openview for Windows are shown in Table 9.9.

9.7.3 Network Analyzers

With the increased use of hubs and switching hubs with built in RMON agents, network analyzers are primarily used to track and understand end-to-end traffic problems. While network analyzers are not platforms they are nevertheless essential tools in managing most sizes of client/server environments. A top-end network analyzer provides three key functions:

- Monitoring traffic at "wire-speeds" or approaching wire speeds. Monitoring provides an accurate count of number of packets, number of broadcast packets and so on. Wire-speed monitoring capability is important for the simple reason that many client/server problems manifest themselves as network load increases or as bursts of network activity.

- Captures actual traffic (rather than statistical views of traffic provided by tools such as the RMON agent) for examination and decode by an intelligent application. Actual traffic views are important when debugging multi-layer infrastructure problems.

- Frame generation to allow stress testing of client/server infrastructure components ranging from devices to servers. For frame generation to be realistic frames have to be unique in size and content. Also the inter-frame gap (or the frequency of frame generation) is an important control parameter.

Table 9.9: *Main Features of HP Openview for Windows*

OV for Windows Feature	Description
Auto-discovery	Discovers both IP and IPX devices. The former by searching ARP cache tables and the latter using Netware services. Auto-discovery can be run periodically to discover new or departed devices. Once devices have been discovered, the devices are periodically polled to see if they are responding.
Maps and layout	Maps are shown as a router topology of IP and IPX devices. Submaps can be created to show different views of the network. All subviews may be displayed simultaneously. Change of state of a device is simultaneously shown on all maps where the device is present.
Trap management	Devices can be monitored for SNMP traps. The traps to monitor can be configured as well as a mapping to a severity level and annotation of a text message to display. A clearing trap which "clears" a trap condition can be defined where relevant.
SNMP manager	The SNMP manager includes an ASN.1 MIB compiler and tools for MIB browsing, polling and setting MIB variables and graphing MIB values. MIB values can also be exported to Microsoft Excel spreadsheets. Custom menu items can be created representing MIB queries. The manager console can be secured when logging out while allowing any application to continue running.
Visual basic controls	Visual basic controls include meters and switches for doing gets and sets, respectively. Simple applications are created by configuring controls and the values they access. This is especially useful for simple types of automation.
Alarm forwarding	Alarms that are received by a manager can be forwarded to another Openview for Windows manager or to the higher-end HP Openview Unix platform. Alarms forwarded by an update to the device in the respective maps at the target Openview console.
Remote control	Openview for Windows includes an application for a central console to "take-over" remote Openview for Windows consoles that are forwarding alarms to it. Once a console has been taken over, it can be used as a local console.

Case Study 9.5: Case Study of a Network Analyzer

Network General Corp's Sniffer is a high-speed analyzer with support for a 100 MBit Ethernet and FDDI (as well as 10 MBit Ethernet, Token Ring, ISDN and ATM networks). Network General sells software and network adapter cards for a range of hardware from laptops to high-end PCs.

For higher speed networks, powerful hardware is needed—otherwise wire-speed capture and generating is unlikely to be achieved. Sniffers can also be distributed to monitor and analyze remote networks or different parts of a client/server application's service delivery path.

The Sniffer has a unique analysis and decode application which makes it a powerful diagnostic tool. The Sniffer has filters to decode between 180 and 200 protocols. These range from SQL to the TCP/IP suite of protocols to common network operating system protocol families (e.g., Novell Netware, Banyan Vines and IBM LAN Server). Decoded informations is shown within a 7-layer model starting with the MAC layer right up to the application layer. Decoded packets are annotated with English text interpretations.

Table 9.10 shows the main features of the Sniffer. The expert system-based application provides two types of information:

- Recognizes common symptoms and produces alerts with explanations and causes.
- When symptoms are repeated or a "well known" problem is recognized a fault condition is produced—with explanation and causes.

In both cases the actual packets associated with the recognized problem is stored and can be recalled to do further manual processing. The collection of expert analysis information can be scheduled and the results saved to hard disk.

To capture actual traffic on high-speed LANs such as FDDI and 100 MBit Ethernet, hardware-based analyzers are required. An FDDI or 100 MBit LAN analyzer often has over 30 MBytes of capture buffer as standard, yet this is often inadequate to capture any meaningful client/server transaction in its entirety—unless the traffic is filtered to capture only specific packets. Filtering can be done in hardware, in which case filters can be dynamically created.

Network analyzers often have at least one intelligent application—to decode and identify captured packets and layer details and to infer relationships between sequences of packets. For example, analyzers can decode NFS and SQL—both culprits in many client/server infrastructure problems.

As network analyzers are generally used relatively rarely, mostly to solve problems when trouble strikes, it is important that the user interface is both intuitive and easy to use.

Table 9.10: *Main Features of the Sniffer*

Sniffer Feature	Description
User interface	A character-based interface. Considered highly intuitive and easy to use. Textual displays of explanations. Multiple windows allow different views of traffic. Statistics are collected and displayed in numerical and graphical formats.
Display filter criteria	Information that is displayed is controlled by the choice of one or more display-filter criteria. Criteria that may be defined include the address level, a station address (e.g., in FDDI), pattern match, error frames.
Capture filter criteria	Information that is captured is controlled by the setting of one or more capture-filter criteria. Criteria that may be defined include LAN protocol type, pattern match, good frames or error frames.
Traffic generator	The network can be injected with traffic. The options are to repeat the same frame at defined intervals or to use user-edited contents of the capture buffer.
Traffic history	Traffic history can be tracked for the network that is being monitored at programmable intervals ranging from seconds to days. Traffic parameters include a time-stamp, number of good frames, number of errors, network utilization.
Alarms	Alarms may set for individual stations or for the network being viewed. Alarms are logged to a printer, disk or made audible. Alarms are on the basis of exceeding pre-set thresholds for rate of error, network utilization, network idle time, rate of broadcast or multicast, oversize frame.
Network statistics	Network statistics that can be stored/displayed include average and peak utilization, number of bytes and frames, number of stations, number of errors. Also network utilization by LAN protocol types, frames and bytes by protocol types as well as frame-size statistics.
Station statistics	Station statistics include traffic received and sent, time of first seen frame, time of last seen frame, average network utilization and total frames sampled.

9.8 Books for Further Reading

Abeck, Sebastian, *et al. Integrated Network and System Management* (Data Communications & Networks). Addison Wesley, 1994.

Terplan, Kornel, and J. Huntington-Lee. *Applications for Distributed Systems and Network Management.* Van Nostrand Reinhold, 1994.

Huntington-Lee, J., and Kornel Terplan. *HP's Openview* (A Practical Guide). McGraw Hill, 1997.

The Technology of Protocols and Interfaces

Areas covered in this chapter

- A brief history of management protocols and their driving forces

- Description of the widely deployed Simple Network Management Protocol (SNMP)

- The strengths and weaknesses of SNMP and evolution to SNMPv2

- Description of the SNMPv2 standard and issues in implementation and deployment

- Introduction to the concepts and models of OSI management standards

- Enumeration and descriptions of commonly used management interfaces

- Use of common application protocols (X11, RPC, SQL) in a management context

- Introduction to intranet protocols with a management dimension

- Key components of the Java management API

Current literature in network management, systems and application management is heavily biased towards aspects of its technology. This primarily consists of the management platform, the management protocols and agents. Secondarily, it includes databases, the user interface and Application Program Interfaces (API) for application development.

This chapter looks at the technology of infrastructure management largely from the perspective of the *protocols* and interfaces between different parts of the systems model described in Chapter 1. This model in many ways sets the limits on how the people, process and architecture aspects of infrastructure management relate to technology.

The functionality provided by the management platform and agent technologies is determined to a large degree by the protocol used between the two. A management protocol is in effect a "proto-language" that puts a bound on the *types of things* the platform and agent can communicate about.

The most dominant protocols by "market share" of network management tools and services are:

- Simple Network Management Protocol (SNMP) defined by the Internet Activities Board (IAB).

- Netview from IBM which started off in the management of SNA but now supports the heterogeneous environments including TCP/IP.

- Common Management Information Protocol (CMIP) defined by the International Organization for Standardization (ISO).

Today, SNMP is ubiquitous in TCP/IP environments while Netview pre-dominates in IBM environments, with CMIP being limited largely to the telecommunications and some utility companies around the world.

While protocols such as SNMP started life specialized for network management, they have found use, almost by default, in managing other layers of the infrastructure. In particular hosts and operating systems, software systems and applications are to varying degrees monitored using SNMP.

Other general purpose protocols such as Remote Procedure Call (RPC) and Structured Query Language (SQL) are also widely used in infrastructure management frameworks, albeit in a proprietary way by each vendor.

The use of general purpose protocols is driven by the expanding scope of infrastructure management, particularly in the era of client/server based computing architectures. This computing model has been adopted by many organizations, to one degree or another, and is used for developing new business applications or specified when buying "off-the-shelf" software.

An infrastructure management system, in common with other complex applications, is limited by the capabilities of the protocol(s) it uses to tie together its components.

Specific characteristics of protocols used in managing the various parts of the infrastructure highlight the requirements to manage the respective point or layer of the infrastructure.

10.1 *Modern History of Management Protocols*

As TCP/IP developed through the 1970s little thought was given to managing networks. The Internet Control Message Protocol (ICMP) in conjunction with tools such as the Packet Internet Groper (PING) in the hand of TCP/IP experts was deemed adequate to "manage" modest-size networks of a few thousand machines—this form of management included the ability to:

- Examine whether an IP addressable device could be reached, and if it were a host, to verify that it was operational.

- Examine whether a subnet could be addressed and return paths existed from the subnet.

- Pinpoint areas of the network where data packets were being lost and diagnose the reasons.

- Observe variations in roundtrip time and hence the variation in loading on the network.

As networks became larger and spread out geographically, problems grew exponentially and more and more experts were need to keep the networks operational. These experts produced ad hoc, individually developed tools for their trade.

A number of initiatives were started in the TCP/IP community by a larger and possibly less skilled population of technicians to define a more standardized way of managing TCP/IP networks. The Simple Network Management Protocol (SNMP) was one result of this quest for a standard protocol.

What distinguished SNMP was its sheer simplicity. This in turn led, very quickly, to reference implementations—launching widespread support for its principles. Meanwhile, ISO started work on defining the Common Management Information Protocol (CMIP). For a while the two communities cooperated.

SNMP was first defined in 1988 at which time the view was that SNMP would be superseded by ISO's CMIP (over TCP/IP). This linkage to CMIP and its management information structure was subsequently removed. The take-up of SNMP by vendors was further accelerated by the removal of, what was viewed by many as the constraint of having to track ISO's very complex work on management object definition and its snail's progress through a standardization process.

Four to five years after SNMP became widely adopted, largely due to its simplicity, its limitations in managing enterprise-size networks became evident. This and competitive factors with respect to the ISO work has led to the SNMPv2 protocol, which provides solutions in the areas of security, manager-to-manager communications and bulk transfer of information (between agents and managers).

Meanwhile, CMIP has gained the market in the larger telecommunications organizations and national government bodies as well as parts of the defense industries worldwide.

While SNMP and SNMPv2 provide management capability for TCP/IP networks and CMIP for OSI networks, the vast majority of networks in the world are actually based on the Intel x86 platform. Transport and network layer protocols vary from PC network to PC network. The kind of information that is useful for managing very large numbers of PCs is however different to UNIX workstations. The Desktop Management Task Force (DMTF) defined an interface and a simple way of representing these classes of PC-related information.

Lately, web-based management schemes are also under development.

10.1.1 Management Protocols, Platforms, and Agents

With the first take up of SNMP by network device vendors, each vendor defined a management station to manage its own products with SNMP agents. The recognition that there were too many management stations, each providing application for only some vendor specific device set, led to a market shake-up and the concept of a management *platform* was born.

The idea behind the network management platform was that any SNMP compatible device could be managed using the basic operations (set, get and trap) from a platform. The platform learned of a device's management variables by compiling and loading the device's Management Information Base (MIB).

The "evolution" of this idea is that management applications should not be concerned about the underlying management protocol that is used (SNMP or CMIP). XMP is a protocol-independent API specified by the X Open consortium. It has been supported by several leading platform vendors. WinSNMP is another API which hides the details of SNMP from management applications.

While network management platforms gained favor with enterprises deploying network devices with SNMP agents, host management became a hot issue. System administrators ruled this area, the best ones deployed good tools in areas such as password and user group management, monitoring for systems thresholds, configuring each machine of a class to standard settings and so on.

The first host management platforms essentially put a graphical front end in a standard systems administrator's toolkit. SNMP was considered unsafe for managing hosts and host-based resources and CMIP was far too complex.

Protocols such as Remote Procedure Call (RPC), X-Windows and Structured Query Language (SQL) have found ready uses in both network management applications and in building infrastructure management frameworks that cover hosts and network services such as network information system NIS, domain name service (DNS) and network file system (NFS).

Management platforms are essentially compute engines and require high-specification hardware. Management platforms exist which encompass the services of SNMP management stations and CMIP manager systems.

They also form a focal point for the launch of "proprietary" manager applications so that several product families and layers can be managed from a single point. While most platforms specialize on the network or host systems, others have integrated the different layers of the infrastructure.

Agents obviously play a pivotal role in the current network and systems management models. While there is no accepted taxonomy of agents, they fall into one of the categories defined in Chapter 11.

10.2 Simple Network Management Protocol (SNMP)

The main architectural goals of SNMP were:

- Protocol simplicity—a standardized protocol, easily learned across a spectrum of skill levels and easy to write applications for.

- Low agent overheads—keeping host processor and memory overheads low to encourage its adoption by a wide variety of vendors.

- Accommodating future additions—to encourage incremental development through a flexible MIB structure and standardized tools to compile and browse through MIBs.

- Independence from specific devices, hosts and operating systems (but not the protocol stack which has to be TCP/IP).

SNMP uses the User Datagram Protocol (UDP) for transport and IP for the network layer protocol. SNMP does not define any manager to agent session or connection management primitives. It is a connectionless protocol—i.e., every SNMP based message exchange between a manager and an agent is a separate and complete transaction. SNMP has the following basic primitives:

- Get—enables station-end to read the value of a management variable at the agent.

- Set—enables station-end to write a value of management variable at the agent.

- Trap—allows an agent to notify the station of any significant events.

Figure 10.1 shows the relationships between the management station-end and the agent-end. The notion of a proxy agent extends the use of SNMP into non-TCP/IP environments by providing a translation of MIB variables to and from the non-TCP/IP environment.

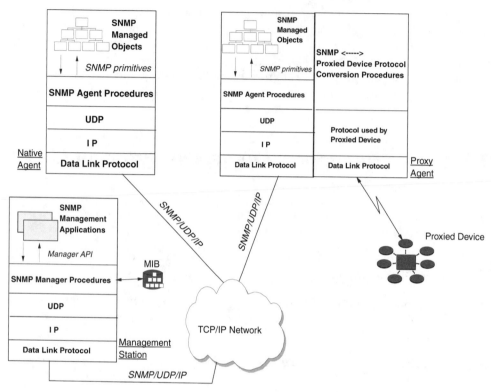

Figure 10.1: *Key elements of the SNMP-based management model*

10.2.1 Management Information Base (MIB)

The MIB represents resources that are to be managed at a device or system. The MIB is useful only under the following conditions:

- The MIB objects used to represent specific resources must be the same (i.e., have the same semantics) at each node (whether instances of managers or devices).

- All nodes need to follow a common representation scheme for these objects so that an unambiguous "traversal" is possible over the representation at each node. A representation scheme includes definitions of:

  — The way in which an object is uniquely named.
  — The way object instances at a node are defined.
  — The way multiple nodes are distinguished.

— The data structure for representing the objects.

— The way in which objects are encoded within the protocol delivery.

With SNMP, the management station can only access information it knows that the agent-end is supporting. Hence the station-end requires access to a central MIB holding all the MIBs relevant to the agents that it manages.

MIB I was the original definition of MIB objects. The aim was to keep the number of objects to around 100 to keep it simple to implement. MIB II is a superset of MIB I. New objects were added to MIB I groups and new groups were defined.

Today, many enterprises define their own MIBs—in proxy agents, for managing client/server systems, etc. MIB definition using agent toolkits is one way of integrating the management of the layers of the client/server infrastructure.

A discussion of the original rationales of the MIB concept is a useful guide to defining new MIB objects. The criteria for adding objects to MIB I to produce MIB II were:

- Only weak control objects were permitted, where their tampering would only result in limited damage. This was in recognition of SNMP's weaknesses as a control protocol.

- Only objects that could not be derived from others in the MIB were permitted.

- An object needed to have immediate or current use, and the utility was essential for fault or configuration management.

Figure 10.2 shows the MIB II structure and the following are very brief descriptions of each of the MIB II groups:

- *system*—provides general information about the system being managed.

- *interfaces*—provide generic information about physical interfaces of the device or system being managed. This group is mandatory in all MIB II implementations.

- *address translator*—included only for backwards compatibility with MIB-I. It provides a mapping from network address to a physical address for each interface.

- *ip*—contains information relevant to the implementation and operation of IP at both hosts and routers.

- *icmp*—contains information relevant to the implementation and operation of ICMP at each node.

- *tcp*—contains information relevant to the implementation and operation of TCP at each node.

- *UDP*—contains information relevant to the implementation and operation of UDP at each node.

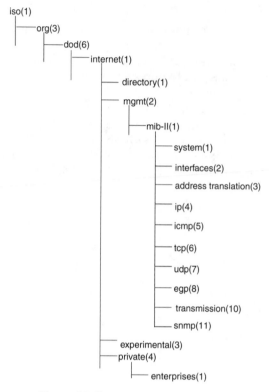

Figure 10.2: The MIB II object groups

- *egp*—contains information relevant to the implementation and operation of EGP at each node.

- *transmission*—intended to contain information specific to transmission media for each interface in the system.

- *snmp*—contains information relevant to the implementation and operation of SNMP at each node.

10.2.2 Information Structures and Encoding

The structure of management information (SMI) or the framework within which a MIB is defined, constructed and used is defined by document RFC 1155.

The MIB is a collection of objects. Each object has a type which defines what kind of managed object it is. An object instance is an *instantiation* of an object type that has been bound to a value. The following data types are allowed to be used to define MIB objects:

INTEGER

OCTET STRING

NULL

OBJECT IDENTIFIER

SEQUENCE

SEQUENCE OF

The first four are building blocks from which to construct other types of objects. SEQUENCE and SEQUENCE OF are constructor types used to define tables. Each object in the MIB has a unique object identifier. This uniqueness is derived from its position in the MIB tree. Since an object can only reside at one (and only one) point of this tree it can be given a unique identity. With reference to Figure 10.2, the identity for an object(x) in the SNMP group is 1.3.6.1.2.1.11.x.

Scalar objects that are read and manipulated by the SNMP protocol are instances of these MIB objects. MIB object instances are defined in a tabular data structure. A concatenation of the object identifier for an MIB object and a set of values of an INDEX object specifies a particular instance in a row of the table defined by that INDEX.

MIB objects are encoded using the basic encoding rules of the Abstract Syntax Notation One ASN.1—a widely used and standardized encoding scheme.

10.2.3 Security Features of SNMP

In the SNMP model, a management station manages a number of agents, some of which may be local to devices and others may act as proxies for devices. There may be multiple management stations that have overlapping responsibility for these agents.

Each agent is responsible for its MIB, in that it decides which station may access the MIB, what part of the MIB may be accessed with the credentials "shown" on access and what may be done to the MIB once access has been granted.

This is in effect *authentication and access control* in security terms. However, since SNMP only provides very trivial security features in these areas, the term "authentication and access control" are hardly ever used to describe it.

The *community* is the security primitive provided by SNMP. A community defines a relationship between an agent and a set of management stations. The relationships from agent to each station are exactly similar. Figure 10.3 shows the community model. At the agent

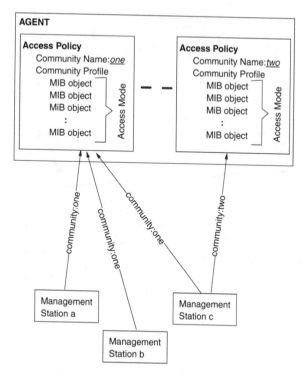

Figure 10.3: SNMP *community concept*

there is one community defined for each desired security combination of authentication and access control. Each community has a name that is unique within the agent. The name of the community must be used in all get and set operations by the station.

Stations may find that different agents use the same community name for different purposes, i.e., community names are not unique across a class of agents or across a general population of agents.

Authentication in SNMP is *trivialized* by the following: the community name functions as a password and the agent assumes the set or get message from a station is authenticated by virtue of knowledge of this password.

This trivial authentication is the main reason network managers are reluctant to allow anything more than monitoring on a network that is manageable using SNMP. It is also the reason why there has been only a limited uptake of SNMP in systems and infrastructure services management.

By defining different communities the agent can provide *views* of the MIB to different management stations. The view defines a subset of MIB objects (set membership need not be confined to any single sub-tree of the MIB). Each community also has an *access mode* associ-

Table 10.1: Reconciliation Results of MIB Object's Access Clause and SNMP Access Mode

MIB Object	Community Access Mode	
Access Clause	Read-only	Read-write
READ-ONLY	**Get** and **trap** operations allowed	**Get** and **trap** operations allowed
READ-WRITE	**Get** and **trap** operations allowed	**Get, set** and **trap** operations allowed
WRITE-ONLY	**Get** (value returned is implementation specific) and **trap** operations allowed	**Get** (value returned is implementation specific), **set** (value allowed is implementation specific and **trap** operations allowed
NOT ACCESSIBLE	Not accessible	Not accessible

ated with it. The access mode defined is applied uniformly to all objects in the community. The access modes are:

- READ-ONLY—where the accessor may only read the variable value.

- READ-WRITE—where the accessor may read and write the variable value.

There is however a potential contention between the access mode applied to the MIB objects in the community and the MIB access clause which is defined as part of each MIB object definition. Table 10.1 shows how this is reconciled and the actual operations allowed on each MIB object.

Communities have a special role to play in the case of proxy agents. A proxy may support any of the following situations:

- A non-SNMP device in a TCP/IP environment.

- A device in a non-TCP/IP environment.

- An SNMP device in a TCP/IP environment.

In the last of the above cases, the proxy plays a filter role to limit the traffic between management station and the agent. Such a proxy is relevant for example when station/agent traffic has to traverse a wide area network. By having an access policy for each device it supports, a single proxy may support all the above contexts.

The proxy can centralize the associated security and in the case of being an intermediary with another SNMP agent, it knows the MIB view defining the objects that may be used to manage the device. This is shown in Figure 10.4.

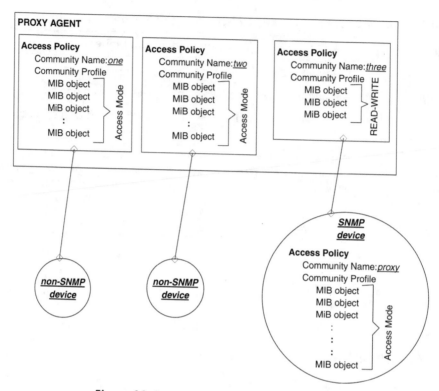

Figure 10.4: Role of communities in proxy agents

10.2.4 Security Threats with SNMP

SNMP is prone to a number of security threats. A listener on a network, depending on relative position, and using a protocol decoder can:

- Record and identify individual messages between a management station and agents. Once the community name is known for SETs, the listener can perform management operations at will. Such an attack is called a masquerade.

- Record a message sequence and replay it some time later. Alternatively, after altering the sequence or values in any message can re-send it to the destination. This is an attack on the integrity of the message between the time of it being originally sent and it being received at the target.

- By observing the flow between management stations and agents, learn of values and events occurring. Hence no information carried in the protocol can be considered to be confidential.

- A human user can send a message and later deny having sent it. This makes it impossible to set up audit trails.

10.2.5 MIB Tools

Most management platforms include two tools for manipulating MIBs:

- MIB compilers—allow new MIBs that are not part of the platform shipment to be added at a later date. A compiler is essential for extensibility of the management platform to manage new devices. Some compilers are more robust than others and is a key differentiator when choosing platforms.

- MIB browsers—allow MIBs to be examined using a user interface that is friendlier that typing in GET and GET-NEXT or SET commands. Browsers use buttons and display widgets to visualize MIB values. Some browsers allow multiple GETs to be serialized through a script and for scripts to be assigned to user-defined buttons or function keys.

10.2.6 Strengths and Weaknesses of SNMP

The main strengths of SNMP are:

- The structure of management information (SMI) for SNMP can be implemented in an economic fashion allowing fairly low-level devices to have an embedded SNMP agent.

- The existence of simple and wide availability of low-cost toolkits and protocol stacks to build agent and station-ends of the protocol stacks.

- Simple interface for management applications to access.

- De facto standard for network management—wide market acceptance, support by almost all types of management platforms.

- Acceptable standard for monitoring from most parts of the infrastructure.

While it is fashionable to air the limitations of SNMP, the fact is that it has made a major difference to the lives of network and systems management groups.

SNMP has contributed to the productivity gains implicit in a constant size team being able to manage expanding networks. It has contributed to improvements in the quality of service. Nevertheless, the weaknesses of SNMP include:

- The burden of management in SNMP is with the station-end, with resultant increase in network traffic as the agents-to-manager ratio increases to above 50 or so (over Ethernet).

- Network traffic also increases on the polling frequency increasing—sometime essential to drill down to a problem area. SNMP is therefore not suitable for large environments—due to the polling architecture which does not scale well.

- Management across wide area links is error prone particularly due to the SNMP traps being lost. The practicality of a polling frequency similar to that on the LAN is limited by the relative low bandwidth of the WAN links.

- A sufficient polling frequency is needed to ensure the management station sees a condition before the users experience its effects. Polling across highly utilized wide area links is often useless as there is not enough polling bandwidth to be effective.

- There is no authentication of the source of the message, hence the scope to build a control framework is severely limited. Such a framework would be prone to both malicious and accidental damage.

- No manager-to-manager protocol, hence it is difficult to implement scalable frameworks or a multi-domain management framework.

10.2.7 Implementation Problems

With thousands of implementations of SNMP now available, the basic problems facing the developers of network management frameworks are:

- The rule that *all objects in a group have to be implemented* or the group cannot be claimed to be implemented has led to the adoption of the so-called *zero value option* by vendors. With this option a vendor's implementation returns the value zero for an un-implemented variable. Since the user is not party to what is not implemented, the value is taken to be a genuine value for the variable. While it allows the vendor to avoid the rule, it can distress the integrity of a management framework.

- Similarly, interpretation of MIB variables varies from vendor to vendor, hence collecting the same information from different vendors devices or even different models from the same vendor is prone to mistakes. Vendors don't have to undergo any certification process before claiming compatibility hence a wide variability in implementation should be expected. Even with a single vendor, variability in implementation across versions of software as well as across devices in a family is not uncommon.

- The insecurity of the protocol has resulted in vendors not developing control variables for manipulation via SET. Apart from omitting a basic requirement of network management, it also makes essential operations such as remote configuration hard during a crisis, when security considerations may be secondary.

- The information carried in SNMP traps is generally useless in large environments where specific identifying values may be duplicated across multiple devices. Hence the trap has to be "normalized" before a decision about which objects to poll can be made at the receiving end. The normalization scheme needs to be driven by vendor-specific mappings that are hard to maintain.

10.3 Simple Network Management Protocol Version 2 (SNMPv2)

SNMPv2 is an evolution of SNMP. Its aim is to overcome the inadequacies of SNMP. Its major enhancements are in the areas of:

- **Security** defined by a party MIB. Three types of security services are provided:

  — Data integrity which ensures that messages are received at the destination "as-and-when-sent" without replays, insertions or modifications. The MD5 message-digest algorithm is used to compute a 128 bit digest over the SNMP message. This digest is included with the message.

  — Data source authentication that provides verifications of the message's origin. A secret value known *a priori* to the sender and recipients of the message is prefixed to the part over which the message digest is computed.

  — Data confidentiality which ensures that the content of the message is not accessible to entities without the appropriate key. The data encryption algorithm (DES) is used.

- **Manager-to-manager** communication capability allowing SNMPv2 manager entities to exchange information. This is defined by the manager-to-manager MIB which defines manager-to-manager exchanges including events.

- **Protocol enhancement** where the SNMP primitives of GET, SET and TRAP is augmented by a number of new functions.

  — INFORM for exchanging information between managers.

Table 10.2: Summary of SNMPv2 Enhancements

Enhancement Area	New Component
Manager-to-manager communication	Manager-to-manager MIB
	INFORM message
Protocol functionality	Get BULK message
	New transport mapping
Structure of Management Information (SMI)	SNMPv2 MIB
	Gauge attribute type (clarification)
	Row creation
Security	Data integrity
	Data confidentiality
	Source authentication
Administration model	Context for MIB views
	Party MIB
	Proxy and native relationships

— Get BULK to access bulk information such as multiple rows in a table without the single request single-response model of SNMP.

— Row creation which is a method of creating objects dynamically.

The structure of management information is a superset of *SMI for SNMP*. SNMPv2 defines a number of new MIBs. For example the Manager-to-Manager MIB defines the mechanism for information exchange. Table 10.2 shows the new components relating to the enhancements above.

10.3.1 New Administration Model

The proposed SNMPv2 standard does not use the community mechanism. Instead it defines through a new set of concepts:

• A context is a collection of managed objects accessible with SNMPv2. A context is a mechanism for defining an access control policy between SNMPv2 parties. A local context is an MIB view. A remote context is a proxy relationship.

• A subject party is an SNMP party that requests management operations to be performed by a target party and identifies the context of the request.

- A target party is an SNMP party performing management operations as requested by a subject party. The operations are performed on a local MIB view or a proxy relationship as defined by the context. Only operations pertaining to the context are performed.

- A privileges parameter of the context defines the list of SNMPv2 protocol data units that may be sent from the subject party to the target party.

10.3.2 Coexistence with SNMP

SNMPv2 defines two models of coexistence with the large installed base of SNMP based technology. This is shown in Figure 10.5 and is described below:

- Coexistence through a proxy agent that mediates between an SNMP agent and an SNMPv2 management station. The SNMPv2 protocol data units are translated by the

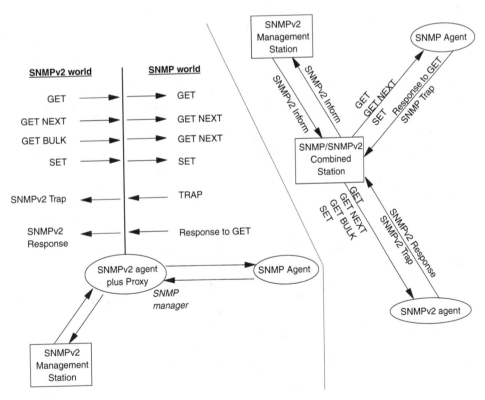

Figure 10.5: SNMP/SNMPv2 coexistence models

proxy agent so that both the SNMPv2 management station and the SNMP agent are unaware of each other's difference. Gets, Sets and GetNext operations are passed unchanged by the proxy. A Jetbead is mapped to a GetNext with the same bindings. The result is that only one row of the bindings list will be retrieved.

In the opposite direction, responses from the SNMP agent are passed unchanged. An SNMP trap is converted to an SNMPv2 trap with additional variables.

- Coexistence by a combined SNMP/SNMPv2 manager is the second model. An SNMPv2 management application is therefore not aware of whether the agent is SNMP or SNMPv2.

The performance implications associated with the proxy agent solution remains to be seen.

10.3.3 Future of SNMPv2

SNMPv2 is a proposed standard. Until very recently it was viewed by many users and observers in the industry as being the long-term successor to SNMP.

However, recent disagreements between various interest groups during the ratification process for the proposed standard has cast serious doubts on this view. Currently, the security features are left out altogether from the published standard.

An industry consortium outside the IETF is to develop products that implement security and administration. This may result in products but they will to all intents and purposes remain proprietary to each consortia.

The migration from SNMP to the new SNMPv2 therefore has little gain for the current users of SNMP. The shaded area in Table 10.2 shows the *net loss* of features from the proposed standard.

Evolving from SNMP is still a key strategic issue for many large organizations. The retention of SNMP till eventual migration to CMIS/CMIP seems to make more sense now.

Evolving from SNMP may in reality turn out to be a lot harder, given that increasing portions of the infrastructure are being monitored using SNMP agents.

SNMP has shown the huge benefits that a *standard* management protocol provides to large organizations in terms of standardization of management requirements in developing RFP's to vendors, training, ability to choose best-of-breed products, etc. The factoring of SNMPv2 into a part that is a published standard and a part that is consortia developed goes against the benefits of a single stakeholder for the whole protocol.

10.4 OSI System Management Standards

The ISO's Open Systems Interconnection (OSI) model of systems management is considerably more complex than the SNMP based model described above.

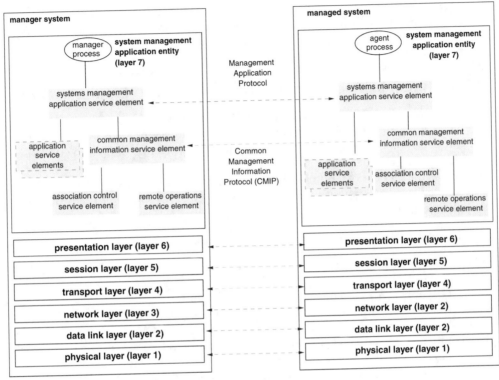

Figure 10.6: *The OSI management model*

Largely due to this complexity, it has moved very slowly through the standardization process. Many large organizations, government bodies and inter-government agencies remain committed to OSI standards for management. The adoption of the standards, when they do become available, on an enterprise-wide basis remain their strategic goal.

Given the recent setbacks with the SNMPv2 security standard being ratified, OSI management standards may be in a stronger position as a natural successor to SNMP for a wider set of large organizations.

The space available in this publication can only provide an overview of the OSI protocols for system management. OSI has its own complex terminology that is used to define components of the OSI standards. OSI uses the term *systems management* to mean network management.

OSI architecture and statements in the standards imply that the full seven layer OSI protocol stack needs to be supported as a managed system before management applications can be run.

Efforts are underway to standardize the details of a "skinny" stack that specifies a simplified state machine and minimal subset of session, presentation and application layers. This partial stack can run on top of a TCP if needed in the managed environment.

10.4.1 Common Management Information Service (CMIS)

The *Common Management Information Service* (CMIS) provides OSI management services to management applications. The common information management protocol (CMIP) provides the information exchange capability to support CMIS. Hence CMIS and CMIP are intimately related.

CMIS uses the services of a number of *application service elements* (ASE). Figure 10.6 shows the interrelated set of ASEs that provide CMIS services. ASEs specific to network management applications are:

- The *common management information service element;* and

- The *systems management application service element.*

In addition the *association control service element* (ACSE) and the *remote operations service element* (ROSE) are generic service elements useful to all types of applications.

The CMIS services are defined terms of a set of primitives. CMIP is the protocol used to exchange information between CMIS elements. There is therefore a direct mapping between CMIS services and CMIP protocol data units, that carry the information.

CMIS services are specified in terms of primitives. A confirmed service requires the "remote" end to send a response indicating receipt and non-confirmed services don't require responses. The CMIS primitives M-GET, M-ACTION and M-DELETE can specify operation on multiple objects. A summary of CMIS services are shown in Table 10.3. Another class of services relevant to CMIS (and not shown) is association service to establish an application association to communicate. CMIS provides a set of tools to define the objects and to control multiple replies to a single request.

Figure 10.7 shows the relationship between CMIS services and applications in the OSI functional areas. System management functional areas (SMFA) describe a vertical area of responsibility and are indeed the basis of application products.

Applications in these functional areas use system management functions (SMFs) to define functionality. This ensures that where SMFAs have common needs (e.g., in event reporting), the SMFs provide consistency and re-usability. There are some 13 such functions defined as OSI standards (X.7XX/ISO 10164-Y). Three of these SMFs are described below:

- *State management function (X.731/ISO 10164-2)*—Defines a model for how the management state of an object is to be represented. the model also specifies how the state of the managed objects are to be monitored.

Table 10.3: *Summary of CMIS Services*

Service Category	Primitive	Service Type	Description
Notification	M-EVENT-REPORT	Confirmed or non-confirmed	Notifications reports are initiated by an agent process in response to a previous request for notification by a manager process.
Operation	M-GET	Confirmed	Retrieves information from instances of managed objects in the MIB. The information may be with respect to a single managed objects or a set of objects
	M-SET	Confirmed/ non-confirmed	Modifies information in the MIB. The value of one or more attributes may be changed. The modification operation can replace value, add to a set of values, remove from a set of values or set to a default value.
	M-ACTION	Confirmed/ non-confirmed	Invokes a predefined action procedure associated with the object class. The type of action and its input parameters are specified in the operation.
	M-CREATE	Confirmed	Creates a new instance of an object class. The conditions to be applied are specified. Alternatively, an existing instance to be used as a reference is specified. Each instance has a unique Id within the MIB tree.
	M-DELETE	Confirmed	Deletes one or more instances from the MIB.
	M-CANCEL-GET	Confirmed	Stops an existing Get operation which may be ongoing.

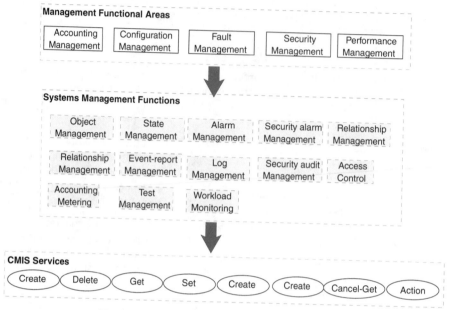

Figure 10.7: Mapping of functional areas to CMIS

- *Relationship management function (X732/ISO 10164-3)*—Defines a model for relationships between managed objects and how different relationships translate to dependencies.

- *Alarm reporting function (X733/ISO 10164-4)*—Defines a model for alarm reporting through generic alarm notification semantics. Alarms are primarily associated with fault management but are not confined to this system management functional area.

10.4.2 OSI Structure of Management Information (SMI)

The SMI defines the data type that can be used to define an MIB and the structure of the MIB in terms of resources and naming. The OSI model is an object oriented one. OO design concepts are used to model the resources to be managed. Each resource is represented by a managed-object in the MIB.

- A single managed-object may represent a single network resource or multiple resources.

- A single network resource may be managed by a single managed-object or several managed-objects (where each separate object specializes in representing different aspects of the resource).

Using object-oriented design terminology, each managed-object is an *instance* of a managed-object *class*. A class defines a template defining attributes, operations, and notifications that all instances of the class share. The class explicitly defines:

- All the attributes visible to management processes (manager or agent) through the interface of the object instance.

- The management operations that can be applied to the object itself (such as create or delete of the instance) as well as on the attributes of the object instance.

- The notifications that the object issues to alert about internal states or about values of attributes or about relationships between attributes.

- Relationships to other objects in the class hierarchy of managed-objects through the notion of inheritance.

The SMI defines all the important aspects of managed objects. These are summarized below:

- The integrity of a managed object is maintained through the principle of *encapsulation*. With encapsulation, the attributes of an object, the operations that can be performed on the attributes, the notifications that can emanate from the object and the object's relationship with other objects remain stable for the lifetime of the object.

- The *datatype* of attributes may be integer, real, Boolean, a string or any composite constructed from the basic types. Sets are also supported.

- New classes can be defined through inheritance—i.e., in terms of an existing class or classes that are further *specialized*. Specialization is achieved through one or more of—(*a*) addition of new attributes, (*b*) addition of new operations and notifications, (*c*) extension of a range of an existing attribute or range of arguments to operations and notifications, (*d*) restriction of a range of an existing attribute or range of arguments to operations and notifications.

- *Multiple inheritance* through the specialization of more than one parent class is possible. However, experience from other OO spheres suggest caution.

- The *behavior* of a managed-object changes with the receipt of CMIP messages invoking an operation. Behavior is also determined by internal events such as time-outs of a timer. All instances of a managed-object class exhibit the same behavior.

- Managed objects send *notifications* when a pre-defined, internal or external occurrence happens. Manager processes may "solicit" to some or all notifications from a managed object. Notifications can also be designated to be sent to a log object. Notifications are contained in an event-report.

- A *conditional package* is a collection of optional attributes, operations, notifications and behavior. The "whole" package is applied if the "triggering condition" for application of the package is present. A condition always reflects a capability of the resource that is modeled by the object. For example, a condition for a managed-object representing a protocol engine may define its major-version. Different packages are applied depending on the specified major-version in a create statement.

- *Containment* is a concept where one object may contain one or more other objects. Containment is achieved by including a reference to the "contained" (subordinate) object in the "containing" (superior) object. This reference is the object identifier of the subordinate object stored as a value of an attribute in the superior object.

- *MIB structures* are trees because a subordinate object is only allowed to be contained in one superior object. A superior object may however be contained in a "more superior" object, allowing a tree of arbitrary depth to be constructed.

10.4.3 OSI Management Information Base (MIB)

As with SNMP the foundation of network management in the OSI model is the management information base (MIB) and the framework for MIB definition is also called the Structure of Management Information (SMI). However, there the similarity with the SNMP world ends.

The OSI MIB is a collection of objects. Objects that refer to an OSI layer are called *N-layer* objects, Objects can also refer to resources that span more than one layer—these are called *system managed* objects. Other objects don't represent resources to be managed but exist solely for supporting management—an example is a log object to capture and store notifications.

There are three distinct tree structures in OSI management:

- The *registration tree*—a naming tree where definitions of managed-object classes, attribute definitions, notifications, actions and packages are registered. Registration essentially ensures that the names and semantics remain consistent.

- The *inheritance tree*—defines class/sub-class relationships of managed-object classes. The inheritance tree ensures the stability of the relationship between object classes.

- The *containment tree*—essentially the MIB structure with the objects and their hierarchy through containment. This defines the relationship between managed-object instances.

Each object class is registered under a unique object identifier. The naming of object instances is however distinct from naming of object classes. Each managed-object class specifies an attribute used for naming instances of the class. The name of an object instance corresponds to a specific value of this naming attribute. This value must be unique among all peer instances. The "distinguished name" of an object instance is the sequence of names from the root of the containment tree to the object instance is question.

The structuring capabilities of the OSI containment trees is a flexible and powerful tool. The hierarchic naming of MIB objects is also powerful, allowing very fine control over accessing and setting attribute values.

10.5 *Management Interfaces*

Network management protocols are *proto-languages* to remotely manipulate managed objects. Management interfaces on the other hand define a level of abstraction closer to actual data structures in the entities being managed.

The actual transport of information to and from the *user programs* of the interface is left as an implementation detail—i.e., it is not part of the interface definition. Hence these interfaces usually reside independently of the protocols and inter-process mechanisms used in the host environment. This section looks at two such interfaces, which are of considerable importance to the network management field:

- The Desktop Management Interface (DMI) allows Personal Computers (PCs), peripheral devices, computer subsystems and applications to participate in the enterprise management framework.

- The XOpen Management Protocol (XMP) is actually an Application Programming Interface (API) supported on management platforms. This allows management applications to be unaware of the actual protocol services used in accessing and managing a system or device. It primary attraction is to third-party tools and application vendors marketing to a dual SNMP/CMIP market.

10.5.1 Desktop Management Interface (DMI)

The Desktop Management Task Force (DMTF) was set up in recognition of the fact that SNMP simply could not cover the spectrum of devices attached to a network.

This included printers, network interface cards and PCs. The DMTF is led by a steering committee composed of representatives from PC hardware and software vendors such as IBM, Hewlett Packard, Microsoft and Novell.

Most networks include many end systems that cannot possibly support SNMP agents—particularly in terms of the memory resources, processing cycles and network bandwidth required.

On the other hand, proliferation of such devices on most networks, leads to severe problems in configuration, troubleshooting, performance tuning and security management.

DMTF sees its role as providing the means to ease this situation. The DMTF defines manageability standards for both networked and stand-alone PC systems and products. Its princi-

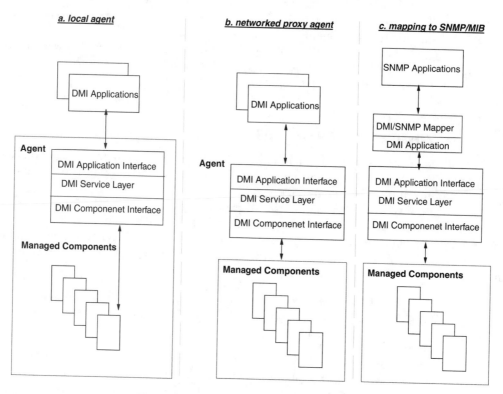

Figure 10.8: *DMI-based management model*

pal mission is to specify and implement the DMI, which is the operating system and protocol independent architecture that will allow physical components and software from participating vendors to communicate with management applications. The Desktop Management Interface (DMI) covers five product types:

- *PC platforms*—such as desktops and servers.

- *Hardware and software subsystems*—such as operating systems, and application software.

- *Network and local management applications*—such as virus checkers.

- *Peripherals*—such as printers and mass storage devices.

- *Management consoles*—with applications for remote management.

Figure 10.8 shows the major components of implementing DMI based management. It involves the following components:

- *Management application* which takes information from or provides information to the agent. An application can retrieve a list of managed components by accessing a local agent on each DMI managed desktop. This agent provides the services for managing the individual components.

- *Local agent* consisting of a service layer with two interfaces, one to the component and the other to the application. The service layer needs to be built for each operating system. The first implementations of agents are for DOS/Windows and those for NT are known to be on the drawing board at the time of writing. No plans have been published for UNIX.

- *Hardware and software components* being managed by an agent. The local agent communicates via the DMI Components Interface using SETs and GETs over the device-attribute variables. The component can also notify the service layer which in turn can notify the management application of events (such as the discovery of a virus, running out of disk space. etc.).

The DMI depends on a Management Information Format (MIF) file to describe the manageable aspects of a particular component. The MIF is an ASCII file that guarantees a basic level of information.

Currently published MIFs include ones for PC systems, network adapters and printers. A vendor may choose to include private groups in addition to DMTF specified groups. For example, the part of the MIF called the *standard component ID group* includes "entries" to describe:

- *Product name*—as defined by the vendor.

- *Version*—a vendor-specified version number.

- *Serial number*—a vendor-specified serial number.

- *Time of last installation*—free format date string.

- *Component name*—a vendor-defined name for the component.

- *Component ID*—a vendor-defined identity value.

- *Component class ID*—a vendor-defined family identity value.

MIFs are structured lists of attributes that are mappable to SNMP/MIBs. The main difference between SNMP/MIB and DMI is that DMI was designed to run on desktops and other systems. Such systems are affected by the following factors:

- Sensitive to the size of the memory footprint needed by an agent.

- Sensitive to the processing cycles to run SNMP and its associated protocol stack.

- Sensitive to running a TCP/IP stack for added cost and added complexity reasons.

For DOS the target is 14 kb of TSR loadable into high memory and for Windows environments a DLL. For a memory-constrained system the local agent can also operate as a networked proxy.

The mapping of MIFs to MIB equivalents leads to the possibility of SNMP management platforms being able to manage DMI compliant components. While definition of a UNIX DMI service layer is unlikely to occur, there are currently several SNMP MIBs for UNIX that are in a prototype stage. These emulate the information in the standard DMTF groups.

This would allow applications such as asset management and asset tracking tools to view all desktops uniformly.

Caveat emptor. One of DMI's original goals was to ease the gathering of management information from PC desktops that in most enterprise constitute the largest population of hosts to be managed.

DMI interfaces the desktop's components, peripherals and eventually its software components to a network management protocol at the service interface. Without a network management protocol to transport the information, only the local user of the desktop has access to the data at the interface.

In this sense DMI and SNMP have complementary roles. However, this relationships goes beyond the transport issue: seamless management of PCs and other workstations is dependent on the same applications and management automation processes being consistently applied. This in turn implies that management information semantics should be common across DMI and non-DMI environments.

In pursuing this requirement of a common semantics, it is doubtful whether it is possible to implement any existing SNMP MIBs using DMI. This is because the DMTF has made some simplifying assumptions about future MIBS that current MIBs cannot possibly fulfill.

This is so because the simplifications are at the most fundamental level of MIB structure—such as scalars are not allowed in a DMI compatible MIB. Without a resolution of this incompatibility or a re-writing of DMI's goals, the original vision of unifying PC and non-PC management will not be fulfilled.

Current indications are that DMTF efforts are at a standstill and that it is looking for new remits such as on the web-based management front.

10.5.2 X-Open Management Protocol (XMP)

The XMP API is a general programming interface and allows management applications to access SNMP and CMIS services. This application-level API is utilized to develop applications that can manage environments modeled on both SNMP and OSI. This is shown in Figure 10.9.

This interface hides the details of the underlying protocol from application developers and is defined in terms of request/response pairs of function calls. Table 10.4 shows a mapping between XMP functions and CMIS/SNMP services. The API supports all seven CMIS services and four SNMP services. The source and destination of a message is identified at the XMP API, either as an OSI fully distinguished name or a network address.

Both synchronous and asynchronous modes of communication are supported for manager-to-agent messages. Agent responses communicated are in synchronous mode only.

XMP employs another standard, the X/Open OSI Abstract Data manipulation API to manage the information objects or arguments, to XMP functions.

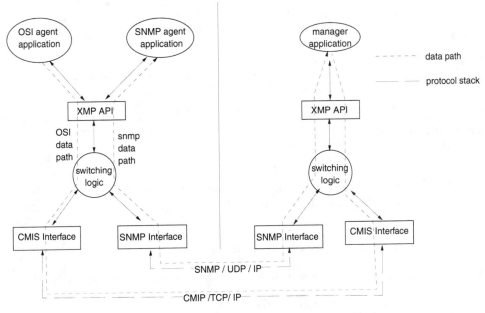

Figure 10.9: *Use of XMP API by management applications*

Table 10.4: XMP API Function's Mappings to SNMP and CMIS Functions

XMP	CMIS/CMIP	SNMP	Description
xmp_action_req xmp_action _rsp	Action		Requests the agent to perform one of the actions defined for a managed object.
xmp_create _req xmp_create _rsp	Create		Requests the agent to create an instance of the specified class of object.
xmp_delete _req xmp_delete _rsp	Delete		Requests the agent to delete an instance.
xmp_get _req xmp_get _rsp	Get		Requests the agent to provide the values of one or more attributes of an object instance.
xmp_get_next _req xmp_get_next _rsp		Get Next	Requests the agent to provide the name of the next SNMP variable in a table.
xmp_cancel_get _req xmp_cancel_get _rsp	Cancel Get		Requests the agent to terminate an earlier, uncompleted Get request.
xmp_set _req xmp_ set_rsp	Set	Set	Requests the agent to set the value of one or more attributes of an object instance.
xmp_event_report _req xmp_event_report _rsp	Event Report	Trap	Requests the issue of any notifications defined for an object.

The XMP interface is used for service request by a manager within a defined *context.* A context defines a bundle of re-usable definitions for communications between manager and agent entities.

- Whether a confirmed or unconfirmed service is needed.

- Whether a synchronous or asynchronous communication mode is required.

- The maximum number of linked responses allowed.

- The maximum period of time to wait for a response to a synchronous request.

Other input parameters are object class and instance information and object attribute lists used for Get and Set type operations. Output parameters of an XMP function include an *invocation handle, result* and *status.* The invocation handle is provided for asynchronous operation to match incoming results. The result shows the result of a request executed in the synchronous mode. The status defines the success or failure of the request.

10.5.3 WinSNMP

WinSNMP establishes an interface to what is essentially an "SNMP service layer." This is significant for several reasons:

- It allows developers to write to a single API that hides details of SNMP and the future evolution of SNMP to SNMPv2.

- It opens up the way for serious management applications for the Windows platform. There are several advantages to this—e.g., the low cost of the platform and the portability of a notebook PC based toolkit that is useful in many situations.

The WinSNMP/Manager API and its relationship to applications and managed devices is shown in Figure 10.10. The API is defined by a relatively small number of functions (summarized in Table 10.5). This layer provides SNMP functionality to management applications

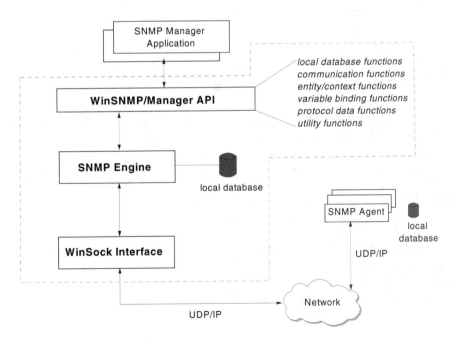

Figure 10.10: *WinSNMP/Manager API functions*

Table 10.5: Summary of WinSNMP/Manager API Functions

Functional Category	Example Functions	Description
Communication	SnmpSendMsg SnmpRcvMsg	Defines messaging operations between the application and the managed environment. The message carries a PDU. Messages are asynchronous.
Protocol Data Unit	SnmpCreatePdu SnmpGetPduData	Defines operations on protocol data units passed across the interface from the application to the managed environment and from the managed agents to the application.
Database	SnmpSetRetry	Defines operations with respect to the local database parameters. These include parameters to control the messaging.
Binding	SnmpCreateVbl	Defines operations on binding between application variables and values passed across the API.
Context	SnmpStrToEntity	Defines operations on creating and freeing context between an application and managed entities.
Utility	SnmpGetLastError	Utility functions supporting the API.

while hiding SNMP details such as packet formatting, operations involving ASN.1 and Basic Encoding Rules (BER), message transmission and message reception.

WinSNMP is typically implemented as a dynamic link library (DLL) of routines, but it could also be implemented as an executable on a local or remote machine (relative to the application). In the latter case RPC is a possible access mechanism.

While at first sight WinSNMP seems to be exclusively associated with the Windows environment, it does facilitate the porting of management applications source from Windows to UNIX, using conversion packages where the application class libraries resolve to WinSNMP/Manager API in Windows and to some other proprietary SNMP API in UNIX.

WinSNMP implementation includes the mechanism for communication with the managed agents. It uses an interface to WinSock API to perform the UDP based communication with managed agents.

The WinSNMP/Manager API consists of six functional categories. Application developers can conform to the API at different levels of compliance. The API allows applications written to the specification to be distributed in binary form to reside at any part of the network. These application can be run from any Windows desktops.

10.5.4 User Network Management Interface

A trend in enterprise networks is to effectively outsource the wide area network (WAN) infrastructure through global services such as public frame relay or subscription with a global virtual private network (VPN) provider.

In managing client/server infrastructures, it is important to understand what is happening in this WAN cloud. One of the key features of an enterprise-wide client/server environment cited in this publication is its geographic extent.

Because the components of an application are distributed geographically, it is the end-to-end network characteristics—delay, latency, throughput and burstiness that are of interest to infrastructure management.

Such end-to-end metrics are impossible to construct without real-time or "near" real-time information from the system interconnecting corporate LANs. Hence remote management of client/server applications remains a black art.

Figure 10.11 shows the role carrier services play in interconnecting different parts of an enterprise. The User Network Management (UNM) interface is an abstract interface between the carrier service provider's domain and the enterprise management domain.

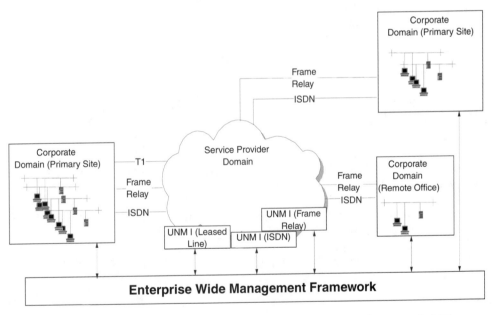

Figure 10.11: *Carrier services as an interconnect system for corporate LANs*

Service providers have always provided management information at various granularity of usefulness, particularly to their most *favored* corporate users.

One of the drivers making such information available to *all* corporate users is global competition in telecommunications. Providing value-added services to the corporate user furnishes competitive advantage to the service provider.

Large enterprises commonly use multiple services from carriers in interconnecting LANs—leased lines, frame relay, SMDS and VSAT services. Keeping track of the cost base and utilization of these diverse services is a complex, time-consuming and error-prone problem. Such costs constitute as much as 30% to 40% of the operating budgets in some enterprises and therefore well worth automating to any degree.

Functionality currently offered across UNM interfaces is very rudimentary. It is usually limited to a command line user interface to view status and control minimal aspects on a service by service basis. This is relatively easy to integrate into a management framework—e.g., through a manager-of-manager interface to the interface or through proxy agents.

Some carriers are busy making the interface easier to integrate with corporate network management systems, e.g., through SNMP or CMIP-SNMP gateways. The real issue is however not interfacing: there is a major gap between information currently provided across a UNM interface and what is required for more effective infrastructure management.

Below are the types of information from the service provider's domain that is of most use to infrastructure management:

- Tracking quality of service against thresholds defining a service level agreement with the provider.

- "Near real-time" billing information and invoicing by user cost center codes provided by the client.

- Service usage profiles of each service subscribed to by the client.

- Service fault notification by the service provider of connectivity problems in specified end-to-end paths.

- Service problem reporting by the client's management system with respect to each of the services subscribed to by the client.

- Service fault resolution tracking for problems reported by the client system.

The UNM interface can also enhance other information flows between the client and the service provider:

- General helpdesk functions.

- Ordering service and changes such as more bandwidth or more service provision.

- Ordering of value added services.

10.6 *General Application Protocols Used in a Management Context*

Several general protocols are used widely in the deployment of management infrastructures. Here we look at three such protocols in terms of their role in infrastructure management:

- X-11 the protocol used in the X-Windows Graphical User Interface systems. X-11 and its variants are useful in viewing conditions at remote sites.

- RPC—Remote Procedure Call is a general-purpose mechanism widely used in building both client/server applications. Increasingly, infrastructure management frameworks are based on a client/server model.

- SQL—Structured Query Language is widely used in accessing relational database systems from client/server applications. As infrastructure management frameworks become industrial strength, relational databases play a key part.

10.6.1 X-11

Network and systems management platforms in enterprise-wide contexts are predominately UNIX workstations. Motif is the most popular windowing system on UNIX workstations. It uses the X-11 protocol at the application level. X-11 is also available on most other platforms and operating systems including MS Windows and Microsoft NT running on a PC.

X-11 is organized as a client/server system. The server runs on the workstation while the clients are the applications the workstation is currently interacting with. The details of X-11 internals is not of much relevance here. X-11 is useful in the infrastructure management context to run remote application servers.

One common use of X-11 is in executing a management application (such as analysis of results from SNMP Remote Monitoring—RMON) on a platform at a remote site. Specific views of the result from the remote execution can then be distributed to multiple destinations using X-11. At these destinations, management workstations can remotely control the application servers. Variants of X-11 such as *Shared X* from HP provide the basis for global solutions to problems such as:

- *Group cooperation*—Use of mechanisms such as electronic whiteboard applications to distribute, in real-time, information that is essential to a community of network management staff cooperating on a problem. A trend in large enterprises is the development of centers of excellence especially in specific application, operating system and security areas. This expertise may be on call to the rest of the enterprise.

- *Application mirrors*—Allow expensive but occasionally very useful applications such as high-end simulation tools to be run and maintained at a central location, but its functionality is shared across an enterprise regardless of distance from the center of excellence or center of computation.

10.6.2 Remote Procedure Call (RPC)

RPC is a network based protocol where a process residing in one host can execute processes on another host on the network. The two hosts can be running different operating systems. RPC is in effect the equivalent of a procedure call across a network.

RPC is a primary building block of the client/server model. RPC is fully integrated into most "first tier" operating systems such as Unix and NT. RPC simplifies client/server communications in several ways:

- Hides network addressing, network transport and naming details from the RPC programmer.

- As an optional service in some environments, such as Sun's Solaris, provides authentication of the client to the server and provides a check of the integrity of contents of the message exchange between the client and server.

- Deployed across multiple platforms, allowing platforms appropriate for given roles to be mixed and matched, e.g., a database server on a Unix platform, workstations on Wintel and compute servers on a mainframe.

The semantics and functionality of RPC have been extended on several fronts, for example, to encompass transactional semantics. These are used by middleware products such as Encina to support multi-platform transaction processing. RPC's use in the infrastructure management context include:

- Client workstation to communicate with server-based application components.

- Server-to-server communication in data distribution and replication.

- "Agent servers" to platform servers in a scaled-up agent-to-platform communication model.

RPC is a "connectionless" mechanism in that the connection disappears once the invocation is complete. An RPC implementation may use one of several "transports" depending on the options chosen by the run-time program.

In the RPC model the location of the remote service (represented by a remote procedure interface) is not known to the client program or process. The first requirement is for the client to find the server where the required service resides. This sometimes involves specialized procedure/server databases or more commonly the directory service available with the client platform. A more recently available alternative is to use an object request broker (ORB) which is beginning to be industrial strength for many classes of applications.

A database or another repository, associated with an intermediary service such as the ORB, has to be populated with the information about services for clients to find the remote server(s) for the requisite service.

Before a service can be used at run-time, the developer has to have created an interface definition using the Interface Definition Language (IDL). A IDL complier can subsequently translate the interface definitions into "stubs."

A "stub" at a client system acts as a substitute for the remote server procedure, while stubs at the server acts as substitutes for clients. The two stubs automate the establishment of the conditions for the client and server to communicate at the service level.

The RPC runtime system provides the integrated services for the client and server to communicate transparently. Transparency is extended to the following areas:

- Independence from network protocols and architecture.

- Independence from naming conventions, addressing schemes and type of look-up or directory services.

- Reliable delivery and recovery mechanism.

- Multi-threading support at the service interface to handle concurrent requests.

- Support across multiple operating systems.

This support of the above levels of transparency makes RPC a genuine piece of middleware. Most client/server systems in existence today use RPC.

10.6.3 Structured Query Language (SQL)

In a relational data model all data is organized into tables. Rows represent records while columns represent fields in the record. Tables are designed to represent real-world models and facts.

A relational database and SQL are intimately related in that SQL is the only means of accessing data in a relational database. SQL is used to define operations that manipulate data in a relational database. SQL provides what is called *non-navigational access* in that users only specify *what* data to access and need not define *how* to reach it. The database management system works out how to satisfy the data-access requests.

SQL has been evolving and most database management products conform to the "SQL-92" as the base "standard." Most SQL database vendors have extended SQL to meet their market segment's requirements (e.g., Sybase in the distributed computing market, Oracle in the OLAP market, etc.) SQL will eventually have object extensions allowing the transparent manipulation of multiple data sources.

Table 10.6 shows a subset of SQL statements and their function. SQL only has a relatively small number of operators, however, this belies its power and complexity. A thorough understanding of a particular relational database management system and relational algebra is required to develop complex databases.

Table 10.6: A Subset of Data Definition and Data Manipulation Operators of SQL

Operator	Functional Subset	Description
Create table	Data definition	Creates a table in the database. Columns can be specified to be unique or to be a primary key into the table.
Select into	Data definition	Allows the creation and population of a table that is similar to an existing base table.
Alter table	Data definition	Allows an existing table to be altered. Options define integrity issues.
Drop table	Data definition	Allows one or more base tables to be dropped from the table catalog.
Select	Data manipulation	The commonest form of this statement is to *"Select specified columns from a specified table where a specified condition is true."* It is used to define most queries including nested queries.
Insert	Data manipulation	A row is inserted into a specified table with the specified values into the specified columns. Alternatively, a specified sub-query is evaluated and the result (which may be multiple rows) is inserted into the specified columns.
Update	Data manipulation	The content of a specified row or set of rows are updated depending on the associated qualifiers.
Delete	Data manipulation	The content of the specified row or set of rows are deleted depending on the associated qualifiers.

This is one of the reasons why a management platform should support multiple relational databases. An enterprise may already have investments in a particular relational database. For it to be forced to support a new database vendor for the management platform is generally not feasible, especially when the management framework is viewed from a strategic context.

SQL is both an interactive language and a language to build database applications. Any SQL structure that is sent over the network can also be embedded in a program. *Interactive* SQL and *embedded* SQL only differ in minor details of syntax.

In-house developed applications front-ending a management database (using an appropriate toolkit) will allow the underlying details of the database to be hidden from the user. The user actions at the application's user interface may be parsed into a stream of SQL statements. These are sent to the database's runtime interface (usually as RPC data).

Instead of sending a stream of SQL over the wire, the database engine can support stored procedures. Each stored procedure has an identity which is specified in a statement sent from the application. Stored procedures define common operations executed from an application in relation to a database.

Triggers are special stored procedures associated with a specific table that are invoked automatically whenever the table is the subject of a "triggering" action such as update, insert or delete operation that changes the content of the table. Triggers cannot be invoked explicitly by naming them as a stored procedure in a statement. Triggers are primarily used to enforce database integrity rules.

SQL is attractive as a development tool in infrastructure management applications. This is provided on condition that management data can be placed in relational databases in the first instance.

This is not always easy, as management platforms sometimes, even today, do not support a relational database, or the supported one is inappropriate for an enterprise.

A point to note is that considerable internal expertise is needed to build and administer SQL based applications and it should not be undertaken lightly. A second point is that investment in SQL based development should be undertaken to solve tactical problems. With the rapid evolution of web languages such as Java and object-oriented databases, SQL's role will change.

10.7 Intranet Protocols in a Management Context

Having an intranet-based application environment introduces at least two protocols which have use in an application management context. These protocols help to realize a new class of management applications.

The base technology of the web is based on the Hypertext Transfer Protocol (HTTP), which is currently undergoing a major re-vamp. HTTP is already a useful protocol for using browsers as management application environments to access and manage infrastructure management information. The management information being viewed with a browser may be generated by the source of the information as HTML pages and act as its own web server. Alternatively, the source may depend on an intermediate web server to convert information—e.g., SNMP table information to HTML.

The second protocol of interest in a management context is the Lightweight Directory Access Protocol (LDAP). LDAP has the potential to help build global infrastructure management frameworks. The ability to store, access and control information about users, application stacks, systems and infrastructure from a single but scalable mechanism is needed to gain global perspectives on infrastructure management. The second advantage is that such a directory mechanism can be used from a browser, reducing both capital and training costs associated with deployment.

10.7.1 Hypertext Transfer Protocol (HTTP)

HTTP is an application level transport protocol optimized for use in navigating through hypertext "jumps." The name of this protocol is misleading—it is in fact capable of transporting any type of application data including graphics, plain text, hypertext, video clips, audio sequences and so on.

HTTP is a client/server protocol. It is also transaction-oriented in the sense that there is the suggestion of a complete transaction being done during any single request-response cycle. HTTP treats each transaction independently and is therefore termed "stateless."

Because HTTP needs to be reliable, it uses TCP as its transport-level protocol. Most implementations today create a new TCP connection for each transaction and terminate the connection on completion of the transaction. HTTP specification allows a TCP connection to be re-used, and some implementations are beginning to use this capability.

HTTP consists of two basic message types—request and response. A request sent by a client to a server to initiate some action. A response message is sent by a server to a client as a result of a request. Table 10.7 shows some of the HTTP commands and results that are possible.

Table 10.7: *Example of HTTP Commands and Results*

Message Type	Command/Result	Description
Request	Get	A command to retrieve information.
	Put	A command to accept the attached entity for storage under the supplied URL.
	Post	A command to accept the attached entity as a new sub-entity at the identified URL.
	Delete	A command to delete an entity.
Response	Entity body	A result carrying retrieved information.
	Informational status	A result carrying informational status only indicating that processing is continuing.
	Success status	A result indicating successful receipt, and execution of the request. Can be accompanied by an entity body.
	Error status	A result indicating client-level request error or server-level error leading to request being unfulfilled.

10.7.2 Use of HTTP in Management Applications

The stateless nature of HTTP is well suited to its use in an infrastructure management application. A typical use of such an application is to view pages of summary information regarding the status of the infrastructure or some part of it. This involves retrieving a set of pages in some logical sequence. The location of the pages may be distributed globally.

Figure 10.12 shows the possible HTTP based relationships between a browser-based management application and the location of the pages containing summary information.

- The browser can establish a direct connection with the server on which the page resides. The client end opens a connection to the server. The name of the server and other details necessary to request information may be accessed from a directory. The client supplies the command, a URL and other parameters specifying content. The server attempts to perform the requested command and returns a response. A response includes status information, information about the server and any content being returned.

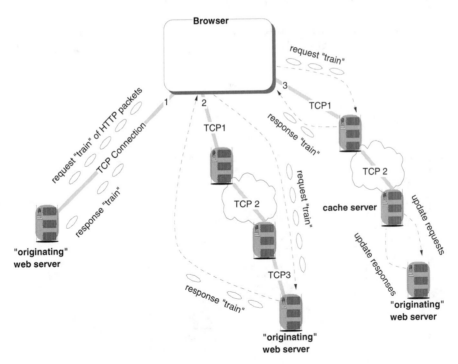

Figure 10.12: *Use of HTTP in browser-based management applications*

- A second relationship between the client and the server through one or more intermediary servers. Intermediary servers allow an automated system of information relationships to be set up.

10.7.3 Intermediary HTTP Servers

Intermediary servers as the name implies mediate between clients and servers. There are several types of intermediary servers envisaged to work with HTTP. Figure 10.13 shows four types of intermediaries:

- A *proxy* is one type of intermediary. A proxy acts on behalf of clients presenting requests from the clients to the server. One use of a proxy is to reconcile different versions of HTTP being used at client and server ends. Such a proxy allows de-coupling between the clients and server versions of HTTP, which is an important consideration when scaling up client numbers. A second use of a proxy is in accessing a server through a firewall. The proxy provides the service of setting up authenticated connections with a server for a client outside the firewall.

- A *gateway* is a second type of intermediary server. A gateway appears to the client as if it were the source of the web pages. A gateway intermediary acts on behalf of servers

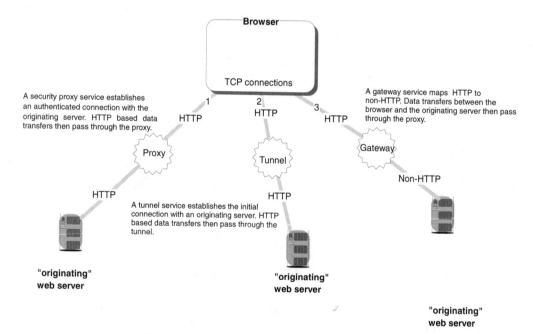

Figure 10.13: Classes of intermediary HTTP servers

giving a single point of access for clients. The servers that a gateway acts for may not be able to handle HTTP. For example, a gateway can give access to SNMP tables from a browser. A gateway therefore extends the multi-protocol ability of the browser. A gateway can also authenticate clients to the servers it services.

- A *cache* is an intermediary server which holds previous requests and responses. If a new request is received then the cache is examined for the results of any matching transactions. A policy script defines under what circumstances to re-request information from a server rather than using cached results.

- A *tunnel* is another type of intermediary server. It is a relay point between two TCP connections. The tunnel does not alter the information travelling through it, however, it may monitor and log each transaction. Tunnels are used to create a single logical HTTP connection in inter-domain scenarios where a direct connection between a client and a server is not possible.

10.7.4 Lightweight Directory Access Protocol (LDAP)

LDAP defines both a directory and an access protocol. LDAP, the protocol, is a reasonably simple mechanism for any corporate application client (including Internet and intranet clients) to access and manipulate an arbitrary database of hierarchical attribute/value over TCP. LDAP is a simplification of the X.500 Directory Access Protocol (DAP).

LDAP has significant vendor and industry support and is defined by RFC 1777. The directory service model (which LDAP allows a user to access) is based on a concept called entries. Entries are organized in trees with entries reflecting countries at the top, with national organizations at a level below that. Lower down in the tree may be levels defining departments, people in the department, resources used, e-mail address, etc. The directory can in fact contain any information that is useful in an enterprise context.

An entry is a collection of attributes that has a name called a distinguished name (DN). The DN is used to refer to the entry unambiguously. Each of the entry attributes has a type and one or more values. The types are predefined and describe classes of concepts such as an e-mail address, a person's name, an image file, etc.

LDAP is used between parties conducting information transfer relating to information held in a hierarchical, attribute-based directory. LDAP therefore also defines a standard for placing entries and attributes in a tree so that a meaningful transaction can be conducted. Figure 10.14 shows the role of LDAP in information exchange between clients and servers.

LDAP defines operations for querying and updating the directory entries. LDAP is primarily used to search for information. For example, a management application can use LDAP to search a part of the directory for an entry defining a specific kind of performance report. The attributes of the entry would point to the home pages that allow the report to be dynamically created.

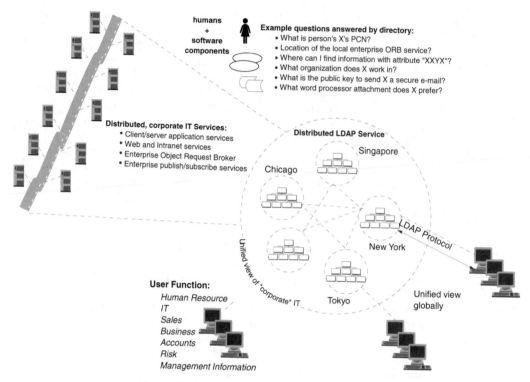

Figure 10.14: *LDAP's role in client/server exchange*

The components of the management report can therefore be changed centrally in one place. All future queries for that type of report would access the update. The directory therefore acts as an information broker for the application.

LDAP's power comes from this ability for a client application to specify dynamically a search filter to search a specific portion of the directory. LDAP also has operations for adding and deleting an entry, changing an existing entry and changing the name of an entry.

LDAP also includes a mechanism for a client to choose an authentication protocol to authenticate itself to a directory server. Hence the information in a directory server can be protected by access control mechanisms relating to users who have been authenticated. Access control typically classifies users according to what they are allowed to do—for example, read, write, search, and delete are common access levels.

The LDAP specification allows the propagation of changes to replicated slave servers. Replicated directory servers are powerful tools for load balancing for queries. Replication is also used to make copies of sub-directories relevant to the local context—such as a business group or an enterprise-wide process.

LDAP however has topological limitations, such as each entry must have a single master, therefore writes to the entry are centralized. When only a few hundred or few thousand write operations are needed, a single server can still cope. Other issues exist such as the referral mechanism used that can be very costly for some types of searches. Due to such limitations, LDAP is probably more ideal for intranet use—which is ideal for management applications.

LDAP provides an API that is simple to use and supports both synchronous and asynchronous communications between a client and the LDAP directory server. An LDAP gateway to an existing X.500 directory is also available as a reference implementation, allowing management applications using LDAP to take information from existing corporate directories.

Access to an LDAP server is through specifying a server name to a Domain Name Service. The most obvious "large-scale" use of LDAP based directories is in building a global view of the users being supported by different parts of the infrastructure. Connecting such a directory with human resources records of joiners and leavers provides a powerful information source to manage add moves and changes.

Hundreds of other "point uses" of LDAP directory-based information will be found once information creation and usage in management processes are centered on a directory.

10.7.5 Java Management API (JMAPI)

The Java Management API is in fact a set of APIs and these are potentially important to the future development of management applications. JMAPI allows Java-based management applications to be developed that can be executed on any browser as a platform.

JMAPI is a rich set of extensible objects that may be used in developing integrated infrastructure management. The JMAPI set includes:

- *Applet integration interfaces*—Specification for seamless integration of Java applets into a JMAPI environment. A number of integration levels are defined including registered links into management pages, registered management pages holding applets and registered applets.

- *Base object interfaces*—Classes that support the construction of objects to represent resources and services in the managed environment. These objects can model data persistence.

- *Managed protocol interfaces*—Classes that implement an infrastructure to perform secure, operations on remote objects. These classes use the existing Java mechanisms for security and distribution.

- *SNMP interfaces*—These classes extend the managed protocol interface classes so that information obtained from existing SNMP agents can be contained within JMAPI base objects.

- *Managed data interfaces*—These classes define mapping from Base Object classes to a relational database. The Java Database Connectivity (JDBC) specification is used to connect to a number of database engines.

- *Managed notification interfaces*—These classes provide a toolset to build asynchronous event management services. Such services can be employed for both inter-application and inter-object notification.

- *Managed container interfaces*—Allows multiple instances of objects to be treated as a single entity to perform operations on. This allows the same operations to be applied to clusters or groups of objects representing resources.

JMAPI is written in Java and is portable to any Java-enabled browser. JMAPI also defines a User Interface Style Guide which provides the baselines for developing the user interfaces for all management applications conforming to JMAPI.

The Admin View Module (AVM) is an extension of the standard Java Abstract Toolkit, that is specifically designed for developing infrastructure management user interfaces. The building blocks provided by the AVM include multi-column lists, a hierarchy browser, a help subsystem and an image canvas. Together these allow rapid development of application user interfaces.

10.8 *Books for Further Reading*

McGovern, D., *et al. Guide to Sybase and SQL Server.* Addison Wesley, 1992.

Plevyak, Thomas, (editor) *et al. Telecommunications Network Management into the 21st Century* (Techniques, Standards, Technologies, and Applications). IEEE, 1994.

Stallings, William. *SNMP, SNMPv2, and CMIP—A Practical Guide to Network Management Standards.* Addison Wesley, 1993.

Townsend, Robert. *SNMP Application Developer's Guide.* Van Nostrand Reinhold, 1995.

11

The Technology of Agents

Areas covered in this chapter

- A classification of agents used in infrastructure management
- The structure of SNMP based MIB agents
- Tools for developing native and proxy agents
- Structure of RMON MIB based agents and autonomous processing
- Management agents for monitoring higher level software such as the operating systems layers
- Life-cycle issues that complicate developing MIB based agents for the application layer
- Extensible agents for modeling complex monitoring environments
- High-level pattern (or regular expression) matching agents and their deployment
- The concept, support framework and roles for mobile agents that travel to target hosts for gathering or processing management information and returning the results
- The concept of service agents that provide scaling-up as a set of services that may be used to deploy agents in a large environment
- Issues and caveats for agent deployment
- Cost factors and cost control of agent deployment
- The changing role of the agent concept within the intranet model

Agents are components that undertake management tasks in a local context. Some agents have relatively simple structures, in others, raw data from the managed environment is locally cached and processed.

The *scope* for an agent's tasks can be limited to a single device such as a router, a single host or a single application component. Scope can encompass, for example, a whole sub-network of some tens of devices. The scope for system management and application management agents is usually limited to a single host.

In the simplest sense agents have functions to compute the values of variables defined in a *schema* called the management information base (MIB). Access to the results of these functions is invoked through the protocol between the agent and its manager.

Agents also play more complex roles, such as monitoring specific types of traffic against a "baseline" model of traffic activity. Only exceptions to these baseline conditions are notified to the manager.

The protocol between the manager and the agent determines the "type of things" an agent can communicate about. The structure of the agents is therefore largely influenced by the protocol. In this chapter we look primarily at agents that communicate using SNMP. SNMP is by far the most prominent protocol at this time and therefore most of the agents that will be built will use SNMP.

Figure 11.1 shows a taxonomy of agents examined in this chapter. The first distinction is between static and mobile agents. The former is permanently associated with a device or host, while the latter forms temporary relationships with executing hosts, which are terminated once a task is completed.

Static agents are further subdivided between MIB-based agents and pattern-matching agents. The former is driven by a predefined MIB specification, including the data encoding values to be used in the manager-agent protocol.

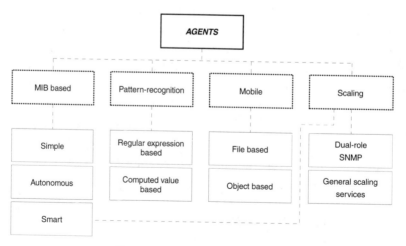

Figure 11.1: *Taxonomy of agents*

Pattern-recognition agents are driven by a database of "patterns" to match against. The manager-agent protocol and encoding rules are proprietary in this instance—they allow the current manager-agent model to be scaled to enterprise levels. In the course of this objective they provide important new functionality. MIB based smart agents can sometimes play the role of a scaling agent.

General scaling agents are strictly speaking enabling mechanisms—they allow the current manager-agent model to be scaled to enterprise levels. In the course of this objective they provide important new functionality. MIB based smart agents can sometimes play the role of a scaling agent.

A representative example of a product in each agent category is briefly described as a product case study in each section. The example product was chosen largely on the basis of illustrating the points described for each category and should not be construed as an endorsement of any product.

11.1 *Simple SNMP Agents*

Simple agents are most commonly seen embedded in network devices such as routers, hubs and switches. By and large they support the MIB-II standard with enterprise specific extensions.

The main behavioral characteristic of simple agents is that they wait to be polled before responding with the current values of the requested MIB objects. This polling is done by the manager through the manager-agent protocol.

In addition, agents can notify the manager through the same protocol of a finite set of internal events. In SNMP these notifications are called traps. One type of trap is an enterprise-specific trap used by vendors to indicate device-specific events.

In many case it is the enterprise-specific MIB objects and enterprise specific trap values that makes most vendors' agents useful in management. These extensions represent device and vendor specifics that cannot be covered by a general standard such as MIB-II.

Such values may therefore be duplicated in different device MIBs, and will vary from vendor to vendor, making them non-unique to the manager station.

The enterprise specific MIB subtree and trap values returned by agents is distributed in a format to be compiled onto specific management platforms.

Simple agents are not always embedded just into network elements and devices. They may be part of a protocol stack such as TCP/IP, or may be part of an operating system. In such cases the agent will be installed onto every host that the stack or the operating system is installed.

Availability of agent building toolkits has resulted in many specialized MIBs being defined and simple agents being developed to solve enterprise-specific management problems.

The agent-manager protocol determines the environment in which the agent may reside. The term *native* agent is used to describe an agent that operates in the native environment of the agent-manager protocol. Hence in the case of SNMP a native agent operates in a TCP/IP environment.

Agents can also be used to develop a management bridge between two environments. A private MIB can be defined to manage a device that does not have a TCP/IP stack. Such an agent is called a *proxy* agent.

11.1.1 Native Agents

These reside and operate in the native environment of the agent-manager protocol. These agents have close inter-process associations with the managed entity and by and large share the computing resources (CPU, memory, interprocess communication and operating system interfaces) of the managed environment.

Native agents are usually developed as part of product development of the managed entity due to the close coupling between the agent and the managed entity. General principles that native agents have to conform to include:

- Its resource footprint (in both memory and CPU cycles) should not impact the functions or performance of the entity being managed.

- It should be able to compute and post results in a timescale where they can be usefully acted on by the management station.

11.1.2 Proxy Agents

Proxy agents have two discernible interfaces. At one it talks the protocol of the manager and at the other it talks the protocol of the managed device in the *alien* environment. Proxy agent software is sometimes executed on a dedicated platform with a physical interface to the proxied device.

Figure 11.2 shows the structure of a proxy agent used to manage a device that does not have a TCP/IP stack (or one that has a TCP/IP stack but does not have an SNMP based management agent).

Proxy agents are still driven by an MIB, given the standard protocol interface with the manager. The MIB is however a private MIB. Private MIBs and the conversion procedures to the proxied device's protocol are developed using toolkits. Guidelines are available on writing MIBs.

Proxy agents are viable as monitoring agents, however, the security issues of SNMP have stopped their use in configuration and control of proxied devices.

11.1.3 Structure of Simple Agents

Simple agents form the basis of more complex types of agents discussed in this chapter. It is therefore worthwhile to look at the logical and service level structures of simple agents.

Figure 11.3 shows and describes the functional components of a simple proxy agent. The services provided by a simple agent are:

- *Status determination*—Most native agents periodically execute relevant procedures to determine values of state variables defined in the MIB. This information is cached in a local MIB database for future reference by a management station through a GET

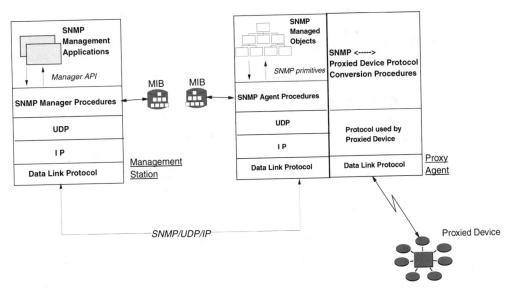

Figure 11.2: *Proxy agent structure*

or GETNEXT command. Depending on the level of internal coupling between the agent process and the managed entity's logic, the managed entity may undertake to inform the agent of any status change.

Determining the status in the case of a proxy agent involves polling the proxied device, processing the response through a mapping to an MIB variable and caching a value for it in the MIB database.

Some state variables define the physical or logical configuration of the managed entity. In the case of native agents, populating such variables may need polling procedures to ensure that configuration changes that occur through causes other than at the agent's behest are reflected in the MIB in a timely manner.

• *Alarm processing*—For native agents, the managed entity usually notifies the agent of its internal exceptions or change of state. The agent may in some cases poll for change of state.

In the case of proxy agents an alarm message sent by the proxied device needs to be parsed and recognized as an alarm.

In either case the agent needs to determine whether the alarm warrants the generation of an SNMP trap. It then generates an appropriate mapping to an SNMP trap including insertion of a value for the *minor trap identifier.*

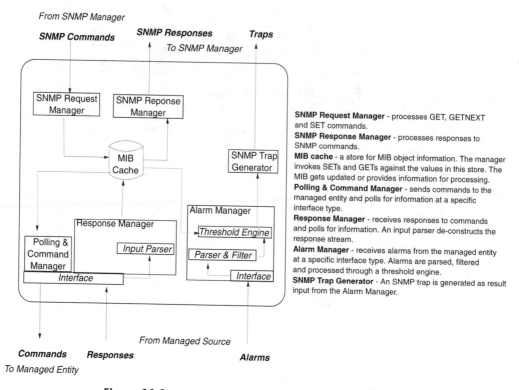

From SNMP Manager

SNMP Commands   **SNMP Responses**   **Traps**

To SNMP Manager

SNMP Request Manager   SNMP Reponse Manager

MIB Cache

SNMP Trap Generator

Response Manager

Alarm Manager

Threshold Engine

Polling & Command Manager

Input Parser

Parser & Filter

Interface   Interface

Commands   **Responses**   **Alarms**

From Managed Source

To Managed Entity

SNMP Request Manager - processes GET, GETNEXT and SET commands.
SNMP Response Manager - processes responses to SNMP commands.
MIB cache - a store for MIB object information. The manager invokes SETs and GETs against the values in this store. The MIB gets updated or provides information for processing.
Polling & Command Manager - sends commands to the managed entity and polls for information at a specific interface type.
Response Manager - receives responses to commands and polls for information. An input parser de-constructs the response stream.
Alarm Manager - receives alarms from the managed entity at a specific interface type. Alarms are parsed, filtered and processed through a threshold engine.
SNMP Trap Generator - An SNMP trap is generated as result input from the Alarm Manager.

Figure 11.3: Functional components of a simple proxy agent

- *Configuration*—In both native and proxy agents the manager initiates configuration change. This is done with an SNMP SET command. In the case of a native agent, it executes a procedure to change the respective parameter at the device.

- In the case of a proxy, it sends the proxied device a message mapping to the SET command on the respective variable.

- *Security*—The manager-agent protocol defines the minimum security functions the agent has to implement. In both native and proxy agents the SNMP *community* scheme needs to be implemented for access control rights to MIB objects and the authentication of the manager to the agent.

Case Study 11.1: Native Agent Toolkit Product

Emanate from **SNMP Research** Inc. is an SNMP agent toolkit for use in developing native agents for a range of host environments including Unix, Microsoft NT and MSDOS. The agent architecture is based on a master agent that provides services to a number of subagents through an internal API. A master agent is required per host. A subagent is defined per MIB supported at the host. The subagent MIBs are "concatenated" into a unified MIB tree view at the master agent.

The manager sees only the master agent, that supports multiple threads of conversation with a manager. The master agent supports the SNMP and a version of SNMPv2. Multiple threads provide high performance when several subagents are supported.

Subagents communicate with the master agent without recourse to ASN.1 encoding, making the interface highly performant. Subagents can also connect to the master agent and disconnect at runtime. At the master agent the portions of the MIB contributed by the subagents are respectively added or deleted from the unified MIB tree. Tables with the master agent can be populated by different subagents.

This is called "run-time extensible" by the vendor and is a powerful mechanism to cope with subagents associated with components that are transient.

The toolkit and libraries allow developers to concentrate on defining MIB structures and the procedures to populate the MIB objects. The toolkit generates stubs for these procedures.

Case Study 11.2: Proxy Agent Toolkit Product

Extensible Proxy Agent Builder (EPA) from **Bridgeway** is a toolkit for developing SNMP proxy agents. Proxy agents collect management information from a source that is a non-SNMP device and presents it to a designated manager station. It also translates commands from the manager station to the non-SNMP device.

The EPA product provides a set of generic services such as an MIB database, processor for messages from the non-SNMP source and processing of commands from the manager station.

This is presented as a set of pre-defined, high level software functions to develop agent services such as those in Section 11.1.4

- *Translating alarms from non-SNMP sources*—Key functions in this category are a sophisticated ASCII message stream parser, support for multiple message streams, support to cascade multiple proxy agents for complex monitoring applications.

- *MIB value population*—Key functions in this category include those for MIB parsing, MIB updating, logging of received messages.

- *Processing SNMP commands from the manager station*—Key functions in this category include processing of SNMP GET, GETNEXT and SET commands, MIB support via a Mibmaster utility, launch of procedure to execute commands and actions on a SET being processed.

The procedures are built using the Event IX Application Generator, a toolkit that should be part of the development environment for infrastructure management.

11.2 Autonomous Agents

The term autonomous agent is used to differentiate behavior from simple agents which are passive in that they wait to be polled for MIB values. Autonomous agents on the other hand, once configured, work independently without the prompting of manager stations.

Infrastructure management that extends over an enterprises's intra-network involves monitoring of each networking component, subnet, host and application. To extend the polling model is clearly not viable when applied to simple agents.

An autonomous agent is exemplified by the RMON standard specified in RFC 1271 by the IETF. This is essentially an MIB definition. However, this standard has had a major influence in the definition of autonomous monitoring agents in other areas such as at the host management and application levels.

For autonomous agents to be really useful in an infrastructure management, applications are needed to take the raw data captured and held by the agents and to process it into easily digestible information for operators. Three different agents that fall into this category are described below.

11.2.1 Remote MONITOR (RMON)

The Internet RMON is a remote monitoring agent that is used as a standard way of monitoring subnetworks and indeed for distributing much of the packet level processing to remote compute engines of the remote monitors. Figure 11.4 shows the multiple points on an enterprise network at which RMON agents are commonly deployed.

Each monitor operates in a promiscuous mode viewing every packet on the subset, analyzing and producing summary statistics such as:

Errors on the network media—e.g., collisions and number of undersize packets.

Performance on the network media—e.g., utilization and packet size distribution.

Prior to capture, packets are filtered on the basis of packet type and other recognizable characteristics in the packet data. In addition to packet capture other processing may be done in the background on previously captured packets of data.

The RMON (defined largely by an MIB specification) has significantly contributed to the acceptance of SNMP as a viable network management protocol. Its main goals are:

- To allow continuous, proactive polling, independent of polling from the manager station. The monitor is configured so that the parameters for pro-active polling are locally available to the monitor.

- The monitor holds local logs of monitoring results, so that it can provide a manager station with local summaries on an infrequent basis. The monitor may be associated with more than one manager station, hence it has mechanisms to recover from potential conflict.

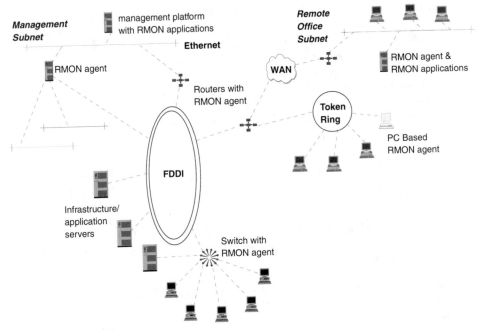

Figure 11.4: Role of RMON components in an enterprise network

- The monitor can run applications to analyze locally collected data so that information returned to the manager station has been processed to add informational value to the raw data.

- The monitor can be configured for exception recognition, where threshold values define exception boundaries. The monitor can also be configured to notify manager stations when exceptions occur.

An interesting side effect of these goals is that an RMON agent can identify all devices on the subnet that use the TCP/IP suite. This can be used to inventory changes to the subnet population. Another use is to identify SNMP based agents for a manager station. Given the possibility of multiple agents on any single host, the RMON plays a role in auto-configuration.

Controlling the RMON. The RMON MIB is organized into nine functional groups defined in the last section. Each remote monitor needs to be configured for data collection. Each such configuration defines baseline conditions in the respective environment.

Within each group there is at least one control table and one data table. In some groups such as *statistics* the two are combined as the control table is very small.

The control tables provide the configuration mechanism of the RMON. They contain parameters that describe the data in the data table. The manager station sets the appropriate parameter in the control table to configure the collection of the associated data.

Information is then collected according to the parameter settings of a control row. This is stored in rows of the corresponding data table.

The parameters are set by adding a new row to the control table or by modifying an existing row. To modify any parameters it is necessary to set the current value to invalid. This deletes the row which in turn causes the deletion of all associated rows in data tables. Deletion of data tables rows allows their resources to be reclaimed.

RMON Groups. The RMON MIB has a subtree identifier 16 in the MIB II definition. The RMON MIB consists of nine groups. All of these are optional, however, some groups are dependent on other groups being implemented:

- *Statistics*—Holds basic statistics for each monitored subnetwork. This is held in a single table with a row for each subnet monitored by the agent. All objects are counters that get zeroed when the row is created.

  The group contains objects for Ethernet. Vendors have defined extensions for other LAN interfaces including Token Ring and FDDI. These two are however likely to be part of the standard definition.

  The statistics group provides a good overview of the load and general health of the subnet.

- *History*—The history group defines the sampling function for the monitor's interfaces. It consists of a control table that defines the sampling function and a data table that stores data for each network medium supported (Ethernet, FDDI, Token Ring).

  The specification recommends that there are at least two sampling activities for each interface: one on a short sampling period such as 30 seconds to monitor sudden changes in traffic behavior. The other to capture the steady state behavior (for possible archival purposes).

- *Alarm*—The alarm group defines the thresholds for network performance. When a defined threshold is crossed in the defined direction an alarm is sent to a manager station. The specification defines a hysteresis mechanism to avoid minor fluctuations triggering alarms.

- *Host*—The host group is used to gather information about specific hosts on LAN. Information is gathered for each interface of the monitor. New hosts are discovered by observing the source and destination addresses at the MAC level of "good" packets seen by the monitor. Statistics are maintained for each host that is seen. (These statistics are also available directly from each host equipped with an SNMP stack and which supports MIB-II.)

- *HostTopN*—The hostTopN group defines a set of hosts at each interface of the monitor that top a list. The criteria for the list is based on a control parameter. The list basis includes data packets, data octets, errors, broadcast and multicast packets.

- *Matrix*—The matrix group records information about traffic between pairs of hosts on the subnet. This is stored as a matrix indexed by source MAC address as well as indexed by the destination MAC address. Traffic statistics captured are number of packets, number of octets and number of errors.

- *Filter*—The filter group allows a manager station to configure an RMON agent to capture statistics on selected traffic. The selection criteria is defined either by a data filter consisting of a bit pattern on a masked portion of the packet or by a status filter consisting of status (good packets, long error, short error) of a packet. The filter group introduces the concept of a channel which is a logical path through one or more filters. Filters may be combined by a logical OR.

- *Packet capture*—The buffer capture group allows the manager station to set up a buffering scheme and to define packet data sent to the manager station or cached locally on the RMON's local environment. Packet capture may be related to a channel in the filter group. Captured packets are stored in a sequence.

- *Event*—The event group allows the manager station to define events to be generated by conditions occurring elsewhere in the MIB. The event may result in an SNMP trap being generated and/or cause the event to be logged in the data table.

RMON Applications. RMON applications take data recorded in RMON data tables and add informational value to it. Applications also ease the problem of managing the life-cycle of RMON configurations.

The usefulness of RMON is largely due to its ability to be configured to recognize nominal conditions in the subnet being monitored. An important role of RMON applications is to provide user interface and scripting tools for the easy configuration of the groups.

However, as the number of RMON agents increase, and they get integrated into managing client/server "service paths," applications that configure one RMON interface at a time become inadequate.

What is needed is the ability to reconfigure arbitrary collections of RMONs that reflect the service paths being managed. The ability to reconfigure RMON groups dynamically makes it viable as a diagnostic tool rather than as a baseline monitoring tool. This is an area of tool development in many mature management organizations.

Applications in this area include analyzers for inter-network traffic, tools to recognize steady state conditions automatically, a time series database engine and query tools to examine data at different "timelines."

While it should theoretically be possible to make RMON probes and applications from different vendors interwork, the fact of life is that this is not the case. Most RMON probes work reliably only with RMON applications from the same vendor.

Future of RMON. The RMON specification is a cornerstone of SNMP based management. The RMON specification is currently under revision and a new specification RMON II is expected soon.

The revisions primarily allow the application layer monitoring and multi-segment monitoring. With these upgrades, applications can be developed that can monitor client/server applications end-to-end.

The ability to see bandwidth utilization or multi-segment traffic patterns by application, by user or user group make the next generation of RMON products better able to support the requirements of infrastructure management.

With the development of sophisticated applications that RMON II would allow, a possible evolution would be the emergence of an *infrastructure analysis server.* This would service the diverse monitoring and analysis needs of a set of LANs or a whole site's infrastructure.

This would also provide a point of integration for additional agents and analysis applications to process *in situ*, the data monitored by the agents.

While RMON has revolutionized the way multi-segmented LANs are managed, many networks are in the process of re-engineering to the use of switch-based designs. The main driver for this is to cope with network bandwidth requirements of powerful workstation and server hosts.

There are essentially two types of switches used: workgroup switches deliver bandwidth to the desktop. Backbone switches connect together workgroup switches.

Some switch vendors have been deterred by the complexity of embedding RMON into their products and have left it out. Others have been deterred by the CPU cycles needed for RMON and either support a limited set of RMON groups or allow data collection on a few ports at a time.

This has serious implications for infrastructure management. Support of just MIB-II without RMON is not very useful for traffic analysis. While stand-alone probes can in theory be attached to every port, this clearly is too expensive for most environments.

The problem is especially acute in network architecture that is specifically designed to cater to the latency and burstiness characteristics of distributed computing (of which the client/server model is but the beginning).

The backbone switch plays a major role in providing low latency for core server-based services such as real-time message distribution to subgroups of users. With the RMON on these backbone switches, end-to-end management is impossible.

11.2.2 Host Management Agents

The concept of a Host Resources MIB was originally developed to inventory hosts and to monitor a host's runtime configurations. This is defined in RFC 1514.

Case Study 11.3: Software-based RMON Product

Netmetrix was one of the earliest serious RMON products and is still one of the best software-based RMON agents. In large networks it also provides one of the most cost-effective solutions.

The power of the HP Netmetrix Power Agent is that it is a UNIX based software product that can be installed on a "spare" workstation on a LAN to be monitored. It can also concurrently monitor multiple, heterogeneous (Ethernet, Token Ring and FDDI) LANs through the respective interfaces.

The Power Agents' data can be used by any manager through SNMP. However another attraction of the product is a highly integrated set of applications that add informational value to the monitored data.

The current application suite consists of analysis and mapping tools—the *Load Monitor* which is an analysis tool for traffic load, the *Protocol Analyzer* that does drill-down analysis of protocols of the protocol stack, the *NFS Monitor* that provides load and performance analysis of NFS servers and clients, the *Traffic Generator* that can be used to simulate loads and generate user defined packets, the *Internetwork Monitor* that combines data from multiple agents to give cross network traffic maps.

Rights to the Netmetrix brand name, its agent technology and applications are currently with HP and as such are likely to be fully integrated into HP Openview. Integration with HP Openview is through SNMP based access. The suite of applications can however be installed and run locally with a Power Agent.

An X Windows interlace with the suite provides a manager station with display and user interface of the installed applications. The product also provides integration through SNMP traps and command line interface.

Case Study 11.4: Integrated RMON Probe

A software-based RMON agent for which suitable hosts have to be found and ultimately administered is not to the taste of all organizations. There are arguments for self-contained RMON based probes.

One of the most innovative product sets in this area is from Frontier Software Development, Inc.—namely the Netscout range of intelligent RMON probes. The RMON is also available as a software agent for Sun SPARC and Intel X86 based machines.

Ethernet, Token Ring and FDDI LANs are supported. In addition there is a WAN probe which can analyze traffic traversing a WAN interface of a router.

The NETscout Manager is a suite of applications that is integrated at the menu level to HP Openview, SunNet Manager and IBM NetView management platforms.

The suite consists of applications that can present information from a selectable subset of probes: *Protocol Monitor*—provides a graphical view of traffic and protocol details for data. *Traffic Monitor*—provides a graphical view of network statistics. *Domain Manager* allows the management of probes in terms of domains of network traffic. *Resource Manager* allows proactive monitoring of IP devices using SNMP Get (and by setting threshold values for selected MIB variables) and Ping.

Several vendors have however developed this MIB into very useful products as far as infrastructure management is concerned. These developments include:

- Implementation of the MIB for multiple operating systems—in effect giving enterprises with the respective environments a *de facto* standard to implement asset management applications.

- Extension of the MIB to include other aspects of a typical UNIX environment—allowing a single source of management information that previously had to be gathered through as many as a dozen or more different means.

- Extension of the MIB with control and thresholding mechanisms—borrowed from the RMON, allowing such agents to be configured with threshold conditions pertaining to capacity and performance states.

Also, several large enterprises have expended development efforts in extending capability around this basic MIB. This has huge payback in terms of streamlining costs of asset management, basic performance monitoring of hosts, understanding usage, related patterns, etc.

The model for several of these orthogonal developments around a standard MIB has been influenced by the utility and success of RMON. As such these MIBs have set very similar goals for continuous monitoring, local caching, presentation of data to value-added applications and configuration for notification thresholds.

Host Resources MIB. Although the Host Resources MIB *does not* define the workings of an autonomous agent, many products built around it are. The Host Resources MIB is therefore briefly described in this category of agents. It has the following six groups.

- *hrSystem*—provides information about the host as system.

- *hrStorage*—defines logical storage structures seen by applications.

- *hrDevice*—defines devices contained by the host and information including status and errors on each device.

- *hrSWRun*—lists the software that is currently running on the host system.

- *hrSWRunPerf*—defines the performance of currently running software.

- *hrSWInstalled*—lists the software currently installed including version informations and list of patches applied.

Value Added Application for Host Resources. Products built around and including the Host Resources MIB offer raw data for a unique set of applications that would otherwise not be possible.

- Asset management of hardware and software resources including software version consistency between hosts, calculation of license adequacy criteria, uptime metrics for SLA management.

- Automated tracking of hosts that move between different parts of the organization. Especially since lifetimes of hosts is in the order of two years, departments are keen to be attributed only proportional costs.

- Host management in terms of failure patterns and processor load management. Also tracking patterns of memory, disk and buffer usage provides early indications of changes in user activity.

11.2.3 Application Management Agents

Application problems usually manifest themselves as network related problems; degradation of service, loss of connectivity, application timeouts, etc. Network management staff are increasingly involved in solving problems associated with applications.

Some studies have shown that 30% to 40% of network management helpdesk resources are expended on such problems. Indeed, it is this very phenomena that has prompted many enterprises to look to extending the remit of network management as described in Chapter 1.

Many enterprises are looking to provide support staff with the information to aid in such problem management. User definition of problems is notoriously difficult to reproduce.

Some enterprises have designed ad hoc tools for the helpdesk to reduce dependency on user definitions of problems. Others have initiated task force type helpdesks with more on-hand expertise of application components.

In any case, specifying manageability as a primary criterion is increasingly common for a distributed application to be considered for enterprise-wide deployment. This is viewed as an area with huge payback to the enterprise. This payback is in terms of controlling the complexity and service elements of deploying client/server applications on an enterprise scale.

Unlike the developing MIBs for host resource management that interfaces with existing operating system functions, application MIB development requires cooperation from in-house developers of applications as well as vendors.

The agent needs to be configured on installation. It can subsequently be dynamically reconfigured. Uses of this agent are in inventorying, aspects of security monitoring and performance management. It really requires the development of a custom application (e.g., written in TCL/TK) that can provide screen-based dialogs for dynamic reconfiguration.

Application functions are not widely published nor easily interfaceable without an API. Also, applications have complex life-cycles. Operating system versions with new features are changed relatively rarely, while application versions have shorter lifetimes. One of the reasons is that vendors and in-house development teams undertake incremental delivery of function.

Case Study 11.5: Extended Host Resources Agent Product

UNIX Systems Management Agent from **Empire Technologies Inc.** is an example of an agent that supports the Host Resources MIB but also includes a widely extended information and function as described below. The agent has the ability to be configured with polling frequencies, relational operator and threshold values. Exceptions against the thresholds are sent as traps to a designated manager. An unusual feature of the agent is the control parameters available as SET parameters. Given SNMP's security inadequacies these need to be examined by each enterprise on a security policy basis. The agent tracks and notifies authentication failure at its manager interface. The agent supports the following groups:

- *system*—contains information about the host name and id, the operating system, CPU and memory details.

- *mounted devices*—contains information about the devices and file systems that are mounted on the UNIX host, including the mount point, block size, number of free blocks and present capacity. A control variable is available to unmount a device in the table.

- *kernel configuration*—contains the kernel configuration such as maximum concurrent processes, maximum number of Inodes, amount of system swap space as well as kernel version and identity.

- *boot configuration*—contains information about partitions used in root, dump file system and swap as well as number of block for each partition.

- *streams*—contains information about the configuration, usage statistics and health of the streams subsystem.

- *user information*—shows the user accounts that have been created on the host, including login name, password, user ID, user home directory.

- *group information*—which user groups have been created on a host.

- *process*—shows the processes currently running, its status, id, name, owner uid and gid and amount of memory and CPU being consumed by the process. Two control variables allow the process's priority to be modified and for a process to be terminated.

- *who*—shows the users currently logged into the host. Information includes user name login device, login time.

- *remote shell*—allows shell scripts to be executed on a remote system by specifying the command, arguments and output file. The status of the command is available.

- *performance*—allows CPU performance monitoring and contains information about idle time, time spent in user and kernel spaces. Monitoring is initiated by a control variable.

- *kernel performance*—allows operating system performance. Collected statistics include information on jobs, paging, processes and open files.

- *message queue, shared memory segment and semaphore* tables define usage of these interprocess communication (IPC) usage, ownership and any size information. Each table has a control variable to delete an instance of current IPC usage.

Case Study 11.5: Extended Host Resources Agent Product *(continued)*

- *mbufAlloc* table shows the message buffer allocation and purpose, count of denied and delayed message buffer request.

- *strbufAlloc* table shows buffer allocation and usage statistics for buffers used by the Streams subsystem.

- *iobuf* table shows the buffer allocation for disk input/output (i/o) operations and cache hits and instances of buffer starvation.

- *monitor table*—this is a control table that allows the agent to monitor and report against the set threshold for any counter, integer, gauge and enumerated integer in the Emipre MIB or the Host Resources MIB.

- *RPC*—shows statistics including errors, of RPC related activity divided into client and server side operations.

- *NFS*—shows statistics relating to NFS related activities, divided into client and server side operations.

Application life-cycle. Application environments differ markedly from each other, however, distributed applications have a life-cycle which makes the population of MIB objects dependent on a number of sources. Figure 11.5 shows a three-stage life-cycle:

- The installation phase is undertaken by a software distribution tool. At this time values of a number of MIB variables can be evaluated. Examples include name of the application, version number, file names.

- The software distribution tool is essentially responsible for transporting images of the applications and other resources such as configuration scripts to each host—setting the stage for integrating it into the operation environment of each host. This is the job of a configuration tool which provides values for another class of MIB objects.

- Once configuration is complete the application is essentially operational. MIB objects reflect values as updated by the interface procedures with the operational environment. This group of objects may also include objects that act as controls for a version control tool.

- The cycle starts again when the application is changed (under a change control process). New versions with incremental features, new deployment design to cope with demand patterns, etc. drive this. The respective MIB objects are updated.

Another life-cycle issue with client/server applications is that some of the agents are as transient as their hosting application components. Components that reside in workstations are controlled by the user. An application is launched, made idle and terminated through these components. Agents reflect these existential states of the hosting component.

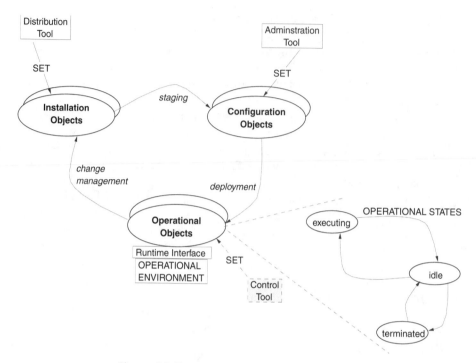

Figure 11.5: *Life-cycle of distributed applications*

The SNMP manager-agent protocol is not designed to handle agents that are transient. The application MIB designer has to take this into account. The transient behavior of application agents needs to be effectively hidden from the manager.

Application MIB information. An application MIB needs to provide different types of information. Client/server applications software consists of many elements that may fail independently or in a cascade manner.

Client/server applications rarely work in self-contained isolation. They interact with other services, database engines, user interfaces and so on by their very definition. The key types of information provided in the MIB are:

- *Inventory type information*—define relatively static information that enables the unambiguous identification and instance details of the application.

- *Existential type information*—define the status objects.

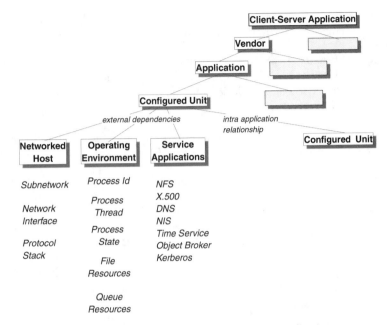

Figure 11.6: *Information tree for client/server applications*

- *Relationship type information*—define intra-application relationships.

- *Dependency information*—define relationships with services and infrastructure external to the application.

Figure 11.6 shows an information tree for a private application MIB developed by a large investment bank. From this model a hypothetical set of MIB groups were defined:

- *Installed Application*—contains information equivalent to DMTF Minimum Interworking Functionality. Information includes vendor name, product name, version number, etc. There is one such table per application. Information is placed into this table by the software distribution application.

- *Configured Unit*—contains information about each part of the application that is discernible as a discrete computing unit. An application consists of a number of these. Some units may be resident on client hosts, while others may be on several hosts. The table has an entry for each unit that gets configured. Columnar objects include the type, name and address of the host on which the unit is resident, the communication stack used at the host, the operating system at the host, existential variables show information on whether the unit has invoked its processes.

- *Configured Resources*—contains information about resources configured for each configured unit. There is a corresponding entry for each entry in the configured unit table. Columnar objects include swap space, memory, file system, operating system objects such as queues.

- *External Services*—contains information about the external services used by a configured unit. There is a corresponding entry for an entry in the configured unit table.

- *Intra Relationships*—contains information about the relationships between configured units.

- *Process*—contains information about processes related to each configured unit. There is one such table for each configured unit. Process Id, process state, current number of threads.

Application Monitor Products. There are currently no known commercial or public domain products based on an SNMP MIB.

11.3 Smart Agents

Smart agents are differentiated from simple and autonomous agents by their ability to process raw data using an internal model. This processing may result in a set of actions being taken.

Smart agents are generally used to monitor "patterns of activity" across multiple agents (or devices) being managed against some internal model of the activity.

Internal models represent relationships that are inherent and unique to an enterprise's network topology or host and application deployment. Smart agents provide the ability to express these tools as stand-alone applications.

They are a means of distributing intelligence to the points on the infrastructure. As such, smart agents are fairly complex applications. One issue is how to maintain these applications in line with the changing environment. This requires serious software engineering abstractions to be applied.

Smart agent technology therefore exists mostly in the form of toolkits to build these agents using prefabricated mechanisms. Common uses of such internal models are in complex monitoring scenarios—for example:

Existential state of application servers—A host responding to Ping only, indicates that the host is reachable on the network and the basic TCP/IP stack is functional. In order to be assured that an application server such as a database server is functional (to actually process application requests), some sequence of operations needs to be executed. These need to return uniquely verifiable results that indicate the target is "live."

A smart agent that periodically executes a script to test and verify functionality of an application service needs an internal model such as a finite state machine as the verification procedure.

Event correlation—Another common area for smart agent capability is using an internal model to find relationships between individual events in an event stream.

A common use of a correlation engine is in managing wide area networks based on meshed leased lines, multiplexers and routers. The serial relationships between the components means that when a fault occurs anywhere in the chain, multiple secondary faults show up.

The automated isolation of the primary cause from the side-effects has major implications for time-to-repair quality metrics. An internal model for this type of correlation requires the explicit definition of the events and dependency between individual parts of the chain in terms of these events. One commercial product (NetCortex from BIM) uses a Prolog based database of facts and relationships.

11.3.1 Smart Agent Products

Given the amount of internal development involved in areas such as the above, the tools used, and the deployment of such agents have important cost implications. There are several smart agent products on the market. Two of these are described below:

11.4 Pattern Recognition Agents

Agents based on pattern recognition are essential for a whole class of monitoring situations where the definition of an MIB is impractical.

Impracticality is partially due to the time cost element of developing MIBs and associated application software. More importantly, some environments that need to be monitored right now are intractable for MIB definition—in many cases because the MIBs are not powerful enough to satisfy the complex structure of the environment.

Most operating systems and applications are capable of logging a variety of information concerning the status and health of respective components. Another case in point is security logs.

However in many enterprises these capabilities are not configured. Certainly, operating systems such as Unix require meticulous crafting of the parameters by knowledgeable systems administrators. Even when these capabilities are well configured, they are often logged

Case Study 11.6: State Machine Based Tool to Model Agent Behavior

The Netlabs/Nerve Center product from Seagate can interface to SNMP agents, essentially masquerading as a management station. It gets data from the agent through traps and by polling MIB objects at the agent.

This raw data is processed through an internal model built up from a number of mechanisms in the toolkit. The output of the processing is some action. Nerve Center provides the following mechanisms:

- *A Trap Mask*—allows traps from an agent to be examined for specific categories and privately specified identifiers within a category. Once a trap has been identified a unique internal trigger is generated. Such triggers are fed to an associated action mechanism or the state machine.

- *A Polling Engine*—allows polling conditions to be defined on an MIB object by object basis. The conditions include polling frequency and values based on a powerful set of relational operators such as "if equal a specified value," "if increased since last poll," "if increased since last poll or equal to specified value." Once a condition is recognized an internal trigger is generated and fed to the state machine.

- *The State Machine*—The evaluation of traps and polls result in unique triggers which are fed to a state machine modeling the further processing of the event. The state machine is created using a graphical tool and there is a state machine for each MIB object that is polled. Associated with the state machine is a predefined set of state values (critical, major, minor, etc.). The state machine processes each event through these states.

- *Actions*—When a state transition occurs in a state machine a number of predefined actions can be taken. These include—logging the information about the event, invoking of scripts or applications, dealing a page with a unique identifier for the event, send e-mail to a distribution list, issue an SNMP command and issue a trap or trigger. The last of these allows state machines to be cascaded or developed into networks to manage complex conditions.

- *Action Router*—A further level of processing can be invoked to aid the decision-making for actions. The action router provides an orthogonal set of criteria by which to make action decisions. These include the day and time at which the event occurs, the node at which it originates and the severity of the alarm state.

One common use of Nerve Center is as a smart agent to monitor remote offices in an enterprise network. The agent takes actions for generic classes of problems. The program for the smart agent is a system or collection of trap masks, polling conditions, state machines, network of state machines, scripts actions and routing criteria.

Nerve Center allows a re-usable model for monitoring of remote offices that can scale to many thousands of managed devices. It allows tight control over the WAN bandwidth budget for remote monitoring. It has also been used, at least in one instance, to automate the management of some 95% of problems found in well-designed remote office networks and some 70% of other infrastructure problems.

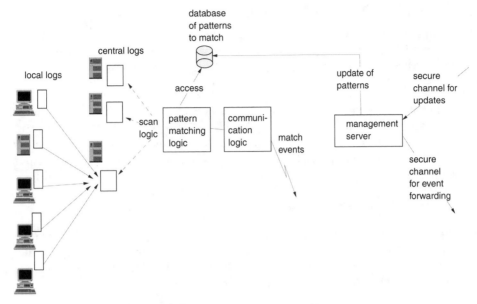

Figure 11.7: *Model for pattern matching agents*

in unsafe places—prone to deletion, modifications or simply being forgotten until some crisis occurs.

In a large enterprise the systems administrator may be responsible for hundreds and sometimes thousands of systems. A system of pattern matching agents can leverage the existing information in these systems to be usable within a broader monitoring framework. Figure 11.7 shows a general model for using pattern matching agents in monitoring log-based messages (and generating events as a result of recognizing predefined patterns).

The agent contains the logic or has access to logic to convert the recognition of a pattern to an event that is communicable as an event to the monitoring framework. There are two types of pattern matching agents evident:

- Agents where the pattern recognition is on the basis of matching a *regular expression* as defined for example in Perl, the scripting language. These are particularly useful in converting log file entries to events.

- Agents that match against a *value* including bit patterns. Such agents are useful in monitoring flag settings in file systems and cryptographic checksums of a software configuration.

11.4.1 Regular Expression Matching Agents

Agents that provide service through matching regular expressions are essentially passive and relatively simple in construct. Regular expression matching agents are widely used to monitor log files, console messages and sometimes for client entities to post a message via an API. Typically they consist of:

- *Configuration source*—this defines the type and number of sources for monitoring. Types include log files, consoles and API. There may be several instances of each at a single host. For each source it points to a set of *pattern | action* pairs. The pattern defines the regular expression to look for and the action defines the corresponding action to take on a match. The pattern | action pair may be augmented by a *timer value* to filter out redundant messages of the given pattern and the option for a *network time stamp* to be added when forwarding the match event.

- *Execution engine for pattern matching*—this defines the process level mechanism for executing the trawl through the configured sources. Design details include the privilege levels to run this daemon, the mechanism for sending a heartbeat for the agent itself, the mechanism for dynamic reconfiguring of source information, procedure to re-start on failure.

- *Library of actions*—this defines the set of actions the agent can do on a match taking place. Typical actions include audible alarm to a defined console, send as e-mail @ a distribution list, send to pager with message, do nothing, send to an event monitoring framework, execute a script.

When such agents are deployed in large environments of hosts, a common practice is to centralize the logging before pattern matching. Copying "important" local log information to a central point provides several advantages:

It provides redundancy and security. Such agents are particularly useful in monitoring system security. Operating systems such as Unix are built up of many utilities, each of which have logging capabilities. These may be localized to a single *syslog* at each host. Such logs are prime targets for intruders who want to remove traces of their sojourn.

Centralizing log information also allows time-ordered patterns to be seen. For example, failed login attempts within a short timeframe, across multiple systems would indicate a breakin attempt. More sophisticated pattern matching algorithms.

Regular expression matching agents provide utility because they can deal with the here and now situations. As such they have important roles in specific areas of continuous, background monitoring, including:

- Security related monitoring has already been mentioned—particularly of super-user activity, login attempts, instances of virus detection by virus checking utilities and firewall status.

- Availability related monitoring is another area—for instances of systems crashes, system re-boots, kick-in of redundant servers. Also messages from disk mirroring and RAID type devices that may be accessible as console messages.

- Environmental monitoring of messages such as temperature rise and power status.

- Procedure status messages from successful operational management procedures such as backup, version upgrade.

11.4.2 Value Matching Agents

Value based agents are active in the sense that they execute a script-based algorithm to compute a value against which to apply a pattern match. Typical components are:

- Configuration database that define for each target, a set of *signature | algorithm(1) | algorithm(n) | +action | -action* tuples that define a sequence of scripts to use to compute a value to match against the *signature* or bit pattern specified in the tuple. The configuration database is usually encrypted to retain the confidentiality of stored signatures.

- Execution engine for computing the defined script-based algorithm and matching. This is usually an interpreter for a scripting language such as TCL or Perl. Safety may be an issue, hence "safe" variants of an interpreter are often used.

- Library of actions defines the actions the agent takes on a match occurring and on a match not occurring. This includes logging the result, sending an e-mail message, send to an event monitoring framework and execute a script.

Example uses of value matching agents include:

- *Host security baseline monitoring*—A security baseline relating to operating system services and networked services such as file systems is expressed in terms of a number of attribute values and bit patterns of flags and data structures. Once a baseline level of security is established, future audit of the host can be done using the representative signatures of these structures.

- *Build integrity monitoring*—Operating systems and applications often have features that are not required by all classes of users. Such software is configured specifically for different types of users in the organization, removing inappropriate functionality and features. One way of ensuring that a "build" has retained its integrity is to compute non-forgeable signatures for key executables at the installation of a particular configuration. Integrity is monitored by re-computing and matching against the stored signatures.

Case Study 11.7: Pattern Matching Agent

Simple WATCHer (*Swatch*) is a public domain program developed at **Stanford University**. It is a good example in two respects—the first as an example of a regular expression-based pattern matching software and secondly as an example of the high quality of software available in the public domain.

Swatch was developed to look through a centralized log—on a batch basis, or as messages were appended to the log and also to examine the standard output of a program. Swatch has three basic parts:

- *A configuration file* which consists of four fields—a regular expression to match against, a set of actions to be taken on the pattern being matched, an optional time interval to filter redundant messages, and an optional time stamp.

- *A set of actions* that can be executed by Swatch:

  echo—to swatch's control terminal.

  bell—to send a bell character to swatch's control terminal.

  ignore—to ignore the current match.

  write—to send a copy of the line via the Write command.

  mail—to send a copy of the line via the mail command.

  pipe—allows the matched line to be used as an input to a command.

  exec—allows the user to execute a command with selected fields from the matched line as its arguments.

- The *watcher process*. This translates the configuration file to a Perl script and then executes it as a watcher process. Two control signals cause the watcher process to terminate, re-read the configuration file and re-start the watcher process. Other signals cause the watcher process to terminate, cleanup and exit.

Multiple Swatch processes can each be specialized to look for different purposes—examples include monitoring for high-priority kernel messages and application messages. Each process is run in the background. The *pipe* and *exec* actions may be used to communicate the matched line to a scaling agent via its API. The scaling agent converts the message to an enterprise specific trap.

Swatch is written in Perl. It has been used by several organizations as a prototype to build expression-matching agents with more functionality—e.g., to read from multiple log files concurrently, to support additional input sources such as an API for applications to write directly to the agent.

11.5 Mobile Agents

Mobile agents are programs that can be transported to a target host, do some set of management tasks on being executed at the host, returning the results to a defined destination.

Mobile agents are distinguished from other types of agents in that they are only temporarily associated with a given host. A mobile agent can be associated with a large number of hosts during its tenure.

Other types of agents are bound to a single device or host by being permanently resident at the one point.

Mobile agents have a distinctive life-cycle. This life-cycle starts when the host grabs the agent software, authenticates it, decrypts its contents, de-compresses it and sets it running in a safe environment.

On being run the agent executes a finite set of transactions at the host, returning the results to destination—usually the source of the invoked agent. The mobile agent then removes itself from the host.

Mobile agent technology is relatively new. It is however sufficiently mature to be useful in a large number of infrastructure management scenarios.

Two types of mobile agents are distinguished by their containment architecture. File-based agents are transported as files to their target hosts where they are executed in a specially secure environment. Object-based agents are transported as recognizable objects and executed in an object-oriented operating system at the target host.

This chapter will primarily look at using file-based agents as they reflect what is possible with current off-the-shelf technology.

11.5.1 Technology Components

The technology of mobile agents consists of the functional components shown in Figure 11.8. Mobile agents need to be transported securely from an acceptable point of origin to the target hosts. The target hosts need to recognize the signature of a mobile agent and its functions. The target host needs an execution environment where the agent may be safely executed.

The transport protocol may be used return results back to the origin of the agent or be indirected to some other destination. Alternatively, the agent may be re-launched from the host carrying the results.

The following subsections describe these components.

The Transportation Component. This component is responsible for transporting the agent from a point of origin to one or more targets. The two transport mechanisms available are objects and files. Objects need to be executed in an object-oriented environment at the targets. This is clearly not feasible in the application domain of infrastructure management.

A widely accepted transport for mobile agents is e-mail. Recent advances in security features applied to e-mail makes this one of the most secure systems of delivery.

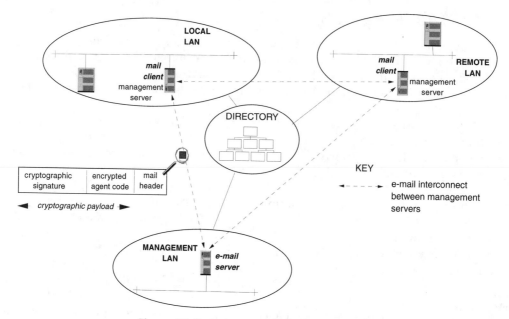

Figure 11.8: Delivery system for mobile agents

One of the management framework recommendations in Chapter 10 is to have a special mail domain for infrastructure management. This would be used solely for management traffic.

A specialized domain allows specific paths to be defined for different types of mobile agents. A directory would orchestrate these paths as e-mail distribution lists. Both the domain and the respective part of the directory can be configured to be accessible only to the infrastructure management organization.

E-mail carrying mobile agents are addressed to the local management server in the first instance for verification and decrypting. It may be then be distributed or forwarded onto other local hosts where execution of the agent code occurs.

The Security Component. Security is clearly a major component of mobile agents. Security mechanisms are needed for several security functions:

- *Secrecy of function and control parameters of a mobile agent.* A key requirement is for the function and controls of a mobile agent to be kept confidential from casual interested parties. Mobile agents have particular utility in managing remote offices.

- *Secrecy of results returned by agent.* A mobile agent may carry results back to a control point or may carry it forward to some other destination. This should be subject to confidentiality, especially in the event of cross-border traversal.

- *Authentication of source of the mobile agent.* A key concern for a host seeing a mobile agent destined for itself is whether the source of the mobile agent is one it expects. This is best done by a set of complementary mechanisms to enhance the strength of the authentication.

- *Integrity of agent functions and purpose at destination.* Another concern is whether the mobile agent has been intercepted and its contents changed between it leaving the source and the destination.

The security components are carried in the security payload.

The Host Environment. Because of the temporary and casual association between the agent and the host, the host needs to protect itself from possible rogue code causing havoc:

- *Protection against viruses.* In an unprotected environment, there is no reason why viruses cannot be transported as mobile agents. Limiting the points from which mobile agents are accepted reduces this risk considerably. Each of the security mechanisms further reduces this risk.

- *Protection against denial of service attacks.* Another form of attack is a mobile agent that uses up memory and CPU resources of the host. One defense against this risk is for a mobile agent to have a finite existence at a host, during which the host environment monitors for undue usage patterns.

  The execution environment at the host will need to be such that the agent cannot alter the specifics of functions such that its own termination is avoided.

- *Access control and indirection of access.* The agent should carry with it some profile about the type of things it is allowed to do. It should be provided access to interfaces and resources based on its generic or looked-up access rights.

  The agent should not be given direct access to resources. Rather, part of the host environment should include an agent-access interface. Other aspects of this interface are a standard semantics for errors, a standard way to kill an agent, a standard way of packaging results.

The Language Component. Mobile agents are likely to be developed to cater specifically to infrastructure management requirements at each enterprise, rather than shrink-wrapped code. This is therefore a potential area of in-house development.

The main requirements of a language for mobile-agent development is that the agent code should execute safely at the target host. While mobile agents are used in infrastructure management tasks their origination and quality can be controlled.

Mobile agents will need to create and manipulate data structures at the target host. However, the overwhelming concern is that the host must be able to protect itself from being memory compromised.

One way to achieve this is to use the powerful partitioning features of operating systems such as Unix. However, potential target hosts for mobile agents may have operating systems that are less secure.

Hence the language itself must provide the safety features. One way of achieving this is to craft a language variant of an existing language base where execution safety is assured.

When an agent gets loaded into the target host environment, it starts to interact with the local environment by executing local functions. This is called dynamic linking.

This is best achieved with an interpreted language, where each variable and function call goes through a look-up process at the interpreter. The interpreter can filter out access to memory and functions that take it outside a prescribed set of behavior.

An agent language would also need to be devoid of pointer-arithmetic functions and logic. While this is much valued in writing conventional programs, the ability for an incoming agent to manipulate pointers at a target host is one of the unsafest characteristics imaginable.

11.5.2 Role of Mobile Agents

Mobile agents have a major role to play in infrastructure management, in that they can be used to logically glue together information from diverse and distributed resources. The main rationales for using mobile agents in an integrative role is described below:

- Proliferation of agents within hosts makes infrastructure management both costly and error prone. The latter because large numbers of interrelated configurations have to be maintained.

  Mobile agents can replace several classes of static agents, including those that hold asset information, those for security baseline audit, and those that hold accounting and usage information. Most of such information is available "free" from the host's operating system or vendor supplied utilities. Such information also has little or no real-time significance.

  Mobile-agent code can be developed relatively simply to collect, consolidate and transport such information reliably to points of processing.

- While fault monitoring provides information after the event, state information can point to emerging problems. Annotating context to state information is a requirement when infrastructures are geared to delivering specific applications. The context of interest being the continued delivery of the application.

  Mobile agents can collect information about the health of essential resources for the delivery task. Such resources are likely to be highly diverse in character and relationships between the resources are likely to change unpredictably. Mobile agents can collect information from diverse sources and better cope with uncertainty by treating unexpected situations as exceptions.

- Client/server environments change in essential characteristics every 3 to 12 months. Mobile agents can be changed faster and their paths altered more quickly than any other agent technology.

  This makes it less likely that a changing infrastructure is going to be left without management visibility during some period. Because mobile agents can utilize existing management information, solutions are easier to find.

11.5.3 A Model System for Mobile Agents

The goal of any model for mobile agents is to develop agents that execute in a controlled environment where they can do no harm. This section describes a system from which the simple types of mobile agents required for management tasks can be created.

The language TCL/TK is an important part of the toolkit for infrastructure management. A variant called Safe-TCL has been developed for mobile agents. This is integrated with the Multipurpose Internet mail Extension (MIME) standard.

MIME is a standard for specifying the contents of a message. This is done in the e-mail header and allows a mailer receiving a message to send it to different applications, depending on the content of the message.

A content tag called application/Safe-TCL identifies the part of the message as a block of code that should be fed to a Safe-TCL interpreter if one is available. Other parts of the message may carry other types of information.

Associated with Safe-TCL is a Safe-Tk which allows a user interface to be distributed as part of the agent code. User interfaces allow the operations of the agent to be viewed locally or remotely. Control through the user interface may also be allowed—e.g., in a configuration agent. Safe-TCL and Safe-Tk are the first and second components.

The third component in this model system is the use of the Pretty Good Privacy (PGP) standard to provide the security mechanisms for encryption (confidentiality), message digest (integrity) and signature (authentication). PGP is briefly described in Chapter 10 as an enabling tool.

The fourth component is a control script that ties the mailer to the PGP service and the PGP service to the mailer and the Safe-TCL interpreter.

This means that mobile agents developed using Safe-TCL can be easily transported using e-mail. PGP is usable free for non-commercial purposes. The chain of events at the target host occurs as follows:

1. When an agent arrives as a message the mailer hands it to a control script.

2. The control script saves the message in a file and invokes the PGP service.

3. This decodes the message and verifies the signature, and returns it to the control script.

4. The control script finds a Safe-TCL interpreter with the required version.

5. The agent gets interpreted depending on any time of evaluation parameters carried in the message.

6. The control script invokes the mailer for returning any results for the agent's work.

11.5.4 Example of Uses of Mobile Agents

The use of mobile agents in this role is relatively new. Some generic uses are described below. Each such agent may be specialized with a profile or personality which defines the basic tasks it may do:

- *Collecting agents.* These can collect information from specific hosts reachable from a central point. A single agent may be made to traverse a set of hosts (in a random or in some sequential path). Alternatively, multiple agents may be released. The results are sent back from each stop-off point or may be concatenated as a results payload within the agent. Collecting agents have numerous uses in infrastructure management; some are described below:

  In periodic collections of metrics from hosts—where local host procedures cache the information for collection. This is also useful in sampling local variables or file systems.

  In consolidating information from heterogeneous sources—by defining a path for a mobile agent, information can be collected, normalized and transported. A mobile agent traversing in a defined path can consistently transport certain classes of events.

  Generally, information collected in this way should have no strict real-time delivery constraints. Even when e-mail is used, the fact that the e-mail domain is strictly confined to management servers provides good delivery characteristics.

- *Configuration agents.* These allow remote configuration at a host. Configuration agents carry information in attached files and can execute code manipulating the content of those files.

  A variation on this is to use a target host as a staging point for configuration of SNMP devices, for example. In this case the configuration script has to be translated to SNMP sets. When TCL is used as the agent language, TCL interface to an SNMP engine is available both commercially and in the public domain. Hence the TCL code in the agent uses the SNMP interface to configure and test each specified or discovered device.

  The secure transport of the configuration script to a local staging point inside a LAN is a sufficient condition for remote configuration. TCL can be used to develop safe configuration scripts that handle exceptions elegantly.

- *Auditing agents.* One use of mobile agents is to carry agents for auditing hosts or to use a target host as a staging post to audit hosts or devices local to the target host.

  Auditing is sometimes carried out on an ad hoc basis so that it cannot be predicted by users. The auditing procedure is also subject to constant change. Both these factors are supportable by mobile agents.

- *Control agents.* A unique feature of TCL is the TK toolkit for developing X-Windows front-ends. Several classes of control operations such as viewing and resetting RMON control variables don't need high levels of source authentication on a per operation basis.

  Secure transport of a mobile agent to a local staging point, and subsequent remote control using an embedded TK front-end is feasible. The X protocol can ride over a secure-RPC transport, making it relatively immune to masquerade-type attacks.

11.6 Scaling Agents

Scaling agents are agents that allow the current generation of agents to be deployed in large environments. The variables associated with scaling up are:

1. Number of agents in the environment—A single polling engine has a finite capacity to poll agents serially.

2. Capacity of the polling engine.

3. Communication bandwidth required for polling.

4. The burstiness of communications from the agents.

An architectural perspective on scaling agents is given in Chapter 7. Scaling agents are highly enterprise specific and individually crafted to enterprise's prevailing architectural perspectives.

Scaling is achieved through introducing a new level between the manager and agent model. Scaling agents can differ widely in complexity, we consider two such classes: dual-role agents and a general scaling services agent. Both classes of scaling agents provide the following services:

Polling service with reduced polling bandwidth—Reduce the bandwidth needed to monitor large population of agents through a divide-and-conquer approach. Each dual-role agent has responsibility for polling a number of agents. A polling engine has controls to allow polling frequency to be varied and relational operators to be applied to polled MIB object values.

Configuration services—Act as a staging post for configuring the lower level agents. The degree to which this is possible is dependent on the coupling between the scaling agent and the polled agents. Coupling is determined by writeable MIB variables at the scaling agents corresponding to configuration parameters at the lower level agents. Strong coupling implies that scaling agents are specifically built to support some finite types of agents. The coupling between the scaling agent and lower level agents can also be dynamic in the sense that the scaling agent/lower agent relationship is defined by configuration data specified at the scaling agent.

Trap forwarding services—Act as a staging post to collect, recognize and forward recognized traps to the higher level manager. A database of traps to match against, including corresponding translation values for notifying the higher level manager, is configured at the scaling agent.

Consolidated data services—scaling agents often include an MIB to record consolidated data from agents with similar properties. This service again implies close coupling between the scaling agent and the lower level agents.

11.6.1 Dual-Role SNMP Agents

These are agents that appear as normal agents to a manager and as a manager to a population of SNMP agents. Chapter 8, Figure 8.3 shows the relationship between the manager-agent model and dual-role agents.

Dual-role agents are largely used to offload responsibility for polling MIB objects of a population of agents, forwarding traps from the same population to a manager and in some cases as a staging post for the configuration of the lower level agents. Only a single such level can be interposed between the manager and agents. Dual-role agents are also called *middle managers* by some vendors.

SNMP dual-role agents are predominantly used in network monitoring. SNMP is the protocol at both service interfaces of the dual-role agent. The security inadequacies of SNMP have stopped most enterprises from using them in a control role. In fact, other than configuration most dual-role agents don't allow any SET operations.

11.6.2 General Scaling Services Agent

General scaling services (GSS) agents provides additional services that are required for infrastructure management. An infrastructure of networks, databases, hosts, and applications services has many different types of agents. GSS agents need to support this diversity. Such agents are likely to be server based and likely to be an in-house developed component.

Case Study 11.8: Dual-Role Agent Product

The *Domain Manager* from **Legent Corporation** (the technology rights of which have been acquired by Computer Associates) is a dual-role, standards-based agent specifically designed with solving scaling problems in large environments of agents.

Domain Manager notionally sits between a management platform and a population of agents to be managed. The product has capabilities for data collection using automated polling, exception-based reporting and trap re-generation.

In addition it provides facilities for analysis, local automation and correlation using user-defined rules.

A powerful feature of the Domain Manager is its support of the notion of data abstraction with respect to data it collects from the lower level agents. This is a tool to define specific contexts for management. Examples of such contexts are a domain that defines a business group's resources or one that defines a specific application.

Abstract resources can map to variables spread across multiple MIBs and at one or more lower level agents. Domain Manager is therefore a building block to develop a layer of software that processes raw data from lower level agents into information that is relevant to the defined management contexts.

This building block feature is especially enhanced by the ability to cascade Domain Managers or to establish a network to do complex processing.

It has two interfaces, one to the manager and one to the lower level agents. It supports SNMP at both these interfaces. It integrates with network management platforms such as HP Openview and SunNet Manager at its manager interface.

- *Support for different agents types*—Simple and autonomous SNMP agents as well as pattern-matching agents and mobile agents are all important to infrastructure management. GSS agents should support the scaling of all these types of "lower level" agents. Such agents may be deployed at any of the layers of the infrastructure and may use a variety of protocols and mechanisms (such as SNMP, RPC and operating system level inter-process communication mechanisms) to communicate with the GSS agent. The GSS agent has to multiplex events from these agents to the monitoring framework. It is also responsible for normalizing events within the enterprise's event classification. In addition the GSS agent is sometimes a staging post from which configuration of lower level agents can be carried out.

- *Support for redundancy*—Failure of a GSS agent can render all the lower level agents communicating with it to be *invisible* to the management framework. A key element of the GSS architecture, especially for remote offices is its survival when such failures occur in the management framework. This is done by having a secondary redundant

GSS agent available to "switchover" if the primary one fails. (This is highly feasible if the GSS agent only needs a low cost platform.) Associated with redundancy is the need to revert to a "normal" state when the failed component has been restored.

- *Support for security*—The GSS agent may need to guarantee confidentiality and integrity of information sent to the management framework. When used as a staging post for configuring agents it requires source authentication of the configuring entity.

- *Auto-discovery of agents*—Agents are added, changed and moved in an environment. Newly configured agents need to be associated with a GSS agent to support it. Part of the installation procedure for an agent should include the creation of the association, including any access parameters used by the GSS agent.

- *Filtering services*—A GSS agent may support hundreds of agents in a local environment. Events forwarded by the GSS agent to the management framework is usually only a subset of the total events received. The forwarding may also be rate-limited to guarantee low impact on the production network. Another common type of filtering is that of the same event from a source being repeated within a time window.

- *Support for multiple transport protocols*—GSS agents need to be able to use different protocols to transport information from lower level agents. Common protocols for this purpose include secure-RPC—a high integrity variant of RPC, any protocol usable as a manager-to-manager protocol (such as SNMPv2 or CMIP). Information for reconfiguring lower level agents may be transported to the GSS agent using different protocols. Secure-RPC and mobile agents over secure e-mail are feasible alternatives.

11.7 General Issues in Agent Deployment

Agents are programs that have a closely coupled relationship with complex software such as operating systems and applications. This section looks at three common issues this coupling raises: the economics of agent deployment, agents as factors that complicate change management and the security implications in agent deployment.

11.7.1 Agent Economics

Agents viewed collectively are the highest cost item in a large environment. This by virtue of the numbers and different types of agents that are typically deployed.

Other than capital cost, the operational and support costs need to be considered. Case Study 11.9 shows typical costing for agent purchase in a global investment bank. This environment is admittedly highly instrumented—but realistically so for the support of a state of the art client/server infrastructure. This cost is especially significant when viewed from the following perspective:

1. On a per unit basis as a percentage of the unit cost of desktops and servers.

2. The typical lifetime of the desktop workstation is in the region of 24 to 30 months. An upgrade cost for the agent can be expected on this cyclic basis.

3. The support fees to the vendor adds an average of 15% of total cost per annum.

4. The sheer number of agents incurs additional internal support cost in terms of installation, reconfiguration, testing, etc. This is about 20% of cost.

Infrastructure management groups that work at enterprise level have several ways of controlling cost elements:

- The first and foremost is to negotiate for enterprise-wide licenses. This is especially valid for enterprises that are at the beginning of a growth cycle for the associated technology. A key factor is the 2- to 3-year life-cycles of hosts.

- Make increasing use of public domain software. In specific areas such as security there is a strong argument that software that has undergone "public" scrutiny is far superior to software developed in "isolation" in vendor labs. Since there are some highly reputable sources of such public domain software it is an option well worth examining. Two key areas are in monitoring the baseline of host security and inventorying the network and host resources. Successful use of public domain software agents, however, requires greater degrees of in-house expertise and skills.

- In-house development of agents becomes an attractive option in certain size environments and in environments that are very security conscious. Given that modern tools make agent software development relatively easy (given good developers and software management skills), in-house development provides a whole set of advantages. This includes control over function, control over change cycles and control over quality. The reasons that more organizations with large infrastructures don't embark on this road is to do with philosophy and not having a full picture of the real costs of agent deployment.

11.7.2 Leveraging Capital Costs

Deploying agents is a major cost item, whether in terms of capital expenditure, buying advanced competencies and skills or running in-house development teams.

A key rationale of instrumenting the infrastructure using agents is to enable operational processes (and the applications that automate these processes), to have a uniform view of the

Case Study 11.9: Cost of Agent Deployment in a Client/Server Environment

Agent Types	Workstations 2,000	General Servers - 130	Database Servers - 50	Total
Host Resource	$100,000	$11,700	$4,500	$116,200
Security Baseline Monitoring	global	license		$70,000
7 layer RMON-II Performance	global	license		$200,000
Application Fault Monitoring		$26,000	$10,000	$36,000
Database monitoring			$30,000	$30,000
Security Event Monitoring		$29,250	$11,250	$40,500
Remote Office Monitoring				$150,000
				$642,700

infrastructure regardless of diversity such as architecture, host platforms, operating system differences, etc.

Hence to get benefit from an investment in agents, a parallel investment is needed in applications for processing data from the agent population.

This is why standards are important in agents technology. A standards-based agent that is deployable across operating systems or across platforms or across software architectures is needed in order to leverage from applications that process data from agents. Unfortunately, there is currently a dearth of such standards. RMON and Host Resources MIB are not enough.

Moreover, most vendors take the opposite view, which is that the value-added parts of the agents supersedes in importance the underlying standard's utility. This allows vendors to differentiate products in admittedly very useful ways—however, this should be recognized as a short-term view.

11.7.3 Agents as Complicating Factors

Another view of agents is that they constitute a distributed layer of software closely coupled to both the management framework at a layer above it and to the entities being managed at a level below it.

This closely coupled relationship complicates operational aspects in several ways.

Installation and reconfiguration of agents in large environments is as we have seen not confined to a single agent type. Multi-agent deployment requires automation tools. When the vendor does provide a configuration tool, it is bundled into a console-based product with a myriad of other functions. The choice is therefore between proliferation of consoles versus in-house development of multi-agent configuration tools. Without simple tools it is a time-consuming, error-prone process to use a half a dozen different console-based applications.

Close coupling necessitates some agents working with root privileges. This may be contrary to internal security policies relating to software from certain sources or types of software. Often, major usefulness of the agent resides in the fact that it allows control of the managed entity. When protocols such as SNMP are used in a control mode, security policies are likely to be breached.

There is an inevitable lag between changes at the two layers, above and below the "agent layer" and the agent itself catering to such changes. The reasons range from the vendor's development cycle not being synchronized with changes at the related layers, to the vendor losing interest in a variant of the agent or the agent vendor going out of business.

This lag compromises the management capability by giving incomplete or inaccurate information, or in the worst case, rendering the agent inoperable.

The severity of compromise depends on the way the agent is coupled; is it through published or standard interfaces or is it manipulating internals of the managed entity through other types of interfaces that are prone to sudden change?

A hidden danger of having multiple agents to hosts is that the performance of the host can suffer under a given configuration and "computational" stress conditions. Also an agent vendor rarely does integration testing, hence changes in system and software versions can impact the stability of a deployment. Agent deployment should follow the same rules of piloting, testing and verification as other types of software.

11.8 *Agents in the Intranet Context*

The availability of low-cost intranet-based infrastructures based on browsers and web servers offers new capabilities for infrastructure management. New capabilities discussed in Chapter 8, "Architecture of Management Frameworks," include:

- The ability to stage information from multiple management agents into a single summary page for use by general users.

- The ability to build a universal form-based client service point to collect information from users and to distribute information back to users through e-mail.

- Pre-set links to key vendor's software and service resources.

The agents discussed until now were constrained by the coupling with their controlling entity. The second limitation is that of the protocol between the controller and the agent. In conjunction with intranets, agents have the potential to break free from such limitations and

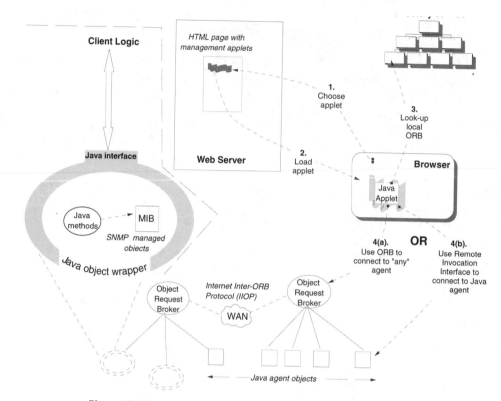

Figure 11.9: *Agents in an intranet-based management framework*

to act as mini-applications in their own right. This is illustrated in Figure 11.9 where an agent is a dynamically loaded application in its own right. It uses a variety of services to find and interact with conventional types of agents.

Locally collected data can be transported to central web server(s) using a variety of options. Using distributed file system functions, using a "file relay" agent or using a mobile agent—are some of the different techniques available.

11.8.1 Intranet-based Mini-Applications

There is currently a gap in the infrastructure management tools market for tools that can consolidate information from multiple sources. One of the reasons is that such tools don't slot cleanly into any single vendor's categories.

Intranet technologies now offer powerful and secure languages such as Java (see Chapter 12, "Tools and Enabling Technologies") to be used to develop mini-applications (applets). These applets are distributed between the web server and the browser. There are two main types of management applets:

- Those that are attached to management data. These attachments are downloaded and executed in the browser when viewing the associated data.

- Those that are executed in the web server as part of the web server's functionality in processing management data. These may have a client counterpart in the browser.

In the infrastructure management context, such applets are a final link in making conventional agent technology work in a cooperative manner. This also applies to operating system utilities that support single functions.

The new economics of software development, offered by environments such as Java and the web, means that there is now a real possibility of totally new sources of management applications.

This source comes from the development of a "cottage industry" for the infrastructure management field. The tools for intranet application development also provide new opportunities for in-house development that is independent of vendor's platforms.

11.8.2 Candidates for Management Applets

There are several areas of client/server infrastructure management where such applets could automate a class of administrative activities that have the potential to provide major benefits when done proactively. Currently, such activities consume a lot of time when done manually and therefore are often postponed due to more immediate concerns.

Applets are also a means of integrating information from the many powerful utilities available for individual operating systems. Applets allow a framework to be built for controlling these utilities. Three such areas are discussed below:

- *Application license metering.* As enterprises provide desktop machines for all employees and in some cases multiple machines, the capital cost and maintenance costs of licenses is a significant item. The active management of licenses has direct benefits to the enterprise. Minimizing costs and meeting legal requirements are two key benefits to be gained.

  As discussed in Chapter 1, the evolution of client/server deployment means that most software currently used in an organization was bought by individual departments. Most organizations have little or no idea about the total number of software licenses they own, even at a departmental level.

  License management is complicated in large client/server environments because multiple departments and multiple servers are involved. The ability to meter and track software usage accurately across "all" servers leads very often to a drastic reduction in software acquisition costs while complying with vendor license agreements.

In the context of an infrastructure management group, licenses across all the predominant operating systems are ideally treated together within one function.

Before license metering can be envisaged, a software inventory needs to be defined. Each package in the inventory needs to have a unique identity. There are often several inventory management applications and utilities (for each operating system) on the market. Other utilities provide license metering and administration functions at each local server. Typically, metering allows the correct number of concurrent usage, the users who access applications, the times when users were denied access due to copies being unavailable.

Consolidating such metrics from multiple servers allow a more rational analysis on where the bottlenecks are, whether licenses can be shifted from one server to another. The power of consolidation is that license-usage patterns can be averaged across a significant number of servers—regardless of where they are sited. In global organizations, license agreements should take into account that a license may be used anywhere in the world.

A web server-based applet for consolidation and distributing usage analysis would make such an exercise a part of the operational function rather than a project.

- *Disk and file usage monitoring.* Machines, especially server class machines need adequate disk space to function. Knowing the patterns of disk-space usage helps to pinpoint potential problem areas. Collecting such information from each server is however both time-consuming and data-intensive.

Operating system utilities, third-party utilities and file-system utilities exist to collect such information from individual machines. In client/server infrastructures, there are dependencies between servers—for example, a file server, a broker server and a database server may all need to work together to deliver a client/server application. Emerging problems in inter-server relationships require analysis across servers in existing delivery relationships.

However, nothing currently exists to automate the analysis, summary and distribution of disk-usage patterns. The data from collection utilities can be staged at a web server. A server-based applet can be driven by browser-based control parameters.

An associated area of monitoring is file-system monitoring. Such monitoring is key to understanding many performance problems. In a client/server environment the monitoring needs to be across all the servers involved in delivering a service. Other reasons for file-system monitoring include security logging of access to key files.

Again, the problem is not that there aren't utilities to collect data about file access. Rather, consolidation from multiple collection points and analysis tools are the missing parts.

- *Procedure scheduling.* Many day-to-day activities of infrastructure management should be defined by procedures. In a client/server environment these procedures are likely to be relatively complex and to span across several machines.

For example, backup may be best done in a specific order, so that all the data relating to an application's service delivery are clustered together. Or file copying and distribution across servers with multiple operating systems may be needed. Other aspects of scheduling are to execute a job at a specified clock time and to repeat an activity at regular intervals.

Such sequences are best run automatically. A web based applet could be built to design common job schedules, execute the individual activities and post events indicating the status of each job in a web page.

The client part of the applet would define the user interface for the tool, manage and control function and data validation. The client would run in the browser, allowing activities for any layer of the infrastructure to be scheduled from one "neutral" point (i.e., independent of any management platform).

11.9 Books for Further Reading

Cockayne, William R., and Michael Zyda. *Mobile Agents.* Manning Publications Co., 1997.

Harrison, Colin G. *Agent Sourcebook.* John Wiley & Sons, 1997 (to be published).

Muller, Jorg P. (editor). *Intelligent Agents III* (Agent Theories, Architectures, and Languages). Springer Verlag, 1997.

Stallings, William. *SNMP, SNMPv2 and RMON* (Practical Network Management). Addison Wesley, 1996.

Wayner, Peter. *Agents Unleashed* (A Public Domain Look at Agent Technology). AP Professional, 1995.

Tools and Enabling Technologies

Areas covered in this chapter

- Third-party applications for management platforms and common levels of integration with the platform

- Strategic areas of infrastructure management needing tool development

- Tool selection criteria in sample areas of infrastructure management (performance and "cluster" configuration)

- Generating "deltas" and "flows" from historical information

- Middleware as an enabling concept/tool to integrate infrastructure management areas

- Uses of warehousing and replication in infrastructure management architecture

- Fundamental role of directory technology and its role in unifying naming needs across an enterprise, including infrastructure management

- Object orientation fundamentals and their role in developing infrastructure management systems

- Java fundamentals and roles in developing infrastructure management systems

The previous chapters have provided a multi-disciplinary perspective of infrastructure management from business, architecture and technology viewpoints. In this final chapter the focus is on looking slightly beyond the conventional technology of management. For infrastructure management to progress towards a discipline, innovative tools are needed.

Infrastructure management users, however, need to look beyond the product offering of traditional vendors in this area, and more towards harnessing some of the technologies used for developing client/server applications.

Infrastructures to support client/server applications cover a wide range of technologies from silicon-based compression in WAN links to artificial intelligence techniques used in event-correlation software. There are several strategic areas of infrastructure management—such as performance management and ticketing. The trends in some of these key areas of management tools suggest that "fusion" of the infrastructure layers is indeed accelerating.

Management platforms provide different degrees of coverage of the infrastructure layers (as discussed in Chapter 9, Section 9.2.1). Third-party tools are available primarily for "open" platforms and "open" platforms predominantly cover network management and also tend to lean towards systems management.

The integrated managers and system managers tend to supply their own suite of "harmonized" applications with much less in the way of third-party offerings. This probably reflects the smaller market size, (and hence the reluctance of vendors to risk their resources), rather than the lack of "openness" of these platforms.

The basic tools on a network management platform are essentially little more than a MIB browser (with a sophisticated user interface) capable of accessing and manipulating MIB objects and mechanisms for staging events. For the raw data in these management objects to be of use operationally, other applications are needed to process this data into useful information. Without processing, the data has limited consumption within network management processes.

Hence the true worth of a management platform is in terms of the third-party application products that are integrated into the platform or can use data on the platform.

While the core technology described in Chapters 9 to 11 more or less define the current status quo, infrastructure management's scope is constantly being extended.

In this concluding chapter we define a set of software technologies that are the building blocks for large, distributed computing frameworks. Such large frameworks are relevant to infrastructure management in integrated enterprises. The two main goals of this chapter are:

- To look at selected, strategic areas of infrastructure management and tool-trends in the area.

- To briefly look at some strategic technologies which are likely "enablers" for achieving progress in the infrastructure management field.

12.1 Third-Party Applications

Many third-party tools provide specialized functionality that is not available from the platform vendor or the tools themselves are "best-of-breed" compared to the platform vendor's offering.

From a user viewpoint, the main issues in the integration of third-party applications with popular platforms (such as HP Openview) are:

- No architectural models management objects beyond the MIB or "containers" for holding other types of management information such as states. This results in the reinvention of the data model by each application. The major side-effect of this is the amount of resources each application takes on the physical host. (Hence in reality the power of the host determines the number of applications that are operationally viable on a management platform.)

- Applications are very task specific and often applicable only to a niche area of the problem domain. Hence while an application may have functionality that is applicable in another area of the problem domain, organizing the information for the purpose is either cumbersome or impossible. An example is that tools for configuring a router backbone, could have been applied to configuring a switch backbone by plugging in a different set of objects for switches. This kind of genericity is however not in the interests of the vendor.

- The customizing and maintenance of multiple applications on the management platform generates a huge overhead in the infrastructure management organization. Given the complexity of each tool, most tend towards an un-optimized state of existence over relatively short periods of time. This is unfortunately generally true even when a vendor's local experts are involved in the process.

Using new releases or versions of applications or platform software, the chances of failure of previously working "family" of applications increases as they interact at the host operating and file system level. This leads to unreliability of the platform, which cannot be solved by any single vendor.

The management tool market is highly fragmented on the one hand with lack of good tools in several key areas of infrastructure. However, tools also have overlapping functionality, making operational choice difficult.

Third-party tools often have proprietary consoles, and integration into management platforms is mostly very superficial (usually the platform merely allows the tool to be launched from the menu and the menu structure of the tool follows the platform's style conventions).

The integration of third-party tools with the management platform can be classified in terms of one of the following levels (where level 1 is the lowest level of integration):

- *Level 1*—The lowest level of integration is at the menu level of the platform. Integration at this level merely means that "navigation" is possible between the platform, the third-party application and back to the platform. This allows an application to be launched from the platform user interface. The only context passed (if any) is at the device level where a referred icon or icon cluster on the platform map is passed to the application in terms of network address(es) for it to communicate with the devices. The use of the platform's protocol engine is rare at this level.

- *Level 2*—The next higher level of integration allows the platform and the third-party application being capable of unilateral or bilateral transfer of status information. This is in addition to common reference to the objects being managed and use of the platform's protocol engine for all communication with the managed environment.

- *Level 3*—The application integrates to the platform console or command line at this level. The application may be able to take or output information to common data structures such as flat files or the operating system's file system. This level of integration extends to use of the platform's event architecture (especially internal state models) and database interfaces (such as a specific SQL server product).

- *Level 4*—The application uses one or more of the services provided by the management platform. By and large this kind of integration occurs only with stronger commercial bonds between the application vendor and the platform vendor (and is therefore relatively rare). The most common additional services used through platform APIs are managed objects, client/server functions such as queuing, more comprehensive use of map and user interface, database services such as replication and synchronization, event mechanisms including filtering and logging.

12.1.1 Tool Evolution in Selected Strategic Areas

The aim of third-party application vendors is sell their applications for as many platforms as possible. This however requires significant development resources and specific platform skills to achieve the higher levels of integration. The resource crunch is determined by the level of abstraction in the software technologies. Typically, the application is built for the most popular platform and then ported to others.

Level 1 is likely to remain the commonest form of integration—as this eases the porting and hence availability on multiple platforms within reasonable time windows. Levels 2 and 3 begin to occur only when the platform vendor and the third-party vendor form some closer business partner relationship.

As client/server systems get complex in function and life-cycle terms and their reach extends over wider geographical areas, certain areas of management get highlighted. These are strategic to the discipline of infrastructure management because without evolution of tools in these specific areas infrastructure management as a discipline cannot evolve. For example, tools to understand and tune the performance of a client/server application are critical to the application's long-term viability in a changing organization.

Table 12.1 lists a subset of such areas that are strategic to managing client/server infrastructures. Platforms have generally fallen behind in catering to strategic issues. A generation of re-vamped integrated platforms such as CA Unicenter TMN and the Tivoli/IBM Systemview merger offer promise. However time is still needed for these promises to come to fruition.

The current status and trends for third-party tools in each area is briefly discussed below in Table 12.1.

Table 12.1: Strategic Areas of Infrastructure Management and of Tools

Sub-area	Trends in Tool Development
Performance management	Covers the network media, hosts and applications. Monitoring for exception to pre-set thresholds remains the model. Definition of more standardized MIBs such as RMON and RMON 2 allow individual parts across the whole infrastructure stack to be monitored. The ability to look at performance on an "infrastructure-as-a-system" level is still in its infancy, with integrated platforms such as CA Unicenter showing the most promise. Performance management is a critical issue because of the multiple systems and layers that have to cooperate in an application's delivery.
Asset management	Covers the network cabling, components, hosts, peripherals, base software and applications. No standard way of collecting or storing information has emerged. Relational databases are appearing for storage, however, the lack of scehemas that cover the whole infrastructure remains a problem. Asset management is increasingly important in recycling equipment within an enterprise and managing the life-cycles of client/server applications. Also in an enterprise context, organizations tend to have global agreements with vendors and suppliers on pricing, service, upgrade paths, etc. Accurate asset information is a precursor to fully benefit from such deals.
Router, switch and hub "cluster" management	Client/server applications are heavily dependent on a robust network architecture—with properties such as self-healing, modularity, bandwidth-as-needed hierarchy being critical to application delivery. A key requirement is in configuring a collection or subsystem of multiple devices (rather than just one device at a time which is highly error prone). Error at the network level often affects end-users very directly. Configuration tools for managing router backbones are beginning to appear although none is generic and have limited use in a heterogeneous router environment. Limited progress in other areas although tools to manage "virtual LANs" are in development with some hub and switch vendors.

Table 12.1: *Strategic Areas of Infrastructure Management and of Tools (continued)*

Sub-area	Trends in Tool Development
Wide area network management	With the global deployment of client/server applications and the intranet phenomena, the wide area networks are critical to some types of client/server application delivery. Monitoring line quality, interface setup (including filters) and capacity monitoring are top priorities in enterprises that use leased line meshes. Other areas are in data compression and encryption, both of which are needed in delivering mission-critical applications in sectors such as banking and finance. Applications have progressed little in all these areas.
	With the emergence of public switched services such as frame-relay and SMDS, many enterprises are moving away from self-managed WANs. In Virtual Private Networks, monitoring the service interface for SLA conformance is the primary focus. Applications are emerging in this area, however, national variances service details have limited the markets for such tools to single countries.
Event visualization and event management	There has been little in the visualization area although the more innovative platforms such as Cabletron's Spectrum provide a fixed set of contextual views and integrated platforms such as CA Unicenter TMN promise to go considerably further. Ticketing remains the primary mechanism of tracking and managing events. Visualizing events and tracking individual events to a closure remain the primary strategy for increasing the service levels of infrastructures for mission-critical applications. Also a process-oriented infrastructure management organization is difficult to build without tools that can automate context identification during a crisis. Ticketing and associated process workflow tools need to span the same geographic extent as the mission-critical client/server applications being supported. There are several industrial strength ticketing systems which complement client/server application deployment.
Simulation and planning	With the requirements of client/server applications changing over each of its mini life-cycles, infrastructure changes are often needed after a number of successive changes. Simulation is a model-based approach to understand the traffic flows at each layer of the infrastructure—i.e., ranging from packets at network interfaces to service requests at servers. The ability to try out what-if scenarios before changes are made would help life-cycle changes to be smoother. In reality however simulation tools are still very difficult to get useful information out of for a variety of reasons, including internal service models that cannot handle country variances, semantic gaps between actual deployment and topologies understood by the tool. Also the often prohibitive cost of the tool is a major inhibitor to wider usage.

Table 12.1: Strategic Areas of Infrastructure Management and of Tools (continued)

Sub-area	Trends in Tool Development
Infrastructure usage and accounting	As infrastructure for client/server applications stabilize and begins to be viewed in terms of a utility, with service provision to different classes of users, several trends emerge. Many enterprises are thinking on charging users for infrastructure services. Charging users directly is also a natural step from outsourcing. Users can buy different classes of service and have a single point of contact for all infrastructure services. Tools in this area are beginning to appear. A market driver is the need to meter communication service provision from telecommunication suppliers. The discrepancy between what is seen at the user-end and what is claimed by the supplier is a useful method for strengthening price negotiations.
Privacy and firewall management	With the deployment of client/server applications globally and the dependence on e-mail-based messaging for global communications in many enterprises, deployment of security is essential to maintain business status quo. E-mail is capable of carrying corporate documents, mini-applications, etc. as attachments. Privacy and safety are therefore key issues. Tools to manage privacy services and firewalls both on an enterprise scale are critical needs. This is similar in some respects to the configuration of device clusters described above, however, here multiple types of components need to be configured. For example, a typical security architecture includes globally deployed firewalls to connect over public links and encryption of all information over the links to stop back-door attacks through a second country. Encryption and firewall services need to be managed in a coordinated fashion.

12.1.2 Performance Management

Performance management is a strategic area in infrastructure management. Performance problems plague client/server infrastructures more than any other class of problems. With prior "intelligence" many problems that hit the infrastructure in sudden and catastrophic ways can be avoided. Proactive performance management includes the following activities:

- Baseline setting for each class of performance agents, sets the scene for viewing performance at the different levels of the stack.

- Exception monitoring against the established baseline.

- Baseline change management.

Performance monitoring is dependent on the quality of data from distributed agents. This in turn is based on the baselines established for each type of agent.

Standardized MIBs include those for Remote Monitoring RMON of network media traffic, and the HOST MIB for monitoring UNIX hosts. RMON 2 agents (of which there are several pre-standard version products) allows higher level protocols such as SQL to be monitored.

Several vendors have extended the HOST MIB to provide process level information. There are also several prototype MIBs to define application-level monitoring.

The main model of performance management is to establish a baseline of performance on a business domain basis. There are two areas of deficit in application functionality around this model, especially in large environments where thousands of elements may be involved:

- Functionality for establishing the baseline all too often still requires each RMON agent or HOST to be individually programmed. Maintenance of the baseline in terms of changes is hard to achieve manually and error prone. Ad hoc applications being developed as part of the customizing process are currently the only remedy to this.

- Maintaining the baseline introduces a new security vulnerability, in that the source of the change cannot be authenticated with currently used protocols. Change of baselining parameters can be used for denial of service type attacks.

Case Study 12.1: Selecting Tools for Client/Server Performance

Client/server communication is at some time or other liable to performance bottlenecks. This could either be due to a problem either in the infrastructure (network, database server or dependent services) or may be due to inefficiencies in the client/server application components.

Especially with an incremental development model, the relationships between client/server components change over the increments. Hence many performance problems tend to occur after software upgrades and well after the application is first deployed.

Trouble shooting client/server performance problems requires good instrumentation—this is often provided by software-based agents that are either permanently placed or downloaded for the purpose. Instrumentation can also be provided by network analyzers. The RMON 2 (pre-standard) products offer one way of collecting application level messages. RMON 2 probes are however even more difficult to configure than RMON probes for the higher group functions. Hence without good configuration tools they are not very useful for application traffic decodes.

Table 12.2 shows questions to guide the development of selection criteria for performance management tools. A key consideration is whether performance management should be a reactive function or a proactive function. Since the latter is more sensible the next question is whether performance management should be viewed in terms of a permanently available capability or whether its should be "portable"—on an application case by application-case basis.

Table 12.2: Key Questions to Ask in Selecting Client/Server Performance Tools

Question	Beware of
Does the product fully support the version of database you are running?	Small under-capitalized vendor.
	Support of too many database products.
	Database vendor has not heard of product.
Does the product scale across the configuration you want to test?	Can it measure across a WAN?
	Can it measure in a multi-tier structure?
Does the product add to existing bandwidth problems?	Simple agents that have to send collected data to a console for storage.
What latency measurements are carried out and how is it done (or can you depend on it)?	Unsynchronized timers between multiple measuring points—timers diverge over time.
	Comparison of internally generated references for queries/responses pairs—wrong responses can be paired to queries.
	Can't handle multi-threading SQL interfaces.
Does the product functionality overlap with database administration tools?	SQL diagnosis toolkit with timed message decode capability.
Does the product use pre-standard RMON 2— what are the plans for upgrade to standard?	Vagueness of product plans (or doubts on need to conform to a standard).
How does the product present data and what configuration facilities does it provide?	No graphical display capabilities.
	Manual configuration of probe parameters.

12.1.3 Asset Management

Asset management is a strategic area in infrastructure management due to the capital "recycling" implications of managing client/server life-cycles. It includes the following areas of functionality:

- Asset discovery is the ability to auto-discover equipment classed as assets. In some organizations details of infrastructure components such as routers are excluded from the discovery process.

- Asset tracking is the ability to track an asset automatically during add, move and change processes.

- Asset journaling is the ability to hold an ad hoc database of annotations about the asset.

Asset discovery and tracking is closely allied to the topology auto-discovery algorithm of the platform although most asset management applications conduct their own discovery process. Some algorithms are dependent on certain types of agents being present in the asset being tracked.

Hence the limitations of topology auto-discovery (namely incomplete coverage, timeliness of discovery, overheads of discovery, controlling extent of discovery) apply to automated asset discovery as well.

Asset discovery and tracking on an enterprise scale can consequently be only partially automated. The following type of assets can be discovered and/or tracked:

- *Desktop and server hosts*—discovery is largely automated through use of local agents, especially with the emergence of DMI for PC systems and similar MIBs for SNMP supported hosts, the information should be more uniformly attainable.

- *Network visible components*—only partial discovery is possible, again due to similar problems to auto-discovery in platform maps (non-IP elements, occlusion by topological details) and the remainder has to be manually entered. Since this class of components tends to be relatively long-lived (2 to 3 years) manual entry is by and large an unavoidable part of any asset survey process.

- *Cable and physical infrastructure*—almost none of this discovery is automated. Survey information is used to draw map representations.

Storage for asset discovery in a large environment requires good underlying database engine support. Since it seems inevitable that some details of most assets have to be filled in "manually," it leads to an argument that a directory-based tool (fronting the relational database) would improve the ability for the asset database to evolve with the changing enterprise.

Asset databases also need to support references to mechanisms for holding "annotations" such as maintenance history and fault log for the asset.

With assets that have a finite life-cycle such as specific versions of client/server software, asset related information may be set up during distribution, during configuration and subsequently on usage.

The information in the asset database can become inconsistent (in some cases resulting in false alarms) unless the asset discovery process is synchronized with the change management process. Automated reporting and financial breakdown of the asset base are usually applications developed internally in the organization. Such development can often be justified on downstream cost savings.

12.1.4 Cluster Management (for Router, Switch, and Hub Backbones)

Router and hub vendors were among the earliest supporters of SNMP and hub vendors also were some of the earliest developers of SNMP stations specifically for their products. These stand-alone stations have either evolved to full-scale management platforms (e.g., Spectrum from Cabletron) or their functionality has been "loosely integrated" into mainstream management platforms. Current router and hub management tools are primarily device-at-a-time management tools for:

- *Configuration*—For setting up and changing configurations on the network. (These tools are, given the complexity of these devices, some of the most essential tools.)

- *Monitoring*—Enterprise-specific MIB variables and traps to identify fault conditions specific to the device.

From the earliest days router and hub tools have adopted a user interface style that reproduced the front panel of the device. Fault presentation with reference to physical modules has a continuing rationale for these components since the remedy for a fault on a physical module often involves replacing or resetting the module. Similarly, configuration is also with respect to physical modules and physical interfaces.

The status of hub ports shows the connectivity to desktop and server hosts. A single hub may support multiple cable media with logical busses forming connectivity between them. Such logical structures are often manipulated during add, moves and changes.

While most management applications in this area work at the single module level, notions such as "virtual LANs" are driving the need for configuring at a logical or subsystem level across multiple physical devices or clusters.

A relatively new component in network design is the use of switching components to enhance the bandwidth and latency characteristics of network protocols. Switches are likely to replace routers in many topologies, especially in single protocol (IP) environments. Current generation of switches have begun the introduction of integral RMON agent to provide traffic information from the switch. Currently, switches in large topologies are both hard to configure and monitor on a system basis.

Case Study 12.2: Selecting Configuration Tools for Routers

Routers are the mainstay of IP based global networks. The management of routers has always been a problem. Without a "healthy" router backbone, corporate traffic is likely to encounter major problems.

Router vendors themselves rather than third parties have been responsible for developing products in this area. Hence most products are specifically for a single family of routers. Key requirements of router configuration tools are defined in Table 12.3.

Configuration tools may however work for only a subset of a vendor's routers. This can sometimes cause problems. Most organizations have given up trying to get routers from multiple vendors to interwork—especially in industrial strength production environments. The subtle differences in the way routing and management algorithms (that support standards) often result in inexplicable side-effects in traffic flow or result in the instability of the router backbone.

12.1.5 WAN Management

WAN management is a critical part of client/server application management when these applications are deployed globally. Most corporate data WANs are still dependent on mesh topologies of leased (and even dial-up) lines. Outside the U.S., however, high capacity lines are still very expensive. Most corporate networks depend on links in the range of 64 KBit/s to 1 MBit/s for inter-site connectivity.

The use of "pre-router" components such as multiplexers are still not uncommon to split bandwidth. Today many organizations outsource voice (and newer video) services to (more cost-effective) Telecom carrier-based transports, while retaining the leased lines to carry data. Tools for network management on the scale of existing WAN include:

- *Element managers for non-SNMP devices*—such as multiplexers and DSUs. Such mangers may be integrated into a manager-of-manager (MOM) platform and monitored and controlled from the MOM.

Table 12.3: Key Questions to Ask in Selecting Router Cluster Management Tool

Key Questions to ask	Notes
Can the tool verify the basic safety of a configuration?	Without some verification or safety checking the tool does not add much value.
Does the tool support configuration templates?	Without pro-formas like templates, the tool will not make complex configurations any simpler or reproducible.
Does the tool support distribution to multiple routers?	Without the ability to distribute "similar" configurations the tool cannot be expected to configure a router backbone any better than a one-at-a-time configuration.
Does the tool support software distribution and asset management relating to routers?	Upgrading router software is a relatively common activity (once every 3 months or so). Software distribution requires similar tool functionality.
Is the tool part of any router monitoring scheme?	Configuration of some parameters can be combined with monitoring their values.
Can the tool be used in any modeling?	What-if models allow configurations to be simulated before actual loading into a router or router backbone. The ability to "export" configuration data to external tools allows such tools to be developed.

- *Managing hardware-based compression*—to maximize the usage of expensive link resources. The failure of these components can severely slow down the network. Hence in addition to link failure, the correct working of these components determines performance design centers in mesh networks.

- *Managing hardware-based encryption*—many organizations prefer all communication exiting the premises into carrier-based leased lines to be encrypted. Such devices have to be monitored to ensure failure does not cause clear text to flow for longer than necessary. Key management is done out of band.

- *Managing hardware-based security firewall*—some links into the premises may be from a Point of Presence on the Global Internet. Hardware-based firewalls are the first line of defense, hence their monitoring and detection of alarms or unexpected patterns are of extreme importance.

- *Managing link failures*—through out-of band dial-up services such as ISDN is a low-cost means of providing link-level redundancy. In some cases redundant links can boost the capacity of a link during peak demands. Secondary links such as ISDN need to be carefully configured so that they kick-in only when "genuinely" required. (For example, certain types of denial-of-service attacks saturate a WAN link, the backup links providing additional bandwidth will contribute to the effectiveness of the attack.)

- *Modeling traffic flows across WAN interfaces*—to understand potential hot spots through capture and analysis of source-destination talkers, application types, packet types, transport characteristics. The models should take into account the fractal nature of network traffic. Performance monitoring of a WAN link against a set of thresholds and the number of hits occurring in the thresholds will indicate change in traffic patterns

- *Monitoring global state-of-the-WAN mesh*—provides network managers with the ability to concentrate energies in solving the right problem or with the right supplier. Many large corporations still deal locally with each service supplier. Others who have been through a mergers and acquisition cycle also have the same problem of a fragmented supplier base. Deploying client/server applications over such a framework introduces significant operational risks. Such monitoring is a first step in mitigating this risk.

The role of WAN connections (relative to client/server applications that use them) is essentially to link together LANs on either side of the WAN. All too often the bandwidth requirements for LAN interconnect, from client/server applications, soon outstrips the ability of the mesh network. This is especially true of client/server application deployment that get scaled-up.

A major cause of network outage at the WAN link level is the sudden changes in user demand for services across a link—for a given configuration of client/server application. Such outage manifests itself in terms of router interface problems. In other cases the interface itself remains up but application elements time-out causing application failure.

Given the order of magnitude mismatches between bandwidth in the LAN and bandwidth across a commercially viable WAN link, slight changes in the LAN can have amplified effect over the WAN link. The fractal nature of traffic complicates the life-cycle of global client/server applications (see Chapter 6, Section 6.7.6).

In many organizations developers and business planners of client/server applications rarely talk to network engineers or managers, let alone involve them in the business planning process.

As the move from the current generation of client/server to truly distributed computing occurs, the WAN connections remain the weakest link in the network topology. To ensure that this link is not the cause of business application outage requires understanding of end-to-end traffic flows.

Given the disproportionate costs of WAN operations, cost re-allocation of costs to business units remains a requirement in many organizations. Most solutions for usage accounting, however, remain *ad hoc* and prone to subjective interpretation of results.

Managed IP data networks are an evolving trend, opening up the possibility of outsourcing all global connectivity services ranging from *e-mail only* to *IP* to *encrytped IP* services. The future WAN management is therefore likely to be very different for many organizations, whether small or large.

12.1.6 Security, Privacy, and Monitoring

Increasingly, security related events have the potential to bring business operations to a standstill. The single most critical danger to client/server environments comes from security breaches. Most organizations however have a blind spot about security and only have superficial capability to deal with real contingency. This unfortunate situation has already been exploited by high technology crime syndicates which move from organization to organization, demonstrating their ability (using some indefensible weakness), to bring down a network, and to collect ransoms for not bringing the networks down.

In large enterprises security-related events ranging from viruses to unauthorized change of workstation addresses have brought down networks before support staff could react, let alone diagnose the problem.

Examples from many other spheres of human intercourse, where rules have been defined for the common good, have shown that relatively simple deterrence measures have dramatic effects on behavior. Being continuously monitored is one such measure.

While many organizations have invested in developing a security policy for the deployment and use of distributed computer resources such as workstations and server hosts, little effort has been expended in automating the monitoring of how those policies are being observed by the employees (and increasingly business partners).

The manual audit of paper logs by "security staff" totally unfamiliar with the technology of client/server and networking is relatively common. In fact such paper trails are a common role for ex-mainframe security staff.

Integrated management platforms such as CA Unicenter TMN already provide the means to generate and transport security events to a common monitoring framework.

A more recent, critical area of security is the real-time monitoring of external firewalls that may be deployed with the outside world as well as internal firewalls to be used for containment of sensitive business areas. The basic principle of a firewall is as a focus of security features including filtering, authentication and authorizing.

Again, the integrated managers such as CA Unicenter and Tivoli seem to be leading the field with an understanding of the need for firewall monitoring applications.

12.2 Determining Flows and Deltas

Event maps show point "status" (at the device and subsystem level), some time "soon" after they occur. Surfaces and other 3D models can show relationships such as the combined status of a set of geographically distributed servers in a single map.

Flow implies a time dimension being added to static information so that information is viewed across a span of time. Visual mechanisms such as surfaces can also be used to "replay" recorded information held in a database. User interfaces allow search parameters to be visually defined, and for simple requests to be dynamically created as a result are relatively easy to build using tools such as Visual Basic and TCL/TK. The requests are generated based on simple rules such as parameter substitution and sent to the database.

Commercially available performance management tools such as HP Netmetrix can show information as traffic "trajectories"—e.g., between a set of workstations and a set of servers. Such trajectories can be shown for any layer protocol—depending on the tool's capabilities to decode the different layers. For example, the standard RMON specification covers only the lower layers (some products extend RMON to cover specific application service protocols such as Network File System (NFS)).

In a wider sense, information that flows through the infrastructure can be perceived at higher levels of abstraction than the packet level. Processes are one such abstraction. Processes use one or more applications and each application uses infrastructure resources. Of particular interest to the infrastructure management organization is information pertaining to the execution of support processes. Metrics on how a client/server application is used by a business process is also important in managing the performance of the process itself.

In a global organization, process-related information flows across geographic and business boundaries. Application servers that support business processes and also service functions such as helpdesks are usually established on a regional basis.

The volume of information into and out of regional "hubs" is dependent on the operational capacity of the hub point. Process-related information is held in "process artifacts"— e.g., a trouble ticket in the case of the problem-management process, a "change request" in the case of a change-management process. In many cases a single ticketing technology provides the basis to define artifacts for all processes—leading to trouble tickets, change tickets, order tickets, etc.

Over a period of time, the volume of "transactions" relating to different processes (problem management, change management, etc.) changes and, hence, also affects the processing capacity needed for each type of transaction. The actual level of change (delta) and the rate-of-change values are important to understand trends. Deltas and rate of change values are used in capacity planning at every level, ranging from network connectivity to staffing levels. Because processes use application and lower level services, inefficiencies at the process level manifest themselves as increased demand for infrastructure resources. Hence a simple scale-up of resources rarely solves such capacity problems.

Traffic-related flow information is provided by performance management tools working together with RMON and RMON 2 agents that continuously monitor network traffic. Process-related flow information however has to be generated from raw data in process artifacts (rather than data packets). Process artifacts are stored in a database.

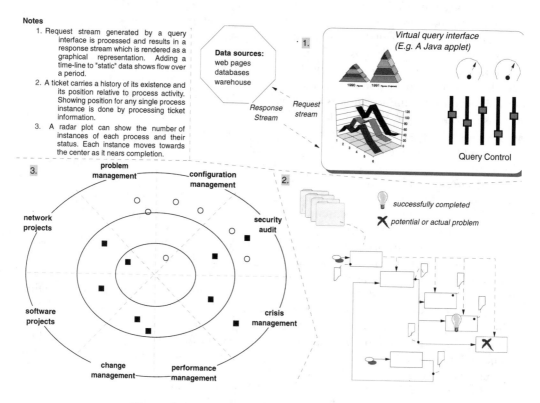

Figure 12.1: *Extracting information to generate flows*

Access to the information fields of a support process's artifact such as a trouble ticket is usually through an SQL interface. Business processes are often deployed using one or more commercial workflow products. Access to information within product specific process artifacts is sometimes only possible through an API, sometimes across an SQL interface and sometimes not at all.

12.2.1 Helpdesk Related Flows

In most enterprises the helpdesk is the central point of contact between users and the support organization. The efficiency of the helpdesk determines the perception users have of the competence of the management organization. A helpdesk in every site is likely to be impractical, especially when the offices are of different sizes.

Requests to a hub helpdesk therefore flows in from remote offices supported by the hub site. The types of requests depend on the services that are available through the helpdesk. Different requests are submitted to the helpdesk using the phone, using electronic forms, or even "hot buttons." Each type of request is recorded in a medium that persists after the execution of the request. Many organizations have standardized on a "ticket" as this persistent medium.

A ticket records all the data relevant to each specific type of submission by the end-user. Hence the ticket associated with a problem report will have generic fields for problem reporting. The values for these fields may be provided directly by the submitter or may be filled-in by the helpdesk staff.

Generic field information is generally augmented with "free form" information such as annotations (created by the people executing a problem management process), current status and escalation path (determined by the specific of the problem management process). A ticket associated with equipment order will have another set of generic fields.

Flows of user to helpdesk and helpdesk to user information allow analysis of service provision, especially to a geographically dispersed user base. The flows generated using information from persistent sources provide a guarantee that the information being used to generate flow information is complete and representative of the actuality.

In global enterprises such as a global investment bank, helpdesks ideally need to be available 24 hours a day. Helpdesks therefore need to share information so that management processes (such as problem resolution) can be "handed over" to different helpdesks—to be worked on a 24-hour basis. This requires global standardization of helpdesk architecture.

Achieving helpdesk standardization is however easier said than done because of intercultural barriers that often need to be overcome. Helpdesks that standardize on the ticket concept and store tickets in an industrial strength relational database can use the powerful storage and replication features of these databases.

Replication allows helpdesk teams to automate the distribution of "persistent" information in process artifacts such as tickets. This distribution is a part of the wider architecture of a corporate helpdesk and occurs in the course of executing management processes.

12.2.2 Simulation and Planning Tools

Simulation is a powerful analytical tool used to study complex systems before they are built as well as to analyze the effect of changes to existing systems. Chapter 2, Section 2.4.3, cites some of the uses of this powerful tool in the gap analysis of infrastructure capability in specific areas.

Using simulation as a tool in the systems development life-cycle would greatly enhance the quality of IT based solutions. Quality of the IT that is delivered is a problem, especially in complex business domains such as investment banking and manufacturing.

The awareness brought by modeling stretches through the life-cycle—from design to deployment and post-deployment. Client/server applications are becoming more complex, are deployed with more components, have wider deployment extent and larger user bases.

Architects, designers and managers responsible for delivering the IT infrastructure and services need intimate understanding of some of the wider issues and their impact on service delivery paths:

- *Impact of application portfolios changing.* The business model of an organization determines the actual use of different classes of applications and the constituencies of users that use the applications. As the number and distribution of these users change, application traffic requirements change.

- *Impact of corporate changes.* An organization undergoing a major change such as business re-engineering or merging with another organization is likely to end up with different application mixes. Many businesses are in the process of re-defining their global roles, most of which have a serious impact on how IT services are delivered.

- *Changing demands on WAN capability.* The globalization of businesses is increasing as well as the use of high bandwidth services such as video conferencing. Global businesses require their mobile staff to have access to corporate resources on a 24-hour basis from wherever in the world. This also puts new requirements on corporate security.

- *Impact of the use of middleware.* Middleware has emerged as a technology to connect up islands of data and generations of technology. It has however also introduced an "opaqueness" to end-to-end delivery of services. New types of integration problems stem from the inability to see part of the IT delivery chain.

Most simulation and planning tools available today are not suitable to modeling the complete service delivery paths. They can however provide indicative information about the impact of changes to an IT environment. Such information is still valuable before the provisions of an infrastructure are changed.

At the lowest parts of the infrastructure, current simulation tools can provide valuable insight to moving from one technology base to another. For example, moving from shared to switched network technologies has implications for how traffic will get "clustered" at different classes of servers such as network files and communication services. Such deltas need to be studied before production environments are moved to newer technologies.

Newer modeling tools will depend on building and looking at different scenarios. Data warehouse-based data and analytical "engines" executed using Java in browsers are two components of newer modeling applications. Scenarios are dynamically built. Currently, however, such tools have to be developed in-house.

12.2.3 Usage and Accounting

The infrastructure provides a set of services—that enables applications to be delivered to business users. In many organizations old divisions have evolved to global business. Each global business usually has a different profit center, but may share IT infrastructure.

In many organizations there is an implicit need to charge different businesses on the basis of actual usage, or proportion of usage. While unit cost of IT has dropped in a large number of components, the overall trend is for IT costs to increase. This is largely because a drop in unit cost tends to increase demand.

For example, decrease in WAN costs is an enabler to use high bandwidth video-conferencing across two sites. Overall the business may benefit through reducing "time to engage" and savings on travel costs.

Charges by IT resources and services (and service levels reached) are likely to become a model for most businesses. Components of IT charging include both activities and assets that provide "IT bandwidth."

Charge-back is likely to be on the basis of IT resources consumed at a business process level. Each business process will be supported by one or more service delivery paths. Some of these paths will be shared with other processes in which case an accounting model will be needed to share costs. Examples of components in a charging model (by business process) include:

- *Data storage quotas allocated by business processes.* Data storage needs constantly increase, and increasingly an overall quota model applied across a hierarchic storage scheme is needed.

- *Application licenses used by business processes.* While licenses are the predominant method of paying for bought in software, in the future other, more granular, "per usage instance" type models are likely to be available. License usage management in the meantime is a major cost component.

- *Number of service paths unique to supporting a business process.* Service delivery paths have different support costs. Some service paths are unique to a business process, others are shared. By costing a service path down to the component level, cost of delivery can be applied to business processes. When business processes change then the service delivery paths are also likely to change.

- *IT quality measurement and SLA monitoring.* Increasingly, many infrastructure services will be bought from service providers. For example, only a few large enterprises can afford to build a global switched ATM backbone. Others will buy the capability as a service—which is equivalent to outsourcing the development and operations of an enterprise's long-haul network capability. An outsourced service is integrated with other outsourced and in-house services to build a service delivery path. Quality and service metrics from each component have to be combined to provide quality of service views of a service delivery path.

At the lower levels of the infrastructure, namely at the switches and routers, the capability to see packet flow in terms of end-to-end characteristics is beginning to emerge. Also the ability to "reserve" bandwidth for different application traffic types will change the way service delivery paths are built and costed.

12.3 Middleware

Middleware is in an important new type of software that was first treated as applications but is increasingly managed as part of infrastructure level service.

Middleware is a layer of software that provides communication, location and data transparency across multiple platforms. This allows a client of the middleware services, to remain unaware of:

- *Where* other parties that it interacts with reside, and

- *How* these parties organize information or distribute the information.

Middleware's origin is from client/server development in large legacy environments and in heterogeneous client/server environments where information from diverse systems on diverse platforms needs to be integrated.

Concurrent to such IT integration, business change is also very often being executed in each environment. For example, middleware is of particular significance to infrastructure management when organizations merge with or acquire other organizations. The application systems and infrastructures of two organizations are rarely similar enough to be of any significance.

The concept of middleware is relevant in the enterprise management context because increasingly information from several significantly "large" management platform have to be integrated to provide a "stacked" view. The drivers for middleware in infrastructure management and include:

- Data essential to infrastructure management processes reside on multiple platforms and *ad hoc* databases in most enterprises. Tactical tools developed in the context of a process engineering support organization are by and large built using off-the-shelf software packages. Middleware can provide a major role in providing various types of transparency described above.

- On a similar theme, there are users looking for a model of strategic re-deployment of network management technology, without loss of enterprise management data gathered by previous generations of tools. Middleware components can bridge the old and the new.

- The reality in many enterprises is that there are multiple management platforms and stand-alone consoles. Each plays useful functions in limited contexts. Middleware to integrate and combine information from diverse sources provides significant improvement in ROI on current investment (especially when the capital discount cycle has not been completed for the investment).

- Integration of information produced by a network management application and critical but loosely integrated third-party application(s) on the platform. Such integration is required for example to manage service delivery paths.

- Enterprises looking for global inter-operability solutions often conclude that in-house development is the only short-term option. Middleware helps to leverage from components on the market.

- Related to in-house development is that developing inter-operability solution requires skill sets not easily found on the market with the infrastructure management domain knowledge. Middleware can help to ease the transition to infrastructure management.

Figure 12.2 shows the conceptual relationship between middleware services and infrastructure management. Middleware increases transparency so that previously closed systems can be integrated together.

12.3.1 Middleware for Infrastructure Management

Middleware is relevant to the field of infrastructure management because the reality in large enterprises is that there is a diversity of management platforms and tools on which the current operational integrity is based. No single platform can replace all these "legacy" tools, neither would most organizations want to de-commission working solutions.

Also, in the context of process engineering within a support organization, information from these diverse operational platforms needs to be intelligently integrated for use in these processes. The use of middleware-based solutions helps to answer the following questions:

- Given the deficit in the tool market for managing the large global enterprises how can in-house solutions be developed now to make the best use of current technology investments, while not locking out promised products?

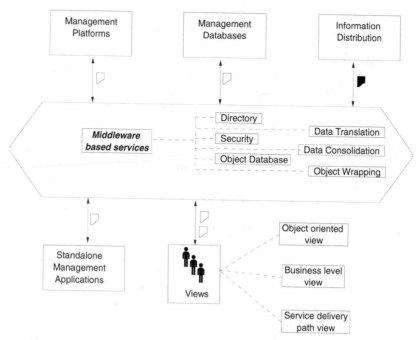

Figure 12.2: *Middleware services pertinent to managing infrastructure*

- Given that the model of management platform being the point of integration for third-party applications, not quite working to the user's advantage, are any other models of integration viable?

Middleware as a software technology is currently touted by many product vendors. Experiences in using middleware have been mixed. (See Case Study 12.3, "Caveats in Using Middleware" for one set of conclusions). Middleware products are based on one of the following:

- *Database and object repository technology*—The most common means of providing middleware services is to integrate data from diverse sources into a relational database or a data warehouse. Database applications then factor and recombine the data to provide different informational views of the data. A future development of this is the use of object-oriented databases where "real" entities can be modeled. Several database vendors provide high quality tools and products for building blocks of this model. Another technique is to put an "object wrapper" around data staged at a data warehouse. The object wrapper allows the data to be manipulated within the context of an object level abstraction. For example, such an object may be built to maintain the complete history of an infrastructure server.

- *RPC and object request broker (ORB) technology*—RPC is a mechanism for peer-to-peer relationships to be formed between client/server parties. Object broker technology provides location transparency and a means of programming the relationships between the parties. RPC is described in Chapter 10, Section 10.6.2, and ORBs are described in Section 12.6.2 of this chapter.

- *Messaging technology*—Messages are a means of distributing data from one or more sources to one or more destinations. Some of the destinations may be applications that selective reprocess data in the messages and re-send it. Messaging as a concept is described in Chapter 6, Section 6.2.

Within the infrastructure management field, the manager-of-managers platform described in Chapter 9, Section 9.6, is a potential candidate to take on the mantle of middleware. Vendors currently provide a point of control integration, however this is a long way away from data integration between lower level platforms.

A database/repository based middleware is probably the easiest approach. No such products currently exist "out-of-a-box," however most of the required components exist. These include data-warehousing building blocks deployable over NT, object request brokers and object wrapping.

12.3.2 Message-Based Middleware

Messaging middleware can be used to establish a stable infrastructure for other high-level application protocols such as RPCs and ORBs. Middleware used in infrastructure management need not be domain specific as suggested so far. As (or if) middleware services becomes

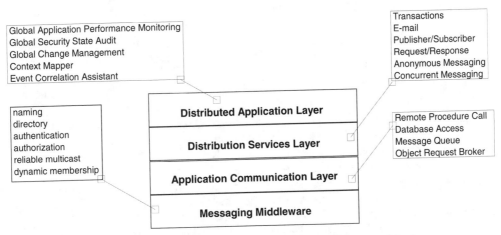

Figure 12.3: Infrastructure management and middleware architecture

established as a method of developing "high-end" distributed applications then the same tools will be applicable in realizing infrastructure management applications.

An abstract relationship between infrastructure management and messaging middleware is shown in Figure 12.3. Middleware's role (and the longevity of that role) in the wider context of distributed application development is currently under debate. Factors include new models of distribution offered by the intranet concept as well as the complexity of working with current middleware products.

A common management software tool that has the characteristics of middleware is a distributed ticketing and workflow system. Such a system can already connect together different

Case Study 12.3: Caveats in Using Middleware

A survey of eight major client/server projects (exceeding 20 man years each), using middleware components, by a small software consultancy, showed six failures of various degrees and two outstanding successes. Within the "successful" project teams, middleware was perceived to have been instrumental in delivering complex product requirements within the time and cost constraints.

Within the failing and failed projects middleware was blamed for many of the unexpected problems that arose. In this survey, the following five common factors distinguished the successful projects:

1. The choice of middleware products was done from an overall architectural perspective. This perspective especially took into account the respective middleware product's life-cycle, and the means by which the vendor's technologists and the client project team could maintain close cooperation during the course of the project.

2. The projects were undertaken within a relatively formal systems development methodology. This included in the one case a risk management framework being developed and managed. The formality allowed problems to be identified and captured early.

3. The middleware vendor agreed to provide direct consultancy specifically to help in overcoming the "occlusion" of the operating system functions by middleware products.

4. Special tools and instrumentation were developed to help debug (and subsequently help operate) applications written over the middleware layer.

5. Special emphasis was given to staffing a performance management function that worked concurrently with application development. This function helped in early understanding of the relationship between middleware, the operating system and the application components.

The overall conclusion of this survey was that while middleware is an enabler for developing sophisticated client/server functionality, a matching degree of sophistication is required in architecture and development processes. Middleware products are not suitable for "out-of-the-box" use. This would suggest that success in the use of middleware may be tied in with the maturity of the development organization.

management platforms for the purpose of raising process "artifacts" and managing these through an infrastructure management process such as fault management.

Current generations of ticketing and workflow systems can also be architected to be high-level messaging passing middleware—connecting together the information flows of infrastructure management processes.

In this model, the ticket is a high-level message medium carrying process-specific information between producers of the information and consumers of information. While basic routing based on content of a ticket is often provided as a function of the ticketing software, other higher level functions are likely to be needed, including security, translating business rules into message routing and message addressing.

Essential concepts of messaging based middleware to consider at the architectural level include:

- Reliably asynchronous messaging so that multiple messages can be concurrently processed.

- Transactional message queuing so that a message can be recognized as part of a transaction sequence of messages. This allows a transaction to survive failures in a service delivery path and for there to be guarantees of delivery of message.

- Translation from one management "world" (e.g., SNMP MIB) to another (e.g., SQL table).

12.4 SQL Databases and Warehousing

The deployment of systems and network management tools results in large quantities of data being produced from the managed environment. In addition, directories are often "back-ended" by SQL databases.

To be useful in management roles and within management processes, data has to be organized and managed in such a way that its value is enhanced to the organization. "Value-enhancing" activities within data management include:

- Compressing information on a time-series basis so that the most detail is for the useful information. Hence in the case of performance databases, past information gets progressively less useful over time.

- Schemas that define how data should be structured and stored on a global level. Developing and managing schemas relevant to the way the organization works with the data rather than generic models developed by vendors.

- Building applications to automate time-consuming or error-prone activities in a management process. Examples include packaging and distributing baseline performance thresholds in a large environment and software version control of network components.

- Define unambiguous responsibility for the maintenance static data (e.g., configurations, skills and competencies) pertaining to infrastructure management.

Enterprise-wide infrastructure management requires a data-engineering viewpoint to be adopted. Most tools on the market today have little concept of a use for the data beyond the tool's functionality. Most of the large and influential tool and platform vendors are opposed to any standards that would allow an "out-of-the-box" data model for infrastructure management. As vendors dominate and manipulate many standards bodies, at least in relation to users, this situation is unlikely to change.

A data warehouse is one of the "meta" tools available to an infrastructure manager for synthesizing enterprise-specific views that cut across functional tool sets and organizational boundaries.

Data warehousing is also a means of defining stepping stones to an object-oriented architecture for infrastructure management. A key question in a future move to an object-oriented architecture is what happens to all the current management data. Once a warehouse is built, parts of the warehouse can be encapsulated within "object wrappers" and migrated to behave as objects.

The logistics of the deployment of database, directory and warehouse engines needs careful consideration as it forms a "data-backbone" of the infrastructure management architecture.

- Putting the database and directory engines onto a dedicated platform for speed advantages. Different databases and directories have different access requirements. Availability of industrial strength directories and database software on the "Intel" platform makes multiple machines in this role feasible in many organizations.

- Resilience at the disk storage subsystem level. Coupled with status monitoring this manages the risk of the commonest hardware cause of database failure in the context of a single geographic site. The static information should also be replicated so that in the event of a site disaster data critical to re-building the environment is not lost.

- Responsibility and skills for administering the database and directory engines should be developed. Training of users to use developed applications.

12.4.1 Consolidating Management Databases

Network and system management applications have for the most part specified their own database structures. Within the network management tool space, most platform vendors now recognize that SQL databases are an essential marketing feature. Most third-party tool vendors still work to proprietary structures.

In many cases the database is the least developed part of a product. Vendors often claim performance reasons for the absence of a database architecture.

Within the system management tool space the situation is much worse. These tools are aimed at a distinct user community, namely systems administrators. Systems administrators have traditionally little or no exposure to data structures outside file systems. Hence the data architecture of systems management tools is often centered around file systems and more recently a notionally object-oriented model.

In most organizations therefore there are a large number of tool-specific data residing in a variety of "data containers" (SQL tables, files, objects) and platforms (stand-alone, network management, system management). Each data structure on each platform is likely to be tool specific. Hence over a decade of packaged-management tool development, the data architecture component is the least improved from a tool-user's perspective.

Within many organizations the consistency of most management data, in whatever form it is stored, is likely to be highly suspect. Data consistency is dependent on the disciplines of capturing and storing that in turn are driven by management processes.

Within an infrastructure management context, management is with respect to "end-to-end" service delivery paths. An end-to-end view requires information in more than one platform and tool databases to be consolidated. Examples of end-to-end views are for asset management, fault management and capacity management of a service delivery path. A service delivery path may be confined to a single LAN or may have a global extent.

Some end-to-end views such as fault management require "near real-time" data about the service delivery path to be available. Data consolidation for end-to-end views can be done on a "just-in-time" basis or be architected as a data warehouse. Recent advances such as the Java language and platform make the former highly feasible (see Section 12.7.2).

Data warehousing is a more immediate (and architecturally stable) alternative for "slow-moving" information. End-to-end capacity management and service-path asset management are two candidates for the warehousing approach. The two key aspects of building a data warehouse are:

- *The design of the interfaces* between the warehouse and the data sources that provide operational data. In the case of the management data sources these may range from SQL based interfaces to scripts for extraction from flat files to extraction across tool APIs.

- *The design of the warehouse* which is likely to evolve in an iterative manner with the evolution of service path itself. For example, a business application may be deployed in an incremental manner. The service delivery path therefore extends over the deployment. The warehouse, its location, its distribution, etc. become design issues.

Extraction of operational data and its subsequent "insertion" into a warehouse is however not enough for generation of future end-to-end views. Some of the complexities likely to be faced before moving data from the various sources to a warehouse environment include:

- *Conditional sources of data.* Some service paths may be "special cases" of the more generic service path. The input source(s) to be chosen, in computing a service path, view differently with the case being viewed. For example, a service delivery of a business application may differ between large offices and small offices. Hence computing views for each will be with respect to using different types of resources.

- *Difficulty in understanding or selecting data.* Many management tools don't define the structure and semantics of their data. Hence selecting operational data for reflection in a warehouse may be difficult and in some cases based on wrong information.

- *Data needs to be normalized.* Different sources will keep data types such as time and date in different formats. These need to be converted to the warehouse standards. Also re-naming of data elements is usually needed.

- *Data needs to be cleansed.* This may range from making data consistent across two "subsources," to filling in missing parts of data sets to correcting for known bugs in the data source. Defaults have to be defined to patch-up data sets.

- *Data needs restructuring.* It is unlikely that the data components of a warehouse designed to provide service path information are going to be satisfied from single sources without restructuring or recombination.

Despite these hurdles, data warehousing provides real opportunities to develop service path views for non real-time views of service path delivery models. Interestingly, even in the case of fault and performance data, where a warehouse generated view is inappropriate for operational management, the views still provide trends for a service path in the respective dimensions.

12.4.2 Replication

Database replication is an important tool in infrastructure management where a database is distributed across multiple database engines. The replicated databases may be "co-located" at one or many sites.

The relative locations of the primary and replicated databases is dependent on the objectives of developing a replicated database.

A replication system copies database tables from a "primary" database into multiple "target" databases. The replicated data is "loosely consistent" with the primary data.

The replicated data essentially lags behind the primary data by the amount of time the replication system takes to distribute changes from the primary to the replicated points. Replication is used to meet the following objectives:

- *Performance*—Multiple copies of the database allow concurrent access to the data. Hence overall performance of certain types of distributed applications is enhanced.

- *High availability*—Because there are multiple copies, the loss of one copy (or even the primary itself) does not make the whole organization incapable of accessing and using the data.

- *Cycling*—Different locations rotate as the primary "site" as part of a business model such as "follow-the-Sun" support or as part of disaster recovery where a replicated site becomes a new primary site if disaster strikes the primary site.

Each database is a replicate database or the primary database. Primary databases are updated by client applications while replicate databases only hold data-replicate data. Replicate data is not updated directly by employing design rules for the application.

Replication provides flexibility in providing redundancy of key databases (such as a ticket database associated with problem management) by the replicated database being a warm standby. The location of the warm standby could be local to the primary or at a remote site.

Replication also provides solutions in global infrastructure management. Each site "owns" its own data while subscribing to data at other sites as data replicated from the sites.

Replication is supported by all major database management systems such as Sybase and Oracle. As replication is done on a subscription basis, where the select statement defines table level subscription, great care is needed in designing replicated databases.

For example, if triggers are embedded within subscribed tables, these can be inadvertently fired at multiple sites with damaging results. Another challenge is to manage concurrent updates through designed mechanisms. Before designing and building replicated databases an architectural framework for security and administration needs to be defined and followed.

The primary aim of such an architecture is to be aware and hence avoid dangerous side-effects from being propagated from the primary to the secondary.

Transformation of a non-replicated database to a replicated one is unlikely to be viable. Replicated databases need to be developed from scratch.

12.4.3 Open Database Connectivity (ODBC)

ODBC is an important component in being able to integrate SQL and non-SQL databases from applications written on the Wintel platform. Prior to this, most infrastructure management applications developed in-house, and needing to access information on multiple databases, were difficult to develop on the Wintel platform.

Where this was possible, it had to be done over Unix and to use Unix workstations. While Unix was feasible in "high-value" environments such as investment banking and utilities, it is less so in IT cost-sensitive environments. Lower cost development tools and platforms are needed for infrastructure management to be viable in these latter environments.

ODBC is based on a standard SQL client call interface specification and therefore has wide industry support. ODBC is accessed by an application, through an API, to talk to many types of data sources. These range from proprietary databases on personal computers to mainframes. The API is supported through a generic driver manager that can control drivers specific to each data source. Drivers are likely to be loadable at run-time. (The ODBC model is in effect very closely related to the Wintel print, where a print manager loads print drivers specific to specific hardware.)

Applications can however access and use multiple driver managers. This is a major advantage in writing applications that integrate multiple data sources as well as applications that apply the same logic to multiple data sources.

Drivers have been developed for a range of sources ranging from SQL databases such as Sybase and Oracle to "desktop" databases such as Access and Paradox. In many organizations such small databases hold personal information that is nevertheless important in building service path models.

ODBC is however not necessarily a strategic tool. Most database management systems however have proprietary extensions. Hence ODBC allows "pass through" for applications to exploit special features of target database engines. Applications which use pass-through functions will not be portable.

Many ODBC drivers are produced by third parties and may also conform in different ODBC compliance levels. When applications connect with more than a few databases, changes at the databases need to be tracked by the respective drivers. Hence such applications are in danger of suddenly stopping when a change is made in one of the contributing data sources.

12.5 Directories

Directories are a special kind of database for storing and accessing information about real-world entities. However, these real-world entities can be organized into logical frameworks to give us context.

Currently, every organization abounds with directories provided by desktop and server-operating systems (e.g., NIS in Unix and NDS in Netware), the network protocol suite (e.g., DNS in TCP/IP suite), messaging systems such as e-mail (Lotus cc:Mail) and even by individual client/server applications.

"Internet" applications need to communicate from both "inside-out" and "outside-in." As applications become network-centric, a general purpose directory service becomes a key enabling technology in unifying internal and external communications.

OSI's X.500 Directory (in its multiple incarnations), has been the key influencer over the last decade for scalable, secure, global directory services. The key protocol of the X.500 standards is the Directory Access Protocol (DAP).

While the X.500 standards provide a foundation architecture, like many of its OSI brethren, DAP is impractical for implementation on most of the world's computers—namely Windows/Intel machines. A result has been the Lightweight Directory Access Protocol (LDAP), developed at the University of Michigan, and which runs over TCP.

LDAP does not require an X.500 compliant directory (however, it can indeed connect to a "genuine" X.500 directory through a LDAP/DAP protocol gateway). LDAP is able to connect to any hierarchical attribute-based directory. LDAP however requires the support of the X.500 naming model including the support of X.500 objects such as country and organization.

The existence of widespread implementations of LDAP has triggered renewed interest and the formation of a vendor-driven bandwagon. Key vendors such as Lotus, Novell, Netscape and even Microsoft have joined. This makes a cross industry, inter-operable directory highly likely at last.

12.5.1 Directories and Infrastructure Management

A single directory model for an organization can transform the way the infrastructure is managed. Directories allow nothing less than the efficient administration of distributed resources. This translates to less errors, better responsiveness and better user relationships.

A directory provides a set of basic services. This includes *naming* and *protecting*. S*earches* to be done for specific information with only partial knowledge of a resource's name, structure or content.

A directory service plays a special role for infrastructure management—it allows an integrated view of data stored in different infrastructure management systems' internal representations through "pulling" information from these diverse databases models to a directory model. This is shown in Figure 12.4.

An industrial strength directory also allows information to be reliably distributed across a global organization from a central point of change. Examples of information that requires global distribution include organization changes and changes to cryptographic keys.

In infrastructure management terms, the type of information that is most suited for storage in a directory is information that is subject to change, but on a relatively infrequent basis: organization, people, IT assets used, sites, and support structure are all liable to change, however, the pace or rate of change is slow.

Hence a person may change names, say, by deed poll or marriage. However name changes are likely to occur only a very few times during the person's spell at the organization.

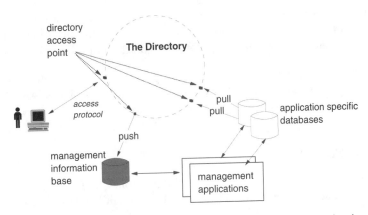

Figure 12.4: Relationship between a directory and management databases

Moreover, the duration of stability between successive name changes is likely to be very long (in directory time). Advantages that directories offer infrastructure management data are:

- *Process integration*—Most organizations suffer from the "disconnect" between infra-structure management processes such as *add, move* and *changes* and related processes such as *hiring* and *firing* or organizational re-structuring conducted at the human resource and upper management levels. A distributed directory service can enable information flow as well as synchronization between processes. The geographic point of control also becomes less relevant allowing truly global business processes to be built.

- *Intranet management*—A corporate directory service is essential to change manage-ment of a corporate intranet. For example, the current hardcoded URLs are at the same stage of maturity as the first client/server applications (where each client "knew" all the servers it could connect to) making changes difficult to manage. A dis-tributed directory could form the basis to locate and manage the global distribution intranet resources such as Java applets, mobile agents and ActiveX controls.

- *Replication of the data*—Data can be replicated so that in the event of site failure com-ponents and processes that depend on information in the directory can still access it from another site (although the price may be a degraded level of service). Replica-tion also allows local copies being accessed, rather than a central source, speeding up access operations.

- *Security*—Only personnel with relevant access rights and passwords to authenticate access to sub-trees can view and manipulate information in the directory. Directories may include security sensitive or personal information when its role is as a central repository or corporate information.

- *User interface*—Consistency for both applications that a human being uses to access the directory and application processes. This allows one set of expertise to be suffi-cient to cater for both management application development and integration work.

- *Scaleability*—A distributed directory can grow and evolve with an organization because it is built from a number of consistent building blocks. Also, different sizes of organizational units can be accommodated as can future mergers and acquisitions

12.5.2 Use of LDAP

LDAP is both an access protocol for human access directory servers as well as an API for pro-grams to communicate with the same servers. LDAP can be utilized in several ways in desktop and server products:

- The initial use of LDAP will be in web browsers to access and search directories. Both Netscape and Microsoft say their browsers will support LDAP.

- Future versions of LDAP (possibly LDAP 3) will support industrial strength authentication mechanisms (e.g., X.509 public key certificates). With strong authentication, LDAP can be allowed to access corporate resources.

- LDAP 2 provides Kerberos-based authentication as the "stronger" option. This is sufficient for limited LDAP server-to-server communications including directory replication and referrals to other LDAP servers in a search path.

See Case Study 12.4, "Three Vendors Approach to LDAP" on projected exploitation of LDAP by three key vendors.

Worries however abound about the lack of explicit specification in key areas of distributed directory usage—including a standard access control mechanism and strong authentication. Other deficit areas are in the search capability for items that need to be referred to another directory server and lack of multi-master replication. The latter two deficit areas and their consequences are described below:

LDAP Referral. When a query is made to a directory server and the query fails due to the absence of the required information at the node, LDAP allows the server to refer the client to one or more servers which may be able to answer the query. The client thus becomes aware of what information is stored where because referring server returns the name of the second server. The LDAP client then connects to the referred server. Referrals are however based on static entries manually made in the directory server. Because servers cannot learn about each others' contents automatically, and cannot process the "historical" state of referrals, simple configuration errors have the potential to set up infinite loops.

LDAP Replication. LDAP assumes a single master which makes all the changes to the directory database. "Slave" servers provide replicas of the master, allowing the access and search operational loads to be distributed. In simple uses of the directory (such as e-mail and intranet), "reads" outnumber directory writes by many orders of magnitude (say 100,000 reads for every write). In more complex uses (such as active agent distribution) this ratio falls. The single master is however a single point of failure—in the sense that its failure means the directory cannot be changed. On an enterprise scale this compromises availability of the full-range directory services.

12.5.3 The LDAP/X.500 Model

Vendors such as those in Case Study 12.4, will enhance LDAP to suit their cross-product strategies. Hence Netscape is developing an extension that allows access-control, while Microsoft is developing integration with its domain management concepts.

Case Study 12.4: Three Vendors Approach to LDAP

Three key players (in terms of market share and influence over the Wintel user population) are Netscape, Novell and Microsoft. All three vendors see a key role for directory services in extending their products to an enterprise scale. Netscape has been a pioneer in the adoption of LDAP. Novell and Microsoft changed their respective stances on directory directions as a result of the momentum behind LDAP.

All three vendors see LDAP as not only providing basic levels of inter-operability in heterogeneous environments but also as being the enabler for intranet and Internet applications. The summary of these three vendors' currently understood position on LDAP is shown below:

Points	Netscape	Novell	Microsoft
Uses of LDAP	Directory browsing Secure access of corporate resources (with access control extensions) LDAP server-to-server	Directory browsing Authenticated client/ server access	Directory browsing over the Internet
Replication	Develop simple replication as per the LDAP V2 specification	Already has multi-master directory replication technology (NDS) which will be used as an extension to LDAP	Develop extensions to LDAP. Within NT the domain will define a replication boundary
Referral	Develop simple referral as per the LDAP V2 specification	Looking to intelligent referral capabilities being added to the Internet standard	Looking to adopt forward indexing and dynamic pruning of referrals
Product with LDAP	Netscape Directory Server		Microsoft Exchange directory
Interoperability baseline	LDAP Version 2. Intends to publish its V2 extensions for inclusion in Version 3	LDAP Version 2. Undecided if baseline will be raised to Version 3	LDAP Version 2

This raises the possibility of product divergence beyond a minimum inter-operability point. LDAP 2 is currently accepted as the inter-operability baseline.

These become more apparent as the use of LDAP is scaled-up, first to enterprise e-mail (consolidation of address), to intranet (integration of directory content) and then to intelligent agents (unification of paths through an enterprise).

While LDAP is simpler and has the power to reach a huge user base, LDAP has the holes discussed in Section 12.5.2. X.500 on the other hand is perceived to be operationally complex, with few products to choose from. Table 12.4 shows a technical comparison of LDAP and X.500.

An alternative in "widely scoped" uses of directory services is to use LDAP to access an industrial strength X.500 directory. Or an X.500 directory may already be deployed in an organization—in which case LDAP can be the access solution.

The X.500 standard defines a directory service that meets the requirement of highly distributed environments. There are several directory vendors who provide industrial strength products. Whether these vendors will continue to develop these products depends on how the market develops.

The contents of an X.500 directory is called a Directory Information Tree (DIT). This consists of a number of sub-trees. Figure 12.5 shows the key components of the X.500 model. Sub-trees are made of a number of objects. The key concepts and the main components of the "foundation" X.500 model and mapping to LDAP are briefly described below:

- *Directory Service Agent (DSA)*—In LDAP terms the *server* on which the directory tree or part of the directory tree resides. Multiple servers are deployed in an organization. (A key issue is solving the hierarchical relationships between Internet naming services such as DNS, vendor concepts such as Microsoft NT Domains and LDAP.)

- *Directory User Agent (DUA)*—In LDAP terms the *client* which uses the services of the directory servers including access, add and search the directory content.

- *Directory Access Protocol (DAP)*—The term "LDAP" describes both a protocol and an API that describes the client/server communication model.

- *Home DSA*—In LDAP terms the local or initial server to which a client initially binds to. In an intranet context, DNS is a logical place to find the local directory server. The local server becomes more important as strong security is implemented as an unambiguous point of reference.

- *Chaining*—In LDAP terms a client request may not be resolvable by the current server. The server can "chain" the request to another server (providing additional state information to avoid duplication and looping). The second server can repeat the chaining process. LDAP however does not define standards for chaining. It is rather left to server implementations to support chaining. LDAP referrals are described in Section 12.5.2.

Table 12.4: *Comparison of LDAP/X.500 on Key Points*

Points	LDAP	X.500
Originators	University of Michigan and IETF. The aim was to develop a simple but powerful model for enterprise-wide directory services.	Part of the Open Systems Interconnection (OSI) suite of protocols. The primary objective was develop a global directory service.
Transport protocol and encoding	TCP for transport. Simplest possible encoding through use of lightweight Basic Encoding Rules (BER).	Full OSI protocol stack as well as application service mechanisms for session. Encoding through use of full Abstract Syntax Notation 1 (ASN.1) and Basic Encoding Rules (BER).
Schema model and scope	Adopts X.500 standard attributes. Other attributes published as part of LDAP standards for inter-operability. LDAP's reduced scope allows mixture of fixed and enterprise specific sub-trees. Provides a simple C function call-based API for software developers.	Fixed, hierarchical data model developed for scaling to a global directory. Largely general hierarchy with lower level specifics undefined by standard. Top-down name resolution. Scope is meant to be global but many enterprises use X.500 in a local context. Provides an object oriented API (with language bindings as defined by vendor/product).
Server-to-server protocol	LDAP is used in server-to-server communication role—e.g., in maintaining server hierarchy and replication.	Servers have a special inter-server protocol—Directory System Protocol (DSP). DSP is used in both "chaining" and referrals.
Client/server protocols	Client may concurrently query multiple servers. Provides various strength of authentication (ranging from clear passwords to SSL to X.509). Does not define encryption or access control.	Supports DAP and DSP level multicasting for concurrent communication. Provides a strong authentication framework (X.509 certification scheme). De facto standard for encryption is RSA.
Bulk transfer	Import and export of LDAP information in text file and text string format.	Not possible outside access protocols.

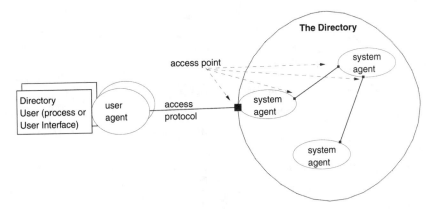

Figure 12.5: *X.500 directory components*

DAP/LDAP Operations. The X.500 standard provides a rich set of functionality for the storage and access of information relating to the real world of users and organizations and devices. The abstract operations of the two directory access protocols (LDAP and DAP) is shown in Table 12.5. The same operations are available through the respective APIs.

12.6 Object-Orientation

The client/server model and object orientation are complementary concepts. In the simplest, structural sense both aim to "break-up" large IT problems into smaller manageable "chunks." Increasingly, client/server applications use object-oriented tools and programming techniques.

Characteristics of client/server applications, such as incremental development of functionality, are a direct consequence of using object-oriented technology. C^{++} has emerged as the predominant language for client/server application development Some of the reasons for this include:

- The number of high quality C^{++} tool vendors.

- The relative "openness" of the language.

- Similarity to C (that is universally taught at undergraduate level).

- Adoption by all major computer platform and operating system vendors and standards bodies.

Table 12.5: LDAP/DAP Operations and API Functions

Operation	Description
Bind	Binds to a directory (server).
Unbind	Unbinds from a directory.
Read	The user can read a variety of information from the directory database—including types of attributes, values of specific types attributes. The returned values are dependent on the permissions the user has to read attribute types and values.
Compare	Compares each attribute that is presented with an entry to the respective values stored for each attribute in the directory. The comparison is done with the "equality matching" rule defined for the attribute type.
List	A search-like operation that lists the subordinates of an entry in the directory. Depending on the position of the entry, the results could be large. The paged results service provides results in a screen-readable size.
Search	A search operation starts a search of the directory from the base object to the scope—that are both defined in the query. This is one of the most complex directory functions.
Abandon	Abandons operations that have previously been started and results of the operations will not be returned to the user. (Abandon does not necessarily mean the directory service stops computing a result. For example a search may have propagated out to offsite servers and a following Abandon may not "catch-up" with the preceding request before it is completed.)
AddEntry	A directory modification operation that adds an entry to the leaf of the directory. The new entry must not exist currently, but the immediate parent must exist at the time of operation. AddEntry is only possible on the "master" directory, i.e., copies cannot be modified. All mandatory attributes must be complete for the operation to succeed.
RemoveEntry	Deletes an entry from the directory. Only leaves can be deleted directly, however, through a sequence of repeated calls sub-trees can be deleted. Only entries authorized to the user for deletion may be removed.
ModifyEntry	Modifies a directory entry through a sequence of additions and deletions from the attribute and attribute values of the entry. The modified entry must conform to the sub-schema for the entry.

Object-orientation however goes beyond C^{++}. Smalltalk and Eiffel are two industrial strength languages. In fact, Java is also an object oriented language. Java is also unique for a number of reasons (described in Section 12.7), and may turn out to be the evolutionary path for C^{++}.

The term object-orientated programming is widely used in the context of building software systems, especially in the software engineering of large or complex systems.

A second force that has shaped object-orientation (in a wider sense), was the research during the late 1970s and early to mid 1980s in modeling human reasoning. This was another area which needed to structure the huge amounts of data required in defining knowledge "concepts" into entities expressible through programming language level constructs.

This latter aspect of object orientation has been exploited by innovative vendors such as Cabletron in its Spectrum management platform. This allows the platform to endow devices it manages with behavior such as event correlation.

12.6.1 Object-Orientation in a Management Context

Object orientation has increasing relevance to infrastructure management. The primary use today is in modeling devices and services being managed by a platform. Hence several products have an object model and an object oriented database (based on the object model) as a central architectural concept (see Case Studies of CA Unicenter and Tivioli Management Environment in Chapter 9, Sections 9.5.1 and 9.3.1, respectively).

The object model has been used to unify a number of disparate models of managed objects:

- Management Information Base (MIB) from SNMP.

- Managed objects from OSI management.

- Unix operating system objects, such as users and passwords.

- Product specific objects such as Kerberos realms.

- Conceptual relationships between communication circuits (or links) and devices they connect.

Object-orientation is therefore relevant to infrastructure management in two distinct ways: Firstly, the managed environment is increasingly going to be based on the object-oriented model. Secondly, the software technology used to develop infrastructure management applications is also likely to be object-based.

Object-oriented programming (and hence applications built as a result) implies a structure defined in terms of objects that relate to physical and logical entities in the real world. Traditionally software deals with procedures and data—these are now hidden or encapsulated within the "object." The object concept (as used in the context of languages such as C^{++} or Smalltalk), and its associated characteristics are shown in Figure 12.6—making it more than just good programming style.

There are however three major classes of object-oriented systems (language families) that have relevance to infrastructure management:

Class-based languages. These define a set of objects with common structure and behavior. The class is essentially a template for generating executable representation of the object. Classes can be refined in a variety of ways. The most common one is successive specialization of a subclass. Hence a hierarchy can be envisaged, where each subclass inherits the methods and data structures of the parent classes.

C^{++} and Smalltalk are well known examples of class-based languages. In the example hierarchy in Figure 12.6, successive specialization is shown by the *a-kind-of* link indicating a bus is a kind of vehicle (as well as being a kind of mass transport mechanism and a kind of wheeled transport).

The bus subclass inherits from three ancestor classes. This is called multiple inheritance—which while being decried by purists is important in fields such as infrastructure management. The subclass minibus is a further specialization of the class bus. The executable

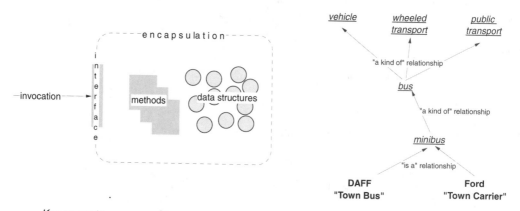

Key concepts
- **object** - the basic unit of object-oriented programming. An object consists of both data and the logic that manipulates the data. Objects have a defined behavior that can be invoked through an interface.
- **encapsulation** - the grouping together of data and the operations that are logically or conceptually related. Operations can be invoked only through the object's interface.
- **inheritance** - the ability to define the behavior of an object as a specialization ("a-kind-of" relationship) of a more general class. Hence "bus" is a subclass of a more general class "vehicle" as well as the class "wheeled transport" and "public transport". "Bus" inherits the properties of all three classes - this is called multiple inheritance.

Figure 12.6: *Summary of object-oriented concepts (for class-based objects)*

representations of the object is called an instance. Hence a Ford minibus *is an* instance of the class minibus.

Class-based languages are primarily used to develop application software. An application consists of sets of class hierarchies. Some parts of the hierarchy are built while others are part of a library.

Frame-based languages. A frame is a prototype, modeling an object or a situation. A frame consists of *slots* with different *facets*. *Declarative* facets associate values to slots, while *procedural* facets associate daemons with slots. A daemon is a procedure that is activated when the slot is accessed (i.e., read from or written to).

Frames are organized hierarchically, but unlike classes, a frame which is executable can generate more specialized frames during its execution. Frames are used primarily for "knowledge" representation and are a useful method for modeling relationships between infrastructure components. There are several industrial strength frame languages built over the language lisp as a foundation.

Actor-based languages. These were originally developed to simulate a "society" of cooperating experts. An actor communicates with other actors it knows as "acquaintances" (in a society), using asynchronous messages.

Actors are not organized hierarchically. An actor, which is in connection with other actors, can delegate the messages it cannot process. An actor is defined by a script which describes the way it should behave when it receives messages from other actors.

Delegation and inheritance are equivalent mechanisms. Actors are suited to developing distributed infrastructure management models—for example across a network of loosely coupled workstations.

Actor-based languages have not been commercially exploited. The model has however been used to provide solution for large-scale compute intensive modeling.

12.6.2 Object Request Brokers

The Common Object Request Broker Architecture (CORBA) is a major milestone in the maturity of the client/server concept and an essential step in the evolution to distributed computing.

CORBA compliant brokers allow applications components to "find" the services they need at runtime through the broker. This is the opposite of having to know *a priori* of the details of each service's point of existence. These server details are either defined by the programmer (and resolved at compile time) or entered as a configuration parameter prior to entering runtime. In either case change involves manual re-mapping.

Brokers essentially allow the de-coupling of servers that provide a service from the clients that use them. De-coupling has major implications, for example, in change management where a server is relocated or upgraded with a new version of the application. Without a bro-

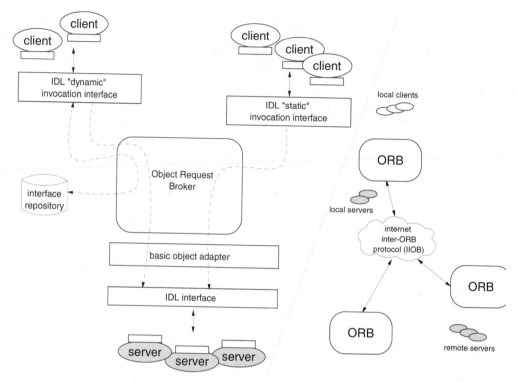

Figure 12.7: *The object request broker model*

ker each client that has "hardcoded" knowledge of the service needs to be reconfigured. With a broker the reconfiguration is more likely to be confined to the broker. The concept of an object request broker is shown in Figure 12.7. The main components are:

- *Static invocation interface*—The simplest interface to use since the object to invoke and the environment are known by the client. The relationship between the client and the object is fixed.

- *Dynamic invocation interface*—Object requests are created at runtime (when they are needed). This interface is more flexible and relevant to component-based models.

- *Interface definition language*—An abstract programming language used to specify an object's service or operations interface to a client. IDL is independent of the programming language used to realize the object (and the language used to realize the client).

- *Language mappings*—CORBA compliant products support language-specific bindings for access to respective objects' services. Currently C, C++, Smalltalk and Java are among the language binding specifications that have been defined.

- *Interface repository*—A database of IDL definitions that are accessed and used by clients needing to access an object's services. Access to the repository is often controlled through access control lists. Client can use the repository to check types and arguments.

- *Basic object adapter*—An interface between the ORB and implementations of objects that provide the services accessed through the IDL. The basic object adapter provides the object with ORB functions such as "create" which allows the object to process requests.

Object request brokers are themselves servers whose function is to act as a "filtering switch" between clients and servers (appropriate for the client request). Both clients and servers can communicate through the server, alternatively they can communicate directly with each other.

A protocol called the Inter Object Request Broker Protocol allows multiple brokers to coexist in an enterprise-wide environment.

12.6.3 Knowledge Representation Using Objects

When an event arrives from the managed environment it is useful to know how it relates to other events that may be occurring at the same time. An arbitrary event may relate to multiple contexts of interest to an enterprise.

Example contexts include risk, the geographic extent of an event's effect and business area affected by the event. Figure 12.8 shows a partial "knowledge base" of a LAN topology. This structure may be used to:

- Correlate between two events (i.e.) cause and effect.

- Identify business area affected.

- Identify the extent of the effect.

The default knowledge (or relationships) to draw such conclusions as correlation between events or classification of an event into a specific context is represented in the knowledge base in a structured, maintainable manner.

One such representation mechanism is based on a special type of object theory called *prototypes*. From this theory a class of languages called *frame based languages* were derived in the late 1980s (briefly described above).

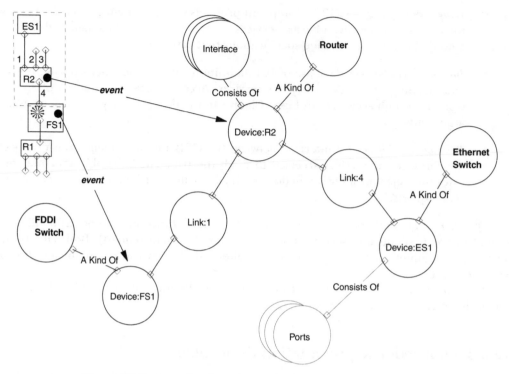

Figure 12.8: *Example of knowledge representation of a LAN topology*

A *frame* represents default information characterizing a family of managed entities such as links or devices and their interrelationships. It is used as a reference for comparing input events to be analyzed, recognized or classified.

The structure of a system of frames should have the capacity to evolve through the changes in the managed environment, including addition and deletion of properties as new types of entities or relationships between entities change.

Frame-based structures essentially define a knowledge base that can hold default values, exceptions, incomplete information, etc. that are not representable using other knowledge representation formalisms such as predicate calculus (e.g., in the Prolog language). As such it is an ideal tool for developing infrastructure management applications in event-correlation, classification.

In the case of the network portion, for example, there may be frames representing *device, link, service,* etc. Such frames represent actual network resources being managed.

Frames consist of a set of predefined "slots" relevant to the resource being modeled. Slots may have procedures attached to them to do localized processing every time the information in the slot is accessed.

Associated with the slots in a frame-based language are facets. Typical facets that are associated with a slot are:

- *Value* facet that gives the current value of a slot.

- *Domain* facet that specifies the set of values admissible for the slot.

- *Default* facet that gives a default value.

Every execution of the frame system is the result of an access slot in one or more frames. Hence in the case of an event that needs to be classified into a context such as security, then writing the event into a slot of the frame system (representing the object from which the event originated) will trigger off procedures attached to slots. Execution of procedures propagate to other related frames in the system as slots in one get associated to slots in another and so on in a chain.

The final result from this could be messages to a mapping drawing object to draw the map representing the matched context (or to pull up predefined maps from a database).

12.6.4 Searching and Developing Front-Ends

Searching for information stored in directories, databases and knowledge bases is a key part of the operations management and infrastructure management processes:

- In directories, searching is attribute-based.

- In databases, search is through executing SQL directly from a user interface (or from front-end tools generating SQL streams).

- In knowledge bases such as frame-based systems the query is the input-trigger (such as the event described above).

Structured Query Language (SQL) based toolkit is a common method for accessing databases. Most industrial strength databases provides a client/server model of interaction. The most commonly developed applications with infrastructure management databases are:

- Report generation.

- Query for historic information.

Reports may be with respect to a management process where information such as data on a metric used for tracking service-level agreements are calculated from the ticketing/resolutions database, and placed in a standard reporting format.

Such access to information in infrastructure management databases is likely to occur from PC platforms, as the responsibility for production of such reports is likely to vary from organization to organization.

Visual BASIC provides a method of developing such applications using a library of common functions used for search and query of popular databases such as Sybase SQL Server.

Dynamic querying is an emerging concept where user interface provides a "visual programming language" to structure queries into a database. These can be built relatively easily with tools such as the Java Management API toolkit.

12.7 Java—The Last Word

Java is an appropriate topic as the "last word" in this book—because Java is probably going to affect everyone connected with client/server infrastructures.

Java is an object-oriented language that is similar to C++—supporting polymorphism, inheritance, encapsulation, dynamic linking and multi-threading. Java is an interpreted language and runs on a virtual machine over a conventional platform. Java is important as an enabler for two reasons:

- There is a good chance that Java will be the language of choice for developing infrastructure management applications.

- Java is also likely to provide the computing model for mainstream computing—the so-called network-centric computing.

Java is establishing itself as an industrial strength programing language. It has caught the imagination and support of the world's most innovative tools makers, software developers and operating system vendors.

Its shortcomings, namely, (*a*) an immature security model, (*b*) lack of run-time performance, (*c*) inadequacy of development tools and environment are largely technical and is more than likely to be solved relatively quickly given the number of innovative minds addressing these problems.

Network-centric computing overcomes a number of major headaches in developing client/server applications:

- *Memory footprint*—The memory footprint (or the size) of a typical application written in a conventional language such as C++ increases with each successive generation. This leads to continuous pressure to increase the computing and memory capability of client machines. While the argument "memory is cheap" is true, increase in application size is often due to gross internal inefficiencies. Java offers a "thin" client model that is almost independent of the overall code size. This is because only the operational logic actually required of a given Java application needs to be resident. A thin client in turn extends the lifetime of client workstations.

- *Distribution of increments*—Most development of client/server applications occurs in an incremental fashion. Incremental functionality has to be distributed, usually to both client and servers in a production environment. This production part of the software life-cycle is difficult to control if the frequency with which increments are produced is such that the service organization cannot manage it. Java-based applications can have increments self-distributed. The application will always run the current version.

- *Capitalization of product development*—To develop a typical management application in the conventional world requires considerable resources—to the order of several million dollars. Java opens up a new world for developing high-quality products on a much lower capital base—because drastically smaller marketing and sales budgets are required if users can try the software before buying it. This allows more talented individuals and start-ups to produce products.

- *Product economics*—Every infrastructure management organization has management software it has bought and then abandoned without gaining much benefit from it. With Java it is already possible to envisage an economic model where the software is paid for on an as-used basis. Hence capitalizing the whole cost of software before its efficacy is understood will be a thing of the past.

- *Portability*—Java applications are portable to any hardware and operating system combination that can run a Java virtual machine. This allows decisions about machines and operating systems to be based more on sound technical and economic reasons.

In the area of infrastructure management the Java Management API (JMAPI) defines functionality to develop management application logic. This is described in Chapter 10, Section 10.7.5.

12.7.1 The Java Virtual Machine

The center of the Java environment is the Java virtual machine (VM). The Java VM is a software emulation of the hardware architecture to execute Java code. The Java VM had simplicity as its central theme. (Java can also be executed on a Java RISC machine implemented in silicon.)

The cycle from Java source code to compiled form (applet) to execution in the target environment is shown in Figure 12.9. The Java VM's instruction categories are also shown.

The Java VM has its own set of instructions. The Java compiler translates the source code of the method into the instructions of this abstract machine (called bytecodes). The Java VM can be ported to use the instruction set of any conventional machine. The just-in-time compiler is an evolving concept where the bytecodes are compiled directly to a conventional machine's instruction set just before its execution.

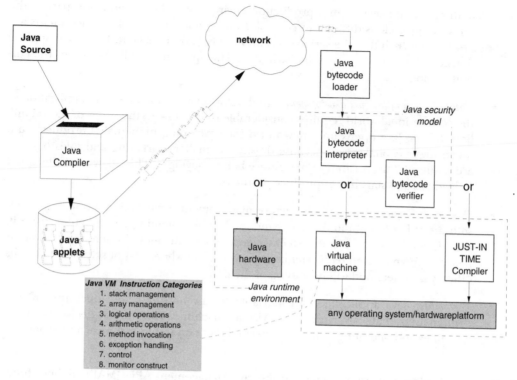

Figure 12.9: Execution life-cycle of a Java applet

12.7.2 Advanced Features of Java

The design goals of Java were to develop a language for robust, secure, distributed application that could run in a heterogeneous environment. Java has taken the better qualities of several modern programming languages—such as concurrency, garbage collection and dynamic linking.

Simplicity was however Java's overriding goal. Java therefore looks very much like C and C++ with most of their complicated features removed—e.g., use of pointers and overloading operators are not allowed in Java.

Java can be used as a conventional language—compiled into stand-alone executable. Microsoft is pushing this view of Java through the definition of a branded language environment J++—in an effort to put Java into a "box" that does not compete with its own ActiveX. Ironically, this is likely to provide high quality, low-cost tools for Java development—the results of which can be run on any machine.

Java's uniqueness however is as a "distributed" language—where applets are downloaded over a network and executed in a Java runtime environment. The advanced features of Java as a network-centric language are described below:

Memory management. The Java runtime environment takes complete responsibility for memory management, thus removing the biggest problem that plagues C^{++} based applications—memory leakage. Memory management in Java is based on a memory manager that keeps track of all object references from the time they are created. When objects are no longer referenced their memory can be collected—this is called garbage collection. The garbage collection algorithm runs in the background using idle cycles. Memory is allocated to an object by the Java "new" statement.

Multi-threading. Java provides built-in support for multiple threads of processing to occur concurrently. This allows more performant code to be written—the code's logic does not have to be serialized to do one thing at a time. Threads are part of the language itself rather than a construct of the operating system.

Java APIs. The Java software platform includes functions seen in a conventional operating system layer. These are defined as APIs to the outside world and implemented as Java classes in the Java platform. Table 12.6 describes a subset of these APIs.

Java runtime security. Java's security model is primarily concerned with execution safety. Since Java applets can be loaded over the network it is difficult to have the same legal assurances as conventional software bought from a vendor. The Java runtime system depends on four basic principles for implementing safety.

1. The language itself disallows any manipulation of memory. Hence back-door access cannot be created through manipulating addresses.

2. The class-loader which loads the runtime environment with an applet's classes and internal reference link is itself always part of a local file system.

3. The bytecode verifier puts all code through a theorem prover before execution, to ensure that a "hostile" compiler has not compromised runtime security.

4. Access control to platform resources such as disk and network interfaces. Hence "untrusted" applets can run in a "sandbox" environment if need be. Current enhancement includes a cryptographic signature to identify the source of an applet (and hence whether it comes from a trusted source).

In the end, however, each implementation of the Java virtual machine has to adhere to Java security principles as a quality issue. Otherwise, dangerous security holes can be left in specific implementations.

Table 12.6: A Sample Set of Java APIs

Java APIs	Description
Java.lang	The fundamental language types such as threads; exceptions as well as the root object and class. This API provides functions primarily accessed by Java runtime systems.
Java.io	Corresponds to stream input/output and file input/output.
Java.net	The network input/output that provides support for a set of intranet protocols including HTTP, FTP, and Sockets.
Java.util	Utility classes such as time, stack and queue.
Java.awt	The abstract windowing toolkit that includes a mechanism for developing user interfaces including scroll bars, buttons and fonts.
Less mature Java APIs have been defined in the following areas:	
JavaManagement	Java Management API (JMAPI) is an emerging API for systems and network management.
JavaSecurity	An API that provides access to authentication and encryption services to Java applications.
Java2D	An API similar to Postscript that provides two-dimensional rendering functions.
Java3D	An API similar in function to Silicon Graphics Open GI for three dimensional modeling.
JavaAnim	An API for two dimensional animation.
JavaMedia	An API for multi-media applications that include audio and video components.
JavaShare	An API for shared and group communication applications.
JavaEC	An API for electronic commerce applications including micro-payment.
JavaTel	An API for telephone integration.

12.7.3 Java Middleware

Middleware allows Java applets to interact directly with conventional sources of information, including databases, object servers and application servers. In addition, a class of objects called "JavaBeans" provides cross-platform component technology. While a component-

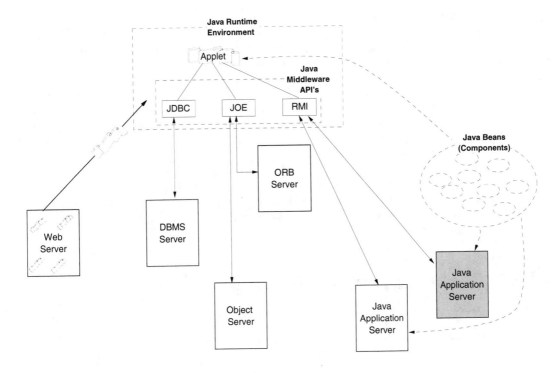

Figure 12.10: *Java middleware*

based architecture *per se*, doesn't provide middleware services, the cross-platform capabilities of Beans provides a typical characteristic of middleware.

Figure 12.10 shows how an applet (loaded from a web server into a Java runtime environment) can use different middleware APIs. These APIs are described below:

Each API provides connectivity to a different class server used in conventional client/server development:

- *Java Data Base Connectivity* (JDBC)—This API allows a Java applet to connect directly to an SQL database. Without JDBC an applet would use a web server and CGI scripts resident in the webserver to interface to a database server. In terms of client/server design the webserver as an intermediary can cause performance problems at the webserver (acts as a bottleneck handling requests from multiple clients), at the database server (unable to handle the high frequency of a single stream of requests from the webserver) and at the client (slow response as many client's queue at the webserver for service). A client applet's direct access to an SQL database allows the database engine to use its native concurrency mechanisms.

- *Java Object Environment* (JOE)—Many large client/server systems are increasingly based on CORBA defined object services (see Section 12.6.2). The JOE API allows existing object-based services to be used as the "back-end" by Java applications (without having a CORBA runtime environment).

- *Java Remote Method Invocation* (RMI)—Java can be used as a conventional client/server development language—with a server-resident components. A client-based component can then access remote functionality on a Java application server using RMI. Without RMI, Java cannot easily be used as a conventional language.

- *JavaBeans*—This is pre-written component software that can work across platforms in building Java programs or applets. Beans have a specialized class file structure and event model. For example, the components in the JDK1.1 Abstract Windowing Toolkit (AWT) are written as Beans. The Beans specification will encourage component libraries for Java-based development.

12.8 Books for Further Reading

Chadwick, David. *Understanding X.500* (the Directory). Chapman & Hall, 1994.

Harkey, Dan, and Robert Orfali. *Client/Server Programming with Java and CORBA.* John Wiley & Sons, 1997.

Inmon, W. H. *Building the Data Warehouse.* John Wiley & Sons, 1996.

Masini, Gerald, *et al. Object Oriented Languages* (The APIC Series, vol. 34). Academic Press, 1991.

Wheeler, Tom, *et al. Open Client/Server Computing and Middleware.* AP Professional, 1995.

Glossary

ActiveX is the latest implementation of Microsoft's OLE technology. It offers a system for embedded controls and their distribution for developing *network centric* applications for the Wintel platform. ActiveX is compatible with existing development tools and existing applications (such as Visual C^{++} and Excel respectively). This provides ActiveX with a major leverage with existing developers on the Wintel platform. It rivals (and corresponds in many ways) to Java-based systems which work on Wintel as well as non-Wintel platforms—ranging from mainframes to RISC platforms.

Activity based costing is a method of costing of projects and processes on the basis of explicitly defined activities involved in delivering a final product or result. Especially relevant to infrastructure projects to track costs and provide cash flow. Also useful in analyzing costs of delivering a process. Chapter 2, Section 2.5.4, provides a description of activity based costing in infrastructure management projects and processes.

Actors—used in the process definition context, define the "participants" in the process. Actors may be human or system-based such as a database or an application. Processes defined in terms of actors and the "use" they have for the process tend to fit the needs of a given environment better than generic processes specialized for an environment. The concept of actors is related to the concept of "use-cases"—which explicitly define the differences in the context in which a process is used. Chapter 2, Section 2.2.2, defines the actor concept for infrastructure management.

Agents are a software component used in the management of individual infrastructure components or layers. Management agents are comprehensively discussed in Chapter 11. Agents also increasingly play a role of "network assistants" to discover answers to "incomplete" queries, in security architecture as intermediaries between clients and security servers and in the deployment of artificial intelligence algorithms.

ATM—Asynchronous Transfer Mode is an emerging network technology based on switching fixed-size cells that can handle data, voice and video traffic over a single infrastructure. The fixed size of the cells and the point-to-point addressing allows switching to occur with minimal delay. ATM is still viewed largely as a backbone technology to connect a **campus** environment or in a **WAN**. Telecom companies and other organizations that own their fiber can run private ATM WANs while most organizations are dependent on public ATM offerings

Authentication—a concept in IT security where a user (or a computer system) is verified to be "genuine." A user name identifies the person (e.g., JONES_H). An addition information token such as a secret password or a "unique" characteristic such as a palm print is associated with each user name. The "production" of the secret or the unique characteristic by a person using a specific id is matched against a matching association in a secure database. This results in the user being authenticated or rejected.

Bandwidth—defines the capacity of a system to carry an ideal workload. When applied to a network it defines its ability to carry traffic. Usable bandwidth defines the actual bandwidth that may be used by a system connected to the network. A higher usable bandwidth allows greater throughput from a connected system. Chapter 6, Section 6.7, covers network considerations including bandwidth-related issues.

Benchmarking—a technique of ranking specific aspects of an organization against data collected from a set of peers. In IT, benchmarking can be applied to costs, skills and competency in specific areas, use of technology and processes, architecture maturity, development methodology, etc. Benchmarking is often driven by a definite methodology and reference databases in specific fields are available from consulting firms. Benchmarking is covered in Chapter 2, Section 2.4.

Best practice—defines a model for reproducing a procedure or technique that is successful for achieving results in some specific, within an industry or within an organization. The model procedure or technique may originate from outside or inside an industry. In Chapter 3, Section 10.3, "best practice" for a set of quality metrics, essentially defines what is being achieved in infrastructure management in "top" organizations.

Burstiness—describes a phenomenon in client/server based application where computing requests for a services occur closely together. When application requests are aggregated and viewed from underlying infrastructure layers such as the networks and the servers, these appear as bursts of traffic followed by zero or nominal activity. Many current networks are incapable of being able to handle bursts without losing information. Chapter 6, Section 6.7, covers network considerations including burstiness of client/server traffic

Business continuity—describes a concept of planning for continuing business activity in the event of a disaster in the normal business environment. Business continuity is disaster planning from a business process perspective, so that all the activities of key business processes can be supported at known levels of scaleability. Chapter 2, Section 2.6, covers the key principles of business continuity planning.

Campus Network also termed Metropolitan Area Network (MAN)—A network connecting multiple buildings in a diameter of some 100 meters to 10 kilometers. The upper range of a campus diameter is continuously increasing with public ATM backbone deployment by Telecom vendors and smaller service companies.

CGI—Common Gateway Interface is essentially a compute engine found on web servers and defines the point where scripts are invoked, as a result of a web client (browser) requesting a service supported by the CGI. Typical services include conversion to **HTML** from a relational table, and just in time calculation of data, both for presentation to the browser.

CMIP—Common Management Information Protocol is the standard OSI management protocol that supports the OSI Common Management Information Services (CMIS) framework for management applications. CMIS and CMIP are still widely supported in the Telecom sector as well as some government sectors in Europe and USA. The OSI management framework is described in Chapter 10, Section 10.4.

Confidentiality—a term used in IT security to ensure the privacy of information that is transported or stored. Implementing confidentiality is the key to using "insecure" transportation systems such as the Internet for global services. It is also the key to outsourcing services such as PC support where organization data has to be secured. The confidentiality concept is further described in Chapter 7, Section 7.3.2.

Correlation—used in the context of correlating one event with other events, to identify chained events. For example, the failure of an IP router interface will inevitably cause failure of higher level protocols in machines connected to that interface. Correlation techniques can use the physical association between the machines and the failed IP subnet to filter out "secondary" events that occur as a result of the primary failure. Correlation techniques can also predict the deterioration of service delivery as a consequence of different types of failure.

Criticality (of service)—a concept in high availability where if high availability features such as one-half of a redundant pair of servers fails, then the criticality of services provided by the server-pair has increased. In this example a further failure, i.e., the working server failing will bring down the service. Criticality can cumulatively be applied to a whole "service path" through multiple layers (i.e., adding up all the subsystems delivering the service).

DCOM or Distributed Common Object Model is a model for distributed computing using objects and was invented by Microsoft. It is a rival standard to the Common Object Request Broker Architecture (CORBA) from which the Object Request Broker (**ORB**) concept was born. Both DCOM and CORBA provide the services for application objects at the desktop to connect to objects distributed on machines elsewhere on the network.

DHCP or Dynamic Host Configuration Protocol—is a protocol for allocating IP addresses dynamically according to different allocation policies such as the lifetime of an allocated address. DHCP solves error-prone manual allocation and recycling of IP addresses. DHCP is a key part of migrating to newer operating systems such as **Windows NT** on an enterprise scale, where coexistence with older internal addressing schemes is a requirement. DHCP is also a key component in designing virtual **LAN**s for global businesses.

Distributed computing—a concept that goes beyond the client/server and three-tier architectures (of presentation, business logic and database) to where computational and service functions are distributed across multiple machines. Services are invoked to operate on information, held in information "containers" such as "documents" and "objects." The concept is described in Chapter 6, Section 6.4.1.

Event classes—a method of developing a classification structure to identify and monitor events produced within a client/server environment. Each organization needs to develop an event classification that corresponds with its client/server architecture. A classification system in particular needs to capture dependency chains between events from different layers of an environment. Chapter 7, Section 7.4, describes key factors in developing a classification system.

Exception management—a concept where only exceptions to a "baseline" are considered as management events. Used in remote management where threshold values define the baseline conditions, such as **Utilization** on an Ethernet connection. When the threshold is exceeded an event is generated. Thresholds can also define a lower limit—when a measured value falls under this limit an event is generated. Exception management is supported by the RMON agent specification which is described in Chapter 11, Section 11.2.1.

Fractal—a term used to define "self-similarity." A key discovery about traffic distribution made in 1993 was that LAN traffic viewed within any time-scale (ranging from milliseconds to months) was similar in nature. This is described in Chapter 6, Section 6.7.6.

Gap analysis is a tool or method for measuring an existing state or condition, defining an ideal or desired state and analyzing the difference or gap between the two. Gap analysis is a powerful problem-solving tool that can be applied to a wide variety of problems, including skills, application of technology, process maturity, performance of technology investment. The results of gap analysis should be a path to filling the gap. The principles for applying gap analysis are covered in Chapter 2, Section 2.4.1.

High availability is a concept for making an IT system available at close to 100% as possible. While techniques for achieving this have been developed for centralized environments, applying the same principles to a client/server environment is not straightforward. In client/server environments multiple techniques have to be applied concurrently and actively managed. Chapter 7, Section 7.7, defines application of the high availability concept.

HTML or Hypertext Markup Language is the mechanism used to define the content and layout of information pages on the web and viewed through a browser. HTML can be a static part of a web page, or more commonly now, HTML is generated on the fly in response to queries generated from a web browser. The raw data depicted in a dynamically created page is often held in a relational database.

HTTP or Hypertext Transfer Protocol is the key protocol used in browser to web (client/server) communication. HTTP is a stateless protocol in that each request/response cycle is independent of the previous and future cycles. HTTP and its uses in infrastructure management are described in Chapter 10, Section 10.7.1.

I-Net is a term that unifies the term Internet and intranet to signify their transparency from the perspective of a "consumer" of services accessed and delivered through these media. An example is a salesperson who can access an up-to-date price catalog through his browser while in his office, and accessing it over a dialup Internet connection while he is on the road. A key implication of I-Net is that of security mechanisms "adapting" to policies governing whether the access to the catalogue came from "outside" or from "inside."

IDL or Interface Definition Language is an abstract programming language for describing the operations interface of an object. Such objects can participate in distributed computing because clients requiring their services can find them through an object request broker or directly by searching an interface repository. IDL is independent of the programming language used to realize the object.

IETF or Internet Engineering Task Force is essentially a standards making body responsible for defining all IP related standards. One of the reasons for the success of the IETF relative to other similar bodies is that reference implementations provided by multiple vendors or institutions are required for the body to start the standards definition process. The IETF represents both vendors and users and hence tends to gain better consensus on policies.

IIOP or Internet Inter-ORB Protocol—is a protocol for "local" Object Request Broker (ORB) to communicate with other ORBs distributed on an enterprise scale. Local ORBs are sometimes deployed as a centralized service. IIOP is an essential protocol when deploying object-oriented applications on a global scale, hence important to specifying ORBs.

IPSEC or Internet Protocol Security workgroup within the IETF responsible for developing Internet security architectures. These architectures aim to be independent of the actual algorithms used in realizing the architecture. IPSEC is likely to have a major influence on the way security is defined and implemented in IP networks.

Java is a new object-oriented language developed by Sun that takes the best features of many modern languages, including concurrency, object orientation, strong typing, etc. Java is however unique in the sense that it is the first of network computing languages where executable parts of an application are downloaded only when functionally needed. Java is often described as a network-centric language. It can be executed in any platform/ operating system environment that has a Java Virtual Machine (JVM). A JVM is usually provided as part of the browser.

JVM or the Java Virtual Machine is an execution engine developed in software for executing Java bytecodes. Java programs are compiled into bytecodes. Bytecodes are therefore hardware and operating-system independent. While the idea of virtual machines has been around for many years, processor speed increases and the download on the demand model of Java makes such virtual machines a key component of network-centric computing.

LAN or Local Area Network is a network that is physically confined to a relatively small diameter of a few hundred meters. LAN architecture determines the type of client/server traffic and loads the network infrastructure should be designed for. Generally, the diameter of a LAN decreases as the speed increases. Hence the diameter possible with a 10 MB Ethernet is a binary order of magnitude more than the diameter possible with a 100 MB Ethernet.

Latency—the delay experienced by a client in gaining service. Latency is a cumulative effect of the operational characteristics of the intermediate layers through which client/server communications have to traverse. Latency and especially variance in latency is a common problem in global deployment of client/server based applications. Latency at the network level is discussed in Chapter 6, Section 6.7.4.

LDAP or Lightweight Directory Access Protocol is used to define a kind of directory as well as to describe a protocol to access directory content. LDAP is defined as an IETF standard. Both LDAP the directory and LDAP the protocol have key roles to play in global infrastructure management. The LDAP protocol's role is described in Chapter 10, Section 10.7.4, while LDAP as a directory is described in Chapter 12, Sections 12.5.2 and 12.5.3.

Manager—also termed a station is used in the context of the "manager-agent" model that defines the current network and systems management operational model. The manager is an application to control and access information from agents. A protocol defines the structure of the communication between the manager and the agent. Managers can be relatively simple or may host more complex functions. See Chapter 9, "The Technology of Platforms"—which is a comprehensive treatment of managers of all types.

Messaging—an "umbrella" term that covers a range of applications including e-mail, voice-mail, "chat," paging, voice-to-text conversion, etc. Messaging can be thought of in terms of: (*a*) a "backbone" that reliably carries message traffic (often on a global scale), and (*b*) individual messaging applications that use the backbone through standard APIs. Messaging has an important transport role in infrastructure management (e.g., in Chapter 11, Section 11.5, a messaging system is discussed as a method for transporting mobile agents). Messaging also refers to a model for client/server communication and is an alternative model to using RPC. This comparison is described in Chapter 6, Section 6.2.1.

MIB or Management Information Base is a key concept in the definition of management protocols such as SNMP and CMIP. The MIB is both a specification of management variables as well as a definition of how these variables get "packed" (and therefore referenced) in a message between a manager and an agent. In addition to standard MIBs (such as the MIB II) vendors provide product specific MIBs. These latter are often the key to manage devices. MIBs are distributed in a format where they can be compiled and incrementally added onto a manager or platform (that manages the devices).

Middleware is a class of software that notionally sits between an application layer and the operating system layer. In distributed systems, middleware provides transparency across multiple platforms, name and address spaces, as well as providing services such as data replication, data translation, transaction and queuing models. Middleware is an enabling technology and includes products such as object request brokers, rpc-based toolkits, and transaction monitors.

Migration is a term used to define a model for transition from one technology base to another. Common examples in the infrastructure are the migration from one network technology to another and from one operating system to another. In this model, both the old and the new technologies have to coexist. This implies that temporary "bridges" have to be built to enable active cooperation between the old and the new environments while transition is in progress. Due to the scale implied by changes such as a new desktop being deployed, migration programs can sometimes take a long time.

MIME—Multipurpose Internet Mail Extension is a standard that allows a mail message to carry different types of content, ranging from simple text to multi-media to executable programs. MIME allows the messaging backbone to transport different types of data. The responsibility of content "unpacking" and processing is the "responsibility" of the recipient of the message. A secure form of MIME called S/MIME allows better safety checks to be maintained on content.

Multicasting—a network carries different types of traffic ranging from very large message files to short requests packets from browsers. Services can be characterized as "pull"—when the service is provided in direct response to a request. Services are of the "push" type when a service is delivered to a client on the basis of some previous subscription to the service. Multicast is a method of addressing groups of users with common interest in a service—and hence have subscribed to the service. Multicast traffic is handled by routers that map packets to ports that have subscribed to a service using the Internet Group Management Protocol (IGMP). Multicast therefore allows "push" type services to scale to enterprise levels without significant increase of network bandwidths.

Network-centric—an emerging model of computing where the network plays the role of providing resources "just-in-time" for it to be made use of in a computational context. An example of this model is using Java applets which are downloaded over a network only when the context for a specific applet is recognized. This is described in Chapter 12, Section 12.7.2. Another example is that of mobile agents that are transported to target hosts for infrastructure management tasks on an as-needed basis. This is described in Chapter 11, Section 11.5.

Object wrapping—a concept of putting an interface "wrapper" recognizable by an object request broker (ORB) around a software function or program written in a non-object oriented language. Through object wrapping, "legacy" applications and their data-sets can be made to look as application level servers and to fully participate in an object-oriented framework of software components. Object wrapping is often an intermediate step in migrating to an object-oriented framework. Object-wrapping toolkits for specific procedural languages are supplied by most ORB vendors.

ORB or Object Request Broker is a technology for objects (generated by an object-oriented development environment) on a client machine to find other compliant objects that provide some service required by the client. "Wrapped" objects can also be found through an ORB. ORBs are largely used for "coarse" grained services such as requests to an application server running a special calculation engine. The ORB is not practical for finding and connecting to "fine grained" objects as the overhead is often too great .

Paradigm shift is a model of technical and scientific revolution described by Thomas Kuhn in his book, "The Structure of Scientific Revolutions." It defines how an "established way" (or model) accepted by most practitioners in a field, is surrounded by paradigms or "different ways" of achieving the same ends. Almost overnight the established way is overtaken by a paradigm that until then tends to be dismissed by the mainstream practitioners. A recent example of a paradigm shift in computing is the move away from procedural languages to the use of object-oriented languages in commercial software development.

Peaky traffic—used in the context of characterizing client/server traffic as consisting of bursts of activity interspersed by relative inactivity. As application servers become more distributed a single (often client generated) transaction can result in many (often orders of magnitude greater) secondary transactions and events being generated. This is as a result of the original transaction being computed by multiple services and the results of each service being distributed. From an infrastructure perspective there should be an underlying capacity by all components (networks, hosts, operating systems, application software) to cope with these bursts of activity. This is discussed in Chapter 6, Section 6.7.3.

Platform—used in the infrastructure management model, the system that provides the manager functions and hosts the management applications layered above the basic protocol engines and display interfaces. These applications provide management functions. The platform plays a centralized role in managing agents distributed in the infrastructure. Chapter 9 is devoted to the different types of platforms.

Process mapper is a term used in the context of an information bus-based client/server architecture, where it is an engine that holds rules about business processes. The process mapper provides a service that maps an application packet, originating from a business process, to the application servers that service the packet. The logic of a process mapper's function is described in Chapter 6, Section 6.4.2.

Process re-engineering is a term used to describe the "micro" re-design of infrastructure management processes using a method of review and analysis. Process re-engineering is relevant to organizations that already have a set of management processes. The term process engineering is used to describe the design of processes in an environment where no processes formally exist.

Quality metrics defines a set of characteristic values to measure the quality of infrastructure management. Definition of quality metrics allow "improvement" to be defined in terms of meeting target values. Organizational quality metrics are described in Chapter 3, Section 3.3, and quality metrics for key processes are described in Chapter 5, Section 5.4.

Replication refers to distributing information in a database, directory or any application repository onto multiple, physically distinct "service points." Replication is an important tool in defining global infrastructure management frameworks—to enhance performance, increase probability of survival after a disaster, optimize sizing to local use of data and for developing 7 x 24 support structure. Chapter 12, Section 12.4.2, describes replication in the context of databases in infrastructure management. Replication can also refer to distributing computational processes and "threads" across multiple "service points"—to achieve load balancing (i.e., performance) and high availability.

RFC or Request for Comment is a term used by the Internet Engineering Task Force (*IETF*) to define Internet standards. A number identifies the specific standard. (IETF is probably the most important standards making body for developing standards that appear in products aimed at the IP market.)

RISC—Reduced Instruction Set Computer is a processing chip architecture that is based on a small number of simple instructions being able to work at high clock speeds and able to exploit concurrent execution techniques. Languages such as C and C^{++} have compilers that can optimize for such instructions. Architecturally, RISC is at the opposite end to Intel processors which are based on a traditional or Complex Instruction Set (CISC).

Risk—when applied to infrastructure management is a concept of a future event that could operationally jeopardize the infrastructure. Also applicable to infrastructure projects where risks are future events and conditions that can affect the progress of the project. Once identified, risks can be actively managed. Risk management is defined in Chapter 2, Section 2.3.

RMON—Remote Monitor is a specification for remotely monitoring LAN segments. RMON specs exist for Ethernet and Token Ring and de facto standards exist for other technologies such as FDDI. RMON agents (which gather the LAN data) are realized in monitoring probes. Such probes may be realized by software running on an off-the-shelf platform or an integrated unit. Both connected to the LAN(s) being monitored. RMON is described in Chapter 11, Section 11.2.1.

RPC—Remote Procedure Call is the commonest method that client code uses to execute remote services. RPC is an extension of the normal function call mechanism and hence widely supported by operating systems on most platforms. RPC is briefly defined in Chapter 10, Section 10.6.2.

Segmentation is a concept in deploying distributed security where users are segmented according to enterprise-specific criteria such as the "need-to-communicate." Within a segments a specific set of policies are applied. At each "inter-segment" boundary, specific policies can be defined. For example, entry from a development environment into a production environment can be controlled by a policy of enforcing strong authentication of users, and access to systems in the production environment to be confined by strong access rights mechanisms.

Service delivery chain is a simple mapping tool for documenting dependency between a given service and the multiple parties involved in its delivery. This allows complex relationships between different internal groups, external parties and multiple external parties to be understood. Such maps are particularly useful in analyzing multi-party relationships and interfaces and in process design that spans across multiple organizations.

Single-point-of-contact is a service concept where users access all IT services through a logical single point. Services available through the point can range from the traditional help-desk functions such as problem reporting and change request to ordering IT kits to general technology queries. This concept allows service levels seen by users and emerging capacity needs for various services to be easily analyzed. Chapter 3, Section 3.4.2, describes an integrated service desk function. The concept can also be extended to provide information on IT capability to be distributed to the user from a single point. Examples include maps showing the current status of key business services such as messaging and advance warning of infrastructure work that may potentially affect services.

Skills portfolio is a concept of analyzing and maintaining the skills necessary to handle infrastructure management tasks in an organization. An explicit process to review skills against needs and to fulfill the "gap" through training or outsourcing is important to meeting infrastructure demands in organizations that have fast-moving business cycles. Chapter 4, Section 4.5.3, defines a process for reviewing skills while Section 4.6 gives tasks commonly undertaken for infrastructure management.

SNMP and **SNMPv2** or Simple Network Management Protocol and its second version defines the protocol used between management agents and management stations. SNMP has been widely deployed, ranging from power supplies to operating systems to network applications. Its relative simplicity is both its strength and its weakness. SNMPv2 was defined to overcome the limitations of SNMP, however its take-up by vendors was slowed down by major disagreements between different interest groups. SNMPv2 has been "partially" deployed in several new products.

SQL or Structured Query Language is an integral part of relational databases. SQL is used to define queries as well as to define procedures for "processing" data in the database tables. Such procedures automate common manipulations specific to a database design at the database engine. SQL is often defined to a baseline standard with vendor specific extensions. SQL is also evolving to support object-oriented databases. SQL is described in Chapter 10, Section 10.6.3.

Station is a term used interchangeably with "Manager" described above. Station is however less used now as "managers" have evolved to mean more centralized management platforms.

Switched networks provide a model for building network infrastructure that better matches the characteristics of client/server traffic. Using an architecture approach, switching can be deployed from the desktop, through a local network backbone, through any campus backbone and out onto the wide area network. ATM is one technology that employs switching techniques and also removes the differences between local area, campus and wide area divisions. ATM is however very new. Switched networks are more commonly built from switched Ethernet at the desktop to backbone, with public switched services (including ATM) at the campus and wide area levels. While higher bandwidth is provided by switching, latency is still an issue for certain types of traffic profiles. Latency is catered for in such networks by allowing servers to be deployed at different "levels" (near the desktop, at the local backbone, at the campus backbone, etc.). Also switched networks still need a routing function to handle multicast and broadcast traffic.

TCP/IP—a suite of protocols that drive the whole field of modern networking. TCP is a transport layer (level 4) protocol, while IP is a network layer (level 3) protocol. The TCP/Ip suite has been steadily evolving to be an industrial strength family of protocols under the guidance of the IETF, with new protocols to handle the steady evolution of networking. The suite also covers management protocols such as SNMP as well as control protocols such as DHCP (address allocation) and IGMP (multicast session subscription).

Trouble ticket is a concept of creating a ticket to mark an event such as a problem (trouble) being reported. The ticket then provides a single point for "commentary" to be maintained about the resolution of the problem. The commentary reflects the paths of a problem management process that it has traversed. The concept of a ticket can be applied to other services requested from an infrastructure management organization, including change requests and ordering IT equipment. Chapter 5, Section 5.4.3, defines some of the quality metrics associated with ticketing.

Use-case is a general concept meaning "use to which something is put." Used in the context of infrastructure management processes, the term defines the actual conditions under which the process is used. Also usable in defining an object's function under different contexts. Chapter 2, Section 2.2.3, defines the use of use-cases in infrastructure management processes.

User awareness is a service-oriented concept defining the "depth of understanding" about the business practices of the user base supported by a support organization. Such knowledge is key to developing proactive management practices that match changing business needs. User awareness development requires a model of the user organization and workflows to be constructed. Chapter 2, Section 2.7, describes a framework for developing user awareness.

Utilization is a measure of the amount of capacity that is actually used. There is a relationship between utilization and throughput (or amount of work done). As utilization increases, throughput increases until a point is reached where further increase in utilization results in throughput falling. This threshold is sometimes called the "knee point," due to the shape of the suddenly falling curve, and is different for different systems. In conventional Ethernet, for example, utilization above 70% means that the collision between the packets is beginning to affect throughput on the LAN segment. Similarly, an application or "infrastructure service" server that is "hit" at a high rate has a threshold beyond which it is more busy handling request queues than providing the requested service.

Visualization is a term used to describe the viewing of monitored events from the perspective of different groups of people who may be interested in the consequences of the event. Event can depict failure of infrastructure components, key outsourced services and activity patterns related to security breaches. The commonest method of presenting events is through maps. By developing different maps for different interests (e.g., for infrastructure support groups, business groups and security management groups) the impact of an event can be concurrently viewed. Visualization allows better value to be gained from monitoring, as all relevant parts of the organization can use the information in day-to-day operations. Chapter 7, Section 7.5, covers the development of visualization for infrastructure management.

WAN or Wide Area Network defines a network that spans geographic distances over several hundred kilometers. WANs can be built from point-to-point leased lines or through the use of a public service such as Frame Relay, SMDS or ATM. An alternative is to use a managed service from global Telecoms or services vendor.

Warehousing is the concept of collecting, cleaning and collating data from different sources into a "warehouse." The main objective of warehousing is for applications that provide management information systems (MIS)—to use the data in a consistent way. Such MIS requirements are often associated sales, marketing and delivery chain functions. MIS is also relevant to infrastructure management—a common example is when managing one or more outsourcers of support services. Chapter 12, Section 12.4, looks at data warehousing in this context.

Web hosting is a concept of using third parties to manage and maintain both the infrastructure and the content of webs. The web is an important channel of communicating with customers for many organizations, and therefore specialist organizations may provide better value for money in establishing reliable web services especially on a global basis. This is a service area that is still maturing. Providers of web hosting often allow both static content as well content that is generated on the fly from "back-end" sources at the client site. This allows the client organization to maintain control of information outflow, while not worrying about issues in reliable delivery.

Web services range from HTML-based pages accessed through browsers to "push" type services for distributing software. In some organizations, web services include any service accessed from a browser, such as Internet Relay Chat and various types of interpersonal message services such as voice-to-text conversion. As the web is often used as a channel to customers, reliability, capacity and quality of web services are key concerns to many organizations.

Windows NT is Microsoft's flagship operating system. Deployed for the Intel platform and a number of "bi-endian" RISC processors. (Bi-endian refers to the fact that a processor's internal logic can handle processing of computer "words" starting from the least significant bit or alternatively from the most significant bit.) NT can be deployed on both servers as well as workstations and is a key component of many organizations' IT strategy. (Microsoft has developed a product strategy of office automation technology that exploits the 32-bit power of NT.) Windows NT is also potentially a strategic component for infrastructure management as it brings down the unit cost-of-ownership of management platforms.

Wintel is an acronym derived from <u>Win</u>dows (Microsoft) and In<u>tel</u> to describe the operating system and hardware platform combination that is the commonest PC specification in existence today. Intel dominates the desktop and server processor markets while Microsoft currently dominates the desktop market. Microsoft is making major inroads into the server/network operating system market with Windows NT as the network operating system of choice in many organizations.

Workflow refers to traversal through a process's activities (i.e., the flow of work) as an "instance" the process gets executed. The precise path through different process actors is determined by the specific conditions that started the process execution. Workflow is a term most often used in the context of automating processes and in being able to track the progress of each instance of a process. Chapter 5, Section 5.5, provides a model for developing automation of business processes.

Index